JEWISH GENEALOGY

GARLAND REFERENCE LIBRARY
OF SOCIAL SCIENCE
(VOL. 214)

JEWISH GENEALOGY
A Sourcebook of Family Histories and Genealogies

David S. Zubatsky
Irwin M. Berent

GARLAND PUBLISHING, INC. • NEW YORK & LONDON
1984

Library of Congress Cataloging in Publication Data

Berent, Irwin M.
  Jewish genealogy.

  (Garland reference library of social science ; v. 214)
  1. Jews—Genealogy—Bibliography. I. Zubatsky,
David S., 1939–   . II. Title. III. Series.
Z6374.B5B47   1984   929′.1′089924   83-16554
[CS31]
ISBN 0-8240-9028-4 (alk. paper)

CS
31
Z79
1984

Cover design by Laurence Walczak

Printed on acid-free, 250-year-life paper
Manufactured in the United States of America

Contents

Foreword

The confluence of Alex Haley's <u>Roots</u> and the American Bicentennial
started millions of Americans in search of their own origins.
Genealogical societies have proliferated to the extent that a guide
to their locations has been revised and enlarged biennially.

Within the Jewish community, the roots-searching phenomenon has
appealed to a rising generation of youth even more than to their
elders, although the latter, too, have joined in the chase. A number
of Jewish "how to" books have been published successfully. All of
them underline the point that the would-be searcher needs to be armed
with family names. But once one has the requisite list of family
names, where shall the search for these names begin?

This comprehensive volume attempts to answer that query. It shows
the researcher, in ready-reference form, what families have been
explored and charted. For Jewish genealogy it is a most invaluable
finding aid for which all "roots-diggers" will forever bless the
compilers.

As one who pioneered in the field of American Jewish genealogy,
and as a consequence has become the best-known searcher in the field,
I am especially grateful to David Zubatsky and Irwin Berent. My desk
stays flooded with queries from Jews and non-Jews alike searching for
their Jewish origins. From now on, with this volume, many an answer
will be at my finger-tips, many a searcher can be told where to begin
his search. Thousands of libraries, public and private, besieged
with genealogical queries, will share my gratitude for this most
helpful research tool.

Malcolm H. Stern
President, Jewish Genealogical Society
Past-president & Fellow, American Society of Genealogists
New York, N.Y. 1983

Introduction

This bibliography is the first attempt since Hermann Meyer's
Bibliographia Genealogica Judaica (1942) to provide a comprehensive
work for published and unpublished Jewish genealogies, family
histories, and individual family names. With some exceptions, books,
newspaper and journal articles, Jewish encyclopedia entries, family
papers, and family trees containing genealogical and/or historical
information about individual Jewish families have been included in
this bibliography. It does not include, however, entries from
biographical directories, such as Who's Who-type works, nor data from
communal, institutional, or governmental records. (For an overview
of sources for the latter-mentioned types of data, see the special
section on "Digging Up Jewish Roots.")

Only material that is available in archival repositories and
libraries are included; there are no items from private collections.
Wherever possible, archival or library locations for each
bibliographic entry have been listed. Most library locations were
found through the published Library of Congress' *National Union
Catalog* series. This source was supplemented by various catalogs and
bibliographies published by both Jewish and non-Jewish libraries and
archival repositories. United States trade publishers were, however,
excluded from this location service. In most instances, their titles
are available in an excellent cross-section of different types of
libraries throughout the United States. In addition, library
locations for most journal articles are not listed since a very large
percentage of the titles cited can be found in the *Union List of
Serials* or the *New Serial Titles*, which are available in most
academic and large public libraries.

The compilers have attempted to include all collections of Jewish
family papers in foreign repositories (mainly English and Israeli).
It is hoped that such inclusions will further aid the professional
historian in locating primary sources on Jewish families of variety
of times, places, and backgrounds, as well as to help fulfill
genealogists' needs for a greater number of sources to complete their
genealogical and historical work. However, because of space
limitations and better bibliographic and physical access, family
papers located in U.S. repositories have not been listed unless it
could be determined that they contained definite genealogical data.

The compilers have tried to avoid listing any entries which are
too limited in content. For example, if an item's coverage of a
family's history/genealogy does not span at least three generations,
it will likely not be listed. Also, no entries have been placed
under insignificant family-name headings. Thus, if an item dealt
with five or ten different families, it would only be listed under
those family-name headings which were significantly covered by the
work, or which were key names in the identification of the family.

The compilers' intention has been to list entries under, at least, all of those family names that are found in the titles of the particular articles, books, chapters, and manuscripts.

Wherever possible, annotations have been provided for the entries in order to further identify place of family origin, progenitor of the family line, name changes, maternal lines, and chronological coverage. For quick reference, brief biographical descriptions have also been provided in many instances.

While no bibliographical work of this type can ever be totally comprehensive, the compilers hope that this work will prompt other researchers to discover those genealogies and family histories which, due to the compilers' access problems and foreign language deficiencies, have not yet been unearthed. Also, before a more complete listing of family histories and genealogies can be produced, more newspapers will have to be searched, as well as such untapped sources as memorial books, compilations of rabbinical biographies, cousin club newsletters, and synagogue records. Additionally, searching for past sources will be difficult enough, but as the ever increasing popularity of Jewish genealogy throughout the world causes genealogies to be compiled at a much greater rate than ever before, an equally formidable task will lie ahead in the compilation of these works as well.

In summary, the compilers believe their bibliography will be helpful to all those who are searching their Jewish ancestry, but at the same time, it is hoped that the "missing parts" of this work will spur others on to further bibliographic study in this field.

MAJOR SOURCES CONSULTED
SOURCES USED IN THIS BIBLIOGRAPHY WHICH LIST JEWISH FAMILY HISTORIES
AND GENEALOGIES

Addis, Patricia K. Through A Woman's "I": An Annotated Bibliography of American Women's Autobiographical Writings, 1946-1976. Metuchin, N.J., and London: Scarecrow Press, Inc., 1983.

American Jewish Archives. Guide to the Holdings of the American Jewish Archives, by James W. Clasper and M. Carolyn Dellenbach. Cincinnati: American Jewish Archives, Hebrew Union College-American Institute of Religion, 1979. 211 p.

American Jewish Archives. "Selected Acquisitions" sections.

American Jewish History. "Judaica Americana" sections.

Bloom, Lynn Z., comp. American Autobiography, 1945-1980. Madison: The University of Wisconsin Press, 1982.

Blumenkranz, Bernhard. Bibliographie des juifs en France. Paris: Edouard Privat, Editeur, 1974. 349 p.

Cogan, Sara G. The Jews of Los Angeles, 1849-1945: An Annotated Bibliography. Berkeley, Calif.: Western Jewish History Center, Judah L. Magnes Memorial Museum, 1980. 237 p.

————, comp. The Jews of San Francisco and the Greater Bay Area, 1849-1919: An Annotated Bibliography. Berkeley, Calif.: Western Jewish History Center, Judah L. Magnes Memorial Museum, 1973. 127 p.

————, comp. Pioneer Jews of the California Mother Lode, 1849-1880: An Annotated Bibliography. Foreword by Moses Rischin. Berkeley, Calif.: Western Jewish History Center, Judah L. Magnes Memorial Museum, 1968.

Ginzei Am Olam Newsletter (The Central Archives for the History of the Jewish People, Jerusalem), nos. 1- ; 1971-   (Annual).

Index of Articles on Jewish Studies (The Jewish National and University Library, Jerusalem), nos. 1- ; 1966-   .

Jacobs, Joseph and Lucien Wolf. Bibliotheca Anglo-Judaica: A Bibliographical Guide to Anglo-Jewish History. London, 1881. 231 p.

Kaganoff, Benzion C. A Dictionary of Jewish Names and Their History. New York: Schocken Books, 1977. 250 p.

Kaminkow, Marion J., compiler and editor. A Compliment to Genealogies in the Library of Congress: A Bibliography: Twenty Thousand Additions from Forty Five Libraries. Baltimore, Md.: Magna Carta Book Co., 1981. 1118 p.

————, ed. Genealogies in the Library of Congress: A Bibliography. Baltimore, Md.: Magna Carta Book Co., 1972. 2 vols.

————. ————. Supplement, 1972-1976. Baltimore, Md.: Magna Carta Book Company, 1977. 285 p.

Kaplan, Louis, comp. A Bibliography of American Autobiographies. In association with James Tyler Cook, Clinton E. Colby, Jr., and Daniel C. Haskell. Madison: The University of Wisconsin Press, 1962.

Lehmann, Ruth Pauline. Anglo-Jewish Bibliography, 1937-1970. London: Jewish Historical Society of England, 1973. 364 p.

Leo Baeck Institute of Jews from Germany. Katalog. Vol. 1. Tübingen: Mohr, 1970.

————. Year Book, 1956-   .

Meyer, Herrmann MZ. Bibliographia Genealogica Judaica: A Brief Introduction to the Pedigrees and Other Sources of Jewish Genealogy. Jerusalem, 1942. 1 vol. CtY, DLC.

Milano, Attilio. Bibliotheca historica italo-judaica. Firenze Sansoni, 1954. 209 p.

————. ————. Supplemento, 1954-1963. Firenze: Sansoni, 1964. National Union Catalog of Manuscript Collections. Washington, D.C.: Library of Congress, 1959-   .

R.R. Bowker Co. Biographic Books, 1950-1980. New York: R.R. Bowker
Co., 1980. 1557 p.

Regenstein, Janice Mendenhall. American Jewish Genealogy: An
Annotated Bibliography of Books on Jewish Local History and Other
Subjects of Use to Genealogists. Wichita, Kansas: Family Heritage
Institute, Inc., 1981. 27 p.

————. Jewish Genealogy Worldwide: An Annotated Bibliography of
Books on Jewish Local History and Other Subjects of Use to
Genealogists. Wichita, Kansas: Family Heritage Institute, Inc.,
1981. 79 p.

Romano, Giorgio. Bibliografia italo-ebraica (1848-1977). Firenze:
Leo S. Olschki Editore, 1979. 208 p. (Biblioteca di Bibliografia
Italiana, 88).

Roth, Cecil. Magna Bibliotheca Anglo-Judaica: A Bibliographical
Guide to Anglo-Jewish History. London: The Jewish Historical
Society of England, 1937. 464 p.

Rottenberg, Dan. Finding Our Fathers: A Guidebook for Jewish
Genealogy. New York: Random House, 1977. 401 p.

Schembs, Otto, ed. Bibliographie Zur Geschichte der Frankfurter
Juden, 1781-1945. Frankfurt am Main: Kramer, 1978. 680 p.

Singerman, Robert. Jewish and Hebrew Onomastics: A Bibliography.
New York: Garland Publishing, Inc., 1977. 132 p. [Of special
interest for genealogists is the "Appendix: Index of Norbert
Pearlroth's 'Your Name' column, Jewish Post and Opinion
(Indianapolis), Sept. 7, 1945 to Sept. 24, 1976," pp. 83-116. This
index, however, is not indexed herein.]

————. The Jews in Spain and Portugal: A Bibliography. New York:
Garland Pub. Co., 1975. 364 p.

Stern, Malcolm, comp. First American Jewish Families: 600
Genealogies, 1654-1977. New York: KTAV Publishing House, 1978.
419 p.

Studemund, Michael. Bibliographie zum Judenspanischen. Hamburg:
Helmut Buske, 1975. 148 p.

Wiener Library, London. German Jewry: Its History, Life and Culture.
London: Valentine, Mitchell, 1958. 279 p. Reprint: Westport,
Conn.: Greenwood Press, 1975. (Its Library Catalogue, No. 3.)

————. German Jewry: Part II: Additions and Amendments to Catalogue
No. 3, 1959-1972. London: Institute of Contemporary History, 1979.
363 p. (Its Library Catalogue, No. 6.)

MAJOR COMPILATIONS OF GENEALOGIES AND FAMILY HISTORIES NOT INDEXED IN
THIS BIBLIOGRAPHY

Béthencourt, L. Cardozo de. "Le trésor des juifs sephardim: notes
sur les familles françaises israélites du rite portugais," Revue des
Études Juifs 20 (1890):287-300; 25 (1892):97-110, 235-45; 26
(1893):240-56.

Jerusalem. Hebrew University. Family Who's Who. Jerusalem: The
Hebrew University of Jerusalem, 1969-1976. 2 vols. Contains brief
lists of forbears and progeny for hundred of Jewish families
world-wide who gave money to establish endowments at the Hebrew
University. The amount of information provided by each family
varies widely. For some reason, Canadian-Jewish families usually
provided the most complete genealogical information. JNUL; Jewish
Public Library of Montreal, Canada.

Levi, Isaia. "Famiglie distinte e benemerite della comunità
israelitica di Montova," Il Vessillo Israelitico, vols. 53-55,
1905-1907.

Wolf, Lucien. "Anglo-Jewish Coats of Arms," Transactions of the
Jewish Historical Society of England 2 (1894/95):153-69.

How To Use
This Bibliography

Most all of the entries in this bibliography are cross-referenced.
That is, upon looking up any particular entry, there will be given
the names of any other family names being significantly discussed in
the particular work. The reader, however, should keep in mind that
the author's surname, each part of hyphenated surnames, and any names
listed in the title itself are all possible additional families
discussed in the work. If the work is not listed separately under
these family-name headings as well, then the family name is probably
not discussed in the work. Furthermore, the reader should be aware
of the fact that since many of the works could not be thoroughly
studied by the compilers, there are likely other families covered in
them which will not be listed in the bibliography.

Since cross-indexing of name variants is mainly given only for
works which specify the changed surname, the reader should also
examine family name headings which are spelled slightly different
from the particular name being researched. For an explanation of how
to identify surname variations, the reader should refer to the
VARIATION GUIDE.

Where an entry contains six or more family names, the entry is not
repeated, but instead a "See" cross-reference is used. Thus, the
statement located under the LOEB family-name heading—"See David
Joseph entry under BEITMAN"—tells the reader where the full citation
of this multi-family-name work is located in the bibliography.
Similarly, the statement under the WEISENFREUND heading, "See MUNI,"
refers the reader to a variation of the particular family's name so
as not to repeat the citation.

General works which contain a multiple number of unrelated
families' genealogies and/or family histories are cited only once in
the MOST FREQUENTLY CITED GENERAL WORKS section of this bibliography;
within the main body of the bibliography, only the author's last name
and the shortened title of the work are repeated under the applicable
family-name heading. Following the annotations of those entries is
the statement, See GENERAL WORKS, which instructs the reader to find
the full citation of the work in the MOST FREQUENTLY CITED GENERAL
WORKS section.

Under each family-name heading, entries are listed alphabetically
in the following order: (1) "See HEADING" entries; (2) encyclopedias
and unsigned manuscript repository holdings, eg. "CFM has a family
tree"; and/or (3) published works, signed and unsigned, and
manuscript repository holdings which either give the compiler's name
or which specify the first name of the family's ancestor.

Variation Guide:
A Guide to Locating Variations
of Jewish Family Names

While the similarity of surnames of different families does not necessarily mean that the families are related, one of the most important ways of locating related-family genealogies is to locate surnames which are the same as, or variations of, the desired name. Thus, whether or not the bibliography has the exact family-name headings being researched, the user should also study the works found under headings of variations of the name. Most name variations are the result of the replacement of letters and/or the deletion of syllables.

Interchanges

The following lists are of the major possible interchangeable combinations of letters. Thus, for example, where the list below the vowel heading has "ai" and "ay," this means that "ay" could be replaced with "ai"; hence, the family name Chait could also be spelled Chayt. Other variations of the name could possibly, but not necessarily, be Cheit, Cheut, Cheyt, Chout, etc. Likewise, for example, where the list below the consonant heading has "h, g" this means that a name such as Hurwitz could possibly also be spelled Gurwitz. And the list beginning with "ch" indicates that Novich could also be spelled Novicz, Novitch, Novits, etc.

VOWELS:
a, e, i, o, u, y, ai, au, ay, ea, ee, ei, eu, ey, ie, oa, oi, oo, ou, oy, uy, ye [ending usually], yi [ending usually], and sometimes: aa, ae, ia, oe, ua, ue, ui
"v" and "w" are interchangeable with "u"

CONSONANTS:
(The first letter in each of these lists also represents the original sound. The proceeding letters may or may not retain the same sound.)

ch, cz, czh, dj, dz, tch, ts, tz, z, and sometimes: c, g, j, s.
    and sometimes interchangeable with: sh, sch, sz, s, z, ch
h, g
k, c, ck, ch, g, gh, gg, and sometimes: kh, kk, q.
l, ll, hl
m, mm
n, nn, kn, hn
r, rr, hr
rt, t (eg., Warter, Water)
s, c, ss, sh, sz, z
sh, sch, sz, s, z, ch
t, d, dd, dt, tt, th.

t, s	x, z, chs, ks
v, w	y, j
v, b, bb, f, ff, pf, p, ph, pp	z, zz

Also, allow for possibility of "e" endings, and remember that any
two consonants side-by-side could become separated by a vowel (eg.,
Horwitz, Horowitz; Handl, Handel; Finkl, Finkel; Brandeis, Barondes;
Berl, Beryl; etc.)

Deletions

As the process of surname alteration progresses, not only letter
interchanging occurs, but also deletion. Most often, a syllable--
usually a name-ending--is deleted. Below are some of the more common
endings. (Also, consider possible variations of these endings--by
using the variation chart above.)

au, auer, bach, bard, baum, berg, blatt, busch, blum, chik, dorf,
dorn, er, es, ev, el, en, farb, fein, feld, fried, garten, gold,
hain, haft, hart, haus, heil, heim, hoff, horn, ig, itz, ke, kin,
kind, koff, krantz, land, laub, le, lein, ler, lich, lieb, lin, litz,
man, mark, meyer, ner, nik, off, ov, ovits, ovna, reich, schein,
schild, schmidt, schutz, sky, son, stadt, stadter, stamm, stein,
stern, stock, stone, strauss, taub, thal, wasser, wein, wald, zweig.

The syllable which is deleted from a name may not always be the
ending. It may even be the first part of the name. Indeed, the
possible variations are almost unlimited. For example, the name
Katzenellenbogen has been altered to form Katzin, Ellenbogen, Ellen,
and Bogen.

Reasons

Remember also that names have been altered by being misspelled and
translated and that many names originated from nicknames and
descriptive words, as well as places of residence, names of
occupations, plants, animals, and objects. Other names are
patrynomics and matronymics, and some are even abbreviations
(acronyms) of Hebrew phrases. Also, names have often been
intentionally altered in order to disguise their typical Jewish
origin and to resemble more closely the popular names of the
non-Jewish citizenry. Therefore, always consider how the name could
have been changed as well as what was its possible origin.

* This topic is also discussed in Benzion C. Kaganoff's A Dictionary
of Jewish Names and their History (New York: Schocken Books, 1970)
and Dan Rottenberg's Finding Our Fathers: A Guidebook to Jewish
Genealogy (New York: Random House, 1977), pp. 141-46.

Digging Up Jewish Roots
Arthur Kurzweil

The family histories and genealogies in this bibliography are, in essence, compilations of oral history and of communal, institutional, and governmental records. To best utilize and expand upon these compilations, it is helpful to be aware of what primary source material is available. Arthur Kurzweil, the author of From Generation to Generation: How to Trace Your Jewish Genealogy and Personal History (New York: William Morrow & Co., Inc., 1980) and co-editor of Toledot: The Journal of Jewish Genealogy, presents here an overview of these sources for tracing Jewish genealogy.

****

Genealogy did not begin with Alex Haley's Roots or the efforts of those wanting to join the Daughters of the American Revolution. In fact, it is fair to say that genealogy itself has its "roots" firmly planted in ancient Jewish tradition.

It is known, for example, that the Temple in Jerusalem had a special room devoted exclusively to the storing and maintaining of family genealogies. Discussions of genealogy are scattered in the Talmud, and one need not be a Biblical scholar to know that hardly a character is introduced into the Biblical drama without being accompanied by a family tree. The famous "begat" paragraphs of Genesis are a crucial part of the first book of the Torah (Old Testament), and there are scores of commentaries on the meanings behind these genealogies.

Jewish Interest in Jewish Genealogy
Jewish interest in genealogy, beginning with early tradition, has continued to the present day. Current Jewish customs and texts reflect the importance which Judaism attributes to a "generational" view of life. Jewish tradition accurately sees Jewish names as two names joined by "ben" or "bat" (son of or daughter of). Thus, for example, Rabbinic literature, Jewish tombstones, and much of Jewish oral history and Jewish communal records record a Jew's name not merely by his or her name but also by the father's, and even sometimes the grandfather's, name as well.

Modern liturgy also reflects the Jewish interest in genealogy. When the phrase "Abraham, Isaac, and Jacob" appears in Jewish prayer, a genealogy is being recited: father, son, grandson. Indeed, many other liturgical references are genealogical as well.

However, while it is quite easy to recognize genealogical interest in Jewish tradition, the question arises: Can the family tree and family history of a present-day Jew be successfully traced?

Investigating Jewish Roots

The answer is a definite "Yes," and the "myth" that all Jewish
records from Europe were destroyed is just that--a misconception.
There are records, there are books, and there are many other sources
which can help the average family trace itself back through the
generations.

Before one is ready to consult the libraries, archives, and record
centers which will provide the bulk of written data for family
history/genealogy research, one must begin the family tree with oral
history research. There is no substitute for interviewing family
members and beginning to plot a family tree simply by drawing from
the memories of family relatives--especially the older ones. It is
not uncommon for a family tree to stretch back five and six
generations simply on the basis of memory. Also, it is important to
remember that a family tree is not just a genealogy which goes back
in time. The names and dates of living cousins should also be
recorded. Likewise, a genealogy of the family should be part and
parcel to a history of the family, and thus relatives should be asked
not only about names, dates, and places, but also about their
experiences, acquaintances, and opinions.

After as many relatives as possible have been contacted, the
researcher is ready to search the records.

Public Records

Most people have a tendency to think that their own families could
never appear in books or records--but this is simply not true. Let
us say, for example, that a grandparent came to the United States in
1848 (which is quite probable if they came from Germany, since this
was the height of German-Jewish immigration). If this is so, then
there is little doubt that the family would appear in the 1850, 1860,
1870, 1880, 1900, and 1910 Federal census records (the 1890 records
were destroyed in a fire). All of the U.S. Census records, from 1910
on back to 1790, are open to the public. [Federal records available
in the National Archives include not only these censuses but also
passport applications, military records, draft registration records,
war pension applications (as recent as World War One), and over a
million other records of virtually every type which may have Jewish
family members recorded. An important inclusion within the latter
category is the recently-discovered records of the Russian
Consulate.]

Citizenship Records and Passenger Lists

Another research variant is the Naturalization record. Most of
the immigrant ancestors (the families' first member to arrive in this
country) became citizens. Often the citizenship records, or more
specifically the applications for citizenship (which are available to
the public) contain important family history information, such as the
ancestors' native town and the name of the boat which brought them to
America. With the name of the boat, steamship passenger lists can be
obtained at the National Archives. [Keep in mind that those persons
who did not become citizens may have filled out alien registration
forms which are also open to the public and which often provide much
of the same information as citizenship papers would provide.]

There are countless other sources in the U.S. alone, such as
birth, death, and marriage records. [The local courts around the

country often house these materials as well as wills, civil and criminal court proceedings, deeds, tax records, and voter registration lists, all of which may provide additional genealogical and historical information about the Jewish family.] Also, early "city directories," which look like, but pre-date, telephone books, may list family relatives.

Unconventional Records
Non-American Jewish records are more difficult, but still possible, to locate. If the family was from Eastern Europe, "Memorial Books," also known as "Yizkor Books," may be useful. Each of the more than one hundred volumes is devoted to a different Eastern European town, and often even the tiniest towns are represented. These books usually deal with the particular Jewish families that resided in the town and often provide photographs and general historical information about the town.

Interestingly, the Mormon Church in Salt Lake City has a great number of Jewish community records from around the world. Genealogy is part of the Mormon religion, and because of this they have set out to microfilm the world's records. At the present time, the Mormons have a collection of Jewish birth, death, and marriage records representing 300 Polish towns, 300 German towns, and 300 Hungarian towns, as well as a few Russian towns.

[Records of Jewish charitable, fraternal, religious, and Zionist institutions are also important potential sources of genealogical and historical data on families as are also the records of Landsmanschaften groups, family circles, family clubs, recent Jewish genealogical and historical societies, regional branches of the Hebrew Immigrant Aid Society, and synagogues. Synagogue records, called Pinkasim, may also include valuable cemetery records, marriage Ketubots, mohel (circumcision) records, and memorial prayers.]

Holocaust Research
A deeply disturbing but vitally important aspect of Jewish genealogy is Holocaust research. While the number 6,000,000 is unfathomable, learning about family members who were killed by the Nazis makes the Event all the more personal. Since there are no graves for the victims, the family trees become their personal memorial.

The International Tracing Service, under the direction of the International Red Cross, is an agency which has attempted to collect all records relating to the Holocaust. By writing to them, one may be able to learn more about the Holocaust victims in the family. [Yad Vashem, Martyrs' and Heroes' Remembrance Authority, located in Israel, has accumulated a vast collection of data, called Pages of Testimony, on each verifiable victim of the Holocaust. Also, there exist Nazi birth and death books and deportation lists which contain names and dates pertaining to many of the victims of the atrocity.]

Entering Jewish History
Sources for researching Jewish genealogy are vast. How large one's family tree is, how far back one can go, is immaterial: the importance of Jewish genealogy cannot be mistaken. Through the Jewish family, the researcher can "enter" Jewish history. Rather than approaching Jewish history from ancient times, working one's way

to the present, genealogy provides the opportunity to do the reverse.
Begin with today, with yourself, and work your way back in an endless
Jewish family chain.

Major Locations of Jewish Genealogical Sources

Federal Census Records, Passenger Lists, and Other Federal Records	National Archives Washington, D.C. 20408
Naturalization Records and Alien Registration Forms	(Locations vary depending upon the year) Immigration and Naturalization Service Washington, D.C. 20536
Mormon Church Records of Jewish Locations	Genealogical Society of Utah 50 East North Temple Street Salt Lake City, Utah 84150
Holocaust Victims and Survivors	International Tracing Service D-3548 Arolsen West Germany and Yad Vashem Har Hazikaron P.O. Box 84 Jerusalem, Israel
German Jewish Families and History	Leo Baeck Institute 129 East 73rd Street New York, N.Y. 10021
Eastern European Jewish History and Memorial Books	YIVO Institute for Jewish Research 1048 Fifth Ave. (at 86th St.) New York, N.Y. 10028

**"Digging Up Jewish Roots" (© Jewish Student Press Service, November
1977) first appeared in American Jewish Times-Outlook (Jan. 1978) and
The Jewish Veteran (Jan.-Feb. 1978). The bracketed comments have
been supplied by the compilers.

Other Jewish Family
Genealogical and Historical Sources

AJA.......American Jewish Archives.
AJHS......American Jewish Historical Society.
AMH.......Albert Montefiore Hyamson Papers, Anglo-Jewish Archives,
         Mocatta Library, University College, University of
         London, Gower Street, London, WC1E 6BT, England. The
         papers of the controversial Hyamson (1875-1954), English
         civil servant, historian, and chief immigrant officer in
         Palestine (1921-1934) under the British Mandate, contains
         genealogical notes and pedigrees of many Anglo-Jewish
         families.
BR........Bibliotheca Rosenthaliana, Amsterdam University Library,
         Amsterdam, The Netherlands.
CAJ.......Central Archives for the History of the Jewish People,
         Jerusalem.
CAJD......Central Archives for the History of the Jewish People, File
         on the Jewish Cultural Reconstruction in Darmstadt.
CFM.......Sir Thomas Colyer-Fergusson Collection of Pedigrees,
         Anglo-Jewish Archives, Mocatta Library, University
         College, University of London, Gower Street, London,
         W.C.1, England. Anglo-Jewish families.
CLU.......University of California/Los Angeles.
CSt.......Stanford University.
CtY.......Yale University.
CU........University of California/Berkeley.
CZA.......Central Zionist Archives Library, Jerusalem.
DLC.......Library of Congress.
G.........Georgia State Library, Atlanta.
ICarbS....Southern Illinois University, Carbondale.
ICJ.......John Crerar Library, Chicago.
ICU.......University of Chicago.
IEN.......Northwestern University.
JGCT......Jewish Genealogical Club of Tidewater Virginia, 560 Roland
         Drive, Norfolk, VA 23509.
JNUL......Jewish National and University Library, Hebrew University
         Campus, Jerusalem.
LBI.......Leo Baeck Institute, New York City.
LBIS......Leo Baeck Institute, Rudolf Simonis Collection.
LU........Louisiana State University, Baton Rouge.
MB........Boston Public Library.
MH........Harvard University.
MWalB.....Brandeis University, Waltham, Mass.
MnU.......University of Minnesota.
N.........New York State Library, Albany.
NB........Brooklyn Public Library.

NcD.......Duke University, Durham, N.C.
NcU.......University of North Carolina, Chapel Hill, N.C.
NHi.......New-York Historical Society, New York City.
NIC.......Cornell University, Ithaca.
NjP.......Princeton University.
NjR.......Rutgers University, New Brunswick, N.J.
NN........New York Public Library.
NNC.......Columbia University.
NNJ.......Jewish Theological Seminary of America, New York City.
OCH.......Hebrew Union College–Jewish Institute of Religion,
          Cincinnati.
OCl.......Cleveland Public Library.
OClW......Case Western Reserve University, Cleveland.
OU........Ohio State University, Columbus.
PD........Paul Diamant Collection at the Central Archives for the
          History of the Jewish People, Jerusalem.
PHi.......Historical Society of Pennsylvania, Philadelphia.
PJAC......Philadelphia Jewish Archives Center, 625 Walnut Street,
          Philadelphia, PA 19106.
PP........Free Library of Philadelphia.
PPDrop....Dropsie University, Philadelphia.
PPRF......Rosenbach Foundation, Philadelphia.
RMJHS.....Rocky Mountain Jewish Historical Society, Center for Judaic
          Studies, University of Denver, University Park, Denver,
          Colorado 80208.
TxU.......University of Texas, Austin.
ViU.......University of Virginia, Charlottesville.
WHi.......State Historical Society of Wisconsin, Madison, Wisconsin.
WJHC......Western Jewish History Center, 2911 Russell Street,
          Berkeley, California 94705.
WU........University of Washington, Seattle.
YIVO......Yivo Institute for Jewish Research, New York City.

MOST FREQUENTLY CITED JOURNAL AND MONOGRAPH ABBREVIATIONS

EJ (1928)...Encyclopaedia Judaica
EJ (1972)...Encyclopaedia Judaica
JE..........Jewish Encyclopedia
JFF.........Jüdische Familienforschung
MGWJ........Monatsschrift für Geschichte und Wissenschaft des
            Judentums
ZGJD........Zeitschrift für die Geschichte der Juden in Deutschland
ZGJT........Zeitschrift für die Geschichte der Juden in
            Tschechoslowakei

Most Cited
General Works

Bałaban, Majer. Dzieje Żydów w Krakowie i na Kazimierzu,
1304-1868. Kraków: "Nadzieja" Towarzystwo ku Wspieraniu Chorej
Młodzieży Żydowskiej Szkół Średnich i Wyższych w Krakowie,
1912-1936. 2 vols. This history of the Jews of Cracow and
surrounding areas includes many brief family genealogies. There
are also detailed name and location indices in each volume. DLC,
MH, NN, OCH, PP. Cited hereinafter as:
Bałaban. Żydów w Krakowie.

Ballin, Gerhard. Geschichte der Juden in Seesen. Hrsg. von der
Stadt Seesen am Harz. Seesen: Flentje-Durck, 1979. 286 p.
Includes a "Genealogische und persönliche Angaben über die
einzelnen jüdischen Familien in Seesen (alphabetisch nach den
Familiennamen)," pp. 153-242. DLC. Cited hereinafter as:
Ballin. Juden in Seesen.

Bermant, Chaim. The Cousinhood: The Anglo-Jewish Gentry. London:
Eyre & Spottiswoode, 1971. 466 p. Genealogical tables. Cited
hereinafter as:
Bermant. The Cousinhood.

Bick-Shauli, Avraham. "Roots and Branches: Genealogical Trees of
Jewish Revolutionary and Communist Leaders," (In Hebrew with
English Summary.) Shevut (Ha-Makhon Le-Heker ha-Tefusot, Tel Aviv)
7 (1980):94-104. Cited hereinafter as:
Bick-Shauli, "Roots and Branches."

Birmingham, Stephen. The Grandees: America's Sephardic Elite. New
York: Harper & Row, 1971. 368 p. Includes "We Are Connected: An
Abbreviated Genealogical Chart of America's Sephardic Elite."
Emphasis on Nathan, Hendricks, de Sola, Mendez, Seixas, Lazarus,
Levy, Lopez, Gomez, Hart, de Lucena, Peixotto, Solis, and Tobias
families. Cited hereinafter as:
Birmingham. The Grandees.

————. Our Crowd: The Great Jewish Families of New York. New York:
Harper & Row, 1967. 404 p. Emphasis on Schiff, Seligman, Kahn,
Loeb, Warburg, Guggenheim, Straus, Lewisohn, Thalmann, Lehman, and
Rothschild families. Cited hereinafter as:
Birmingham. Our Crowd.

Chelminsky-Lajmer, Enrique. "London, Berlin and Other Jewish
   Surnames," Names 23 (Mar. 1975):59-60. Cited hereinafter as:
Chelminsky-Lajmer, "Jewish Surnames."

Droege, Geart B. "Frisian Family Names Borne by Jews Only," Names 26
   (Mar. 1978):27-39. Cited hereinafter as:
Droege, "Frisian Names."

Eisenstadt, Israel Tobiah and Samuel Wiener. Da'at-Kedoschim.
   German title page: Materialen zur Geschichte der Familien
   Eisenstadt, Bachrach, Günzburg, Heilprin, Hurwitz, Minz, Friedland,
   Katzenellenbogen, Rapoport und Rokeach. Welch ihre abstammung von
   dem im jahre 1659 im litthaulsen stadtchen Rushani in folge einer
   blutbeschuldigung als märtyer gefallenen herleiten.... St.
   Petersburg, 1897-98. Various paging. DLC, NcU. Cited hereinafter
   as:
Eisenstadt and Wiener. Da'at Kedoschim.

Encyclopaedia Judaica: das Judentum in Geschichte und Gegenwart.
   Berlin: Eschkol, 1928-1934. 10 vols. Only "A" to "LYRA"
   published. Cited hereinafter as:
EJ (1928).

Encyclopaedia Judaica. Jerusalem: Encyclopaedia Judaica; New York:
   Macmillan, 1971-1972. 16 vols. Only entries with family trees are
   listed in this bibliography. Cited hereinafter as:
EJ (1972).

Familieminder Tilegnet vore Efterkommere. København, 1920. CAJ.
   Cited hereinafter as:
Familieminder Tilegnet.

Frank, Fedora Small. Beginnings on Market Street: Nashville and Her
   Jewry, 1861-1901. Nashville, Tenn.: By the Author, 1976. 227 p.
   The family trees are indexed in this bibliography. CtY, DLC, MH,
   NcD, NIC, NjP, NN, OCH, TxU, WU. Cited hereinafter as:
Frank. Nashville Jewry.

Gold, Hugo, ed. Die Juden und Judengemeinden Mährens in
   Vergangenheit und Gegenwart, ein Sammelwerk. Brünn: Jüdischer
   Buch-und Kunstverlag, 1929. 623 p. This history of the Jews and
   Jewish communities in Moravia contains a section on prominent
   Moravian Jeweish families. The family history articles and the
   genealogical tables are indexed in this bibliography. DLC, ICU,
   MH, NN, OCH, OU. Cited hereinafter as:
Gold. Juden Mährens.

Gronemann, Selig. Genealogische Studien über die alten jüdischen
   Familien Hannovers. Berlin: Lamm, 1913. 160, 146 p. Families of
   Hannover. CtY, MH, NN, OCH, PPDrop. Cited hereinafter as:
Gronemann. Genealogische Hannovers.

Harris, Leon. Merchant Princes: An Intimate History of Jewish
    Families Who Built Great Department Stores. New York: Harper &
    Row, 1979. 411 p. Cited hereinafter as:
Harris. Merchant Princes.

Jewish Encyclopedia. New York: Funk & Wagnalls Co., 1901-1906.
    12 vols. Only entries with family trees are listed in
    bibliography. Cited hereinafter as:
JE.

Kahan, Samuel. 'Anaf 'ez avoth. Krakau: Verlag des Verfassers,
    1903. 70 p. Added title page: Anaf ez aboth; Familienstammbaum
    der bekannten jüdischen familien: Horowitz, Heilprin, Rappaport,
    Margulies, Schorr, Kaznelnbogen, etc. von deren ursprung bis zur
    gegenwart aus druckwerken und handschriften gesammelt und mit
    kritischen Anmerkungen u. erlecterungen versehen von Samuel Kahan.
    CtY, DLC. Cited hereinafter as:
Kahan. 'Anaf 'ez avoth.

Kempelen, Béla. Magyarországi Zsidó és zsidó eredetü Családok
    [Hungary's Jewish and Jewish-Origin Families]. Budapest: Szerzö
    saját Kiadása, 1937-1939. 3 vols. This very rare work contains
    genealogies for hundreds of Hungarian Jewish families. Length and
    time period coverage of individual families vary widely. CtY, MH.
    Cited hereinafter as:
Kempelen. Magyarországi Zsidó.

Keneseth Israel Congregation, Philadelphia. "Biographical Sketches."
    n.d. AJA. Biographical sketches of members of this Philadelphia
    congregation, written by pupils and under the supervision of Rabbi
    Dr. Bertram W. Korn. Included are certificates of birth,
    confirmation, citizenship, marriage, and death; family trees;
    genealogies; and other documents of various families. Cited
    hereinafter as:
Keneseth Israel.

Kopp, August. Die Dorfjuden in der Nordpfalz, dargestellt an der
    Geschichte der jüdischen Gemeinde Alsenz ab 1650. Meisenheim am
    Glan, 1968. 458 p. This work reconstructs the growth of some of
    the thirty Jewish families that lived at Alsenz during the 17th to
    19th century. North Palatinate region of Germany. Includes
    genealogical tables. CU, CtY, DLC, ICU, MH, MnU, NNC, OU. Cited
    hereinafter as:
Kopp. Jüdischen Alsenz.

Leslie, Donald. "The Chinese-Hebrew Memorial Book of the Jewish
    Community of K'aifeng," Abr-Nahraín (University of Melbourne,
    Australia, Department of Semitic Studies) 4 (1963/64):19-49; 5
    (1964/65):1-28; 6 (1965/66):1-52. Includes family trees for
    several Jewish Chinese clans. Cited hereinafter as:
Leslie, "Chinese-Hebrew K'aifeng."

Narell, Irena. Our City: The Jews of San Francisco. San Diego:
    Howell-North Books, 1981. 424 p. Cited hereinafter as:
Narell. Our City.

Pudor, Heinrich. Die internationalen verwandtschaftlichen
  Beziehungen der jüdischen Hochfinanz. Leipzig: By the Author,
  1933-   . This multi-volume work on the history of Jews within
  the international financial community contains sections on
  prominent and influential families. DLC, NN, OCH. Cited
  hereinafter as:
Pudor. Internationalen Hochfinanz.

Rachel, Hugo and Paul Wallich. Berliner Grosskaufleute und
  Kapitalisten. Berlin: Verlag von Gsellius, 1934-1939. 3 vols.
  Reprint: Berlin: de Gruyter, 1967. 3 vols. This history of
  prominent Berlin merchants and other "Capitalists" includes
  sections on Jewish families. The family history articles and the
  genealogical tables are indexed in this bibliography.
  Original-edition library locations: CU, DLC, ICJ, NNC, OCH.
  Reprint-edition library locations: CSt, CtY, CU, DLC, MH, NIC, NjP,
  NjR, NNC. Cited hereinafter as:
Rachel and Wallich. Berliner Grosskaufleute.

Reychman, Kazimierz. Szkice genealogiczne. Serja I. Warszawa:
  F. Hoesick, 1936. 212 p. Only part ever published. The work
  includes genealogies (mainly 19th and 20th centuries) of a group of
  Jewish plutocratic families in Warsaw and the Kingdom of Poland.
  MH. Cited hereinafter as:
Reychman. Szkice genealogiczne.

Rose, Karl. Geschichte der Gemeinde Schöninger Juden. Schöningen,
  1959/66. 36 p. Rose studied the life and fate of 44 Schöningen
  Jewish families and, whenever possible, that of their descendants.
  Covers 18th to 20th century. DLC, MH. Cited hereinafter as:
Rose. Schöninger Juden.

Rosenstein, Neil. The Unbroken Chain: Biographical Sketches and the
  Genealogy of Illustrious Jewish Families from the 15th-20th
  Century. New York: Shengold Publishers, Inc., 1976. 716 p. Cited
  hereinafter as:
Rosenstein. Unbroken Chain.

Rothschild, Lazarus von. Det Svenska Israel: Från Aaron Isaac till
  Marcus Ehrenpreis. Stockholm: B. Wahlströme Bokförlag, 1933.
  239 p. This brief history of Jews in Sweden includes chapters on
  prominent Jewish families from the 18th century to time of
  publication. Many of these families were originally from Germany.
  Cited hereinafter as:
Rothschild. Svenska Israel.

Schnee, Heinrich. Die Hoffinanz und der moderne Staat. Geschichte
  und System der Hoffaktoren an deutschen Fürstenhöfen im Zeitalter
  des absolutismus, nach archivalischen Quellen. Berlin: Duncher &
  Humboldt, 1953-1967. 6 vols. Family studies and family
  genealogies of the prominent German "Court Jews" are indexed in
  this bibliography. CtY, IEN, MH, NN, OCH. Cited hereinafter as:
Schnee. Hoffinanz und Staat.

Schulte, Klaus H.S. Bonner Juden und ihre Nachkommen bis um 1930:
Eine familien-und sozialgeschichtliche Dokumentation. Bonn: Ludwig
Röhrscheid Verlag, 1976. 724 p. Pages 83-550 contain genealogies
of major Jewish families of Bonn through 1930. There is also a
"Verzeichnis der Personnenamen" index on pages 631-703. DLC, NIC,
NjP, NNC, OCH, ViU. Cited hereinafter as:
Schulte. Bonner Juden.

Semi-Gotha. Från Ghetton till Riddarhuset. En rasbiologisk studie
med förord av Elof Eriksson [Semi-Gotha: From Ghetto to Nobility, A
"Race Biology" Study with a Foreword By Elof Eriksson]. Stockholm:
Nationens Förlag, 1939-1941. 2 vols. Includes genealogies of
Swedish Jewish families, mainly those of the aristocracy. Many
families are of Germanic origin. Somewhat anti-Semitic in nature.
DLC, MH, NN. Cited hereinafter as:
Semi-Gotha.

Semigothaisches genealogisches Taschenbuch, aristokratisch-jüdischer
Heiraten mit Enkel-Listen (Deszendenz-Verfolgen). München:
Kyffhauser-Verlag, 1914. Includes genealogies of German Jewish
noble and other aristocratic families. This work appears
anti-Semitic in nature. Only the genealogical charts are indexed
in this bibliography. Cst, CU, DLC, NN, NNC, OCH, OU. Cited
hereinafter as:
Semigothaisches Taschenbuch.

Shapiro, Jacob Leib. Mishpachot Atikot Beyisrael [Ancient Jewish
Families]. Tel Aviv: Holiot, 1981. 414 p. Includes family
genealogies. JNUL. Cited hereinafter as:
Shapiro. Mishpachot Atikot.

Stern, Malcolm, comp. First American Jewish Families: 600
Genealogies, 1654-1977. New York: KTAV Publishing House, 1978.
419 p. Cut-off date for arrival of Jewish family in U.S. is 1840.
Includes all of their descendants, and descendants' spouses,
through 1977. The index contains 40,000 names. The foreign
city/country which is given in this bibliography indicates that of
the earliest ancestor for whom FAJF has specified the ancestor's
surname and geographic location. The Roman numeral corresponds to
title of the particular family tree, and to its relative location,
in FAJF. Thus "(IV) Hamburg" under the COHEN entry indicates that
"Cohen IV" is the title of the family tree, upon which the earliest
ancestor listed was from Hamburg, and that it is the fourth Cohen
family tree listed in FAJF, being located after "Cohen III" and
before "Cohen V." Cited hereinafter as:
Stern. FAJF.

Tänzer, Aaron. Die Geschichte der Juden in Jebenhausen und
Göppingen. Berlin: W. Kohlhammer, 1927. 573 p. "Stammbäume,"
pp. 287-388. Towns in Württemberg. Jebenhausen families are
indexed in this bibliography. DLC, ICU, MB, MH, NN, OCH. Cited
hereinafter as:
Tänzer. Juden in Jebenhausen.

————. Die Geschichte der Juden in Tirol und Vorarlberg. Teil 1
und 2: Die Geschichte der Juden in Hohenems und im übrigen
Vorarlberg. Meran: F.W. Ellmenreich's Verlag, 1905. 2 vols.
Towns are in present-day Austria. Family genealogies are indexed
in this bibliography. DLC, MH, NN, NNC, OCH, OU, WU. Cited
hereinafter as:
Tänzer. Juden in Tirol.

Universal Jewish Encyclopedia. New York: Universal Jewish
Encyclopedia Inc., 1941-1948. 10 vols. All family name entries
are indexed under "Families and Family Trees" in The Seven-Branched
Light: A Reading Guide and Index to The Universal Encyclopedia (New
York: The Universal Jewish Encyclopedia, Inc., 1944). This
bibliography, however, lists only the family names for which
neither EJ (1972) nor JE (see above) have genealogical,
biographical, or historical entries. Cited hereinafter as:
UJE.

Wolf, Lucien. "Old Anglo-Jewish Families," in his Essays in Jewish
History (London: Jewish Historical Society of England, 1934),
pp. 203-29. Cited hereinafter as:
Wolf, "Anglo-Jewish Families."

Yaoz, Chana. Album Shel Mishpachot Udmiot Yehudiot Yeduot Badorot
Ha'acharonim: Abulafia, Ohanah, Eliashar, Gordon, Michlin, Asael,
Kovalsky, Koppel-Reich, Stein. Translation: Album of Well-Known
Jewish Families and Individuals in Recent Generations (followed by
names of families). Tel-Aviv: Aked, 1976. 98 p. The book deals
with families living in Israel, pictures of individuals,
considerable biographical material, bibliography of outstanding
figures in each family across a number of generations. Page 58 is
a vertical genealogy showing the leading rabbis in 13 generations
of the Yaffe family. JNUL. Cited hereinafter as:
Yaoz. Album Shel.

Zapf, Lilli. Die Tübinger Juden: eine Dokumentation. Tübingen:
Katzmann Verlag, 1974. 288 p. Contains genealogical information
on Jewish families of Tübingen. DLC, MiU, NcU, NjP, NN, NNJ, OCH,
WU. Cited hereinafter as:
Zapf. Tübinger Juden.

Zielenziger, Kurt. Juden in deutschen Wirtschaft, 1930. Berlin:
Welt-Verlag, 1930. 287 p. This work includes chapters on
prominent Jewish banking families and financiers in Germany. All
articles on families are indexed in this bibliography. Cited
hereinafter as:
Zielenziger. Deutschen Wirtschaft.

JEWISH GENEALOGY

BIBLIOGRAPHY OF JEWISH GENEALOGIES
AND FAMILY HISTORIES

AARON
AMH has family records.
CFM has family records.
LBIS has family tree of family
of Mecklenburg.
Schnee. Hoffinanz und Staat,
1:47-77. "Die Familie
Aaron-Schulhoff-Liebman in
brandenburgisch-preussichen
Diensten." Includes
genealogical information on
family for 17th to 18th
century. See GENERAL WORKS.

AARONS
AJA has family tree from
Holland, beginning 18th
century.
AMH has family records.
Stern. FAJF. Aarons family
trees beginning in:
(I) Haarlen, Netherlands; (II
and IV) U.S.; and (III) Cape
François, Guadeloupe.

AARONSON
AMH has family records.

ABACASIS
AMH has family records.

ABAFFY
Kempelen. Magyarországi Zsidó,
2:105. See GENERAL WORKS.

ABARBANEL
See ABRAVANAL, ABRAVANEL.
AMH has family records.
CFM has family records.

ABAZ
AMH has family records.

ABECASES
AMH has family records.

ABECASIS
CFM has family records.

ABECASSIS
AMH has family records.

ABEL
LBIS has family tree.
AJA has family tree compiled by
Mrs. Joseph Abel, Washington,
D.C., 1837-1953. Typescript.
Kempelen. Magyarországi Zsidó,
3:44. See GENERAL WORKS.

ABELES
Kempelen. Magyarországi Zsidó,
2:35. See GENERAL WORKS.

ABEL-GYAGYOVSZKY
Kempelen. Magyarországi Zsidó,
2:63,64. See GENERAL WORKS.

ABELSON
AMH has family records.

ABENAKER
CFM has family records.

ABENARDUT
Cardoner Planas, Antonio and
Francisca Vendrell Gallostra.
"Aportaciones al estudio de
la familia Abenardut, médicos
reales," Sefarad 7
(1947):303-348. Family of
Spain.

ABENASER
CFM has family records.

ABENDANA
AJA has genealogical files for
Abendanone-Abendana families.
AMH has family records.
CFM has family records.
Wolf, "Anglo-Jewish Families."
See GENERAL WORKS.

ABENDANONE
Stern. FAJF. Abendanone
family tree beginning in U.S.
See GENERAL WORKS.

ABENMENASSE
Romano, David. "Los
Abenmenassé al servicio de
Pedro el Grande," in Homenaje
a Millás-Vallicrosa
(Barcelona, 1956), 2:243-92.
Aragón.

ABENSUR
CFM has family records.

ABERLE
AMH has family records.

ABISDID
CFM has family records.

ABISTID
AMH has family records.

ABOAB
EJ (1972), 2:91. Genealogical
table, 14th to 17th century.
Family of Italy, Portugal,
and Spain. See GENERAL
WORKS.
Löwenstein, Leopold. Die
Familie Aboab. Pressburg:
Druck von A. Alkalay, 1905.
41 p. Off-print from
Monatsschrift für Geschichte
und Wissenschaft des
Judentums 48 (1904):661-701;
50 (1906):374-75. NN.
Révah, I.S. "Fondo de
manuscritos pour l'histoire
des nouveaux-chretiens
portugais: la relation
généalogique d'Isaac de
Mathatias Aboab," Boletim
Internacional de Bibliografia
Luso-Brasileira 2
(abril/junho de
1961):276-312. Includes
genealogical tables and other
documents, 15th to early 18th
century.
CFM has family records.

ABONYI
Kempelen. Magyarországi Zsidó,

3:26. See GENERAL WORKS.

ABRABANEL
See ABRAVANAL, ABRAVANEL.

ABRAHAM
Abraham Family. London,
England, and Cincinnati,
Ohio. Genealogical Chart of
the Abraham and Related
Families, 1729-1947. MS and
typescript. AJA.
AMH has family records.
CAJ has family tree beginning
1804.
CFM has family records.
LBI has family tree.
Abraham, Florence K.
Genealogical files. AJA.
Abraham, Levy family,
1769-1935. Genealogical
files. AJA.
Kopp. Jüdischen Alsenz,
pp. 138-40. See GENERAL
WORKS.
Schulte. Bonner Juden, p. 83.
See GENERAL WORKS.
See Stern, FAJF (III) entry
under HENRY.
See Stern, FAJF entry under
WATERMAN.
Stern. FAJF. Abraham family
trees beginning in:
(I) London; and
(II) Portsmouth, England. See
GENERAL WORKS.

ABRAHAMFFY
Kempelen. Magyarországi Zsidó,
1:13. Abrahámffy family. See
GENERAL WORKS.

ABRAHAMS
AMH has family records.
CFM has family records.
Abrahams Family, Savannah,
Georgia, 1819-1935. Vital
statistics. AJA.
Gluckstein, Joseph.
Genealogical Tables of the
Gluckstein-Salomon-Joseph-
Abrahams Families, etc.
London: By the Author, 1925.
Stern. FAJF. Abrahams family
trees beginning in:
(I) Brest-Litovsk;

(II) Berkhoff, near Bremen;
(III, V, VI, and VII) U.S.;
and (IV) London. See GENERAL
WORKS.

ABRAHAMSEN
Fischer, Joseph. Abraham Elias
og Hans-Efterkommere
(Familien Abrahamsen) påa
Foranledning af Grosserer
Nic. Abrahamsen.
København: O. Fraenckel,
1918. 41 p. Printed as MS.
1 genealogical table. Family
of Denmark. CAJ, OCH.

ABRAHAMSON
LBIS has family tree.
Semi-Gotha, 1:122. See GENERAL
WORKS.

ABRAMS
AMH has family records.
See Stern, FAJF (III) entry
under ABRAHAMS.

ABRAMSON
JGCT has genealogy of family
originally from Ligum(?),
Lithuania.
AJA has genealogical files for
Samuel Abramson family.
Gray, Betty Anne. Manya's
Story. Minneapolis: Lerners,
1978. 127 p. An account of
the Abramson and Polevoi
families' ordeal in
Revolutionary Russia,
1917-1922. Author's mother,
Manya Polevoi Abramson
(d. 1975), and her father,
Israel Abramson, were from
the Tolne, Ukraine area and
came to U.S. in 1925. This
work includes many photos of
the Abramson and Polevoi
families. DLC.

ABRAVANAL, ABRAVANEL
EJ (1972), 2:103. Genealogical
table, 12th to 16th century.
Sephardic family names used
in Italy, Portugal, and
Spain. See GENERAL WORKS.
JE, 1:126. Family tree, 15th
to 18th century. Abarbanel,

Abravanal, Abravanel families
of England, Holland, and
Turkey. Also, EJ (1928),
1:583-88. See GENERAL WORKS.
LBIS has Abrabanel, Abravanel
family tree.
Abravanel-Mickleshanski-
Freedman-London Families,
1762-1948. Printed and
handwritten. AJA.
Blondheim, David Simon. "Notes
étymologiques et
lexicographiques," in
Mélanges de linguistiques et
de littérature offerts à M.
Alfred Jeanroy, (Paris,
1928), pp. 71-80. Includes
Abravanel name.
Margulies, Samuel Hirsch. "La
Famiglia Abravanel in
Italia," Rivista Israeltica
(Firenze) 3 (1906):97-107,
147-54.
Polacco, Bruno. "Rafanellum,"
Anuario di Studi Ebraica
(1963/64):53-63.
"The True Orthography of
Abravanel's Name," The
Menorah (New York) 27 (Nov.
1899):287-90.

ABRENSBEY
AMH has family records.

ABUDARHAM
CFM has family records.

ABUDIENTE-GIDEON
Friedman, Lee M. "Rowland
Gideon, An Early Boston Jew
and His Family," Publications
of the American Jewish
Historical Society 35
(1939):27-37.

ABULAFIA
Yaoz. Badorot Ha'acharonim.
See GENERAL WORKS.

ACHERN
Semi-Gotha, 2:15. See GENERAL
WORKS.

ACHIMAAZ
Kaufmann, David. "Der
Stammbaum des Achimaaz von

Oria," in his Ges. Schriften
(1915), 3:53.

ACKERMAN
AMH has family records.

ACSADI
Kempelen. Magyarországi Zsidó,
1:125. Acsádi family. See
GENERAL WORKS.

ACZEL
Kempelen. Magyarországi Zsidó,
1:106; 2:90; 3:34, 36. Aczél
family. See GENERAL WORKS.

ADAMS
AJA has genealogical file.
Gorin, Sadie Novich. "History
of the Novice-Adams Families,
Waco, Texas." AJA.

ADELSBERG
Kempelen. Magyarországi Zsidó,
2:61, 63. See GENERAL WORKS.

ADELSHEIMER
Tänzer. Juden in Jebenhausen,
pp. 289-90. See GENERAL
WORKS.

ADELSON
See George M. Gross entry under
GROSS. Family originally
from Minsk gubernia.

ADELSTEIN
Reychman. Szkice
genealogiczne, pp. 9-10. See
GENERAL WORKS.

ADLER
AJA has birth and marriage
records.
AMH has family records.
CFM has family records.
EJ (1972), 2:269. Genealogical
table, from Nathan Adler of
Frankfurt (d. 1707) to 1950.
English and German branches
of family only. See GENERAL
WORKS.
Adler, Marcus Nathan. The
Adler Family: An Address
Delivered at the Jewish
Institute on June 6, 1909, on

the Occasion of the Jubilee
of the Chief Rabbi Nathan
Marcus Adler. London: Office
of the Jewish Chronicle,
1909. OCH.
Adler, Robert S., comp. The
Family of Max and Sophie R.
Adler. Chicago: White Hall
Co., 1972. 177 p. History
of the Adler family of
Chicago. ICN, AJA, AJHS.
Ettlinger, Shlomo.
"Altfrankfurter jüdische
Familiennamen,"
Jüdisches/Israelistisches
Gemeindeblatt (Frankfurt am
Main, U.A.T.) 3, no. 11
(1957):7.
Fruchter, Shlomo ben Yisrael.
Egeret Shlomo. Jerusalem,
1960. 138 p. The lineage of
3 brothers: Rabbi Shlomo
Fruchter, Rabbi Mordechai
Stern, and Rabbi Avraham
Adler. JNUL.
Kempelen. Magyarországi Zsidó,
1:70, 125; 2:95; 3:83, 91,
139. See GENERAL WORKS.
Rosenstein. Unbroken Chain,
pp. 265ff. Adler descendants
of R. Jacob Shor. See
GENERAL WORKS.
Schulte. Bonner Juden, p. 83.
See GENERAL WORKS.
Wolf. "Anglo-Jewish Families."
See GENERAL WORKS.
Zapf. Tübinger Juden, p. 45.
See GENERAL WORKS.

ADLERSBERG, ADLERSBURG
Shmarler, Binyamin. Magen
Avot. Stanislawów: Grafika,
1936. 17 p. About family of
Shaul Adlersberg or
Adlersburg (d. 1810) from
Radzin, near Stanislawów,
Poland. JNUL.

ADOLPHUS
AJA has family tree beginning
Germany, 18th century.
AMH has family records.
CFM has family records.
Stern. FAJF. Adolphus family
tree beginning in Bonn,
Germany. See GENERAL WORKS.

ADRET
EJ (1928), 1:906. Family of
  Spain. See GENERAL WORKS.

ADSCHIMAN
EJ (1928), 1:919-20. Family of
  Turkey. See GENERAL WORKS.

AEHRENTHAL
Wank, Solomon. "Aehrenthal's
  Jewish Ancestry," Journal of
  Modern History 41 (Sept.
  1969):319-26. Graf Alois von
  Aehrenthal, Austro-Hungarian
  diplomat and government
  offical, 1899-1912.

AFFACHINER
CAJ has family records.

AFLALO
CFM has family records.

AGLOBLIN
CAJ has family records.

AGNEW
Burke's Peerage and Baronetage.
  Anglo-Jewish family.

AGOSTON
Kempelen. Magyarországi Zsidó,
  2:96, 97. See GENERAL WORKS.

AGUILAR, AGUILLAR
AMH has Aguilar family records.
CFM has Aguilar family records.
Kandel, Edward M. "The Arms of
  de Aguilar," Sephardi
  Bulletin 34, no. 1
  (1980):3-5.
Lehmann, Marcus. Die Familie y
  Aguillar. Frankfurt am Main:
  Sänger & Friedberg, 1922.
  2 vols. (Sänger und
  Friedberg's jüdische
  Volksbucher für Jung und Alt,
  Bd. 2.) OCH, BR.

AHARONISKY
Gabow, Lois and Beverly Murphy,
  comps. "Aharonisky,
  Saltzberg, (Shultzberg):
  Family History." Edited by
  Alvin Shultzberg.
  Philadelphia, 1982. PJAC.

AHLFELD
See Ludwig Herz entry under
  REICHENHEIM.

AHRON
CAJ has family tree from
  Germany.

AI
Leslie, Donald. "The
  Chinese-Hebrew Memorial Book
  of the Jewish Community of
  K'aifeng," Abr-Naharaîn
  (University of Melbourne,
  Australia, Dept. of Semitic
  Studies) 4 (1963/64):19-49; 5
  (1964/65):1-28; 6
  (1965/66):1-52. Includes
  family trees for the
  following clans: Ai, Chang,
  Chao, Chin, Kao, Li, Shih.
————. The Survival of the
  Chinese Jews: The Jewish
  Community of K'aifeng.
  Leiden: E.J. Brill, 1972.
  Genealogical chart of Ai
  clan, 11 generations,
  ca. 1400-1600, plate IV.

AIGNER
Kempelen. Magyarországi Zsidó,
  2:90. See GENERAL WORKS.

AILION
CFM has family records.

AINSA
Kempelen. Magyarországi Zsidó,
  1:125. See GENERAL WORKS.

AIRTH
Semi-Gotha, 1:38. See GENERAL
  WORKS.

AITKEN
AMH has family records.

AKAY
Kempelen. Magyarországi Zsidó,
  1:100. See GENERAL WORKS.

AKERHJELM
Semi-Gotha, 1:83, 87; 2:38,
  161. See GENERAL WORKS.

AKERMAN
Semi-Gotha, 1:16, 17, 92. See
GENERAL WORKS.

AKSELROD
Bick-Shauli, "Roots and
Branches." Includes
genealogy of Lyubov Isaakovna
Akselrod (b. Bunilovichi,
Vilnius Province, 1868;
d. 1946), Marxist philosopher
and literary historian. See
GENERAL WORKS.

ALAGEM
CFM has family records.

ALAPI
Kempelen. Magyarországi Zsidó,
3:64. See GENERAL WORKS.

ALATRI
CFM has family records.

ALBAHARI
Kempelen. Magyarországi Zsidó,
2:58. See GENERAL WORKS.

ALBERT
AMH has family records.

ALBO, ALBU
AMH has Albu family records.
CFM has Albu family tree.
LBI has family tree.

ALBURY
AMH has family records.

ALCAZAR
Alcázar, Baltasar de Poesías.
Madrid: Librería de los Suc.
de Hernando, 1910. Includes
a family tree of this
converso family. CU, DLC,
ICU, MH, NcD, NcU, NIC, NjR,
NN, TxU.
Pike, Ruth. "The Converso
Family of Balthasar del
Alcázar," Kentucky Romance
Quarterly 14 (1967):349-65.
Family of Spain.

ALDASSY
Kempelen. Magyarországi Zsidó,
1:69. Aldássy family. See

GENERAL WORKS.

ALDOR
Kempelen. Magyarországi Zsidó,
2:95. See GENERAL WORKS.

ALEX
AMH has family records.
CFM has family records.

ALEXANDER
Alexander Family. Genealogies
of the Alexander and Ernst
Families, 1824-1956. MS.
AJA.
AMH has family records.
CFM has family records.
Alexander, Charles C. and
Virginia W. Alexander.
Alexander Kin. Columbia,
Tenn., 1965. 173 p. NN.
Alexander, Henry Aaron. Notes
on the Alexander Family of
South Carolina and Georgia
and Connections. Atlanta,
Ga?: By the Author, 1954.
142 p. Genealogical table.
Descendants of Abraham
Alexander (1743-1816), who
settled in Charleston, S.C.,
ca. 1760. DLC, NN, OCH.
Ehrlich, Richard A. Fünf
Generationen der Familie
Alexander-Ehrlich. Cambridge,
Mass., 1964. 10 p. Family
from Rogasen and Wollestein.
MS. LBI.
Kempelen. Magyarországi Zsidó,
2:73; 3:24. See GENERAL
WORKS.
Phillips, Marcia Bowdish, comp.
Genealogies of Two Early
California Families, Selig
Alexander and Marie Levy.
N.p., 1968. 42 p.
Typescript. WJHC.
Skaller, Ulrich. The Family
History of Nicholas Paul
Alexander. London, 1972.
34 p. YIVO.
Stern. FAJF. Alexander family
trees beginning in:
(I) London, England; and
(II) England. See GENERAL
WORKS.

ALFANDARI
JE, 1:373. Genealogical table
of this Middle East family's
chief members, 17th to 18th
century. See GENERAL WORKS.

ALFAWWAL
EJ (1928), 2:281-82. See
GENERAL WORKS.

ALGAZI
EJ (1928), 2:292. Middle
Eastern family. See GENERAL
WORKS.

ALLAN
AMH has family records.

ALLATINI
CFM has family records.
Milhaud, Darius. Notes without
Music. New York: Alfred A.
Knopf, 1953. 355 p.
"Origins," pp. 3-8; "My
Childhood," pp. 9-20.
Autobiography of the French
composer (1892-1974), a
descendant of an old family
from Aix-en-Province.
Milhaud's mother, who was
born in Marseilles, was a
member of the Allatini family
which originated in Modena,
Italy.

ALLEN
AMH has family records.
Guiterman, Vida Lindo. The
Allen Ancestry: An
Illustrated Family Tree. MS.
Family tree beginning in
England, 1762. AJA.
Stern. FAJF. Allen family
tree beginning in England.
See GENERAL WORKS.

ALMANZA
CFM has family records.

ALMANZI
EJ (1928), 2:369. See GENERAL
WORKS.
JE, 1:429. "Sketch Pedigree of
the Almanzi Family, 18-19th
Centuries." Family of Italy.
See GENERAL WORKS.

Gottheil, R. "The Family
Almanzi," Jewish Quarterly
Review 5 (1893):500-505.

ALMASI
Kempelen. Magyarországi Zsidó,
3:63. Almási family. See
GENERAL WORKS.

ALMASY
Kempelen. Magyarországi Zsidó,
3:27. Almásy family. See
GENERAL WORKS.

ALMEIDA, ALMEYDA
Jewish Quarterly Review 16
(1904):opp. p. 712.
Genealogical table of Spanish
family, 16th to 17th century.

ALMOSNINO
AMH has family records.
CFM has family records.
EJ (1972), 2:668. Genealogical
table, 15th to 17th century.
Sephardic family, originating
in Spain and prominent later
in Morocco, Salonika,
Gibraltar, and England. See
GENERAL WORKS.
Carmoly, Eliakim. La famille
Almosnino. Paris, 1850.
31 p. MH, NN, OCH.

ALNAQUA
JE, 1:437. Genealogical table,
12th to 15th century. Family
first in Spain, 12th century,
and then more prominent in
Turkey and Northern Africa.
See GENERAL WORKS.

ALOOF
CFM has family records.

ALPALHAO
CFM has family records.

ALPAR
Kempelen. Magyarországi Zsidó,
1:122. Alpár family. See
GENERAL WORKS.

ALPINER
AJA has family tree.
Felsenthal Family. Family tree

of Descendants of Benjamin
Wolf Felsenthal and Agatha
Hart Felsenthal; birth
certificate of Helen Leah
Alpiner, Chicago, Ill.; "Aunt
Mimi's Story," written by
Amelia Darling Alpiner, An
Autobiography Written, June,
1967; Newspaper articles
Concerning Members of the
Alpiner Family, a Branch of
the Felsenthal family. AJA,
Box No. 955.

ALSBERG
Schulte. Bonner Juden, p. 83.
See GENERAL WORKS.
Wallach, Laura. Die Familien
Alsberg und Löwenstein.
Israel, 1964. 29 p. MS.
LBI.

ALSCHULER
Alschuler family tree,
1791-1938. AJA.

ALSTROMER
Semi-Gotha, 1:82. Alströmer
family. See GENERAL WORKS.

ALTER
Kempelen. Magyarországi Zsidó,
3:34. See GENERAL WORKS.

ALTMAN
AMH has family records.
CFM has family records.

ALTSCHUL
Asaf, S. "Megillat juḥasin
šee mišpaḥat Altsul,"
Rešumot (Tel Aviv) 4 (1947).
Hebrew genealogy.

ALTSCHULER
AJA has family tree beginning
1791.
LBI has family tree.
Straunch, Ralph. The
Altschuler Family Tree: The
Descendants of Moses and
Sarah Altschuler; A
Genealogical Survey. New
York: Ludwig-Field-Altschuler
Family Circle, 1975. NN,
YIVO.

ALVAERENGA
AMH has family records.

ALVAERES
AMH has family records.

ALVARENGA
AMH has family records.
CFM has family records.

ALVARES
AMH has family records.
CFM has family records.

ALVARES-CORREA
Alvares-Corrêa, Herbert-Marius.
The Alvares-Corrêa Families
of Curaçao and Brazil. La
Haye, 1965. AJHS.

ALVES
CFM has family records.

ALVIN
CFM has family records.

AMADIOS
AMH has family records.

AMARILLO
EJ (1928), 2:550-51. Family of
Saloniki. See GENERAL WORKS.

AMBACH
AJA has family tree beginning
in Bavaria, 1807.
Cone, Sydney M. "Cone Family
Genealogy, 1755-1974."
Genealogy of family of
Baltimore, Md., including
Herman Cone, who arrived in
Baltimore in 1845. Family
originally from Bavaria.
Deals with Ambach, Burgunder,
Cone, Frank, Guggenheimer,
and Skutch families. AJA.

AMDURSKY
Amdursky-Shamberg Family.
Papers, 1868, 1964, 1969.
1 folder. Genealogy, 1969,
and photocopies, 1868, 1964,
of information about members
of Amdursky and Shamberg
families. PJAC.

AMINOFF
Semi-Gotha, 1:80. See GENERAL
WORKS.

AMSCHEL
Schiff, Adelheid. Die Namen
der Frankfurter Juden zu
Anfang des 19. Jahrhunderts.
Inaug. Dissertation ...
Universität Freiburg.
Freiburg, 1917. 81 p.
Includes genealogical table
of Amschel family.

AMSTER
Viertel, Salka. The Kindness
of Strangers. New York:
Holt, Rinehart and Winston,
1969. 338 p. Autobiography.
Information concerning
Amster, Rafalovicz, and
Steuermann families of
Czernowitz and Sambor near
the town of Wychylowka in
Galicia, pp. 1-9 especially.

ANAKLET
JFF, no. 23. Family history.

ANAW
EJ (1928), 2:789. Genealogical
table, 11th to 14th century.
See GENERAL WORKS.
JE, 1:566-67. Two genealogical
tables of Italian family,
11th to 19th century. See
GENERAL WORKS.

ANCKER
Stern. FAJF. Ancker family
tree beginning in England.
See GENERAL WORKS.

ANCONA
AMH has family records.
CFM has family records.

ANDAHAZY-KASNYA
Kempelen. Magyarországi Zsidó,
3:63. Andaházy-Kasnya
family. See GENERAL WORKS.

ANDERSON
AMH has family records.

ANDRADE
AMH has family records.
CFM has family records.

ANDREWS
AJA has family tree beginning
1753. Stern. FAJF. Andrews family
trees beginning in: (I and
II) U.S. See GENERAL WORKS.

ANDRIESSE
JNUL has family trees (in Dutch
and English) of family from
Brabant, a province of
Holland.
"Het Geslacht Andriesse," Gens
Vostra (Amsterdam), no. 8/9
(1975):237-46; no. 10
(1975):292-98.

ANES
CFM has family records.

ANGEL
AMH has family records.
EJ (1928), 2:830-33. Family of
Turkey and Palestine. See
GENERAL WORKS.

ANGELI
CAJ has family records.

ANGELO
AMH has family records.

ANGERTHAL
LBI has family tree.

ANGYAL
Kempelen. Magyarországi Zsidó,
2:15; 3:33. See GENERAL
WORKS.

ANHAUCH
LBI has family tree.

ANHORI
EJ (1928), 2:945-46. Family of
North Africa. See GENERAL
WORKS.

ANKERBERG
PD has family records.

ANNENBERG
Cooney, John. The Annenbergs:
The Salvaging of a Tainted
Dynasty. New York: Simon &
Schuster, 1982. 428 p.
Descendants of Tobias and
Moses Annenberg (1878-1942).
Tobias came to U.S. from
Kalwichen, hamlet of East
Prussia, in 1882.

ANSCHEL
Auerbach, Siegfried Moritz,
comp. The Descendants of
Herz Anschel of Bonn. London,
1964. 57 p. Genealogical
tables. DLC.
Schulte. Bonner Juden, p. 83.
See GENERAL WORKS.

ANSEL
AMH has family records.

ANSELL
AMH has family records.
CFM has family records.

ANTAL
Kempelen. Magyarországi Zsidó,
3:71. See GENERAL WORKS.

ANTHONES
CFM has family records.

ANTICI-MATTEI
Kempelen. Magyarországi Zsidó,
1:44. See GENERAL WORKS.

ANTOKOLSKI
CAJ has family records.

ANYOS
Kempelen. Magyarországi Zsidó,
3:91. See GENERAL WORKS.

ANZALAK
AMH has family records.

APFALTERN
Kempelen. Magyarországi Zsidó,
1:51. See GENERAL WORKS.

APFEL
AMH has family records.
Kempelen. Magyarországi Zsidó,
3:65. See GENERAL WORKS.

Schulte. Bonner Juden,
p. 91. See GENERAL WORKS.

APPEL
LBI has family tree.
Phillips, Marcia Bowdish, comp.
"Genealogies of Two Early
California Families--Selig
Alexander and Marie Levy;
Nathan Davis, and Rosa
Appel." WJHC.
Schulte. Bonner Juden, p. 93.
See GENERAL WORKS.

APPELZWEIG
CAJ has family tree of family
from Hungary.

APPLEYART
AMH has family records.

APPONYI
Ello, Anton. "Interessantes
aus dem Stammbaum der
gräflichen Häuser Apponyi und
Klebelsberg," Jüdisches
Archiv 2, no. 5 (1929):3-4.

APT, APTA
AJHS has eulogy of Shmuel Shaul
Apt, grandfather of Samuel
Apt Marks (b. 1903), "showing
descendancy from both 'The
Apter Tsadik' (Heschel?) and
'RASHBAM' (and therefore,
'RASHI')."
LBI has family tree.
Rosenstein. Unbroken Chain,
pp. 512ff. Genealogical
chart. See GENERAL WORKS.

ARANYI
Kempelen. Magyarországi Zsidó,
1:69; 2:122; 3:71. Arányi
family. See GENERAL WORKS.

ARBIB
Raccah, Babriele di Vittorio.
Appunti per un archivi delle
famiglie ebraiche della Libia
"Arbib." S.l., n.d.,
(1944?). 21, 2 p. OCH.

ARCH-SMITH
AMH has family records.

ARDIT, ARDITE, ARDITI
EJ (1928), 3:300-303. See
  GENERAL WORKS.

ARDUT
EJ (1928), 3:304-5. Family of
  Spain. See GENERAL WORKS.

AREDES
CFM has family records.

ARENDT
Young-Bruehl, Elizabeth. Hannah
  Arendt: For Love of the
  World. New Haven: Yale
  University Press, 1982.
  563 p. Especially, pp. 5-26.
  Arendt (1906-1975) was born
  in Königsberg, East Prussia
  (now Kaliningrad, U.S.S.R.),
  the daughter of Paul
  (d. 1913) and Martha Cohn
  Arendt and the granddaughter
  of Max (d. 1913) and Joanna
  Arendt and Jacob Cohn
  (1838-1906).

ARENSBERG
Schulte. Bonner Juden, p. 100.
  See GENERAL WORKS.

ARIA
AMH has family records.
CFM has family records.

ARIAS
CFM has family records.

ARMSTRONG
AMH has family records.

ARNDT
See Ludwig Herz entry under
  REICHENHEIM.

ARNHEIM
Ballin. Juden in Seesen,
  p. 155. See GENERAL WORKS.

ARNHOLD
LBI has family tree.

ARNIM
Semigothaisches Taschenbuch.
  Genealogical table 1. See
  GENERAL WORKS.

ARNOLD
AJA has family tree beginning
  18th century.
AMH has family records.
Arnold, Edward, Brooklyn, N.Y.
  "Recollections of the Early
  20th Century in the Life and
  Times of Edward Arnold."
  Autobiography and family
  history, 1978. Typescript
  and Xerox copies. AJA.
Stern. FAJF. Arnold family
  tree beginning in Ibenhausen,
  Württemberg. See GENERAL
  WORKS.
Tänzer. Juden in Jebenhausen,
  pp. 291-95. See GENERAL
  WORKS.
Zapf. Tübinger Juden, pp.
  123-25. See GENERAL WORKS.

ARNOLDSON
Semi-Gotha, 1:147. See GENERAL
  WORKS.

ARNSTEIN
AMH has family records.
EJ (1928), 3:489. Genealogical
  table, 18th to 19th century.
  Family of court purveyors and
  financiers in Vienna. See
  GENERAL WORKS.
Grünwald, Max. Zur
  Familiengeschichte einiger
  Gründer der wiener Chewra
  Kadischa. Die Familie
  Arnstein. Wien, 1910. 19 p.
  Off-print from Mitteilungen
  zur jüdischen Volkskunde,
  Heft 33.
———. "Familienurkunden und
  Stammtafelframente zur
  Geschichte der Familie
  Arnstein-Eskeles-Daniel
  Itzig," JFF, no. 1.
Heinrich, Gerd, genealogist.
  Die Grafen von Arnstein.
  Köln: Böhlau, 1961. 568 p.
  (Mitteldeutsche Forschungen,
  21.) Includes genealogical
  tables. CU, DLC, ICU, MH,
  NIC, NjP, NN, NNC, WU.
Jäger-Sunstenau, Hanns. "Der
  genealogische Hintergrund des
  Bankhauses Arnstein & Eskeles
  in Wien," Veröffentlichungen

des Verbandes österr.
Geschichtsvereine (Wien) 22
(1979):300-304.
Spiel, Hilde. Fanny von
Arnstein oder die
Emanzipation. Ein
Frauenleben ander
Zeitenwende, 1758-1818.
Frankfurt: S. Fischer, 1962.
537 p. Includes genealogical
table for Arnstein, Itzig,
and Pereira families. CLU,
CST, MH, MnU, MWalB, NcU,
NjR, NIC, NN, NNC, OU, WU.

ARON
AMH has family records.
Aron Family, New Orleans.
Genealogical Information on
the Aron and Schwabacher
Families, 1700-1964. MS.
AJA.
Kempelen. Magyarországi Zsidó,
1:7. See GENERAL WORKS.

ARONSBURG
AMH has family records.

ARONSON
AJA has genealogical files.
Aronson-Rosenthal Family
Papers, 1878-   . Include
Solomon Rosenthal-David
Aronson Family Tree. WJHC.
Aronson, Chaim. A Jewish Life
under the Tsars: The
Autobiography of Chaim
Aronson, 1825-1888.
Translated from the Original
Hebrew and Edited by Norman
Marsden. Totowa, N.J.:
Allanheld, Osmun and Co.,
Publishers, 1983. 352 p. The
author (1825-1893) was born
in Serednike on the rivers
Nieman and Dubsia between
Yurburg and Kovno, the son of
Aaron [Aronson or Ashkenazi]
and the grandson of Mendel
Ashkenazi. Chaim Aronson was
an inventor, clockmaker, and
photographer, and lived or
studied in Vilna,
St. Petersburg, and Telz
(Telsiai) before emigrating
to U.S. in 1888.

ARONSTEIN
Aronstein, Fritz. Stammbaum
der Familie Aronstein aus
Büren. Groitzsch, 1929.
16 p. Seven family trees
contain 648 descendants of
Aron b. Samuel (b. Büren,
Westfalen, ca. 1730). DLC,
NN.
————. "Die Familie
Aronstein," JFF, no. 25
(1931):338-44.
Aronstein, Raphael Fritz.
"Philipp Aronstein.
4. Dezember 1862 bis
24. September 1942."
Nahariya, Israel, 1944.
182 p. English language
philologist who was murdered
at Theresienstadt. The work
has brief genealogy of
Philipp Aronstein's family,
from beginning of the 18th
century. Family originally
from Büren/Westfalen. LBI.
Braun, Siegfried. "Aus der
Geschichte einer
westfalischen Familie
(Aronstein in Büren),"
Mitteilungsblatt
Wochenzeitung des Irgun Olej
Merkas Europa (Vereinigung
der Einwanderer aus
Mitteleuropa,
Tel-Aviv-Deutschsprachiges
Wochenblatt in Tel-Aviv)
vom. 1, vol. 25, no. 44
(Nov. 1957):4.

ARRHENIUS
Semi-Gotha, 1:22. See GENERAL
WORKS.

ARROW
AMH has family records.

ARTHNER
Kempelen. Magyarországi Zsidó,
1:101. See GENERAL WORKS.

ARTHUR
AMH has family records.

ASAEL
Yaoz. Badorot Ha'acharonim.
See GENERAL WORKS.

ASBOTH
See TOTHVARADJAY-ASBOTH.

ASCH
LBI has family tree beginning
1495.
[Berliner, Abraham]. Zur
Familiengeschichte Asch ...
Ein 200 jähriges Gedenkblatt
(1713-1913). Berlin: Druck
von H. Itzkowski, 1913. 16 p.
Notes on the descendants of
Meyer b. Josef, who removed
in 1713 from Meseritz, Posen,
to Stargard (Pommern), and of
Leiser Asch, Rabbi in Brätz,
1800. MH, NN, PP, YIVO.
Stern. FAJF. Asch family tree
beginning in Poland. See
GENERAL WORKS.

ASCHER
LBI has family tree beginning
1801. Family of Poland and
Germany.
Ascher, Charles S. Family
Reminiscences of Charles S.
Ascher of New York Written in
France, August 12, 1967, for
Norton B. Stern. France,
1967. Typescript. 6 p.
Leaves 5 and 6 contain family
genealogical chart. Charles
Stern Ascher (b. New York,
1899; d. ?), a public
administrator, the son of
Ernest and Josephine Ascher.
AJA.
Freimann, Alfred. "Die
Ascheriden (1267-1391),"
Jahrbuch der
Jüd.-literarischen
Gesellschaft 13
(1920):142-254.
Gold. Juden Mährens,
pp. 547-48. Ascher family
from Triesch. See GENERAL
WORKS.

ASCHERSON
CFM has family records.

ASCHKENASY
Teutsch, Albert. Geschichte d.
Juden d. Gemeinde Venningen
in Baden, bes. d. Familie

Teutsch, 1590-1936.
Karlsruhe, 1936. 112, 23 pp.
13 trees. Descendants of
Gerson Aschkenasy. LBI.

ASCHNER
Kempelen. Magyarországi Zsidó,
2:38. See GENERAL WORKS.

ASCOLI
AMH has family records.

ASHENHEIM
AMH has family records.

ASHER
AMH has family records.
CFM has family records.

ASHKENASI
EJ (1928), 3:461-93. See
GENERAL WORKS.
JFF, no. 21. Family tree.

ASHKENAZI
See Chaim Aronson entry under
ARONSON.
Rosenstein. Unbroken Chain,
pp. 456ff. See GENERAL
WORKS.

ASHTON
AMH has family records.

ASIMOV
Asimov, Isaac. In Memory Yet
Green: The Autobiography of
Isaac Asimov, 1920-1954. New
York: Doubleday, 1979. 732
p. "My Birthplace," pp. 3-7;
"My Ancestors," pp. 8-17; "My
Parents," pp. 18-29. Family
from Petrovichi, 75 miles
west of Mogilyov and 55 miles
north of Smolensk on the
Upper Dnieper River. Spelling
was changed from Azimov to
Asimov in U.S.

ASPINALL
AMH has family records.

ASSER
AMH has family records.
CFM has family records.

ASSER-LEVIN
Feilchenfeldt, K. "Die
Beziehungen der Familie Carel
und Rose Asser-Levin zu ihren
Berliner Verwandten," Studia
Rosenthaliana 4
(1970):181-212.

ASSON
AMH has family records.

ASTRUC
JE, 2:253. "Genealogical Tree
of the Astruc Family." French
and Spanish family, 17th to
19th century. See GENERAL
WORKS.

ASYL
LBI has family tree beginning
1740.

ATHERSTONE
See GRABOWSKY-ATHERSTONE.

ATHIAS
Athias Family. "Genealogical
Chart of the Athias-Robles
Family." 1971. AJA.
CFM has family records.

ATKINSON
AMH has family records.

ATLAS
Chelminsky-Lajmer, "Jewish
Surnames." See GENERAL
WORKS.

ATTEMS
Kempelen. Magyarországi Zsidó,
1:52. See GENERAL WORKS.

ATWELL
AMH has family records.

ATZEL
Kempelen. Magyarországi Zsidó,
1:43. Atzél family. See
GENERAL WORKS.

AUBER
Kempelen. Magyarországi Zsidó,
1:74. See GENERAL WORKS.

AUER
Auer Family, Cincinnati, Ohio.
Family Tree, 1826-1964.
Typescript; printed. AJA.
Kempelen. Magyarországi Zsidó,
1:101; 2:58; 3:106. See
GENERAL WORKS.
Klein, Stanley S. "Auer Family
Tree." Cincinnati?, 1966?
36 p. Allen County Public
Library, Fort Wayne, Indiana.

AUERBACH
AMH has family records.
Auerbach Family. Family Tree,
1800-1950. Typescript. AJA.
CAJ has family trees from
Germany, 1740-1954.
EJ (1972), 3:841-42.
Genealogical table of
descendants of David Tevele
Auerbach, 1575 of Vienna to
20th century. Includes
Austrian and German branches.
See GENERAL WORKS.
EJ (1928), 3:648-64.
Descendants of Moses Auerbach
of Hessen-Darmstadt. See
GENERAL WORKS.
JE, 2:305. Descendants of Juda
Loeb Rofe, Rabbi of Cracow,
16th to 19th century. See
GENERAL WORKS.
LBI has family trees beginning
1600 and 1745.
Auerbach, Jerold. How Goodly
Are Thy Tents O Jacob: The
Auerbach Family in History.
N.p., 1978. 24 p. Family of
Jacob Auerbach, who died in
Pittsburgh in 1923.
Auerbach, Siegfried Moritz. The
Auerbach Family: The
Descendants of Abraham
Auerbach. London: Perry
Press Producations, 1957.
171 p.
————. ————. Supplement.
London?, 1960-1965. 3 vols.
MH, NN, NNJ, OCH.
Fraenkel, Abraham Adolf.
Lebenskreise. Aus den
Erinnerungen eines jüdischen
Mathematikers. Stuttgart:
Deutsche Verlagsanstalt,
1967. 207 p. "Meine

Vorfahren," pp. 13-55.
Genealogical information on
the Auerbach, Fraenkel, and
Neuburger relatives of the
author (1891-1965) who was
born in Munich. His
relatives were from Fürth,
Nürnberg, and Munich. Abraham
Fraenkel's father was Sigmund
Fraenkel (1860-1925),
grandfather was Wilhelm
[Wolf] Fraenkel (1830-1907),
and great-grandfather was
Abraham Fraenkel (1792-1858).
CSt, DLC, NIC, NjP.
Hirsch, Joseph. R. Binyamin
Hirsch. Jerusalem, 1947.
91 p. Includes genealogical
tables. Benjamin Hirsch,
1840-1911; Benjamin Hirsch
Auerbach, 1808-1872. Family
of Halberstadt. DLC, NN.
Kempelen. Magyarországi Zsidó,
2:86. See GENERAL WORKS.
Rosenstein. Unbroken Chain,
pp. 433ff. See GENERAL
WORKS.
Schulte. Bonner Juden, p. 101.
See GENERAL WORKS.
Seckbach, Markus. Eine
Ahnentafel von 27
Generationen bis zum Jahre
1290. Betr. die Familien
Seckbach, Meyer, Auerbach,
Hirsch, Marx. Bodenheimer u.
a. Hamburg: Laubhutte, 1936.
22 p. OCH.

AUGENFELD
Kempelen. Magyarországi Zsidó,
3:85. See GENERAL WORKS.

AUSCHER
CAJ has family tree.

AUSLANDER
Kempelen. Magyarországi Zsidó,
1:46, 128, 138; 3:69.
Ausländer family. See
GENERAL WORKS.

AUSPITZ
LBI has family tree beginning
1663.
Kempelen. Magyarországi Zsidó,
2:96, 97. See GENERAL WORKS.

Winter, Josefine. Fünfzig
Jahre eines wiener Hauses.
Wien: W. Braumöller, 1927.
104 p. Includes genealogical
tables. ICarbS, MH, MnU, NN.

AUSTEN
AMH has family records.

AUSTERLITZ
Kempelen. Magyarországi Zsidó,
2:8, 9, 10; 3:102. See
GENERAL WORKS.
Munkácsi, Bernát. A Nyitrai,
Magyváradi És Budapesti
Munk-Család Valamint A
Nyitrai, Nagytapolcsányi,
Balassagyarmati,
Nagykanizsai, Szentesi És
Budapesti Felsenberg-Család
Genealógiája: Ösök És
Ivadékok. Budapest:
F. Gerwürcz, 1939. 230 p.
Includes Austerlitz,
Felsenberg, Lerner, Munk,
Spitz, Stein, and Weisz
families of Hungary. JNUL,
MH.

AUSTIN
AMH has family records.

AUTOR
CAJ has family records.

AVELLIS
Stammbaum der Familie des Jacob
Levin Levinstein, 1772-1820,
Märk Friedland. By the
Author, 1910. Hereinafter
cited as Stammbaum
Levinstein. Includes
Avellis, Haac, Hunefeld,
Klein-Chevalier, Lehmann,
Riess, and Wolff families.

AVES
Samuel, E.R. "Portuguese Jews
in Jacobean London,"
Transactions of the Jewish
Historical Society of England
18 (1958):181. Pedigree
chart of Anglo-Jewish Aves
family.

AVIGDOR
AMH has family records.
Pribłuda, A.S. "Imia i
familiia Perez ... Avigdor,"
(In Russian.) Onomastica 18
(1973):261-65.

AVILA
AMH has family records.
Cantera Burgos, Francisco.
Pedraria Dávila y Cota,
capitán general y gobernador
de Castilla del Oro y
Nicaragua: Sus antecedents
judíos.... Madrid:
Universidad de Madrid,
Cátedra de Lengua Hebrea e
Historia de los Judíos, 1971.
44 p. 16th and 17th
centuries. DLC.
CFM has family records.

AYLING
AMH has family records.

AYRE
AMH has family records.

AYRTON
AMH has family records.

AZARIA DE FANO
Kaufmann, David. "Menachem
Azaria de Fano et sa
famille," Revue des Études
Juives 35 (1897):84-90.

AZEBI
CFM has family records.

AZIMOV
See ASIMOV.

AZRIEL
Gaon, Moshe David. 9 Dorot
Le-Mishpachat Azriel
Beyerushalaim, 1725-1950.
Jerusalem: Azriel Press,
1950. 160 p. Includes
genealogy of the nine
generations of the family in
Jerusalem. JNUL.

AZUBY
Stern. FAJF. Azuby family

tree beginning in Holland.
See GENERAL WORKS.

AZULAI
EJ (1972), 3:1017. Genealogical
table of the descendants of
Mordecai Azulai, 1500 to 19th
century. Family of scholars
and Kabbalists of Castilian
origin which settled in Fez,
Hebron, and Jerusalem after
their expulsion from Spain.
See GENERAL WORKS.
EJ (1928), 3:805-6. See
GENERAL WORKS.
JE, 2:375-77. Includes
genealogical table. See
GENERAL WORKS.

AZULAY
CFM has family records.

BAAZOV
Baazov, Faina. Prokazhennie.
(In Russian.) Hebrew title:
Hametsoraim. Hebrew edition
by Davida Carol. Cherikover,
1979. 214 p. Describes the
experiences of Baazov family
which helped found the
Zionist movement in the
Russian area of Georgia. CZA.

BABAD
Rosenstein. Unbroken Chain,
pp. 409ff. Genealogical
chart. See GENERAL WORKS.

BABICZ
YIVO has chart of family of
Warsaw.

BABIN
Raphael, Marc L. A Family
Story: Fifty Years in Los
Angeles. Los Angeles, 1964.
Typescript. iii, 36, (6) p.
AJA. Includes Babin family.

BABITZKY
CAJ has family records.

BACH
AJA has family tree beginning
1854.
LBI has family trees beginning
1540, 1726, and 1730.
Bach, H.J. "Zur Geschichte
einer schwäbisch-jüdischen
Familie," in
Pessach-Festschrift, 5731,
April/Nissan 5731
(Israelitsche
Religiongemeinschaft
Württemburg), Stuttgart,
1971, pp. 26-28.
————. ————, in Rosh
Hashana, 5732/1971
(Israelitsche
Religionsgemeinschaft
Württemburg), Stuttgart,
1971, pp. 37-49.
Stern. FAJF. Bach family tree
beginning in Germany. See
GENERAL WORKS.

BACHARACH, BACHRACH
AMH has Bachrach family
records.
CFM has Bacharach family tree.
Keneseth Israel. Includes
Bachrach family information.
See GENERAL WORKS.
Birnbaum, Walter. Stammbaum
der Familie Birnbaum.
Frankfurt am Main-London,
1938. Also contains
information on Bachrach
family.
Eisenstadt and Wiener.
Da'at-kedoschim. See GENERAL
WORKS.
Flesch, Heinrich. "Die Familie
Bachrach in Wien, Trebitsch,
Triesch und Kanitz," ZGJT 2
(1931/32):229-35.
Kaufmann, David. "Jair Chayim
Bacharach, A Biographical
Sketch (1638-1702)," in
Arthur Ellis Franklin's
Records of the Franklin
Family and Collaterals
(London: G. Routledge, 1915),
pp. 127-66. The Franklins
are descended from Bacharach
family. CLU, MH, NN, TxU.
————. "Die Kinder R. Jair
Chajjim Bacharach," MGWJ 43

(1899):37-48. I. Tobias
ben Joseph Solomon Bacharach,
d. 1659. II. Löw ben
Bezalel, d. 1609.
————. R. Jair Chajjim
Bacharach (1638-1702) und
seine Ahnen. Trier: S.
Mayer, 1894. 139 p. (Zur
geschichte jüdischer
familien, 2). A genealogical
study of Rabbi Löw's
descendants. DLC, NN, OCH,
PP, PPDrop.
Kempelen. Magyarországi Zsidó.
Bacharach family, 1:120, 121;
Bachrach family, 1:20. See
GENERAL WORKS.
Rose. Schöninger Juden. See
GENERAL WORKS.
"Stammreihe," in Wiener
Genealogisches Taschenbuch, 8
(1937).

BACHER
LBI has family tree beginning
1799.
Kempelen. Magyarországi Zsidó,
1:90, 100, 120; 2:13. See
GENERAL WORKS.

BACHMAN
Tänzer. Juden in Tirol,
p. 685. See GENERAL WORKS.

BACHMANN
AJA has family tree in German.
LBI has family tree beginning
1790.

BACHRACH
See BACHARACH, BACHRACH.

BACHRUCH
Kempelen. Magyarországi Zsidó,
1:119. See GENERAL WORKS.

BACHSCHUTZ
Kempelen. Magyarországi Zsidó,
1:111. Bachschütz family.
See GENERAL WORKS.

BACK
Hajdu, Miklós. Szeniczei
Savuót; A Hönig-Hönig-és
Backcsalád Történetéböl.
Budapest: Mult és jövö, 1939.

110 p. Includes genealogical
table and bibliography.
Family of Hungary. JNUL.
Kempelen. Magyarországi Zsidó,
1:56, 57, 127; 2:101; 3:140,
59. See GENERAL WORKS.

BACRI
Eisenbeth, M. "Les juifs en
Algérie et en Tunisie à
l'époque turque (1516-1830),"
Revue Africaine 96
(1952):372-84. On Bacri and
Busnach families.
Hildesheimer, Françoise.
"Grandeur et décadence de la
Maison Bacri de Marseille,"
Revue des Études Juives 136,
no. 3/4 (1977):389-414.

BADCHAN
See BADHAN (BADCHAN).

BADDELEY
AMH has family records.

BADER
CAJ has family records.

BADHAN (BADCHAN)
Lowe, Heinrich. "The Name
Badḥan," (In Hebrew.)
Yeda'-'am no. 31/32
(1967):66-71.

BADT
Baehr, Jacob. "Badt," JFF,
no. 21 (1930):222.
Klibansky, Erich. "Zum
Stammbaum der Familie Badt,"
JFF, no. 14 (1928):35-37.

BAECK
LBI has family tree beginning
1785.
Bato, Y.L. "Vorfahren und
Familienangehörige von
Rabbiner Dr. Leo Baeck,"
Zeitschrift für die
Geschichte der Juden (Tel
Aviv), no. 1/2
(Apr. 1965):65-68.
Biermann, Hildegard. "Vorfahren
und Familiengehörige von
Rabbiner Dr. Leo Baeck:
Berichtigung und

Erganzungen," Zeitschrift für
die Geschichte der Juden (Tel
Aviv) 4 (1967):257.

BAER
Baer Family, St. Louis, Mo.
Family History, 1972.
Typescript. AJA. Begins in
1787.
JGCT has two family trees.
LBI has family tree beginning
1600 and 1785.
Ettlinger, Shlomo.
"Altfrankfurter jüdische
Familiennamen,"
Jüdisches/Israelistisches
Gemeindeblatt (Frankfurt am
Main, U.A.T.) 3, no. 11
(1957):7.
Homeyer, Fritz. Deutsche Juden
als Bibliographilen und
Antiquare. Tübingen: Mohr,
1963. 151 p. Includes the
antiquarian bookseller family
of Baer from Frankfurt,
pp. 27-28. DLC, MH, NN, OCH.
Schwarz, Friedrich Hermann.
"Zur Geschichte der Firma
Joseph Baer & Co.
(1785-1944)," Antiquariat
(Frankfurt am Main) 29, no. 9
(1973):A415-A418.

BAERWALD
Baerwald, Lesser. Geschichte
des Hauses Baerwald.
Festschrift zur goldenen
Hochzeit von Lesser und
Pauline Baerwald. Nakel, 17.
März 1913. Nakel, 1913.
112 p. Family tree begins
with 1770. LBI, YIVO.

BAGGE
Semi-Gotha, 1:30, 112; 2:16.
See GENERAL WORKS.

BAGHY
Kempelen. Magyarországi Zsidó,
3:79. See GENERAL WORKS.

BAGRATIDEN
JFF, nos. 32 and 34. Family
histories.

BAGSHAW
AMH has family records.

BAHR
Semi-Gotha, 1:152. See GENERAL
WORKS.

BAIERSDORF
Kempelen. Magyarországi Zsidó,
3:138. See GENERAL WORKS.

BAINES
AMH has family records.

BAIRD
AMH has family records.

BAJOR
See Kempelen entry under BAYOR.

BAK
See BACK.
Kempelen. Magyarországi Zsidó,
3:107. See GENERAL WORKS.

BAKACH-BESSENYEY
Kempelen. Magyarországi Zsidó,
1:45. Bakách-Bessenyey
family. See GENERAL WORKS.

BAKER
AMH has family records.

BAKONYI
Kempelen. Magyarországi Zsidó,
3:118. See GENERAL WORKS.

BALAKLEISKY
See BELKOV.

BALAS
Kempelen. Magyarországi Zsidó,
3:34. Balás family. See
GENERAL WORKS.

BALASHAZI, BALASHAZY
Kempelen. Magyarországi Zsidó,
3:93. Balásházi, Balásházy
family. See GENERAL WORKS.

BALAZS
Kempelen. Magyarországi Zsidó,
3:30, 61. Balázs family. See
GENERAL WORKS.

BALINT
Kempelen. Magyarországi Zsidó,
3:114. Bálint family. See
GENERAL WORKS.

BALKANYI
Kempelen. Magyarországi Zsidó,
2:59; 3:87. Balkányi family.
See GENERAL WORKS.

BALL
Ball-Kaduri, Kurt. Jüdisches
Leben einst und jetzt das
Calaver Judenhaus; erlebtes
Israel. München: Ner-Tamid
Verlag, 1961. 128 p.
Includes genealogical
information on Ball family.
LBI, MH, NIC, OCH.

BALLA
Kempelen. Magyarországi Zsidó,
3:123. See GENERAL WORKS.

BALLAGI
Kempelen. Magyarországi Zsidó,
3:97. See GENERAL WORKS.

BALLIN
AJA has family tree.
AMH has family records.
CAJ has family tree.
CFM has family records.
Ballin, Gerhard. "Die Familie
des Hamburger Reeders Albert
Ballin und ihre Herkunft,"
Norddeutsche Familienkunde
26, no. 11 (juli-sept.
1977):65-69.
Ballin, Jakob Moritz. "Der
Familienname Ballin," JFF,
no. 5 (1926):113-14.
Ballin, Oscar. Die Familie
Ballin mit besonderer
Berücksichtigung ihres
Hannoverisch-Braunschweigisch
n Zweiges. Gandersheim,
1913. 74 p. LBI, PPDrop.
Cohn, John Magnus. The Cohn
Family Tree. Swan Hill,
Australia: n.p., Mar. 1963.
32 p. Genealogical table,
1751-1962. Lists over 400
relatives. Cohn family is
related to Ballin family of
Denmark. Four Cohn brothers

migrated to Australia from
Denmark in the mid-19th
century. CAJ, Call No. 1676.
Neumann, Norbert Collection,
York, Pa. "Genealogies of
the Ballin, Lazarus, Schäfer,
and Neumann Families, 11th
Century to Date." AJA.
Rothschild, Samson. "Die
Familie Ballin," Heimat am
Rhein, no. 3 (2.7.1927):18.
————. "Die Familie Ballin,"
Vom Rheim 13 (1914):7.

BALSER
JGCT has family tree for family
originally of Ligum?,
Lithuania.

BALTZAN
Baltzan, P. Ha'olam
She-neḫerav (The World That
Was Destroyed). Vol. 1
title: Ner Neshama. Herzelia,
Israel, 1965. 327 p.
Includes genealogy fold-out
chart of Baltzan family from
Kishinev, Bessarabia.

BALVANYI
Kempelen. Magyarországi Zsidó,
2:47. Bálványi family. See
GENERAL WORKS.

BAMBERGER
CAJ has family tree, 1692-1933.
LBI has family tree beginning
1561.
Bamberger, Elisabeth. Die
Geschichte und Erlebnisse
unserer Familie während der
Hitlerzeit in Deutschland.
N.P., n.D. 196 p. Family of
Frankfurt-am-Main. Some of
the family fled to South
America in 1940. LBI.
Bamberger Family: The
Descendants of Rabbi Seligman
Bär Bamberger the "Würzberger
Rav" (1807-1878). 2d ed.
Jerusalem: The Bamberger
Family, 1979. 112, 56 p.
Kempelen. Magyarországi Zsidó,
1:40; 3:36, 74, 101. See
GENERAL WORKS.
Stern. FAJF. Bamberger family

tree beginning in Hessdorf,
Bavaria. See GENERAL WORKS.
Stern-Bamberger Families.
"Genealogical Chart of the
Ancestors of Morris Stern and
the descendants of both Stern
and His Wife, Mathilda
Bamberger, Compiled and
Charted by Howard Stern,
grandson of Morris Stern,
Germany, Delaware, and
Philadelphia, Pa., Feb. 16,
1973." AJA.

BAMMERSCHLAG
Kempelen. Magyarországi Zsidó,
2:9. See GENERAL WORKS.

BAN
Kempelen. Magyarországi Zsidó,
3:35. Bán family. See
GENERAL WORKS.

BANARRABI
CAJ has family tree.

BANETH
Brilling, Bernhard. "The Name
'Baneth,'" (In Hebrew.)
Yeda'-'am 1, no. 10
(1953):99-101.
Kempelen. Magyarországi Zsidó,
1:90. See GENERAL WORKS.

BANO
Kempelen. Magyarországi Zsidó,
1:96. Bánó family. See
GENERAL WORKS.

BANOCZI
Kempelen. Magyarországi Zsidó,
1:115-16. Bánóczi family.
See GENERAL WORKS.

BANYAI
Kempelen. Magyarországi Zsidó,
3:58. Bányai family. See
GENERAL WORKS.

BAR
LBI has family tree beginning
1787.
"Isascher Bär, gen. Behrend
Cohnen, Gründer der Clause in
Hamburg und seine Kinder,"
MGWJ, 1896, p. 220.

BARABAS
Kempelen. Magyarországi Zsidó,
2:39. Barabás family. See
GENERAL WORKS.

BARACH
Kempelen. Magyarországi Zsidó,
2:96, 130. See GENERAL
WORKS.

BARACK
AMH has family records.

BARACS
Kempelen. Magyarországi Zsidó,
2:96. See GENERAL WORKS.

BARASCH
AJA has genealogical files.
Barasch Family. "Genealogical
Charts, 1815-1976."
Birmingham, Alabama, 1976.
AJA.
CAJ has family records.

BARAT
Kempelen. Magyarországi Zsidó,
1:62; 3:37. Barát family.
See GENERAL WORKS.

BARBANELLO
Kempelen. Magyarországi Zsidó,
1:92. See GENERAL WORKS.

BARBARIN
Kempelen. Magyarországi Zsidó,
1:73. See GENERAL WORKS.

BARCLAY
AMH has family records.
Semi-Gotha, 1:39. See GENERAL
WORKS.

BARCSAI
Kempelen. Magyarországi Zsidó,
2:126. See GENERAL WORKS.

BARCZA
Kempelen. Magyarországi Zsidó,
3:95. See GENERAL WORKS.

BARCZUOSKY
AMH has family records.

BARD
Kempelen. Magyarországi Zsidó,

3:37. Bárd family. See
GENERAL WORKS.

BARDEN
De Beer, Esmond S. Genealogy
of Hallenstein, Hart, and
Associated Families. London,
n.p., 1976. 55 p. Includes
genealogical tables. Family
originated in Germany and
spread out to England,
Australia, New Zealand, and
U.S. in the 19th century.
Includes above families and
Barden, Benjamin, Benson,
Blaubaum, Brasch, Cianchi,
Cohen, Danglow, Fels,
Forsyth, Friedlander,
Gotthelf, Hyams, Isaacs,
Israel, Jonas, Keesing, Kohn,
Lazarus, Lowenstein, Marks,
Meinrath, Michaelis, Milns,
Mohr, Moss, Mountain,
Philips, Prior, Raphael,
Reeves, Robertson, Selby,
Smith, Theomim, Thompson, Van
de Walde, and Wallach
families. JNUL, Manuscript
and Archives Dept., Call
No. V.2197.

BARED
CFM has family records.

BARENBLOOM
See Albert Barmatz entry under
BLOOM.

BARENTZ
CFM has family records.

BARHUN
Poznánski, Samuel. "Il nome
Barhun," Rivista Israelitica
7 (1910):66-71.

BARING
AMH has family records.

BARISCH
Kempelen. Magyarországi Zsidó,
2:130. See GENERAL WORKS.

BARISER
AMH has family records.

BAR KOKBA, BAR KOZEBAI
Zeitlin, Solomon. "Bar Kokba
and Bar Kozebai," Jewish
Quarterly Review, n.s., 43
(1952/53):77-82.

BARLA
Kempelen. Magyarországi Zsidó,
2:136. See GENERAL WORKS.

BARNA
Kempelen. Magyarországi Zsidó,
3:26. See GENERAL WORKS.

BARNARD
See LEWIS-BARNARD.
AMH has family records.

BARNATO
AMH has family records.
Jackson, Samuel. The Great
Barnato. London: Heinemann,
1970. 278 p. Includes
genealogical table. Barnett
Isaacs (Barney) Barnato was a
South African financier and
mining magnate, b. London,
1852; d. 1897.

BARNED
AMH has family records.

BARNEKOW
Semi-Gotha, 1:44, 140. See
GENERAL WORKS.

BARNET
AMH has family records.
CFM has family records.
Stern. FAJF. Barnet family
tree beginning in U.S. See
GENERAL WORKS.

BARNETT
AMH has family records.
CFM has family records.
Kohn, Walter A. Illustrated
Family Tree of the Kohn,
Barnett, and Other Related
Families of Albany, N.Y.
Philadelphia, 1946. AJA.
Stern. FAJF. Barnett family
trees beginning in: (I, II,
V, and VI) U.S.; (III and
IV) Holland; and

(VII) England. See GENERAL
WORKS.

BARNSLEY
AMH has family records.

BARON
Kempelen. Magyarországi Zsidó,
3:81, 84. Báron family. See
GENERAL WORKS.

BARONYI
Kempelen. Magyarországi Zsidó,
3:139. See GENERAL WORKS.

BAROSS
Kempelen. Magyarországi Zsidó,
1:102. See GENERAL WORKS.

BARRAH
CFM has family records.

BARRETT
AJA has genealogical files.
Stern. FAJF. Barrett family
tree beginning in U.S. See
GENERAL WORKS.

BARROW
AMH has family records.
CFM has family records.

BARTA, BARTHA
Kempelen. Magyarországi Zsidó,
1:82; 2:126. See GENERAL
WORKS.

BARTH
Kantor, Harvey A. "The Barth
Family: A Case Study of
Pioneer Immigrant Merchants,"
Missouri Historical Review 62
(July 1968):410-430. Study
of German immigrant family.
Moses Barth, b. Illingen,
Prussia, 1824; d. 1890; son
of Michael and Sarah Barth.

BARTHA
See BARTA.

BARTHOLOMEW
AMH has family records.

BARTOK
Kempelen. Magyarországi Zsidó,

3:36. Bartók family. See
GENERAL WORKS.

BARTOLUCCI
AMH has family records.

BARTON
AMH has family records.

BARUC
Stern. FAJF. Baruc family
tree beginning in Germany.
See GENERAL WORKS.

BARUCH
AJA has family tree for family
of U.S. financier Bernard
Baruch.
CFM has family records.
Baruch, Bernard Mannes. Baruch:
My Own Story. New York:
Holt, 1957. 337 p.
Genealogical information on
relatives of Baruch's
parents, pp. 3-4, 13-21.
Simon Baruch, Bernard's
father, was the son of
Bernhard Baruch and was born
in Schwersenz, near Posen.
The relatives of Bernard's
mother, Isabelle Wolfe
Baruch, were the Marques,
Marks, Cohen, and Wolfe
families.
Coit, Margaret L. Mr. Baruch.
Boston: Houghton Mifflin,
1957. 784 p. "American
Family Tree of Bernard M.
Baruch," opp. p. 1. Includes
mainly the relatives of
Bernard Baruch's mother, the
Marques, Marks, Wolfe, and
Cohen families of the West
Indies and South Carolina.
Corwin, Henry M.
Baruch-Berendsen, Van den
Bergh. Oldenzaal: n.p.,
Apr. 1960. 17 p. Three
pictures of the cemetery in
envelope. Genealogy starts
with Moses Berends (Mausje
ben Baruch) in late 1700s and
continues to 1960. Family
originated in the
Netherlands. BR; CAJ, Call
No. 1017.

Kempelen. Magyarországi Zsidó,
2:97. See GENERAL WORKS.
Olcovich, Joseph. Miscellaneous
Papers. Contain diary with
four pages of genealogical
information on Olcovich's
family and his wife Hattie's
family, the Isaac Baruchs of
Coulterville, California.
Historical Society Library,
San Francisco.
Schulte. Bonner Juden, p. 107.
See GENERAL WORKS.
Stern. FAJF. Baruch family
trees beginning in: (I) U.S.;
and (II) Schwersenz, Poland.
See GENERAL WORKS.

BARUCHSON
CFM has family records.

BARZILAI
Poznánski, Samuel. "Nochmals
der name Barzilai,"
Orientalistische
Literaturzeitung 23
(1920):128-29.

BARZILAY
CFM has family records.

BAS
CAJ has family tree from the
Netherlands.

BASCH
See Siegfried Porta entry under
FALKENSTEIN.
Kempelen. Magyarországi Zsidó,
1:42, 135; 2:131, 146; 3:72,
92, 124. See GENERAL WORKS.

BASCHWITZ
JE, 2:567. Family tree of
family of German printers,
descendants of Ƶebi (Hirsch)
ben Meîr, 1701 to early 19th
century. See GENERAL WORKS.
Brilling, Bernhard. "Jüdische
Druckerfamilien in
Frankfurt/Oder," Archiv für
Geschichte des Buchwesens 1
(1956/57):570-81. "Die
Familie Baschwitz,"
pp. 573-77. 18th to early
19th century.

BASELLI
Kempelen. Magyarországi Zsidó,
2:133. See GENERAL WORKS.

BASEVI
AMH has family records.
CFM has family records.
Roth, Cecil. "La famiglia
Basevi e le sue vicende," La
Rassegna Mensile di Israel
36, no. 7/9 (1970):359-62.
Wolf, "Anglo-Jewish Families."
See GENERAL WORKS.

BASILEA
AMH has family records.
Levi, Isaia. "La famiglia
Basilea," Il Vessillo
Israelitico 52 (1904):43-44.
From Mantova, Italy.

BASIVA
AMH has family records.

BASS
Schulte. Bonner Juden, p. 116.
See GENERAL WORKS.
Ullmann, Elias.
Familien-Register und
Stammtafeln des Seligmann
Sulzbach aus Fürth, des Ruben
Juda Beyfuss des Moses Isaac
Ochs und des Isaac Jacob Bass
aus Frankfurt am Main und
deren Nachkommen. Frankfurt
am Main, 1875.

BASSANO
CFM has family records.

BASSEVI
LBI has family tree beginning
1545.
PD has family records.
Kisch, Bruno. "Ein Jüdmaler
Leone Bassevi aus Verona,"
JFF, no. 44 (1937):811-12,
36.
Polák-Rokycana, Jaroslav. "Die
Häuser des Jakob Bassevi von
Treuenburg," ZGJT 1
(1930):253-66.
Porto, L.S. "Die erste
Nobilitierung eines deutschen
Juden, meines vorfahren Jakob
Bassevi von Treuenburg," JFF,

no. 1 (1924):12-15.
Roth, Cecil. "Der Ursprung der
Familie Bassevi in Prag und
Verona," JFF, no. 4
(1928):57-60.

BASSEWITZ
Semigothaisches Taschenbuch.
Genealogical table 2. See
GENERAL WORKS.

BASTO
Basto, Artur Carlos de Barros.
Linhagem de Arthur Ben-Rosh.
Pôrto, 1920. 52 p. Ben-Rosh
was author's Hebrew name
after he converted to
Judaism. His family,
however, were historically
Marranos. The author lived
from 1877-1961 and was well
known not only in Portugal
but also in Jewish
intellectual and cultural
circles abroad.

BATTAT
Battat, Ezra Moses, comp.
Battat: A Genealogy of the
House of Battat. Jerusalem:
Hemed Press, 1972. 125 p. in
English; 113 p. in Hebrew.
JNUL, WJHC.

BATTHYANY
Kempelen. Magyarországi Zsidó,
2:38, 78; 3:27. Batthyány
family. See GENERAL WORKS.

BAUER
AJA has genealogical files for
Lehmann-Bauer family.
CAJ has family tree from
Germany.
PD has family records.
Kempelen. Magyarországi Zsidó,
2:76, 89; 3:61, 75, 94. See
GENERAL WORKS.

BAUERSDORF
PD has family records.

BAULAND
Tänzer. Juden in Jebenhausen,
p. 296. See GENERAL WORKS.

BAUM
Baum Family. Claremont,
California, 1849-1956. Vital
statistics. AJA.

Baum, Vicki [Hedwig]. It Was
All Quite Different: The
Memoirs of Vicki Baum. New
York: Funk and Wagnalls,
1964. 372 p. Especially,
pp. 3-102. The famous
novelist (1888-1960) was born
in Vienna, the daughter of
Hermann (1850?-1943) and
Mathilde Donat Baum. Her
father was born in Novi Sad,
Yugoslavia. The author came
to U.S. in 1932.

Crohn, Lawrence W. We
Remember: Saga of the
Baum-Webster Family Tree,
1842-1964. New York?, 1964.
105 p. Includes genealogical
tables. OCH.

Dickler, Ruth. We Remember:
Saga of the Baum-Wedster
Family Tree, 1842-1979. N.p.,
1979. iv, 115 p. AJHS.

Kempelen. Magyarországi Zsidó,
1:123. See GENERAL WORKS.

See Nathan M. Reiss entry under
EDELMUTH. Includes Baum
family of Lichenroth.

Schulte. Bonner Juden,
pp. 117, 120. See GENERAL
WORKS.

BAUMANN
AMH has family records.
CFM has family records.
Kempelen. Magyarországi Zsidó,
2:56. See GENERAL WORKS.

BAUMGARTEN
Baumgarten, Franziska. Heimat
und Schicksal: Die Geschichte
einer Familie. Bern, n.d.
147 p. Family of Germany and
Poland. Author was a doctor
of philology at the
University of Bern,
Switzerland. LBI.

Breitbard, Gail A.J.
Baumgartner/Baumgarten
Family: Biographical
Sketches. Miami, Fla.: By
the Author, 1969. 20 p.

Allen County Public Library,
Fort Wayne, Indiana.
Kempelen. Magyarországi Zsidó,
2:21, 58, 68, 142, 144; 3:83,
107, 112. See GENERAL WORKS.

BAUMGARTNER
See Gail A.J. Breitbard entry
under BAUMGARTEN.

BAYER
LBI has family tree beginning
1783.

BAYERTHAL
LBI has family tree beginning
1730.

BAYOR
Kempelen. Magyarországi Zsidó,
3:55. See GENERAL WORKS.

BEARSTED
AMH has family records.

BECHMANN
LBI has family tree beginning
1666.

BECK, BEKK
Feibelman, Julian B. The
Making of a Rabbi. New York:
Vantage Press, 1980. 508 p.
Autobiography of this Reform
Rabbi (1897-1981) who served
at New Orleans' Temple Sinai
from 1936 to 1967. Pages
15-20 contain a brief
discussion of his mother's
family, the Beck family of
Lissa, Prussia. The author's
grandfather, Gabriel Julius
Beck (1842-1890), came to
U.S. in 1859.
Kempelen. Magyarországi Zsidó,
1:65; 2:26, 119; 3:105, 117.
See GENERAL WORKS.

BECKER
Kempelen. Magyarországi Zsidó,
2:133. See GENERAL WORKS.

BECK-FRIIS
Semi-Gotha, 1:24. See GENERAL
WORKS.

BECKH
Semi-Gotha, 2:135. See GENERAL
WORKS.

BEDDINGTON
AMH has family records.
CFM has family records.

BEECHAM
See BISCHHEIM.

BEELER
Kempelen. Magyarországi Zsidó,
2:48. See GENERAL WORKS.

BEER
See Kempelen entry under
LOW-BEER.
AMH has family records.
CAJD has family tree of German
family.
CFM has family records.
LBI has family trees beginning
1767 and 1823.
Ballin, Gerhard. "Die Ahnen
des Komponisten Giacomo
Meyerbeer," Musikgeschichte
und Genealogie 8, no. 6
(1966):228-34. Meyerbeer
(1791-1864), German composer,
known mainly for his
compositions of French grand
opera. His real name was
Jacob Liebmann Beer, and he
was born in Berlin within a
banking family.
"Dr. Bernhard Beer," MGWJ,
1862, p. 41.
Heymann, Josef. "Die Familie
des Hofjuden Aaron Abraham
Beer und ihre Bedeutung f. d.
Gesch. Ostfrieslands und
Auriche," JFF, no. 14,
pp.43-47.
Ettlinger, Shlomo.
"Altfrankfurter jüdische
Familiennamen,"
Jüdisches/Israelistisches
Gemeindeblatt (Frankfurt am
Main, U.A.T.) 3, no. 11
(1957):7.
Hoffmann, Paul. Urkundliches
von Michael Beer und über
seine Familie. 1908. LBI.
Kempelen. Magyarországi Zsidó,
1:12, 63; 3:22. See GENERAL

WORKS.
Rachel and Wallich. Berliner
Grosskaufleute, 3:129-33.
Merchant family of Berlin.
See GENERAL WORKS.
Schulte. Bonner Juden, p. 121.
See GENERAL WORKS.

BEER-HOFFMANN
LBI has family tree beginning
1713.

BEHR
AMH has family records.
Kempelen. Magyarországi Zsidó,
2:121; 3:139. See GENERAL
WORKS.
Levy, Arnold. The Behr Tree
(1683-1949). Taunton,
England: Printed for Private
Circulation by the Wessex
Press, 1949. 130 p. MB,
NjR, NN, NNJ, YIVO.

BEHREND
AJA has family tree beginning
17th century.
AMH has family records.
CFM has family records.
Behrend, Moses. Papers, 1962.
1 folder. Biography, 1962,
of Dr. Moses Behrend
(1877-?), written by his
daughter on the occasion of
his 85th birthday. Dr.
Behrend was a
Philadelphia-born physician.
Biography includes
information about his family.
PJAC.
Behrend-Sonneborn Family.
Papers, 1907, 1911, 1940,
1942, 1978-79. 1 folder.
Family papers, including
genealogies, newspaper
clippings, and correspondence
of Sonneborn and Behrend
families. Behrend family
genealogy, 1942. Sonneborn
family, 1978. PJAC.
Behrend, Helmut. "Ergänzungen
und Berichtigungen zur
Stammfolge Behrend in Band
126 (1. Westpreussen),
pp. 1 +," Westpreussen
Geschlechterbuch 3

(1964):619-26.
Behrend, Itzig. The Family
Chronicle. Foreward and
Translated into English by
William Bonwitt. London,
1978. 23 p. Includes
genealogical table. Covers
through 1842. Itzig Behrend,
b. 1765; d. 1845, Rodenberg,
near Hannover. LBI.
Holland, Samuel H. "The
Behrends: Six Generations of
a Washington Family," The
Record (The Jewish Historical
Society of Greater
Washington) 3 (Nov.
1968):36ff.
Kohn, Magnus. "Unsere
Familien-Chronik geführt vom
seligen Grosspa Itzig
Behrend," Jahrbuch für
Jüdische Geschichte und
Literatur 12 (1909):110-134.
Valentin, Bruno. Geschichte
der Familien Valentin, Loewen
und Manheimer-Behrend. Rio
de Janeiro, 1963. 82 p. LBI.

BEHRENDS
CFM has family records.

BEHRENS
AMH has family records.
CFM has family records.
LBI has family tree beginning
1570.
Kempelen. Magyarországi Zsidó,
1:39. See GENERAL WORKS.
Schnee. Hoffinanz und Staat,
2:13-46, 58-63. "Die Familie
Behrens." Includes
genealogical information on
this family of Hannover, 16th
to 18th century. See GENERAL
WORKS.
Schnee, Heinrich. "Der Hof-u.
Kammeragent Leffmann Behrens
als Hoffinanzier der Welfen.
E. Beitr. zur Gesch. d.
Beziehungen zwischen
jüdischer Hochfinanz u.
Modernem Staat. nach
archivalischen Quellen,"
Niedersächsisches Jahrbuch
für Landesgeschichte 23
(1951):116-57.

BEHRMAN
Alperin, Richard J. Rimmonim
Bells: Generations of the
Behrman, Drucker, Hahn,
Stockler and Sztynberg
Families Plus Ten Related
Families. Philadelphia:
Richard J. Alperin, 1980.
249 p. Includes above
families and Judek, Netgen,
Paricer, Schneyer, Schnitzer,
Schugleit, Solomon, and
Szmeidler families.

BEINESCH
See Heinrich Kurtzig entry
under KUHLBRAND.

BEIT
CAJ has family tree.
Lassally, Oswald. Geschichte
d. Familie Beit von Speyer.
1936.

BEITH
Kempelen. Magyarországi Zsidó,
1:39. See GENERAL WORKS.

BEITMAN
Joseph, David. Family Tree for
the Children of Joseph and
David. Jerusalem, 1978.
62 p. Most of the family
branches are traced to
various parts of Germany.
Includes Beitman, David,
Joseph, Isenberger, Loeb,
Mayer, Nusbaum, Nussbaum,
Oppenheimer, Rothschild, and
Stern families. CAJ.

BEKE
Kempelen. Magyarországi Zsidó,
2:119. See GENERAL WORKS.

BEKESI
Kempelen. Magyarországi Zsidó,
1:32. Békési family. See
GENERAL WORKS.

BEKK
See Kempelen entry under BECK,
BEKK.

BELAFFSKY
See BELKOV.

BELASARIO
AMH has family records.

BELASCO
Belasco Family. Los Angeles.
Family Tree and Biographical
Information Concerning the
Belasco Family. MS and
typescript. AJA.
CFM has family records.

BELCHER
AMH has family records.

BELFORTE
CFM has family records.

BELICOS
AMH has family records.

BELIFANTE, BELINFANTE
CFM has Belinfante family
records.
JE, 2:660. Family tree of
Sephardic family, 1526 to
early 19th century.
Descendants of Joseph Cohen
Belinfante, a fugitive from
Portugal to Turkey in 1526.
See GENERAL WORKS.

BELILIOS
CFM has family records.

BELINFANTE
See BELIFANTE, BELINFANTE.

BELISARIO
AMH has family records.

BELISHA
AMH has family records.

BELKIND
EJ (1972), 4:439. Genealogical
table of Israeli family of
the first aliyah. Descendants
of Meir Belkind (1827-1898),
Hebrew teacher, originally
from Russia. See GENERAL
WORKS.

BELKOV
Balakleisky-Belkov-
Belaffsky-Bell Family Tree.
Compiled by Michael Reynolds.

Each branch changed its name
from the original
Balakleisky, whose name was
derived from hamlet of
Balakleya, adjacent to Smela
in Kiev Province, Ukraine.
Family migrated from there to
Odessa in 1880s, then from
Odessa to Chicago, Illinois
and Norfolk, Virginia in
early 20th century. JGCT.

BELL
See BELKOV.
AMH has family records.

BELLACHINI
Kronthal, A. "Die Bellachini,
eigentlich Berlach aus
Posen," Posener
Heimatsblätter, 1935.

BELMONT, BELMONTE
AMH has family records.
CFM has Belmonte family
records.
JE, 2:663. Family tree of
German family. Descendants
of Simhah ben Ephraim
(d. 1685), 17th to end of
19th century. See GENERAL
WORKS.
JE, 2:664. Family tree of
Portuguese Dutch Marrano
family, which traces its
descent from Don Iago
Sampayo, to whom in 1519 King
Manuel of Portugal gave the
city of Belmonte, allowing
him to take the name of the
city and to transmit to his
descendants. Table is
through 18th century. Another
genealogical table is for the
Dutch Marrano family,
descendants of Jacob Belmonte
(1570-1630), through
beginning of 18th century.
See GENERAL WORKS.
Gottheil, Richard James
Horatio. The
Belmont-Belmonte Family. A
Record of Four Hundred Years
Put Together from the
Original Documents in the
Archives and Libraries of

31 BENEDEK

Spain, Portugal, Holland,
England, and Germany as from
Private Sources. New York,
1917. 244 p. DLC, ICN, MB,
NN, OCH.
Liebeschütz, Rahel.
Feist-Belmont History,
1775-1837. Leeds, England:
By the Author, 1971.
Genealogical tables.
————. Feist-Belmont History.
Part II: 1842-1859. Leeds,
England: By the Author, 1973.
54, 37 p.
————. "The Wind of Change,
Letters of Two Generations
from the Biedermeir Period,"
Leo Baeck Institute Yearbook
12 (1967):227-56.
Genealogical chart of
descendants of Elias Simon
(d. 1795) and Isaac Simon
Belmont (d. 1813), p. 239.
Family of Germany, New York,
and Chicago.

BENARIO
Eschelbacher, Max. "Leopold
Benario, 1822-1906. Hrsg. von
Hermann Ehmer. Mit einem
Stammbaum der Famile Benario
von Erich Langguth,"
Wertheimer Jahrbuch
(Wertheim/Main), 1980,
pp. 113-30.
Schwabacher, Alfred. "Meine
Lebengeschichte." New York,
1951. 34, [6] p. Schwabacher
family from Fellheim/Bavaria
and the Benario (author's
mother) family from Wertheim
in Baden. Includes Benario
family tree.

BENAS
AMH has family records.
CFM has family records.
Wolf. "Anglo-Jewish Families."
See GENERAL WORKS.

BENCZE
Kempelen. Magyarországi Zsidó,
2:119. See GENERAL WORKS.

BENDA
Oppenheimer, Franz. Erlebter,

Erstrebtes, Erreichtes,
Lebenserinnerungen.
Düsseldorf: Joseph Melzer
Verlag, 1964. 372 p.
"Elternhaus," pp. 33-44.
Franz Oppenheimer
(1864-1943), German and
American sociologist and
economist, was born in
Berlin. His mother's family
was the Benda family of
Berlin. CSt, CtY, CU, DLC,
ICU, NcU, NjP, NNC, OCl.

BENDAHON
AMH has family records.
CFM has family records.

BENDEDACK
CFM has family records.

BENDER
Meyer, Karl. Die Geschichte
der Familie Bender. Jüdische
Familiengeschichte aus dem
Moselland. Hrsg. v. Bruno
Bender. Tel Aviv, 1960.
Typed MS. LBI.

BENDIT
LBI has family tree beginning
1746.

BENDIX
Maser, Karl. Nachkommen des
Gompertz Hertz Bendix (Lünen
1768). Gedruckter Stammbaum.
Verlag J. Blömeke,
Gelsenkirchen (o.J.). LBI.
Rachel and Wallich. Berliner
Grosskaufleute, 3:116-18.
Merchants and bankers of
Berlin. See GENERAL WORKS.
Semi-Gotha, 1:92ff.
Bendix-Benedicks-Bleichröder
family. See GENERAL WORKS.

BENDIXON
Semi-Gotha, 1:136ff. See
GENERAL WORKS.

BENDON
AMH has family records.

BENEDEK
Kempelen. Magyarországi

Zsidó, 3:49. See GENERAL
WORKS.

BENEDICKS
See Semi-Gotha entry under
BENDIX.

BENEDICT
AMH has family records.
CFM has family records.
Benedict, Avraham. Yesh Sḥar.
Jerusalem: n.p., 1974.
History and genealogy of
Benedict and Bennet families.
JNUL.
Kempelen. Magyarországi Zsidó,
3:74, 75. See GENERAL WORKS.
Raphael, Jacob. "Die
Stuttgarter Familie Benedict
im 19. Jahrhundert," Bulletin
des Leo Baeck Instituts (Tel
Aviv) 11, no. 41
(1968):32-37.

BENEDICT-GOMPERTZ
Schulte. Bonner Juden, p. 124.
See GENERAL WORKS.

BENESCH
Kempelen. Magyarországi Zsidó,
1:101. See GENERAL WORKS.

BENET
See HIRSCHFELD-BENET.
CAJ has family records.
EJ (1928), 5:91. See GENERAL
WORKS.
Färber, Rubin. Pe'er
Mordekhai. Tel-Aviv, 1951.
218 p. Benet family,
descendants of Mordecai Benet
(1753-1829), talmudist and
chief rabbi of Moravia.
Kempelen. Magyarországi Zsidó,
3:47, 49. Benét family. See
GENERAL WORKS.

BENEVISTE
Roth, Cecil. The House of
Nasi: Doña Gracia.
Philadelphia: Jewish
Publications Society of
America, 1948. 208 p. Family
tree, p. 82. Gracia
Mendesia, ca. 1510-1569?

BENHAM
AMH has family records.

BENJAMIN
AJA has genealogical files.
AMH has family records.
CFM has family records.
See Esmond S. De Beer entry
under BARDEN.
Schulte. Bonner Juden, p. 126.
See GENERAL WORKS.
See Stern, FAJF (V) entry under
PHILLIPS.
Stern. FAJF. Benjamin family
trees beginning in: (I) St.
Eustatius; and (II) Canada
and London. See GENERAL
WORKS.
Stern, Malcolm H. "Myer
Benjamin and His
Descendants," Rhode Island
Jewish Historical Notes 5
(Nov. 1968):133-144. 18th to
19th century.

BENNET
AMH has family records.
Benedict, Avraham. Yesh Sḥar.
Jerusalem: n.p., 1974.
History and genealogy of
Benedict and Bennet family.
JNUL.
Semi-Gotha, 1:46. See GENERAL
WORKS.

BENNETT
AMH has family records.
Keneseth Israel. See GENERAL
WORKS.

BENOZIEL
CFM has family records.

BENSABAT
AMH has family records.

BENSAKEN
Stern. FAJF. Bensaken family
tree beginning in U.S. See
GENERAL WORKS.

BENSAUDE
AMH has family records.
Mode, Gabriele A. "The
Bensaudes of Lisbon," Jewish

Chronicle (London),
Mar. 1949, p. 19.

BENSBACH
Löwenstein, Leopold. Stammbaum
des August Oppenheim.
Mannheim, 1908. Folio.
Includes Bensbach family.

BENSON
AMH has family records.
See Esmond De Beer entry under
BARDEN.

BENSUSAN
CFM has family records.
Bensusan, Arthur David, comp. A
Short History of the Bensusan
Family. Johannesburg, 1935?
6 p. OCH.

BENSUSON
AMH has family records.

BENT
Bent, A.A. "Essay Delivered at
the Golden Wedding of Mr. and
Mrs. Hyman Bent, with an
Appendix (Genealogy)."
Fitchburg, 1967. 24 p. Long
Island Historical Society,
Brooklyn, N.Y.

BENTULO
AMH has family records.

BENTWICH
AMH has family records.

BENUSAN
AMH has family records.

BENVENISTE
EJ (1928), 4:142-43. See
GENERAL WORKS.
EJ (1972), 12:838. Genealogical
table of Nasi and Benveniste
families, 16th century. See
GENERAL WORKS.
Benayahu, Meir. "A Group of
Documents on Jerusalem in the
18th and 19th Centuries," (In
Hebrew.) Yerushalayim 1
(Tevet-Adar 1948):74-88. Part
of article deals with history
of Benveniste family.

BENZAKEN
Stern. FAJF. Benzaken family
tree beginning in U.S. See
GENERAL WORKS.

BENZAQUEN
CFM has family records.

BENZECRY
AMH has family records.

BENZIAN
LBI has family tree beginning
1762.

BENZIMRA
AMH has family records.

BEN-ZVI
See Zevi Shimshi entry under
SHIMSHELEWITZ.

BER
Freud, Jechiel. Stammtafel der
Abkömmlinge von Aba
Gabua-Stern, Meier
Jaffa-Scheiner und Moses Abr.
Abisch Margulies-Ber.
Entworfen: Max Besner.
Buczacz: Verein Rodzina,
1914. 1 genealogical table.
Includes Ber family. DLC,
NN.

BERAHO
CFM has family records.

BERCHTOLD
Kempelen. Magyarországi Zsidó,
1:145. See GENERAL WORKS.

BERCINSKY
Zunser, Miriam Shomer.
Yesterday: A Memoir of a
Russian Family. New York:
Harper & Row, 1978. 274 p.
Originally published in 1939
by Stackpole Sons. The story
of three generations of
family life in Pinsk and New
York. DLC, NN, PPDrop.

BERCOFF
AMH has family records.

BERCZELLY
Kempelen. Magyarországi Zsidó,
2:126. See GENERAL WORKS.

BEREGI
Kempelen. Magyarországi Zsidó,
2:98. See GENERAL WORKS.

BEREND
See Ludwig Herz entry under
REICHENHEIM.
Kempelen. Magyarországi Zsidó,
2:57, 71. See GENERAL WORKS.
Wallich, Paul. "Gebr. Berend
u. Co., Berliner
Heereslieferanten, Bankiers
und Industrielle aus dem
Anfang des 19. Jahrhunderts,"
Forschungen zur
Bradenburgischen und
Preussischen Geschichte 33
(1921):77-115; 369-407.

BERENDI
Kempelen. Magyarországi Zsidó,
3:83. See GENERAL WORKS.

BEREND LEVY
Gronemann. Genealogische
Hannovers. Includes
genealogical table of Berend
Levy family: "Stammtafel der
Nachkommen des Landrabbiners
Berend." See GENERAL WORKS.

BERENDSEN
Corwin, Henry M.
Baruch-Berendsen, Van den
Bergh. Oldenzaal: n.p.,
Apr. 1960. 17 p. Three
pictures of the cemetery in
envelope. Genealogy starts
with Moses Berends (Mausje
ben Baruch) in late 1700s and
continues to 1960. Family
originated in Netherlands.
BR; CAJ, Call No. 1017.

BERENS
AMH has family records.
CFM has family records.
Jost, J.M. "Eine
Familien-Megillah aus der
erster Hälfte des 18. Jh.
(Bericht über die Schicksale
der Gebrüder Berens in

Hannover)," Jahrbuch für die
Geschichte der Juden und des
Judentums (Leipzig) 1 (1861).

BERENSTEIN
Rosenstein. Unbroken Chain,
pp. 439ff. See GENERAL
WORKS.

BERENT
Berent Family Tree. Compiled
by Irwin M. Berent. Family
of Chorzelle, Poland and U.S.
Covers early 19th to 20th
century. JGCT.

BERETVAS
Kempelen. Magyarországi Zsidó,
1:140; 2:146. See GENERAL
WORKS.

BERFET
Bloch, Isaac. "Le nom
patronymique de Ribasch,"
Revue des Études Juives 10
(1885):255.

BERG
Kaufman, Louis, Barbara
Fitzgerald, and Tom Sewell.
Moe Berg: Athlete, Scholar,
Spy. Boston: Little, Brown
and Co., 1975. 274 p. "The
Family," pp. 29-39. Moe Berg
(1902-1972) was born in New
York City, the son of Bernard
and Rose Tashker Berg.
Bernard was the son of Mendel
Berg of Kamnets, Ukraine, and
Rose was the daughter of
Simon Tashker of Zaleschiki.
Keneseth Israel. See GENERAL
WORKS.
Kempelen. Magyarországi Zsidó,
3:85, 120. See GENERAL
WORKS.

BERGEL
CFM has family records.

BERGER
CAJD has family tree from
Germany.
Kempelen. Magyarországi Zsidó,
1:109, 146; 2:98, 128; 3:117.
See GENERAL WORKS.

BERGH (VAN DEN)
AMH has Bergh family records.
CFM has family records.
Bergh, Samuel van der Wielen.
The Life of Simon Van den
Bergh and Elisabeth van der
Wielen. Portrayed for Their
Descendants. London, 1911.
The Van den Bergh family
originally came to the
Netherlands from Prussia in
late 18th century. They own
various industrial concerns.
BR.
Corwin, Henry M.
Baruch-Berendsen, Van den
Bergh. Oldenzaal: n.p.,
Apr. 1960. 17 p. Three
pictures of the cemetery in
envelope. Genealogy starts
with Moses Berends (Mausje
ben Baruch) in late 1700s and
continues to 1960. Family
originated in Netherlands.
BR; CAJ, Call No. 1017.
Hoynck van Papendrecht, J.C.
"De Tilburgsche
Fabrikanten-familie van den
Bergh," Nedederlandsche
Leeuw. 58 (1940):32-37.
Mid-18th to 20th century.
Signal, M.C. "De Tilburgsche
Fabrikantenfamilie van den
Bergh," Nederlandsche Leeuw.
58 (1940):85-86. 20th
century.

BERGHEIM
CFM has family records.

BERGMAN
Bergman, Gerson (1893-).
Interview, 1976. 1 cassette
tape. Includes genealogical
information. PJAC.
Cohn, Rose B. Stein, Bergman,
and Cohn Families
(1787-1954). Baltimore: Ida
Charles Wilkins Foundation,
1954. 21 p. Includes
genealogical tables. NN.

BERGMANN
LBI has family tree beginning
1800.
Bergmann, I. "Wie unsere

Familiennamen entstanden
sind," Jahrbuch für Jüdische
Geschichte und Literatur 28
(1927):34-72.
Tänzer. Juden in Tirol,
p. 686. See GENERAL WORKS.

BERGSON
Reychman. Szkice
genealogiczne, pp. 11-18. See
GENERAL WORKS.

BERGTHEIL
CFM has family records.

BERIA
CFM has family records.

BERKOVITS
Kempelen. Magyarországi Zsidó,
2:53. See GENERAL WORKS.

BERKOWITZ
AJA has genealogical files.
Berkowitz Family. "Letter and
genealogy charts sent to
Rabbi Malcolm H. Stern by his
grandmother, Clara Landman
Berkowitz, Philadelphia, Pa.,
March 19, 1956." AJA.

BERLANDIA
CFM has family records.

BERLANDINA
Stern. FAJF. Berlandina
family tree beginning in
London. Family tree is
listed in FAJF under
"Bensaken." See GENERAL
WORKS.

BERLIN
See BRODY-BERLIN.
AMH has family records.
LBI has family trees beginning
1700 and 1738.
Blachman-Berlin Reunion,
November 24-26, 1977.
Norfolk, Va., 1977. Includes
family tree of Berlin family
members, originally from
Ligum, Lithuania, who married
into Blachman and Kanter
families in America, ca. 1830
forward. AJHS, JGCT.

Chelminsky-Lajmer, "Jewish
Surnames." See GENERAL
WORKS.
Duckesz, Eduard.
Familiengeschichte des Rabbi
Lase Berlin im Hamburg.
Hamburg: Max Täschner Nachf.,
1929? 146 p. Genealogical
tables. OCH.
Malachi, Eliezer Raphael. "The
Berlin Family and the
Yishuv," in Eliezer Raphael
Malachi's Perakim be-toldot
ha-yishuv ha-yashan [Studies
in the History of the Old
Yishuv], (Tel-Aviv, 1971),
pp. 253-62.
Schulte. Bonner Juden, p. 127.
See GENERAL WORKS.
Stammbaum und genealogische
Notizen zu dem Stammbaum der
Familie Berlin in Fürth.
N.p., n.d. 33 p. JNUL,
Manuscript and Archive Dept.,
Call No. V.1959.

BERLINER
AMH has family records.
LBI has family trees beginning
1750, 1761, 1776, and 1816.
Berliner, Kurt. Meine
Familiengeschichte. São
Paulo, Brazil, 1962. 11 p.
Family history begins in 1780
with founding of the David
Berlin Co. in Flatow, West
Prussia. Author went to
Brazil in 1936. LBI.
Rosenstein. Unbroken Chain,
pp. 414ff. See GENERAL
WORKS.

BERLINGER
CAJ has family tree and family
records.
Risch, Izhak. Megilat
Mishpaḥtenu. Added title
page: Records Concerning the
Ancestry of the Levi,
Berlinger, and Ellinger
Families of the Zvi branch.
1974. 88 p. CLU, DLC, MB,
NN, WU.

BERLOWITZ
Berton, William K. "In Search

of the Berlowitz Family,"
Toledot: The Journal of
Jewish Genealogy 1 (Summer
1977):4, 11-14.
Lithuanian/Prussian family.
———. "Berlowitz Revisited,"
Toledot: The Journal of
Jewish Genealogy 4, no. 1/2
(1981):23-25.
———. Tol'dot Mishpahat
Berlowitz: The Generations of
the Berlowitz Family.
Saginaw, Mich., 1981. Lists
members of family found in
the Western Hemisphere;
traced to two small East
Prussian villages dating back
to the 17th century. AJHS.

BERMAN
AMH has family records.
Berman, Alexander and Sarah,
Minneapolis. "Sarah and
Alexander Berman: A Family
Chronicle by Their Chilren."
1973. AJA.
Berman, Morton Mayer. For
Zion's Sake: A Personal and
Family Chronicle. Prescott,
Ariz.: Typ. Prescott
Graphics, 1980. 550 p. DLC.
Berman, Susan. Easy Street:
The True Story of a Mob
Family. New York: Dial
Press, 1981. 224 p. David
Berman, hotelier, was the
mob's man in Las Vegas,
Nevada.

BERMANN
LBIS has family tree.
Tänzer. Juden in Tirol,
p. 687. See GENERAL WORKS.

BERMANT
Bermant, Chaim Icyk. Coming
Home. London: Allen & Unwin,
1976. 220 p. Emphasis of
this autobiography is on the
author's family's life in
Breslev and Barouke,
Lithuania, and Scotland.
Bermant, the Anglo-Jewish
novelist and historian, was
born in Breslev in 1929, the
son of a rabbi.

37

BERNAL
AMH has family records.
CFM has family records.

BERNARD
"Descendants of Abraham Levy
and Rachel Cornelia Bernard
of Richmond, Va." AJA.
Wilson, Nelly. Bernard-Lazare:
Antisemitism and the Problem
of Jewish Identity in Late
Nineteenth-Century France.
Cambridge: Cambridge
University Press, 1978.
348 p. "Roots...," pp. 3-5.
Bernard-Lazare (real name
Lazare Marcus Manassé
Bernard; 1865-1903), French
writer and supporter of
anarchist and socialist
movements, was born in Nîmes,
the son of Jonas Bernard,
grandson of Lazare Bernard,
great-grandson of Marcus
Bernard, and
great-great-grandson of
Abraham Lazare, who had come
to France in 1793 from
Creglingen, Brandenburg.
Original family name was
Lazare.

BERNARDI
Bernardi, Jack. My Father the
Actor. New York:
W.W. Norton, 1971. 233 p.
Story of the Yiddish actor,
Berel Bernardi (born Berel
Torfin) and his family,
originally from Lemberg in
Galicia.

BERNAT
Kempelen. Magyarországi Zsidó,
3:121. Bernát family. See
GENERAL WORKS.

BERNAUER
Bernauer, Rudolf. Das Theater
Meines Lebens: Erinnerungen.
Berlin: Lothar Blanvalet
Verlag, 1955. 411 p. "Die
Eltern," pp. 13-22. Bernauer
(1880-1953) was a theater
director and stage manager in
Vienna and Germany. The

family came to Vienna from
Bavaria and Hungary. DLC,
MiU, NN, OCl.

BERNAYS
AJA has family tree.
CAJ has family tree from
Germany and family records.
CFM has family records.
Schulte. Bonner Juden, p. 128.
See GENERAL WORKS.

BERND
AJA has family tree beginning
1760.
Frank, Helen Bernd Klein. This
is the Saga of the Bernd,
Bloch, and Blum Families in
the United States of America.
N.p., 1961. 54 p. Genealogy
of three Southern Jewish
families. Levi Bernd,
b. Hohensolms, Germany, 1788;
Ferdinand Bernd, b. Giessen,
1823. AJHS.

BERNFELD
Kempelen. Magyarországi Zsidó,
3:24. See GENERAL WORKS.

BERNHEIM
AMH has family records.
CAJ has family tree of Bernheim
family of Berlin. Call
No. 3418.
Keneseth Israel. See GENERAL
WORKS.
Bernheim, Isaac Wolfe. The
Story of the Bernheim Family.
Louisville: J.P. Morton and
Co., Inc., 1918. 145 p.
AJHS, DLC, MH, OCH, PPDrop.
Frank. Nashville Jewry,
p. 132. Family originally
from Württemberg, arrived in
U.S. in 1850s. See GENERAL
WORKS.
Picard, Jacob. "Childhood in
the Village: Fragment of An
Autobiography," LBI Yearbook
(1959):273-93. The author
was born in Wangen Am
Bodensee, Baden, the son of
Simon Picard and the
great-grandson of Isac
Bigard. Picard traces his

relatives back to the middle
of the 18th century. Some of
his family moved to
Constance, Switzerland,
before W.W.II. The Bernheim
family was author's mother's
family. Stern. FAJF. Bernheim family
trees beginning in:
(I) Hechingen, Germany; and
(II) U.S. See GENERAL WORKS.

BERNHEIMER
Bernheimer Family Papers, 1858,
1890-1898, n.d. 1 box.
Include family tree of Leo G.
Bernheimer (1876-1941) of
Philadelphia. PJAC.
Bernheimer, Ernst. Familien-und
Geschäftschronik der Firma L.
Lehmann Bernheimer K.G.
München. 1950. 211 p.
Family of Munich. LBI.
Tänzer. Juden in Jebenhausen,
pp. 297-98. See GENERAL
WORKS.
Tänzer. Juden in Tirol,
pp. 688-91. See GENERAL
WORKS.

BERNRIEDER
Kempelen. Magyarországi Zsidó,
1:101. See GENERAL WORKS.

BERNSTEIN
AMH has family records.
LBI has family tree beginning
1648.
Bernstein, Burton. Family
Matters: Sam, Jennie, and the
Kids. New York: Summit
Books, Distributed by S. &
S., 1982. 200 p. Narrative
of the immigrant parents of
composer-conducter Leonard
Bernstein, theatrical
producer Shirley, and
author-writer Burton, and
their respective generation.
Family of Russia.
Bernstein, Eduard. Eduard
Bernstein von 1850 bis 1872:
Kindheit und Jugendjahre.
Berlin: Erich Reiss Verlag,
1926. 219 p. "Herkunft und
Eltern," pp. 4-17. Eduard

Bernstein (1850-1932) was a
German Socialist. CtY, DLC,
ICarbS, MB, OCH.
"Bernsteins of Baja California:
A Gallery Story," Western
States Jewish Historical
Quarterly 7
(Jan. 1975):108-115. Includes
information on Max Bernstein
(b. Germany, 1854; d. 1914)
and his descendants. He was
the son of Joseph and Bertha
Bernstein of Nuremberg.
Draznin, Yaffa. It Began with
Zade Usher: The History and
Record of the Families
Bernstein-Loyev/Lewis-Mazur.
Los Angeles: Jamy
Publications, 1972? 255 p.
Includes genealogical tables.
Includes the above families
and Boyarsky, Chalidenka,
Ehrlichman, Fishelson,
Gellman, Karsunsky, Lander,
Mastow, Nathanson, Nodler,
Rabinowitz, Ritzwoller,
Rojok, Rosen, Savetsky,
Sheftman, Sher, Spector,
Spivak, Tetievsky,
Wishnipolsky, Yampolsky, and
Zimbler families. CU, DLC,
MH, N, OU, ViU.
Kempelen. Magyarországi Zsidó,
2:23. See GENERAL WORKS.
Kurtzig, Heinrich. Ostdeutsches
Judentum. Tradition einer
Familie. Stolip: Eulitz,
1927. 164 p. DLC, MH, NN,
OCH. 2nd ed. Leipzig:
G. Engel, 1930. NN, PPDrop.
Includes information on
Bernstein family of Austria.
Louis, Julius (1833-1892)
Collection, 1778-1965.
1 folder. Includes
genealogical material dealing
with Pollack family,
1778-1943, and Bernstein and
Louis families, 1840-1965.
Baltimore, Maryland and
Norfolk, Virginia. AJA.
Namier, Julia. Lewis Namier: A
Biography. London: Oxford
University Press, 1971.
347 p. "Ancestry and Birth"
section, pp. 3-10. Sir Lewis

Bernstein Namier (real
surname, Namierowski; b. Wola
Okrzejska, Eastern Galicia,
1888; d. 1960), famous
English social historian,
philosopher, and Zionist. He
arrived in England in 1908.
Reychman. Szkice
genealogiczne, pp. 19-20. See
GENERAL WORKS.
Stern, Norton B. Baja
California: Jewish Refuge and
Homeland. Los Angeles:
Dawson's Book Shop, 1973.
Contains information on Max
Bernstein and his family,
pp. 21-22, 33-38.

BEROLDINGEN
Semigothaisches Taschenbuch.
Genealogical table 3. See
GENERAL WORKS.

BEROLZHEIM, BEROLZHEIMER
LBI has family trees beginning
1516, 1684, 1747, etc.

BERR
Ginsburger, Moses. Cerf Berr
et son époque. Guebwiller,
1908.
————. "Les familles Lehmann
et Cerf Berr (de Bischheim),"
Revue des Études Juives 59
(1910):106-130.
Godechot, Jacques.
"Berr-Isaac-Berr et sa
famille," La Revue Juive de
Lorraine 1
(1925):122-25, 41-44. Nancy,
France, 18th century.
Neher-Bernheim, René. "Cerf
Berr de Medelscheim: le
destin d'une famille durant
la Révolution," Revue des
Études Juives 137
(1978):60-75.
————. "Cerf Berr et sa
famille," Saisons d'Alsace
(Strasbourg), no. 55/56
(1975):47-61.
Notes et documents concernant
la famille Cerf Berr,
recueillis par un de ses
membres. 3 pts. in 3 vols.

Paris: Topographie
Plon-Nourrit, 1902-1906. NNJ.
BERSON
Reychman. Szkice
genealogiczne, pp. 21-24. See
GENERAL WORKS.

BERSTINGEL
AMH has family records.

BERTRAM
AMH has family records.

BERVIN, BERWIN
Bervin (Berwin) Family. Vital
Statistics, 1827-1876. In
Hebrew and Yiddish. AJA.

BESELS
Michael Berolzheimer.
Collection. Includes family
tree. LBI.

BESSENYEY
See BAKACH-BESSENYEY.
Kempelen. Magyarországi Zsidó,
1:45. See GENERAL WORKS.

BESSO
AMH has family records.

BETHLEN
Kempelen. Magyarországi Zsidó,
1:56; 3:45, 88. See GENERAL
WORKS.

BETHUN
Semi-Gotha, 2:20. See GENERAL
WORKS.

BETHUNE
AMH has family records.

BETTELHEIM
EJ (1928), 4:443. Family of
Hungary. See GENERAL WORKS.
Kempelen. Magyarországi Zsidó,
1:12-18, 74; 2:10-11, 92;
3:62, 67. See GENERAL WORKS.
Kohut, Rebekah Bettelheim. My
Portion: An Autobiography.
Introduction by Henrietta
Szold. New York: Thomas
Seltzer, 1925. 301 p.
Especially, pp. 4-12. Family

of Hungary. Author
(1864-1951), a noted American
Jewish communal leader was
born in Kaschau (Kosice), the
daughter of Albert Siegfried
Bettelheim, a noted rabbi,
who came with his family to
U.S. in 1867. Mrs. Kohut was
the second wife of Alexander
Kohut (1842-1894), famous
Hungarian-U.S. rabbi and
scholar. CU, MB, NcD, NcU,
NN, OCH, OCl, PP.

BETTMAN
Bettman, Dr. Adalbert G.,
Portland, Oregon. Interview
Collection. Includes copy of
his biography and family
history, 1963. AJA.

BETTSACK
Brilling, Bernhard. "The Names
Lachmann, Bettsack, Sanwil,"
(In Hebrew.) Yeda'-'am 2,
no. 1 (1953):13-15.

BEUTUM
Kempelen. Magyarországi Zsidó,
2:118. See GENERAL WORKS.

BEYER
AMH has family records.
Kempelen. Magyarországi Zsidó,
3:55. See GENERAL WORKS.

BEYFUS
AMH has family records.
CFM has family records.

BEYFUSS
Ullmann, Elias.
Familien-Register und
Stammtafeln des Seligmann
Sulzbach aus Fürth, des Ruben
Juda Beyfuss, des Moses Isaac
Ochs und des Isaac Jacob Bass
aus Frankfurt am Main und
deren Nachkommen. Frankfurt
am Main, 1875.

BIACH, BICH
Flesch, Heinrich. "Die Familie
Bich (Biach), Feilbogen,"
JFF,no. 45 (1927):826-29.
Kempelen. Magyarországi Zsidó,

1:12. Biach family. See
GENERAL WORKS.

BIBO
Bibo Family, Albuquerque, New
Mexico. Genealogy;
Documents; and Printed Matter
Tracing Family History,
1820-1969. MS and typescript
in English, Hungarian,
Spanish, German, and Yiddish.
Family can be traced back to
Hungary in 1582. AJA.
Bibo Family, Albuquerque, New
Mexico. Family Tree,
1807-1961. AJA.
Fierman, Floyd S. The Impact
of the Frontier on a Jewish
Family: The Bibos. El Paso?:
Texas Western College Press,
1961. 32 p. On the
descendants of Nathan and
Simon Bibo, brothers,
emigrants from Germany in
1866, settlers in New Mexico
as traders with the Indians.
————. "Nathan Bibo's
Reminiscences of Early New
Mexico," El Palacio 68
(Winter 1961):231-57; 69
(Spring 1962):40-60.

BICH
See BIACH, BICH.

BICKART
Mirwis, L. Stammbaum der
Familie Bickart. N.p., 1925.
30 p. Family originated in
Eichstetten, Germany in early
1700s. Genealogy ends in
1925. CAJ, Call No. 5315.

BICKERMANN
Bickermann, Joseph. Two
Bickermans: Autobiographies
by Joseph and Jacob J.
Bickerman. New York: Vantage
Press, 1975. 209 p.
Especially, pp. 1-16, 77-83.
Joseph Bickermann
(1867-1942), the father;
Jacob J. Bickerman
(1898-   ), the son.
Descendants of Menashe
Bickermann (1825/27-1901) and

Baer Bickermann from Podolia
Province. CtY, DLC, MnU, NN,
NNC, OCH.

BIDERMAN
Yizraeli, Meir. Mishpachteinu.
Jerusalem: Otzaat Tikva,
1980. 394 p. 6 genealogical
tables. Calendar for
yahrzeits of family members.
Includes Biderman, Broda,
Eidlish, Eliah, Epstein,
Halevi, Hellman, Horowitz,
Idilish, Israelish, Katz,
Levi, Nishri, Parlov, Reich,
Ruttenberg, Sirkis, and
Yizraeli families. JNUL.

BIDERMANN
Shapiro. Mishpachot Atikot,
pp. 197-226. See GENERAL
WORKS.

BIEDERMANN
CFM has family records.
PD has family records.
Kempelen. Magyarországi Zsidó,
1:39, 41-52, 54; 2:52, 93;
3:62, 127. See GENERAL
WORKS.
Jäeger-Sunstenau, Hanns. "Die
geadelten Judenfamilien im
Vormärzlichen Wien." Ph.D.
dissertation, Universität
Wien, 1950. Hungarian family
of nobility, pp. 111-112.
Michigan State University
(East Lansing) Library.
Tänzer. Juden in Tirol,
p. 692. See GENERAL WORKS.

BIELEFELD
LBI has family tree beginning
1670.

BIELSCHOWSKY
LBI has family tree.

BIEMA
See VAN BIEMA.

BIGARD
Picard, Jacob. "Childhood in
the Village: Fragment of An
Autobiography," LBI Yearbook
(1959):273-93. The author

was born in Wangen Am
Bodensee, Baden, the son of
Simon Picard and the
great-grandson of Isac
Bigard. Picard traces his
relatives back to the middle
of the 18th century. Some of
his family moved to
Constance, Switzerland,
before W.W.II. The Bernheim
family was author's mother's
family.

BIGGS
AMH has family records.

BIHARI
Kempelen. Magyarországi Zsidó,
3:89. See GENERAL WORKS.

BIKARD
Tänzer. Juden in Tirol,
p. 693. See GENERAL WORKS.

BIKERMAN
See BICKERMANN.

BILANZ
Schay, Rudolf. Juden in der
Deutschen Politik. Berlin:
Der Heine-Bund, 1929. 319 p.
Includes genealogical
information on Bilanz family.
DLC, ICU, IEN, MH, NN, NNC.

BILDT
Semi-Gotha, 1:83. See GENERAL
WORKS.

BILLIGHEIMER
LBI has family tree beginning
1765.

BILLITZER
Kempelen. Magyarországi Zsidó,
1:82. See GENERAL WORKS.

BILSKY
Figler, Bernard. Lillian and
Archie Freiman. Biographies,
etc. Montreal: Northern
Printing & Lithography Co.,
1962. 331 p. Lillian Bilsky
Freiman, 1885-1940; Archibald
Jacob Freiman, 1880-1944.

BINDER
CAJ has family tree of family
of Berlin. Call No. 3418.

BINDMAN
Cramer, Sidney. Lineages of
Bindman, Kramer, Kaplin,
Linn, Wellins, Cousins, and
Half Cousins. Edinburgh,
Scotland, n.p., 1975. 7 p.
Genealogical table showing
descendants of "Solomon
Blacher [who] married Hoda
Reise Mandelowitch about 1852
in Rumania or Russia or
Latvia or Lithuania." Hoda
Reise died in Scotland. Most
of present-day family is
located in England. Includes
the above families and
Blacher, Copeland, Gold, and
Mandelowitch families. CAJ,
Call No. 4918.

BING
AMH has family records.
EJ (1928), 4:806. See GENERAL
WORKS.
LBI has family trees beginning
1713 and 1814.
Frank, Wilhelm and Rudolf
Frank. Stammwald im Westen:
Fünfundzwanzig jüdische
Generationen im Rheingebiet.
N.p., n.d. 64 p. Family
table beginning with Abraham
de Sunnesheim (1240-1316).
Includes Bing, Emden, Frank,
Honig, Sunnesheim,
de Sunnesheim, Sinsheim, and
Sinzheim families. Last
entry on family table is
1962. Bibliography, p. 64.
CAJ, Call No. 5506.
Kempelen. Magyarországi Zsidó,
3:140. See GENERAL WORKS.
Loewengart, Stefan. "Aus des
Geschichte der Familie Bing,"
Bulletin des Leo Baeck
Instituts, no. 59
(1981):29-54. Family from
Nürnberg.
————. Aus der Geschichte
meiner Familie. Die Familie
Bing. Der Familienname
Loewengart. Kiryat Bialik,

Israel: By the Author, 1973.
23 p. Inludes genealogical
tables. The Bing, Rav
Abraham-Loewengart family.
LBI, OCH.
————. From the History of My
Family: The Bing Family of
Nuremberg (From the Songs of
Songs to the Diesel Motor).
Kiriath Bialik, Israel: By
the Author, April 1980.
32, 5 p. Includes
genealogies. LBI.
Tuchmann, Friedrich Carl.
Stammbaum und Chronik d.
Familie Tuchmann aus Uhlfeld
bei Neustadt A. D. Aisch,
Feiner enth. D. Fam. Hopf,
Winkler, Reitzenberger, Bing,
und Iglauer nach dem Stande
vom 1.1 1928. 47 lfs. Folio.
AJA.
Ullmann, Elias.
Familien-Register und
Stammtafel des Michael Isaac
Bing und seiner Nachkommen.
Nebst beigefügtem auszuge aus
dem Testamente seiner
Enkelin, Gütche Worms geb.
Mendler-Oetingen, die
Stiftung eines
Brautvermächtnisses zu
Gunsten ihrer Anverwandten
betreffend. Frankfurt am
Main, 1864. 42 p. Family of
Frankfurt, 1625-1864. LBI.
————. Eine frankfurter
jüdische Familie von Jahre
1550 bis zur Gegenwart.
Frankfurt, 1880. 49 p. OCH,
YIVO.

BINGEN
Friedericks, Henry F.
"Frankfurter Ahnen von
Anthony Armstrong-Jones,"
Hessiche Familienkunde 5,
no. 3 (1960/61):156-58.
Bingen and Stern families.
Laurence, Alfred. "Zwei alte
Soester Portraits," Soester
Zeitschrift 83
(1971):101-109. On Süsskind
Stern, 1610-1687, and his
descendants. Family of
Frankfurt. Includes Bingen

family.
Lejeune, Fritz W. and Eckart
Lejeune. "Die Frankfurter
Judenfamilien Bingen und
Stern," Hessiche
Familienkunde 7, no. 2
(1964/65):75-83.
Schulte. Bonner Juden, p. 129.
See GENERAL WORKS.

BINNES
Schulte. Bonner Juden, p. 132.
See GENERAL WORKS.

BINSWANGER
Binswanger family. "Come with
Us through a Modern Looking
Glass--Diamond
Jubilee--Seventy-fifth
Anniversary--Binswanger and
Co., Inc.--Founded in 1872."
Richmond, 1947. Pamphlet.
Beth Ahabah Archives,
Richmond, Virginia.
Solis-Cohen, Myer. The
American Descendants of
Samuel Binswanger.
Philadelphia, 1957. 44 p.
AJA, NHi, NNJ, PPRF.
Stern. FAJF. Binswanger
family tree beginning in U.S.
See GENERAL WORKS.

BIRGIER
See Richard J. Alperin entry
under BEHRMAN.

BIRINGER
Kempelen. Magyarországi Zsidó,
2:91. See GENERAL WORKS.

BIRKETT
AMH has family records.

BIRNBAUM
AMH has family records.
CAJ has family tree.
CAJD has family tree.
CFM has family records.
Birnbaum, Walter. Stammbaum
der Familie Birnbaum.
Frankfurt am Main-London,
1938. 4, 58 p. LBI.
Kempelen. Magyarországi Zsidó,
2:22. See GENERAL WORKS.

Lind, Jakov. Counting My
Steps. New York: MacMillan,
1970. 223 p. Recollections
of the author's youth, pp.
31-38. Author (1927-   )
was born in Vienna, the son
of Simon Lind and the
grandson of Jacob and Maria
Lind. Simon was born in
Rabka in the Zakopane on the
Polish side of the Tatra
Mts., near the Czech border.
The Birnbaums of Snyatin on
the Pruth, between Kolomea
and Czernowitz, were the
family of the author's
mother.

BIRO
Kempelen. Magyarországi Zsidó,
2:42; 3:61. Biró family.
See GENERAL WORKS.

BIRSTEIN
Birstein, Ann. The Rabbi on
Forty-Seventh Street: The
Story of Her Father. New
York: The Dial Press, 1982.
202 p. Rabbi Bernard (Beril)
Birstein, b. Brest Litovsk,
1892; d. 1959; and his
family. He graduated from
the Slobodka Yeshiva in
Lithuania and eventually
became the rabbi of West Side
Hebrew Relief Association
(Congregation Ezrath Israel,
"The Actors' Temple") in New
York City.

BIRSTINGL
CFM has family records.

BIRSTINGLE
AMH has family records.

BISCHHEIM
Bischheim, Simon. The
Bischheim-Beecham Family.
Merchants Family. Merchants
in Frankfurt A/M, Manchester,
Hamburg, London. London: By
the Author, 1969. 98 p.
Genealogical tables.
———. (Meine

Familiengeschichte.) London,
1963. 126 p. MS. LBI.

BISCHOFFSHEIM
CFM has family records.
EJ (1972), 4:1056.
Genealogical table of the
descendants of Raphael Nathan
Bischoffsheim through first
quarter of 20th century. See
GENERAL WORKS.
JE, 3:227. "Genealogy of the
Bischoffsheim Family."
Descendants of Raphael
(Nathan) Bischoffsheim
(b. Bischofsheim-on-the-Taube,
1773; d. Mayence, Jan. 22,
1814). Genealogical table
includes Belgian, French,
English, and German branches
of family. See GENERAL
WORKS.
Schulte. Bonner Juden, p. 133.
See GENERAL WORKS.

BISCHOPPHEIM
AMH has family records.

BISCO
AMH has family records.
Bisco and Blackman family
records. Manuscript notes
and clippings. New York?
19-. 1 vol. NN.

BISHOP
AMH has family records.

BISNO
AJA has genealogical files.

BISSINGER
Frank. Nashville Jewry,
p. 128. See GENERAL WORKS.

BITTNER
Kempelen. Magyarországi Zsidó,
3:74. See GENERAL WORKS.

BJORKENHEIM
Semi-Gotha, 1:77, 80.
Björkenheim family. See
GENERAL WORKS.

BLAAUW
Semi-Gotha, 2:126. See GENERAL
WORKS.

BLACHER
See Sidney Cramer entry under
BINDMAN.

BLACHMAN
Blachman-Berlin Reunion,
November 24-26, 1977.
Norfolk, Va., 1977. Family
tree of Blachman family of
Latvia which married into
Berlin and Kanter families in
America, ca. 1830 forward.
AJHS, JGCT.

BLACK
AMH has family records.
Loveman-Black Family;
Cleveland, Ohio and
Nashville, Tenn. Genealogy,
1811-1845. MS, typescript,
and printed. AJA.

BLACKMAN
Bisco and Blackman family
records. Manuscript notes
and clippings. New York?,
19-. 1 vol. NN.

BLACKWOOD
AMH has family records.

BLAINE
AMH has family records.

BLANCKENSEE
AMH has family records.

BLANKENSEE
AMH has family records.

BLASCHCZIK
Kempelen. Magyarországi Zsidó,
1:73. See GENERAL WORKS.

BLASKOVICH
Kempelen. Magyarországi Zsidó,
2:19. See GENERAL WORKS.

BLATHY
Kempelen. Magyarországi Zsidó,

2:21. Bláthy family. See
GENERAL WORKS.

BLAU
Kempelen. Magyarországi Zsidó,
2:134, 135; 3:35, 123, 124.
See GENERAL WORKS.

BLAUBAUM
See Esmond De Beer entry under
BARDEN.

BLAUSCHAUL
Kempelen. Magyarországi Zsidó,
2:73. See GENERAL WORKS.

BLAW
CFM has family records.

BLEICHER
Bleicher, A. "Istoria unei
familii evreieşti din
România; arborele genealogic
al neamului Bleicher,"
Toladot 11, no. 4
(1975):20-24.

BLEICHRODER
Kempelen. Magyarországi Zsidó,
1:53. Bleichröder family.
See GENERAL WORKS.
Rachel and Wallich. Berliner
Grosskaufleute, 3:126-28.
"Bleichröder." See GENERAL
WORKS.
Semi-Gotha, 1:92ff.
Bendix-Benedicks-Bleichröder
family. See GENERAL WORKS.
Zielenziger. Deutschen
Wirtschaft, pp. 64-74. "Das
Haus Bleichröder." Banking
family of Berlin. See
GENERAL WORKS.

BLES
CFM has family records.

BLEYER
Kempelen. Magyarországi Zsidó,
3:21, 48, 114. See GENERAL
WORKS.

BLIX
Semi-Gotha, 2:78. See GENERAL
WORKS.

BLOCH
AJA has family trees beginning
1650 and 1652.
AMH has family records.
CAJ has family tree from
Vienna.
LBI has family trees beginning
1650 and 1652.
Orgler Family. "Genealogy of
the Orgler Family, Including
Some Information on Bloch,
and Gratz Families, Tracing
the Ancestry of Rebecca
Gratz, Germany and the United
States, 1650-1939." AJA.
Simon, Steinman and Block
Families' Tree (1798-   ).
WJHC.
Bachrach, Samuel and Babette.
Collection of Correspondence,
Memoirs, and Genealogical
Material Concerning the
Bloch, Wise, Tandler, and
Mack Families, 1851-1940. In
German and English. AJA.
Bloch, Sidney. No Time for
Tears: Childhood in a Rabbi's
Family. London: Kimber,
1980. 176 p. Family of
London. Covers
ca. 1930-1942. DLC.
Flesch, Heinreich.
"Genealogical Notes on the
Descendants of Israel Isaac,
17th Century," JFF, no. 3
(1925):64-70.
Frank, Helen Bernd Klein. This
is the Saga of the Bernd,
Bloch and Blum Families in
the United States of America.
N.p., 1961. 54 p. Genealogy
of three Southern Jewish
families. AJHS.
Kempelen. Magyarországi Zsidó,
2:66; 3:76, 97, 139, 140.
See GENERAL WORKS.
Reychman. Szkice
genealogiczne, pp. 21-24.
See GENERAL WORKS.
Rosenstein. Unbroken Chain,
pp. 300ff. Bloch descendants
of R. Ari Lieb Katz. See
GENERAL WORKS.
Stern. FAJF. Bloch family
tree beginning in U.S. See
GENERAL WORKS.

BLOCK
Block Family; Arkansas.
Genealogical Data, 1810-1916;
Typescript. AJA.
Rosenwaike, Ira. "Eleazer
Block: His Family and
Career," American Jewish
Archives 31 (Nov.
1979):142-49. The family of
Eleazer Block, 1797-1886,
originally came from Bohemia
and later settled in
Richmond, Va.
Schulte. Bonner Juden, p. 134.
See GENERAL WORKS.
Stern. FAJF. Block family
trees beginning in: (I) U.S.;
and (II) Rousnty, Bohemia.
See GENERAL WORKS.

BLOMFIELD
AMH has family records.

BLOOM
AJA has genealogical files.
AMH has family records.
Barmatz, Albert. Bloom Family
Reunion, Denver, 1982, 1 vol.
Illustrated. "A brief
history of the descendants of
Zev Barenbloom, born in
Russia between 1800 and 1830;
includes a directory of where
all the members of the family
are at present located."
AJHS.

BLOOMINGDALE
AMH has family records.
Stern. FAJF. Bloomingdale
family tree beginning in U.S.
See GENERAL WORKS.

BLOOMSTEIN
Frank. Nashville Jewry,
p. 129. Family originally
from Poland, arrived in U.S.
in 1850s. See GENERAL WORKS.

BLUCH
Gratz-Sulzbacher Family Papers,
1747-1961. Contain family
tree of Bluch and Henry
families of Philadelphia and
New York. AJA.

BLUEN
See BLUN.

BLUM
Frank. Nashville Jewry,
p. 130. See GENERAL WORKS.
Frank, Helen Bernd Klein. This
is the Saga of the Bernd,
Bloch, and Blum Families in
the United States of America.
N.p., 1961. 54 p. Genealogy
of three southern Jewish
families. AJHS.
Kempelen. Magyarországi Zsidó,
2:74, 96, 92. See GENERAL
WORKS.
Blum Family; Galveston, Texas.
"The Blum Saga, 1836-1968,"
by Hennie B. Kempner, 1968.
Typescript. AJA.
Lacouture, Jean. Léon Blum.
Paris: Seuil, 1977. 596 p.
Genealogical information on
family of Léon Blum
(1872-1950), the famous
French Socialist political
leader, pp. 13-20.
Lutz, Robert. "La communauté
juive de Westhoffen: les
familles Blum et Debré,"
Société d'Histoire et
d'Archéologie de Saverne et
Environs (Saverne), no. 79/80
(1972):67-71.

BLUMBEY
AMH has family records.

BLUMENFELD
AMH has family records.
CAJ has family tree for
Bachrach, Blumenfeld, Katz,
Klebe, and Meierstein
families of Bremke and Rhina,
Germany, Israel, and U.S.
covering 1650-1975.

BLUMENTHAL
AMH has family records.
CFM has family records.
Ballin. Juden in Seesen,
pp. 156-58. See GENERAL
WORKS.
Kempelen. Magyarországi Zsidó,
2:39. See GENERAL WORKS.

BLUMSTEIN
Keneseth Israel. See GENERAL
WORKS.

BLUN, BLUEN
AJA has genealogical files.
Blun (Bluen) Family.
"Scheuer-Blun Family
Genealogical Chart." 1952.
AJA.

BLYTHMAN
AMH has family records.

BOAS
AMH has family records.
CFM has family records.
Brilling, Bernhard. "Die
Vorfahren des Prof. Franz
Boas," Mitt. d. Mindener
Geschichte-und Museumsvereins
38 (1966):103-112. Columbia
University anthropologist,
Franz Boas, b. Minden,
Westphalia, Germany, 1858;
d. 1942.
Kann, Eleazar. Autobiographia
van Eleazar Kann. By the
Author, n.d. 62 p. Contains
family trees of Kann and Boas
families.
Zuiden, D.S. van. Proeve eener
genealogie van der Haagsche
familie Boas. Den Haag,
1939. 5 p. OCH.
──────. De val van een Haagsch
bankiershuis. Den Haag,
1919-20. 15 p. Reprinted
from Die Haage Jaarboek,
1919/20. OCH.

BOBELLE
PD has family tree.
Kempelen. Magyarországi Zsidó,
2:35. See GENERAL WORKS.

BOCARRO FRANCES
Azevedo, Pedro A. d'. "O
Bocarro Francês e os judeus
de Cochim e Hamburgo,"
Arquivo Histórico Portugues 8
(1910):15-20, 185-98.
Includes genealogical
information, as well as
inquisition proceedings, on
family, 17th to 18th century.

Révah, I.S. "Une famille de
'nouveaux-chrétiens': les
Bocarro Francês," Revue des
Études Juives 116
(1957):73-87. 17th century;
includes genealogical table.

BOCHORY
Kempelen. Magyarországi Zsidó,
2:24. See GENERAL WORKS.

BOCIAN
Bałaban. Żydów w Krakowie
1:180. Genealogy table of
the descendants (17th
century) of Wolf Bocian. See
GENERAL WORKS.

BOCK
AMH has family records.
Schulte. Bonner Juden, p. 136.
See GENERAL WORKS.

BODENHAUSEN
Semi-Gotha, 1:140. See GENERAL
WORKS.

BODENHEIMER
CAJ has family records.
CFM has family records.

BODROGH
Kempelen. Magyarországi Zsidó,
1:122. See GENERAL WORKS.

BOERNE
LBI has family trees beginning
1635 and 1665.

BOGDAN
Kempelen. Magyarországi Zsidó,
2:23. Bogdán family. See
GENERAL WORKS.

BOHM
Kempelen. Magyarországi Zsidó,
2:17. Böhm family. See
GENERAL WORKS.

BOIJE
Semi-Gotha, 1:99. See GENERAL
WORKS.

BOILEAU
AMH has family records.

BOJNITZER
Kempelen. Magyarországi Zsidó,
3:121. See GENERAL WORKS.

BOKOR
Kempelen. Magyarországi Zsidó,
3:72. See GENERAL WORKS.

BOLDNER
Kempelen. Magyarországi Zsidó,
1:92. See GENERAL WORKS.

BOLLAG
Guggenheim-Grünberg, Florence.
"Michael Polag, der
Stammvater der Endiger
Bollag-Familien,"
Israelitisches Wochenblatt
(Zürich) 64, no. 36
(4.IX.1964):41-47.

BOMEISLER
Stern. FAJF. Bomeisler family
tree beginning in Bavaria.
See GENERAL WORKS.

BONAS
AMH has family records.

BONDE
Semi-Gotha, 1:90. See GENERAL
WORKS.

BONDI
AJA and LBI have family trees
beginning 1603.
Auman, Reiner J., ed. The
Family Bondi and Their
Ancestors. Jamaica?, New
York, 1966. 100 p.
2 genealogical tables.
Descendants of Rabbi Jona
Marcus Bondi of Mainz. DLC,
NN.
See Jonas Marcus Bondi entry
under LUCKA.
Jakobovits, Tobias. "Die
Verbindung der Prager
Familien Oettinger-Spira
(Wedeles)-Bondi," MGWJ 76
(1933):511-19.
Bondi Family; Genealogy; MS.
The genealogy of the Bondi,
Eybeschutz, and Wise
Families, compiled by Isaac

M. Wise, grandson of Rabbi
Isaac Mayer Wise. AJA.

BONDY
Kempelen. Magyarországi Zsidó,
2:8. See GENERAL WORKS.

BONFIL
CFM has family records.

BONFILS
AMH has family records.

BONIS
Kempelen. Magyarországi Zsidó,
1:123. Bónis family. See
GENERAL WORKS.

BONN
Bonn, Moritz Julius. Wandering
Scholar. New York: The John
Day Co., 1948. 403 p. "My
Father's People," pp. 12-18;
"My Mother's People" [Brunner
family], pp. 18-24. Author
(1873-1965), German
economist, was born in
Frankfurt-am-Main. Brunner
family lived in Hohenems, a
large village in Vorarlberg.
DLC, ICU, MB, NcD, NNJ, OU.

BONNIER
LBIS has family tree for
German/Swedish family.
Rothschild. Svenska Israel.
See GENERAL WORKS.
Semi-Gotha, 2:30ff. See
GENERAL WORKS.
Simonis, Rudolf. Genealogisk
förteckning över ättlingar
till Gerhard Bonnier med
familje-porträtt av medlemmar
ur de äldre generationera.
Stockholm: Alb. Bonnier,
1956. 84, 1, 82 p., plus
40 pages of pictures and
explanations. Descendants of
Gerhard Bonnier (b. Dresden,
Germany, 1778; d. 1862).
Family eventually developed
one of the largest publishing
firms in Sweden. CtY, OCH.

BORCHARDT
AMH has family records.

49

BORCHHEIM
LBI has family tree beginning
1655.

BORGENICHT
Borgenicht, Louis. The
Happiest Man: The Life of
Louis Borgenicht as Told to
Harold Friedman. New York:
G.P. Putnam's, 1942. 414 p.
Real name Leon Borgenicht
(1860-?). A large part of
the book deals with family
life in Rzegocina, Lonkta,
Wishnicz, and
Zacliczyn-am-Dunajec,
Galicia. His father was
Nathan David Borgenicht
(1818?-?), a rabbi and
merchant in Zacliczyn. The
author came to U.S. in 1888,
where he eventually became a
leader in the infants' and
childrens' wear industry in
New York.

BORN
Born, Max. My Life:
Recollections of A Nobel
Laureate. New York: Charles
Scribner's Sons, 1975.
308 p. Genealogical
information about the Jacobi,
Lipstein, and Kauffman
relatives of the author,
pp. 3-28. The German
physicist (1882-1970) was
born in Breslau.
Kempelen. Magyarországi Zsidó,
1:19. See GENERAL WORKS.

BORNEMISZA
Kempelen. Magyarországi Zsidó,
2:24, 45. See GENERAL WORKS.

BORNSTEIN
Rose, Leesha. The Tulips Are
Red. Cranbury, N.J.: A.S.
Barnes, 1978. 275 p. Work
describes Bornstein family's
experiences in Holland during
the Holocaust. Author
(1922-   ) is the daughter
of Yeshayahu and Chanah
Bornstein. The father was
born in Poland. Her parents

BOTON

and brothers did not survive
the war.

BORSODI
Kempelen. Magyarországi Zsidó,
2:56. See GENERAL WORKS.

BORVENDIG
Kempelen. Magyarországi Zsidó,
3:102. See GENERAL WORKS.

BOSCHAN
Kempelen. Magyarországi Zsidó,
3:136. Boschán family. See
GENERAL WORKS.

BOSCHWITZ
Zielenziger, Georg. Stammbaum
der Familien Pagel und
Boschwitz. Ausgeführt von
Karl Hacker. Berlin, 1907.
BR.

BOSKOWITZ
Kempelen. Magyarországi Zsidó,
2:8, 10, 35, 36, 139; 3:31.
See GENERAL WORKS.

BOSS
AMH has family records.

BOSSANYI
Kempelen. Magyarországi Zsidó,
2:88. Bossányi family. See
GENERAL WORKS.

BOSSANYI-HAVAS
Kempelen. Magyarországi Zsidó,
1:19. Bossányi-Havas family.
See GENERAL WORKS.

BOSZORMENYI
Kempelen. Magyarországi Zsidó,
1:134; 3:79. Böszörményi
family. See GENERAL WORKS.

BOTON
JE, 3:339. Genealogical chart
of Spanish family which
immigrated to Salonica,
Turkey in 1492 and which
produced many eminent rabbis
and talmudists, especially
during 16th to 18th century.
See GENERAL WORKS.

BOTOSANI
CAJ has family tree.

BOTTENHEIM
AMH has family records.

BOUMAN
CAJ has family tree from the
Netherlands.

BOWYER
Cohen, Evelina Gleaves. Family
Facts and Fairy Tales.
Wynnewood, Pa., 1953. 115 p.
Descendants of Joseph Cohen
(1745-1822). Includes Bowyer
family. DLC, NN, PHi,
PPDrop.

BOYARSKY
See Yaffa Draznin entry under
BERNSTEIN.

BOZNER
Tänzer. Juden in Tirol,
p. 694. See GENERAL WORKS.

BOZO
Kempelen. Magyarországi Zsidó,
3:100. Bozó family. See
GENERAL WORKS.

BRACHFELD
Kempelen. Magyarországi Zsidó,
1:14, 54, 90, 137. See
GENERAL WORKS.

BRACKMAN
AMH has family records.

BRADLEY
AMH has family records.

BRADSHAW
AMH has family records.

BRAHAM
AMH has family records.
CFM has family records.

BRAK
Kempelen. Magyarországi Zsidó,
3:26. See GENERAL WORKS.

BRAKEL
Semi-Gotha, 1:79. See GENERAL
WORKS.

BRALIA
AMH has family records.

BRANDEIS
Keneseth Israel. See GENERAL
WORKS.
PD has family tree.
De Haas, Jacob. Louis D.
Brandeis: A Biographical
Sketch. New York: Bloch
Publishing Co., 1929. 296 p.
Author mentions the judge's
ancestors on both sides of
his family. DLC, MH, NcD,
MB, NN, NNC, OCH, OCl, OU,
PP, PPDrop.
Goldmark, Josephine. Pilgrims
of '48: One Man's Part in the
Austrian Revolution of 1848,
and a Family Migration to
America. New Haven: Yale
University Press, 1930.
311 p. Pt. 2, pp. 167-296:
"The Forty-Eighters in the
United States. Account of
the Emigration of Several
Jewish Families (Goldmark,
Wehle, and Brandeis) to
America in 1849."
JFF, no. 10. Family history.

BRANDENSTEIN
WJHC has family tree.
McDougall, Ruth Bransten.
Under Mannie's Hat. San
Francisco: Hesperian Press,
1964. 172 p. Traces the
history of the San Francisco
Brandenstein (now Bransten)
family, founders of the
M.J. Brandenstein coffee
firm, from 1906 to time of
publication. Author's
grandfather, Joseph
Brandenstein, came to
California from Germany in
1850. CU, DLC, N, NIC, NN,
WHi.

BRANDES
Simonsen, David. "Name und
Abstammung von George

Brandes," JFF, no. 10
(1927):231-32.

BRANDON
AMH has family records.
CFM has three family trees
related to Brandon, Fonseca,
Israel, and Rodrigues
families.
Bull, William. "Fortiter et
Recte" Short History of the
Brandon Family (1492-1935).
London, 1935. 20 p. AJA.
Stern. FAJF. Brandon family
trees beginning in:
(I) London; and
(II) Barbados. See GENERAL
WORKS.
Wolf, "Anglo-Jewish Families."
See GENERAL WORKS.

BRANDT-MEYER
Conway, J.S. "The Last Letters
of the Brandt-Meyer Family
from Berlin," Yad Vashem
Studies 11 (1976):91-130.
The letters of Oscar Ludwig
Brandt (real last name
Meyers; 1889-1943?), and his
wife, Margarete Jacoby
Brandt. Oscar Brandt was
born in Cologne.

BRANDUS
AMH has family records.
Sommerguth, Ludwig. Chronik
der Familien Somerguth,
Weinzig, Brandus. Berlin,
1933. 18 p. folio. LBI.

BRANSTEN
See BRANDENSTEIN.

BRASCH
Japha Family Tree. Unpublished
family tree of Japha family
compiled by Max Japha or one
of his relatives. Includes
Brasch family. Family
originally from Fraustadt,
Germany. Related to
descendants of Mordechai ben
Abraham ben Josef Jeffe
(Jaffe?) of Posen, b. 1530.
JGCT.

See Esmond S. De Beer entry
under BARDEN.

BRATT
Semi-Gotha, 1:37, 128, 150.
See GENERAL WORKS.

BRAUDE
Rosenstein. Unbroken Chain,
pp. 456ff. See GENERAL
WORKS.

BRAUER
AJA has genealogical files.
Stern. FAJF. Brauer family
tree beginning in U.S. See
GENERAL WORKS.

BRAUMAN
Reychman. Szkice
genealogiczne, pp. 28-31.
See GENERAL WORKS.

BRAUN
AMH has family records.
Kempelen. Magyarországi Zsidó,
1:104, 106; 2:87, 136; 3:68,
115. See GENERAL WORKS.
See Daniel Nathan Leeson entry
under LEESON.

BRAV
AJA has family tree.

BRAVO
AMH has family records.
CFM has family records.

BRAWN
AMH has family records.

BREHMER
Semi-Gotha, 2:19. See GENERAL
WORKS.

BREIDENBACH
Schnee. Hoffinanz und Staat,
3:156-60. "Stammreihe-Wolf
Breidenbach." Wolf
Breidenbach, b. Kassel,
Aug. 1750; d. Offenbach am
Main, Feb. 27, 1829. 18th to
early 20th century. See
GENERAL WORKS.

BREIT
LBI has family tree beginning
1394.
Richter, John Henry. The
Neisser Families. The
Descendants of Aron and
Catharina (Breit) Neisser of
Katscher, District of
Leobschütz, Upper Silesia,
Germany. In Memoriam Prof.
Dr. Med. Max Neisser
(1869-1938), First Collector
of Genealogical Data. Ann
Arbor, Mich., 1958. 74 p.

BREITENBACH
Breitenbach-Ehrlich Family.
"Family Records Contained in
Prayer Book Owned by Sarah
Breitenbach Ehrlich,
Bainbridge, Ga., 1849-1974."
AJA.

BREITNER
Kempelen. Magyarországi Zsidó,
2:102, 103, 130. See GENERAL
WORKS.

BREMER
CAJ has family tree.
LBI has family tree beginning
1768.
Ballin. Juden in Seesen,
pp. 159-65. See GENERAL
WORKS.

BRENDON
AMH has family records.

BRENER
JGCT has family tree. Some
family members in Lancaster,
Pennsylvania.

BRENNEMAN
Frank, Ivie A. The Wenger
History: Descendants of Jacob
Wenger and Hannah Brenneman
Wenger. N.p., 1970. 66 p.
NN.

BRENNER
Hechter, Ruth Kaaplander.
Brenner-Sattenstein-
Kaaplander (Caplan)-Hoff

Family Tree. Brooklyn, N.Y.,
1982. PJAC.

BRENTANO
Tänzer. Juden in Tirol,
pp. 695-96. See GENERAL
WORKS.

BRESH
See BRUSH.

BRESLAU, BRESLAUER
LBI has Breslau family tree
beginning 1711.
Brilling, Bernhard.
"Breslau(er) als jüdischer
Familienname," Breslauer
Jüdisches Gemeindeblatt,
nos. 7, 9 (1937).
———. "Eine Hebraïsche
Handschrift auf Warendorf,"
Westfalen 40, no. 3
(1962):333-41. Contains
Breslau family history.
Schnee. Hoffinanz und Staat,
6:153-69. "Der münstersche
Hoffaktor Michael Meyer
Breslauer und der
gesellschaftliche Aufstieg
seiner Nachkommen." 18th to
20th century. See GENERAL
WORKS.

BRESSELAU
CAJ has family tree from
Germany.

BREST
AMH has family records.

BRETTAUER
Tänzer. Juden in Tirol,
pp. 697-700. See GENERAL
WORKS.

BRETTHOLZ
CAJ has family records.

BREUER
Kempelen. Magyarországi Zsidó,
1:62; 2:58, 133, 139; 3:118.
See GENERAL WORKS.

BREWSTER
AMH has family records.

BRICE
AMH has family records.

BRICHTA
Kempelen. Magyarországi Zsidó,
2:51. See GENERAL WORKS.

BRICKNER
AJA has genealogical files.
Stern. FAJF. Brickner family
tree beginning in Welbhausen,
Bavaria. See GENERAL WORKS.

BRIDGES
AMH has family records.

BRIEDEMANN
AMH has family records.

BRIETSCHE
AMH has family records.

BRIGHT
AMH has family records.
CFM has family records.
Lipson, Eric. "The Brights of
Market Place," Hunter
Archaeol. Soc. Transactions
6, pt. 3 (Aug. 1947):117-25.
Family of Sheffield, England.

BRILIN
PD has family records.
Michael Berolzheimer.
Collection. Includes Brilin
family tree. LBI.

BRILL
Kempelen. Magyarországi Zsidó,
1:7; 2:91; 3:25. See GENERAL
WORKS.

BRILLMAN
AMH has family records.

BRISK
CAJ has family tree.

BROD
Jakobovits, Tobias. "Die
Abstammung (Max Brod's),"
Jüdischer Almanach, 5695
(1934), pp. 202-206.

BRODA
PD has family records.

Braude, Azriel Meier.
Mišpaḥat Broda, toledot
ha-Rabbanim ... Šemoş 'am
mi-mišpaḥa zo. Warszawa,
1938. YIVO.
See Meir Yizraeli entry under
BIDERMAN.

BRODE
Kempelen. Magyarországi Zsidó,
1:27. See GENERAL WORKS.

BRODER
"The Los Angeles Broders: A
Picture Story," Western
States Jewish Historical
Quarterly 13 (Apr.
1981):225-29. Descendants of
Jacob and Mildred Kaplan
Broder, originally of Odessa,
Russia.

BRODI, BRODY
AJA has Brody genealogical
files.
Brody Family. "Genealogy of
the Brody-Seiferth Family,
1764-1976." New Orleans,
La., 1976. AJA.
Kempelen. Magyarországi Zsidó,
1:63; 2:91, 94, 122, 123;
3:87. Bródi, Bródy family.
See GENERAL WORKS.

BRODRICK
AMH has family records.

BRODSKY
Brodsky, Pinchas (1827-1924).
Papers, 1896, 1975.
1 folder. Copy of an 1897
photograph and a letter,
1975, containing biographical
information about Pinchas
Brodsky written by his
great-grandson, Mitchell
Snyderman. Born in Russia,
he immigrated to Philadelphia
in 1911 and died in New York.
PJAC.
Rosenstein. Unbroken Chain,
pp. 430ff. Related to Babad
family. See GENERAL WORKS.

BRODY
See BRODI, BRODY.

BRODY-BERLIN
Semi-Gotha, 1:116ff. See
GENERAL WORKS.

BROGLIE
Semigothaisches Taschenbuch.
Genealogical table 4. See
GENERAL WORKS.

BRONFMAN
Hayes, Saul. "The Bronfman
'Dynasty': A Friend's
Reminiscence," Viewpoints 10,
no. 1 (1979):45-49. Family
of Canada.
Newman, Peter C. King of the
Castle: The Making of a
Dynasty: Seagram's and the
Bronfman Empire. New York:
Atheneum, 1979. 304 p.
Family of Canada. Story of
Sam Bronfman, 1891-1971, and
his family. They are
descendants of Ekiel and
Minnie Bronfman who came to
Canada in 1889.
Siekman, Peter. "The
Bronfmans: An Instinct for
Dynasty," Fortune 74, no. 6
(1966):144-49, 196-210; 74,
no. 7 (1966):176-79, 198-208.

BRONNER
Bronner, Barbara. "The
Bronners and the
Verschvovskys: Genealogy of
the Bronner-Verschvovsky
Family." Louisville, Ky.,
1975. AJA.

BROOKER
AMH has family records.

BROOKS
Morris, Jo Ann. "Genealogy of
the Morris-Brooks Family."
Louisville, Ky., 1975. AJA.

BROOK-SMITH
AMH has family records.

BROWN
See HOWARD-BROWN.
AMH has family records.

BRUCK
Bruck, Alfred Julius. "The
Bruck Family: A Historical
Sketch of a Jewish Family
through a Thousand Years,"
Historia Judaica 9
(Oct. 1947):159-77.
————. The Bruck Family. A
Historical Sketch of a Jewish
Family through a Thousand
Years. London, etc., 1946.
288 p. folio, typescript.
Descendants of Abba Mari
Perlhefter founder of Bruck
family. When he settled in
Vienna in 1626 he adopted the
family name of Bruck after
the Austrian city, Bruck an
der Leitha, where he had
leased the customs and excise
tax concessions. LBI, NN.
Kopp. Jüdischen Alsenz,
pp. 119-21. Brück family.
See GENERAL WORKS.

BRUEHL
Reychman. Szkice
genealogiczne, pp. 32-35.
See GENERAL WORKS.

BRUGLER
Kempelen. Magyarországi Zsidó,
2:88. Brügler family. See
GENERAL WORKS.

BRUHL
CAJ has family records.

BRUKNER
Kempelen. Magyarországi Zsidó,
1:82. Brükner family. See
GENERAL WORKS.

BRULL
Kempelen. Magyarországi Zsidó,
1:86, 88, 113, 129; 2:44, 46,
68, 74, 146. Brüll family.
See GENERAL WORKS.
"Verschwägerung der Familie
Brüll mit dem Pressburger
Stammhause Heines," Judaica
(Pressburg) 3, no. 19/20
(1936):19-20.

BRUML
Bruml Family; St. Louis, Mo.

Genealogical Information,
1746-1977. MS and printed.
In German and English. AJA.

BRUNAUER
Kempelen. Magyarországi Zsidó,
3:65, 70. Brünauer family.
See GENERAL WORKS.

BRUNNEN
Rosenstein, Conrad. Der
Brunnen. Eine
Familienchronik. Israel,
1958. 64 p. MS. Posen,
Lithuania. LBI.

BRUNNER
AJA has genealogical files for
family of Barbar Brunner.
LBI has family tree beginning
1685.
Bonn, Moritz Julius. Wandering
Scholar. New York: The John
Day Co., 1948. 403 p. "My
Father's People," pp. 12-18;
"My Mother's People" [Brunner
family], pp. 18-24. Author
(1873-1965), German
economist, was born in
Frankfurt-am-Main. Brunner
family lived in Hohenems, a
large village in Vorarlberg.
DLC, ICU, MB, NcD, NNJ, OU.
Kempelen. Magyarországi Zsidó,
3:139. See GENERAL WORKS.
Reychman. Szkice
genealogiczne, pp. 37-44.
See GENERAL WORKS.
Tänzer. Juden in Tirol,
pp. 701-703. See GENERAL
WORKS.

BRUNT, VAN
See VAN BRUNT.

BRUSH
Stern. FAJF. Brush family
tree beginning in Goshlin
(Prussia? or Poland?). Also
originally Bresh. See
GENERAL WORKS.

BRUSSEL-SCHAUBECK
Kempelen. Magyarországi Zsidó,
1:54. See GENERAL WORKS.

BRUST
Kempelen. Magyarországi Zsidó,
3:100. See GENERAL WORKS.

BRYSK
AJA has genealogical files for
family of Eric Brysk.

BUBER
Rosenstein. Unbroken Chain,
pp. 321ff. Genealogical
chart. See GENERAL WORKS.

BUCHHEIM
Buchheim, Wilhelm. The Story
of the Buchheim Family. New
York, 1957. 16, 18, 5 p.
MS. Family from Hessen and
Westphalen. LBI.

BUCHSBAUM
MGWJ 41 (1897):128. Buchsbaum
family history.

BUCHWALD
Kempelen. Magyarországi Zsidó,
2:15, 66. See GENERAL WORKS.

BUCKLEY
AMH has family records.

BUCKSTEIN
AJA has genealogical files.
AJA also has family tree of
Kaven-Buckstein family.

BUDAY-GOLDBERGER
Kempelen. Magyarországi Zsidó,
3:129. See GENERAL WORKS.

BUENO
CFM has family records.

BUFF
Deutsch, Hermann. Stammbäume
der Familien Buff und Riegel
Wild und Martin. Cronheim,
n.p., 1936? 4 pts. Pt. I:
Erlauterungen zur Stammtafel
der Familie Buff aus
Cronheim, 1635-1936. 42 p.
CAJ, Call No. 2771/3.

BUJANOWSKA
See ZUKER.

BULL
AMH has family records.

BULLER
AMH has family records.

BULYI
Kempelen. Magyarországi Zsidó,
3:48. See GENERAL WORKS.

BULYOVSZKY
Kempelen. Magyarországi Zsidó,
2:73. See GENERAL WORKS.

BUN
Kempelen. Magyarországi Zsidó,
2:37. See GENERAL WORKS.

BUNZL
PD has family records.

BURCHARD
LBI has family tree beginning
1843.

BURG
LBIS has family tree.

BURGAUER
Tänzer. Juden in Tirol,
pp. 704-705. See GENERAL
WORKS.

BURGEL
Kempelen. Magyarországi Zsidó,
2:75. Bürgel family. See
GENERAL WORKS.

BURGER
LBI has family tree beginning
1600.
Kempelen. Magyarországi Zsidó,
2:127. See GENERAL WORKS.
Levison, Wilhelm. Die
Siegburger Familie Levison
und verwandte Familien.
Bonn: Röhrscheid, 1952.
187 p. Family history and
genealogical tables. CSt,
DLC, LU, NN, NNJ.

BURGOS
CFM has family records.

BURGUNDER
AJA has genealogical files.

See Sydney M. Cone entry under
AMBACH.

BURIAN
Kempelen. Magyarországi Zsidó,
1:56; 2:126. Burián family.
See GENERAL WORKS.

BURKHARDT
Kempelen. Magyarországi Zsidó,
2:38. See GENERAL WORKS.

BURLEY
AMH has family records.

BURNHAM
AMH has family records.

BURNS
AMH has family records.

BURSCH
AJA has family tree for
Chasker-Bursch family
beginning 1758.

BUSBY
Busby, Gladys J.L. The Blood
of Abraham: A Genealogy and
Temple Record of Abraham John
Busby. Mesa, Ariz.: Printed
by H.M. Roy, 1958? 174 p.
Includes genealogical tables.
NN.

BUSH
AJA has Isidor Bush (1822-1898)
family tree beginning 1722.
Bush born in Prague, came to
live in St. Louis, Mo.
Stern. FAJF. Bush family tree
beginning in Prague. See
GENERAL WORKS.

BUSNACH
Eisenbeth, M. "Les juifs en
Algérie et en Tunisie à
l'époque turque (1516-1830),"
Revue Africaine 96
(1952):372-84. On Bacri and
Busnach families.

BUSSE
CFM has Bussé family tree.

BUTENHEIM
AMH has family records.

BUTENWIES
"Elkan Henler Butenwies,
1761-1833," MGWJ, 1918,
p. 223.

BUTLER
AMH has family records.

BUTSUM
Kempelen. Magyarországi Zsidó,
2:46. See GENERAL WORKS.

BUTTENWIESER
Buttenwieser Family Tree,
1780-1975; and American
Jewish Archives
Autobiographical
Questionnaire of Sadie
Klingenstein Klau, 1975;
Printed. AJA.

BUXBAUM
CAJ has family tree.
Kaufmann, David. "Eine Frank.
Arztefamilie," MGWJ 41
(1897):128-35. 17th to 18th
century.
Kempelen. Magyarországi Zsidó,
3:95. See GENERAL WORKS.

BUZAGLO
AMH has family records.
CFM has family records.

BUZGABO
Roth, Cecil. "The Amazing Clan
of Buzgabo," Transactions of
the Jewish Historical Society
of England 23 (1971):11-21.
Descendants of Abraham ben
David, called Abuzgalo. 16th
to early 19th century in
Holland.

BYDESKUTHY
Kempelen. Magyarországi Zsidó,
2:76. See GENERAL WORKS.

BYE
AMH has family records.

BYNG
CFM has family records.

CABALLERIA
See CAVALLERIA.

CABRIT
Cardoner Planas, A. "El linaje
de los Cabrit en relación con
la medicina del siglo XV,"
Sefarad 16 (1956):357-68.

CACERAS, CACERES
JE, 3:482. Genealogical table
of Amsterdam branch of
family. Family members have
lived in Spain, Portugal,
Holland, England, Mexico,
Surinam, the West Indies, and
U.S. Name also spelled
Caceras, Carceres, Carcerts,
Casares, Casseras, and
Cazares. See GENERAL WORKS.

CADET
Stern. FAJF. Cadet family
tree beginning in Lyons,
France. See GENERAL WORKS.

CAFFAROLLI
Kempelen. Magyarországi Zsidó,
1:44. See GENERAL WORKS.

CAHEN
CFM has family records.
Schulte. Bonner Juden, p. 139.
See GENERAL WORKS.

CAHN
AJA has family record book,
1700-1915.
CAJD has family tree from
Germany.
CFM has family records.
LBI has family tree beginning
1742.
LBIS has notes of family from
Frankfurt.
Schulte. Bonner Juden,
pp. 147, 170, 173, 177. See
GENERAL WORKS.

CAILLARD
AMH has family records.

CAILLE
AMH has family records.

CALDER
Calder Family; Wilmington, N.C.
"Records and Recollections of
the Calder Family, Including
Information About the Lazarus
and Mordecai Families of
Charleston, S.C., 1757-1959."
Typescript. Xerox copy.
AJA.

CALE
Chapiro, José, ed. Für Alfred
Kerr. Ein Buch der
Freundschaft. Berlin:
S. Fischer. 181 p. Contain
information on his
ascendants, the Kempner and
Calé families, pp. 162ff.
CtY, DLC, IEN, MH, NN, NNC,
WU.

CALLMANN
Schulte. Bonner Juden, p. 178.
See GENERAL WORKS.

CALMAN-LEVY
LBI has family tree beginning
1720.

CALMANN
Kempelen. Magyarországi Zsidó,
1:14; 2:10, 11. See GENERAL
WORKS.

CALMS
See KALM-CALMS.

CALVARISKI
Simon, Fritz. Schalscheleth
ha-Juchasin
Eger-Margoliouth-Calvariski-
Simon. Jerusalem, 1941.
1 leaf folio. Family trees
of the above families.

CALVERLEY
AMH has family records.

CALVO DE SILVA
Filippini, Jean-Pierre. "Une
famille juive de Livourne au
service du Roi de France au
XVIII siécles: les Calvo de

Silva," Revue des Études
Juives 138 (1979):255-89.

CAMONDO
Levy, M.E. "Une famille de
Mécènes sépharadis en France:
Les Camondo," Message
Sépharadi (Paris), 1952,
pp. 157-58.

CAMPBELL
AMH has family records.

CAMPOS
CFM has family records.

CANCO
CFM has family records.

CANETTI
Canetti, Elias. The Tongue Set
Free: Remembrance of a
European Childhood.
Translated from the German by
Joachim Neugroschel. New
York: Seabury, 1979. 268 p.
The Nobel Prize-winning
author (1905-   ) was born
in Ruschuk, Bulgaria, of a
Sephardic family. His
parents were Jacques and
Mathilde Canetti, and his
grandparents were Elias and
Lacra Canetti. Family moved
to England when the author
was six. Autobiography
covers 1905-1921.

CANSINO
AJA has family tree of
Spanish/North African family,
1440-1967.
AMH has family records.
CFM has family records.
EJ (1928), 5:23. See GENERAL
WORKS.

CANTARINI
Albero genealogico della
famiglia Cantarini Casale,
Monferratto, Paolo Bertero.
1875. 1 p. Large fold-out
genealogical chart of
Cantarini family, 1492-1875;
in Italian; includes names of
important rabbis. JNUL.

CANTER
Stern. FAJF. Canter family
tree beginning in Denmark.
See GENERAL WORKS.

CANTOR
AMH has family records.
LBIS has family notes.
Familieminder Tilegnet. Cantor
family, pp. 88-89. See
GENERAL WORKS.

CAPADOSE
AMH has family records.
CFM has family records.
Da Costa, Isaac. Noble
Families among the Sephardic
Jews. By Isaac da Costa.
With Some Account of the
Capadose Family (Including
their Conversion to
Christianity). By Bertram
Brewster. And an Excursus on
their Jewish History. By
Cecil Roth. London: Oxford
University Press, 1936.
219 p. CtY, CU, DLC, NB,
NcD, NNC, NNJ, PPDrop.

CAPADOZA
CAJ has family tree.

CAPLAN
AJA has genealogical files.
Caplan Family Tree. Compiled
by Irwin M. Berent. Family
originally from Ligum?
(Lygumai?), Kovno Gubernia,
Lithuania.
Hechter, Ruth Kaaplander.
Brenner-Sattenstein-
Kaaplander (Caplan)-Hoff
Family Tree. Brooklyn, N.Y.,
1982. PJAC.

CAPULA
AMH has family records.

CARAVAGLIO
CFM has family records.

CARAVITA
Sobrequés Vidal, Santiago.
"Contribución a la historia
de los judíos de Gerona.
Familias hebreas gerundenses:

Los Zabarra y los Caravita,"
Anales del Instituto de
Estudios Gerundenses 2
(1947):68-98.

CARCERES, CARCERTS
See CACERAS, CACERES.

CARDELL
Semi-Gotha, 2:47. See GENERAL
WORKS.

CARDOSO
AMH has family records.

CARDOZA
AMH has family records.
De Leon Family, Charleston,
S.C. Biographical and
Genealogical Records,
Indicating the Relationships
between the Seixas, Cardoza,
and De Leon Families,
1708-1888; Photostats. AJA.
See Stern, FAJF entry under
CARDOZO.

CARDOZO
CFM has family records.
EJ (1972), 5:162. American
descendants of Aaron Nuñez
Cardozo (d. 1800). See
GENERAL WORKS.
Cardozo, Francis Lewis
(1836-1903). Family Papers,
1864-1968. Black educator,
Congregational clergyman, and
public official.
Genealogical information
about his ancestry,
particularly the connection
between this family and the
Jewish Cardozo family of
South Carolina. LC,
Manuscript Division.
Cardozo, Michael H., IV.
Leaves from a Family Tree.
2d ed. [Washington, D.C.],
1976. 18 ll. Genealogical
charts on Nathan, Seixas, and
Cardozo families. AJHS.
Cardozo Family; New York and
Washington, D.C. "Family
Tree of the New York City law
firm of Cardozo and Cardozo,
Covering the Years 1864-1980;

and Family Tree Prepared by
Michael H. Cardozo IV, and
Related Correspondence,
1976-1980." MS, typescript
and printed. AJA.
Hellman, George S. Benjamin N.
Cardozo, American Judge
(1870-1938). New York:
Whittlesey House, 1940.
339 p. DLC, NcD, NIC, NN,
NNJ, OCH, PP, PPDrop, TxU.
Contains genealogical
information.
Cardozo, Benjamin Nathan.
Genealogy of the Supreme
Court Justice, prepared by
Walter Max Kraus. AJA.
Stern. FAJF. Cardozo family
tree beginning in London.
Also spelled Cardoza in later
generations. See GENERAL
WORKS.

CARLEBACH
EJ (1972), 5:182. Genealogical
table of rabbis of family.
Descendants of Joseph Hirsch
Carlebach (d. 1881). Family
members in Germany, U.S.,
Israel, Canada, and England.
See GENERAL WORKS.
Carlebach, Naphtali. The
Carlebach Tradition: The
History of My Family. 1973.
AJHS.

CARLSTON
Kempelen. Magyarországi Zsidó,
1:125. See GENERAL WORKS.

CARMINHA
CFM has family records.

CARMON
See Zevi Shimshi entry under
SHIMSHELEWITZ.

CARNEGY
AMH has family records.

CARO
AMH has family records.
Caro, Abraham. Caro Family
Pedigree; Translated from the
Hebrew of Rabbi Abraham Caro
of Krotoschin (from

1864-1888), by the Rev. Dr.
David De Sola Pool, Annotated
and Extended from Jewish
Encyclopedia and Other
Sources, by Ella F.
Mielziner, and with
Geographic Names Located by
Dr. Boas Cohen.... New York,
1928. Genealogical tables.
MS. NN, OCH.
Caro Family; Highland Park,
Illinois. "From These
Roots," A Family Chronicle by
Joseph H. Caro, 1966.
Typescript and printed. AJA.

CAROLINA
CFM has family records.

CARR
AMH has family records.

CARRACOSA
CFM has family records.

CARRASCO-SANCHEZ
AJA has genealogical files of
Carrasco-Sánchez family.

CARRENCE
CAJ has family tree of family
of Paris. Call No. 5267.

CARRERAS
AMH has family records.

CARRION
CFM has family records.

CARTAGENA
Cantera, Francisco. "El poeta
Cartagena del 'cancionero
general' y sus asciendentes
los Franco," Sefarad 28
(1968):3-39. Includes
genealogical table. Spanish
Marrano family.

CARTE
AMH has family records.

CARVAJAL
EJ (1972) 5:220. Genealogical
table of 16th century Mexican
converso family. Descendants
of Gaspar de Carvajal,

d. ca. 1550. See GENERAL
WORKS.
Cohen, Martin A. The Martyr:
The Story of a Secret Jew and
the Mexican Inquisition in
the Sixteenth Century.
Philadelphia: Jewish
Publication Society of
America, 5733-1973.
xviii, 373 p. Family
history, 16th century.
Family tree, early 16th to
early 17th century,
p. [xviii].
Kohut, George Alexander. The
Martyrdom of the Carabajal
[sic] Family in Mexico,
1590-1601. Portland, Oregon,
1904. CtY, NN, OCH, OCU.
"The Carvajals and Their
Contemporaries," in Seymour
B. Liebman's The Jews in New
Spain: Faith, Flame, and the
Inquisition, (Coral Gables,
Florida: University of Miami
Press, 1970), pp. 159-82.
Toro, Alfonso. La familia
Carvajal. Estudio histórico
sobre los judíos y la
Inquisición de la Nueva
España en el siglo XVI basado
en documentos originales y en
su mayor parte inéditos que
se conservan en el Archivo
General de la Ciudad de
México. México: Editorial
Patria, S.A., 1944. 2 Vols.

CARVALHO
AJA has genealogical files.
AMH has family records.
CFM has family records.
Stern. FAJF. Carvalho family
tree beginning in London.
See GENERAL WORKS.

CARY
Warfield, N. Chart of the
Gist-Cary Family Tree, 1903.
Revised 1959. AJA.

CASARES
See CACERAS, CACERES.

CASELBERG
AMH has family records.

CASELLA
CFM has family records.

CASES
Levi, Isaia. "La famiglia
Cases," Il Vessillo
Israelitico 51 (1903):391-93.
From Mantova, Italy.

CASHMAN
Weaner, Arthur. History and
Genealogy of the German
Emigrant Johan Christian
Kirschenmann (Anglicised
Cashman), with References to
Other Cashman Surnames in
America of German, Irish,
Jewish, and Other Unknown
Origins. Gettysburg, Pa.: By
the Author, 1957. 1 vol.
NN, PHi, OCl, WHi.

CASHMORE
AMH has family records.

CASPER
AMH has family records.
Rothmann, Adolph Abraham.
Familiengeschichte.
Karkur/Palästina, 1940.
12 p. Family of Posen.
Also includes Rothmann,
Michalowski, Munderstein, and
Wolff families. LBI.

CASSEL
CAJ has family records.
CFM has family records.
LBI has family trees beginning
1720 and 1782.
Burke's Peerage and Baronetage,
1970. Family of England.
Prijs, Joseph. Pedigree of the
Family Goldsmit-Cassel of
Amsterdam (1650-1750).
Translated from the Dutch by
Oscar Schmeiler. Basle: By
the Author, 1937. 20 p.
Genealogical table. NN.
————. Stammboom der familie
Goldsmit-Cassel te Amsterdam,
1650-1750. Bazel, Uitg. Van
den auteur, 1936. 22 p.
Genealogical table. OCH, OU.
Schulte. Bonner Juden, p. 179.
See GENERAL WORKS.

CASSERAS
See CACERAS, CACERES.

CASSIRER
LBI has family tree beginning
1857.

CASTANO
CFM has family records.

CASTAYNE
AMH has family records.

CASTELAZZO
David, A. "Mišpaḥat
Castelazzo," (In Hebrew.)
Sinai 64, no. 5/6 (1969); 65,
no. 5/6 (1970).

CASTELLAZZO
Kaufmann, David. "La famille
Castellazzo," Revue des
Études Juives 22 (1890):290;
23 (1891):139-43.
————. "Der Maler Mose del
Castellazzo," Allg. Ztg. D.
Judentums 56 (1892):465ff.

CASTELLO
AMH has family records.
CFM has family records.

CASTILLO
AJA has family tree beginning
15th century.

CASTLE
AMH has family records.

CASTLE-LEVY
AMH has family records.

CASTRO
See DE CASTRO.
See OROBIO DE CASTRO.
AMH has family records.
CAJ has family tree.
EJ (1928), 5:90-95. See
GENERAL WORKS.
JE, 3:608-613. Genealogy of
Dutch family. Descendants of
David Henríquez de Castro
(d. 1779), through mid-19th
century. See GENERAL WORKS.
Castro, Carlos de. Grundriss
der Geschichte der Familie de

Castro. Berlin: Im
Selbstverlage des Verfassers,
1934. 23 p. DLC.
Millás y Vallicrosa, José
María. Estudios sobre
historia de la ciencia
española. Barcelona,
C.S.I.C., Instituto "Luis
Vives de Filosofía," 1949.
499 p. "La obra médica de la
familia toledana de los
Castro," pp. 443-54. CtY,
DLC, ICU, MH, NcD, NN,
PPDrop.
————. "Sobre el supuesto
judaísmo de la familia de
médicos toledanos, los
Castro," Sefarad 11
(1951):111-14.
Révah, I.S. "Orobio de Castro
et sa famille aux prises avec
l'Inquisition espagnole,"
Berichten en Mededelingen
v.h. Genootschap voor Joodse
Wetenschappen 9 (1965):87-90.
17th-century, Dutch-Jewish
family, originally Marranos
from Portugal.
Schoeps, Hans Joachim. Ein
Weites Feld: Gesammelte
Aufsätze. Berlin (West):
Haude und Spener, 1980.
403 p. Includes a section on
"Die sephardische Arztfamilie
de Castro." A Portuguese
Marrano family of physicians
which first settled in
Hamburg in 17th century.
DLC, JNUL.

CATELLA
CFM has family records.

CATTAUIS
Grunwald, Kurt. "On Cairo's
Lombard Street," Tradition
(West Germany) 17, no. 1
(1972):8-22. Includes three
genealogical tables on four
Jewish banking families:
Cattauis, Hararis, Mosseris,
and Suares, ca. 1800-1952.

CATTELA
AMH has family records.

CAUFFMAN
Stern. FAJF. Cauffman family
tree beginning in U.S. See
GENERAL WORKS.

CAUFFMAN-CLAVA
AJA has genealogical files.

CAUSTON
AMH has family records.

CAVALLERIA
EJ (1972), 5:263. Genealogical
table of de la Cavallería
family. Descendants of Judah
de la Cavallería, bailiff of
Saragossa, d. 1276, through
early 15th century. See
GENERAL WORKS.
Serrano y Sanz, M. "El linaje
hebraico de la caballería,
según el Libro Verde de
Aragón y otros documentos,"
Boletín de la Real Academia
de la Historia 73
(1918):160-84. Caballería or
Cavallería families, 14th to
16th century.

CAYN
CAJ has family tree beginning
16th-century Germany.

CAZARES
See CACERAS, CACERES.

CEDERCREUTZ
Semi-Gotha, 1:81. See GENERAL
WORKS.

CEDERHJELM
Semi-Gotha, 1:84. See GENERAL
WORKS.

CEPEDA
See SANCHEZ DE CEPEDA.

CERF
AMH has family records.
Pudor. Internationalen
Verwandtschaftlichen.
Volume 2 contains a section
on Cerf family. See GENERAL
WORKS.

CHACON
CFM has family records.

CHADAS
See COHODAS.

CHAGAL, CHAGALL
Chagall, Marc. My Life.
Translated from the French by
Elisabeth Ahbeltt. New York:
Orion Press, 1960. 173 p.
Author (1887-   ) was born
in Vitebsk on the Dvina
River. He is the son of
Zakhar and Fega-Ita Chagal
and the grandson of David and
Bachewa Chagal. When Marc
Chagall went to France he
added a second "l" to the
name. The original family
name was Segal. CLU, CSt,
CtY, CU, DLC, ICU, NcD, NIC,
NjP, NNC, OCH, OCl, TxU.

CHAGIS
EJ (1928), 5:153. See GENERAL
WORKS.

CHAIM
Crammer, Simon. "The Origin of
Chaim," Jewish Digest, June
1974, pp. 58-60.

CHAJES
Rosenstein. Unbroken Chain,
pp. 427ff. Related to Babad
family. See GENERAL WORKS.

CHALEPSKY
Lepsky, Harry and Nellie. Our
Family Tree: The
Chalepsky-Lipsky-Lepsky-
Mogalevitch-Malowitz-
Molevitz-Molle,
Lebensohn-Levison and Related
Families. Cincinnati, Ohio,
N.d. AJA.

CHALFAN
Englemann, Bernt. "Die Familie
Chalfan," JFF, no. 44
(1937):803-805.

CHALFON
EJ (1928), 5:208-209. See
GENERAL WORKS.

CHALIDENKA
See Yaffa Draznin entry under
BERNSTEIN.

CHALIVA
EJ (1928), 5:210. Family of
Spain and Morocco. See
GENERAL WORKS.

CHALMERS
AMH has family records.

CHAMBERLAIN
AMH has family records.

CHAN
Schulte. Bonner Juden, p. 185.
See GENERAL WORKS.

CHANDERS
Keneseth Israel. See GENERAL
WORKS.

CHANDLER
AMH has family records.

CHANG
Leslie, "Chinese-Hebrew
Kaifeng." Chang clan. See
GENERAL WORKS.

CHANNING
AMH has family records.

CHAO
EJ (1972), 5:335. Genealogical
table of most important
family of the former Jewish
community of Kaifeng, China.
Descendants of Chao Ch'eng
(fl. 1421-1423), through late
17th century. See GENERAL
WORKS.
Leslie, "Chinese-Hebrew
Kaifeng." Chao clan. See
GENERAL WORKS.
Leslie, Donald D. The Survival
of the Chinese Jews; The
Jewish Community of Kaifeng.
Leiden: E.J. Brill, 1972.
270 p. "Chao Ying-Ch'eng and
His Family," pp. 44-47. 17th
century.
————. "The K'aifeng Jew Chao
Ying-Ch'eng and His Family,"
T'oung Pao 53 (1967):147-79.

CHAPELLIER
AMH has family records.

CHAPMAN
AMH has family records.

CHARIF
EJ (1928), 5:308-312. Family
of Poland. See GENERAL
WORKS.

CHARIG
See Max and Erwin Krieg entry
under KRIEG.

CHARLAP
"Die Familien Charlap und
Don-Jachia," JFF, no. 11
(1927):261-64.
"König David und die Familien
Charlap," JFF, no. 30
(1932):457-62.
Marx, Alexander. "Die Familien
Charlap," JFF, no. 33
(1933):538.
Neuman, Otto. "Eine Deszendenz
von König David bis auf die
Jetztzeit," JFF, no. 32
(1932):486-97.

CHARMAK
Conrich, J. Lloyd, comp.
"Louis Charmak/Annie Shemasky
Family Tree, 1965." WJHC.

CHASAN
EJ (1928), 5:330-36. See
GENERAL WORKS.

CHASKER
LBI has family tree for
Chasker-Bursch family
beginning 1758.

CHASSON
EJ (1928), 5:390. Family of
Salonica. See GENERAL WORKS.

CHAZAL
AMH has family records.

CHAZAN
See HAZAN, HAZZAN.

CHELBO
Poznánski, Samuel. "Der Namen

Chelbo," Zeitschrift für
Hebräische Bibliographie 8
(1904):158-59.

CHEMERINSKY
Chemerinsky Family; New York.
"A Life to Live Is Not Like
Crossing a Field," A Family
History by Mollie Seletsky;
1973-1974; typescript. AJA.

CHERMSIDE
Semi-Gotha, 1:142. See GENERAL
WORKS.

CHESTER
AMH has family records.

CHIN
Leslie, "Chinese-Hebrew
Kaifeng." Chin clan. See
GENERAL WORKS.

CHODAS
See COHODAS.

CHOLMONDELEY
AMH has family records.

CHORIN
PD has family records.
Kempelen. Magyarországi Zsidó,
1:93, 94. See GENERAL WORKS.

CHOTZINOFF
Chotzinoff, Samuel. A Lost
Paradise. New York: Knopf,
1955. The author,
b. Vitebsk, Russia, 1889;
d. 1964; the son of Mayshe
Bear and Rachel Traskenoff
Chotzinoff. The family came
to U.S. in 1896.

CHOTZNER
AMH has family records.

CHRAMBACH
Kempelen. Magyarországi Zsidó,
1:27. See GENERAL WORKS.

CHYET
AJA has family tree.

CIANCHI
See Esmond S. De Beer entry
under BARDEN.

CIENER
AJA has gnealogical files.

CIMPONERIU
Kempelen. Magyarországi Zsidó,
2:116. See GENERAL WORKS.

CINNER
Kempelen. Magyarországi Zsidó,
2:137. See GENERAL WORKS.

CIPPERL
Kempelen. Magyarországi Zsidó,
2:43. See GENERAL WORKS.

CITROEN
Citroën, K.A. The
Spanjaard Family: A Survey of
the Descendants of Salomon
Jacob Spanjaard (1783-1861)
and Sara David van Gelder
(1793-1882). 2d rev. and
augmented ed. Borne,
Holland: Family Association
"Berith Salom," 1981. 286 p.
AJHS.

CLAR
"The Clars of Colorado and
California: A Picture Story,"
Western States Jewish
Historical Quarterly 12
(Apr. 1980):209-214.
Descendants of Melamed Max
Clar (1859-1943); family
originally from Kiev.

CLARK
AMH has family records.

CLARKE
AMH has family records.

CLAVA
See CAUFFMAN-CLAVA.
Stern. FAJF. Clava family
tree beginning in U.S. See
GENERAL WORKS.

CLAY
AMH has family records.

CLAYTON
AMH has family records.

CLEVE
AMH has family records.
CFM has family records.
Cohen, Daniel J. Geschichte
der Familie Cohen-Walsrode.
N.p., n.D. Microfilm.
Includes Cleve, Cohen, David,
Goldschmidt, Melrich, Moses,
Norden, Oldenburg, Popert,
Salomon, Wagner, Wallich,
Walsrode, and Worms families.
Discussion of Cleve family
from Altona, pp. 88-90.
Family tree, early 1600s to
1786, p. 119. CAJ, Call
No. HM 2800.

CLIFF
AMH has family records.

CLINE
Frank. Nashville Jewry,
p. 132. Polish family, came
to U.S. in 1851. See GENERAL
WORKS.

CLUTTERBACK
AMH has family records.

COBB
AMH has family records.

COBLENZ
AMH has family records.

COBURN
AMH has family records.

CODRINGTON
AMH has family records.

COEN
Angelini, Werther. Gli ebrei
di Ferrara nel settecento: I
Coen e altri mercanti del
rapporto con le pubbliche
autorità. Urbino: Argalià,
1973. 330 p. DLC.

COHEN
GENERAL

See D'AZEVEDO-COHEN.
See MEYER-COHEN.
See SAX-COHEN.
Cohen, Baruch. Sefer
Ha-Zikaron. New York, 1920.
AJHS.
Stern. FAJF. Cohen family
trees beginning in:
(I) Swansea, Wales;
(II) Oberdorff, Germany;
(III) Elberfeld, Westphalia;
(IV, X, and XII) U.S.; (V and
VIII) England; (VI) Wartha,
Poland; (VII) Zamosc, Poland;
(IX) London, England; and
(XI) Bristol, England. See
GENERAL WORKS.

ENGLAND

AMH has family records.
EJ (1972), 5:659-60.
Genealogical table of
Anglo-Jewish family of Levi
Barent Cohen and
Cohen-Wally. Descendants
of Levi Barent Cohen
(1747-1808), through
mid-20th century. See
GENERAL WORKS.
Bermant. The Cousinhood.
Genealogical table. See
GENERAL WORKS.
Burke's Landed Gentry, 1937.
Family of Barwythe.
Burke's Peerage and Baronetage,
1970. Family of
Birkenhead.
Burke's Peerage and Baronetage,
1967. Family of Brighton.
Burke's Peerage and Baronetage,
1970. Wally-Cohen family.
Cohen, Hannah Floretta.
Changing Faces: A Memoir of
Louisa Lady Cohen, by Her
Daughter Hannah F. Cohen.
London: M. Hopkinson, 1937.
383 p. Includes
genealogical table. Lady
Louisa Emily (Merton)
Cohen, 1850-1931. CtY,
DLC, OCl, TxU.

Cohen, Lionel Leonard (Baron Cohen). "Levi Barent Cohen and Some of His Descendants," Transactions of the Jewish Historical Society of England 16 (1952):11-24. Includes genealogical tables of descendants of Benjamin Cohen (fl. ca. 1660) to time of article and descendants of Levi Barent Cohen (fl. ca. 1747) to time of article.

[Cohen, Lucy.] Arthur Cohen, a Memoir by His Daughter for His Descendants. London: Bickers, 1919. 215 p. Pedigree table and family history. MH. See Esmond S. De Beer entry under BARDEN. Family of England.

Emden. Jews of Britain, pp. 529-30. "The Cohen Family of Liverpool and Lewis's Stores." See GENERAL WORKS.

Joseph, Anthony. "The Genealogy of Some 19th Century Australian Jewish Families," Journal and Proceedings of the Australian Jewish Historical Society 6, pt. 7 (1969):377-91. Also, Burke's Colonial Gentry includes Cohen families of Australia.

FRANCE

Roback, Abraham Aaron. "The Tribe of Levy in France," in his Jewish Influence in Modern Thought (Cambridge, Mass., 1929), pp. 98-123. On the modern Jewish names of Levy and Cohen in France and other countries, and the fame they have achieved.

GERMANY

Cohen, Arthur. Geschichte der Familie Cohen mit Berücksichtigung der Familien Marx und Pflaum. Mit ergänzenden Anmerkungen und

einem Stammbaum (1558-1940) versehen von Willy Cohn. München, 1934-1935 und New York, 1956. 29 p. MS. Families of Munich. LBI. See Daniel J. Cohen entry under CLEVE. German family from Hanau, Altona, pp. 91-97. Family tree, early 1600s to 1764, p. 120.

Kaufmann, David. "Issachar Bär, genannt Berend Cohen der Gröuder der Klause in Hamburg, und seine Kinder," in his Gesammelte Schriften (Frankfurt am Main, 1915), vol. 3, pp. 108-137. Appeared originally in MGWJ 40 (1896).

"Liepmann Cohen und seine Söhne, Kammeragenten in Hannover," MGWJ, (1864), p. 161.

Schnee. Hoffinanz und Staat, 2:63-67. "Die Hoffaktorenfamilie Cohen." Includes genealogical information, 17th to 19th century. Family of Hannover. See GENERAL WORKS.

Schulte. Bonner Juden, pp. 187, 191. See GENERAL WORKS.

Wiener, M. "Liepmann Cohen und seine Söhne, Kammeragenten zu Hannover," MGWJ 13, no. 5 (1864):161-84. 18th to early 19th century.

HUNGARY

Kempelen. Magyarországi Zsidó, 1:77. See GENERAL WORKS.

THE NETHERLANDS

Corwin, Henry Max. Geslacht Hartz Samson Cohen. Oldenzaal, Netherlands, N.p., 1960. 41 p. Family history starting with Hartz Samson, 1735/40-1808, and his son Hartz Samson Cohen, 1768-1839. BR; CAJ, Call No. 1053.

UNITED STATES

See BARUCH. Cohen family of
South Carolina.
Cohen Family; Charleston, S.C.,
and New York, N.Y.
Genealogy, 1732-1940. MS.
AJA.
Cohen Family, S.C. Record of
the Cohen Family in the
Confederate Army, 1862-1864.
AJA.
Cohen Family; Baltimore. Vital
Records of the Cohen, Etting,
and Related Families of
Baltimore. MS. AJA.
Cohen Family of Philadelphia.
Papers, 1807-1867. Include
genealogical charts and
biographies. AJA.
Cohen Family Papers, 1802-1945.
Include genealogical data on
Cohen, Gratz, Etting, and
Nathan families of Maryland.
Maryland Historical Society
Library.
"Cohen-Etting Cemetery
Inscriptions." Typescript,
n.d. Maryland Historical
Society, Baltimore.
Baroway, Aaron. "The Cohens of
Maryland," Maryland
Historical Magazine 18
(1923):357-76; 19
(1924):54-77. Article
reprinted in Maryland
Genealogies: A Compilation of
Articles from the "Maryland
Historical Magazine"
(Baltimore: Genealogical
Publishing Co., 1980),
vol. 1, pp. 295-338.
Descendants of Meyer Cohen,
b. ca. 1700 in Oberdorf, near
Nordlingen, in the district
called the Riess, not far
from Ansbach, Bavaria.
Colonial period through 1920.
Includes genealogical table.
Cohen Family. "Genealogical
Chart of the Descendants of
Alex Cohen and Anna Ringold."
N.p. Covers 1852-1959.
Cohen, Caroline. Genealogical
files. AJA.
Cohen, Eleanor. Genealogy of

the Cohen Family of
Baltimore. MS. AJA.
Cohen, Evelina Gleaves. Family
Facts and Fairy Tales.
Wynnewood, Pa.: By the
Author, 1953. 115 p.
Descendants of Joseph Cohen,
b. 1745, d. 1822. DLC, NN,
PHi, PPDrop.
Cohen, Jodi. Genealogical
files. AJA.
Cohen, Morris Raphael.
Dreamer's Journey:
Autobiography. Boston: The
Beacon Press, 1949. 318 p.
"My Parents," pp. 6-14;
"Neshwies (1887-1890)--The
Old Piety," pp. 25-40; and
"Neshwies Revisited and the
Journey to America,"
pp. 56-62. Following a
description of childhood in
Kletsk and Neshwies in Minsk
gubernia and adolescence in
New York's east side, the
book primarily describes the
author's development as a
philosopher and teacher at
New York City College and
Harvard. The author
(1880-1947) came to U.S. in
1892. His parents were
Abraham Mordechai Cohen
(1847-1937) and Bessie Farfel
Cohen (1848-1936). DLC, ICU,
MB, OU, PU, TxU, ViU.
Cohen, Octavus Roy.
Genealogical files. AJA.
Cohen, Oscar J.; Mobile, Ala.
"Record Book Recording
Marriages, Births, Deaths,
and Genealogical Information,
1888-1898." MS. Xerox copy.
AJA.
Cohen, Simon. Genealogical
files. AJA.
Cohen Family Papers, 1841-1913.
Include genealogical material
for Solomon A. Cohen
(1802-1875), merchant and
businessman in South
Carolina, blockade runner,
and Confederate spy, and
other members of Cohen
family. AJHS.
Cowan, Paul. An Orphan in

History: Retrieving a Jewish
Legacy. New York: Doubleday,
1982. 246 p. Author is the
son of Louis Cowan, former
President of CBS-TV, and the
great-grandson of Jacob
Cohen, a rabbi in Litvinova,
Lithuania. Author's mother's
family was famous Spiegel
family of Chicago.
"Genealogical Chart of the
Descendants of Moses Cohen,
First Jewish Priest in
America, 1710. Married Dinah
Conque." New York?, 1926?
24 X 34 in. Moses Cohen,
1709-1762, was born in
England and came to
Charleston, S.C. by 1750. He
was the first
"Rabbi"--probably a volunteer
hazzan--of Congregation Beth
Elohim in Charleston. NN.
Lipton, Ann Lynn. "Anywhere,
So Long as It Be Free: A
Study of the Cohen Family,
Richmond and Baltimore,
1773-1826." Master's thesis,
College of William and Mary,
1973.
Nurnberg, Maxwell.
"(Cohen-Kagan)," Names 14
(Sept. 1966):192. On the
identity of these two names.
See Daniel Jay Rottenberg entry
under ROTTENBERG. Includes
Cohen family.
Silverman, Albert J. "They Ate
Kosher at Fort Mc Henry,"
Generations (Jewish
Historical Society of
Maryland) 1, no. 2
(1979):2-9. On the
well-known Cohen and Etting
families of Maryland.

COHEN D'AZEVEDO
See Stern, FAJF entry under
D'AZEVEDO.

COHEN DELMONTE
See Stern, FAJF entry under
DELMONTE.

COHEN-WALSRODE
See Daniel J. Cohen entry under

CLEVE. Family from Altona,
pp. 5-28. Family tree, 16th
to 20th century, pp. 109-110.

COHN
See ARENDT.
AMH has family records.
CAJ, Call No. 3553, has a
wall-size chart of Marcus and
Cohn families, 16th century
to 1923. Descendants of
Rabbi Moses ben David
Hacohen, who lived in Deutz,
Germany in 1627 and also in
Cologne in first half of
1600s.
Ballin. Juden in Seesen,
pp. 167-73. See GENERAL
WORKS.
[Cohn, Alfred]. Familientafel
des Rabbiners Dr. Salomon
Cohn sel. And. Hamburg, 1910.
LBI.
Cohn, Cilla. En Jødisk
Families Saga. København:
Nyt Nordisk Forlag Arnold
Busck, 1960. 190 p. Family
of Denmark. Emphasis of book
is on W.W.II. DLC, OCH.
Cohn, Frederick. Genealogical
files. AJA.
Cohn, John Magnus. The Cohn
Family Tree. Swan Hill,
Australia: n.p., Mar. 1963.
32 p. Genealogical table
from 1751-1962. More than
400 relatives listed. Cohn
family is related to Ballin
family of Denmark. Four Cohn
brothers migrated to
Australia from Denmark in the
mid-19th century. CAJ, Call
No. 1676.
Cohn, Rose B. Stein, Bergman,
and Cohn Families
(1787-1954). Baltimore: Ida
Charles Wilkins Foundation,
1954. 21 p. Includes
genealogical tables. NN.
Duckesz, Eduard.
Familiengeschichte Rabbi
Jekev Cohn in Altona.
Abgeschrieben von Daniel
Cohen, 25-8-44, Tel Aviv.
11 p., plus 2 pages of family
tree, 1627-1902.

Reproductions of writings on
grave monuments. CAJ, Call
No. 2787, microfilm.
Kempelen. Magyarországi Zsidó,
1:49, 92. See GENERAL WORKS.
Schulte. Bonner Juden,
p. 191-92. See GENERAL
WORKS.
Semi-Gotha, 2:38. See GENERAL
WORKS.

COHNREICH
Conrich, J. Lloyd, comp. "The
German Branch of the
Cohnreich Family." 1967.
WJHC.
————. "The Cohnreich Family
(San Francisco Branch)."
1964. WJHC.

COHODAS
Treloar, Wilbert H. Cohodas:
The Story of a Family.
Marquette: Northern Michigan
University Press, 1977.
256 p. Story of Polish
immigrant family which has
developed one of America's
largest produce distribution
companies and banking
corporations of the Midwest.
Work discusses the
descendants of Aaron Cohodas
(1860-1904) of Kobylnik (now
Narach) on the Syrmiez River,
White Russia. Aaron Cohodas
came to the Upper Peninsula
of Michigan in late 1890s.
His first wife was Leah Mendl
(1860?-1887), and his second
wife was Eva Mansfield (d.
1931), the daughter of Bessie
and Max Mansfield.

COLACO
CFM has family records.

COLCHESTER
AMH has family records.

COLCUTT
AMH has family records.

COLEMAN
AMH has family records.
CFM has family records.

Stern. FAJF. Coleman family
tree beginning in U.S.
Originally Kohleman. See
GENERAL WORKS.

COLEMAN-CONTENT
AJA has genealogical files.

COLLAS
Kempelen. Magyarországi Zsidó,
1:65, 3:122. See GENERAL
WORKS.

COLLET
AMH has family records.

COLLINS
AMH has family records.
CFM has family records.

COLLIS
AMH has family records.

COLLOREDO-MANSFELD
Kempelen. Magyarországi Zsidó,
1:82. See GENERAL WORKS.

COLMAN
AMH has family records.
Colman Family; Los Angeles.
Genealogical Notes on the
Schwarzenburg and Colman
Families, 1959 and 1964;
Typescript and MS. AJA.

COLN
AMH has family records.

COLORNI
Colorni, Vittore. "Genealogia
della familigia Colorni
(1477-1977)," in Scritti in
memoria di Umberto Nahon:
Saggi sull'Ebraismo Italiano
(Jerusalem, 1978), pp. 43ff.

COLUMBUS
Alperin, Charles. "Christopher
Columbus--A Jew," Midstream
25, no. 3 (1979):35-48.
Provides evidence dating to
late 14th century that
Columbus was a Jew.
Cantera y Burgos, Francisco.
"El origen de Colón y el
monograma de su firma,"

COLYER-FERGUSSON
AMH has family records.

COMERFORD
AMH has family records.

COMORNER
Schulte. Bonner Juden, p. 193.
See GENERAL WORKS.

CONE
Cone Family, North Carolina.
    Genealogy, 1828-1965;
    Typescript. AJA.
Cone, Sydney. Genealogy of the
    Guggenheimer, Cone and
    Related Families.
    Greensboro, N.C., 1960.
————. "Cones from Bavaria."
    Greensboro, N.C., 196?
    145 p. Allen County Public
    Library, Fort Wayne, Indiana.
See Sydney M. Cone entry under
    AMBACH.

CONEGLIANO
Kaufman, David. Dr. Israel
    Conegliano und S. verdienste
    um die Republik Venedig bis
    nach dem frieden von
    Carlowitz. Wien: C. Konegan,
    1895. Various paging. CtY,
    DLC, MH, OCH, PPDrop, WU.

CONITZER
LBI has family tree beginning
    1789.

CONRAD
AMH has family records.
Kempelen. Magyarországi Zsidó,
    2:52. Conrád family. See
    GENERAL WORKS.

CONRADI
AMH has family records.

CONRICH
Conrich, J. Lloyd. The Family
    Photograph Album (with
    genealogies and birth
    certificate). 2 vols. WJHC.

CONSTATT
AMH has family records.

CONTENT
See COLEMAN-CONTENT.
AMH has family records.
Stern. FAJF. Content family
    tree beginning in Holland.
    See GENERAL WORKS.

COOK
AMH has family records.

COOKE
AMH has family records.

COOPER
AMH has family records.

COPELAND
See Sidney Cramer entry under
BINDMAN.

COPPENHAGEN
Schulte. Bonner Juden, p. 194.
See GENERAL WORKS.

CORBETT
AMH has family records.

CORCHO
CFM has family records.

CORCOS
AMH has family records.
JE, 4:263. "Genealogical Tree
of the Corcos Family."
Descendants of Abraham Corcos
(fl. second half of 13th
century), through early 18th
century. Family lived in
Spain, Italy, Morocco, and
Gibraltar. See GENERAL
WORKS.
CFM has family records.
Avital, Michael. Mishpachat
Corcos Vehahistoria Shel
Morocco Bizmaneinu. French
title: Temoins et Acteurs.
Les Corcos et L'histoire du
Maroc contemporain.
Jerusalem: Machon Ben Zvi,
1978. 30 p. in Hebrew; 42 p.
in French. Includes fold-out
chart of family, 1492 to
present. JNUL.

CORIAT
EJ (1928), 5:668-69. See
GENERAL WORKS.

CORN
Semi-Gotha, 2:41. See GENERAL
WORKS.

CORNISH
AMH has family records.

CORONEL
CFM has family records.
EJ (1928), 5:671. See GENERAL
WORKS.
Peñalosa, Luis Felipe de.
"Juan Bravo y la familia
Coronel," Estudios Segovianos
1 (1949):73-109.

CORREA
See ALVARES-CORREA.
CFM has family records.

CORTELLO
AMH has family records.

CORTISSOS
AMH has family records.
CFM has family records.

COSETTE
Kempelen. Magyarországi Zsidó,
1:73. See GENERAL WORKS.

COSSMANN
Schulte. Bonner Juden, p. 199.
See GENERAL WORKS.

COSTA
See DA COSTA.
See MENDES DA COSTA.
AMH has family records.
CFM has family records.

COSTELLO
AMH has family records.

COSTER
AMH has family records.
CFM has family records.

COTA
Cantera Burgos, Francisco. La
familia judeo-conversa de los
Cota de Toledo. Lección
inaugural del curso de 1969
leída en día 21 de enero,
Academia de Doctores de
Madrid. Madrid, 1969.
————. "B'nai Cota
M'Toledot." [History of the
Sons of Cota.] In Hayyim
Schirmann Jubilee Volume, ed.

Schragn Abramson (1970),
pp. 319-45.
────────. Pedraria Dávila y
Cota, capitán general y
gobernador de Castilla del
Oro y Nicaragua: Sus
antecedents judíos....
Madrid: Universidad de
Madrid, Cátedra de Lengua
Hebrea e Historia de los
Judíos, 1971. 44 p. 16th to
17th century. DLC.
────────. El poeta Ruy Sánchez
Cota (Rodrigo Cota) y su
familia de judíos conversos.
Madrid: Universidad de
Madrid, Cátedra de Lengua
Hebrea e Historia de los
Judíos, 1970. 155 p.
Genealogical tables. Rodrigo
de Cota, fl. 15th century.
DLC, MH.

COTTEREL
AMH has family records.

COUDRILLES
Kempelen. Magyarországi Zsidó,
1:73. See GENERAL WORKS.

COURCY-MAC
Kempelen. Magyarországi Zsidó,
1:129. See GENERAL WORKS.

COUSSERI
Kaufmann, David. "La famille
Cousseri á Riva," Revue des
Études Juives 16
(1888):270-71; 30 (1895):292;
33 (1896):311-14; 35
(1897):302-304.

COUTINHO
CFM has family records.

COWAN
AMH has family records.
CFM has family records.
Cowan, Evelyn. Spring
Remembered: A Scottish Jewish
Childhood. Edinburgh:
Southside, 1974. 160 p.
Work covers family of Glasgow
through the Depression. CtY,
DLC, MB, MH, OCH, OU.

See Paul Cowan entry under
COHEN.

COWEN
AMH has family records.

COWLAND
AMH has family records.

COX
AMH has family records.

CRAMER
CAJ has family tree from
Germany, 18th to 19th
century.
Cramer, Sally David. The
Cramer Family Tree. London:
n.p., 1974, 1975, 1976, 1977.
393 p. 64-page index.
Covers eight generations
beginning with Hirsch Cramer,
b. Thundorf, a small hamlet
in Upper Franconia, 1759;
d. 1835. Includes Cramer,
Eisemann, Feuchtwanger,
Forchheimer, Fordsham,
Hirsch, Joel, Kaplin,
Oppenheimer, and Schwarzchild
families. JNUL, Manuscript
and Archive Dept., Call
No. V.1934.
See Sidney Cramer entry under
BINDMAN.

CRAVEN
AMH has family records.

CRAWCOUR
AMH has family records.
CFM has family records.

CRESQUES
Fajarnés y Tur, Enrique. Los
Cresques: médicos, judíos
mallorquines del siglo XIV.
Palma de Mallorca: Imprenta
de la hija de J. Colomar,
1929. 28 p. DLC.

CRICHTON-STUART
Semi-Gotha, 1:152. See GENERAL
WORKS.

CROHN
Crohn Family, New York.

"Memoirs of Ninety Fruitful
Years," by Burrill B. Crohn.
N.d. Family history,
including anecdotes and
personal recollections.   AJA.

CROHN-UHLMANN
AJA has genealogical files.

CROMELIEN
AJA has family tree beginning
1780.
Stern. FAJF. Cromelien family
tree beginning in Holland.
See GENERAL WORKS.

CRONBACH
AJA has family tree.

CRONHJELM
Semi-Gotha, 1:81. See GENERAL
WORKS.

CRONSTEDT
Semi-Gotha, 1:83. See GENERAL
WORKS.

CROW
AMH has family records.

CROWCHER
AMH has family records.

CROZA
CFM has family records.

CSAKY
Kempelen. Magyarországi Zsidó,
1:44, 83, 145; 2:38, 103.
Csáky family. See GENERAL
WORKS.

CSANYI
Kempelen. Magyarországi Zsidó,
2:64. Csányi family. See
GENERAL WORKS.

CSATARY
Kempelen. Magyarországi Zsidó,
2:47. Csatáry family. See
GENERAL WORKS.

CSATHO
Kempelen. Magyarországi Zsidó,
3:34. Csathó family. See
GENERAL WORKS.

CSEMEGI
Kempelen. Magyarországi Zsidó,
1:147. See GENERAL WORKS.

CSEPELI
Kempelen. Magyarországi Zsidó,
1:103. See GENERAL WORKS.

CSERGHEO
Kempelen. Magyarországi Zsidó,
1:100. Csergheő family. See
GENERAL WORKS.

CSERHALMI
Kempelen. Magyarországi Zsidó,
1:146. See GENERAL WORKS.

CSIKES
Kempelen. Magyarországi Zsidó,
3:137. See GENERAL WORKS.

CSILLAG
Kempelen. Magyarországi Zsidó,
3:122. See GENERAL WORKS.

CSURY
Kempelen. Magyarországi Zsidó,
3:129. See GENERAL WORKS.

CUFF
Kempelen. Magyarországi Zsidó,
1:51. See GENERAL WORKS.

CULLEN
AMH has family records.

CUNHA
CFM has family records.

CURIEL
CAJ has family tree.
CFM has family records.
EJ (1928), 5:718-19. See
GENERAL WORKS.
CAJ (Call No. 1882) has
genealogical chart of the
descendants of Abraham
Curiel, 16th to mid-20th
century. Family originated
in Amsterdam.

CURLENDER
AMH has family records.

CURTIS
AMH has family records.

CZACZKES
Berman, Myron, ed. "Joseph
Joel: My Recollections and
Experiences of Richmond,
Virginia, U.S.A., 1884-1892,"
Virginia Magazine of History
and Biography 87, no. 3
(1979):344-56. The narrative
focuses mainly upon the
experiences of Joseph Joel's
father, Salomon Czaczkes
(1853-1934; the name was
changed to Joel in U.S.), in
Richmond from 1884-1892. The
family was from Proskurov and
Podwoloczyska, Galicia, and
returned to Galicia in 1892.
Joseph Joel (1882-1960)
returned to Richmond in 1914.
A list of the names and fates
of Salomon Joel's children is
on page 345.

CZANK
Kempelen. Magyarországi Zsidó,
1:42. See GENERAL WORKS.

CZAPKAI
Kempelen. Magyarországi Zsidó,
2:99. See GENERAL WORKS.

CZAPSKI
Czapski, Maria. Une Familie
d'Europe Central, 1772-1914.
Texte adapté du polonais par
A.M. Bohomeles et l'auteur.
Paris: Plon, 1972. 32 p.
CU, DLC, NjP.

CZARNIKOW
CFM has family records.

CZARTORISKI
CAJ has family records.

CZELLITZER
Czellitzer, Arthur. Geschichte
meiner Familie. Holland,
1942. 121, 7 p. MS
genealogy beginning 1815.
Family from Breslau and
Chrzelitz bei
Zülz/Oberschlesien. Arthur
Czellitzer (1871-1943?) was
an ophthalmic surgeon and the
founder of the Gesellschaft

für jüdische
Familienforschung in Berlin.
This work also includes a
history of the Schlesinger
family, the author's mother's
family. LBI.
JFF, no. 2 (1925):38.

CZIGANY
Kempelen. Magyarországi Zsidó,
3:72. Czigány family. See
GENERAL WORKS.

CZIGLER
Kempelen. Magyarországi Zsidó,
3:111. See GENERAL WORKS.

CZINA
Kempelen. Magyarországi Zsidó,
3:124. See GENERAL WORKS.

CZIRAKY
Kempelen. Magyarországi Zsidó,
1:145. Cziráky family. See
GENERAL WORKS.

CZONICZER
Kempelen. Magyarországi Zsidó,
2:101. See GENERAL WORKS.

CZUCZKA
Kempelen. Magyarországi Zsidó,
2:142. See GENERAL WORKS.

DABYMPH
AMH has family records.

DA COSTA
AJA has genealogical files.
AMH has family records.
CFM has five family trees
related to Mendes, Gomes,
Nunes, Athias, and Rodrigues
families.
JE, 4:288-89. Contains "Da
Costa Pedigree" of family of
Holland, 18th to 19th
century. Also, "Genealogical
Tree of Da Costa Family of
England," 18th to 19th
century, p. 290. See GENERAL
WORKS.

Da Costa, Moses. Genealogical
files. AJA.
"The Families of Mendes and Da
Costa," Gentleman's Magazine,
January 1812, pp. 21-24.
Stern. FAJF. Da Costa family
trees beginning in:
(I) London; and
(II) Portugal. See GENERAL
WORKS.

DA FONSECA
See Stern, FAJF (II) entry
under LOPEZ.

D'AGUILAR
CFM has family records.

DAHAN
Canetti, Elias. Die Stimmen
von Marrakesch;
Aufzeichnungen nach einer
Reise. München: C. Hanser,
1967. 106 p. "Die Familie
Dahan," pp. 53-79. CLU, CSt,
CtY, DLC, ICU, MB, NjP, WU.

DAHLHEIM
LBIS has family notes.

DAHLSHEIMER
Dahlsheimer Family.
Genealogical Records,
1810-1859. In English and
Hebrew. Photostats.
Extracted from prayer book.
AJA.

DAICHES
Daiches, David. Two Worlds: An
Edinburgh Jewish Childhood.
2d ed. Sussex: At The
University Press, 1974. 152
p. The author (1912-   ),
an English scholar and
literary critic, is the son
and grandson of Lithuanian,
Orthodox rabbis who emigrated
to England from Vilna. His
father was Dr. Salis Daiches
(1881-1945), and his
grandfather was Israel
Ḥayyim Daiches (1850-1937).
The grandfather was born in
Darshunishek or Darshonishok

(now Darsuniskis; near
Kovno), Lithuania. DLC.

DAJKOVICH
Kempelen. Magyarországi Zsidó,
3:35. See GENERAL WORKS.

DALLOS
Kempelen. Magyarországi Zsidó,
2:73. See GENERAL WORKS.

D'ALMEDA
AMH has family records.

DALMEIDA
CFM has family records.

DALTON
AMH has family records.

DAN
CAJ (Call No. 5044) has the
following large family trees:
"Family of Philip 'Phievel'
Dan," "Family of Pere Libba
'Lizza' Solomon Dan," and
"History of the Den and
Leibowitz Families." Also
included are a 2-page copy of
1900 census; notes on Philip
Dan and family in Memphis,
Tenn.; and pictures of Philip
Dan and brother Solomon Den.
Perre Dan, 1862-1944, was the
wife of Philip Dan. David
King Den and his wife, Kala
Bossel Den, lived in
Tavirick, Lithuania, and had
two sons who came to America:
Philip Dan, 1852-1926, and
Solomon Den, 1858-1940.
Kempelen. Magyarországi Zsidó,
2:50. Dán family. See
GENERAL WORKS.

DANCKWARDT
Semi-Gotha, 1:143. See GENERAL
WORKS.

DANDSON
AMH has family records.

DANGLOW
See Esmond S. De Beer entry
under BARDEN.

DANIEL
CFM has family records.
Daniel, Max. Meine
Familiengeschichte. San
Francisco, 1963. 155 p. MS.
Family from
Bublitz/Pommerania
originally. Covers
1765-1963. LBI.
Kempelen. Magyarországi Zsidó,
1:105, 124. Dániel family.
See GENERAL WORKS.
Schulte. Bonner Juden, p. 200.
See GENERAL WORKS.

DANIELS
AMH has family records.

DANN
AMH has family records.
Dann, Albert. Erinnerungen.
Ramot-Haschawim, Israel,
1944. 23 p. MS. Includes a
Familienstammbuch. Family
from Frankfurt am Main and
Augsburg.
See Wilhelm Dann entry under
LEVI.

DANNENBERG
Hart, Neustadter, and
Dannenberg Families' Tree.
WJHC.
Ballin. Juden in Seesen,
p. 174. See GENERAL WORKS.

DANNHAUSER
Tänzer. Juden in Tirol,
pp. 706-707. See GENERAL
WORKS.

DANOFF
Danoff, Hyman O. "Indian
Traders of the Southwest: The
Danoffs of New Mexico,"
Western States Jewish
Historical Quarterly 12,
no. 4 (July 1980):291-303.
Covers 1900 to 1960. Family
from Vilna. Samuel, Simon,
and Louis Danoff came to New
Mexico in early 1900s.

DANON
EJ (1928), 5:784-85. See
GENERAL WORKS.

DANVERS
AMH has family records.

DARDEL
Semi-Gotha, 1:100, 155. See
GENERAL WORKS.

DAREL
Darel, Sylva. A Sparrow in the
Snow. Translated from the
Russian by Barbara Norman.
New York: Stein and Day,
1973. A story, through 1953,
of the author's family exile
in Siberia. The family,
originally from Riga and
Libau (now Liepaja), began
their exile in 1941.

DARSCHAU
"R. Abraham Darschau von Wien
und die Familie Heler," MGWJ,
(1898), p. 223.

DARVAS
Kempelen. Magyarországi Zsidó,
2:71. See GENERAL WORKS.

DA SILVA
See SILVA.
AMH has family records.
See Stern, FAJF entry under
SOLIS.

DA SILVA ROSA
See SILVA.
"Genealogische Dienst ten
behoeve den leden der
Portugeesch-Isr. Gemeente."
Genealogical table of Da
Silva Rosa family in the
Netherlands, early 1600s to
20th century, appears on some
loose papers, handwritten.
Originally came to Holland
from Portugal. CAJ, Call
No. 3893.
CFM has family records.

DA SOLA
AMH has family records.

DA SUZA
CFM has family records.

DATTELZWEIG
Diamant, J.B. Glaser. "Zur
Geschichte der Familie
Dattelzweig," ZGJT 2
(1931):155-59.

DAVEGA
AJA has genealogical files.
Stern. FAJF. Davega family
tree beginning in U.S. See
GENERAL WORKS.

DA VEIGA
CFM has family records.

DAVENPORT
AMH has family records.

DAVID
AJA has genealogical files.
AMH has family records.
CAJ has family tree beginning
18th century.
"Abriss und Stammliste,"
Schweizerisches
Geschlechterbuch (Almanach
Généalogique Suisse) 6
(1936/37):137-42.
Citroën, K.A. The Spanjaard
Family: A Survey of the
Descendants of Salomon Jacob
Spanjaard (1783-1861) and
Sara David van Gelder
(1793-1882). 2d rev. and
augmented ed. Borne,
Holland: Family Association
"Berith Salom," 1981. 286 p.
AJHS.
See Daniel J. Cohen entry under
CLEVE. Family tree of family
from Braunschweig, 1600s to
1826; pp. 79-87, 118.
Gronemann. Genealogisce
Hannovers. "Michael David
und seine Nachkommen,"
pp. 91ff. See GENERAL WORKS.
JFF, nos. 29, 32, and 34.
Family histories.
See David Joseph entry under
BEITMAN.
Katz, Irving I. "Moses David
of Windsor and His Family,"
Michigan History 47 (June
1963):156-60. General study
of the well-known David
family of Montreal, Canada,

pioneers of the Jewish
settlement in Canada. Family
had immigrated from England.
Moses David (1768-1814) was
the first Jewish settler in
Windsor, Canada.
Sallis-Freudenthal, Margarete.
Ich habe mein Land gefunden;
Autobiographischer Rüchlbick.
Frankfurt-am-Main: Josef
Knecht, 1977. 207 p.
Pp. 1-15 and "Familienchronik
aus meiner mütterlichen
Familie," pp. 166-74. Author
was born in Speyer, Germany
in 1893. Mother's family,
the Regensburger family, was
from Eppingen, Baden. DLC.
Schnee. Hoffinanz und Staat,
2:67-80. "Die Familie David
im Dienste der Welfen."
Includes genealogical
information, 17th to 18th
century. Family of
Braunschweig, Hannover. See
GENERAL WORKS.
Schulte. Bonner Juden,
pp. 203, 207, 211, 213. See
GENERAL WORKS.
Stern. FAJF. David family
tree beginning in Swansea,
Wales. See GENERAL WORKS.

DAVIDOV
CAJ has family records.

DAVIDS
AMH has family records.
CFM has family records.
See Stern, FAJF (II) entry
under DAVIS.

DAVIDSON
AMH has family records.
CFM has family records.
Frank, E.N. Die Familie
Davidsohn. 1924. YIVO.
Rothschild. Svenska Israel.
See GENERAL WORKS.

DAVIES
AJA has family tree beginning
in New York, 1787.
Stern. FAJF. Davies family
tree beginning in Germany.
See GENERAL WORKS.

D'AVIGDOR
AMH has family records.
CFM has family records.

DAVILA
CFM has family records.

DAVIS
AJA has genealogical files.
AMH has family records.
CFM has family records.
Davis, Beverley. Be Fruitful
and Multiply: The Family
History Showing Direct and
Collateral Relationships of
John Mark Davis, a Fourth
Generation Jewish Australian.
Adelaide: Lutheran Publishing
House, 1979. 245 p.
Includes genealogical tables.
DLC.
Isaacs, Nathan. Cambridge,
Mass. Correspondence.
Contains miscellaneous
materials concerning Isaacs
and Davis families,
1812-1942. AJA.
Phillips, Marica Bowdish, comp.
"Genealogies of Two Early
California Families--Selig
Alexander and Marie Levy;
Nathan Davis and Rosa Appel."
Typescript. WJHC.
See Stern, FAJF entry under
MENKEN.
Stern. FAJF. Davis family
trees beginning in: (I and
II) London. The latter Davis
family was originally Davids.
See GENERAL WORKS.

DAVISON
AMH has family records.

DAWIDOWICZ
David, Janina. A Square of Sky
and A Touch of Earth: A
Wartime Childhood in Poland.
New York: Penguin Books,
1981. 349 p. The author
(1930-   ) was from
Krzyzowki, Poland.

DAWIDSON
Reychman. Szkice

genealogiczne, pp. 45-47. See
GENERAL WORKS.

DAY
AMH has family records.

DAYAN
Dayan, Moshe. Moshe Dayan: The
Story of My Life. New York:
Morrow, 1976. "Roots," pp.
21-31. Author's family
originally came from Zaskow,
Kiev District. His father
was Shmuel, his grandfather
Reb Abraham, his
great-grandfather Reb Pinhas,
and his
great-great-grandfather Reb
Eliyahu Dayan.
Teveth, Shabtai. Moshe Dayan:
The Soldier, The Man, The
Legend. Boston: Houghton
Mifflin, 1973. 372 p.
Especially, pp. 1-6.

D'AZEVEDO
CFM has family records.
Stern. FAJF. D'Azevedo family
tree beginning in Holland.
See GENERAL WORKS.

D'AZEVEDO-COHEN
AJA has genealogical files.

DEACON
AMH has family records.

DEAK
Kempelen. Magyarországi Zsidó,
2:71. Deák family. See
GENERAL WORKS.

DEAS
AMH has family records.

DEBEDORDO
CAJ has family records.

DE BEER
See Esmond S. De Beer entry
under BARDEN.

DEBORIN
Bick-Shauli, "Roots and
Branches." Includes
genealogy of Abraham Deborin

(Joffe), (1881-1963), Russian
Marxist philosopher. See
GENERAL WORKS.

DEBRE
Lutz, Robert. "La communauté
juive de Westhoffen: les
familles Blum et Debré,"
Société d'Historie et
d'Archéologie de Saverne et
Environs (Saverne), no. 79/80
(1972):67-71.
Szapiro, E. "Archives Debré,"
Archives Juives 12, no. 1
(1976):12. Family documents
of family from France, 18th
to 20th century.

DE BRITTO
CFM has family records.

DE CASTRO
See OROBIO DE CASTRO.
AMH has family records.
CFM has family records.

DE CAZERES
CFM has family records.

DE CHAVES
CFM has family records.

DECHY
Kempelen. Magyarországi Zsidó,
2:53. Déchy family. See
GENERAL WORKS.

DE CORDOVA
AJA has genealogical files.
CFM has family records.
Stern. FAJF. De Cordova
family tree beginning in
Constantinople. See GENERAL
WORKS.

DE CRASTO
CFM has family records.
Stern. FAJF. De Crasto family
tree beginning in London.
See GENERAL WORKS.

DE ESPINOZA
CFM has family records.

DE FARO
CFM has family records.

DE FLORIS
CFM has family records.

DE FRIES
AMH has family records.

DEGENER
PD has family tree.
Semi-Gotha, 1:140. See GENERAL
WORKS.

DEGENFELD
Kempelen. Magyarországi Zsidó,
1:55, 145. Dégenfeld family.
See GENERAL WORKS.

DEGGINER
Zapf. Tübinger Juden, pp.
44-46. See GENERAL WORKS.

DE GRANADA
CFM has family records.

DE GROOT
AMH has family records.

DE HAIZE
CFM has family records.

DE JONGH
CFM has family records.
See I. Rosenwaike entry under
DE YOUNG.
Woolf,, Leonard Sidney.
Sowing: An Autobiography of
the Years, 1880-1904.
London: The Hogarth Press,
1960. 206 p. Especially,
pp. 11-26. The author
(1880-1969), an English
publisher and writer, was the
son of Solomon Rees Sydney
Woolf (1844-1892) and Marie
De Jongh Woolf and the
grandson of Benjamin
(1808-1870) and Isabella
Woolf (1808-1878). Author's
mother was born in Amsterdam
of an old Dutch Jewish
family. CLU, CSt, CtY, DLC,
ICN, MnU, NcD, NjR, NN, NNC,
TxU.

DELACOUR
AMH has family records.

DE LA MARE
CFM has family records.

DE LA MOTTA
Stern. FAJF. De La Motta
family tree beginning in St.
Eustatius. See GENERAL
WORKS.

DELANCEY
AMH has family records.
Newman, Katherine Rideout.
"Brigadier General Oliver and
Phila Franks Delancey and
Their Descendants," The Saint
Charles 1 (Jan. 1935):131-48.

DE LANGE
Stern. FAJF. De Lange family
tree beginning in Amsterdam.
See GENERAL WORKS.

DE LANGE-DE LA TORRE-DELEGADO
AJA has genealogical files.

DE LA PAZZA
CFM has family records.

DE LA PENHA
AMH has family records.
CFM has family records.
Friedman, Lee Max. Early
American Jews. Cambridge,
Mass.: Harvard University
Press, 1934. 238 p.
Includes a chapter on the De
la Penha family and its
Labrador grants.

DE LA PITTE
AMH has family records.

DE LARA
AMH has family records.

DE LA SILVERA
AMH has family records.

DE LA TORRE
See DE LANGE-DE LA
TORRE-DELEGADO.

DELBACO
Fischer, Josef. Jacob Simonson
og Hastru Rose fodt Hahn og
deres Forfaedre. Hundrede

Aar efter Jacob Simonsen
fodsel, udgivet af S.H.
Simonsen born. København,
1927. Includes Delbaco
family. NN, OU.

DELBANCO
CAJ has family trees.
LBIS has family tree and notes.

DEL BANCO
CFM has family records.

DE LEAO
See Stern, FAJF entry under DE
LYON.

DE LEDESMA
See Stern, FAJF entry under
LEDESMA.
Stern. FAJF. De Ledesma
family tree beginning in
Portugal. See GENERAL WORKS.

DE LEEMO
CFM has family records.

DE LEEUW
CFM has family records.

DELEGADO
See DE LANGE-DE LA
TORRE-DELEGADO.

DE LEMOS
CFM has family records.

DE LEON
CFM has family records.
De Leon Family; Charleston,
S.C. Biographical and
Genealogical Records,
Indicating the Relationships
between the Seixas, Cardoza,
and De Leon Families,
1708-1888. AJA.
Marcus, Jacob R. "Military
Record of the De Leon Family
and of Captain Perry M. de
Leon by Perry M. de Leon,"
Publications of the American
Jewish Historical Society 50
(1961):332.
Stern. FAJF. De Leon family
trees beginning in:
(I) Amsterdam ("probably")

and (II) U.S. See GENERAL
WORKS.

DELEVAN
CFM has family records.

DELGADO
AMH has family records.
CFM has family records.
Stern. FAJF. Delgado family
tree beginning in Kingston,
Jamaica. See GENERAL WORKS.

DELI
Kempelen. Magyarországi Zsidó,
1:122. See GENERAL WORKS.

DE LIMA
CFM has family records.
De Lima, Arthur. The De Limas
of Frederick Street.
Trinidad: Imprint Caribbean
Ltd. Publishers, 1975. 170
p. Includes genealogical
table for Sephardic family,
most of whose members have
converted to Catholicism.
Present family members live
in Trinidad and Venezuela.
University of
Illinois/Urbana-Champaign.

DE LIS
CFM has family records.

DELISSA
AMH has family records.

DE LISSA
AMH has family records.
CFM has family records.

DE LISSER
AMH has family records.
CFM has family records.

DELLAR
AJA has genealogical files.

DELMAR
CFM has family records.
Schnee. Hoffinanz und Staat,
1:230-44. "Die
Hoffaktoren-Familie
Levy-Delmar." Includes
genealogical information,

17th to 19th century, family
of Brandenburg-Prussia. See
GENERAL WORKS.
Stern. FAJF. Delmar family
tree beginning in Kingston,
Jamaica. See GENERAL WORKS.

DELMEDIGO
EJ (1928), 5:915-16. Family of
Crete. See GENERAL WORKS.
Bercovy, D. "La famille
Delmédigo," Revue d'Histoire
de la Médecine Hébraïque 22
(1969):13-20.
Eisenstein-Barzilay, Isaac.
Yoseph Shlomo Delmedigo
(Yashar of Candia [Crete]):
His Life, Works and Times.
Leiden: Brill, 1974. 379 p.
Some of the ancestors and
descendants of Delmedigo
(1591-1655) are mentioned on
pages 24-28. DLC.

DELMONTE
AMH has family records.
CFM has family records.
Stern. FAJF. Delmonte family
tree beginning in U.S.
Family tree is listed in FAJF
under "Abendanone."

DELMONTE-DE LUCENA
AJA has genealogical files.

DELSOTTO
CFM has family records.

DE LUCENA
See DELMONTE-DE LUCENA.
Birmingham. The Grandees. See
GENERAL WORKS.
AJA has Abraham de Lucena
family tree beginning 1635.
See Stern, FAJF entry under
NUNEZ.
Stern. FAJF. De Lucena family
tree beginning in New
Amsterdam. See GENERAL
WORKS.

DELVALLE
CFM has family records.

DE LYON
Stern. FAJF. De Lyon family

tree beginning in Portugal;
also spelled De Leao. See
GENERAL WORKS.

DE MATTOS
AMH has family records.
CFM has family records.

DEMBO
CAJ has family records.

DE MEDINA
AMH has family records.

DE MERCADO
AMH has family records.

DE MESQUITA
CFM has family records.
AJA has Bueno de Mesquita
genealogical files.
Stern. FAJF. De Mesquita
family tree beginning in
Brazil. See GENERAL WORKS.

DE METZ
AMH has family records.
CFM has family records.

DE MEZA
CFM has family records.

DE MITZ
AMH has family records.

DE MOLINA
Stern. FAJF. De Molina family
tree beginning in Portugal.
See GENERAL WORKS.

DE MORAIS
AMH has family records.

DE MORRAIS
CFM has family records.

DEN
See DAN.

DENTZ
CFM has family records.

DEPAS
Locker, Zvi. "Membres de la
Famille Depas (ou de Paz) à
St. Domingue," Conjunction:

Revue Franco-Hatienne,
no. 133
(mar./apr. 1977):126-131. A
listing of the various
members of family, what is
known about them, and the
source of the information.
Family of Santo Domingo.

DE PASS
AJA has genealogical files.
AMH has family records.
CFM has family records.
Stern. FAJF. De Pass family
trees beginning in:
(I) Bordeaux and (II) London.
See GENERAL WORKS.

DE PAZ
See DEPAS.

DE PINNA
AMH has family records.
CFM has family records.

DE PINNER
AMH has family records.

DE PINTO
Salomon, H.P. "The 'De Pinto'
Manuscript; a 17th Century
Marrano Family History,"
Studia Rosenthaliana 9
(1975):1-62.

DE PIZA
CFM has family records.

DERENBERG
CFM has family records.

DERENNE
Kempelen. Magyarországi Zsidó,
1:73. See GENERAL WORKS.

DERERA
Kempelen. Magyarországi Zsidó,
2:24. See GENERAL WORKS.

DERKHEIM
AJA has genealogical files.
Stern. FAJF. Derkheim family
tree beginning in U.S. See
GENERAL WORKS.

D'ERLANGER
CFM has family records.

DERNBURG
LBI has family tree.
Semi-Gotha, 1:101ff. See
GENERAL WORKS.

DE ROSSI
CFM has family records.
Levi, Isaia. "La famiglia
De-Rossi," Il Vessillo
Israeltico 49 (1901):382-84.
From Mantova.

DE SALAS
CFM has family records.

DE SAXE
AMH has family records.

DE SHIRA
AJA has Judith Hart de Shira
genealogical files.

DE SOLA
AJA has birth and marriage
records, 1798-1821, for
family of Kingston, Jamaica.
CFM has family records.
Birmingham. The Grandees. See
GENERAL WORKS.
Lazaron, Anita de Sola. De
Sola Odyssey: A Thousand and
One Years. Richmond, Va.:
Dietz Press, 1966. 63 p.
Narrative poem to which is
added some biographical items
on the leaders of de Sola
family starting with Don
Bartolomé of Navarre, Spain
in the 9th century. MH, Vi,
Norfolk Public Library.
Stern. FAJF. De Sola family
trees beginning in:
(I) Navarre and (II) Barbary
States. See GENERAL WORKS.

DESSARRE
Dessarre, Ève. Mon enfance
d'avant le deluge. Paris:
Libraire Arthéme Fayard,
1976. 255 p. Family of
Saarbruck. Author (b. 1926)
covers to the outbreak of
W.W.II.

DESSAUER
CAJ has family trees,
1763-1961, 1715-1962,
1710-1960, and 1735-1900.
Hämmerle, Albert, ed.
Stammtafel der Familie
Dessauer aus Aschaffenburg.
N.p., 1962. 241 p. LBI.
Zapf. Tübinger Juden, pp.
47-48. See GENERAL WORKS.

DESSLER
Dessler, Julia Shapiro. Eyes
on the Goal. New York:
Vantage, 1954. 54 p.
Autobiography. Dessler
family of Lithuania. DLC,
NN, PPDrop.

DE STEIN
CFM has family records.

DE STERN
AMH has family records.

DE SUNNESHEIM
See Wilhelm and Rudolf Frank
entry under BING.

DE SYMONS
CFM has family records.

DETASSICHE
CAJ has family records.

DETMOLD
Banniza von Bazan, Heinrich.
"Der erste jüdische
Reichminister und seine
Ahnen," Volk und Rasse 14
(1939):178-80.
————— and Richard Müller.
"Johann Hermann Detmold,"
Deutsche Geschichte in
Ahnentafeln 2 (1942):322-23.
Includes genealogical table.
Johann Hermann Detmold,
German diplomat, b. Hannover,
1807; d. 1856. As a child he
was baptized.

DE TORRES
AJA has genealogical files.
Stern. FAJF. De Torres family
trees beginning in:
(I) Jamaica and

(II) Portugal. See GENERAL
WORKS.

DETSENYI
Kempelen. Magyarországi Zsidó,
3:57. Detsényi family. See
GENERAL WORKS.

DETTELBACHER
Tänzer. Juden in Jebenhausen,
pp. 299-300. See GENERAL
WORKS.

DETTRICH
Kempelen. Magyarországi Zsidó,
3:76. See GENERAL WORKS.

DEUTSCH
Jastrow, Marie. A Time to
Remember: Growing Up in New
York before the Great War.
New York: W.W. Norton & Co.,
1979. Author nostalgically
recalls her family's life in
Yarac, Serbia, and immigrant
life in New York City,
1905-1917. Daughter of
Julius Grunfeld (1869-?).
Her mother's maiden name was
Deutsch.
See Kempelen entry under
HATVANY-DEUTSCH.
Kempelen. Magyarországi Zsidó,
1:58, 75, 122; 2:35, 53, 61,
62, 89, 102, 126, 134; 3:44,
88, 92, 113. See GENERAL
WORKS.

DEUTSCHER
Bick-Shauli, "Roots and
Branches." Includes
genealogy of Isaac Deutscher,
Marxist historian and
political scientist,
b. Cracow, 1907; d. 1967.
See GENERAL WORKS.

DE VAHL
AMH has family records.
CFM has family records.
Wolf, "Anglo-Jewish Families."
See GENERAL WORKS.

DEVAS
AMH has family records.

DE VEIL, DE VEILLE
See WEIL.

DEVRIENT
LBI has family tree beginning
1669.

DE VRIES
CFM has family records.
Droege, "Frisian Names." See
GENERAL WORKS.

DEVRIES
LBI has family tree beginning
1798.

DE WEILLE
See WEIL.

DE WORMS
Ullman, Elias. Genealogical
History of the Family of De
Worms. Frankfurt am Main,
1886. 16 p.

DE YOUNG
AMH has family records.
Rosenwaike, I. "The Parentage
and Early Years of M.H. de
Young; Legend and Fact,"
Western States Jewish
Historical Quarterly 7
(1975):210-17. Family of
Michael Henry de Young, the
famous San Francisco
publisher and civic leader.
Family originally from
Holland; originally spelled
"de Jongh."

DEZSENYI
Kempelen. Magyarországi Zsidó,
3:121. Dezsényi family. See
GENERAL WORKS.

DIAMANT
PD has family records.
Brilling, Bernhard. "Einer der
ersten jüd. Genealogen: Zur
Erinnerung an Dr. Paul J.
Diamant (Wien/Jerusalem),"
Allgemeine Wochenzeitung der
Juden in Deutschland
(Düsseldorf), Aug. 5, 1966.
Paul Joseph Diamant, Israeli
genealogist and historian of

Austrian Jewry, b. Vienna,
1887; d. 1966. He was
related to both the Heine and
Herzl families. Minna
Diamant was his mother.
Diamant, Paul J. Minna
Diamant, 1815-1840: Ihre
Freunde und Verwandten. Tel
Aviv: Olamenu, 1964. 102 p.
CAJ, LBI.
————. Herzls väterliche und
mütterlich Vorfahren; eine
familiengeschichtliche Studie
mit einer Ahnentafel.
Jerusalem: Bamberger &
Wahrmann, 1934. 19 p.
Jeanette Diamant, 1836-1911,
the mother of Herzl. NN,
PPDrop.
Kempelen. Magyarországi Zsidó,
1:62; 2:50, 58. See GENERAL
WORKS.

DIAMANTSCHLEIFER
AMH has family records.

DIAS
AMH has family records.
CFM has family records.

DICK
Kempelen. Magyarországi Zsidó,
3:55. See GENERAL WORKS.

DICKER
Dicker, Herman. A Jewish
Family Trail; the Dickers and
Their Mates. New York:
Express Printing Co., 1977.
44 p. Genealogical tables.
CtY, DLC, MH, NN, OU.

DICKSON
Semi-Gotha, 1:38, 148. See
GENERAL WORKS.

DIENEMANN
Dienemann, Max and Siegfried
Guggenheim. Stammbaum der
Familie Guggenheim aus Worms.
(Rothschild-Dienemann-Guggenh
im). Offenbach a.M.:
H. Cramer, 1926. 21 p.
7 genealogical tables. DLC,
NN, OCH.

DIETL
Kempelen. Magyarországi Zsidó,
1:82. See GENERAL WORKS.

DIETRICH
Kempelen. Magyarországi Zsidó,
3:120. See GENERAL WORKS.

DIETRICHSTEIN
Kempelen. Magyarországi Zsidó,
1:68, 69. See GENERAL WORKS.

DIGHT
AMH has family records.

DILLON
"Genealogical Information on
the Lapowski-Dillon Family."
AJA.

DIMSHITS
Bick-Shauli, "Roots and
Branches." Includes Binyamin
Dimshits, Soviet economist
and Deputy Prime Minister of
the USSR, b. Fiodosia,
Crimea, 1910. See GENERAL
WORKS.

DINER
CAJ has family records.
Kain, Pollack. "A Diner
Csaladrol," Magyar-Zsidó
Szemle (Budapest), no. 12
(1895):366-67. Family of
Hungary.
Kempelen. Magyarországi Zsidó,
3:135. See GENERAL WORKS.

DINKELSPIEL
Simon, Carl. "Aus der
Geschichte f. Familien
Dinkelspiel in Mannheim,"
JFF, no. 3 (1925):61-64; 4
(1925):86-89.

DIOSI
Kempelen. Magyarországi Zsidó,
2:45; 3:20. Diósi family.
See GENERAL WORKS.

DIRNHUBER
Kempelen. Magyarországi Zsidó,
2:150. See GENERAL WORKS.

DIRSZTAY
Kempelen. Magyarországi Zsidó,
1:87-88, 130, 134; 2:21. See
GENERAL WORKS.

DISCOMBE
AMH has family records.

DISRAELI
AMH has family records.
CFM has family records.
EJ (1972), 6:109. Includes
genealogical table,
descendants of Isaac Israeli,
16th to mid-20th century.
See GENERAL WORKS.
JE, 4:622. "Disraeli
Pedigree." Descendants of
Benjamin D'Israeli
(1730-1816). See GENERAL
WORKS.
Wolf, Lucien. "The Disraeli
Family," Transactions of the
Jewish Historical Society of
England 5 (1908):202-218.
Also, see Wolf, "Anglo-Jewish
Families," under GENERAL
WORKS.

DITTENHOEFFER
Dittenhoeffer Family Tree,
compiled by Moses
Dittenhoeffer in 1932,
revised by Henry M. Loewy in
1953. Family of Bavaria,
covers from 1774. AJA.

DOBAY
Kempelen. Magyarországi Zsidó,
2:27; 3:92. See GENERAL
WORKS.

DOBIAS
Kempelen. Magyarországi Zsidó,
3:34. Dóbiás family. See
GENERAL WORKS.

DOBINSKA
PD has family records.

DOBLHOFF
Kempelen. Magyarországi Zsidó,
2:46. See GENERAL WORKS.

DOBRAI
Kempelen. Magyarországi

Zsidó, 2:43. See GENERAL
WORKS.

DOBRIN
Dobrin, Paul. Stammbaum der
Familien Dobrin. Breslau,
1910. Descendants of Levin
Michael Dobrin, d. 1810.
LBI.

DOBRUSKA
LBI has family tree beginning
1715.
Ruzieka, Leon. "Stammtafel der
Familie Dobruska," JFF,
no. 23 (1930):287-89. Family
of Schonfeld.

DOBRZENSKY
Dobrzensky Family, Inglewood,
California. "Letter from
Mrs. Dorothy R. Millard to
Norton B. Stern, Giving
Information on the Dobrzensky
Family, 1967." Typescript
copy. AJA.
Robert E. Levinson Papers.
Contain David Abraham
Dobrzensky family tree.
WJHC.

DOBSON
AMH has family records.

DOCZY
Kempelen. Magyarországi Zsidó,
1:63-65; 3:122. Dóczy
family. See GENERAL WORKS.

DOLFS
LBI has family tree beginning
1725.

DOMBOVARY
Kempelen. Magyarországi Zsidó,
1:126. Dombováry family.
See GENERAL WORKS.

DOMOKOS
Kempelen. Magyarországi Zsidó,
2:136. See GENERAL WORKS.

DOMONY
Kempelen. Magyarországi Zsidó,
1:112, 129-30; 2:48. See
GENERAL WORKS.

DOMONY-BRULL
Kempelen. Magyarországi Zsidó,
2:48. Domony-Brüll family.
See GENERAL WORKS.

DONATH
Kempelen. Magyarországi Zsidó,
2:106-16. See GENERAL WORKS.

DONCET
AMH has family records.

DONINGTON
AMH has family records.

DONN
AMH has family records.

DONNENBAUM
Tobias ben Juda. "Haus
Donnenbaum. Studien zur
Geschichte einer jüdischen
Patrizierfamilie," Jüdisches
Archiv 1, N.F., no. 1/2
(1927/28):12-16. Mähren.

DONOVAN
AMH has family records.

DO PORTE
CFM has family records.

DORFMAN
Knetzer, Leean and David.
Dorfman Family, Genealogy,
1851-1962. N.d. AJA.

DORMIDO
CFM has family records.

DORY
Kempelen. Magyarországi Zsidó,
1:76; 3:126. Dőry family.
See GENERAL WORKS.

DORZBACHER
Tänzer. Juden in Jebenhausen,
pp. 301-302. See GENERAL
WORKS.

DOUGLAS
AMH has family records.
Semi-Gotha, 1:139, 140, 142.
See GENERAL WORKS.

DO VALLE
CFM has family records.

DOW
AMH has family records.

DOWLER
Lybarger, Donald Fisher. The
Story of the
Dowler-Hartshorne,
Fisher-Lybarger Families.
Cleveland, 1938, 1962, 2d ed.
63 p. DLC, OCl.

DRACHMAN
Fierman, Floyd S. "The
Drachmans of Arizona,"
American Jewish Archives 16
(1964):135-60. Family
originally from Petrokov,
Russian Poland.

DRACHS
AMH has family records.

DRAGE
AMH has family records.

DRAGO
CFM has family records.

DRECHSEL
Kempelen. Magyarországi Zsidó,
3:94. See GENERAL WORKS.

DRECHSLER
Kempelen. Magyarországi Zsidó,
2:89. See GENERAL WORKS.

DREIFUSS
Tänzer. Juden in Jebenhausen,
p. 303. See GENERAL WORKS.

DRESDEN
CFM has family records.

DREYDEL
CFM has family records.

DREYER
LBI has family trees beginning
1545 and 1735.

DREYFOUS
"Dreyfous Family Genealogy,
Cincinnati, Ohio and New

Orleans, La., 1779-1962."
AJA.
"Dreyfous Family, New Orleans,
La., Scrapbook, 1830-1960."
In French and English.
Microfilm. AJA.
Genealogy of Felix Julius
Dreyfous, New Orleans,
Louisiana. AJA.

DREYFUS, DREYFUSS
AMH has Dreyfus family records.
Breal, Michel. "Que signifie
le nom de Dreyfuss?" Revue
Bleue 49, no. 1
(1911):417-18.
"Der Familienname Dreifuss,"
Der Israelit (Frankfurt am
Main) 53, no. 22 (1912):3.
CAJ, Call No. 3418, has two
Dreyfuss family trees: Family
tree for descendants of
Abraham Dreyfuss, b. 1746,
the great-great grandfather
of Edgar Dreyfuss, b. Berlin,
1911; family trees showing
forbears of Edgar Dreyfuss.
Dreyfus, Pierre. "Album de
famille," L'Arche 20 (Juin
1977):32-35. Recollections
of Captain Alfred Dreyfus'
family.
Kaufmann, David. "Zur
Geschichte d. Familien
Dreyfuss," MGWJ 42
(1898):424-29.
See Daniel Nathan Leeson entry
under LEESON.
Millner, Joseph. "Les grandes
familles juives de France,"
Le Monde Juif 5, no. 29
(1950):17-19.
Pudor. Internationalen
Verwandtschaftlichen. Vol. 3
contains a section on Dreyfus
family. See GENERAL WORKS.

DRIELSMA, DRILSMA
Droege, "Frisian Names." See
GENERAL WORKS.

DROSTE ZU HULSHOFF
Semigothaisches Taschenbuch.
Genealogical table 5. See
GENERAL WORKS.

DRUCKER
CAJ has family trees beginning
18th century.
LBIS has notes for families
from Hamburg and Kassel.
See Richard J. Alperin entry
under BEHRMAN.
Herz, Heinrich. Zur Geschichte
der Familie Herz in Weilburg.
Aachen, 1906. 67 p.
Genealogical table for the
descendants of Herz Feist,
1710-1746. Includes Drucker
and Groedel families. YIVO.
Kempelen. Magyarországi Zsidó,
1:47; 2:42, 90. See GENERAL
WORKS.

DRUIFF
AMH has family records.

DRUITT
AMH has family records.

DRUKKER
AMH has family records.

DRUMMOND
Kempelen. Magyarországi Zsidó,
1:81. See GENERAL WORKS.

DRUSELLO
AMH has family records.

DRYFOOS
Dryfoos Family. Records of
Births, Marriages, and
Deaths, 1814-1920. AJA.

DRYFUSS
See Daniel Nathan Leeson entry
under LEESON.

DUBNOW
Belinson, Moses Eliezer.
Shelume Emune Yisrael.
Odessa, 1898-1901. 3 vols.
Includes Dubnow family of
Poland and Russia. DLC.
Horodetzky, S.A. "The
Genealogy of Simon Dubnow,"
(In Yiddish.) Yivo Studies in
History 2 (1937):1-8.

DUCKESZ
CAJ has family records.

DUDAS
Kempelen. Magyarországi Zsidó,
2:90. Dudás family. See
GENERAL WORKS.

DUENKELSBUEHLER
LBI has family tree beginning
1610.

DUFF
AMH has family records.

DUFFIELD
AMH has family records.

DUFFY
AMH has family records.

DUFWA
Semi-Gotha, 2:18. See GENERAL
WORKS.

DUKA
Kempelen. Magyarországi Zsidó,
2:51. See GENERAL WORKS.

DUKES, DUKESZ
PD has family records.

DULKEN
CAJ has genealogy.
LBI has family tree beginning
1808.

DUMREICHER
Kempelen. Magyarországi Zsidó,
1:45. See GENERAL WORKS.

DUNN
AMH has family records.

DUPONT
AMH has family records.

DU PONT
Du Pont Family; Wilmington,
Delaware. Genealogical
Information, 1935.
Typescript. AJA.
Du Pont Family; Wilmington,
Delaware. "The Du Ponts'
Jewish Ancestry," by Malcolm
H. Stern, 1967. Typescript.
AJA.

DURKHEIMER
Glazer, Michele. "The
Durkheimers of Oregon: A
Picture Story," Western
States Jewish Historical
Quarterly 10 (1978):202-209.

DURLACHER
AMH has family records.
CFM has family records.
Kempelen. Magyarországi Zsidó,
1:106. See GENERAL WORKS.
Löwenstein, Leopold. Nathanael
Weil, Oberrabbiner in
Karlsruhe und seine Familie.
Frankfurt am Main: Kauffmann,
1898. 85 p. (Beiträge zur
Geschichte der Juden in
Deutschland, 2.) Includes
Durlacher family history.
Nathanael Weil, 1687-1769.

DUSCHINSZKI
Kempelen. Magyarországi Zsidó,
1:86. See GENERAL WORKS.

DUSSELDORF
Gronemann. Genealogische
Hannovers, pp. 29-43. "Die
Familie Düsseldorf."
Genealogical tables. See
GENERAL WORKS.

DUTCH
AMH has family records.

DUVEEN
AMH has family records.
Behrman, Samuel Nathaniel.
Duveen. New York: Random
House, 1952. 302 p.
Anglo-Jewish family of art
dealers. Family originally
from Netherlands.
Duveen, James Henry. The Rise
of the House of Duveen.
London: Longmans, Green,
1957. 252 p. CSt, DLC, NN.

DUX
CFM has family records.
Kempelen. Magyarországi Zsidó,
1:63; 3:122. See GENERAL
WORKS.

91   ECKSTEIN

DWINGERSMA
Droege, "Frisian Names." See
GENERAL WORKS.

DWORZACZEK
Dworzaczek, Włodzimierz.
Genealogia. (Wyd. 1).
Warszawa: Panstowowe Wydann.
Naukowe, 1959. 181 p.
10 genealogical tables.
─────. Tablice. (Wyd. 1).
1959. 31 p.
183 genealogical tables.
CAJ, CtY, CU, ICU, NcD, NjP,
ViU, WU.

DYAS
AMH has family records.

DYER
Stern. FAJF. Dyer family tree
beginning in Alzey, near
Mainz. See GENERAL WORKS.

DYNER
See Nathan M. Reiss entry under
EDELMUTH. Includes Dyner
family of Olkusz.

DYRSSEN
Semi-Gotha, 2:110. See GENERAL
WORKS.

DYTE
CFM has family records.

DZIALYNSKI
Dzialynski Family; Florida.
"The History of the
Dzialynski Family," by Ruth
Hope Leon, n.d. Typescript.
AJA.

DZIOKOWSKI
See MLOCKI-DZIOKOWSKI.

EASTWOOD
AMH has family records.

EATON
Eaton, Edwin, Fresno,
California. "Letter from

Edwin M. Eaton to Norton B.
Stern, Giving Biographical
Information Regarding His
Family." 1966. Typescript
copy. AJA.

EBER
Kempelen. Magyarországi Zsidó,
3:43. See GENERAL WORKS.

EBERHARDT
AMH has family records.

EBERS
"Die Berliner Familie
Ephraim-Ebers und ihre
gräflichen Nachfahren,"
JFF, no. 2.

EBERSON
AMH has family records.

EBERSTADT
AMH has family records.
CFM has family records.

EBERT
Faris, Alexander. Jacques
Offenbach. London: Faber
and Faber, 1980. 275 p.
"Family Tree," pp. 14-15,
includes descendants of
Juda Ebert (d. ca. 1794) of
Offenbach-am-Main, Germany.
When some of his children
moved to Cologne, the
family name Offenbach was
adopted.

EBHARD
Kempelen. Magyarországi Zsidó,
3:87. See GENERAL WORKS.

ECKENBERG
Kempelen. Magyarországi Zsidó,
3:40. See GENERAL WORKS.

ECKSTEIN
CAJ (Call No. P/123) has the
following: (1) Family album
giving history of Eckstein
family from Lavenförde,
ca. 1806-1982. Dates of
births and deaths of family
members, pp. 1-108 in

German, pp. 111-40 in
English; (2) Family trees
showing forbears of Marie
Therese Weisz (formerly
Eckstein), b. Berlin, 1912;
(3) Eckstein, Henriette
(formerly Stern): Chronik der
Familie Stern, Vlotho a.
Weser, 36 p; (4) Family tree
of descendants of Moses
Kempenich, b. ca. 1795;
d. Neheim, 1870; (5) Articles
on Jacob Freudenthal
(1839-1907), a biographer of
Spinoza (he was born in
Bodenfelde); (6) Loose
pictures of members of
Eckstein and Freudenthal
families.
Eckstein, Hugo. Stammbaum der
Familie Eckstein. Berlin,
1925. 1 leaf, 52 x 77cm.
Descendants of Abraham and
Moses Eckstein of Lavenförde.
Kempelen. Magyarországi Zsidó,
1:69. See GENERAL WORKS.

ECSERY
PD has family records.
Kempelen. Magyarországi Zsidó,
1:139. Ecséry family. See
GENERAL WORKS.

EDEL
Bühler, Hans Eugen. "Die
Wasenmeisterfamilie Edel aus
Düsseldorf:
historisch-genealogische
Hintergründe der Begegnung
Heinrich Heines mit Josepha
Edel," Genealogie
(Neustadt/Aisch) 29, no. 2
(Feb. 1980):33-43.

EDELMUTH
Reiss, Nathan M. Some Jewish
Families of Hesse and
Galicia. Highland Park,
N.J.: By the Author, 1980.
229 p. Includes Edelmuth
family of Beuren and
Reiskirchen. Also includes
Baum, Dyner, Freylich,
Goldblum, Krieger,
Lilienstein, Lippmann, May,

Meyerfeld, and Reiss families.
YIVO.

EDELSTEIN
Berg, Gertrude. Molly and Me,
With Cherney Berg. New York:
McGraw-Hill, 1961. 278 p.
Especially, pp. 3-17, 28-37.
Molly Berg (1899-1966), the
famous American actress, was
the daughter of Jacob and
Dinah Edelstein Goldstein and
the granddaughter of Harris
and Czerna Goldstein and
Mordecai Edelstein. The
Edelstein family was from
Lublin.
Green, Cathy. "My Ancestors: A
Genealogy of the
Green-Edelstein Family."
Louisville, Ky., Jan. 1975.
AJA.
Kempelen. Magyarországi Zsidó,
2:88. See GENERAL WORKS.
Kurzweil, Arthur. "Hizzoner's
Roots," New York,
29 Oct. 1979, pp. 46-48.
About the forebears of New
York City Mayor Edward I.
Koch. Yisroel Edelstein of
Skala, Poland.
Schulte. Bonner Juden, p. 215.
See GENERAL WORKS.

EDERER
Kempelen. Magyarországi Zsidó,
2:103. See GENERAL WORKS.

EDERSHEIM
CFM has family records.

EDGAR
AMH has family records.

EDGLEY
AMH has family records.

EDLER
Kempelen. Magyarországi Zsidó,
2:8. See GENERAL WORKS.

EDWARDS
AMH has family records.

EFROYMSON
"Efroymson Family Genealogical
Chart, 1775-1971." MS. AJA.

EGAN
AMH has family records.

EGER
CAJ has family tree.
JE, 5:52. Genealogical table
listing descendants of R.
Meyer Ginsmann
(d. Halberstadt, Germany,
1674), through late 19th
century. See GENERAL WORKS.
LBI has family trees beginning
11th century, 1572, 1600,
1609, and 1695.
Meyer, Walther. "Zur
Geschichte der Familie
Eger-Gans-Gansmann," JFF,
no. 48/50 (1938):890-96,
914-20, 938-43.
Schreiber, Benjamin. Ketov zot
Zikaron. New York, 1957.
350 p. Genealogical table.
Includes Eger family. CLU,
MH, NN.
Simon, Fritz. Schalscheleth
ha-Juchasin Eger,
Margoliouth, Calvariski,
Simon. Jerusalem, 1941.
1 lf., gr. folio. Includes
genealogical tables.

EGG
Tänzer. Juden in Tirol,
pp. 708-709. See GENERAL
WORKS.

EGGER
Kempelen. Magyarországi Zsidó,
2:97. See GENERAL WORKS.

EGGMANN
Tänzer. Juden in Tirol,
p. 710. See GENERAL WORKS.

EGRY
Kempelen. Magyarországi Zsidó,
3:55. See GENERAL WORKS.

EGYED
Kempelen. Magyarországi Zsidó,
1:116; 3:119. See GENERAL
WORKS.

EHRENBERG
LBI has family tree beginning
1680.
Ballin. Juden in Seesen,
pp. 175-76. See GENERAL
WORKS.
Ehrenberg, Felipe. Generación.
Cullompton, England: Beau
Geste Press, 1973. Book 1:
Spanish and English Text.
64 leaves of plates. Family
of Mexico.
Zunz, Leopold. Samuel Meyer
Ehrenberg, Inspector der
Samsonschen Freischule zu
Wolfenbüttel, ein Denkmal für
angehörige und Freunde. Als
manuskript gedruckt.
Braunschweig, 1854: Gebr.
Meyer. 50 p. 1 genealogical
table. Samuel Myer
Ehrenberg, educator,
b. Brunswick, Germany, 1773;
d. Wolfenbüttel, Germany,
1853. A graduate of the
Samson School in
Wolfenbüttel, he became its
inspector. It was his
intention to change it from a
traditional Yeshiva to a
modern Jewish high school.
OCH.

EHRENFELD
Kempelen. Magyarországi Zsidó,
1:30, 78, 82, 83-84; 2:17,
28, 54; 3:24, 32, 68. See
GENERAL WORKS.

EHRENFELD-POP
Kempelen. Magyarországi Zsidó,
1:81. See GENERAL WORKS.

EHRENFELS
Semigothaisches Taschenbuch.
Genealogical table 16.
Normann-Ehrenfels family.
See GENERAL WORKS.

EHRENPREIS
Rothschild. Svenska Israel.
See GENERAL WORKS.

EHRENREICH
The Krensky-Ehrenreich
"Time-Line," Heder Hadorot,

Spertus Museum of Judaica,
2nd floor, 618 S. Michigan
Ave., Chicago, Illinois.
"This permanent exhibit is a
documentary and pictorial
history of the
Krensky-Ehrenreich family,
with pictures and diagrams
tracing back 200 years, on
the walls of the Milton J.
Krensky and Rosemary
Ehrenreich Krensky Conference
Room."
Kempelen. Magyarországi Zsidó,
2:43; 3:30. See GENERAL
WORKS.

EHRENSTAMM
LBI has family tree beginning
1695.
Heilig, Bernhard. Aufstieg und
verfall des Hauses Ehrenstamm
1752-1852. Vortrag gehalten
in Prag, Nov. 1932. 13 p.
MS. Wiener Library, London.
————. "Aktuelles aus der
Geschichte des Hauses
Ehrenstamm," Zeitschrift des
Deutschen Vereines für Gesch.
Mährens und Schlesiens 37
(1935):9-28. Family of
pioneering textile
manufacturers in the Hapsburg
Empire in the 18th and 19th
centuries.
————. "Aufstieg und Verfall
des Hauses Ehrenstamm,"
Bulletin für die Mitglieder
der Gesellschaft der Freunde
des Leo Baeck Instituts,
no. 10 (Juli 1960):101-122.

EHRLICH
AMH has family records.
Breitenbach-Ehrlich Family.
"Family Records Contained in
Prayer Book Owned by Sarah
Breitenbach Ehrlich,
Bainbridge, Ga., 1849-1974."
AJA.
CAJ has family trees and
records.
LBI has family trees beginning
1600, 1737, and 1820.
"Ahnentafel von Paul Ehrlich,
1854-1915, dem Bezwinger der

Syphilis," JFF, no. 34
(1933):549.
Ehrlich, Richard A. Fünf
Generationen der Familie
Alexander-Ehrlich.
Cambridge, Mass., 1964.
10 p. MS. Family from
Rogasen and Wollstein. LBI.
Kempelen. Magyarországi Zsidó,
2:10. See GENERAL WORKS.
Knoche, Gerd. "Paul Ehrlich's
Ahnen," JFF, no. 41
(1936):734-37.
Gold. Juden Mahrens,
pp. 547-48. Family from
Triesch. Sigmund Ehrlich,
b. Gross-Beranau (bei
Triesch), 1852. See GENERAL
WORKS.

EHRLICHMAN
See Yaffa Draznin entry under
BERNSTEIN.

EHRMANN
Ehrmann, Herbert Brutus,
1891-1970. Papers,
1913-1970. Include
genealogical material.
Mr. Ehrmann was a lawyer from
Brookline, Mass. AJHS.
Tänzer. Juden in Tirol,
p. 711. See GENERAL WORKS.

EIBENSCHUTZ
See EYBESCHITZ, EYBESCHUTZ.

EICHEL
Fischer, Josef. Stamtavlen
Eichel. Udarbejdet af
J. Fischer. København:
Trier, 1904. Printed as MS.
CAJ, OCH.

EICHELBERG
CAJ has family records.

EICHELSTEIN
Saglio, J. "L'origine du nom
de Eichelstein," Revue
Internationale d'Onomastique
11 (Sept. 1959):211-16.

EICHELGRUN
Eichelgrün, Gustav. Die
Familie Eichengrün, ein

Beitrag zur Geschichte der
Westfälischen Juden. By the
Author, 1935. Family tree
beginning 1785. Descendants
of Rafal Eichengrün,
b. Beringhausen, 1794;
d. Tangermönde, 1870. LBI.

EICHENBAUM
Sonder, Alfred. Ahnentafel der
Kinder des Nathan Weill (Sohn
des Löw Weill) in Kippenheim.
Frankfurt am Main: Schirmer &
Mahlau, 1935. 50 p.
Genealogical tables.
Includes Eichenbaum family.
NN.

EICHENGRUN
See EICHELGRUN.

EICHENSTEIN
Rosenstein. Unbroken Chain,
pp. 618ff. Discussion of the
Eichenstein and Safrin
Chassidic dynasties of
Zhidachov and Komarno. See
GENERAL WORKS.

EICHMANN
Rülf, Moses. Stammbaum der
Familie Eichmann, 1660-1931.
Detmold, 1931. 34 p.

EICHTHAL
Semigothaisches Taschenbuch.
Genealogical table 6. See
GENERAL WORKS.

EIDLISH
See Meir Yizraeli entry under
BIDERMAN.

EIDLITZ
Kempelen. Magyarországi Zsidó,
2:10. See GENERAL WORKS.

EIGENE
PD has family tree.

EIGER
AMH has family records.
CAJ, Call No. 4318, has the
following family trees:
(1) Simon, Menashe. The
Genealogical Tree of the

Eiger, Margoliot-Kalvaryski
and Simon Families (begins
with Katzenellenbogen,
Germany, 1312 and ends in
1937) on one side and (2) on
the opposite side:
Margolis-Jahrblum, Laura
(Tel-Aviv), Continuation of
the Genealogical Tree of the
Margoliot-Kalvaryski Family,
19th and 20th Century.
"Margoliot" also written
"Margolis."

EILENBURG
Kempelen. Magyarországi Zsidó,
1:73. See GENERAL WORKS.

EINHORN
Kempelen. Magyarországi Zsidó,
2:43. See GENERAL WORKS.

EINSTEIN
Clark, Ronald William.
Einstein: The Life and Times.
London: Hodder & Stoughton,
1973. 670 p. Includes
genealogical information.
Einstein, Albert. Papers,
1920-1969. Contain family
tree and other family
records. LBI.
Tänzer, A. "Stammbaum von
Professor Albert Einstein,"
JFF, no. 28 (1931):419-21.
Tänzer. Juden in Jebenhausen,
pp. 304-308. See GENERAL
WORKS.
Weil, Emma. Chronik der
Familien Weil, Gutmann und
Einstein. London, 1962.
102 p. Stuttgart. LBI.

EISEMANN
See Sally David Cramer under
CRAMER.

EISENBERG
Eisenberg, Gershon Hanoch.
Sefer Hazichronot: Divrei
Yemay Michpachteinu. Holon,
Israel, 1976. JNUL.
La Zebnik, Edith. Such a Life.
Boston: G.K. Hall & Co.,
1979. 528 p. Deals with
Eisenberg family life in

Minsk gubernya. Author is
the daughter of David
Eisenberg and granddaughter
of Gershon Eisenberg.
Schunk, Betty. Aus alten
Tagebüchern und Erinnerungen
der Familien Hirsch, (Worms),
Strupp, Eisenberg.
Abgeschrieben, illustriert
und mit vier Stammtafeln
versehen von Alexander
Eisenberg. Meiningen, 1924.
24 p. Begins in 1770.

EISENMENGER
CAJ has family records.

EISENSTADT
AMH has family records.
Rosenstein. Unbroken Chain,
pp. 237ff. Eisenstadt
descendants of R. Solomon
Zalman Katzenellenbogen. See
GENERAL WORKS.

EISENSTADTER
Kempelen. Magyarországi Zsidó,
1:57; 3:119, 138, 139.
Eisenstädter family. See
GENERAL WORKS.

EISENSTATTER
PD has family records.

EISLER
PD has family records.
Kempelen. Magyarországi Zsidó,
1:57, 86, 87; 2:51. See
GENERAL WORKS.

EISNER
Eisner, Jake. The Survivor.
Edited by Irving A. Leitner.
New York: William Morrow,
1980. 320 p.
Autobiographical account of a
Warsaw Ghetto youth and his
family. The dedication page
of this work lists the the
names of his cousins who died
in the Holocaust. His
parents were Aron and Zlatka
Eisner of Warsaw.
See Ludwig Herz entry under
REICHENHEIM.

EKENSTJERNA
Semi-Gotha, 1:84. See GENERAL
WORKS.

ELBOGEN
Chajes, Saul. "Die
Verlassenschaft der Frau
Reich Elbogen," Jüdisches
Archiv, Jg. 1, Heft 4/5,
pp. 12-18. Includes family
tree.

ELCAN
Elcan, Marcus. "Genealogy of
Marcus Elcan." Beth Ahabah
Archives, Richmond, Virginia.

EL-DIN
AMH has family records.

ELEK
PD has family records.
Kempelen. Magyarországi Zsidó,
1:82; 3:101, 117. See
GENERAL WORKS.

ELEKES
Kempelen. Magyarországi Zsidó,
2:88. See GENERAL WORKS.

ELFFENSTEIN
Kempelen. Magyarországi Zsidó,
2:8. See GENERAL WORKS.

ELIACHAR, ELYACHAR
CAJ has Elyachar family
records.
An Exhibition of the History of
the Elyachar Family.
Jerusalem: Printed at the
Hadassah Apprentice School of
Printing, 1966? 4 p. in
Hebrew + 4 p. in English
translation. Listing of 24
exhibits and their origins.
Family is descended from
Rabbi Joseph Elichar who left
Spain and came to the Holy
Land between 1492 and 1502.
JNUL.
Efrati, Nathan. Mispaṭat
Elyashar be-Tokhekhe
Yerushalayim. [The Role of
the Eliachar Family in
Jerusalem.] Jerusalem, 1974
or 1975. 318 p. CLU, CtY,

CU, DLC, ICU, MB, MH, NjP,
NNC, WU.

ELIAH
See Meir Yizraeli entry under
BIDERMAN.

ELIAS
AMH has family records.
CFM has family records.
Stern. FAJF. Elias family
tree beginning in Dedesdorf,
Germany. See GENERAL WORKS.

ELIAS-ELIZER
Elias Family. Family record
found in Bible of Eleanor C.
Elias. 1845-1962. AJA.

ELIASH
Alfasi, Yitzhak, comp.
Genealogy of the Eliash
Family. Jerusalem, 1975.

ELIASHAR
Yaoz. Album Shel. See GENERAL
WORKS.

ELIASON
AMH has family records.
CFM has family records.

ELIASSON
Rothschild. Svenska Israel.
See GENERAL WORKS.

ELIJAH
Joseph, A. and M.K. Ireland.
"The Family of Nathan ben
Elijah," Journal and
Proceedings of the Australian
Jewish Historical Society 7
(1974):513-23.

ELISHAR
Elmaleh, Abraham. Ha-rishonim
le-tsiyon Lemishpachat
Elishar. Jerusalem: Reuven
Mass, 1970. Elishar family,
pp. 283-352. NjP.

ELIZER
See ELIAS-ELIZER.
Stern. FAJF. Elizer family
tree beginning in U.S. See
GENERAL WORKS.

ELKAN, ELKEN
AMH has Elkan family records.
CAJD has Elken family tree from
Germany.
Frank. Nashville Jewry,
p. 147. Elkan family. See
GENERAL WORKS.

ELKIN
AJA has genealogical files.
AMH has family records.
CFM has family records.
Stern. FAJF. Elkin family
trees beginning in:
(I) Breslau and (II) Jamaica;
also spelled Elkins
originally. See GENERAL
WORKS.

ELKINS
See Stern, FAJF (II) entry
under ELKIN.

ELLEKER
AMH has family records.

ELLENBERG
Rosenstein. Unbroken Chain,
pp. 252ff. Ellenberg
descendants of R. Naftali
Katz. See GENERAL WORKS.

ELLENBERGER
Kempelen. Magyarországi Zsidó,
1:73. See GENERAL WORKS.

ELLENBOGEN
Rosenstein. Unbroken Chain,
pp. 92ff. See GENERAL WORKS.

ELLER
CFM has family records.

ELLERN
LBI has family tree beginning
1600.

ELLINGER
CFM has family records.
Risch, Izhak. Megilat
Mishpaḥtenu. Added title
page: Records Concerning the
Ancestry of the Levi,
Berlinger, and Ellinger
Families of the Zvi Branch.

1974. 88 p. CLU, DLC, MB, NN, WU.

ELLIOT
Semi-Gotha, 1:106ff. See GENERAL WORKS.

ELLIOTT
AMH has family records.

ELLIS
AMH has family records.
CFM has family records.
Chapman, Margaret. The Humanist Jew: The Family of Elias and Rebecca Ellis, Early Anglo-Jewish Migrants to Australia. Brighton Beach, Victoria: By the Author, 1981. 94 p. Includes genealogical table, 1813-1980. National Library of Australia.
Stern. FAJF. Ellis family trees beginning in: (I and II) U.S. See GENERAL WORKS.

ELLIS-EMANUEL
AJA has genealogical files.

ELLISSEN
AMH has family records.
CFM has family records.

ELMALEH
Galante, Abraham. "Origine de la famille Elmaleh," in Abraham Elmaleh 70th Birthday Book (1959), pp. 22 and 56ff.

ELOESSER
AJA has family tree of Lewisohn-Eloesser family.

ELSAS
Elsas, Adolf. Skizze zum Elsas'schen Stammbaum, gewidmet meinem Bruder Max. Ludwigsburg, 1918. 6 p. MS. Ludwigsburg. LBI.
————. Das Rösle von Wankheim. Ein Familienbild aus dem Jahre 1861 im Elsas'schen Hause in Ludwigsburg. LBI.

ELSBACH
Marsden, Edward Arthur. "Elsbach: Die Geschichte einer Familie und eines Unternehmens in Herford," Herforder Jahrbuch 17 (1976/77). 18 p.

ELSNER
AMH has family records.
CAJ has family records.

ELTZBACHER
Eltzbacher, Hans (1893-1969). Family Papers, 1781-1971. Include genealogical information on Hans Eltzbacher, Belgian painter, whose family was originally from Cologne. LBI.
Eltzbacher, Paul. Aus der Geschichte meiner Familie. Berlin-Grunewald (Aldus Druck), 1928. 58 p. Genealogical tables. Descendants of Jakob Loeb Eltzbacher in Neuenkirchen, 1755-1825. Rheinland. LBI, NN.
Schulte. Bonner Juden, p. 216. See GENERAL WORKS.

ELVES
AMH has family records.

ELVIRO
AMH has family records.

ELY
AMH has family records.

ELYACHAR
See ELIACHAR, ELYACHAR.

EMANUEL
See ELLIS-EMANUEL.
AMH has family records.
CAJ has family records.
CFM has family records.
Emanuel-Sanquinetti-Stein Family. Papers. Include a partial family tree of this family of Philadelphia, prepared in 1981. PJAC.
"The Ancestry of the Children of Henry Phillips Moses and

Charlotte Virginia Emanuel,"
St. Charles 1
(Jan. 1935):83-117. Article
never completed. 18th to
early 19th century.
Schulte. Bonner Juden, p. 220.
See GENERAL WORKS.
Stern. FAJF. Emanuel family
trees beginning in:
(I) England; (II) Weisendorf,
Germany; (III) London; and
(IV) Frankfort am Main. See
GENERAL WORKS.

EMBDEN
See VAN EMBDEN.
CFM has family records.
JE, 5:146. Includes
genealogical table,
descendants of Mortiz Embden
of Germany (1790-1866). See
GENERAL WORKS.
Raphael, J. "Über die
Nachkommen der Charlotte
Embden aus Hamburg,"
Zeitschrift für die
Geschichte der Juden (Tel
Aviv) 7, Nr. 2/3
(1970):65-72. Descendants of
Moritz Embden and Charlotte
Heine Embden, 1820s through
1960s.

EMDEN
AMH has family records.
CAJ has family tree.
CFM has family records.
PD has family records.
See Wilhelm and Rudolf Frank
entry under BING.

EMDIN
CFM has family records.

EMERICK
AMH has family records.

EMMEL
Schulte. Bonner Juden, p. 225.
See GENERAL WORKS.

EMMERICH
LBI has family tree beginning
1649.

EMRIK
AMH has family records.

EMS
LBI has family tree beginning
1770.

ENGEL
AMH has family records.
CAJ has family tree and family
records.
PD has family records.
Kempelen. Magyarországi Zsidó,
1:21, 22, 86; 2:54, 66, 90,
94, 133; 3:31, 33, 63, 101,
116, 124. See GENERAL WORKS.
Richter, John Henry. The
Ancestry and Descendance of
Nancy Egers Engel.
Washington, 1954. 8 p. DLC,
NNJ, OCH.

ENGELHARDT
Semi-Gotha, 1:78. See GENERAL
WORKS.

ENGEL-JANOSI
Engel-Janosi, Friedrich. ...
Aber ein stolzer Bettler.
Erinnerungen aus einer
verlorenen Generation. Graz,
Wien, Köln: Verlag Styria,
1974. 316 p. The historian
and author (1893-   )
returned in 1949 to his
nativee Vienna from an
American exile. "Jugend in
der Hofzeile," pp. 9-32, has
genealogical information.
Family came to Vienna from
Pécs (Fünfkirchen), Hungary.
CtY, CU, MB, NjP, NN, OU, WU.

ENGELMANN
Kempelen. Magyarországi Zsidó,
3:69. See GENERAL WORKS.

ENGELSKIRCHEN
PD has family records.

ENGELSTROM
Kempelen. Magyarországi Zsidó,
1:53. Engelström family.
See GENERAL WORKS.

ENGL
Kempelen. Magyarországi Zsidó,
2:90; 3:33. Engel, Engl
family. See GENERAL WORKS.

ENGLAND
AMH has family records.

ENGLANDER
Kempelen. Magyarországi Zsidó,
2:35 or 36? Engländer family.
See GENERAL WORKS.

ENGLERT
Kempelen. Magyarországi Zsidó,
1:71. See GENERAL WORKS.

ENHORNING
Semi-Gotha, 2:110, 141, 154.
Enhörning family. See
GENERAL WORKS.

ENIS
AMH has family records.

ENNIS
Kurzweil, Arthur. The Kurzweil
Family History and Genealogy.
New York, 1976. Includes
Ennis family of Dobromil,
Galicia. AJA, AJHS.

ENOCH
CAJ has family records.

ENRIQUEZ GOMEZ
Révah, I.S. "Le destin des
Marranes espagnols illustré
par l'histoire de la famille
de l'ecrivain Antonio
Enríquez Gómez," Revue
d'Histoire des Religions 167
(1965):109-127.

ENTHOVEN
CFM has family records.

ENTICKNAP
AMH has family records.

ENTWHISTLE
AMH has family records.

ENYEDY
Kempelen. Magyarországi Zsidó,
3:119. See GENERAL WORKS.

EPENSTEIN
PD has family records.
Prowe, Max. "Enkelliste nach
Louis Epenstein (1769-1837),
Schutzjuden zu Berlin," Der
Deutsche Juden, Jg. 25
(1937):105-106.

EPHRAIM
CAJ has family records and a
family tree beginning in
Germany, 1776.
EJ, 6:810. Genealogical table
for the descendants of Heine
(Ḥayyim) Ephraim of Germany
(1665-1748), through first
half of 19th century. See
GENERAL WORKS.
LBI has family tree beginning
1665.
"Die Berliner Familie
Ephraim-Ebers und ihre
gräflichen Nachfahren," JFF,
no. 2.
Ephraim, Benjamin Veitel. Uber
meine Verhaftung und einige
andere Vorfälle meines
lebens. 2d. verm. aufl.
Dessau, 1808. 264 p. MH,
PP.
Fischer, Josef. En Nakskov
slaego; påa foranledning af
grosserer Nathan Philip, ved
Josef Fischer. København,
1949. 63 p. Descendants of
Philip Jacob Ephraim,
1758-1818. Includes Ephraim
family of Denmark and
Germany. MnU.
"Ephraim," in Ferdinand Meyer's
Berühmte Männer Berlins und
ihre Wohnstätten, 2:109-131.
Michaelis, Dolf. "The Ephraim
Family," Leo Baeck Institute
Yearbook 21 (1976):201-228;
24 (1979):225-46. Discusses
family of Heine Ephraim,
1665-1748, through 1970s.
Family of Prussia.
Papritz, Rachel, Hugo, and
Johannes; and Paul Wallich.
Berliner Grosskaufleute und
Kapitalisten. Berlin:
Verlaguon Gsellius,
1934-1935. 3 vols. Includes
chapter on Ephraim family.

Also, family tree in book's appendix. CU, DLC, ICJ, NNC, OCH.

Rachel and Wallich. Berliner Grosskaufleute, 2:288-353. "Die Ephraim." Genealogical table (No. 7), 1665-1884, appears at the end of this volume. See GENERAL WORKS.

Rosenstein. Unbroken Chain, pp. 81ff. See GENERAL WORKS.

Schnee. Hoffinanz und Staat, 1:145-69. "Die Familie Ephraim." Includes genealogical information, 17th to 19th century. Family of Brandenburg-Prussia. See GENERAL WORKS.

————, vol. 3. "Stammtafel der Hoffaktorenfamilie Ephraim." Descendants of Marcus Heine Ephraim, 1692-1768, and Heine Ephraim, 1665-1748, through late 19th century. See GENERAL WORKS.

Stern, Moritz. "Die Ephraims in der Berliner Liste der im Jahre 1812 angenommener Familiennamen," JFF, no. 1 (1924):6-10, 31-32; no. 4 (1925):82-86.

EPHRUSSI
LBI has family tree beginning 1792.
PD has family records.

EPPINGER
Kempelen. Magyarországi Zsidó, 3:75. See GENERAL WORKS.

EPPSTEIN
"Genealogical data of the Eppstein, Kander, and Ulman Families." June 1974. AJA.

EPSTEIN
EJ, 5:195-99. See GENERAL WORKS.
LBI has family tree beginning 1771.
PD has family records.
Epstein, Baruch. Makor Baruch. 1954. AJHS.
Epstein, Louis H. Family; Records of Births, Marriages,

and Deaths, 1840-1872; In German and Yiddish; MS. AJA.

Ettlinger, Shlomo. "Altfrankfurter jüdische Familiennamen II," Jüdisches/Israelistisches Gemeindeblatt (Frankfurt am Main) 3, no. 12 (1957):9.

Kempelen. Magyarországi Zsidó, 3:55. See GENERAL WORKS.

Mirwis, L. Geschichte der Familie Epstein. N.p., 1927. 80 p. Family table of family from Eichstetten, Germany, mid-1700s-1920s. Includes dates of birth, marriage, and deaths, pp. 23-80. Also descendants of Rabbi Eljakim Picard in Randegg (His wife, Marie Epstein, was born in 1838 in Eichstetten.) and descendants of Herri Kahn (1848-1922) in Freiburg. CAJ, Call No. 5434.

Reychman. Szkice genealogiczne, pp. 49-55. See GENERAL WORKS.

Worms, Daniel August. Stammtafeln der Familien Epstein aus Hofgeismar und Isenberg aus Gilserberg. Frankfurt am Main, 1922. See Meir Yizraeli entry under BIDERMAN.

ERDODY
See SZECHENYI-ERDODY.
Kempelen. Magyarországi Zsidó, 2:98. Erdődy family. See GENERAL WORKS.

ERDOS
Kempelen. Magyarországi Zsidó, 3:65. Erdős family. See GENERAL WORKS.

ERFURT
Berlinson, Moses Eliezer. Shelume Emune Yisrael. Odessa, 1898-1901. 3 vols. Includes Erfurt family of Poland and Russia. DLC.

ERGAOS
AMH has family records.

ERGAS
CFM has family records.

ERHARD
CAJ has family records.

ERKELES
PD has family records.

ERLACH
Tänzer. Juden in Tirol,
p. 712. See GENERAL WORKS.

ERLANGER
LBI has family tree beginning
1780.
PD has family records.
Gothaisches Genealogisches
Taschenbuch der
Freiherrlichen Häuser
(Leipzig) 47 (1897):217-19.
Includes Erlanger family.
Tänzer. Juden in Jebenhausen,
p. 309. See GENERAL WORKS.
Zapf. Tübinger Juden, pp.
128-32, 195-98. See GENERAL
WORKS.

ERLICH
CFM has family records.
Erlich Family. Papers, 1980.
1 folder. Photocopies of
family tree; ancestor chart;
correspondence; legal
documents; history and other
genealogical data dating back
to about 1840. PJAC.

ERNST
Alexander Family. Genealogies
of the Alexander and Ernst
Families, 1824-1956; MS.
AJA.
Kempelen. Magyarországi Zsidó,
2:136. See GENERAL WORKS.

ERNUST
Kempelen. Magyarországi Zsidó,
3:128. See GENERAL WORKS.

EROSS
Kempelen. Magyarországi Zsidó,
1:79; 2:13. Erőss family.
See GENERAL WORKS.

ERVIN
Kempelen. Magyarországi Zsidó,
3:99. See GENERAL WORKS.

ESCARTINO
CFM has family records.

ESCHEL
Schmidt-Ewald, W. "Vom
rabbiner zum thür.
Landpfarrer. Rabbi Josua ben
Abraham Eschel gennant
Augusti u. seine
Nachkommenschaft,"
Thüringische Sippe 2
(1936):57-64.

ESHER
AMH has family records.

ESKELES
LBI has family tree beginning
1718.
Grunwald, M. "Familienurkunden
und Stammtafelfragmente zur
Geschichte der Familie
Arnstein-Eskeles-Daniel
Itzig," JFF, no. 1.
Jäger-Sunstenau, Hanns. "Der
genealogische Hintergrund des
Bankhauses Arnstein & Eskeles
in Wien," Veröffentlichungen
des Verbandes österr.
Geschichtsvereine. (Wien) 22
(1979):300-304.
JFF, no. 11. Family history.
Rosenstein. Unbroken Chain,
pp. 410ff. Related to Babad
family. See GENERAL WORKS.
Schulte. Bonner Juden, p. 226.
See GENERAL WORKS.

ESKELL
AMH has family records.

ESPER
AMH has family records.

ESSEN
Semi-Gotha, 1:107. See GENERAL
WORKS.

ESTLANDER
Semi-Gotha, 1:82. See GENERAL
WORKS.

ESZTERHAZY
Kempelen. Magyarországi Zsidó,
3:126. Eszterházy family.
See GENERAL WORKS.

ETLINGER
AMH has family records.

ETTING
AMH has family records.
Vital Records of the Cohen,
Etting, and Related Families
of Baltimore. MS. AJA.
"Cohen-Etting Cemetery
Inscriptions." Typescript,
n.d. Maryland Historical
Society, Baltimore, Maryland.
Cohen Family Papers, 1802-1945.
Includes genealogical data on
Cohen, Gratz, Etting, and
Nathan families of Maryland.
Maryland Historical Society
Library.
Silverman, Albert J. "They Ate
Kosher at Fort Mc Henry,"
Generations (Jewish
Historical Society of
Maryland) 1, no. 2
(1979):2-9. On the
well-known Cohen and Etting
families of Maryland.
Solis, Elvira Nathan, d. 1963.
"Correspondence and research
notes for genealogical
studies of the Etting,
Menken, Nathan, and Nones
Families." AJHS.
Stern. FAJF. Etting family
tree beginning in Frankfort
am Main. See GENERAL WORKS.

ETTINGER
AMH has family records.
CAJD has family tree from
Germany.
Margolioth, Ephraim Zalman.
Ma'aloth ha-Yuḥasin. Edited
by Abraham Segal Ettinger.
Lemberg: A.B. Krochman, 1900.
83 p. Includes Ettinger
family. DLC, MH.
Rosenstein. Unbroken Chain,
pp. 456ff. See GENERAL
WORKS.

ETTINGHAUSEN
CFM has family records.
Ettinghausen, Maurice L. Rare
Books And Royal Collectors:
Memoirs of An Antiquarian
Bookseller. New York: Simon
and Schuster, 1966. 220 p.
Especially, pp. 12-18.
Author (1883-   ) was born
in Paris, but the family
moved to England when he was
five. He was a descendant of
Judah Oppenheim, who left
from Heidelberg in 1531 to
move to Frankfurt-am-Main.
Later, the family changed its
name to Oppenheimer. Other
members of the family went to
Paris in 19th century. They
were dealers in precious
stones.

ETTLINGER
CAJ has two family trees,
1599-1930 and 1692-1933.
Compiled by Dr. Shlomoh Fritz
Ettlinger. Family of
Frankfurt-am-Main.
LBI has family tree beginning
1733.
[Freimann, Aron]. Aus des
Stammbaum der Familien
Ettlinger, Freimann und
Horovitz. Berlin: Marx &
Co., 1925. 3 genealogical
tables. OCH.
Frintrop, H.W.F. Stammboom
Wormser-Ettlinger. 1954.
4 p. The two families came
to the Netherlands from
Worms. Family tree starts
with Samuel Dudenhofen
(d. 1590) from Dudenhofen.
Gemeente Archief Amsterdam,
Amstelkade, Amsterdam,
Private Archive
No. 578, 8 G6.

EUCKEN
CAJ has family records.

EVANS
AMH has family records.

EWIGTREU
Crasemann, Franz Josef. "Ein

Beitrag zur jüdischen
Namengebung," Zeitschrift für
Niedersächsische
Familienkunde 15 (1933):101.
Georg Ewigtreu.

EYBESCHITZ, EYBESCHUTZ
Brilling, Bernhard.
"Eibenschütziana II: Die
Nachkommen des R. Jonathan
Eibenschütz," Hebrew Union
College Annual 35
(1964):255-73. 18th to early
19th century. Also spelled
Jonathan Eybeschütz or
Eybeschitz. German rabbi and
talmudist, b. Cracow,
ca. 1690; d. Altona,
18 Sept. 1764. Family
members from Hamburg, Altona,
and Dresden.
Kempelen. Magyarországi Zsidó,
3:65. Eibenschütz family.
See GENERAL WORKS.
Rabi, Simon. Sefer Toledot
B'nei Yehonatan. St.
Petersburgh, 1899. 32 p.
Genealogy of Rabbi Jonathan
Eybeschitz (also spelled
Eybeschütz), 1690/95-1764,
was a talmudist and
kabbalist. From 1715-1741 he
lived in Prague, and from
1741 to his death he served
in Metz, Altona, Hamburg, and
Wandsbek. JNUL, MH.
Bondi Family; Genealogy; MS.
The Genealogy of the Bondi,
Eybeschütz, and Wise
Families, compiled by Isaac
M. Wise, grandson of Rabbi
Isaac Mayer Wise. AJA.

EZEKIEL
AMH has family records.
Ezekiel Family; Richmond, Va.,
Washington, D.C., and
Cincinnati, Ohio. Entries of
Births, Marriages, and Deaths
of the Family Taken from the
Family Bible, 1812-1919. MS.
AJA.
Ezekiel Family; Notes in the
Family Bible, 1835-1899.
AJA.
Family Tree of Ezekiel-Levy

Families, Richmond, Virginia.
AJA.
CFM has family records.
Ezekiel, Moses Jacob, Sir
(1844-1917). Papers,
1864-1974. Include
genealogies of Ezekiel
family. Moses Ezekiel was an
American sculptor from
Virginia. He received
knighthoods from both the
Italian king and the German
emperor. AJA.
Stern. FAJF. Ezekiel family
tree beginning in Holland.
See GENERAL WORKS.

EZRA
AMH has family records.
CFM has family records.

FABIAN
LBI has family tree beginning
1773.

FABISCH
LBI has family tree beginning
1781.

FABRI
Kempelen. Magyarországi Zsidó,
2:81, 91, 102. Fábri family.
See GENERAL WORKS.

FABRICZKY
Kempelen. Magyarországi Zsidó,
3:44. See GENERAL WORKS.

FABRIKANT
CAJ has family records.

FACKENHEIM
LBI has family tree beginning
1735.

FADGYAS
Kempelen. Magyarországi Zsidó,
3:107. See GENERAL WORKS.

FAGAR
AMH has family records.

FAHRMAYER
Kempelen. Magyarországi Zsidó,
1:84. See GENERAL WORKS.

FAI, FAY
Kempelen. Magyarországi Zsidó,
1:79, 131; 3:139. Fái, Fáy
family. See GENERAL WORKS.

FAJANSO
Reychman. Szkice genealogiczne
pp. 61-67. See GENERAL
WORKS.

FALCK
CFM has family records.

FALCO
Sobrequeś Vidal, Santiago.
"Contribución a la historia
de los judíos de Gerona.
Familias hebreas gerundenses:
Los Falcó," Anales del
Instituto de Estudios
Gerundenses 3 (1948):113-26.

FALES
See Walter Fales entry under
FEILCHENFELD.

FALK
AMH has family records.
CAJ has family tree beginning
1530 in Germany.
CFM has family records.
Falk, Laurence L. Genealogy of
the Falk Family of Georgia.
Tampa, Florida. MS. Family
tree beginning 18th century.
AJA.
Friedländer, Josua. "Der Name
Falk bei den Juden in
Märkisch, Friedland," JFF,
no. 8 (1926):184-88.
Kempelen. Magyarországi Zsidó,
1:87, 96, 149. See GENERAL
WORKS.

FALKE
AMH has family records.

FALKENAU
LBI has family tree beginning
1782.

FALKENBERG
Semi-Gotha, 1:17, 72, 155. See
GENERAL WORKS.

FALKENSTEIN
Porta, Siegfried. Chronik der
Familie Löwenstein-Porta
sowie der Synogogengemeinde
Neuenkirchen im zusammenhang
mit der Geschichte der
Grafschaft Rietberg und des
israelitischen Konsistoriums
zu Cassel. Nach amtlichen
Quellen bearb. Bielefeld,
1903. 103 p. Family trees.
Includes Basch, Falkenstein,
Goldsmith, Levi, Löwenstein,
Porta, Rosenberg, Schönberg,
and Steinheim families. LBI,
NNJ.

FALKMANN
CAJ has family tree beginning
1768.

FALKSON
LBI has family tree beginning
1773.

FANO
AMH has family records.
CAJ has family tree beginning
in 19th-century Italy.
CFM has family records.
Kaufmann, David. "Menahem
Azarya de Fano et sa
famille," Revue des Études
Juives 25 (1897):84-90.

FANTY
AMH has family records.
LBI has family tree beginning
1646.

FARESOL
Gaster, Moses. "Faresol, nicht
Feritsol," MGWJ 80
(1936):489-90.

FARFEL
Cohen, Morris Raphael.
Dreamer's Journey:
Autobiography. Boston: The
Beacon Press, 1949. 318 p.
Following a description of
childhood in Kletsk and

Neshwies in Minsk gubernia
and adolescence in New York's
east side, the book primarily
describes the author's
development as a philosopher
and teacher at New York City
College and Harvard. Note
especially, "My Parents,"
pp. 6-14; "Neshwies
(1887-1890)--The Old Piety,"
pp. 25-40; and "Neshwies
Revisited and the Journey to
America," pp. 56-62. The
author (1880-1947) came to
U.S. in 1892. His parents
were Abraham Mordechai Cohen
(1847-1937) and Bessie Farfel
Cohen (1848-1936). DLC, ICU,
MB, OU, PU, TxU, ViU.

FARJEON
AMH has family records.
CFM has family records.

FARKAS
Kempelen. Magyarországi Zsidó,
1:134; 2:73, 89; 3:79, 99.
See GENERAL WORKS.

FARKASCH
CAJ has family tree from
Hungary.

FARKASHAZY
Kempelen. Magyarországi Zsidó,
1:132, 133. Farkasházy
family. See GENERAL WORKS.

FARO
AJA has genealogical files.
AMH has family records.

FASS
CFM has family records.
Deutsch, Helene [Hala].
Confrontations with Myself:
An Epilogue. New York:
Norton, 1973. 217 p.
Especially, pp. 19-92. The
author (1884-   ), the noted
psychoanalyst and
psychiatrist, was born in
Przemyśl, Galicia, the
daughter of Wilhelm
Rosenbach, a lawyer and
Jewish community leader, and

Regina Fass Rosenbach. She
settled in U.S. in 1935.

FAUDEL
CFM has family records.

FAUDELL
AMH has family records.

FAUNA
AMH has family records.

FAY
See FAI, FAY.

FEATHERSTONEHAUGH
AMH has family records.

FEBOS
CFM has family records.

FECHENBACH
Fechenbach, Hermann. Die
letzten Mergentheimer Juden
und die Geschichte der
Familie Fechenbach. Mit
Holzschnitt-illustrationen
von Hermann Fechenbach.
Stuttgart: W. Kohlhammer,
1972. 216 p. Includes
genealogical tables. DLC,
MH, MWalB, NjP, NNJ, OCH, WU.

FECHHEIMER
AJA has family trees beginning
1680 and 1797.
Fechheimer, Richard. Genealogy
of the Fechheimer Family.
Highland Park, Illinois.
n.d. AJA.

FECHNER
PD has family records.

FECHTIG
Kempelen. Magyarországi Zsidó,
3:95. See GENERAL WORKS.

FEDAK
Kempelen. Magyarországi Zsidó,
2:70. Fedák family. See
GENERAL WORKS.

FEIBELMAN
Feibelman, Julian B. The
Making of a Rabbi. New York:

Vantage Press, 1980. 508 p.
Especially pages 11-34.
Autobiography of this Reform
Rabbi (1897-1981), who was
born in Jackson, Mississippi,
and who served as Rabbi of
New Orleans' Temple Sinai
from 1936 to 1967. His
grandfather, Judas Feibelmann
(1837-1906) came to Jackson
in 1867 or 1868 from the
Rheinfalz village of
Ingenheim, near Rülzheim.
Rabbi Feibelman's father was
Abraham Feibelman, a Jackson
merchant, and his mother was
Eva Beck Feibelman.

FEIBELMANN
AJA has family tree beginning
1732.
"The Feibelmanns from
Rülzheim." Family chart
which lists more than 880
descendants of Jakob
Feibelmann (1732-1796). CAJ,
Call No. 4318.
Kopp. Jüdischen Alsenz,
pp. 127-29.
Hayum-Feibelmann-Haym-
Haymann-Heymann family of
Alsenz. See GENERAL WORKS.

FEIBES
Feibes, J., Hrsg. Stammbaum
der Familien Itzig (aus
Burgstein) und Feibes
(Lengerich). Münster, 1887.
46 p. Family tree begins
1720. LBI.

FEIGELSTOCK
Kempelen. Magyarországi Zsidó,
3:44. See GENERAL WORKS.

FEIGENBAUM
CAJ has family records.
LBI has family tree beginning
1746.

FEIGL
Kempelen. Magyarországi Zsidó,
1:62; 2:24, 25. See GENERAL
WORKS.

FEILCHENFELD
Feilchenfeld Family Records,
1745-1950. AJA.
Fales, Walter. The Descendants
of Wolf Fales: A Chronicle of
the Feilchenfeld Family. New
York, 1947. LBI.

FEILER
Batkin, Stanley I., ed. The
Tenzer Family Tree Including
the Feiler and Zahl Families.
New Rochelle, N.Y.: S.I.
Batkin Co., 1977. 1
portfolio, 54 leaves. Family
originated in Southern
Galicia. Covers 1690-1978.
AJA, DLC, MH, NN.

FEIN
Efrati, Mosheh Zevi; ed.
Bimsilat Rishonim: Toledot
Mishpachat Fein. Tel Aviv,
1969? 136 p. Includes
pictures and portraits.

FEINBERG
Feinberg, Abraham L. Storm the
Gates of Jericho. Toronto:
McClelland & Stewart, 1964.
344 p. The author sketches
his family background in the
shtetl of Grinki-Shok. CtY,
DLC, MH, NN, OCH.

FEIS, FEISENBERGER, FEIST
AMH has Feist family records.
CFM has Feist family records.
LBI has Feisenberger family
tree beginning 1495.
Kopp. Jüdischen Alsenz,
pp. 121-22. Genealogical
information on Feis, Feist,
and Feisenberger family of
Alsenz. See GENERAL WORKS.
Liebeschütz, Rahel.
Feist-Belmont-History,
1775-1837. Leeds, England:
By the Author, 1971.
Genealogical tables.
————. Feist-Belmont-History.
Part II: 1842-1859. Leeds,
England: By the Author, 1973.
54, 37 p.
Schulte. Bonner Juden, p. 230.

Feist family. See GENERAL
WORKS.

FEITS
LBIS has family tree.

FEIVALAVITZ
Schragai, Shlomo Zalmen and
Miriam Shragai. Min Hayamim
Hahame Ad Hazmin Hazeh.
Jerusalem, 1978. 52 p.
Traces authors' descendants
and forbears. JNUL.

FEJER
Kempelen. Magyarországi Zsidó,
2:79, 88; 3:118. Fejér
family. See GENERAL WORKS.

FEJERVARY
Kempelen. Magyarországi Zsidó,
1:54-56; 2:53. Fejérváry
family. See GENERAL WORKS.

FEKETE
Kempelen. Magyarországi Zsidó,
3:69. See GENERAL WORKS.

FELBEL
AJA has genealogical files.
Stern. FAJF. Felbel family
tree beginning in Germany.
See GENERAL WORKS.

FELDHEIM
Kempelen. Magyarországi Zsidó,
1:112; 3:47, 48. See GENERAL
WORKS.

FELDMAN
"Feldman Family History
Traced," The Historical
Scribe of the Jewish
Historical Society of Oregon,
Fall 1980, pp. 6, 8. Family
of Philip Feldman,
b. Altenmuhr, Bavaria, 1864;
d. 1939; raised in Fürth,
arrived in Portland, Oregon,
June 1880. Eventually became
owner of the Mt. Hood Soap
Co. (now Mt. Hood Chemical
Co.) in 1905.

FELDMANN
Kempelen. Magyarországi Zsidó,

2:90; 3:107, 124. See
GENERAL WORKS.

FELEDY
Kempelen. Magyarországi Zsidó,
2:103. See GENERAL WORKS.

FELEKI
Kempelen. Magyarországi Zsidó,
3:34, 82. See GENERAL WORKS.

FELLHEIMER
Tänzer. Juden in Jebenhausen,
pp. 310-11. See GENERAL
WORKS.

FELLNER
PD has family records.
Kempelen. Magyarországi Zsidó,
2:125; 3:97. See GENERAL
WORKS.

FELMAN
Felman, Abraham. Pioneers of
Hebrew Citrus Culture in
Erets-Israel. Tel-Aviv,
1940.

FELS
See Esmond De Beer entry under
BARDEN.
Phalen, Dale. Samuel Fels of
Philadelphia. Philadelphia:
Samuel S. Fels Fund, 1969.
100 p. "Youth and Family,"
pp. 1-6, and "The Fels
Family," p. 99. Samuel Fels
(1860-1950), philanthropist,
financier, and manufacturer
("Fels Naptha" soap), was
born in Yanceyville, N.C.,
the son of Lazarus and
Susanna Fels of
Kaiserlautern, Bavaria. CLU,
DLC, ICU, MH, NcD, NjP, WHi.
Wolf Family. Papers,
ca. 1970-1977. 1 folder.
"Biographical material, 1976,
of Howard A. Wolf (1900-)
and genealogical information
about his ancestors and those
of his wife, Martha Rosenthal
Wolf, including members of
Wolf, Rosenthal, Loeb, Fels,
and Price families, dating
back to 18th century." PJAC.

FELSENBERG
Munkácsi, Bernát. A Nyitrai,
Nagyváradi Es Budapesti
Munk-Család Valamint A
Nyitrai, Nagytapolcsányi,
Balassagyarmati,
Nagykanizsai, Szentesi Es
Budapesti Felsenberg-Család
Genealógiája: Osök Es
Ivadékok. Budapest:
F. Gerwürcz, 1939. 230 p.
Families of Hungary. JNUL,
MH.

FELSENBURG
Kempelen. Magyarországi Zsidó,
2:74; 3:95. See GENERAL
WORKS.

FELSENSTEIN
CAJ has family tree beginning
in 18th-century Prague.

FELSENTHAL
AJA has family tree,
descendants of Benjamin Wolf
and Agatha Hart Felsenthal.
Felsenthal Family. Family tree
of Descendants of Benjamin
Wolf Felsenthal and Agatha
Hart Felsenthal; birth
certificate of Helen Leah
Alpiner, Chicago, Ill.; "Aunt
Mimi's Story," written by
Amelia Darling Alpiner, An
Autobiography Written, June,
1967; Newspaper articles
Concerning Members of the
Alpiner Family, a Branch of
the Felsenthal family. AJA,
Box No. 955.

FELSOVANYI
Kempelen. Magyarországi Zsidó,
2:97. Felsőványi family.
See GENERAL WORKS.

FENTLAM
AMH has family records.

FENYES
Kempelen. Magyarországi Zsidó,
1:146; 2:128. Fényes family.
See GENERAL WORKS.

FENYO
Kempelen. Magyarországi Zsidó,
3:58. Fenyő family. See
GENERAL WORKS.

FENYVES
Kempelen. Magyarországi Zsidó,
2:144; 3:107. See GENERAL
WORKS.

FENYVESSY
Kempelen. Magyarországi Zsidó,
1:150; 2:22. See GENERAL
WORKS.

FERENCZY
Kempelen. Magyarországi Zsidó,
3:65. See GENERAL WORKS.

FERGUSSON
See COLYER-FERGUSSON.

FERNANDES
CFM has family records.
Samuel, E.R. "Portuguese Jews
in Jacobean England,"
Transactions of the Jewish
Historical Society of England
18 (1958):181. Includes
pedigree chart of
Anglo-Jewish family of
Fernandes, originally from
Antwerp.

FERNANDEZ
AMH has family records.
CAJ has family tree.

FERREIRA
CFM has family records.

FERRI
Kempelen. Magyarországi Zsidó,
1:43. See GENERAL WORKS.

FESTETICS
Kempelen. Magyarországi Zsidó,
2:76. See GENERAL WORKS.

FEUCHTWANGER
AMH has family records.
Brilling, Bernhard. "Die
Geschichte der Familie
Feuchtwanger,"
Mitteilungsblatt,
Wochenzeitung des Irgun Olej

Markas Europa (Tel Aviv),
16 Oct. 1953.
See Sally David Cramer entry
under CRAMER.
[Feuchtwanger, Felix].
Stammbaum der Familie
Feuchtwanger, 1786-1910.
München, 1911. 18 p. LBI,
OCH, PP.
Feuchtwanger, Martin. The
Feuchtwanger Family. The
Descendants of Seligmann
Feuchtwanger. Tel-Aviv:
Olympia, 1952. 151 p.
Genealogical charts.
Seligmann Feuchtwanger
(1786-1852) was born in Fürth
and later moved to Munich.
NN.
Grunwald, Kurt. "The
Feuchtwangers. A Family of
Bankers," AJR Information 23,
no. 6 (June 1968).
Hartig, Angelika. "Die
Familiendynastie
Feuchtwanger," pp. 269-72, in
Hans Lamm's Vergangene Tage:
Jüdische Kultur in München
(München: Langen Müller,
1982). Covers 16th to 20th
century.
Kahn, Lothar. Insight and
Action: The Life and Work of
Lion Feuchtwanger.
Rutherford, N.J.: Fairleigh
Dickinson University Press,
1975. 392 p. Genealogical
information, pp. 24-36.
Feuchtwanger (1884-1958), the
famous German novelist, was
born in Munich, the son of
Sigmund (1854-?) and Johanna
Feuchtwanger and the grandson
of Elkan Feuchtwanger
(1823-1902). The family
originally came from Fürth.
Lamm, Hans. "Die
Feuchtwangers. Geschichte
einer münchner Familie,"
Münchner Stadtanzeiger, no. 6
(12 Febr. 1965).
Waldo, Hilda. "Lion
Feuchtwanger: A Biography,"
in John M. Spalek's Lion
Feuchtwanger: The Man, His
Ideas, His Work: A Collection

of Critical Essays (Los
Angeles: Hennessey & Ingalls,
1972). A letter to Walter
Berendsohn, June 16, 1957,
written by Lion Feuchtwanger,
providing the results of his
own family studies, is quoted
on page 2. DLC, ICU, MH,
NIC, NjR, NNC, OU.

FEUER
Kempelen. Magyarországi Zsidó,
2:78. See GENERAL WORKS.

FEYLE
AMH has family records.

FIDANQUE
CAJ has family tree, 1700-1962.
Fidanque Family Tree; Notes in
the Family Bible;
Philadelphia, Pa. Begins
17th century. AJA.
Salomon, Herman P. "The
Fidanques, hidalgos of
Faith," American Sephardi 4,
no. 1/2 (Autumn 1970):14-36.
Saragossa.

FIELD
Straunch, Ralph. The
Altschuler Family Tree: The
Descendants of Moses and
Sarah Altschuler; A
Genealogical Survey. New
York: Ludwig-Field-Altschuler
Family Circle, 1975. NN,
YIVO.

FIENBURG
AMH has family records.

FIEST
AMH has family records.

FIGADOR
PD has family records.

FINALI
Kempelen. Magyarországi Zsidó,
1:71-78; 2:35. Fináli
family. See GENERAL WORKS.

FINBERG
AMH has family records.

FINCI
Mander, Anica Vesel with Sarika
Finci Hofbauer. Blood Ties:
A Woman's History. Berkeley
and New York: Moon Books and
Random House, Inc., 1976.
297 p. Feminist
autobiography focusing on the
author's birth (1934-   )
and early childhood in
Sarajevo, Yugoslavia; the
family's escape to Italy in
1943; and their emigration to
California in late 1940s.
Interspersed are chapters on
reminiscences of Sarika Finci
Hofbauer, the author's
grandmother, about World Wars
I and II. CtY, DLC, ICarbS,
MB, MH, NN, NNC, OCl, OU,
TxU.

FINKELSTEIN
Rosenstein. Unbroken Chain,
pp. 252ff. Finkelstein
descendants of R. Naftali
Katz. See GENERAL WORKS.

FINZI
AMH has family records.
CFM has family records.
EJ (1928), 6:1010ff. See
GENERAL WORKS.

FIORINO
Fiorino, Alexander. Der
Miniaturmaler Jeremias David
Alexander Fiorino, 1797-1847
und seine Familie. Cassell:
Gedruckt von der
Aktiengesellschaft für Druck
und Verlag, 1926. Family
from Cassel, Germany. LBI,
MH.

FIRMAN
JFF, no. 20. Family history.

FIRMIAN
Kempelen. Magyarországi Zsidó,
3:51. See GENERAL WORKS.

FIROZ
"Die Karäische Familie Firoz,"
MGWJ, (1913), p. 44.

FIRUZ
Poznánski, Samuel. "Die
karäische Familie Firuz,"
MGWJ 57 (1913):44-58.
————. "Zweiter Nachtrag zur
karäische Familie Firuz,"
MGWJ 60 (1916):149-52.

FISCH
Kempelen. Magyarországi Zsidó,
1:106, 108; 2:95; 3:48, 124.
See GENERAL WORKS.

FISCHBEIN
CAJD has family tree from
Germany.
Kempelen. Magyarországi Zsidó,
1:139. See GENERAL WORKS.

FISCHEL, FISZEL
AMH has Fischel family records.
CFM has family records.
PD has family records.
Bałaban. Żydów w Krakowie,
1:40, 400. Genealogical
table of the descendants of
Efraim Fiszel, 15th to 16th
century. See GENERAL WORKS.

FISCHER
Gold. Juden Mährens,
pp. 547-48. Family of Albert
Fischer (b. Triesch, 1836;
d. Vienna, 1914). See
GENERAL WORKS.
Kempelen. Magyarországi Zsidó,
1:122, 131, 132; 2:78, 87,
88, 134, 136; 3:50, 51, 77,
96, 124. See GENERAL WORKS.
Rose. Schöninger Juden. See
GENERAL WORKS.

FISCHHOFF
CAJ has Fischhoff-Kalisch
family tree. Family from
Galanta in Rumania.

FISCHL
Kempelen. Magyarországi Zsidó,
1:87. See GENERAL WORKS.

FISCHLER
Kempelen. Magyarországi Zsidó,
3:25. See GENERAL WORKS.

FISCHMANN
Kempelen. Magyarországi Zsidó,
1:146. See GENERAL WORKS.
Vadász, Ede. Adalékok A
Wahrmann-, gorlicei Weiss-,
Szófer-(Schreiber)-Es
Fischmann-Családok.
Budapest: Atheneum, 1907.
32 p. JNUL.

FISCHOF
Kempelen. Magyarországi Zsidó,
1:128. See GENERAL WORKS.

FISHEL
Fishel, Morris, fl. 1865.
Papers, 1846-1928.
1 microfilm reel.
"Nashville, Tennessee,
businessman.... Also
included is information on
the Fishel family of Germany,
Ohio, and Tennessee." AJA;
Tennessee State Library and
Archives, no. 432.

FISHELSON
See Yaffa Draznin entry under
BERNSTEIN. Family history.

FISHER
AJA has genealogical files.
AMH has family records.
Fisher Family. "Genealogical
Chart of the Fisher-Plaut
Family." N.p., n.d.
Applebaum, Philip. The
Fishers: A Family Portrait.
Detroit: Harlo Press, 1982.
xi + 153 p illus. Family of
Detroit. "A major portion of
the work is devoted to the
prominent Jewish communal
leader, Max M. Fisher."
Fisher (1908-   ) was born
in Pittsburgh, grew up in
Salem, Ohio, and started his
business career in Detroit.
He is the son of William and
Mollie Fisher.
Lybarger, Donald Fisher. The
Story of the
Dowler-Hartshorne,
Fisher-Lybarger Families.
Cleveland, 1938, 1962, 2d ed.
DLC, OCl.

Fisher-Hecht Family Papers,
Cincinnati, Ohio and
Wheeling, W. Va., 1845-1852.
Include genealogical material
on Fisher, Hecht, and
Rindskopf families. AJA.

FISKE
AMH has family records.

FITCH
AMH has family records.

FITZGERALD
AMH has family records.
Kempelen. Magyarországi Zsidó,
1:51. See GENERAL WORKS.

FITZHERBERT
AMH has family records.

FITZMAURICE
AMH has family records.

FLANDERS
AMH has family records.

FLASCHNER
Kempelen. Magyarországi Zsidó,
2:10. See GENERAL WORKS.

FLATAW
Reychman. Szkice
genealogiczne, pp. 69-71.
See GENERAL WORKS.

FLATTERLEY
AMH has family records.

FLECK
Schulte. Bonner Juden, p. 233.
See GENERAL WORKS.

FLECKELES
Kaufmann, David. "Der
Stammbaum des R. Eleasar
Fleckeles, seine Ahnenprobe
Moritz Hartmanns," MGWJ 37
(1893):378-92.

FLECKER
AMH has family records.

FLEETWOOD
Semi-Gotha, 1:20. See GENERAL
WORKS.

FLEGMANN
Kempelen. Magyarországi Zsidó,
2:45. See GENERAL WORKS.

FLEISCHER
LBI has family tree beginning
1864.
Kempelen. Magyarországi Zsidó,
2:120, 130. See GENERAL
WORKS.
Schindler, Walter. [Uberlebt
in Berlin 1941-1945.]
Berlin-Charlottenburg 1945.
11 + 13 p. Includes
Fleischer family (Schlesien)
tree from 1780. LBI.
Tänzer. Juden in Jebenhausen,
pp. 312-17. See GENERAL
WORKS.

FLEISCHHACKER
Ballin. Juden in Seesen,
p. 177. See GENERAL WORKS.

FLEISCHMANN
Kempelen. Magyarországi Zsidó,
2:45; 3:32, 58. See GENERAL
WORKS.

FLEISHER
Stern. FAJF. Fleisher family
tree beginning in U.S. See
GENERAL WORKS.

FLEISSIG
Kempelen. Magyarországi Zsidó,
1:47. See GENERAL WORKS.

FLEMING
AMH has family records.

FLERSHEIM
AMH has family records.

FLES
AMH has family records.

FLESCH
Flesch, Heinrich. Die Familie
Flesch. Hrsg. aus Anlass des
100. Geburtstages des Herrn
Adolf Flesch in dankbarer
Erinnerung von seinem Sohne
Adolf Flesch in Brünn.
Brünn: Verlag des Verfassers,
1914. 68 p. 2 genealogical

tables. Family of Frankfurt
am Main, Vienna and
Neu.-Rauchnitz. DLC, LBI,
MH, OCH.
Kempelen. Magyarországi Zsidó,
1:142; 3:21, 25, 87. See
GENERAL WORKS.

FLIESS
LBI has family tree.
Cohn, Warren I. "The Moses
Isaac Family Trust," Leo
Baeck Institute Yearbook 18
(1973):267-79. From 17th
century, the Fliess and
Sussmann families. The Moses
Isaac Fideikommiss, Berlin,
ca. 1680. Includes
genealogical table of persons
directly involved with the
trust.
Semi-Gotha, 2:47ff. See
GENERAL WORKS.

FLINN
AMH has family records.

FLITTER
JNUL has a 5-page genealogy of
the descendants of Beryl
(Dov) Flitter, who died at
the age of about 98 shortly
after 1910. Compiled in 1978
by Melvin Flitter of
Philadelphia. The family
came from Mizocz, between
Dubno and Rovno. Some
members later lived in
Zbolbunov. Manuscript and
Archive Dept., Call
No. V.2239.

FLOERSHEIM
CFM has family records.

FLORANCE
AJA has genealogical files.
Meyer, Annie Nathan. "Papa,
Mama, and Grandfather
Florance; From a Family Album
of the 1870s," Commentary 11
(Mar. 1951):273-79. Memoirs
of Mrs. Meyer's childhood;
includes large amount of
family history. Family
originally came from Portugal

to Charleston, S.C. early in
the 18th century, and later
went to New Orleans. Related
to Seixas family.
Stern. FAJF. Florance family
tree beginning in London
("perhaps"). Name was
changed from Levy to
Florance. See GENERAL WORKS.

FLORSHEIM
CAJ has family records.
CAJD has family tree from
Germany.
Ullmann, Elias. Die Familie
Worms. Frankfurt am Main,
1886. Includes genealogical
table of the descendants of
Hirsch Amshel Mendler
Ottingen (1644-1720) and
Ester Flörsheim (1654-1728).

FLOTRON
Kempelen. Magyarországi Zsidó,
1:56, 57. See GENERAL WORKS.

FLUSS
Kempelen. Magyarországi Zsidó,
1:95, 106. See GENERAL
WORKS.

FOA
AMH has family records.
CFM has Foà family tree.
EJ (1928), 6:1043-44. See
GENERAL WORKS.

FODOR
Kempelen. Magyarországi Zsidó,
1:32; 2:92. See GENERAL
WORKS.

FOLDES
Kempelen. Magyarországi Zsidó,
3:90. Földes family. See
GENERAL WORKS.

FOLDI
Kempelen. Magyarországi Zsidó,
2:91. Földi family. See
GENERAL WORKS.

FOLDIAK
Kempelen. Magyarországi Zsidó,
2:140. Földiák family. See
GENERAL WORKS.

FOLDVARY
Kempelen. Magyarországi Zsidó,
1:83. Földváry family. See
GENERAL WORKS.

FOLIGNO
AMH has family records.
CFM has family records.

FOLLICK
AMH has family records.

FOLLMAN
Rosenstein. Unbroken Chain,
pp. 104ff. See GENERAL
WORKS.

FONAGY
Kempelen. Magyarországi Zsidó,
1:19. Fónagy family. See
GENERAL WORKS.

FONSECA
AJA has genealogical files.
AMH has family records.
CFM has family records.
See Stern, FAJF entry under
LOPEZ.
Stern. FAJF. Fonseca family
tree beginning in Jamaica.
See GENERAL WORKS.

FONYO
Kempelen. Magyarországi Zsidó,
2:39. Fonyó family. See
GENERAL WORKS.

FORBATH
Kempelen. Magyarországi Zsidó,
3:137. Forbáth family. See
GENERAL WORKS.

FORCHHEIMER
See Sally David Cramer entry
under CRAMER.

FORDE
AMH has family records.

FORDSHAM
See Sally David Cramer entry
under CRAMER.

FOREMAN
AJA has genealogical files.

FORGACH
Kempelen. Magyarországi Zsidó,
2:103, 104. Forgách family.
See GENERAL WORKS.

FORGACS
Kempelen. Magyarországi Zsidó,
2:66; 3:50. Forgács family.
See GENERAL WORKS.

FORMES
Kempelen. Magyarországi Zsidó,
2:18. See GENERAL WORKS.

FORNHEIM
"Die Ahnen," Judaica
(Pressburg) 2, no. 9/10
(1935):21-22. Joachim
Fornheim, 1841-1910.

FORSTER
Kempelen. Magyarországi Zsidó,
1:55; 2:52. See GENERAL
WORKS.

FORSYTH
See Esmond S. De Beer entry
under BARDEN.

FORTI
See SEBOK-FORTI.

FORTUNA
CAJ has family records.

FORTUNATUS
Kempelen. Magyarországi Zsidó,
2:80. See GENERAL WORKS.

FOULD
CAJ has family tree from
Germany.
LBI has family tree beginning
1800.

FOULIS
AMH has family records.

FOX
AJA has genealogical files.
AMH has family records.

FRACKLAND
Frank. Nashville Jewry,
pp. 145-46. Family of Posen,

arriving in U.S. in 1850s.
See GENERAL WORKS.

FRAENCKEL
Maurois, André. Memoirs,
1885-1967. Translated from
the French by Denver Lindley.
New York: Harper & Row, 1970.
439 p. Genealogical
information on Fraenckel and
Herzog (author's real family
name) families of Elbeuf,
Ringendorf, and Bischwiller,
pp. 6-15.

FRAENKEL
Bato, Y.L. "Koppel Fraenkel
and His Descendants. The
Fate of a German-Jewish
Family," AJR Information 19
(July 1964). 17th century
onward.
Fraenkel, Abraham Adolf.
Lebenskreise. Aus den
Erinnerungen eines jüdischen
Mathematikers. Stuttgart:
Deutsche Verlagsanstalt,
1967. 207 p. "Meine
Vorfahren," pp. 13-55.
Genealogical information on
the Auerbach, Fraenckel, and
Neuburger relative of the
author (1891-1965) who was
born in Munich. His
relatives were from Fürth,
Nürnberg, and Munich.
Abraham Fraenkel's father was
Sigmund Fraenkel (1860-1925),
grandfather was Wilhelm
[Wolf] Fraenkel (1830-1907),
and great-grandfather was
Abraham Fraenkel (1792-1858).
CSt, DLC, NIC, NjP.
Fraenkel, Louis and Henry.
Forgotten Frgments of the
History of an Old Jewish
Family. Translated from the
Danish by Malene Woodman.
Vol. 1: Texts and Indexes.
Vol. 2: Ten family trees.
Copenhagen: By the Author,
1975. DLC, OCH.
Reychman. Szkice
genealogiczne, pp. 73-74.
See GENERAL WORKS.

Schulte. Bonner Juden, p. 234.
See GENERAL WORKS.

FRAKNOI
Kempelen. Magyarországi Zsidó,
1:79, 117, 118. Fraknói
family. See GENERAL WORKS.

FRANCHETTI
CFM has family records.

FRANCIA
EJ (1928), 6:1064. See GENERAL
WORKS.

FRANCK
AMH has family records.
CAJ has family records.
Millner, Joseph. "Les grandes
familles juives de France,"
Le Monde Juif 5, no. 28
(1950):3-4.
Schulte. Bonner Juden, p. 236.
See GENERAL WORKS.

FRANCIA
CFM has family records.

FRANCKEL
JFF, no. 1 (1925):77-78.
Fränckel of Breslau;
descendants of Saul Wahl.
Rachel and Wallich. Berliner
Grosskaufleute, 3:112-15.
Fränckel family. See GENERAL
WORKS.

FRANCO
AMH has family records.
CFM has family records.
Cantera, Francisco. "El poeta
Cartagena del 'cancionero
general' y sus asciendentes
los Franco," Sefarad 28
(1968):3-39. Also on
Cartagena family.
Genealogical table. Marrano
origin according to author.
Carrete Parrondo, C.
"Descendientes del 'Martirio
del Niño de La Guardia.'"
Helmantica (Spain) 28,
no. 85/87 (1977):51-61.
Table of descendants of
Alonso Franco who was burned
at the stake along with his

brothers in 1491.
Franco, Arnold G. "An Inquiry
into the Origin and
Derivation of the Spanish
Surname: Franco," Judaïsme
Sephardi, n.s., no. 32
(juillet 1966):21-22.
May, Harry S. "The Origins of
the Franco Family," in The
Sephardic and Oriental Jewish
Heritage Studies, ed.
Issachar Ben-Ami (Jerusalem:
The Magnes Press, The Hebrew
University, 1982), pp.
145-53. Author presents
documents which imply that
the family of Francisco
Franco, the late Spanish head
of state, was of Jewish
origin.

FRANK
CFM has family records.
LBI has family tree beginning
1787.
See Sydney M. Cone entry under
AMBACH.
See Wilhelm and Rudolf Frank
entry under BING.
Frank Family, Boston, Mass.
"Biographical Material
Concerning Mrs. Daniel Frank,
Mrs. Jacob H. Hecht, and
Other Family Members,
1881-1932." In French,
German, and English. AJA.
Frank Family. Genealogical
Notes, 1819-1964; and
Obituaries of William R.
Frank. 1964. MS;
typescript; and printed.
AJA.
Harris. Merchant Princes.
Department store Franks
family of Oregon. See
GENERAL WORKS.
Kempelen. Magyarországi Zsidó,
1:12, 42; 3:60. See GENERAL
WORKS.
Stern. FAJF. Frank family
tree beginning in Sulzdorf,
Germany. Family tree is
listed in FAJF under "Mayer
II."
Tänzer. Juden in Jebenhausen,

pp. 318-19. See GENERAL
WORKS.

FRANKAU
AMH has family records.
CFM has family records.

FRANKEL
AMH has family records.
CAJ has family tree from
Munich.
JE, 5:478. Family tree of the
descendants of Koppel Fränkel
of Vienna, 17th century. See
GENERAL WORKS.
LBI has family trees beginning
1508, 1641, and 1691.
Bato, Y. "Koppel Fränkel und
seine Nachfahren. Die
Schicksale einer
deutsch-jüdischen Familie im
Wandel von mehr als drei
Jahrhunderten,"
Israelitisches Wochenblatt
(Zürich) 64, no. 2
(3.VII.1964):39, 41. Koppel
Fränkel (d. 1670), the
richest man in Vienna, was
born in Baiersdorf and
settled in Vienna around
1635.
See Y.L. Bato entry under
FRAENKEL.
See Jonas Marcus Bondi entry
under LUCKA.
Brann, Markus. "Die Familie
Fränkel," MGWJ 45
(1901):193-213.
————. "Die Grabschriften der
Familie Fränkel-Spira in
Prag," MGWJ 45
(1901):193-213; 46
(1902):450-73, 556-60.
————. "Geneal. übersicht
über die Nachkommenschaft des
Jacob Koppel Fränkel aus
Wien," in Gedenkbuch zur
Erinnerung an David Kaufmann.
(Breslau, 1900). Family
tree, opp. p. 399.
Brilling, Bernhard. "Jüdische
Druckerfamilien in
Frankfurt/oder," Archiv für
Geschichte der Buchwesens 1
(1956/57):570-81. "Die
Familie Fränkel," pp. 577-79.

18th to 19th century.
Frankel Family; Cincinnati. "A
Recent History of the Frankel
Family," by Edward M.
Frankel, 1937-1938.
Typescript. In English and
German. AJA.
"Joseph Jonas Theonim-Fränkel,
Rabbi in Krakau, 1742," MGWJ,
1917, pp. 51, 166.
Kaufmann, David. "Die Fränkel
in Worms," Magazin f. d.
Wissenschaft d. Judentums 17
(1890):87-92.
————. "Die wormser Fränkel
in Breslau," Magazin f. d.
Wissenschaft d. Judentums 17
(1890):175-76.
Lazarus, L. "Neue Beiträge zur
Geschichte der Familie
Fränkel-Spira," MGWJ, N.F.,
20 (1912).
Löwenstein, L. "Stammbaum der
Familie Mirels," Blatter für
Jüdische Geschichte und
Literatur (Mainz) 4
(1903):1-5, 33-37, 49-54,
113-20, 129, 159-60.
Includes Heller and Fränkel
families.
Nebel, Abe L. "Genealogy of
the Frankel Family of Prague,
Bohemia, Descendants of Which
Are Now Living in Cleveland,
Ohio." AJA.
See Rachel and Wallich entry
under FRANCKEL.
Rubinstein, Mordechai. Neta'ai
Ne'emana. Jerusalem, 1910.
71 p. Lineage of author,
includes important rabbis and
family links with Horowitz,
Landau, Rokeach, Shapiro,
Fränkel, and Schor families.
DLC, JNUL, MH.
[Unger, Helen F.W.] Herman
Frankel, 1838-1916. Los
Angeles, 1961. 44 p.
Minnesota Historical Society.

FRANKEL-HIRSCHHORN
Rosenstein. Unbroken Chain,
pp. 197ff. See GENERAL
WORKS.

FRANKENBURG
AMH has family records.

FRANKENSTEIN
AMH has family records.
Reychman. Szkice
genealogiczne, pp. 75-77.
See GENERAL WORKS.

FRANKFURTER
PD has family records.
Ballin. Juden in Seesen,
p. 178. See GENERAL WORKS.
Kempelen. Magyarországi Zsidó,
1:12. See GENERAL WORKS.

FRANKL
Frankl, August. "Zur
Geschichte der Familie
Frankl," ZGJT 2
(1931/32):67-80.
Kempelen. Magyarországi Zsidó.
Frankl family, 1:79, 106,
117, 118; 2:9, 79; 3:88, 91,
94. Fränkl family, 2:118;
3:127. See GENERAL WORKS.

FRANKLIN
AMH has family records.
CFM has family records.
Franklin, Arthur Ellis, comp.
Pedigrees of the Franklin
Family, and Lists of
Collateral Relations....
London: G. Rutledge & Sons,
Ltd., 1915. 91 p. CtY, G.
————. Records of the
Franklin Family and
Collaterals. London:
G. Rutledge, 1915. 166 p.
CLU, MH, NN, TxU. 2nd ed.
London, 1935. 210 p. MH,
OCH, OClW.
Stern, Norton B. "Franklin
Brothers of San Diego,"
Journal of San Diego History
21 (Summer 1975):32-42.
Lewis Abraham Franklin,
1820-1879, and Maurice
Abraham Franklin, 1817-1874,
were prominent citizens of
San Diego in the 1850s. They
were descendants of Menachem
Mendel Franckel, the rabbi of
Wroclaw (Breslau) Poland.
His son, Benjamin Wolf

Franklin, emigrated to London
in 1763.

FRANKS
AMH has family records.
CFM has family records.
EJ (1972), 7:106. Contains
genealogical table listing
descendants of Abraham
(Naphtali Hart) Franks
(d. London, 1708 or 1709),
through early 19th century.
American and European
branches. See GENERAL WORKS.
Gardner, Albert. An Old New
York Family. New York, 1963.
Includes Franks, Friedman,
and Gardner families. AJHS.
Genealogy of the Family of Mary
Davidson (Mrs. Isaac) Franks.
Daughters of the American
Revolution Library,
Washington, D.C.
Oppenheim, Samuel.
"Genealogical Notes on Jacob
Franks from Official
Records," Publications of the
American Jewish Historical
Society 25 (1917):75.
————. "Supplemental Notes on
the Jacob Franks Genealogy,"
Publications of the American
Jewish Historical Society 26
(1918):260-66.
Solomons, Israel. "The
Genealogy of the Franks
Family," Publications of the
American Jewish Historical
Society 18 (1909):213.
Stern. FAJF. Franks family
trees beginning in:
(I) Hannover?; (II) U.S.; and
(III) England. See GENERAL
WORKS.

FRANKS-JUDAH
AJA has genealogical files.

FRANZMAN
AMH has family records.

FRATER
Kempelen. Magyarországi Zsidó,
2:78. Fráter family. See
GENERAL WORKS.

FREDERICK
CFM has family records.
Semi-Gotha, 1:142. See GENERAL
WORKS.

FREED
AMH has family records.

FREEDMAN
AMH has family records.
Abravanel-Mickleshanski-
Freedman-London Families,
1762-1948. Printed and
handwritten. AJA.

FREEMAN
LBI has family tree beginning
1740.

FREI
Tänzer. Juden in Tirol,
pp. 715-16. See GENERAL
WORKS.

FREIBERG
AJA has family tree beginning
18th century for American
family originally from
Germany.

FREIDEN
AJA has genealogical files.

FREIDENFELT
Semi-Gotha, 1:29. See GENERAL
WORKS.

FREIHERR
PD has family records.

FREIMAN
Figler, Bernard. Lillian and
Archie Freiman. Biographies,
etc. Montreal: Northern
Printing & Lithography Co.,
1962. 331 p. Lillian Bilsky
Freiman, 1885-1940; Archibald
Jacob Freiman, 1880-1944.

FREIMANN
CAJ has family records.
LBI has family tree beginning
1733.
[Freimann, Aron]. Aus des
Stammbaum der Familien
Ettlinger, Freimann und

Horovitz. Berlin: Marx &
Co., 1925. 3 genealogical
tables. OCH.
Tänzer. Juden in Tirol,
p. 717. See GENERAL WORKS.

FREINDL
Kempelen. Magyarországi Zsidó,
3:74. See GENERAL WORKS.

FREIRE
CFM has family records.

FREISTADT
PD has family records from
Prague and elsewhere.

FREISTADTER
Kempelen. Magyarországi Zsidó,
2:93, 94. Freistädter
family. See GENERAL WORKS.

FRENCKEL
Kempelen. Magyarországi Zsidó,
2:136. See GENERAL WORKS.

FRENDENSTEIN
AMH has family records.

FRENKEL
Frenkel, Elias Karl, comp.
Family Tree of R. Moshe
Witzenhausen. Ancestors and
Descendants, Collected by His
Great-Great-Grandson Elias
Karl Frenkel. Jerusalem:
Polypress, 1969. 65, 19 p.
Genealogical tables,
bibliography. Rabbi
Witzenhausen of Westphalia
changed his name to Frenkel
at the time of Napoleon.
CLU, DLC.

FREUD
Aaron, W. "Notes sur les
ancêstres de Sigmund Freud et
leurs contacts juifs," Revue
d'Histoire de la Médecine
Hebraïque 93 (1971):73-77.
Aron, Willy. "The Genealogies
of Professor and Mrs. Sigmund
Freud," The Jewish Forum (New
York), Apr. 1957, pp. 50-51.
Clark, Ronald W. Freud: The
Man and the Cause. New York:

Random House, 1980. 652 p.
Includes a genealogical chart
of descendants of Kallamon
Jacob Freud (b. 1815,
Tysmenits; d. 1896, Vienna),
the father of Sigmund Freud
(b. 1856, Freiberg; d. 1939,
London).
"Discussion Regarding Sigmund
Freud's Ancestry," YIVO
Annual of Jewish Social
Sciences 12
(1958/59):297-300.
Freud, Jechiel. Stammtafel der
Abkömmlinge von Aba
Gabua-Stern, Meier
Jaffa-Scheiner und Moses Abr.
Abisch Margulies-Ber.
Entworfen: Max Besner.
Buczacz: Verein Rodzina,
1914. 1 genealogical table.
DLC, NN.
Gicklhorn, R. "The Freiberg
Period of the Freud Family,"
Journal of the History of
Medicine and Allied Sciences
24 (Jan. 1969):37-43.
Kempelen. Magyarországi Zsidó,
1:89; 2:56. See GENERAL
WORKS.
Rainey, Reuben M. Freud as
Student of Religion;
Perspectives on the
Background and Development of
His Thought. Missoula,
Montana: American Academy of
Religion, 1975. 174 p.
(Dissertation Series, 7).
Columbia University
Dissertation, 1971. Includes
chapter on "The Judaism of
Freud's Family."

FREUDENBERG
CAJ has family tree.
Ballin. Juden in Seesen,
p. 179. See GENERAL WORKS.
Hannam, Charles. A Boy in that
Situation: An Autobiography.
New York: Harper and Row,
1978. 215 p. Brief
genealogical chart, opp. p.
7. Karl Hartland, the
author's real name, was born
in Essen, Germany, the son of
Max (d. 1943) and Gertrude

Freudenberg (d. 1937)
Hartland. His mother's
parents were Louis and
Ernestina Freudenberg. His
grandfather was Joseph
Hartland, and his
great-grandfather was Levi
Hartland. Autobiography
covers author's life in
Germany and England through
late 1940s.
Kempelen. Magyarországi Zsidó,
1:110. See GENERAL WORKS.

FREUDENTHAL
AJA and LBI have family trees
beginning 1787 and 1790.
AMH has family records.
See CAJ (Call No. P/123) entry
under ECKSTEIN.
Ballin. Juden in Seesen,
p. 180. See GENERAL WORKS.
Fierman, Floyd S. "Jewish
Pioneers in the Southwest: A
Record of the
Freudenthal-Lesinsky-Solomon
Families," Arizona and the
West 2 (Spring 1960):54-72.
On Julius Freudenthal, his
nephew Henry Lesinsky, and
their mercantile partnership
in Las Cruces, New Mexico;
Henry's development of the
Longfellow Copper Mining
Company, Clifton, Arizona;
Isador Elkan Solomon who
settled in Arizona at Pueblo
Viejo and expanded from
merchant to banker; and other
members of the family.
———. Some Early Jewish
Settlers on the Southwestern
Frontier. El Paso: Texas
Western Press, 1960. 58 p.
Lesinsky, Solomon, and
Freudenthal families.

FREUDIGER
Kempelen. Magyarországi Zsidó,
2:134. See GENERAL WORKS.

FREUND
"Genealogy of the Freund
Family, 1765-1935, Mitwitz,
Bavaria." AJA.
Jacob de Sourdis Freund,

Genealogy and Life History,
1765-1935. AJA.
Kempelen. Magyarországi Zsidó,
2:26; 3:87, 117. See GENERAL
WORKS.

FREUNDLICH
Levison, Wilhelm. Die
Siegburger Familie Levison
und verwandte Familien.
Bonn: Rührscheid, 1952.
187 p. Includes Freundlich
family. CSt, DLC, NN, NNJ.
Levinson, Wilhelm (1876-1947).
Papers, 1898-1968. Include
genealogical material on
Levison and Freundlich
families of England and
Germany. LBI.

FREXINAL
Beinart, Haim. "Three
Generations, Members of One
Family Tried by the
Inquisition," (In Hebrew.)
Tarbiz 30 (1960):46-61.
Family of Spain, 16th
century.

FREYHAN
CAJ has family tree from
Breslau compiled by Bernhard
Brilling. Covers 1720-1935.

FREYLICH
Reiss. Hesse and Galicia.
Includes Freylich family of
Olkusz. See GENERAL WORKS.

FREYSTADTLER
Kempelen. Magyarországi Zsidó,
2:92. Freystädtler family.
See GENERAL WORKS.

FRIDBERG
LBI has family tree beginning
1776.

FRIEBE
Rachel and Wallich. Berliner
Grosskaufleute, 3:112-115.
See GENERAL WORKS.

FRIEBEISZ
Kempelen. Magyarországi Zsidó,
1:56. See GENERAL WORKS.

FRIED
Brandmark, Bernice. Fried
Cousins Club. [Manhasset,
N.Y., 1975]. 26 ll. illus.
"A genealogy of the
descendants of Jacob and
Channa Fried; Jacob was born
about 1830 and lived near
Mielec, Galicia." AJHS.
Kempelen. Magyarországi Zsidó,
1:120; 2:91; 3:44, 48, 124.
See GENERAL WORKS.

FRIEDBERG
LBI has family tree beginning
1503.

FRIEDBERGER
LBI has family tree beginning
1794.
"History of the Friedberger
Family." [Stockton, Calif.,
March 1967]. Typescript, 3
p. "Work begins with the
immigration of Arnold
Friedberger to California in
1852 and his establishment of
a general store in San
Andreas, California in 1857,
where five of his six sons
were born." WJHC.
Kempelen. Magyarországi Zsidó,
2:70. See GENERAL WORKS.

FRIEDEBERG
AMH has family records.
CFM has family records.

FRIEDENHEIM
PD has family records.

FRIEDENWALD
The Friedenwald Family,
1762-1950. Family of
Baltimore, descendants of
Jonas Friedenwald
(b. Germany, 1801). AJA.

FRIEDHEIM
Poizer, Anne. "Die Geschichte
einer Familie. Aus dem Leben
einer deutsche Jüdin," Aufbau
(New York), Apr. 29, 1960.
Hedwig Lesser Friedheim.

FRIEDLAENDER
Friedlaender, Kurt. Papers,
1851-1952. Judge and labor
mediator, of Germany and
England. Include family
trees and other family
papers. LBI.

FRIEDLAND
JE, 5:514. Contains family
trees for family of Prague,
descendants of Nathan
(d. ca. 1670), through
mid-18th century; and for
family of Russia, descendants
of Abraham of Slutzk, 18th
through late 19th century.
See GENERAL WORKS.
Ballin. Juden in Seesen,
p. 181. See GENERAL WORKS.
Eisenstadt and Wiener. Da'at
Kedoschim. Includes
Friedland family of Poland
and Russia. See GENERAL
WORKS.
Livai, Abraham. Sons of Jonah:
The History of a Family in
Israel for 100 Years
(1859-1959). Tel Aviv, n.d.
On the descendants of Jonah
Friedland.

FRIEDLANDER
AMH has family records.
CAJ has family tree and
records, 1760-1912.
Friedländer family.
See Esmond S. De Beer entry
under BARDEN.
Friedländer, Ernst, ed. Das
Handlunghaus Joachim Moses
Friedländer & Sohne zu
Königsberg. Hamburg: Grafe,
1913. 58 p. Includes family
tree. LBI.
Gebrüder Friedländer: Gold-und
Silberwaren, Berlin.
Gebrüder Friedländer,
1829-1929. Berlin, 1929.
30 p. A jewellry firm
founded by Z.L. Friedländer
(b. 1801). LBI.
Friedländer, Saul. When Memory
Comes. Translated from the
French by Helen R. Lane. New
York: Farrar, Straus, Giroux,

1979. 186 p. Memoirs of
family that fled to France
from their native Prague
during W.W.II. The author
(1932-   ) is the son of Jan
and Elli Glazer Friedländer,
both of whom died in the
Holocaust. The mother was
the daughter of Gustav and
Cécile Glazer from Rochlitz,
near Gablonz, Czechoslovakia.
Friedländer, Siegfried.
Geschichte der Familie
Friedländer. 1-2. Breslau
1912 und Potsdam 1921.
110, 111 p. MS. Includes
Friedländer and Skutsch
families of Schlesien. LBI.
Friedländer-Prechtl, Robert.
"Oppeln Aus einem
Lebensrückblick." Starnberg,
1950. 10 p. The author, a
dramatist (b. Vienna, 1874;
d. Starnberg, 1950), briefly
traces history of his
merchant family from
Oppeln/Oberschlesien. LBI.
Kempelen. Magyarországi Zsidó,
2:147; 3:52. Friedländer
family. See GENERAL WORKS.
Perlich, Alfons. "Zur
Geschichte der Firma
Friedländer," Mitteilungen
des Beuthener Geschichte-und
Museumsvereins, no. 15/16
(1954/55):39-42. Dortmund.
Philippsohn, Molly. Chronik
der Familie
Friedländer-Lowenherz,
1760-1912. 51 p. CAJ.
Stern, Moritz. "Ungedruckte
Gutachten und Briefe
Friedländers," ZGJD 6
(1935):113-30. Family of
Berlin.

FRIEDLIEBER
Kempelen. Magyarországi Zsidó,
1:32; 3:124. See GENERAL
WORKS.

FRIEDMAN
AMH has family records.
Chelminsky-Lajmer, "Jewish
Surnames." See GENERAL
WORKS.

Friedman, Lee M. Ancestry of
Lee M. Friedman. Boston,
Mass. AJA, AJHS.
Friedman, Colonel Max;
Pennsylvania. Genealogical
Record of the Friedman
Family; typescript. AJA.
Gardner, Albert. An Old New
York Family. New York, 1963.
Includes Franks, Friedman,
and Gardner families. AJHS.
Josephy, Maria Reines. "The
Social Structure of a Jewish
Family Organization."
Master's thesis, Columbia
University, 1967. Discusses
the Friedman Family Circle of
New York City, organized in
1910. Descendants of Pincus
Friedman and Chanaleid
Glicksman Friedman, both of
whom lived in Poland near the
Nida and Vistula Rivers and
in or near the cities of
Chmelnik and Nowi Korczin,
county of Stobnica in the
year 1790. Includes family
tree and chart.
Rosenstein. Unbroken Chain,
pp. 510ff. Friedman
Chassidic Dynasty of Ruzhin.
See GENERAL WORKS.

FRIEDMANN
Gold. Die Juden und
Judengemeinden Mährens,
p. 108. Genealogical table
of the descendants of Wilhelm
Friedmann, d. Vienna, 1852.
Jackson, Livia E. Bitton.
Elli: Coming of Age in the
Holocaust. New York: Times
Books, 1980. 248 p.
Description of Friedmann
family life during the
Holocaust, 1939-1945. The
family was from Somorja on
the Danube River
(Czechoslovakia; during
W.W.II occupied by Hungary).
The author, Livia Elvira
"Elli" Friedmann, was
daughter of Márkusz
Friedmann, who owned a
grocery store in Somorja.
Kempelen. Magyarországi Zsidó,

1:27, 105; 2:73, 91, 92, 145;
3:125. See GENERAL WORKS.
Schulte. Bonner Juden, p. 239.
See GENERAL WORKS.

FRIES (DE)
See DE FRIES.

FRIESLANDER
CAJ has Friesländer family
records.

FRIIS
See BECK-FRIIS.

FRIJDA
Droege, "Frisian Names." See
GENERAL WORKS.

FRISCH
Kempelen. Magyarországi Zsidó,
3:139. See GENERAL WORKS.

FRITZ
Kempelen. Magyarországi Zsidó,
3:72. See GENERAL WORKS.

FROCKT
Morris, Margie. "My Family."
Genealogical information
concerning Morris-Frockt
family. Louisville, Ky.
AJA.

FROELICH
PD has family records.

FROHLICH
Kempelen. Magyarországi Zsidó,
1:122; 3:96. Fröhlich
family. See GENERAL WORKS.

FROHMAN
AJA has family tree beginning
1755.

FROMMER
Kempelen. Magyarországi Zsidó,
2:100. See GENERAL WORKS.

FRUCHTER
Fruchter, Shlomo ben Yisrael.
Egeret Shlomo. Jerusalem,
1960. 138 p. The lineage of
three brothers: Rabbi Shlomo
Fruchter, Rabbi Mordechai

Stern, and Rabbi Avraham
Adler. JNUL.

Rosenstein. Unbroken Chain,
pp. 517ff. See GENERAL
WORKS.

FRUMET
AMH has family records.

FRUMKIN
Bick-Shauli, "Roots and
Branches." Includes
genealogy of Mariya Yakovlena
(pseud. Ester) Frumkin(a),
(1880-?), Russian Communist
party leader, b. in Minsk
area. See GENERAL WORKS.

FRYDA
Droege, "Frisian." See GENERAL
WORKS.

FRYDMAN
Twerski, Aaron. Sefer Ha-yahas
mi-Tshernobil ve-rosin.
Jerusalem, 1966. On Frydman
and Twerski families. AJHS.

FUCHS
Kempelen. Magyarországi Zsidó,
1:21, 22; 2:94, 103, 133,
134; 3:25, 123. See GENERAL
WORKS.

FUCHSL
Kempelen. Magyarországi Zsidó,
3:83. See GENERAL WORKS.

FUENN
Rosenstein. Unbroken Chain,
pp. 150ff. See GENERAL
WORKS.

FUERST
LBI has family tree beginning
1550.

FULD
CAJ has list of family of
Mannheim.
Benjamin, Heinrich. Chronik
der Familie
Herz-Salomon-Fuld.
Jerusalem, 1944. 36 p. MS.
Families of Frankfurt am
Main. LBI.

FULDA
CFM has family records.
Berliner, Moritz. Stammbaum
der Samonschen Familie.
3. Aufl. Hannover, 1912.
31 p. 14 family trees
containing more than 3,000
names. Samson family of
Wolffenbüttel; descendants of
Marcus Gumpel Moses Fulda
(16?-1733). MWalB, OCH.
Schulze, Hans. Beitrage zur
Geschichte der jüdischen
Gemeinde in Wolfenbüttel.
Wolfenbüttel, 1964. 87 p.
Genealogies of Fulda, Gumpel,
and Samson families,
pp. 4-36, 81-84. LBI.

FULEP
Kempelen. Magyarországi Zsidó,
2:16, 17. Fülep family. See
GENERAL WORKS.

FULTON
AMH has family records.

FUNCK
Semi-Gotha, 1:85. See GENERAL
WORKS.

FURST
Kempelen. Magyarországi Zsidó,
1:26, 74, 85, 105, 130;
2:146; 3:63. Fürst family.
See GENERAL WORKS.

FURSTENBERG
Rothschild. Svenska Israel.
Includes Fürstenberg family.
See GENERAL WORKS.

FURTADO
AMH has family records.
CFM has family records.

FURTH
PD has family records.

GAAL
Kempelen. Magyarországi Zsidó,

125

3:35. Gaál family. See
GENERAL WORKS.

GABAY
AJA has genealogical records.
AMH has family records.
CFM has family records.

GABISCHON
See GAVISON.

GABISON
Sirat, R.S. "Omer ha-šikha et
la famille Gabišon," in
Fourth World Congress of
Jewish Studies Papers 4,
no. 2 (1968):65-67.

GABLENZ-ESKELES
Semigothaisches Taschenbuch.
Genealogical table 7. See
GENERAL WORKS.

GABOS
Kempelen. Magyarországi Zsidó,
2:94. See GENERAL WORKS.

GABRIEL
AMH has family records.
CFM has family records.
Kempelen. Magyarországi Zsidó,
2:8. Gábriel family. See
GENERAL WORKS.

GABUA
See Jechiel Freud entry under
BER.

GADD
Semi-Gotha, 1:97. See GENERAL
WORKS.

GAGE
AMH has family records.

GAGGSTATTER
AJA has family tree beginning
1700.

GAJARY
See KUCHINKA-GAJARY.
Kempelen. Magyarországi Zsidó,
1:16; 3:45. Gajáry family.
See GENERAL WORKS.

GAL
Kempelen. Magyarországi Zsidó,
3:35. Gál family. See
GENERAL WORKS.

GALANO
CAJ has family records.

GALANTE
JE, 5:547. Contains family
pedigree for family of Italy,
descendants of Mordecai
Galante (d. 1540). See
GENERAL WORKS.

GALEWSKY
Sokobin, Samuel, comp.
[Biographical Data on the
Galewsky and Goodman
Families, St. Helena,
California]. Typescript.
3 p. AJA, WJHC.

GALINDO
CFM has family records.

GALLICKI
CFM has family records.

GALLINGER
Deutsch, Hermann. Stammbaum
der Familie aus Wittelshofen.
1964? 4 p. Family table
starts with Jehuda Löw (b. in
Wittelshofen) and his son
Josef Gallinger (1751-1847),
and continues to 1964. CAJ,
Call No. 2773.
Gallinger, Joseph S. Data on
the Gallinger Family of
Wittelshofen. Birmingham,
Ala., 1970. 2 p. CAJ, Call
No. 2773.

GAMBETTA
CAJ has family records.

GAME
AMH has family records.

GAMIE
AMH has family records.

GANS
See GAUSS.
AMH has family records.

LBI has family trees beginning
14th and 16th centuries, and
1774.
Ballin. Juden in Seesen,
p. 182. See GENERAL WORKS.
Gothaisches Genealogisches
Taschenbuch der Briefadeligen
Häuser (Gotha), 1915,
pp. 276ff.; 1923, pp. 194ff.
Genealogy of family of
Frankfurt am Main.
Gronemann. Genealogische
Hannovers. Family tree of
Salman Gans of Hannover,
pp. 21-29. See GENERAL
WORKS.
Herz, Ludwig. Die
sechshundertjährige
Geschichte der Familie Gans,
1330-1930. Berlin, [1930].
45 p. Includes genealogical
tables.
Kempelen. Magyarországi Zsidó,
2:138. See GENERAL WORKS.
Meyer, Walther. "Zur
Geschichte der Familie
Egar-Gans-Gansmann," JFF,
nos. 48-50 (1938):890-96,
914-20, 938-43.
Stern. FAJF. Gans family tree
beginning in Natzingen,
Westphalia. See GENERAL
WORKS.

GANZ
Wagner, Günter. Die Musiker
familie Ganz aus Weisenau.
Ein Beitrag zur
Musikgeschichte der Juden am
Mittelrhein. Mainz: Schott's
Söhne, 1974. 127 p.
Includes genealogical tables.
CU, DLC, ICN, NcD, NN.

GAON
AMH has family records.
CFM has family records.

GARA
Kempelen. Magyarországi Zsidó,
2:123; 3:51. See GENERAL
WORKS.

GARAI
Kempelen. Magyarországi Zsidó,

1:85; 3:118. See GENERAL
WORKS.

GARCIA
AMH has family records.
CFM has family records.
Emden. Jews of Britain,
p. 549. "The Garcias." See
GENERAL WORKS.

GARCIA DE SANTA MARIA
Cantera Burgos, Francisco.
Alvar García de Santa María y
de sus conversos más
egregios. Madrid: Instituto
Arias Montano, 1952. 624 p.
Includes genealogical tables.
15th and 16th centuries.
CtY, ICN, NcD, NN, NNC, OCH,
OClW, OU, TxU.

GARDIE
Semi-Gotha, 1:104. See GENERAL
WORKS.

GARDNER
AMH has family records.
Gardner, Albert. An Old New
York Family. New York, 1963.
Includes Franks, Friedman,
and Gardner families. AJHS.

GARDONYI
Kempelen. Magyarországi Zsidó,
3:78. Gárdonyi family. See
GENERAL WORKS.

GARFEIN
AJA has family tree.
"Information on the Garfein
Family and Brief Genealogy."
Feb. 2, 1962. AJA.

GARGYI
Kempelen. Magyarországi Zsidó,
3:60. See GENERAL WORKS.

GASPAR
Kempelen. Magyarországi Zsidó,
2:104, 144; 3:52, 78, 80.
Gáspár family. See GENERAL
WORKS.

GASTER
AMH has family records.
CFM has family records.

GAUSS
Gauss (Gans), Isaac.
Genealogical data, including
mention of receipt of a Civil
War Congressional Medal of
Honor. AJA.

GAVISON (GABISCHON)
EJ (1928), 7:111-12.   Family of
Spain originally.   See
GENERAL WORKS.

GAY
AMH has family records.

GAYFORD
AMH has family records.

GAZEL
AMH has family records.

GEBER
LBIS has family tree and notes.
Kempelen.   Magyarországi Zsidó,
2:20.   Géber family.   See
GENERAL WORKS.
Rothschild.   Svenska Israel.
See GENERAL WORKS.

GEDIDYA
CFM has family records.

GEER
Semi-Gotha, 1:42.   See GENERAL
WORKS.

GEIGER
CAJ has family records.
CAJ has family tree of German
family compiled by Siegfried
Moritz Auerbach.
"Familie Geiger," (In Hebrew.)
Ha-enṣiqlopedja ha-'ibrit
10:637-42.   Family of
Frankfurt.
Kempelen.   Magyarországi Zsidó,
1:137; 3:77.   See GENERAL
WORKS.
Worms, Daniel August.
Stammtafeln der Familie
Geiger zusammengestellt im
Auftrag des Herrn Alfred S.
Geiger.   Frankfurt am Main,
1903.   Family tree begins
1632.   LBI.

GEIJERSTAM
Semi-Gotha, 1:126.   See GENERAL
WORKS.

GEISLER
Schulte.   Bonner Juden, p. 240.
See GENERAL WORKS.

GEIST
Kempelen.   Magyarországi Zsidó,
3:53.   See GENERAL WORKS.

GEITEL
CAJ has family tree from
Prague, beginning 1787.

GELDER
CAJ has family tree from
Netherlands.
Citroën, K.A.   The Spanjaard
Family: A Survey of the
Descendants of Salomon Jacob
Spanjaard (1783-1861) and
Sara David van Gelder
(1793-1882).   2d rev. and
augmented ed.   Borne,
Holland: Family Association
"Berith Salom," 1981.   286 p.
AJHS.

GELDEREN (VON)
AMH has family records.

GELDERN
"Simeon von Geldern's Stammbaum
der Familie Geldern," in
David Kaufmann's Aus Heinrich
Heine's Ahnensaal (Breslau:
Schottländer, 1896),
pp. 297-303.   CtY, IEN, NjP,
OCH, PP, PPDrop.
Löwenstein, Leopold.   Stammbaum
des August Oppenheim....
Mannheim, 1908.   Folio.
Includes Geldern family of
Breslau.   Also, MGWJ (1907),
pp. 205ff., has the author's
genealogical table of the
family.
Simons, Carl W., ed.   Stammbaum
des gelehrten R. Simon von
Geldern aus Jerusalem.
Düsseldorf, 1905.

GELLMAN
Keneseth Israel.   See GENERAL

WORKS.
See Yaffa Draznin entry under
BERNSTEIN.

GEMMINGER
Tänzer. Juden in Jebenhausen,
p. 320. See GENERAL WORKS.

GENESE
AMH has family records.

GENFANSTEIN
See George M. Gross entry under
GROSS. Family originally
from Polotsk and Kublitch.

GENTILI
EJ (1928), 7:255-56. See
GENERAL WORKS.

GENTILLI
AMH has family records.

GEORGII
Semi-Gotha, 1:53ff. See
GENERAL WORKS.

GERBER
Kempelen. Magyarországi Zsidó,
3:61. See GENERAL WORKS.

GERGELY
Kempelen. Magyarországi Zsidó,
1:70; 2:15. See GENERAL
WORKS.

GERGO
Kempelen. Magyarországi Zsidó,
2:132. Gergő family. See
GENERAL WORKS.

GERLICZY
Kempelen. Magyarországi Zsidó,
1:55; 2:52. See GENERAL
WORKS.

GERLOCZI
Kempelen. Magyarországi Zsidó,
1:62. Gerlóczi family. See
GENERAL WORKS.

GERMAIN
Ashby, Harriet. "The Germains
of Los Angeles," Western
States Jewish Historical
Quarterly 2 (July

1970):217-27. Family
emigrated to Los Angeles from
Switzerland in the 1870s.

GERMAN
Kempelen. Magyarországi Zsidó,
3:55. Germán family. See
GENERAL WORKS.

GERNSHEIM
Gernsheim, Helmut. "The
Gernsheims of Worms," Leo
Baeck Institute Year Book 24
(1979):247-57. Descendants
of Salomon Gernsheim
(d. 1620).

GERO
Kempelen. Magyarországi Zsidó,
1:85, 146; 3:26. Gerő
family. See GENERAL WORKS.

GEROTHWOHL
AMH has family records.

GERSHOMS
Mac Leod, Celeste, comp.
"Seixas Gershoms Solomons
Family Tree." 1969. WJHC.

GERSHOVITZ, GERSHVIN, GERSHWIN
Ewen, David. A Journey to
Greatness: The Life and Music
of George Gershwin. New
York: Henry Holt & Co., 1956.
384 p. "The Gershvins," pp.
29-37. Name was originally
Gershovitz, changed to
Gershvin in U.S. George
Gershwin's parents, Morris
(1870/71-1932) and Rose
(1875/76-1948) Gershvin, were
both born in St. Petersburg.
Morris emigrated to U.S.
about 1891.

GERSICH
Kempelen. Magyarországi Zsidó,
3:43. See GENERAL WORKS.

GERSON
CAJ has family history and
records.
Ballin. Juden in Seesen,
p. 183. See GENERAL WORKS.
Flesch, Heinrich. "Nachkommen

des Gerson in Mähren," JFF,
no. 21 (1930):215-17.

GERSTENBERG
AMH has family records.
CFM has family records.

GERSTL
Kempelen. Magyarországi Zsidó,
2:9, 128. See GENERAL WORKS.

GERSTLE
LBI has family tree beginning
1810.
Greenbaum and Gerstle
Genealogy, 1740-1954. These
families were pioneer San
Francisco families. WJHC.
Mack, Lewis Gerstle. Lewis and
Hannah Gerstle. San
Francisco?, 1953. 131 p.
Includes genealogical charts
and portraits of family
members of pioneer San
Francisco family. CU, WJHC.
Narell. Our City. Includes
genealogical charts of
Gerstle family. See GENERAL
WORKS.

GERSTLEY
"Gerstley Family Tree,
1670-1860," Typescript. AJA.
Gerstley-Loeb Family. Papers,
1868-1976. 2 Boxes and
photographs. Records of four
generations of Philadelphia
family of German origin.
Includes genealogical
information. PJAC.
WJHC has James Gerstley family
charts, 1866-1972.

GERTZ
Gertz, Elmer. To Life. New
York: McGraw-Hill, 1974. 252
p. Genealogical information,
pp. 1-12. Autobiography of
the prominent Chicago lawyer
(1906-   ) who has fought
for civil rights and civil
liberties. Gertz is the son
of Morris and Grace Gertz and
the grandson of Aaron Gertz
of Lithuania.

GETTING
AMH has family records.
CFM has family records.

GEWER
LBIS has family notes.

GHILLANY
Kempelen. Magyarországi Zsidó,
2:24. Ghillány family. See
GENERAL WORKS.

GIBBES
AMH has family records.

GIBSON
Semi-Gotha, 1:147; 2:62. See
GENERAL WORKS.

GIDEON
AMH has family records.
CAJ has family tree from
Germany.
CFM has family records.
Burke's Extinct and Dormant
Baronetcies. English family.
Emden. Jews of Britain,
pp. 521-22. "The Descendants
of Samson Gideon." See
GENERAL WORKS.
Friedman, Lee M. "Rowland
Gideon, An Early Boston Jew
and His Family," Publications
of the American Jewish
Historical Society 35
(1939):27-37.
Zapf. Tübinger Juden, pp.
49-50. See GENERAL WORKS.

GIFFORD
AMH has family records.

GIKATILA
EJ (1928), 7:407-408. See
GENERAL WORKS.

GILBERT
LBI has family tree beginning
1748.
Salomon, Jerry. "History of
the Gilbert Family." N.p.,
n.d. Typescript. 4 p.
Descendants of Michael
Gilbert (d. 1892) of San
Francisco, a California
pioneer. WJHC.

GILDER (VAN)
AMH has family records.

GIMBEL
Harris. Merchant Princes.
Gimbel department store
family. Descendants of Adam
Gimbel who arrived in U.S. in
1835 from Bavarian village of
Rhein-Pfaltz. See GENERAL
WORKS.

GINSBERG, GINSBURG
CFM has Ginsburg family tree.
Ballin. Juden in Seesen,
p. 184. See GENERAL WORKS.
Ginsburg, Sigmar. "Die
Geschichte unseres Zweiges
der Familie Ginsburg." Tel
Aviv, 1946. 64, 40 p. MS.
LBI. Family from Schwaben
and Vilna.
Pudor. Internationalen
Verwandtschaftlichen. Vol. 2
contains a section on
Ginsberg family. See GENERAL
WORKS.
Rosenstein. Unbroken Chain,
pp. 144ff. Discussion of the
"Descendants of R. Naftali
Hirsch Ginsburg (Gunzburg)."
See GENERAL WORKS.

GINZBERG
Ginzberg, Eli. Keeper of the
Law: Louis Ginzberg.
Philadelphia: Jewish
Publication Society of
America, 1966. 348 p.
Genealogical information on
Ginzberg and Jaffe ancestors
of Louis Ginzberg
(1873-1953), the
world-renowned Talmud and
Jewish law scholar, pp.
12-34. Louis was born in
Kovno, the son of Isaac Elias
and Zippe Jaffe Ginzberg and
the grandson of Rabbi Asher
Ginzberg. He emigrated to
U.S. in 1899. CLU, DLC, NjP,
OCH.

GINZBURG
Maggid, Hillel Noah. 'Ir
Vilna. Vilna, 1900. 304 p.

Includes genealogy, extended
to 16 generations, of Gabriel
Yakov Ginzburg (1793-1853), a
merchant who left Vilna to
live in Vitebsk, Komenitz,
and Simferopol, returning
finally to Vilna. DLC.
Rosenstein. Unbroken Chain,
pp. 150ff. See GENERAL
WORKS.

GISBORNE
AMH has family records.

GISIKO
"Gisiko Family Genealogy,
1729-1883." In German and
English. AJA.

GIST
Warfield, N. "Chart of the
Gist-Cary Family Tree, 1903;
Revised 1959." AJA.

GITELSON
AJA has Moses Leo Gitelson
family tree.
Gitelson-Komaiko Family
Association. The Chronicle.
1961-? YIVO.

GLANZ
Kempelen. Magyarországi Zsidó,
2:136. See GENERAL WORKS.

GLASBERG
CAJ has family records.

GLASER
See GLASSER.
Ballin. Juden in Seesen,
p. 185. See GENERAL WORKS.
Press Family Tree. Compiled by
Gladys Glaser Gould. Covers
ca. 1820-1982. Descendants
of Moses Press of Trisig
(Latvia or Lithuania?), a
glazier who apparently
changed his name to Glaser.
Some descendants retained
Press surname. JGCT.
Schulte. Bonner Juden, p. 241.
See GENERAL WORKS.

GLASNER
Kempelen. Magyarországi Zsidó,

2:74, 97, 103. See GENERAL
WORKS.

GLASS
Kempelen. Magyarországi Zsidó,
2:56. See GENERAL WORKS.

GLASSER
Glasser Family Trees. Compiled
by Irwin M. Berent, Morton
Glasser, and Roslyn Leitman.
Covers ca. 1810-1982. Family
originally from Ligum
(Lygumai), Kovno Gubernia,
Lithuania; settled in Norfolk
and Berkley, Virginia and
other American cities as well
as Australia. Originally
spelled Glaser. JGCT.

GLAZER
Friedländer, Saul. When Memory
Comes. Translated from the
French by Helen R. Lane. New
York: Farrar, Straus, Giroux,
1979. 186 p. Memoirs of
family that fled to France
from their native Prague
during W.W.II. The author
(1932-   ) is the son of Jan
and Elli Glazer Friedländer,
both of whom died in the
Holocaust. The mother was
the daughter of Gustav and
Cécile Glazer from Rochlitz,
near Gablonz, Czechoslovakia.

GLAZIER
AMH has family records.
Glazier Family, Marysville and
San Francisco. Papers.
"This collection includes
photocopies of biographical
data and newspaper clippings
concerning Isaac Glazier and
family, as well as a copy of
the Glazier family tree."
WJHC.

GLAZMAN
Rusinek, Alla. Like a Song;
Like a Dream: A Soviet Girl's
Quest for Freedom. New York:
Scribner's Sons, 1973. 267
p. Story of Alla Milkin
Rusinek's discovery of her

Jewish identity and her
efforts to emigrate to
Israel. Her mother was
Polina Glazman (1910-?), the
daughter of Abram and Sarah
Glazman from Dvinsk and
Vologda. Her father was
Tsalik Milkin (1901-1960)
from Tchardjow, Turkmenia.
Author married Yosif Rusinek,
whose family came from
Liepaja, Lithuania.

GLENNIE
AMH has family records.

GLESINGER
AMH has family records.

GLICKSMAN
Josephy, Maria Reines. "The
Social Structure of a Jewish
Family Organization."
Master's thesis, Columbia
University, 1967. Discusses
the Friedman Family Circle of
New York City, organized in
1910. Descendants of Pincus
Friedman and Chanaleid
Glicksman Friedman, both of
whom lived in Poland near the
Nida and Vistula Rivers and
in or near the cities of
Chmelnik and Nowi Korczin,
county of Stobnica, in 1790.
Includes family tree and
chart.

GLUCK
AJA has family tree.
Kempelen. Magyarországi Zsidó,
2:68, 87, 92, 142, 143, 144;
3:43, 83, 107. Glück family.
See GENERAL WORKS.

GLUCKSMANN
Kempelen. Magyarországi Zsidó,
2:55. Glücksmann family.
See GENERAL WORKS.

GLUCKSTEIN
AMH has family records.
Gluckstein, Joseph.
Genealogical Tables of The
Gluckstein-Salmon-Joseph-

Abrahams Families, etc.
London: By the Author, 1925.

GLUCKSTHAL
Kempelen. Magyarországi Zsidó,
2:144. Glücksthal family.
See GENERAL WORKS.

GLUECK
AJA has genealogical files.
Bernstein, Charles B. "Some
Little-Known Aspects of the
Genealogy of Nelson Glueck."
Chicago, Ill., 1974. Nelson
Glueck, Near-East
archaeologist and president
of Hebrew Union College,
b. Cincinnati, Ohio, 1900;
d. 1971. AJA.

GLUECKSBERG
Reychman. Szkice
genealogiczne, pp. 79-82.
See GENERAL WORKS.

GLUGE
AMH has family records.

GODCHAUX
Godchaux, Paul L. "The
Godchaux Family of New
Orleans." Typescript, 1971.
Printed copy. AJA.

GODDARD
AMH has family records.

GODEFROI
CFM has family records.

GODES
AJA has genealogical files.

GODMANCHESTER
AMH has family records.

GODSCHALK
CAJ has family tree published
in Averbuch in 1901.

GOES
Semi-Gotha, 2:15. See GENERAL
WORKS.

GOETSCHLIK
Kopp. Jüdischen Alsenz,

pp. 124-27. See GENERAL
WORKS.

GOETZ
CFM has family records.
Birnbaum, Eduard. "Der
Eigenname 'Goetz.'" Jüdisches
Litteratur-Blatt 23
(1894):132.

GOKESCH
AMH has family records.

GOLD
See Sidney Cramer entry under
BINDMAN.

GOLDBERG
AMH has family records.
CFM has family records.
Keneseth Israel. See GENERAL
WORKS.
Fierman, Floyd S. "The
Goldberg Brothers: Arizona
Pioneers," American Jewish
Archives 1 (1966):3-19.
Family originally from
Piotrkow (Petrikov), Russian
Poland.
Frank. Nashville Jewry,
p. 134. Family originally
from Bremen, arrived in U.S.
in 1850s. See GENERAL WORKS.
Hirsch, Freida. Chronik der
Familien Moses Goldberg-Mainz
und Albert Hirsch-Goldberg.
Kirjath-Ono, Israel, 1965.
55 p. Family originally from
Karlsruhe. LBI.

GOLDBERGER
PD has records of family from
Budapest.
Kállai, László. A 150-éves
Goldberger gyar, Magyar
textilipar-történelem,
1784-1934. Budapest:
"Textilipar ujság," 1935.
History of Goldberger family
of Hungary and the textile
works it founded at Obuda.
NN.
Kempelen. Magyarországi Zsidó,
1:69; 2:31; 3:43, 127. See
GENERAL WORKS.

GOLDBLUM
See Nathan M. Reiss entry under
EDELMUTH. Includes Goldblum
family from Olkusz.

GOLDENSTEIN
See Louis L. Goldstein entry
under GOLDSTEIN.

GOLDING
AMH has family records.

GOLDKETTE
Ballin. Juden in Seesen,
p. 186. See GENERAL WORKS.

GOLDMAN
AMH has family records.
Keneseth Israel. See GENERAL
WORKS.

GOLDMANN
Goldmann, Nahum. The
Autobiography of Nahum
Goldmann: Sixty Years of
Jewish Life. Translated by
Helen Sebba. New York: Holt,
Rinehart & Winston, 1969.
357 p. "Visznevo, Childhood
in the Shtetl," pp. 1-9;
"Home and School Life in
Frankfurt," pp. 10-34. The
author (1895-1983), a Jewish
scholar and world Zionist
leader, was the son of
Solomon and Rebecca Goldmann
and the grandson of Avigdor
Leibmann Goldmann.

GOLDMARK
Goldmark Family, Pest, Hungary
and Philadelphia, Pa.
"Goldmark-Stern Letters,
1845-1870." Pamphlet.
Contains family letters and
genealogical information.
AJA.
LBI has family tree beginning
1799.
Goldmark, Josephine. Pilgrims
of '48: One Man's Part in the
Austrian Revolution of 1848,
and a Family migration to
America. New Haven: Yale
University Press, 1930.
311 p. "The Forty-Eighters

in the United States; Account
of the Emigration of Several
Jewish Families (Goldmark,
Wehle, and Brandeis) to
America in 1849," pt. 2,
pp. 167-296.
Kempelen. Magyarországi Zsidó,
2:29. See GENERAL WORKS.

GOLDREI
AMH has family records.

GOLDSCHIDT
CFM has family records.

GOLDSCHMIDT
AMH has family records.
CAJ has family tree from
Germany, 1621-1925; also
family tree, 1657-1872.
LBI has family trees beginning
1397, 1520, 1621, 1732, 1758,
1764, 1777, and 1812.
Ballin, Gerhard. "Die Familie
Goldschmidt-Oldenburg: Ein
Beitrag zu ihrer Geschichte
im 18. Und 19. Jahrhundert in
Oldenburg," Oldenburgische
Familienkunde 17, no. 1
(1975):123-54.
Ballin. Juden in Seesen,
pp. 187-90. See GENERAL
WORKS.
Brøndsted, Mogers. Meïr
Goldschmidt. København:
Gyldendals Forlagstrykkeri,
1965. 203 p. "Af Levi
Stamme," pp. 25-34. Meir
Aron Goldschmidt (1819-1887),
Danish novelist, political
writer, and journalist, was
the son of Aron (1792-1848)
and Lea (1797-1870)
Goldschmidt. Family
originally came to Denmark
from Hamburg.
See Daniel J. Cohen entry under
CLEVE. Goldschmidt family
history, pp. 48-53. Family
tree of family from Altona,
Germany, late 1500s to 1929,
p. 114.
Deeg, Peter. Hofjuden.
Nürnberg: Verlag Der Stürmer,
1938. 547 p. Includes
genealogical table of the

descendants of the Hofjuden,
Benedict Salomon Goldschmidt
(d. 1812). Goldschmidt
family of Frankfurt. MH.
1939 reprinting: DLC, NcD,
NjP, NN, NNC, OU.
Geadelte jüdische Familien.
Salzburg, 1891. Family of
Frankfurt, p. 30.
CAJ has list of the descendants
of Meyer Goldschmidt from
Eschwege.
Gronemann. Genealogische
Hannovers.
Hameln-Goldschmidt family.
Horowitz, Ludwig. "Hofjuden in
Kurhessen," Hessenland
(Kassel) 23 (1909):291-93,
307-309, 325-27. Mainly
deals with Benedikt
Goldschmidt from Frankfurt,
the first Hoffaktor.
JFF, nos. 7 and 26. Family
histories.
Kempelen. Magyarországi Zsidó,
2:9, 19. See GENERAL WORKS.
Kopp. Jüdischen Alsenz,
pp. 122-23. See GENERAL
WORKS.
Levison, Wilhelm. Die
Siegburger Familie Levison
und verwandte Familien.
Bonn: Röhrscheid, 1952.
187 p. CtY, DLC, NN, NNJ.
Meyer, Richard Moritz.
Verzeichnis der von Salomon
Benedict aus Frankfurt am
Main; stammenden Familien
Goldschmidt. Frankfurt am
Main: Druck von
R. Morgenstern, 1879. 55 p.
DLC, OCH.
Meyer, Stefan and Wilhelm
Pappenheim.
Ascendenz-Stammbaum von
Benedict Salomon Goldschmidt,
1769-1826 und seinen beiden
Ehefrauen, den schwestern
Bella und Sprinze (Sabine),
Braunschweig aufgestellt von
zweien ihrer Urenkel. Wien,
1909. Folio.
Majer-Leonhard, Hans.
Vorfahren und Nachfahren.
Eine genealogische Studie.
Frankfurt am Main: Limpert,

1929. 132 p. "Nachkommen
des Salomon Benedikt
Goldschmidt in Frankfurt,
d. 1821," pp. 53-132.
———. Querschnitt durch zwei
Stammbäume. [1. Franz Herzog
von Sachsen-Coburg und
Nachkommen. 2. Benedikt
Salomon Goldschmidt,
Kuchenbäcker in der
Frankfurter Judengasse--um
1800--und Nachkommen.]
Frankfurt am Main:
Genealogisches Gesellschaft,
1931. 4 p. OCH.
Schulte. Bonner Juden,
pp. 243-44. See GENERAL
WORKS.
Robert E. Levinson Papers.
Contain Joseph
Goldschmidt/Fromet Saumelin
Family Tree, prepared by Jon
Stedman, 1967. Families of
California. WJHC.
Stern. FAJF. Goldschmidt
family tree beginning in
Hamburg, Germany. See
GENERAL WORKS.
Worms, Daniel August.
Stammbaum der Familie
Goldschmidt. Frankfurt am
Main, 1902. 55 p. Includes
four family trees of family
from Cassel. LBI.

GOLDSCHMIDT-ROTHSCHILD
Deeg, Peter. Hofjuden.
Nürnberg: Verlag Der Stürmer,
1938. 547 p. Includes
genealogical table of the
descendants of the Hofjuden,
Benedict Salomon Goldschmidt
(d. 1812). Goldschmidt
family of Frankfurt. MH.
1939 reprinting: DLC, NcD,
NjP, NN, NNC, OU.
Gothaisches Genealogisches
Taschenbuch der
Freiherrlichen Häuser
(Gotha), 1917, pp. 313ff.;
1933 R.B.S., pp. 161ff.
Family of Frankfurt.
Wickenburg, Erik G.
"Frankfurter Familien. III.
Goldschmidt-Rothschild,"

Frankfurter Zeitung,
8.1.1933, p. 7.

GOLDSCHNEIDER
Josephthal, Hans. Stammbaum
der Familie Josephthal.
Berlin: L. Lamm, 1932.
10, 13 p. Twelve family
trees. Includes
Goldschneider, Josephthal,
Kleefeld, Neumann, Oser,
Schönberg, Sutro, and Ullmann
families. Descendants of
Lazarus Josephthal of Ansbach
(b. 1657). LBI, NN, NNJ,
OCH.

GOLDSHEDE
CFM has family records.

GOLDSMID
AMH has family records.
CFM has family records.
EJ (1972), 7:735-36.
Genealogical table,
descendants of Aaron Goldsmid
(1715-1782), through mid-20th
century. English family.
See GENERAL WORKS.
Bermant. The Cousinhood.
Genealogical table of
Anglo-Jewish family. See
GENERAL WORKS.
Cohen, Lucy. Some
Recollections of Claude
Goldsmid Montefiore,
1858-1938. London: Faber &
Faber, 1940. 277 p.
Includes genealogical tables.
DLC, MH, NcD, NN, OCl,
PPDrop.
Emden. Jews of Britain,
pp. 83ff. "The Great
Goldschmids." See GENERAL
WORKS.
Hyamson, Albert M. "An
Anglo-Jewish Family,"
Transactions of the Jewish
Historical Society of England
17 (1951/52):1-10. Includes
genealogical table,
descendants of Moses Simon
Levi of Cassel, d. before
28 Feb. 1678. Migrated to
Holland, then to England.

Wolf, "Anglo-Jewish
Families." See GENERAL
WORKS.

GOLDSMIT
AMH has family records.

GOLDSMIT-CASSEL
Prijs, Joseph. Pedigree of the
Family Goldsmit-Cassel of
Amsterdam (1650-1750).
Translated from the Dutch by
Oscar Schmeiler. Basel: By
the Author, 1937. 20 p.
Includes genealogical table.
NN.
————. Stammboom der familie
Goldsmit-Cassel te Amsterdam,
1650-1750 Bazel: Uitg. Van
den auteur, 1936. 22 p.
Includes genealogical table.
OCH, OU.

GOLDSMITH
AMH has family records.
CFM has family records.
Keneseth Israel. See GENERAL
WORKS.
Goldsmith, Joseph; Family Data,
1865-1871. In Hebrew and
German. Extracted from a
prayer book. AJA.
Goldsmith, Phillip. "Family
Record, 1844-1917." AJA.
Harris. Merchant Princes.
Goldsmith department store
family. Family is descended
from Isaac and Jacob
Goldsmith, originally from
Hainstadt in Baden. See
GENERAL WORKS.
Porta, Siegfried. Chronik der
Familie Lowenstein-Porta
sowie der Synagogengemende
Neuenkirchen im zusammenhang
mit der Geschichte der
Graftschaft Rietberg und
Israelitischen Konsistoriums
zu Cassel. Nach amtlichen
Quellen bearb. Bielefeld,
1922. 103 p. LBI.
Rosenbaum, Jeanette
(Whitehill). Myer Myers
Goldsmith, 1723-1795.
Philadelphia: Jewish
Publication Society of

America, 5714-1954. 141 p.
"Genealogy," pp. 60-64.
Family of New York.
Stern. FAJF. Goldsmith family
tree beginning in Rotterdam.
See GENERAL WORKS.
Stryker-Rodda, Harriet, ed.
Price-Goldsmith-Lowenstein
and Related Families,
1700-1967. From the
Collected Notes of Katherine
Goldsmith Lowenstein. New
York, 1967. 49 p. Includes
genealogical tables. DLC.

GOLDSTAND
Reychmann. Szkice
genealogiczne, pp. 83-84.
See GENERAL WORKS.

GOLDSTEIN
AJA has family tree beginning
1840.
LBI has family tree.
"Our Family (approx.
1840-1974)." A genealogical
record of the Goldstein
Family, including charts and
other documents. Chicago and
New York. 1974. AJA.
Berg, Gertrude. Molly and Me,
With Cherney Berg. New York:
McGraw-Hill, 1961. 278 p.
Especially, pp. 3-17, 28-37.
Molly Berg, the famous
American actress (1899-1966),
was the daughter of Jacob and
Dinah Edelstein Goldstein and
the granddaughter of Harris
and Czerna Goldstein and
Mordecai Edelstein. The
Edelstein family was from
Lublin.
Goldstein, Louis L. "The
Goldstein Family History," in
Jewish Life in Indiana (Fort
Wayne, Ind.: Indiana Jewish
Historical Society, Inc.,
November 1980), pp. 19-42.
Author is descendant of Max
Goldenstein of Savron, Russia
and Hannah Teper of Teraspol,
Rumania. Author's father was
David Goldstein, 1878-1963.
Family settled in
Indianapolis and Rushville,

Indiana in 1904 or 1905.
Goldstein, Shlomo. Mizlatopol
to Givataim (From Zlatopol to
Givataim, Israel). 1964.
299 p. Essentially an
autobiography, but with some
genealogical value. JNUL,
MH.
Henderson, Leslie M. The
Goldstein Story. Melbourne,
Australia: Stockland Press,
1973. 189 p. Genealogical
table. CtY, DLC, NN, OCH,
TxU, WU.
Kempelen. Magyarországi Zsidó,
2:136; 3:97, 140. See
GENERAL WORKS.
Keyssner, ? "Die fränkische
Familie Goldstein,"
Familienkunde (Würzburg),
no. 4 (Nov. 1935):3.
See Daniel Jay Rottenberg entry
under ROTTENBERG.
Sher, Eva Goldstein. Life with
Farmer Goldstein. New York:
Funk & Wagnalls, 1967. 247
p. Story of the author's
Russian immigrant family
which settled in New Jersey
to farm and deal in
livestock.
Skeller, Ulrich. "Die
Geschichte der Familie
Goldstein V. der
Oberschlesischen
Holz-Industrie A.G. Beuthen
O/S," Mitteilungen des
Verbandes ehemaliger
Breslauer und Schlesier (Tel
Aviv), no. 45 (April/Mai
1979):9-10.

GOLDSTICK
Goldstick, Julie. The
Goldstick Family Tree. New
York, 1978. AJHS.

GOLDSTOFF
Rosenstein. Unbroken Chain,
pp. 228ff. Descendants of
Zalman Goldstoff. See
GENERAL WORKS.

GOLDSTONE
AMH has family records.
"Genealogical Data Pertaining

to the Hiller-Goldstone
Family." AJA.
Goldstone, Lafayette.
"Genealogy of Several Old New
York Families, Arranged with
Particular Reference to the
Ancestry of John Lewis, Lewis
Goldstone, and Herman
Hendricks Goldstone, also
Showing the True Relationship
of Some of their Cousins,
Aunts, Uncles, and Other
Family Connections;
Illustrated by Vida Lindo
Guterman." AJA.
Stern. FAJF. Hiller family
tree beginning in Kurnick,
Germany. Later generation
changed name to Goldstone.
See GENERAL WORKS.

GOLDSTUCKER
Kopp. Jüdischen Alsenz,
pp. 137-38. Genealogical
information on Goldstücker
family. See GENERAL WORKS.

GOLDSTUCKER-LOB
Kopp. Jüdischen Alsenz,
p. 123. Genealogical
information on
Goldstücker-Löb family. See
GENERAL WORKS.

GOLDSZMIDT
See KORCZAKS.

GOLDWATER, GOLDWASSER
AMH has Goldwater family
records.
Goldwater, Barry M. "Three
Generations of Pants and
Politics in Arizona," Journal
of Arizona History 13 (Autumn
1972):141-58. Descendants of
Hirsch and Elizabeth
Goldwasser of Konin, Poznan
Province, Poland.
———. With No Apologies: The
Personal and Political
Memoirs. New York: William
Morrow· and Co., 1979. 320 p.
"Roots," pp. 17-24. The
famous U.S. Senator from
Arizona is the great-grandson
of Hirsch and Elizabeth

Goldwasser of Konin, Poznan
Province, and the grandson of
Michael and Sarah Nathan
Goldwasser (later Goldwater).
Michael immigrated to
California and Arizona.
Goldwater, Jerrold. "Report of
An Interview with Mr. Jerrold
Goldwater ... Los Angeles,
Calif., October 25, 1967, by
Norton B. Stern." [Santa
Monica, Calif.] 1967.
Typescript, 3 p. "This
report traces the Goldwater
family history starting with
Jerrold's grandfather,
Joseph, who came to Los
Angeles in 1850." AJA, WJHC.
Harris. Merchant Princes.
Goldwater department store
family of Arizona. See
GENERAL WORKS.
Kramer, William M. and Norton
B. Stern. "Early California
Associations of Michel
Goldwater and His Family,"
Western States Jewish
Historical Quarterly 4 (July
1972):173-96.
Stocker, Joseph. "The Dynasty
of Goldwater," in Jewish
Roots in Arizona: Journal of
the Tercentenary Committee of
the Phoenix Jewish Community
Council, Nov. 1954, pp. 7-13.

GOLDZIHER
Kempelen. Magyarországi Zsidó,
1:109, 121. See GENERAL
WORKS.

GOLLANCZ
Gollancz, Samuel Marcus.
Biographical Sketches and
Selected Verses by the Rev.
Rabbi Samuel Marcus Gollancz;
Translated and Edited from
the Original German by His
Son Sir Hermann Gollancz.
London: Oxford University
Press, 1930. 219 p.
Includes genealogical tables.
Anglo-Jewish family
originally from Bremen area
in Germany. Sir Samuel
Marcus Gollancz, 1820-1900;

Sir Hermann Gollancz,
1852-1930. CSt, DLC, NIC,
OCH, PPDrop, TxU.

GOLLAS
Kempelen. Magyarországi Zsidó,
3:122. See GENERAL WORKS.

GOLLEWSKI
AMH has family records.

GOLLIN
AMH has family records.

GOLODETZ
Golodetz, Lazar. History of
the Family Golodetz. New
York, 1954. 44 p. YIVO.

GOLSTEIN
AMH has family records.

GOLTZ
CAJ has family records.
Shanberg, R. Brock (lives in
Arkansas). The Descendants
of Nissen Shanberg and
Related Families. N.p.,
1981. 115 p. Family trees,
pp. 58a, 64, 80. Much of the
book, however, is a family
table. Family came from
Jałowka and Swisłocz near
Bialystok. It begins in late
1700s or early 1800s with
"Nissen Shanberg
[1830/34-1920] who was the
son of Yehuda Benyomin (Labie
Binnie) Kurkin...." The
descendants are now located
in U.S. Includes Goltz,
Kaplan, Kurkin, Provus,
Sakol, Sakolsky, Serlin,
Shamberg, and Shanberg
families. CAJ.

GOMBASZOGI
Kempelen. Magyarországi Zsidó,
1:85. Gombaszögi family.
See GENERAL WORKS.

GOMES
AMH has family records.

GOMEZ
CFM has family records.

JE, 6:41. "Genealogical Tree
of the Gómez Family."
French, Spanish, and U.S.
descendants of Isaac Gómez
(b. Madrid, d. France), 17th
to mid-19th century. See
GENERAL WORKS.
Birmingham. The Grandees. See
GENERAL WORKS.
Gómez, Isaac. Genealogical
files. AJA.
"Luis Moses Gomez (Family
Tree)." [New York?, 1982?]
1 genealogical table. "Luis
Gomez established a trading
post near Newburgh, New
York." AJHS.
Phillips, N. Taylor.
"Genealogy of the Gomez
Family in America,"
Publications of the American
Jewish Historical Society 17
(1907):197.
————. "Items Relating to the
Gomez Family in America, New
York," Publications of the
American Jewish Historical
Society 27 (1920):279.
"Lineage of Members of the
Gomez Family Mentioned in
These Records," in David de
Sola Pool's Portraits Etched
in Stone: Early Jewish
Settlers, 1682-1831 (New
York: Columbia University
Press, 1952), p. 220. Family
of New York, covers 18th
through early 19th century.
Stern. FAJF. Gomez family
trees beginning in:
(I) Spain; and (II) Bordeaux.
See GENERAL WORKS.

GOMPERS
AMH has family records.

GOMPERTZ
AMH has family records.
CFM has family records.
Rachel and Wallich. Berliner
Grosskaufleute, 2:42-65.
"Die Gompertz." Also,
Genealogical Table No. 1 at
end of vol. 1, covers
1664-1851. See GENERAL
WORKS.

Schulte. Bonner Juden,
pp. 247-48, 252-53.

GOMPERZ
EJ (1972), 7:771. Genealogical
table of branches of family
in Brno, Berlin, Budapest,
Vienna, and Prague. See
GENERAL WORKS.
Kaufmann, David and Max
Freudenthal. Die Familie
Gomperz. Frankfurt am Main:
J. Kauffmann in Komm., 1907.
437 p. (Zur Geschichte
jüdischer Familien, 3.)
Family of Austria, Germany,
and Hungary. LBI, MH, NN,
OCH, OU, PP.
Kempelen. Magyarországi Zsidó,
1:39, 83, 84; 3:66. See
GENERAL WORKS.
Nathan, N.M. "Besprechung des
Werkes von
Kaufmann-Freudenthal, Die
Familie Gomperz," MGWJ
(1907).
Schnee. Hoffinanz und Staat,
1:78-96. Includes
genealogical information and
chart on family of
Brandenburg-Prussia, 17th to
19th century. "Die Familie
Gomperz in Dienste der
Hohenzollern." See GENERAL
WORKS.
————, vol. 3. Descendants of
Mardocha Gumpel (d. 1664),
through mid-19th century.
"Stammtafel der Hoffaktoren
familie Gomperz." See
GENERAL WORKS.
Wolf, Ernest. Verzeichnis der
Nachkommen des Leopold Wolf,
1800-1866, Eisenstadt, Rosa
Spitz., 1800-1882, Eisenstadt.
Wien, 1924. 123 p. Includes
six family trees. Includes
Wolf, Gomperz, Latzko,
Oppenheimer, and Wertheimer
families. NN, OCH.

GONOSZ
Kempelen. Magyarországi Zsidó,
2:88. See GENERAL WORKS.

GONSALES
CFM has family records.

GONZALEZ
Beinart, Haim. "Three
Generations, Members of One
Family Tried by the
Inquisition," (In Hebrew.)
Tarbiz 30 (1960):46-61.
Includes González family of
Spain, 16th century.

GOODHART
AJA has genealogical files.

GOODMAN
AJA has family tree from
Philadelphia.
AMH has family records.
CFM has family records.
Sokobin, Samuel, comp.
[Biographical Data on the
Galewsky and Goodman
Families, St. Helena, Calif.]
Typescript. 3 p. AJA, WJHC.

GOODYEAR
AMH has family records.

GOOTMAN
Gootman Family, Cincinnati.
Gootman, Yosef. Memories of
Our Parents, Isaac and Rachel
Gootman, Their Children and
Their Families. N.p., n.d.
In Hebrew and English. AJA.

GORDON
AMH has family records.
Blaustein, Esther. When Momma
Was the Landlord. New York:
Harper and Row, 1972. 201 p.
Family of Newark, New Jersey;
originally came from Polanov,
Russia.
Book of the Descendants of Dr.
Benjamin Lee and Dorothy
Gordon. Contributors: Gordon
Philo Baker and others.
Ventnor, N.J.: Ventnor
Publishers, 1972. 176 p.
AJHS.
Chelminsky-Lajmer, "Jewish
Surnames." See GENERAL
WORKS.
Davis, M. "The Name of

Gordon," Jewish Chronicle
(London), Sept. 1, 1905,
p. 15.
AJA has Aaron Gordon
genealogical files.
Gordon, Benjamin. Between Two
Worlds: The Memoirs of a
Physician. New York: Bookman
Associates, 1952. 354 p.
"The Story of a Name,"
pp. 42-62. DLC, ICJ, NN,
OCH.
Rapoport, Rollin A. "The Name
'Gordon' Among Jews," Jewish
Chronicle (London), June 1,
1934, p. 21. Also see
subsequent issues of the
Chronicle for rejoinders by
M. Sanders (June 22, 1934,
p. 36), M. Kliman (July 6,
1934, p. 37), and
M.G. Liverman (July 20, 1934,
p. 30).
Shick, Maete Gordon. The
Burden and the Trophy: An
Autobiography, translated by
Mary J. Reuben. New York:
Pageant, 1957. 209 p. The
author (1885-   ) discusses
her Lithuanian childhood and
adolescence in order to
provide cultural roots for
her grandchildren. DLC, OCH.
Waldman, Bess. The Book of
Tziril: A Family Chronicle.
Marblehead, Mass.: Micah
Publications, 1981. 250 p.
In narrative form, this book
covers the life of some of
the descendants of Zalman
Yitchok and Dvera Esther
Gordon from 1840-1890s in
Russia and Jersey City, N.J.
Includes the Gordon family of
Kafkaz (near Tiflis in the
Caucasus region); the
Rosenblum family of Kovno
(Chana Gordon and Reb Yosef
Rosenblum); Yosef Yacov and
Tziril Miriam Gordon
Wilkimirsky (changed to
Friedman in U.S.) of Wilki
near Kovno; and Abraham
(Alte) and Hinda Dvera
Friedman Lipschutz of New
Jersey. Abraham Lipschutz

was the son of Reb Yeheschel
and Rivka Lipschutz of
Vienna. The author is the
daughter of Abraham and Hinda
Lipschutz. AJA, AJHS, DLC.
Yaoz. Album Shel. See
GENERAL WORKS.

GOROVE
Kempelen. Magyarországi Zsidó,
1:100; 2:31. See GENERAL
WORKS.

GOSDORFER
Berolzheimer, Michael. Family
tree beginning 1503. LBI.

GOSLA
AMH has family records.

GOTFRED
Margolinsky, Julius. "Abraham
Gotfred de Meza og hans
familie," Jødisk Samfund,
Jan. 1955. Family of
Denmark. YIVO.

GOTTESMANN
Kempelen. Magyarországi Zsidó,
2:47. See GENERAL WORKS.

GOTTFRIED
Rosenblum, Davida. Relatives.
New York: The Dial Press,
1979. 201 p. Family of
Brooklyn, N.Y.

GOTTHEIMER
CFM has family records.

GOTTHELF
See Esmond S. De Beer entry
under BARDEN.

GOTTHELFT
Gotthelft, Richard.
Erinnerungen aus guter alter
Zeit. Kassel: By the Author,
1922. 74 p. Family of
Kassel. Descendants of Abr.
Herz (b. 1757) and his son
Herz Gotthelft (1790-1871).
LBI.
Sichel, Frieda and Karl
Hermann. The Gotthelft

Family Tree, 1670-1966.
Johannesburg, South Africa,
1966. 12 p. A large portion
of family are Americans.
LBI, AJHS.
————. Challenge of the Past:
A Memoir. Johannesburg: By
the Author, 1975. 117 p.
Includes Gotthelft family
tree. Family originally from
Kassel area. DLC, LBI, OCH.

GOTTLIEB
AJA has Leo Gottlieb
genealogical files.
Kempelen. Magyarországi Zsidó,
1:134. See GENERAL WORKS.
Kurzweil, Arthur. From
Generation to Generation: How
to Trace Your Jewish
Genealogy and Personal
History. New York: William
Morrow and Company, Inc.,
1980. Family of Borgo Prund,
Transylvania, pp. 37-53.

GOTTSCHALK
Chelminsky-Lajmer, "Jewish
Surnames." See GENERAL
WORKS.
Korn, Bertram W. "A Note on
the Jewish Ancestry of Louis
Moreau Gottschalk, American
Pianist and Composer,"
American Jewish Archives 15
(1963):117.
Lewin, A. "Die Gottschalke von
Bachrach und Kreuznach,"
Frankf. Israel Gemeindeblatt,
July 1933, pp. 279-80.
Covers 1400-1933.
Marrocco, W. Thomas.
"Gottschalkiana: New Light on
the Gottschalks and the
Bruslés," Louisiana History
12 (Winter 1971):59-66.
Family of Louis Moreau
Gottschalk.
Rose. Schoinger Juden. See
GENERAL WORKS.

GOTTSCHAU
Kopp. Jüdischen Alsenz,
pp. 124-27. See GENERAL
WORKS.

GOTTSCHO
Kopp. Jüdischen Alsenz,
pp. 124-27. See GENERAL
WORKS.

GOUGUENHEIM
Guggenheim-Grünberg, Florence.
"Die rabbiner Familie
Gouguenheim von Metz-aus
Lengnau stammend,"
Israelitisches Wochenblatt
(Zürich) 51, no. 29
(1951):35; no. 30
(1951):13-14.

GOULD
AMH has family records.
"Items Relating to the Gould
Family and the Jews of
Newport," Publications of the
American Jewish Historical
Society 27 (1920):423.

GOULSTON
AMH has family records.

GOZONY
Kempelen. Magyarországi Zsidó,
1:48. Gózony family. See
GENERAL WORKS.

GRAAN
AMH has family records.

GRAANBOOM
"De Zweedse familie Graanboom;
een Hebreeuwse
familiegeschiedenis,
Inleiding, Hebreeuwse tekst
en summary door L. Fuks,"
Studia Rosenthaliana 1, no. 2
(1967):85-106.
Mulder, Sam. Isr. Het Geslacht
Graanboom. Rotterdam, 1858.
Offprint from Israëitische
Almanak voor het Jaar 5619,
1858. BR.

GRABMANN
Kempelen. Magyarországi Zsidó,
2:134. See GENERAL WORKS.

GRABOWSKY-ATHERSTONE
AMH has family records.

GRADE

GRADE
Davies, Hunter. The Grades:
The First Family of British
Entertainment. London:
Weidenfeld & Nicolson, 1981.
268 p. "The [Baron] Grade
Family Tree," pp. 246-47.
Real name was Winogradsky.

GRADENWITZ
LBI has family tree beginning
1796.

GRADIS
JE, 6:63. Descendants table
from David Gradis of Bordeaux
(1650-1750). See GENERAL
WORKS.
Carmoly, Elkiam. "Galerie
Israélite Française," Archives
Israélites de France 22
(1861):610-14, 685-88; 23
(1862):29-34.
Gradis, Henry. Notice sur la
famille Gradis et sur la
Maison Gradis et fils de
Bordeaux. Bordeaux, 1875.
Graetz, Heinrich. "Die Familie
Gradis," MGWJ 24
(1875):447-59; 25
(1876):78-85.

GRADIZ
AMH has family records.

GRADWOHL
Gradwohl Family. "The Story
that Blanche Told,"
genealogical and biographical
information concerning the
Gradwohl family, 1870-1974,
by Barbara Mc Kinlay. Los
Angeles, Calif., 1974. AJA.

GRAETZ
AJA has family tree of German
historian Heinrich Graetz
(1817-1891).
AMH has family records.

GRAETZER
LBI has family tree.

GRAFENBERG
Gräfenberg, Selig.
Stammbaumblätter der Familie

Gräfenberg. Frankfurt am
Main, 1916. 20 p. YIVO.
Family Tree Revised by Carl
H. Grafenberg of San
Francisco, 1975. N.p.
Descendants of Selig Nathan
Gräfenberg, born in Adelebsen
in 1752 and died there in
1834. LBI.

GRALNICK
See Daniel Jay Rottenberg entry
under ROTTENBERG. Includes
Gralnick family.

GRANADIER, GRAND
Doroshkin, Yitzchak Yankl.
Roots of the Granadier
(Grand) Family: From
Zhitkovitch (A Shtetl in
White Russia) to America.
Translated from the Yiddish
by Mindy C. Gross. West Palm
Beach, Fla., 1978. 205 p.
AJHS. JNUL has the Yiddish
edition: Vortsalen foon der
Mishpache Granadier foon
Zhitkovitch biz Amerika.

GRANER
Kempelen. Magyarországi Zsidó,
2:35. See GENERAL WORKS.

GRANICHSTADTEN
Kempelen. Magyarországi Zsidó,
2:58. Granichstädten family.
See GENERAL WORKS.

GRANT
AJA has Rosa Mayer Grant
genealogical files.

GRAPF
See Daniel Jay Rottenberg entry
under ROTTENBERG. Includes
Grapf family.

GRATZ
Cohen Family Papers, 1802-1945.
Includes genealogical data on
Cohen, Gratz, Etting, and
Nathan families of Maryland.
Maryland Historical Society
Library.
Gratz-Moses Family,
Philadelphia. Biographical

Information, 1883, 1898,
1900, 1945, 1962, 1980.
Includes family history
(Xeroxed). PJAC.
EJ (1972), 7:858. Descendants
of Solomon Gratz (Shelomo
Zalman of Langendorf) to late
19th century. See GENERAL
WORKS.
JE, 6:82. "Genealogical Tree
of the Gratz Family."
Descendants of Michael Gratz
(b. Germany, 1740;
d. Philadelphia, 1811),
through mid-19th century.
Family of U.S. See GENERAL
WORKS.
Brilling, Bernhard. "Die
ersten (Schlesischen) Juden
in USA," Jüdischen
Nachrichtenblatt (Berlin),
3.24.1939. Family originally
from Langendorf OS.
Fish, Sidney M. "The Ancestral
Heritage of the Gratz
Family," in Gratz College
Anniversary Volume,
(Philadelphia, 1971),
pp. 47-62.
Gratz Family Papers, n.d.
1 chart. Genealogical chart
listing the descendants of
Michael and Miriam Simon
Gratz, including birth,
death, and marriage dates.
Not all of the information is
complete. PJAC.
Orgler Family. "Genealogy of
the Orgler Family, Including
Some Information on Bloch,
and Gratz Families, Tracing
the Ancestry of Rebecca
Gratz, Germany and the United
States, 1650-1939." AJA.
Gratz, Thomas B. "Various
Letters and Articles
Pertaining to Gratz and His
Family, Including Some
Genealogical Material."
Avalon, N.J. March 1-Dec. 4,
1975. AJA.
"Genealogies of the Hendricks
Family, Including: (1)
Ancestors of Henry Solomon
Hendricks and Rosalie Gratz
Hendricks; (2) Illustrated

Family Tree by Vida Lindo
Guiterman." AJA.
Stern. FAJF. Family tree of
Gratz descendants of Rabbi
Jonathan of Cracow whose son
took name of Gratz. See
GENERAL WORKS.

GRATZE
Kempelen. Magyarországi Zsidó,
1:51. See GENERAL WORKS.

GRAUER
Kempelen. Magyarországi Zsidó,
2:55. See GENERAL WORKS.

GREDITZ
AMH has family records.

GREEN
AJA has Cathy Green
genealogical files.
AMH has family records.
CFM has family records.
Green, Cathy. "My Ancestors: A
Genealogy of the
Green-Edelstein Family."
Louisville, Ky., Jan. 1975.
AJA.

GREENBAUM
Barbe, Lizzie J,
"Autobiography," 1934.
Includes family tree
beginning in Germany,
1719-1931. AJA.

GREENBERG
See Meyer Ellenbogen entry
under KATZENELLENBOGEN.
Genealogical table.
Rosenstein. Unbroken Chain,
pp. 104ff. See GENERAL
WORKS.

GREENEBAUM
AJA has genealogical files.
Greenebaum and Gerstle
Genealogy, 1740-1954. These
families were pioneer San
Francisco families. WJHC.
Narell. Our City. Includes
genealogical charts of
pioneer San Francisco family,
descendants of Herman
Greenebaum (b. Münchweiler,

1826; d. 1883). See GENERAL
WORKS.

GREENHOOD
Neumann, Dorothy. "The
Greenhoods of San Bernardino
[California]: A Memoir,"
Western States Jewish
Historical Quarterly 15
(Apr. 1983):203-213. Family
of Ralph [Rudolph] Greenhood
(1868-1941), who was born in
Niederstetten, Württemberg,
Germany, and Fanny Gusky
Greenhood (1872-1963), who
was born in Wieruszow,
Poland.

GREENHUT
AJA has family tree beginning
1290.

GREENWOOD
AMH has family records.

GREGORY
AMH has family records.

GREIF
Whitehill, Milford H.
"Greif--One of Baltimore's
Great Names in the Clothing
Industry", Generations (Jewish
Historical Society of
Maryland, Baltimore) 3
(June 1982).

GRELLING
LBI has family tree beginning
1746.

GREN
Semi-Gotha, 1:22. Gren af
Rossö family. See GENERAL
WORKS.

GRENVILLE
AMH has family records.

GRIESHABER
Kempelen. Magyarországi Zsidó,
1:93. See GENERAL WORKS.

GRIFF
AJA has family tree beginning
18th century.

GRIFFITH
AMH has family records.

GRILL
Kempelen. Magyarországi Zsidó,
3:122, 123. See GENERAL
WORKS.

GRINFELD
Kempelen. Magyarországi Zsidó,
1:31, 32. See GENERAL WORKS.

GROAK
Kempelen. Magyarországi Zsidó,
2:66. Groák family. See
GENERAL WORKS.

GRODEL, GROEDEL
LBI has family trees beginning
1782 and 1818.
Herz, Heinrich. Zur Geschichte
der Familie Herz in Weilburg.
Aachen, 1906. 67 p.
Descendants table of Herz
Feist, 1710-1746. Contains
information on Drucker and
Groedel families.
Kempelen. Magyarországi Zsidó,
1:130. Groedel family. See
GENERAL WORKS.
Ullmann, Elias.
Familien-Register und
Stammtafeln des Ephraim
Grödel und des Lob Cassel
(Cassella) und deren
Nachkommen als Verwandschafts
Nachweis behufs erhebung v.
Ansprüchen an die Moritz
Kaufmann'sche
Familien-Stiftung in Fürth im
Königreich Bayern. Frankfurt
am Main, 1872. Grödel, Baron
Richard. Stammbaum. 3.,
verb. aufl. Wien, 1926.
1 p. 59 x 40cm. Descendants
of Ephraim and Baruch David
Grödel of Friedberg, Hessen.

GROOMSFELT
AMH has family records.

GROOT, DE
See DE GROOT.

GROSS
Gross, George M. "The

Ancestors of George M.
Gross," Virginia Tidewater
Genealogy (Hampton, Va.), 6
(1975):101-104; 7
(1976):23-33. Includes
Adelson, Genfanstein, Gross,
Malofsky, Mermelstein,
Pildes, and Shapiro families.
Norfolk Public Library,
Norfolk, Virginia.
Spear, M.E. "Genealogy of
Isaac Gross and His
Descendants." N.p., 1957.
11 p. Allen County Public
Library, Ft. Wayne, Indiana.
Kempelen. Magyarországi Zsidó,
1:39, 130; 2:47, 88, 125,
126; 3:21, 115. Gross, Grosz
family. See GENERAL WORKS.
Rosenstein. Unbroken Chain,
pp. 664ff. See GENERAL
WORKS.

GROSSMAN
Chelminsky-Lajmer, "Jewish
Surnames." See GENERAL
WORKS.

GROSSMANN
Kempelen. Magyarországi Zsidó,
2:17, 90, 91, 92. See
GENERAL WORKS.

GROSZ
See Kempelen entry under GROSS.
Kempelen. Magyarországi Zsidó,
2:126. See GENERAL WORKS.

GROSZMANN
Segal, Lore Groszmann. Other
People's Houses. New York:
Harcourt, Brace and World,
1964. 312 p. Story of
family of Vienna that fled
Austria just before W.W.II
for England, then Dominican
Republic, and finally to U.S.
after W.W.II.

GROTTE
Grotte, Alfred. "Zur
Genealogie der Familie
Grotte," JFF, no. 9
(1927):206-210. From 1500.
Family of Prague and
Sulzbach.

————. "Hermann Mayer aus
Kuttenplan," JFF, no. 30
(1932):545-546.

GRUBER
Kempelen. Magyarországi Zsidó,
3:105. See GENERAL WORKS.

GRUISEN
See VAN GRUISEN.
AMH has family records.

GRUM
Kempelen. Magyarországi Zsidó,
2:38. See GENERAL WORKS.

GRUMME
Semi-Gotha, 1:140. See GENERAL
WORKS.

GRUN
Kempelen. Magyarországi Zsidó,
1:85; 2:35; 3:51. Grün
family. See GENERAL WORKS.

GRUNBAUM
LBI has Grünbaum family tree
beginning 1490.
Kempelen. Magyarországi Zsidó,
1:150; 3:51. Grünbaum
family. See GENERAL WORKS.

GRUNEWALD
Grünewald, Simon.
Erinnerungen. N.p., n.d.
18, 8 p. Includes family
history of the author
(1868-1962), a hauptlehrer in
Königshütte/Oberschlesien.
LBI.

GRUNFELD
Grünfeld, Heinrich. Falk
Valentin Grünfeld und sein
Werk. Geschichte der Firma
und Familie ab Jechiel
Grünfeld, Lehrer in Kempen,
1767-1827. By the Author,
1932. LBI.
Jastrow, Marie. A Time to
Remember: Growing Up in New
York before the Great War.
New York: W.W. Norton, 1979.
The author nostalgically
recalls her family's life in
Yarac, Serbia, and immigrant

life in New York City,
1905-1917. Daughter of
Julius Grunfeld (1869-?).
Her mother's maiden name was
Deutsch. Kempelen. Magyarországi Zsidó,
1:31, 32; 2:124. Grünfeld
family. See GENERAL WORKS.

GRUNHUT
AMH has family records.
Kempelen. Magyarországi Zsidó,
2:123. Grünhut family. See
GENERAL WORKS.

GRUNSFELD
LBI has family tree beginning
1749.

GRUNWALD
AMH has family records.
CAJ has family records.
Kempelen. Magyarországi Zsidó,
3:48, 62, 94. Grünwald
family. See GENERAL WORKS.

GRUSIN
Heimovics, Rachel. "A Family
Affair: Marking 60 Years that
Go Back to One Woman," Jewish
Chicago 1, no. 4 (July
1982):9, 11, 13. Discusses
the B'nais Dena Cousin's Club
of Chicago. Dena Grusin
arrived in U.S. from Riga,
Latvia, in 1904.

GRUSSNER
Kempelen. Magyarországi Zsidó,
3:26. Grüssner family. See
GENERAL WORKS.

GRUSZCYNSKY
CAJ has family records.

GRUZENBERG
CAJ has family records.

GRYNSZPAN
Walters, Judith A. Documents
and Charts Relating to
Certain Jewish Families....
In Particular, Grynszpan,
Kmiotek, Melcer, Mycenmacher,
Pyszna, Rozen, and Wejntrop;
In the Towns of Przasnysz and

Ciechanow, Warsaw, Poland.
Washington, D.C.: By the
Author, 1978. 58 p.
Contains introduction,
documents, translations, map,
family group sheets,
photographs, index, and
large, fold-out genealogical
chart.

GRZIMISH
AMH has family records.

GUBAY
CFM has family records.

GUBBAY
AMH has family records.

GUDELSKI, GUDELSKY
See Daniel Jay Rottenberg entry
under ROTTENBERG.

GUDEMANN
CAJ has family records.

GUDENUS
Kempelen. Magyarországi Zsidó,
1:56; 2:53. See GENERAL
WORKS.

GUEDALLA
AMH has family records.
CFM has family records.

GUEST
AMH has family records.

GUGGENBERGER
Kempelen. Magyarországi Zsidó,
2:36. See GENERAL WORKS.

GUGGENHEIM
AMH has family records.
CFM has family records.
EJ (1972), 7:967. A
genealogical table of
descendants of Simon
Guggenheim (1792-1869) of
U.S. Family originally from
Switzerland. See GENERAL
WORKS.
Arends, Dorothea Anne. "The
Guggenheims in Alaska."
Master's thesis, Columbia
University, 1973. 73 p.

Birmingham. Our Crowd. See
GENERAL WORKS.
Brilling, Bernhard. "Der Name
Maram, Marum. Zur Geschichte
der Familien Guggenheim, Weil
und anderer Nachkommen des
Meir von Rothenburg," in
Forschung am Judentum.
Festschrift zum 60.
Geburtstag von Lothar
Rothschild, (Bern, 1970),
pp. 99-125. DLC, ICU.
Chatwin, Bruce. "The
Guggenheim Saga," The Sunday
Times Magazine (London),
Nov. 23, 1975, pp. 34-40,
54-67. Family of U.S.
Davis, John H. The
Guggenheims: An American
Epic. New York: William
Morrow, 1978. 608 p.
Dienemann, Max and Siegfried
Guggenheim. Stammbaum der
Familie Guggenheim aus Worms.
(Rothschild-Dienemann-Guggenh
im). Offenbach a.M.:
H. Cramer, 1926. 21 p.
7 genealogical tables. DLC,
NN, OCH.
Great American Families. New
York: W.W. Norton, 1977.
192 p. "Guggenheim,"
pp. 90-123.
Guggenheim-Grünberg, Florence.
"Die Lengnauer Vorfahren der
'Kupfer-Guggenheim' in
Amerika," Israelitisch
Wochenblatt (Zürich), no. 32,
Aug. 27, 1953, pp. 49-51;
no. 33, p. 34.
————. "Der Pinkas Guggenheim
von Lengnau," Schweizerisches
Archiv für Volkskunde (Basel)
49 (1953):201-206.
Hoyt, Edwin Palmer. The
Guggenheims and the American
Dream. New York: Funk &
Wagnalls, 1967.
Kahn, Ludwig David. Die
Nachkommen des Simon
Guggenheim (1730-1799) von
Endingen. Genealogie einer
schweizerisch-jüdischen
Familie. Basel, 1969.
118 p. Genealogical tables.
DLC.

Lomask, Milton. Seed Money:
The Guggenheim Story. New
York: Farrar, Straus, 1964.
307 p.
Lyll, Eugene P. "Founding the
House of Guggenheim,"
Hampton's Magazine 24
(1910/11):256-67.
O'Connor, Harvey. The
Guggenheims: The Making of an
American Dynasty. New York:
Covici, Friede, 1937. 496 p.
Includes genealogical table.
Tänzer. Juden in Tirol,
p. 719. See GENERAL WORKS.

GUGGENHEIMER
"Guggenheimer Family Tree,
1779-1953." Typescript and
printed. AJA.
Cone, Sydney. Genealogy of the
Guggenheimer, Cone and
Related Families.
Greensboro, North Carolina,
1960.
See Sydney M. Cone entry under
AMBACH.
Miedel, Julius. Die Juden in
Memmingen. Aus Anlass der
Memminger Synagoge verfasst.
Memmingen: Otto, 1909.
117 p. Includes genealogical
chart of Guggenheimer family.
DLC, LBI, NN, OCH, OU,
PPDrop.
Stern. FAJF. Guggenheimer
family tree beginning in
Germany. See GENERAL WORKS.
Untermeyer, Sophie Guggenheimer
and Alix Williamson. Mother
is Minnie. Garden City,
N.Y.: Doubleday, 1960.
213 p. Biography of Mrs.
Charles S. Guggenheimer.
Family of New York.

GUHRAUER
CAJ has family tree, 1788-1921.

GULSTON
AMH has family records.

GUMPEL
Berliner, Moritz. Stammbaum
der Samonschen Familie.
3. Aufl. Hannover, 1912.

31 p. 14 family trees
containing more than 3,000
names. Samson family of
Wolffenbüttel; descendants of
Marcus Gumpel Moses Fulda
(16?-1733). MWalB, OCH.
Raphael, J. "Die Hamburger
Familie Gumpel und der
Dichter Heinrich Heine,"
Zeitschrift für die
Geschichte der Juden (Tel
Aviv) 6, no. 1 (1969):33-38.
Schnee. Hoffinanz und Staat,
vol. 3. "Stammtafel der
Hoffaktoren familie Gomperz."
Descendants of Mardocha
Gumpel (d. 1664), through
mid-19th century.
Schulze, Hans. Beiträge zur
Geschichte der jüdischen
Gemeinde in Wolfenbüttel.
Wolfenbüttel, 1964. 87 p.
Includes Gumpel and Samson
families' genealogies. LBI.

GUMPERTZ
AMH has family records.
CAJ has family records.
LBI has family tree beginning
1653.

GUMPERZ
Gumperz, Sigmund.
Familien-Register der Lion
Gumperz und s. Nachkommen.
Budapest, 1888. Beginning
17th century. LBI.

GUMPLOWICZ
Bałaban. Żydów w Krakowie.
Genealogical table of the
descendants of Abraham
Gumplowicz, 19th to 20th
century. See GENERAL WORKS.

GUNDERSCHEIMER
AJA has genealogical files.

GUNSBERG
AMH has family records.

GUNSBURGER
Günsberger, Moses. Die
Günsberger im Elsas,
Guebwiller-Strasbourg, 1913.

GUNZBERG
Belinson, Moses Eliezer.
Shelume Emune Yisrael.
Odessa, 1898-1901. 3 vols.
Includes Günzberg family of
Poland and Russia. DLC.
Berlin, Moisei Iosofovich. Ein
Wort über die Familie
Günzberg. St. Petersburgh:
M. Ettinger, 1858. 12 p.
Günzberg noble family of
Russia. JNUL.
Eisenstadt. Da'at Kedoschim.
Günzberg family of Poland and
Russia. See GENERAL WORKS.
Pudor. Internationalen
Verwandtschaftlichen.
Vol. 2 has a section on
Günzberg family. See GENERAL
WORKS.

GUNZBURG, GUNZBURGER
JE, 6:110. Contains
"Genealogical Tree of the
Günzburg Family."
Descendants of Simeon
Ulma-Günzburg (d. 1586). See
GENERAL WORKS.
Friedberg, Bernhard. Zur
Genealogie der Familie
Günzburg. Frankfurt a.M.:
J. Kauffmann, 1903. 8 p.
Hebrew Text. Reprinted from
Zeitschrift f. Hebr.
Bibliographie, Jahrgang 6.
MH, NN, OCH.
Kahn, Ludwig David. Die
Nachkommen des Nathan
Günzburger (1720-1775) aus
Uffheim elsässisch-jüdischen
Familie. Basel: By the
Author, 1971. 58 p. DLC,
NN, OCH.
Löwenstein, L.
"Model-Ottingen," Jahrbuch
für Jüdische Literatur und
Gesellschaft 8
(1970):202-203. Descendants
of Simon Günzburg (d. 1585).
Maggid, David. Sefer Toldoth
Mishpeḥoth Günzburg. St.
Petersburg: Verlag des
Autors, 1899. 306 p.
Genealogical tables. Added
title page: Zur Geschichte
und genealogie der Günzburg.

Von den ältesten stammen
dieser familie in Deutschland
(anfang des XVI Jahrhunderts)
bis zum tode des berühmten
Jacob-Gabriel Günzburg aus
Kamenetz in Russland ...
(1853). Aus initiative
meines Vaters, Herrn H.-N.
Maggid nach einem teil
weisen conspecte dessel....
See Rosenstein, Unbroken Chain,
entry under GINSBERG,
GINSBURG.

GURALNIK
See Daniel Jay Rottenberg entry
under ROTTENBERG.

GUSKY
Neumann, Dorothy. "The
Greenhoods of San Bernardino
[California]: A Memoir,"
Western States Jewish
Historical Quarterly 15
(Apr. 1983):203-213. Family
of Ralph [Rudolph] Greenhood
(1868-1941), who was born in
Niederstetten, Württemberg,
Germany, and Fanny Gusky
Greenhood (1872-1963), who
was born in Wieruszow,
Poland.

GUSSOW
Gussow, Dan. Chaia Sonia: A
Family's Odyssey: Russian
Style. New York: Cherry and
Scammel Books, Inc., 1980.
251 p. Life of family from
Pumpian, Lithuania
originally. Chaia Sonia
(Luria) and Simche Gussow
(originally from Kharkov,
Russia).

GUTENBERG
Rosenfeld, H. "Gutenbergs
Wappen, seine Entstehung und
die angeblich jüdischen ahnen
Gutenbergs," Gutenberg
Jahrbuch, 1974, pp. 35-46.

GUTH
CAJ has family tree from
Germany.

GUTKIND
Ballin. Juden in Seesen,
p. 191. See GENERAL WORKS.

GUTMAN
AMH has family records.
Kempelen. Magyarországi Zsidó,
1:105; 2:27, 141, 146; 3:76.
See GENERAL WORKS.
See Daniel Nathan Leeson entry
under LEESON.
Reychmann. Szkice
genealogiczne, pp. 85-86.
See GENERAL WORKS.

GUTMANN, GUTTMANN
LBI has family trees beginning
1600, 1756, 1760, 1784, and
1807.
Bab, Arturo. "Gutmann-Guzmán,"
JFF, no. 28 (1931):421.
Gutmann, Ludwig. "Von
Owos-Owosenu. Aus Alten
Papieren und Erinnerungen
fränkischer Juden." Even
Yehuda/Israel, 1956. 40 p.
Family from Fürth/Bavaria
from 1800. LBI.
Tänzer. Juden in Jebenhausen,
pp. 321-26. Gutmann family
of Jebenhausen. See GENERAL
WORKS.
Tänzer. Juden in Tirol,
pp. 720-21. Gutmann family.
See GENERAL WORKS.
Kempelen. Magyarországi Zsidó,
1:14, 79, 113, 146; 2:10, 58,
88, 103; 3:51, 139. Gutmann
family. See GENERAL WORKS.
Weil, Emma. Chronik der
Familien Weil, Gutmann und
Eisenstein. London, 1962.
102 p. Families of
Stuttgart. LBI.

GUTTERES
AMH has family records.
CFM has family records.

GUTTMANN
See GUTMANN, GUTTMANN.

GUTWILLIG
Kempelen. Magyarországi Zsidó,
3:55. See GENERAL WORKS.

GUZMAN
See Arturo Bab entry under
GUTMANN, GUTTMANN.

GYAGYOVSZKY
See ABEL-GYAGYOVSZKY.

GYEMANT
Kempelen. Magyarországi Zsidó,
2:67. Gyémánt family. See
GENERAL WORKS.

GYLLENHAMMAR
Semi-Gotha, 1:72. See GENERAL
WORKS.

GYONGYOSI
Kempelen. Magyarországi Zsidó,
3:136. Gyöngyösi family.
See GENERAL WORKS.

GYOZO
Kempelen. Magyarországi Zsidó,
3:32. Győző family. See
GENERAL WORKS.

GYSSER
Semi-Gotha, 2:18. See GENERAL
WORKS.

GYULAHAZI
Kempelen. Magyarországi Zsidó,
3:112. Gyuláházi family.
See GENERAL WORKS.

HAAC
See Stammbaum Levinstein under
AVELLIS. Includes Haac,
formerly Isaac, family.

HAAGEN
Kempelen. Magyarországi Zsidó,
1:101. See GENERAL WORKS.

HAAN (DE)
Haan, Mies de. De Kinderen van
de Gazzan: Jacob Israël de
Haan, mijn broer, Carry Van
Bruggen, mijn zusster.
Amsterdam: Uitgeverij
Heijnis, 1966? 60 p. Jacob
Israël de Haan, 1881-1924,

Dutch poet and journalist,
younger brother of the Dutch
novelist and philosophical
writer, Carry (de Haan) Van
Bruggen. They were the
brother and sister of the
author. BR.

HAARTMAN
Semi-Gotha, 1:77. See GENERAL
WORKS.

HAAS
AJA has genealogical files.
Dalin, David G. "Florine and
Alice Haas and their
Families: A Picture Story,"
Western States Jewish
Historical Quarterly 13
(Jan. 1981):135-41. San
Francisco pioneer Jewish
family.
"Haas Brothers of San
Francisco: 127 Years of
Business," Western States
Jewish Historical Quarterly
15 (Oct. 1982):25-30. The
Haas brothers were originally
from Reckendorf, Bavaria.
CAJ (Call No. 3191) has family
history and chart of the
descendants of David (Hirsch)
Haas (b. Fuchsstadt, 1834;
d. Würzburg, 1910), rabbi of
Uffenheim, Germany, compiled
by Alfredo Otto Haas. Last
date on the chart is 1968.
Narell. Our City. Includes
genealogical charts for
pioneer San Francisco family,
originally from Reckendorf in
Bavaria. See GENERAL WORKS.
Kempelen. Magyarországi Zsidó,
2:66. See GENERAL WORKS.
Rosenthal, B. "Ahnentafel des
Haas," JFF, no. 24
(1930):311. Ascendants and
descendants of Ludwig Haas
(1875-1930).
Rothmann, Frances Branstein.
The Haas Sisters of Franklin
Street: A Look Back with
Love. Berkeley: Judah L.
Magnes Museum, 1979. 83 p.
Family of San Francisco.
Stern. FAJF. Haas family tree

beginning in Arnheim,
Holland. See GENERAL WORKS.

HABER
LBI has family trees beginning
1768 and 1801.

HABERMANN
Kempelen. Magyarországi Zsidó,
2:90. See GENERAL WORKS.

HABROFSKY
Gold. Juden Mährens,
pp. 532-35. Includes history
of Dr. Moriz Habrofsky's
family of Trebitsch. See
GENERAL WORKS.

HABSBURGER
JFF, no. 23. Family history.

HACHENBURGER
LBI has family tree beginning
1700.

HACKENBURG
AJA has genealogical files.
Stern. FAJF. Hackenburg
family tree beginning in
Coblentz. See GENERAL WORKS.

HACOHEN
Molho, Michael. La famille
Perahia à Thessaloniki.
Thessaloniki, Salonika:
Imprimèrie Acquarone, 1938.
83 p. 69 p. in French; 14 p.
in Hebrew. Page 67: "Arbre
généalogique de la Familie
Ha-Cohen" starting with
Samuel Perahia (d. 1548) of
Italy. Family of Greece and
Italy. JNUL, NN, PPDrop.
Sopher, Ira. "Sequence of the
Generations for the Hacohen
Family from Which Mr. Sopher
is Descended." 1922. AJA.

HADAS
See COHODAS.

HADDIN
Kempelen. Magyarországi Zsidó,
1:101. See GENERAL WORKS.

HADRA
Hadra, Edmund G. Unsere
Familiengeschichte. Berlin,
1939. 207 p. History covers
150 years of this Prussian
family of physicians and
writers from Berlin. LBI.

HAEBER
Kempelen. Magyarországi Zsidó,
3:51. See GENERAL WORKS.

HAES
AMH has family records.
CFM has family records.

HAGEDORN
"Family Tree, 1753-1969." MS.,
Xerox. AJA.

HAGELBERG
LBI has family tree.

HAGELFELDT
Semi-Gotha, 1:113. See GENERAL
WORKS.

HAGENOW
LBI has family tree beginning
1806.

HAGER
Rosenstein. Unbroken Chain,
pp. 512ff. Hager Chassidic
dynasty of Vizhniz. See
GENERAL WORKS.

HAGIN
Jacobs, Joseph. "Three
Centuries of the Hagin
Family," Jewish Quarterly
Review 3 (1891):776-80.
English family.

HAGSTROMER
Semi-Gotha, 1:99. Hagströmer
family. See GENERAL WORKS.

HAHN
AMH has family records.
See Richard J. Alperin entry
under BEHRMAN.
Fischer, Josef. Jacob Simonsen
og Hustru Rose fodt Hahn og
deres Forfaedre. Hundrede aar
efter Jacob Simonsen fodsel,

udgivet af S.H. Simonsen
born. K$\emptyset$benhaven, 1927.
Founder of family was Simon
David Levy, the so-called
"Holländer," 1760-1833.
Jacob Simonsen, 1821-1880,
and Rose (Hahn) Simonsen,
1826-1869. NN, OU.
Kempelen. Magyarországi Zsidó,
3:127. See GENERAL WORKS.
Lisch, Georg Christian
Friedrich. Geschichte und
Urkunden des Geschlechts
Hahn. Schwerin: In Com. in
der Stiller'schen Hofbuch,
1844-1858. 5 vols. MH.
"Prof. David Simonsen's
Vorfahren," in Festskrift in
anledning af David Simonsen
70 aarige fodselsdag
(K$\emptyset$benhavn, 1923),
pp. 311-79. Includes family
tree.

HAHR
Semi-Gotha, 1:78. See GENERAL
WORKS.

HAIJ
Semi-Gotha, 1:129, 130, 131.
See GENERAL WORKS.

HAIM
AMH has family records.

HAIMANN
Bernheimer, Ernst.
Familien-und Geschäftschronik
der Firma L. Bernheimer K.G.
München, 1950. 211 p.
Includes family of author's
mother, the Heimanns, from
Buchau in Württemberg. LBI.

HAJDU
Kempelen. Magyarországi Zsidó,
3:60, 68. See GENERAL WORKS.

HALASI
Kempelen. Magyarországi Zsidó,
3:18. See GENERAL WORKS.

HALASZ
Kempelen. Magyarországi Zsidó,
3:77, 109. Halász family.
See GENERAL WORKS.

HALBERSTADT
AMH has family records.
LBI has family tree beginning
1754.

HALBERSTAM
Halberstam, Solomon. Siah
Yizhaki. Lemberg, 1882. The
author traces eminent rabbis
on both sides of his family.
Rosenstein. Unbroken Chain,
pp. 485ff. "Ancestry of R.
Haim Halberstam of Sanz"
genealogical chart. See
GENERAL WORKS.

HALDENSTEIN
AMH has family records.

HALDIN
AMH has family records.

HALDINSTEIN
CFM has family records.

HALEVI
AMH has family records.
Schochet, Elijah Judah. "TAZ,"
Rabbi David Halevi. New
York: Ktav, 1979. 79 p.
Contains genealogical
information on Rabbi David
ben Samuel Halevi (ca.
1586-1667), known as the TAZ,
who was born in
Vladimir-Volynski (Lodomerik)
in the Ukraine. DLC, NNJ,
OU.
See Meir Yizraeli entry under
BIDERMAN.

HALEVY
Cahen, Isidore. "Grands noms
du judaïsme français: les
Halévy, les Péreire,"
Archives Israélites (de
France) 47 (1886):57-58.
Halévy, Daniel. "Notes de
famille," Revue de France, 15
de Juillet 1929, p. 740.
Katan, Moshe. "La famille
Halévy," Evidences 6, no. 46
(1955):7-13.
Millner, Joseph. "Les grandes
familles juives de France,"
Le Monde Juif 5, no. 31

(1950):16-17. Halévy family.
Reichel, O. Asher. Isaac
Halevy, 1847-1919: Spokesman
and Historian of Jewish
Tradition. New York: Yeshiva
University Press, 1969. 17
p. Genealogical information
on the Ivenecer, Kovner, and
Rabinowitz ancestors of Isaac
Halevy, pp. 15-16. Isaac
Halevy (Rabinowitz) was born
in Ivenets, Province of
Minsk, near Vilna, the son of
R. Eliyahu and Rahel Kovner
Halevy Ivenecer Rabinowitz.
CLU, CSt, CtY, CU, ICU, MB,
MH, NcD, NIC, NjP, NN.
Rivlin, Benjamin. "Ilan
Hayahas" [in Hebrew], in
Sefer Zikaron le-Rabi
Yitshak Aizik Halevi, Moses
Auerbach, ed. (Jerusalem,
1964), pp. 74-79. Contains
genealogical information
concerning Isaac Halevy.
DLC.
Silvera, Alain. Daniel Halévy
and His Times: A
Gentleman-Commoner in the
Third Republic. Ithaca,
N.Y.: Cornell University
Press, 1966. 251 p. "The
Family," pp. 1-40. The
family of Daniel Halévy
(1872-1962) arrived in Paris
from Würzburg, Germany, at
the end of the eighteenth
century.

HALFON
CAJ has family records.
CFM has family records.

HALFORD
AMH has family records.
CFM has family records.

HALIBURTON
AMH has family records.

HALIC, HALICZ
Hebermann, A.M. "The Sons of
Hayyim Halicz, A Family of
Hebrew Printers," (In
Hebrew.) Kirjath Sepher
(Jerusalem) 33 (1958):509-20.

Family of printers in Cracow
in 16th century. Samuel,
Asher, and Elyakim Halicz
established Poland's first
Jewish press there in about
1530. Surname also spelled
Helic or Helicz.

HALL
See KING-HALL.
AMH has family records.

HALLE
See VON HALLE.
AMH has family records.

HALLENCREUTZ
Semi-Gotha, 1:46. See GENERAL
WORKS.

HALLENSTEIN
AMH has family records.
See Esmond S. De Beer entry
under BARDEN.

HALLER
Hancke, Erich. Max Liebermann:
Sein Leben und seine Werke.
Berlin: Bruno Cassirer, 1923.
"Abstammung," pp. 11-14.
Haller and Liebermann
families of Berlin. Max
Liebermann (1847-1935),
German painter, was the son
of Louis Liebermann and the
grandson of Joseph
Liebermann, who came to
Berlin in 1824 from the state
of Märkisch-Friedland. The
Haller family was Max
Liebermann's mother's family.
CSt, CtY, CU, DLC, MH, NIC.
Kempelen. Magyarországi Zsidó,
1:75; 2:100, 127. See
GENERAL WORKS.

HALLIDAY
AMH has family records.

HALLO
AJA has family tree beginning
1680.
LBI has family trees beginning
1736, 1763, and 1860.
Hallo, Rudolf. Geschichte der
Familie Hallo. 350 Jahre aus

dem Leben einer deutschen
Hofjuden-und
Handwerker-familie
aktenmässig dargestellt,
erläutert und mit abbildungen
versehen. Kassel:
Privatdruck, 1930. 170 p.
Family of Kassel. Includes
family trees. DLC, LBI, MH,
NN, PPDrop, WU.
Jakobovits, Tobias. "Zur
Geschichte der Familie
Hallo," ZGJD 6 (1935):54-56.

HALMI, HALMY
Kempelen. Magyarországi Zsidó.
Halmy, Halmi family, 2:21;
3:92. Halmi family, 3:28.
See GENERAL WORKS.

HALMOS
Kempelen. Magyarországi Zsidó,
2:99, 136; 3:65. See GENERAL
WORKS.

HALMY
See HALMI, HALMY.

HALMY-DEUTSCH
Kempelen. Magyarországi Zsidó,
3:92. See GENERAL WORKS.

HALOM
Kempelen. Magyarországi Zsidó,
3:70. See GENERAL WORKS.

HALPERA
Kempelen. Magyarországi Zsidó,
3:64. See GENERAL WORKS.

HALPERIN
See Shapiro, Mishpachot Atikot,
entry under HEILPRIN.

HALPERN
Belinson, Moses Eliezer.
Shelume Emune Yisrael.
Odessa, 1898-1901. 3 vols.
Includes Halpern family of
Russia. DLC.
Rosenstein. Unbroken Chain,
pp. 601ff. See GENERAL
WORKS.
See Shapiro, Mishpachot Atikot,
entry under HEILPRIN.

HALPERT
Reychmann. Szkice
genealogiczne, pp. 87-89.
See GENERAL WORKS.

HALSTEAD
AMH has family records.

HAM
CAJ has family tree from
Germany.

HAMBRO
AMH has family records.
CFM has family records.
Bramsen, Bo and Kathleen Wain.
The Hambros, 1779-1979.
London: Michael Joseph, 1979.
457 p. Includes genealogical
chart. Major historical
study of the descendants of
Calmer Joachim (1750?-1806)
and Thobe Levi (1756-1820).
"Levy" in Denmark, Norway,
and England. Calmer Joachim
Levy changed his name to
Hambro after arrival in
Copenhagen in 1779 from
Hamburg. Thobe Levi was born
in Denmark. Most descendants
converted to Christianity.
Semi-Gotha, 2:51. See GENERAL
WORKS.

HAMBURG
AMH has family records.

HAMBURGER
AMH has family records.
LBI has family trees beginning
1600 and 1772.
Arcy, Hart, R.J. d'. "The
Family of Mordechai Hamburger
and Their Association with
Madras," Miscellanies of the
Jewish Historical Society of
England 3 (1937):57-75.
Berney, Albert. "The Isaac
Hamburger Family."
Westcliffe, Colorado, 1975.
3 p. Listing of the
descendants of Isaac and
Betty Hamburger. AJA, AJHS.
Familiengeschichte
Hamburger-Schlesinger. Teil
1: Familie [Adolf] Hamburger.

Teil II: Familie Schlesinger.
O.O. Privatdruck, 1974.
58 p. Verfasser der
Aufzeichnungen: Adolf
Hamburger (1841 Hanau-1920
Frankfurt a.M.) Ros'chen
Schlesinger geb. Hamburger
(1844 Hanau-1932 Berlin).
Sofie Diamant geb.
Schlesinger (1880 Mainz-1972
Kibbuz Yawne). LBI.
Hamburger, Karl. Legende zum
Stammbaum der Familien
Hamburger-Singer. Wien,
1928. 29 p. Family
originally from Prossnitz.
LBI.
Kempelen. Magyarországi Zsidó,
2:92. See GENERAL WORKS.
Reis, Victor. Chronik der
Familie Wolf. Schlüchtern,
1932. 8 p. 5 genealogical
tables.
Stern. FAJF. Hamburger family
tree beginning in Breslau.
Name later became Levy and
Hart. See GENERAL WORKS.

HAMELBURG
AMH has family records.

HAMELN
Gronemann, S. Genealogische
Hannovers.
Hameln-Goldschmidt family.
See GENERAL WORKS.
Hameln, Glückel von. Die
Memorien der Glückel von
Hameln. Nach der Ausgabe v.
David Kaufmann übertr. v.
Bertha Pappenheim. Wien,
1910. 16, 320 p. Includes
genealogical tables. MH.
————. Denkwurdigkeiten der
Glückel von Hameln, aus dem
jüdisch-deutschen übersetzt,
mit erläuterungen versehen
und hrsg. von dr. Alfred
Feilchenfeld. Berlin:
Jüdischer Verlag, 1920.
328 p. "Genealogisches,"
pp. 326-28. MB, PPDrop.
Lewinski, Abraham. Die Kinder
des Hildesheimer Rabbiner:
Samuel Hameln. Hildesheim,
1901. 26 p. LBI, OCH.

Rosenstock, Werner. "The
Descendants of Jente Hameln:
An Interesting Genealogy,"
AJR Information 22, no. 11
(Nov. 1968).

HAMILTON
AMH has family records.
Semi-Gotha, 1:44, 105, 123,
148. See GENERAL WORKS.

HAMIS
AMH has family records.

HAMLIN
Barbe, Lizzie J.
"Autobiography, 1934."
Incudes family history. AJA.

HAMM
Ballin. Juden in Seesen,
pp. 192-205. See GENERAL
WORKS.

HAMMARSKJOLD
Semi-Gotha, 2:114.
Hammarskjöld family. See
GENERAL WORKS.

HAMON
AMH has family records.
Gross, Henri. "La famille
juive des Hamon (Contribution
á l'histoire des juifs de
Turquie)," Revue des Études
Juives 56/57
(1908/1909):1-26, 55-78.

HAMOS
Kempelen. Magyarországi Zsidó,
1:27. Hamós family. See
GENERAL WORKS.

HAMPO
Kempelen. Magyarországi Zsidó,
3:128. Hampó family. See
GENERAL WORKS.

HANAU
LBI has family tree beginning
1700.

HANAUER
Ballin. Juden in Seesen,
pp. 207-208. See GENERAL
WORKS.

HANDEL
Kempelen. Magyarországi Zsidó,
3:21. See GENERAL WORKS.

HANDS
AMH has family records.

HANF
Noren, Catherine Hanf. The
Camera of My Family. New
York: Knopf, 1976. 240 p.
100-year album of Hanf and
Wallich families. Hanf
family, descendants of Alfred
Hanf (b. Mönchen-Gladbach,
Germany, 1872; d. Friesland,
the Netherlands).

HANGEBROEK
Van Eeghen, I.H. "De Kindern
van Hansken Hangebroek" [The
Children of Hansken
Hangebroek]. Studia
Rosenthaliana 11
(1977):33-39. 16th to 17th
century. H.H. was recorded
as being Jewish in 1620, but
he had married in a church in
1590 and his children were
later baptized; possibly he
converted to Judaism.

HANNOVER
Hannover, Martin Adolph.
Adolph Hannovers faedrene og
mødrene slaegt. Udg. i
anledning af hundredaarsdagen
for hans fødsel. Tillige
indeholdende Adolph Hannovers
autobiografi samt en
fortegnelse over hans
videnskabelige arbejder m.m.
1814-1914. København: Trykt
hos J. Jørgensen, 1914.
207 p. Adolph Hannover
(1814-1894), Danish scientist
and physician, was the son of
Moses Abraham Hannover
(1790-1834), who came to
Copenhagen from Altona,
Germany. DLC, OCH, OU.

HANOVER
AMH has family records.

HANS
Kempelen. Magyarországi Zsidó,
2:121. See GENERAL WORKS.

HANSEMANN
Daebritz, Walter. David
Hansemann und Adolph v.
Hansemann. Düsseldorf:
Rheinisch-Westf. Bank, 1954.
165 p. (Männer der Deutschen
Bank und der
Dicsconto-Geselschaft.)
David Justus Ludwig
Hansemann, 1790-1864, and
Adolph von Hansemann,
1826?-1903. Bankers of
Berlin. CtY, DLC, MH, WU.

HANSFORD
AMH has family records.

HANSLICKS
Kisch, Bruno. "Eduard
Hanslicks jüdische
Abstammung," JFF, no. 6
(1930):210-11. Family of
Prague.
Sokoll, Josef. "Noch einmal
Eduard Hanslicks jüdische
Abstammung," JFF, no. 8
(1932):456-57.

HANTKE
Reychmann. Szkice
genealogiczne, pp. 91-93.
See GENERAL WORKS.

HANTOS
Kempelen. Magyarországi Zsidó,
2:20. See GENERAL WORKS.

HANZELY
Kempelen. Magyarországi Zsidó,
1:100. Hanzély family. See
GENERAL WORKS.

HARANGI
Kempelen. Magyarországi Zsidó,
2:127; 3:121. See GENERAL
WORKS.

HARARIS
Grunwald, Kurt. "On Cairo's
Lombard Street," Tradition
17, no. 1 (1972):8-22.
Ca. 1800-1952. Banking

157

HART

family of Cairo. Includes
genealogical table.

HARASZTY
Kempelen. Magyarországi Zsidó,
3:79. See GENERAL WORKS.

HARBEN
AMH has family records.

HARBY
"Traditional Genealogy of the
Harby Family, Traced to
England and Morocco." Family
of U.S. 18th century
forward. AJA.
Stern. FAJF. Family tree of
descendants of Isaac Harby,
"Lapidary to Emperor of
Morocco." Isaac Harby's
children were born in
England. See GENERAL WORKS.

HARDEGG
Kempelen. Magyarországi Zsidó,
2:51. See GENERAL WORKS.

HARDT
Gudenus, Philipp Georg. "Die
jüdische Herkunft der Familie
'Hardt' (1793)," Wiener
Geschichtsblätter 28, no. 4
(·1973):118-20. Family of
entrepeneurs in 18th- and
19th-century Austria was of
Jewish origin, as proved by
documents.

HARDY
CFM has family records.

HARFF
Schulte. Bonner Juden,
pp. 255-56. See GENERAL
WORKS.

HARKANYI
Kempelen. Magyarországi Zsidó,
1:143; 2:38. Harkányi
family. See GENERAL WORKS.

HARKAVY
Harkavi, Zvi. Le-bekr
mishpabot. Jerusalem, 1953.
Includes Harkavy and
Maskileison families.

Harkavy, Elhanan. Dor
yesharim. A Righteous
Generation: a genealogical
account of the Harkavy family
and biographical sketches of
its distinguished members in
the past and present. New
York, 1903. 101 p.

HARMON-HENDRICKS-GOLDSTONE
AJA has genealogical files.

HARRACH
CAJ has family records.

HARRIS
AJA has family tree from
Dallas, Texas.
AMH has family records.
CFM has family records.
Lipman, Rowena Dorothy. The
Family of Isaac and Rebecca
Harris. Berkeley, Calif.:
Western Jewish History
Center, 1970. 8 p.
Genealogy of an early San
Francisco family, descendants
of Isaac Harris (1833-1879).
CU, WJHC.
Lipman Family Papers and
Documents. Contain
genealogical chart and
history of the families of
Isaac and Rebecca Harris,
compiled by Rowena Lipman,
1969. Family of California.
WJHC.
Moss, Sanford. Moss-Harris
Pedigree. Somerville, Mass.,
1934, 1937, 1940, 1943.
AJHS.
Stern. FAJF. Harris family
trees beginning in:
(I) London; and (II) Holland.
See GENERAL WORKS.

HARRISON
AMH has family records.

HARSANYI
Kempelen. Magyarországi Zsidó,
2:90, 91; 3:26. Harsányi
family. See GENERAL WORKS.

HART
AJA has family tree for family

of Memphis, Tennessee.
AMH has family records.
EJ (1928), 7:1909. Family of
Canada. See GENERAL WORKS.
Felsenthal Family. Family tree
of Descendants of Benjamin
Wolf Felsenthal and Agatha
Hart Felsenthal; birth
certificate of Helen Leah
Alpiner, Chicago, Ill.; "Aunt
Mimi's Story," written by
Amelia Darling Alpiner, An
Autobiography Written, June,
1967; Newspaper articles
Concerning Members of the
Alpiner Family, a Branch of
the Felsenthal family. AJA,
Box No. 955.
EJ (1972), 7:1353. Descendants
of Bernard Hart (1763-1855),
through mid-20th century.
American/English family
probably originally from
Fürth. See GENERAL WORKS.
Hart and Judah Families;
Biographical Material,
1724-1954. Photostats.
Includes genealogical
information. AJA.
Hart Family, Richmond, Va.
"Records of Births,
Marriages, and Deaths,
1819-1854." Extracted from
the Leeser Bible owned by
Leonora Levy, 1866. AJA.
WJHC has Hart, Neustadter, and
Dannenberg families' tree.
Families of California.
Birmingham. The Grandees. See
GENERAL WORKS.
See Esmond S. De Beer entry
under BARDEN.
"The Descendants of James
Pettigrew," The St. Charles 1
(1935):133-37. Article
includes the descendants of
Lt. James Pettigrew and
Judith Hart (1762-1844), the
daughter of Myer Hart
(d. 1791), early
Jewish-American merchant and
founder of the town of
Easton, Penn. in 1752. The
male line continued to be
Christian while most of the
female line were Jewish.

Douville, R. "Années de
jeunesse et vie familiale de
Moses Hart," Cahiers des Dix
(Montreal) no. 23
(1958):195-216. Moses Hart,
1768-1852, of Hart family of
Canada.
Douville, Raymond. Aaron Hart,
récit historique.
Trois-Rivières: Ed. du Brien
Public, 1938. 194 p. Aaron
Hart, 1724-1800. Canadian
family from Quebec. CtY, MH,
NN.
Hart, Arthur Wellington.
Genealogical files. AJA.
Hart, David. Genealogical
files. AJA.
Hart, Nathan. Davenport, Iowa.
Genealogical information,
n.d.; typescript; Xerox.
AJA.
Joseph, Anthony P. "Jewry of
South-west England and Some
of its Australian
Connections," Transactions of
the Jewish Historical Society
of England 24 (1975):24-37.
Includes genealogical tables
of descendants of Zender
Moses Eliezer Hart and
Eliezer Levy. 18th century
forward.
Rome, David. On the Early
Harts. Montréal: Canadian
Jewish Congress, 1981.
425 p. (Coll. "Canadian
Jewish Archives," New Series,
Nos. 15-18.)
————. On the Early
Harts--Their Contemporaries,
Part I. Montréal: Canadian
Jewish Congress, 1981.
(Coll. "Canadian Jewish
Archives," New Series,
No. 19.)
See Stern, FAJF entry under
HAMBURGER.
Stern. FAJF. Hart family
trees beginning in: (I and
II) London; (III) Hamburg;
(IV) Fürth, Germany; (V) The
Hague, Netherlands;
(VI) Mannheim, Germany;
(VII) Whitechapel, London;
(VIII) Hannover; (IX) Fürth,

Bavaria (descendants of
Samuel Hart or Herz);
(X) Niederweisel, Wetterau;
(XI and XIV) Germany; and
(XII and XIII) U.S.   See
GENERAL WORKS.
Sulte, Benjamin. "La maison
Hart," Mélanges historiques
19 (1932):47-56. Family of
Canada.

HARTEL
Kempelen. Magyarországi Zsidó,
1:80; 2:28. See GENERAL
WORKS.

HARTENSTEIN
Kempelen. Magyarországi Zsidó,
3:112. See GENERAL WORKS.

HARTIG
LBI has family tree beginning
1726.

HARTLAND
Hannam, Charles. A Boy in that
Situation: An Autobiography.
New York: Harper and Row,
1978. 215 p. Brief
genealogical chart, opp. p.
7. Karl Hartland, the
author's real name, was born
in Essen, Germany, the son of
Max Hartland (d. 1943) and
Gertrude Freudenberg Hartland
(d. 1937). His mother's
parents were Louis and
Ernestina Freudenberg. His
grandfather was Joseph
Hartland, and his
great-grandfather was Levi
Hartland. Autobiography
covers author's life in
Germany and England through
late 1940s.

HARTLEY
AMH has family records.

HARTMANN
Kaufmann, David. "Der
Stammbaum des R. Eleasar
Fleckeles, seine Ahnenprobe
Moritz Hartmanns," MGWJ 37
(1893):378-92.

HARTNELL
AMH has family records.

HARTOG
AMH has family records.
CAJ has family tree from
Germany and Holland,
1720-1959.

HARTOGENESIS
See MENKO-HARTOGENESIS.

HARTOGENSIS
Kempelen. Magyarországi Zsidó,
1:134. See GENERAL WORKS.

HARTSHORNE
Lybarger, Donald Fisher. The
Story of the
Dowler-Hartshorne,
Fisher-Lyberger Families.
Cleveland, 1938, 1962, 2d ed.
63 p. DLC, OC1.

HARTSTEIN
Kempelen. Magyarországi Zsidó,
3:48. See GENERAL WORKS.

HARTVIG
Hartvig, Michael. Levin Marcus
Hartvigs efterkommende:
Stamtavle over slaegten
Hartvig. Kóbenhavn: Levin &
Minksgaard, 1928. 58 p.
CAJ, MH.

HARTZELL
See Ruth Harzell Goldstein
entry under HERZOG.

HARVEY
AMH has family records.

HASENFELD
Kempelen. Magyarországi Zsidó,
1:95; 2:50. See GENERAL
WORKS.

HASIDA
Hasida, Yisrael Yitzchok.
Mishpachteinu. N.p., 1980.
49 p. Covers 7 generations,
1820-1980. JNUL.

HASSE
Hasse, Hermann. Familientafeln

der bisher bekannten
Namensträger Hasse, nebst
angeheirateter und
Töchterlinien; zugleich als
Fortsetzung des vierbändigen
Werkes von Regierungsrat
Erdmann Hasse....
Berlin-Friedenau: By the
Author, 1937. 2 vols. NN.
————. "Hasse Stammfolge,"
Deutsche Stammfolgen, 1935,
pp. 17-32.

HASTESKO
Semi-Gotha, 1:29. Hästesko
family. See GENERAL WORKS.

HASTINGS
AMH has family records.

HATCHWALL
AMH has family records.

HATTBURG
See TERNES.

HATTENBACH
Hattenbach Family, Sioux City,
Iowa. "Excerpts from
History: The Godfrey
Hattenbach Family," n.d.;
"Letter Giving Additional
Information," 1969.
Typescript; Xerox copies.
AJA.

HATVANY
Kempelen. Magyarországi Zsidó,
2:27, 61. See GENERAL WORKS.

HATVANY-DEUTSCH
UJE, 5:249-51. Family of
"Hungarian barons,
landowners, industrialists
and art patrons." Originally
Deutsch de Hatvan.
Kempelen. Magyarországi Zsidó,
1:38; 2:61. See GENERAL
WORKS.

HAUGERMANN
Neumann, Robert. Mein Altes
Haus in Kent. Erinnerungen
an Menschen und Gespenster.
Wien: Verlag Kurt Desch,
1957. 338 p. Especially,

pp. 32-48. Austrian novelist
and satirist (1897-   ).
Original family name was
Haugermann, the family coming
to Vienna from Miechow, north
of Cracow. CLU, CtY, DLC,
MH, NIC, NN, WU.

HAUPT
CAJ has family records.

HAUSEN
Fisher, Josef. Familien
Hausen. København: Levin,
Munksgaard, 1917. 29 p.
Danish family, originally
from Hamburg. JNUL.
Nathanson, Joel Levin.
"Optegnelser om Familien
Hausen m.m. meddelt og
forsynet med Anmaerkninger af
Josef Fischer," Tidsskrift
for Jødisk Historie og
Literatur 1 (1917): 51-59,
117-21, 174-81, 230-35.

HAUSER
Tänzer. Juden in Tirol,
p. 722. See GENERAL WORKS.

HAVAS
See BOSSANYI-HAVAS.
Kempelen. Magyarországi Zsidó,
3:21, 92. See GENERAL WORKS.

HAVELBURG
CAJ has family records.

HAWKER
AMH has family records.

HAWKINS
AMH has family records.

HAY
Kempelen. Magyarországi Zsidó,
3:64. See GENERAL WORKS.

HAYES
AMH has family records.

HAYM, HAYMAN, HAYMANN, HAYUM
AMH has Hayman family records.
Kopp. Jüdischen Alsenz,
pp. 127-29.
Hayum-Feibelmann-Haym-

Haymann-Heymann family of
Alsenz. See GENERAL WORKS.
Zapf. Tübinger Juden, pp.
132-35. Hayum family. See
GENERAL WORKS.

HAYS
AJA has genealogical files.
CAJ has some family records.
JE, 6:270. Family of U.S.,
descendants of Michael Hays
of Holland, 17th to end of
19th century. See GENERAL
WORKS.
Myers Family Papers, 1790-1900.
Include genealogical data on
Myers, Mordecai, Hays, and
other Jewish families of
Virginia. Virginia
Historical Society Library.
Cohen, Caroline Myers. Records
of the Myers, Hays, and
Mordecai Families from
1707-1913. Washington, D.C.:
By the Author, 1913? 57 p.
Hays family originally from
Holland. Descendants of
Moses Michael Hays
(1738-1805). AJHS, DLC, NN,
OCH, PPDrop.
Myers-Mordecai-Hays Collection.
Includes genealogy of Judah
Hays family, Virginia, n.d.
AJA.
Hays, Judith. Genealogical
files. AJA.
"Items Relating to the Hays
Family, New York,"
Publications of the American
Jewish Historical Society 27
(1920):318.
Stern. FAJF. Hays family tree
beginning in Storndorf,
Bavaria. Hays family tree is
listed in FAJF under
"Thorman."
————. Hays family tree
beginning in Holland. See
GENERAL WORKS.

HAYUM
See HAYM, HAYMAN, HAYMANN,
HAYUM.

HAYUTIN
RMJHS has family tree of

Denver, Colorado family
originally from Russia.
Family members emigrated to
U.S. in 1890s.

HAZAI
Kempelen. Magyarországi Zsidó,
3:71. See GENERAL WORKS.

HAZAN, HAZZAN
JE, 6:289. Contains family
pedigree, descendants of
Joseph Hazan (1741-1819),
through late 19th century.
Oriental Hazan, Hazzan
family. See GENERAL WORKS.

HECHT
AMH has family records.
CFM has family records.
Fisher-Hecht Family Papers,
Cincinnati, Ohio and
Wheeling, W. Va., 1845-1852.
Includes genealogical
material on Fisher, Hecht,
and Rindskopf families. AJA.
Hecht Family. "Family Tree and
History." Santa Fe, N.M.,
1976. AJA.
Hecht Family Papers, 1976.
Contain family tree. AJA.
Frank Family, Boston Mass.
"Biographical Material
Concerning Mrs. Daniel Frank,
Mrs. Jacob H. Hecht, and
Other Family Members,
1881-1932." In French,
German, and English. AJA.
Hecht, Otto. Einige
Erinnerungen der Familie
Hecht. Haifa: Skikmona
Publ., 1973. 277 p.
Includes family tree. Hecht
and Mannheim families. LBI.
Kempelen. Magyarországi Zsidó,
1:146; 3:139. See GENERAL
WORKS.
Stern. FAJF. Hecht family
tree beginning in Hamburg.
See GENERAL WORKS.

HECKSCHER
CAJ has records and family
history.
LBIS has family tree and notes.
Heckscher, Albert. Stammtafel

(oder Thurnauer) Koppel.
Copenhage: S.B. Salomon,
1883. 24 p. OCH.
Semi-Gotha, 2:62ff. See
GENERAL WORKS.

HECKSHER
AMH has family records.

HEDENBERG
Semi-Gotha, 1:76, 78, 118. See
GENERAL WORKS.

HEDIN
JFF, no. 27. Family history.
Semi-Gotha, 1:117. See GENERAL
WORKS.

HEIDENHAIN
Zapf. Tübinger Juden, pp.
50-52. See GENERAL WORKS.

HEIDLBERG
Kempelen. Magyarországi Zsidó,
2:20. See GENERAL WORKS.

HEIDRICH
CAJ has family records.

HEIDT
CAJ has family tree from
Prague.

HEIDUSCHKA
Kempelen. Magyarországi Zsidó,
2:70. See GENERAL WORKS.

HEIL
Kempelen. Magyarországi Zsidó,
3:96. See GENERAL WORKS.

HEILBRON
AMH has family records.
Stern. FAJF. Heilbron family
tree beginning in U.S. See
GENERAL WORKS.

HEILBRON-HEINEMAN
AJA has genealogical files.

HEILBRUNN
LBI has family tree beginning
1683.

HEILBUT
AMH has family records.

CFM has family records.
LBIS has family tree and notes.

HEILBUTH
AMH has family records.
See Stern, FAJF entry under
Helbert.

HEILPRIN
JE, 6:322-23. Contains family
trees for German and Russian
branches of family. See
GENERAL WORKS.
Biber, Menachem Mendel.
Mazkereth li-gedole Ostrah.
Berdichev, 1907. 346 p.
Includes information on
Heilprin family of Ostrog.
DLC.
Eisenstadt and Wiener. Da'at
Kedoschim. Includes Heilprin
family of Russia. See
GENERAL WORKS.
Kahan. 'Anaf 'ez avoth. See
GENERAL WORKS.
Pollack, Gustav. Michael
Heilprin and His Sons: A
Biography. New York: Dodd,
Mead, 1912. Michael Heilprin
(b. Piotrkow, Poland, 1823;
d. 1888) went to Hungary,
then to U.S. Angelo
Heilprin, 1853-1907; Louis
Heilprin, 1851-1912. DLC,
ICJ, MB, MH, NcD, NN, OCH,
PP, PU, TxU, ViU.
Kempelen. Magyarországi Zsidó,
3:88. See GENERAL WORKS.
Pudor. Internationalen
Verwandtschaftlichen. Vol. 3
contains a section on
Heilprin family. See GENERAL
WORKS.
Rosenstein. Unbroken Chain,
pp. 265ff. Heilprin
descendants of R. Jacob Shor.
See GENERAL WORKS.
Shapiro. Mishpachot Atikot.
Includes genealogy of
Halpern, Halperin, Heilprin
family, pp. 304-322, as well
as Shapiro family. See
GENERAL WORKS.

HEIMANN
LBI has family tree beginning

1815.
Schulte. Bonner Juden, p. 258.
See GENERAL WORKS.

HEINE
Heine Family. "Genealogical
Chart." 1900. AJA.
JE, 6:326. Includes family
tree of Heine family,
descendants of Isaac Heine,
17th to mid-19th century.
See GENERAL WORKS.
LBI has family trees beginning
1614, 1682, 1722, and 1745.
Ballin. Juden in Seesen,
p. 209. See GENERAL WORKS.
Brilling, Bernhard. Heinrich
Heines Berliner Verwandte und
deren Vorfahren: Ein Beitrag
zur Heineforschung. Berlin:
Arnai-Verlag, 1955. LBI,
OCH. Reprinted from Der Bär
von Berlin: Jahrbuch des
Vereins für die Geschichte
Berlins, (Berlin), Folge 5
(1955):33-52.
————. "Die Familie Stieglitz
aus Arolsen: Unbekannte
Heine-Nachkommen,"
Mitteilungsblatt,
Wochenzeitung des Irgun Olej
Merkas Europa (Tel-Aviv),
5.3.1957.
Büchler, A. "Zum Pressburger
Stammbaume Heinrich Heines,"
Judaica (Pressburg) 3,
no. 19/20 (1936):6-7.
Bühler, Hans Eugen. "Die
Wasenmeisterfamilie Edel aus
Düsseldorf:
historisch-genealogische
Hintergründe der Begegnung
Heinrich Heines mit Josepha
Edel," Genealogie
(Neustadt/Aisch) 29, no. 2
(Feb. 1980):33-43.
Heymann, Fritz. "Heinrich
Heines Ahnentafel," Jüdisches
Archiv 1, no. 11/12 (1928);
N.F., no. 5/6:7-9.
Karpeles, Gustav. Heinrich
Heines Stammbaum
väterlicherseits. Breslau:
Schottländer, 1901. LBI.
Reprinted from Gedenkbuch an
David Kaufmann (Breslau,

1901), pp. 487-505.
Kaufmann, David. Aus Heinrich
Heines Ahnensaal. Breslau:
S. Schottländer, 1896.
312 p. LBI.
Raphael, J. "Über die
Nachkommen der Charlotte
Embden aus Hamburg,"
Zeitschrift für die
Geschichte der Juden (Tel
Aviv) 7, no. 2/3
(1970):65-72. Descendants of
Moritz Embden and Charlotte
Heine Embden, 1820s through
1960s.
Rosenbacher, M. "Heinrich
Heines Vater," Mitteilungen
d. Vereins für Hamburger
Geschichte 13 (1920):231-237.
Schnee, Heinrich. "Heinrich
Heines väterliche Ahnen als
lippische Hoffaktoren. Ein
Beitrag zur Geschichte der
Familie Heine und der
Institution des
Hoffaktorentums an kleinen
Fürstenhöfen im Zeitalter des
Absolutismus," Zeitschrift
für Religions-und
Geistesgeschichte 5, no. 1
(1953):53-70.

HEINEMAN
See HEILBRON-HEINEMAN.
Stern. FAJF. Heineman family
tree beginning in Foschstadt,
Bavaria. See GENERAL WORKS.

HEINEMANN
CAJ has family tree.
CFM has family records.

HEINSHEIMER-WESTHEIMER
AJA has genealogical files and
genealogy, 1679-1931.

HEISLER
Kempelen. Magyarországi Zsidó,
2:137. See GENERAL WORKS.

HELBERT
AMH has family records.
Stern. FAJF. Family tree of
descendants of Samuel
Heilbuth of London, who

changed name to Helbert. See
GENERAL WORKS.

HELBERT-HENRY
AJA has genealogical files.

HELD
CAJ has family records.

HELER
Kaufmann, David. "R.
Abraham-Darschau von Wien und
die Familie Heler," MGWJ 42
(1898):366-71.

HELFMANN
AMH has family records.

HELFY
Kempelen. Magyarországi Zsidó,
2:59. See GENERAL WORKS.

HELIC, HELICZ
See HALIC, HALICZ.

HELLENS
Semi-Gotha, 1:135. See GENERAL
WORKS.

HELLER
Heller Family. "Genealogy."
Dallas, Texas and New York,
N.Y. N.d. AJA.
RMJHS has family tree which
covers 1744-1982. Heller
family emigrated to Denver in
1927 from Ratno, and Ludmir,
Poland.
Heller Family. Two Letters
from Isaac S. Heller, New
York, N.Y., to Irving K.
Heller, Cleveland, Ohio,
Regarding Their Family
Genealogy, 1956. Typescript
and MS. Includes family tree
beginning 1780. AJA.
Heller, Isaac Family.
"Genealogy, 1780-1942." New
York, N.Y. 1942. AJA.
Kempelen. Magyarországi Zsidó,
1:118; 2:59, 60. See GENERAL
WORKS.
Levy, Edwin L. The Descendants
of Emanuel Straus and Fanny
Heller Straus. Richmond,
Va., 1972. 11 p. AJHS.

Löwenstein, L. "Stammbaum der
Familie Mirels," Blätter für
jüdische Geschichte und
Litteratur 4 (1903):1-5,
33-37, 49-54, 113-20, 129,
159-60.
Schick, Salamon. Mi-Mosheh 'ad
Mosheh. Added title page:
Der Stammbaum der Familie
Schick mit den Hauptzweigen
Wallerstein, Heller.
Munkács, 1903. Includes
genealogical tables. DLC.

HELLMAN
Hellman, Jack. "Report of An
Interview with Jack
Hellman ... Los Angeles, by
Norton B. Stern, November 1,
1967." [Santa Monica,
Calif.] 1967. Typescript.
4 p. "This report contains
biographical data on Samuel
(1836-1896) and Maurice S.
(1865-1942) Hellman, the
interviewee's grandfather and
father, as well as data on
his mother, Alice
Schwarzchild Hellman of San
Francisco, his siblings, and
his own wife and children."
AJA, WJHC.
"The Hellmans of California,"
American Hebrew 117
(1925):676. Family
originally from Bavaria.
Some family members arrived
in Los Angeles in 1859.
See Meir Yizraeli entry under
BIDERMAN.

HELLMUTH
CFM has family records.

HELTAI
Kempelen. Magyarországi Zsidó,
2:58; 3:34. See GENERAL
WORKS.

HEMMERDINGER
See Daniel Nathan Leeson entry
under LEESON.

HEMMING
AMH has family records.

HENDRICKS
AMH has family records.
CFM has family records.
JE, 6:346. Contains
"Genealogical Tree of the
Hendricks Family,"
descendants of Aaron
Hendricks, d. 1771, through
early 20th century. Family
of U.S. See GENERAL WORKS.
"Genealogy of the Hendricks
Family, Including: (1)
Ancestors of Henry Solomon
Hendricks and Rosalie Gratz
Hendricks; (2) Illustrated
Family Tree by Vida Lindo
Guiterman." AJA.
Birmingham. The Grandees. See
GENERAL WORKS.
Goldstone, Lafayette.
"Genealogy of Several Old New
York Families, Arranged with
Particular Reference to the
Ancestry of John Lewis, Lewis
Goldstone, and Herman
Hendricks Goldstone, Also
Showing the True Relationship
of Some of their Cousins,
Aunts, Uncles, and Other
Family Connections;
Illustrated by Vida Lindo
Guterman." AJA.
Stern. FAJF. Hendricks family
tree beginning in Holland.
See GENERAL WORKS.
Whiteman, Maxwell. Copper for
America: The Hendricks Family
and a National Industry,
1755-1939. New Brunswick,
N.J.: Rutgers University
Press, 1971. 353 p.
Wolff, Frances Nathan. Four
Generations. New York:
Colonial Press, 1939. 192 p.
Also includes Nathan and
Wolff families.

HENDRIKS
AMH has family records.
CFM has family records.

HENEL
Kopp. Jüdischen Alsenz,
pp. 122-23. See GENERAL
WORKS.

HENGELMULLER
Kempelen. Magyarországi Zsidó,
1:54. Hengelmüller family.
See GENERAL WORKS.

HENIKSTEIN
Piotrowski, Ludwik. Szlachta
Mojżeszowa. Krakow: n.p.,
1938-1939. 2 vols. Vol. 1
contains genealogical chart
of Marii i Alfreda br.
Henikstein. The family was
an Austrian banking and
military family, many members
of which converted to
Christianity. CtY, DLC, MH,
NN, NNC.
Semigothaisches Taschenbuch.
Genealogical table 9. See
GENERAL WORKS.

HENLE
AMH has family records.
CFM has Henlé family tree.

HENLER
MGWJ 62 (1918):223. Family
history.

HENNEFELD
Kempelen. Magyarországi Zsidó,
3:28. See GENERAL WORKS.

HENNIG
AMH has family records.

HENNIGSON
LBI has family tree beginning
1800.

HENOCHOBEY
AMH has family records.

HENRIK
PD has family records.

HENRIQUES
AMH has family records.
JE, 6:348. Contains
"Genealogical Tree of the
Henriques Family,"
descendants of Jacob
Henriques, Kingston, Jamaica,
d. 1758. Family of U.S. See
GENERAL WORKS.
LBIS has family tree.

Familieminder Tilegnet.
  Henriques family, p. 85. See
  GENERAL WORKS.
Henriques, Bendix Moses.
  Stamtavlen Henriques,
  1725-1948. København, 1949.
  CAJ.
Henriques, Henry. "History of
  the Henriques Family," 1978.
  Typescript. Family of New
  York. AJA.
Semi-Gotha, 1:86ff. See
  GENERAL WORKS.
Stern. FAJF. Henriques family
  trees beginning in:
  (I) Spain; (II) London; and
  (III) Portugal. See GENERAL
  WORKS.

HENRIQUEZ
CFM has family records.
Henriquez Family. "Genealogy,
  and Miscellaneous Material
  Regarding the Family,
  1831-1920." AJA.
Locker, Zvi. "Simon Isaac
  Henriquez Moron: Homme
  d'affaires de la Grand'Anse;
  Esquisse," Revue de la
  Société Hatienne d'Histoire
  de Géographique et de
  Géologie, no. 125 (decembre
  1979):56-59.

HENRY
See HELBERT-HENRY.
AMH has family records.
CFM has family records.
Gratz-Sulzberger Family Papers,
  1747-1961. Include family
  tree of Bluch and Henry
  families of Philadelphia and
  New York. AJA.
AJA has family tree for Bernard
  Henry family.
Stern. FAJF. Henry family
  trees beginning in: (I and
  II) U.S.; and (III) Ramsgate,
  England, descendants of Levi
  Abraham, whose father's
  surname was Loew and whose
  children's surname became
  Henry. See GENERAL WORKS.

HENRY-HERZOG
AJA has genealogical files.

HENSHAW
AMH has family records.

HEPPNER
CAJ has family records.

HERCZEG
Kempelen. Magyarországi Zsidó,
  3:123. See GENERAL WORKS.

HERCZEL
Kempelen. Magyarországi Zsidó,
  1:137. See GENERAL WORKS.

HERLITZ
CAJ has family records.

HERMANN
Grange, Henry-Louis de la.
  Mahler. Garden City, N.Y.:
  Doubleday & Co., 1973. 982
  p. Genealogical information
  concerning the relatives of
  Gustav Mahler (1860-1911),
  the Austrian composer, pp.
  5-12. Mahler was the son of
  Bernhard (1827?-1889) and
  Marie Hermann (d. 1889)
  Mahler and the grandson of
  Simon (1793-1865) and Maria
  Mahler and Abraham and
  Theresa Hermann. The Hermann
  family was from Sniet and the
  Mahler family was from
  Lipnitz (Lipnice), Iglau
  (Jihlava), and Kaliste
  (Kalischt).
Stern. FAJF. Hermann family
  tree beginning in Roedelheim,
  Germany. See GENERAL WORKS.

HERRMANN, HERRMANNS
Schulte. Bonner Juden,
  pp. 262-63. See GENERAL
  WORKS.

HERMANNS-HIRSCH
Schulte. Bonner Juden, p. 261.
  See GENERAL WORKS.

HERMANSON
Semi-Gotha, 1:102. See GENERAL
  WORKS.

HERON
AMH has family records.

HERRING
AMH has family records.

HERSCHALL
AMH has family records.

HERSCHELL
AMH has family records.
CFM has family records.
Burke's Peerage and Baronetage,
1970. Family of Britain.
Kempelen. Magyarországi Zsidó,
1:97. See GENERAL WORKS.
Schulte. Bonner Juden, p. 265.
See GENERAL WORKS.

HERSCHKOVITS
Kempelen. Magyarországi Zsidó,
1:110. See GENERAL WORKS.

HERSCHLIKOWITZ
Aaron and A. Leah
Herschlikowitz Family
Association. History Book
and Family Tree Issued in
Commemoration of Our Silver
Jubilee. New York: N.p.,
1938. 47 p. DLC, NN.

HERTZ
AJA has genealogical files.
AMH has family records.
CFM has family records.
Hertz, Hans W. "Wilhelm Ludwig
Hertz, ein Sohn des Dichters
Adelbert von Chamisso. Ein
genealogischer Beitrag,"
Börsenblatt für den Deutschen
Buchhandel, no. 51 (27 Juni
1969):1495-1514. Includes
genealogical table. Wilhelm
Ludwig Hertz, publisher,
1822-1901.
CAJ has family tree. CAJ also
has genealogical notes on the
descendants of the physicist
Heinrich Rudolph Hertz
(b. Hamburg, 1857; d. 1894).
He became professor at Bonn
in 1889.
Schulte. Bonner Juden, p. 268.
See GENERAL WORKS.
Stern. FAJF. Hertz family
trees beginning in: (I and
II) U.S.; (III) Hamburg,

Germany; and (IV) Hildesheim,
Germany. See GENERAL WORKS.

HERTZBERG
Keesing, N. "The Story of
Miriam and Adolphus
Hertzburg," Journal and
Proceedings of the Australian
Jewish Historical Society 7
(1974):524-29.

HERTZFELD
AMH has family records.

HERTZKA
Kempelen. Magyarországi Zsidó,
1:27, 28, 86; 2:130. See
GENERAL WORKS.

HERVAY
Kempelen. Magyarországi Zsidó,
1:49. See GENERAL WORKS.

HERXHEIMER
CAJ (Call No. 3454) has family
tree of Isaac Herxheimer of
Herzheim, Germany (d. 1833),
which includes 5 generations
of his descendants. In
addition, the family tree
includes 4 generations of the
descendants of Israel
Strauss. Last date on family
tree is 1931.

HERYING
Reychmann. Szkice
genealogiczne, pp. 95-97.
See GENERAL WORKS.

HERZ
CFM has family records.
Auerbach, Siegfried. The
Descendants of Anschel Herz
of Bonn. London, 1964.
57 p. CAJ.
Benjamin, Heinrich. Chronik
der Familie
Herz-Salomon-Fuld.
Jerusalem, 1944. 36 p. LBI.
Czellitzer, Arthur. "Die
Abstammung von Heinrich
Herz," JFF, no. 6 (1926):148.
Heinrich Herz, Austrian
pianist and composer,
b. Vienna, 1802; d. 1888.

———. "Zur Abstammung von
Heinrich Herz," JFF, no. 15
(1928):63-64.
Gebhart, Peter von.
"Ahnentafel des Heinrich
Herz," JFF, no. 19
(1929):171-72.
Herz, Heinrich. Zur Geschichte
der Familie Herz in Weilburg.
Aufgezeichnet von Heinrich
Herz ... im Jahre 1863, erg.
und bis A. Gegenwart fortgef.
von George Struch. Aachen:
Aachener Verlag und
Druck.-Gesellschaft, 1906.
66 p. Includes 15
genealogical tables;
descendants table of Herz
Feist (1710-1746). BR, YIVO.
Herz, Ludwig. "Fünfhundert
Jahre Familiengeschichte,
1430-1930." 1934. LBI.
See Ludwig Herz entry under
REICHENHEIM.
Kempelen. Magyarországi Zsidó,
1:69, 110, 118; 2:90, 3:120.
See GENERAL WORKS.
Schulte. Bonner Juden,
pp. 269-78. See GENERAL
WORKS.
See Stern, FAJF (IX) entry
under HART.

HERZBERG
Ballin. Juden in Seesen,
p. 210. See GENERAL WORKS.
Herzberg, Abel Jacob. Brieven
aan mijn kleinzoon. De
geschiedenis van een Joodse
Emigrantenfamilie. Den Haag:
B. Bakker, Daamen, 1965.
192 p. DLC, MH, NNC. The
following libraries have 1967
reprinting: DLC, MH, NjP, NN,
NNC. Also, a German
translation was published in
1967: Haus der Väter: Briefe
eines Juden an seinen Enkel.
Übersetzung: Bernhard
Blutmann. Salzburg:
D. Müller, 1967. 171 p.
DLC. Herzberg was born in
Amsterdam of
Russian-immigrant parents.
In these "Letters to My

Grandson," author discusses
his childhood recollections.

HERZEL
Herzel Family, Denver. Herzel,
George Nathan. "Heritage of
the Family--A Family of Some
Status." 1934. AJA.

HERZFELD
CAJ has family records.

HERZFELDER
Kempelen. Magyarországi Zsidó,
2:21. See GENERAL WORKS.

HERZL
EJ (1972), 8:410. Contains
genealogical tables for
Diamant and Herzl families up
to Theodor Herzl and his wife
Jeanette Diamant. See
GENERAL WORKS.
Berlin, Alex. Thedor Herzl:
Biographie. Mit 63 bildern
und einer Ahnentafel. Wien:
Fiba-Verlag, 1934. 736 p.
"Ahentafel Theodor Herzl
(1860-1904)," pp. 699-701.
CtY, DLC, MH, NN, PPDrop.
Diamant, Paul J. Theodor
Herzl's väterliche und
mütterliche Vorfahren; eine
familiengeschichtliche Studie
mit einer Ahnentafel.
Jerusalem: Bamberger &
Wahrmann, 1934. 19 p. NN,
PPDrop.
Fraenkel, J. "Theodore Herzl's
Ancestors," Le Judaïsme
Sephardi (London), n.s., 10
(Mar. 1956):440-41, 449-50.
Kempelen. Magyarországi Zsidó,
2:13, 58. See GENERAL WORKS.
Leuner, H.D. "The Tragedy of
the Herzl Family," Judaica
(Switzerland) 33, no. 3
(1977):101-104.
Nedava, J. and S. Braun. "Die
Tragödie der Familie Herzl,"
Zeitschrift für die
Geschichte der Juden (Tel
Aviv) 4 (1967):141-46.
Molho, M. "Antecedentes
sefardíes de los líderes
sionistas Theodor Herzl y Max

Nordau," Le Judaïsme Sephardi (London), n.s., 19 (Feb. 1960):843-45.

Stern, Arthur. "The Genetic Tragedy of the Family of Thedor Herzl," The Israel Annals of Psychiatry and Related Disciplines 3 (Apr. 1965):99-116.

————. Die genetische Tragödie der Familie Theodor Herzl: eine soziologisch-psychiatrische Studie. Vortrag von Arthur Stern; gehalten am 11. Jan. 1965 in der David Yelling Lodge. Jerusalem: Achwa, 1965. 37 p. JNUL.

Stewart, Desmond. Theodor Herzl. Garden City, N.Y.: Doubleday and Co., Inc., 1974. 395 p. "Theodor Herzl's Ancestors, Connections, and Descendants," front and rear inside covers of this work. "Herzl's Marriage," appendix II, pp. 373-75.

HERZOG
See HENRY-HERZOG.

Goldstein, Ruth Hartzell. Herzog and Lambert Genealogy.... Santa Barbara, Calif.: ABC-Clio, 1971. 41 p. Genealogical tables. Genealogy of family of Germany. The first Herzog arrived in U.S. in 1845, the name subsequently changed to Hartzell. AJHS, DLC, OCH.

Herzog, Paul. Three Generations: The Dispersion of a Jewish Family. London: By the Author, 1973. 64 p. Genealogical tables. Herzog family of Posen; descendants of Jakob Herzog (1758-1833), Schwersenz/Posen. LBI.

Kempelen. Magyarországi Zsidó, 1:89, 127, 138; 2:64; 3:79, 95. See GENERAL WORKS.

Maurois, André. Memoirs, 1885-1967. Translated from the French by Denver Lindley. New York: Harper & Row, 1970.

439 p. Genealogical information on Fraenckel and Herzog (author's real family name) families of Elbeuf, Ringendorf, and Bischwiller, pp. 6-15.

Schwartz, Helene E. "A Photograph Comes to Life: A JGS Directory Success Story," Jewish Genealogical Society Newsletter (New York) 1, no. 5 (Feb. 1980):1-2. Brief genealogical information on the children of Yitzchak and Chana Wiesenthal Herzog of Skala and Jagielnica, Galicia.

Stern. FAJF. Herzog family tree beginning in U.S. See GENERAL WORKS.

HESCHEL
Rosenstein. Unbroken Chain, pp. 434ff. "Descendants of R. Saul, Son of R. Abraham Joshua Heschel of Cracow" genealogical chart. See GENERAL WORKS.

————, pp. 383ff. "Descendants of R. Abraham Joshua Heschel of Cracow." See GENERAL WORKS.

————, pp. 530ff. Heschel Chassidic Dynasty of Apt. See GENERAL WORKS.

HESS
CFM has family records.
Cramer, Jenny. Geschichte der Familie Hess von Aufhausen. O.O., 1931, und Nahariya, Israel, 1941. 172 p. Genealogy begins 1742. LBI.

Kempelen. Magyarországi Zsidó, 2:8. See GENERAL WORKS.

Schulte. Bonner Juden, pp. 279-83. See GENERAL WORKS.

Silberner, Edmund. Moses Hess, Geschichte seines Lebens. Leiden: E.J. Brill, 1966. 692 p. "Familie und Jugend," pp. 1-4. Moses [Moritz] Hess (1812-1875), Socialist and "prophet of Zionism," was born in Bonn, the son of

David Hess, the grandson of
Nathan David Hess, and the
great-grandson of David Hess,
who came to Bonn from
Hessen-Nassau. CtY, CU, MH,
NIC, NjP, NjR, NN, OU.
Tänzer. Juden in Jebenhausen,
p. 328. See GENERAL WORKS.

HESSE
CFM has family records.

HETEES
Kempelen. Magyarországi Zsidó,
3:62. Heteés family. See
GENERAL WORKS.

HETENYI
Kempelen. Magyarországi Zsidó,
2:137. Hetényi family. See
GENERAL WORKS.

HETES
Kempelen. Magyarországi Zsidó,
2:120. Hetés family. See
GENERAL WORKS.

HETSCH
Kempelen. Magyarországi Zsidó,
2:70. See GENERAL WORKS.

HETSEY
Kempelen. Magyarországi Zsidó,
2:52. Hétsey family. See
GENERAL WORKS.

HEUMANN
Kempelen. Magyarországi Zsidó,
2:91; 3:119. See GENERAL
WORKS.
Schulte. Bonner Juden, p. 284.
See GENERAL WORKS.
Tänzer. Juden in Jebenhausen,
pp. 329-30. See GENERAL
WORKS.
Tänzer. Juden in Tirol,
p. 723. See GENERAL WORKS.

HEVESI
Kempelen. Magyarországi Zsidó,
1:31, 63; 3:46. See GENERAL
WORKS.

HEYMAN
Heyman Family, Atlanta, Ga.
Heyman, Joseph K. "My

Children's Roots." N.d.
Typescript; Xerox copy.
Covers 1755-1978. AJA.
Semi-Gotha, 1:111ff. See
GENERAL WORKS.

HEYMANN
AMH has family records.
CFM has family records.
LBI has family trees beginning
1790 and 1804.
LBIS has family tree and notes
from Göteburg, Sweden.
Heymann, Aron Hirsch.
Lebenserinnerungen nach
seiner Niederschrift im
Aufträge seiner Kinder hrsg.
Von Heinrich Loewe. Berlin:
Eigentum der Familie, 1909.
476 p. LBI, MB, OCH, OU, PP.
"Heymann," JFF, no. 1
(1925):78. Descendants of R.
Lewin Heymann, Breslau,
1747-1810.
Schulte. Bonner Juden,
pp. 286-95. See GENERAL
WORKS.
See Kopp, Jüdischen Alsenz,
entry under HAYM, HAYMAN,
HAYMANN, HAYUM.

HEYMANS
AMH has family records.

HEYNEMANN
CFM has family records.

HICHENBERG
CAJ has family tree from
Germany.

HIERONYMI
Kempelen. Magyarországi Zsidó,
1:145; 3:115. See GENERAL
WORKS.

HIERRO
CFM has family records.

HIFFAM
AMH has family records.

HIGHAM
CFM has family records.

HILB
Zapf. Tübinger Juden, pp.
135-38. See GENERAL WORKS.

HILDESHEIM
CFM has family records.

HILDESHEIMER
CAJ has family records.

HILL
AMH has family records.

HILLER
See AJA and Stern entries under
GOLDSTONE.
Hiller, Kurt. Leben Gegen die
Zeit. v. 1: Logos. Reinbek
bei Hamburg: Rowohlt Verlag,
1969. 422 p. "Herkunft und
Kindheit," pp. 11-23. The
author (1885-1972) was a
German socialist
theoretician. He was born in
Berlin, the son of Hartwig
Hiller (1854-1897) and Ella
Singer Hiller (1862-1936) and
the grandson of Joel Hiller
and Julius and Sophie Singer.
The Hiller family came to
Berlin from Bentschen
(Posen). CLU, CSt, CtY, CU,
DLC, ICU, IEN, MH, NIC, NjP.

HILLMAN
Hillman, Sidney. "Genealogical
Information, 1915-1946."
Typescript. AJA.

HILSNER
CAJ has family records.

HILZHEIMER
AMH has family records.

HIMES
AMH has family records.

HIMMELREICH
Keneseth Israel. See GENERAL
WORKS.

HIMMLER
Kempelen. Magyarországi Zsidó,
3:96. See GENERAL WORKS.

HINRICHSEN
Schnee. Hoffinanz und Staat,
2:295-313. "Die Familie
Hinrichsen." Includes
genealogical information,
17th to 19th century. Family
of Mecklenburg. See GENERAL
WORKS.

HIRSCH
AJA has family trees from
Cincinnati and Memphis. AJA
also has genealogical files
of Schlesinger-Hirsch family.
AMH has family records.
CAJ (Call No. 3418) has family
tree for family of Berlin.
Ballin. Juden in Seesen,
p. 211. See GENERAL WORKS.
See Sally David Cramer entry
under CRAMER.
Duckesz, E. "Zur Genealogie
von Samson Raphael Hirsch,"
Jahrbuch für Judische
Literatur und Gesellschaft,
1926. German rabbi,
b. Hamburg, 1808;
d. Frankfurt, 1888.
Duckesz, Eduard. Zur
Genealogie Samson Raphael
Hirsch's. N.p., 191-? 30 p.
Samson Raphael Hirsch, rabbi
and writer, leader and
foremost exponent of
Orthodoxy in Germany in 19th
century, b. Hamburg, 1808;
d. 1888. From 1851 to his
death he served as the rabbi
of the Orthodox congregation
in Frankfurt am Main. OCH.
Frank. Nashville Jewry,
pp. 134-35. See GENERAL
WORKS.
Fuchs, Peter P. "Die Familie
Hirsch und Hirsch von
Duinofels," Zeitschrift d.
Deut. Vereins für Geschichte
Mährens und Schlesiens 37
(1935):141-58.
Hartmann, Werner. "Aron Hirsch
und die Familie Hirsch:
Weltwertes Unternehmertum,
1783-1842," Nachrichtenblatt
der Jüd. Gemeinde von Berlin
und des Verbandes der Jüd.
Gemeinden in der DDR

(Berlin/Dresden), Juni 1980,
pp. 3-4. On Aaron Hirsch &
Co. in Halberstadt and Hirsch
Kupfer-und Messingwerke AG in
Ilsenburg/Eberswalde. Family
of Halberstadt. Aron Hirsch
was founder of the famous
metal firm.
Hirsch, Arnold. Stammtafel der
Familie Hirsch aus Lübeck.
Koblenz, 1968. 24 p. 17th
century onwards.
Hirsch, Frieda. Die Familie
von Hirsch auf Gereuth.
Erste quellenmässige
Darstellung ihrer Geschichte.
München: Selbstverlag, 1931.
112 p. Genealogical table,
coat of arms. CtY, DLC, LBI,
MH, NN, OCH, OU, PPDrop.
———. "Mein Weg von
Karlsruhe über Heidelberg
nach Haifa, 1890-1965."
Kirjath-Onol Israel, 1965.
169 p. LBI.
Hirsch, Helmut. "Yankees from
the Rhine." Chicago,
ca. 1951. Helmut Hirsch
(1907-   ), professor of
European History at Roosevelt
University in Chicago.
Family originally from
Wuppertal-Barmen, Germany.
LBI.
Hirsch, Joseph. R. Binyamin
Hirsch. Jerusalem, 1947.
91 p. Includes genealogical
tables. Benjamin Hirsch,
1840-1911; Benjamin Hirsch
Auerbach, 1808-1872. Family
of Halberstadt. DLC, NN.
Hirsch, Louis.
"Familiengeschichte und
Lebenserinnerungen."
Stuttgart, 1937. 149 p.
Family of Stuttgart.
Includes forbears and
children of Louis Hirsch
(1858-1941) and his wife
Helene Reiss. LBI.
Kempelen. Magyarországi Zsidó,
1:38, 93; 2:17, 18, 51, 64,
127; 3:19, 23, 61, 63. See
GENERAL WORKS.
Prÿs, Josef. Die Familie von
Hirsch auf Gereuth. Erste

quellenmässige Darstellung
ihrer Geschichte. München:
Selbstverlag, 1931. 112 p.
Genealogical table, coat of
arms. CtY, DLC, LBI, MH, NN,
OCH, OU, PPDrop.
———. "Zum Anteil der
Familie von Hirsch auf
Gereuth am Kampfe um die
bayerische
Judenemanzipation," ZGJD 5,
no. 1 (1935):69-72.
Pudor. Internationalen
Verwandtschaftlichen. Vol. 2
includes a section on Hirsch
family. See GENERAL WORKS.
Rose. Schöninger Juden. See
GENERAL WORKS.
Rothschild. Svenska Israel.
See GENERAL WORKS.
Schulte. Bonner Juden, p. 297.
See GENERAL WORKS.
Scholem, Gershom. From Berlin
to Jerusalem: Memories of My
Youth. Translated from the
German by Harry Zohn. New
York: Schocken Books, 1980.
178 p. "Background and
Childhood (1897-1910)," pp.
1-20. Includes genealogical
information on the Scholem
family and the families of
the author's mother: Hirsch
and Pflaum. The Scholem
family came to Berlin from
Glogau, Lower Silesia, in the
second decade of the
nineteenth century, while the
Hirsch and Pflaum families
came to Berlin from Reetz,
Rawicz, and Lissa.
Schunk, Betty. Aus alten
Tagebüchern und Erinnerungen
der Familien Hirsch, [Worms],
Strupp, Eisenberg.
Abgeschrieben, illustriert
und mit vier Stammtafeln
versehen von Alexander
Eisenberg. Meiningen, 1924.
24 p. LBI.
Schwab, Hermann. Die Familie
Hirsch in Halberstadt,
1780-1927. N.p., n.d. 26 p.
LBI.
Seckbach, Markus. Eine
Ahnentafel von 27

Generationen bis zum Jahre
1290. Betr. Die Familien
Seckbach, Meyer, Auerbach,
Hirsch, Marx. Bodenheimer
U.A. Hamburg: Laubhütte,
1936. 22 p. OCH.
Semi-Gotha, 1:119ff. See
GENERAL WORKS.
Semigothaisches Taschenbuch.
Genealogical table 11. See
GENERAL WORKS.
Tänzer. Juden in Tirol,
p. 724. See GENERAL WORKS.
Zapf. Tübinger Juden, pp.
52-53, 138-41, 198-203. See
GENERAL WORKS.

HIRSCHALL
AMH has family records.

HIRSCHBERG
Lövinson, Siegfried. 50 Sterne
am Himmel meiner
Kindheitsjahre. Berlin,
1905. Also on Moses Levin
Hirschberg, 1768-1833, his
wife Johanna, née Marcuse,
1803-1871, and their
children.
Mayer, Richard. "Aus der
Geschichte der Familien Mayer
und Hirschberg." N.p., 1970.
15 p. JNUL.

HIRSCHEL
Kempelen. Magyarországi Zsidó,
1:111; 2:60. See GENERAL
WORKS.
Wolf, "Anglo-Jewish Families."
See GENERAL WORKS.

HIRSCHFELD
LBI has family trees beginning
1767, 1771, 1780, 1817, and
1829.
Hirschberg, Steve. Term paper,
"The History of My Family,"
submitted to Hebrew Union
College-Jewish Institute of
Religion, Cincinnati, Ohio,
May 17, 1976. AJA.
Hirschfeld, Alfred.
"Erinnerungen." Berlin,
1916. 52 p. Includes brief
histories of the Hirschfeld
banking family of Berlin and

the Thorsch banking family
(author's mother's family) of
Vienna and Prague . LBI.
Kempelen. Magyarországi Zsidó,
1:119; 3:106. See GENERAL
WORKS.
Schulte. Bonner Juden, p. 298.
See GENERAL WORKS.
Tänzer. Juden in Tirol,
pp. 725-28. See GENERAL
WORKS.

HIRSCHFELD-BENET
Birth and Death Records,
1832-1963. AJA.

HIRSCHFIELD
AMH has family records.

HIRSCHHAUSER
Kempelen. Magyarországi Zsidó,
2:89. See GENERAL WORKS.

HIRSCHHORN
"The Family Tree of Hirschhorn
and History of the Hirschhorn
Family," in Edward Jessup's
Ernest Oppenheimer: A Study
in Power (London: Rex
Collings, 1979), pp. 330-32.
Forebears of Nancy Hirschhorn
Oppenheimer (1841-1912), the
mother of Ernest Oppenheimer
(1880-1957), the South
African diamond and gold
financier. Family from
Fauerbach and Friedberg in
Hessen. Genealogy covers
18th to early 20th century.
Hyams, Barry. Hirschhorn:
Medici from Brooklyn. New
York: E.P. Dutton, 1979.
206 p. Genealogical
information, pp. 28-31.
Joseph Hirschhorn, art
collector and financier, was
born in 1900 in the village
of Jokst, Latvia, 100 miles
southwest of Riga, and about
the same distance from Libau,
the Baltic port to the north.
Kempelen. Magyarországi Zsidó,
3:123. See GENERAL WORKS.

HIRSCHLAND
Phiebig, Albert. Die Familie

Hirschland. Berlin, 1937.
Begins 1545. LBI, YIVO.
Simon Hirschland Bankhaus,
Essen und Hamburg. 100 Jahre
Simon Hirschland,
Essen-Hamburg. N.p., 1938.
62 p. Simon Hirschland,
1807-1885. LBI.

HIRSCHLER
Kempelen. Magyarországi Zsidó,
1:142; 2:126; 3:139. See
GENERAL WORKS.

HIRSCHS
LBIS has family tree.

HIRSHFELD
"The Hirshfelds of Kern County
[California]," Western States
Jewish Historical Quarterly
15 (Apr. 1983):223-31. The
story of Herman (1844-1902),
Marcus (1852-1924), Lesser
(1853-1917), David
(1854-1924), and Bertha
(1848-1915) Hirshfeld, who
were born in the Prussian
town of Strausberg, near the
Polish border, the children
of Lewin and Dora Hirshfeld.

HIRST
AMH has family records.

HIRZEL
Weisz, Leo. Aus dem Leben des
Bürgermeisters Salomon
Hirzel, 1580-1652. Zürich:
Schulthesz, 1930. 354 p.
(Veröffentlichungen aus d.
Archive d. Familie Hirzel in
Zürich, Bd. 1.) Family of
Switzerland. MH, NN.

HITLER
Rennick, Robert M. "Hitlers
and Others Who Changed Their
Names and a Few Who Did Not,"
Names 17 (1969):199-207.

HJARNE
Semi-Gotha, 2:15. Hjärne
family. See GENERAL WORKS.

HOCHGELERHTER
Rosenstein. Unbroken Chain,
pp. 303ff. See GENERAL
WORKS.

HOCHSCHILD
Berney, Albert. "Descendants
of Zodik Hochschild, Born
1792, Died 12-26-1858,
Married Rikkel Steiermann."
Westcliffe, Colorado, 1977.
9 p. AJHS.

HOCHSINGER
Kempelen. Magyarországi Zsidó,
2:60. See GENERAL WORKS.

HOCHSTAEDTER
LBI has family tree beginning
1760.

HOCHSTETTER
Sonder, Alfred. Ahnentafel der
Kinder des Nathan Weill, Sohn
des Löw Weill, in Kippenheim.
Frankfurt: Schirmer & Mahlau,
1935. 50, 6 p. Genealogical
tables. "Ahnentafel der
Jeanette Hochstetter." NN.

HOCKEN
AMH has family records.

HODAS
See COHODAS.

HODGSON
AMH has family records.

HODOSI
Kempelen. Magyarországi Zsidó,
1:102. See GENERAL WORKS.

HOEXTER
Kern, Janet. Yesterday's
Child. Philadelphia:
J.B. Lippincott Co., 1962.
239 p. Story of author's
family life in Chicago to
W.W.II. Kern family
originally came from
Bohorodczany in Galicia.
Author is daughter of
Maximilian (1890-   ) and
Elaine Hoexter (1901-   )
Kern. Elaine Kern was born

in Chicago of German-Jewish
parents.

HOFBAUER
Mander, Anica Vesel with Sarika
Finci Hofbauer. Blood Ties:
A Woman's History. Berkeley
and New York: Moon Books and
Random House, Inc., 1976.
297 p. Feminist
autobiography focusing on
author's birth (1934-   )
and early childhood in
Sarajevo, Yugoslavia;
family's escape to Italy in
1943; and their emigration to
California in late 1940s.
Interspersed are chapters of
reminiscences of Sarika Finci
Hofbauer, the author's
grandmother, about World Wars
I and II. CtY, DLC, ICarbS,
MB, MH, NN, NNC, OC1, OU,
TxU.

HOFER
Kempelen. Magyarországi Zsidó,
2:141. See GENERAL WORKS.

HOFF
Hechter, Ruth Kaaplander.
Brenner-Sattenstein-
Kaaplander (Caplan)-Hoff
Family Tree. Brooklyn, N.Y.,
1982. PJAC.

HOFFE
AMH has family records.

HOFFENBERG
Kempelen. Magyarországi Zsidó,
3:124. See GENERAL WORKS.

HOFFER
See HOFHEIMER.
Kempelen. Magyarországi Zsidó,
3:34. See GENERAL WORKS.

HOFFMAN
AMH has family records.
Keneseth Israel. See GENERAL
WORKS.
Zelinger, Robert. "Loyal
Family Circle: A History of
Sinai and Dora Hoffman and

Their Families, 1825-1980."
RMJHS.

HOFFMANN
Kempelen. Magyarországi Zsidó,
2:94, 99, 118, 127, 129, 131,
132, 137; 3:46, 79. See
GENERAL WORKS.

HOFFNUNG
AMH has family records.
Bergman, G.F.I. "Sigmund
Hoffnung and the Firm of S.
Hoffnung & Co., Ltd," Journal
and Proceedings of the
Australian Jewish Historical
Society 7 (1973):269-76.
Davis, L.D. "The Hoffnungs,"
Journal and Proceedings of
the Australian Jewish
Historical Society 7
(1973):261-69.
CFM has family records.

HOFHEIMER
Stern, Malcolm H. The
Descendants of Moses, Son of
Naphtali or Hofheim or Moses
Hofheimer (Moshe Hoffer),
1781-1862. Norfolk, Va.,
1964. Genealogy of prominent
family of Norfolk. AJA,
AJHS, JGCT.

HOFMANN
LBI has family tree beginning
1802.
ZGJT 2 (1931). Family history.

HOFMANNSTAHL
JFF, no. 19. Family history.

HOFSTEN
Semi-Gotha, 1:23, 27. See
GENERAL WORKS.

HOHENBERG
AJA has genealogical files.

HOHENEMSER
AMH has family records.

HOHENFELS
Stern. FAJF. Hohenfels family
tree beginning in Germany.
See GENERAL WORKS.

HOHENSTAUFEN
JFF, no. 23. Family history.

HOINEL
Kopp. Jüdischen Alsenz,
pp. 122-23. See GENERAL
WORKS.

HOJER
Semi-Gotha, 1:109. Höjer
family. See GENERAL WORKS.

HOLDERN (VON)
AMH has family records.

HOLDHEIM
CAJ has family records.

HOLLAND
AMH has family records.

HOLLANDER
AMH has family records.
CFM has family records.
CAJ has family records. CAJ
also has history of family of
Altona, Germany, end 17th
century to 1921. Compiled by
Rabbi Eduard Duckesz.
Register betreffende de
Families Hollander en Moerel,
1770-1929. [Semengest. door
Magdalena Esther
Polak-Hollander.] Groningen,
1929. Family of Holland.
BR.
Kempelen. Magyarországi Zsidó,
1:137; 2:91. Holländer
family. See GENERAL WORKS.
Tergit, Gabriele. "Die
Holländers. Geschichte einer
Künstlerfamilie," AJR
Information 12, no. 10
(1957).

HOLLENDER
CFM has family records.

HOLLINWORTH
AMH has family records.

HOLLITSCHER
Kempelen. Magyarországi Zsidó,
1:142; 2:35; 3:101. See
GENERAL WORKS.

HOLLOS
Kempelen. Magyarországi Zsidó,
2:128. Hollós family. See
GENERAL WORKS.

HOLLOWAY
AJA has genealogical files.

HOLST
Semi-Gotha, 1:28. See GENERAL
WORKS.

HOLT
AMH has family records.

HOLTZER
Kempelen. Magyarországi Zsidó,
3:105. See GENERAL WORKS.

HOLZ
CAJ has family records.
LBI has family tree beginning
1773.

HOLZMAN
Gold. Juden Mährens, p. 182.
"Stammbaum Holzmann-Natzler."
See GENERAL WORKS.

HOMBERG
CAJ has family records.
CAJD has family tree from
Germany.

HOMBURGER
LBI has family tree beginning
1694.

HOMONNAY
Kempelen. Magyarországi Zsidó,
2:76. See GENERAL WORKS.

HONCHIN
AMH has family records.

HONECK
CFM has family records.

HONICH
Kempelen. Magyarországi Zsidó,
2:27. Hönich family. See
GENERAL WORKS.

HONIG
PD has family records.
See Wilhelm and Rudolf Frank

177   HOROWITZ

entry under BING.
Kempelen. Magyarországi Zsidó,
3:57, 59. Hőnig family. See
GENERAL WORKS.
Kopp. Jüdischen Alsenz,
p. 129. See GENERAL WORKS.

HONYWOOD
AMH has family records.

HOPF
See Friedrich Carl Tuchmann
entry under BING.

HOPSTEIN
Rosenstein. Unbroken Chain,
pp. 655ff. See GENERAL
WORKS.

HORN
Kempelen. Magyarországi Zsidó,
2:43. See GENERAL WORKS.
Semi-Gotha, 1:26. See GENERAL
WORKS.

HORNER
Kempelen. Magyarországi Zsidó,
2:37. See GENERAL WORKS.

HORNSTEIN
Kempelen. Magyarországi Zsidó,
2:135. See GENERAL WORKS.

HORODEZKY
"Genealogisches von Samuel Abba
Horodezky mit einer
Ahnentafel," in
Gedächtnisschrift zum zehnten
Todestage von Micha Josef bin
Gorion [Berdyczewski], 18.
November 1931, Hrsg. von
Rachel und Emanuel bin
Gorion. (Berlin:
Morgenland-Verlag, 1931).
Horodezky, scholar and
historian of Jewish mysticism
and Hasidism, b. Malin (Kiev
region), 1871; d. 1957. NN.

HOROVITZ
[Freimann, Aron]. Aus des
Stammbaum der Familien
Ettlinger, Freimann &
Horovitz. Berlin: Marx &
Co., 1925. 3 genealogical
tables. OCH.

HOROWITZ
Bałaban. Żydow w Krakowie,
1:150, 156. Genealogical
chart of the descendants of
Jezajasz Horowitz (16th to
17th century) of Poland. See
GENERAL WORKS.
Brilling, Bernhard. "Jüdische
Druckerfamilien in
Frankfurt/oder," Archiv für
Geschichte der Buchwesens 1
(1956/57):570-81. "Die
Familie Horowitz,"
pp. 571-73. 18th to 19th
century.
Friedberg, Bernhard. Toldoth
Mishpaḥat Horowitz. Added
title page: Geschichte der
Familie Horowitz, ihr Leben
und Literarisches Wirken von
Beginn des 16. Jahrhunderts
bis auf die Gegenwart. Nach
den Quellen bearb. Frankfurt
am Main: Sanger & Friedberg,
1911. 24 p. 2 verb. aufl.
Antwerpen, 1928. 32 p.
Includes genealogical table.
CLU, DLC, NN.
Horodezky, Samuel Abba. "The
Age of Ascetic Morality:
Isaiah Horowitz ... and his
Family (XVI-XVII)," (In
Hebrew and Russian.)
Evreiskaia Starina 6
(1913):145-61, 367-83,
455-68. On Rabbi Isaiah b.
Shabbetai Sheftel Horowitz,
1632-1689, and his son, Rabbi
Abraham b. Isaiah Horowitz,
1671-1744, and their
families.
Horowitz, H. "Die Familie
Horowitz in Prag im 16.
Jahrhundert," ZGJT 2
(1931/32):89-105, 127-131,
225-28; 3 (1932/33):127-31,
221-24.
Kahan. 'Anaf 'ez avoth. See
GENERAL WORKS.
Kempelen. Magyarországi Zsidó,
3:27, 48, 70. See GENERAL
WORKS.
Newman, Eugene. Life and
Teachings of Isaiah Horowitz.
London: By the Author, 1972.
216 p. "Parents of Isaiah

Horowitz," pp. 13-15; "Wife of Isaiah Horowitz," pp. 32-34; and "Family [descendants] of Isaiah Horowitz," pp. 69-72. Isaiah Horowitz (ca. 1570-1625/30), rabbi, Kabbalist, and communal leader, was born in Prague, but lived for many years in Poland. CU, DLC, MB, NcD, NIC, NjP, NNJ.
Pesis, Phinehas. 'Atereth ha-Lewiyim. Warsaw, 1902. 80 p. Horowitz family in Poland; descendants of Isaiah Horowitz. DLC.
Rosenstein. Unbroken Chain, pp. 575ff. Horowitz family of Stanislan. See GENERAL WORKS.
————, pp. 551ff. Genealogical chart. See GENERAL WORKS.
See Mordechai Rubinstein entry under FRANKEL.
Shapiro. Mishpachot Atikot. Horowitz, Hurwitz family, pp. 160-94. See GENERAL WORKS.
Sonder, Alfred. Ahnentafel der Kinder des Nathan Weill (Sohn des Löw Weill) in Kippenheim. Frankfurt am Main: Schirmer & Mahlau, 1935. 50 p. Genealogical tables. NN.
See Meir Yizraeli entry under BIDERMAN.

HOROWITZ-MARGARETEN
Margareten, Joel et al. Directory and Genealogy of the Horowitz-Margareten Family. Los Angeles and New York: Horowitz-Margareten Family Association, 1955.
Rosenstein. Unbroken Chain, pp. 568ff. See GENERAL WORKS.

HORT
AMH has family records.
CFM has family records.

HORVAT, HORVATH
Kempelen. Magyarországi Zsidó. Horvát, Horváth family, 1:17,

110; 3:126. Horváth family, 2:95. See GENERAL WORKS.

HORVITZ
CAJ has family tree.

HORWICH
Horwich, Bernard [Beril]. My First Eighty Years. Chicago: Argus Books, 1939. 426 p. "My Boyhood in Poniemon," pp. 1-50. Poniemon is across the river from Kovno (now Kaunas), Lithuania. The author (1861-?) was the son of Jacob Horwich (1819-1906) and the grandson of David Horwich. His brothers were Arye (Aron), Hirsch (Harris), Henach (Henry), David, and Samuel Baruch. The author and his five brothers came to Chicago in the 1880s and 1890s. Bernard Horwich was an active Zionist and Jewish communal leader.

HORWITZ
AJA has genealogical files.
Stern. FAJF. Horwitz family tree beginning in U.S. See GENERAL WORKS.

HOSELITZ
Kempelen. Magyarországi Zsidó, 1:139. See GENERAL WORKS.

HOSKYNO
AMH has family records.

HOWARD
AMH has family records.

HOWARD-BROWN
Kempelen. Magyarországi Zsidó, 1:113. See GENERAL WORKS.

HOXTER
CAJ has family tree from Germany.

HOYOS
Kempelen. Magyarországi Zsidó, 3:31. See GENERAL WORKS.

HUBERT
Kalisch, Simon. A Builder of
Judaism: The Story of Arthur
Hubert and His Family.
Manchester: Boaz House, 1978.
144 p.
Kempelen. Magyarországi Zsidó,
2:136. See GENERAL WORKS.

HUBSCH
Kempelen. Magyarországi Zsidó,
2:120. Hübsch family. See
GENERAL WORKS.

HUFFNAGLE
AMH has family records.

HUGHES
AMH has family records.

HUILLIER
Kempelen. Magyarországi Zsidó,
1:74. See GENERAL WORKS.

HULDSCHINSKY
LBI has family tree beginning
1864.

HULENYI
Kempelen. Magyarországi Zsidó,
2:66. Hulényi family. See
GENERAL WORKS.

HUME
AMH has family records.

HUNEFELD
See Stammbaum Levinstein entry
under AVELLIS. Includes
Hünefeld family.

HUNKAR
Kempelen. Magyarországi Zsidó,
1:102. See GENERAL WORKS.

HUNT
AMH has family records.
Stern. FAJF. Hunt family tree
beginning in Amsterdam. See
GENERAL WORKS.

HUNTER
AMH has family records.

HURWITZ
AMH has family records.

Eisenstadt and Wiener. Da'at
Kedoschim. Includes Hurwitz
family of Russia. See
GENERAL WORKS.
Löwenstein, L. "Hurwitz,"
Jahrbuch für Jüdische
Literatur und Gesellschaft 6
(1908):214.
See Shapiro, Mishpachot Atikot
entry under HOROWITZ.
Unger, Menaše. "The Genealogy
of Haikl Hurwitz," (In
Yiddish.) Publications of the
Yiddish Scientific Institute,
Studies in Philology (Vilno)
3 (1929):83-88.

HUSZAR
Kempelen. Magyarországi Zsidó,
1:44; 2:92; 3:60, 88. Huszár
family. See GENERAL WORKS.

HUTTENBAUER
Levy, Emilie Jane. "My Family,
The History of the
Huttenbauer Family. Bavarian
Immigrants, and Early
Residents of Cincinnati,
Ohio, ca. 1857, Written by
Ms. Levy, 1945." Typescript;
Xerox copy. AJA.

HUTZLER
Hutzler, Charles S. [Genealogy
of the Hutzler Family of
Richmond, Va.], 1957. 18th
century forward. AJA.

HUVOS
Kempelen. Magyarországi Zsidó,
2:69. Hüvös family. See
GENERAL WORKS.

HYAM
AMH has family records.
CFM has family records.

HYAMS
AMH has family records.
CFM has family records.
Hyams Family. "Records of
Births, Marriages, and Deaths
from Family Bibles;
Obituaries; Family Memoirs;
and Notes. Charleston, S.C.;
New Orleans, La.; and San

Antonio, Texas, 1805-1936."
Also includes Nordhaus
family. AJA.
See Esmond S. De Beer entry
under BARDEN.
Solomon Hyams Family;
Genealogical Material. MS
and Typescript. AJA.
Stern. FAJF. Hyams family
tree beginning in Poland.
See GENERAL WORKS.

HYE
CAJ has family tree from
Austria, beginning 19th
century.

HYEEM
CFM has family records.

HYMAN
AMH has family records.
CFM has family records.
Hyman Family, Louisville, Ky.
"Information Regarding the
Hyman Family, Taken from the
Louisville, Ky. City
Directory, for the Period,
1832-1860." Typescript.
AJA.
Frank. Nashville Jewry,
p. 139. See GENERAL WORKS.
Stern. FAJF. Hyman family
trees beginning in:
(I) Kelin, Bohemia; and
(II) England. See GENERAL
WORKS.

HYNEMAN
Hyneman Family. Birth,
Marriage and Death Records.
AJA.
Stern. FAJF. Hyneman family
trees beginning in:
(I) Holland and
(II) Hofgeismar,
Hesse-Cassel. See GENERAL
WORKS.

IBN DANAN
Slouschz, Nahum. "The History
of Fez and the Ibn Danan

Family," (In Hebrew.) Sura
(Israel-American Annual,
Yeshiva University, Sura
Institute for Research and
Publications) 3
(1957/58):163-91.

IBRANYI
Kempelen. Magyarországi Zsidó,
2:46; 3:126. Ibrányi family.
See GENERAL WORKS.

IDANIA
CFM has family records.

IDELMAN
Bernstein, Jeanette Warshawsky.
"Biography: The Life of Max
Idelman, Pioneer Citizen of
Wyoming, and of His Relatives
and Descendants," 1954.
Family originally from
Poland. AJA.

IDILISH
See Meir Yizraeli entry under
BIDERMAN.

IFFLA
AMH has family records.

IGLAUER
See Friedrich Carl Tuchmann
entry under BING.
Genealogical table of Iglauer
family begins 1805.

IHRE
Semi-Gotha, 1:82. See GENERAL
WORKS.

IKLE
LBI has family tree.

ILFELD
O'Grady, Janet. "The Pioneer
Ilfelds: Working Hard, Long,
and Smart," New Mexico
Magazine 60 (Oct. 1982):2-4,
6, 40-41. Family of Germany
which became pioneer
merchants in mid-19th-century
New Mexico.

ILLES
Kempelen. Magyarországi Zsidó,

2:51. Illés family. See
GENERAL WORKS.

ILLYES
Kempelen. Magyarországi Zsidó,
3:98. Illyés family. See
GENERAL WORKS.

INCZE
Kempelen. Magyarországi Zsidó,
2:15, 73. See GENERAL WORKS.

INTRATER
See SPRING.

INWALD
Kempelen. Magyarországi Zsidó,
3:177. See GENERAL WORKS.

IRSAI
Kempelen. Magyarországi Zsidó,
2:78, 102. See GENERAL
WORKS.

ISAAC
AMH has family records.
CFM has family records.
LBI has family trees beginning
1787 and 1808.
Isaac, Franz K.L. Family Tree,
Abraham Isaak, 1852-1938.
Rosenort, Manitoba: Lark
Printing, 1970. 30 p.
Isaac, Isaak family. Allen
County Public Library, Ft.
Wayne, Indiana.
Rachel and Wallich. Berliner
Grosskaufleute, 2:381-89.
"Moses Isaac (1708-1776) und
seine Nachkommen." See
GENERAL WORKS.
Schulte. Bonner Juden, p. 299.
See GENERAL WORKS.

ISAACKS
Stern. FAJF. Isaacks family
tree beginning in Emden,
Germany. See GENERAL WORKS.

ISAACS
AMH has family records.
CFM has family records.
"Isaacs Family Genealogy,
1815-1968;" MS. AJA.
"The Bible of Joshua Isaacs the
Second; a Grandsonn of Joseph

Isaacs, Made a Freeman at New
York in 1698," St. Charles 1
(Jan. 1935):125-130. 18th
century. Also includes
genealogical tables.
See Esmond S. De Beer entry
under BARDEN.
Debrett's Peerage and
Baronetage, 1980, pp. 973-74.
Frank. Nashville Jewry,
p. 136. See GENERAL WORKS.
Isaacs, M. Hyman. "John
Isaacs--Actor, and His
Family," The Jewish Monthly
(London) 3, no. 4
(1949):239-44.
Isaacs, Moses, Cincinnati,
Ohio. "Family History."
AJA.
Isaacs, Nathan. Cambridge,
Mass. Correspondence.
Contains miscellaneous
materials concerning the
Isaacs and Davis families,
1812-1942. AJA.
Reading, Gerald Rufus Isaacs,
2nd Marquis of. Rufus
Isaacs: First Marquess of
Reading. New York:
G.P. Putnam's Sons, 1940.
324 p. Early history of
Isaacs family in England,
pp. 3-7. Descendants of
Michael Isaacs who came to
England from Central Europe
in first decade of 18th
century.
Stern. FAJF. Isaacs family
trees beginning in:
(I) Emden, Germany (listed in
FAJF under Isaacks);
(II) U.S.; (III) Amsterdam;
descendants of Isaac Gerrat
Pront (b. 1772;
d. Philadelphia, 1842), who
changed his name to George
Isaacs. He was the son of
Gatzel Isaac Pront (Van
Brunt) who was born in
Amsterdam. Later generations
changed name to Van Brunt.
(IV) Hamburg; (V) Germany;
(VI) Leeuwarden, Netherlands;
(VII) Amsterdam; and
(VIII) Poland. See GENERAL
WORKS.

Wade, Stuart C. The Isaacs
Genealogy. New York, n.p.,
1902. NN.

ISAACSON
CFM has family records.

ISAAK
See Franz Isaac entry under
ISAAC.
Neumann, O. "Aron Isaak, ein
jüdischer Petschierstecher
vor 200 Jahren," JFF, nos. 22
and 23. Aron Isaak (Aaron
Isaac), founder of the Jewish
community in Stockholm,
Sweden, b. Treuenbrietzen,
Duchy of Mecklenburg, 1730;
d. 1816.
Rothschild. Svenska Israel.
See GENERAL WORKS.

ISAK
CAJ has family trees.
JFF, nos. 22 and 23. Family
histories.

ISENBERGER
See David Joseph entry under
BEITMAN.

ISERLISH
Moshe Iserlish Family. Papers,
1927. 1 folder. Genealogy,
1927, translated from
Yiddish, of a rabbinic family
that lived in Eastern Europe.
PJAC.

ISIDRA
AMH has family records.
CFM has family records.

ISKANDARI
EJ (1928), 8:564-65. Family of
Egypt. See GENERAL WORKS.

ISRAEL
AMH has family records.
CFM has family records.
See Esmond S. De Beer entry
under BARDEN.
Fischer, Josef. Baruch Israel
efterkommere. København:
H. Jensen, 1913. Printed as
MS. Baruch Israel,

b. Schlochern, 1748;
d. København, 1813. OCH.
Friedrich, Susanne Berger.
"Die Chirurgenfamilie Israel
von Mundgut in Eibaun,"
Zittauer Geschichtsblatt 13
(1936):9.
Gronemann. Genealogische
Hannovers, pp. 118ff. "Die
Familie Isaak Israel." See
GENERAL WORKS.
AJA has family tree of
Midshipman Joseph Israel,
beginning 1692.
Markus, Simon. Toldoth
ha-Rabbanim le-mishpaḥath
Yisrael mi-Rodos me-Rhodos.
Jerusalem: R. Mass, 1935.
92 p. Added title page: De
claris qui ex Rhodia Israel
familia erant rabbinis
scripsit dr. Simon Markus.
Includes genealogical table.
DLC.
Seeliger, E.A. "Abeitung des
Familiennamens Israel in der
Oberlausitz," Archiv für
Sippenforschung 13, no. 4
(1936):124-25.
See Stern, FAJF (XVIII) entry
under LEVY.
Stern. FAJF. Israel family
trees beginning in: (I) U.S.
and (II) Amsterdam. See
GENERAL WORKS.
Weatherall, David. David
Ricardo: A Biography. The
Hague: Martinus Nijhoff,
1977. 201 p. "The Jewish
Heritage," pp. 1-7, deals
with the Israel and Ricardo
ancestors of David Ricardo
(1772-1823), the famous
English economic theorist.
His father, Abraham Israel
Ricardo, came to England
about 1759 from Amsterdam.
The Israel family originated
in Livorno, Italy.

ISRAEL BA'AL SHEM TOV (Besht)
EJ (1972), 9:1051. "Israel
Ba'al Shem Tov's Family
(1698-1760)." Through
mid-19th century. See
GENERAL WORKS.

ISRAELISH
See Meir Yizraeli entry under
BIDERMAN.

ISRAELIT
Israelit, Avraham Yitschok.
Zichron Larishonim. Jaffa,
1914. Work divided into 3
sections of 48 p., 30 p., and
10 p. Author includes his
genealogy. He came from
Novogrudok. JNUL.

ISRAELSOHN
Carton, Lawrence Howard.
"Notes on the Descendants of
the Kirschen [,] Samuels and
Other Related Families Who
Immigrated to America."
1983. 1 vol. Computer
printout of a short history
of the Kirschen family
(originally of Seduva, Kovno
Gubernia, Lithuania; later
settled in Baltimore,
Maryland; Pennsylvania; North
Carolina; and elsewhere) and
of genealogical charts of the
Kirschen (also spelled Kirsh,
Kerson, and Kirson),
Israelsohn, and Samuels
families. AJHS.

ISSERL, ISSERLES
CAJ has family tree from
Cracow, Poland, beginning
16th century.
Bałaban. Żydów w Krakowie,
1:75, 410-411. Genealogical
chart of the descendants of
Izrael Isserl (16th century).
See GENERAL WORKS.
Freudenthal, Max. Aus der
Heimat Moses Mendelssohns.
Moses Benjamin Wulff und
seine Familie, die Nachkommen
Moses Isserles. Berlin: E.F.
Lederer, 1900. 304 p. One
genealogical table. DLC, MH,
OCH, NN, PP, PPDrop.
————. "Aus der Heimat Moses
Mendelssohns," 11-40 in
Gedenkbuch für Moses
Mendelssohn. Hrsg. v.
Verbände der Vereine für
jüdische Geschichte und

Literatur in Deutschland.
Berlin: M. Poppelauer, 1929.
171 p. CtY, DLC, MH, NN,
OCH, OU, PPDrop.
Shapiro. Mishpachot Atikot,
pp. 351-68. Isserles family.
See GENERAL WORKS.

ISSERLEIN
"Rabbi Israel Isserlein," MGWJ,
1869, pp. 130, 177, 224, 269,
315.

ISTVANFFY
Kempelen. Magyarországi Zsidó,
3:137. Istvánffy family.
See GENERAL WORKS.

ITALIANDER
AMH has family records.

ITTNER
Kempelen. Magyarországi Zsidó,
2:91. See GENERAL WORKS.

ITZIG
EJ, 9:1151. "Itzig Family."
Descendants of Isaac b.
Daniel Itzig, 1679-1741,
through mid-19th century.
See GENERAL WORKS.
LBI has family trees beginning
1200, 1500, 1609, 1679, and
1720.
Feibes, J., Hrsg. Stammbaum
der Familien Itzig (aus
Burgsteinfurt) und Feibes
(Lengerich). Münster, 1887.
46 p. Family tree begins
1720. LBI.
Grunwald, M. "Familienurkunden
und Stammtafelfragmente zur
Geschichte der Familie
Arnstein-Eskeles-Daniel
Itzig," JFF, no. 1.
————, no. 11. Family
history.
Rachel and Wallich. Berliner
Grosskaufleute, 2:354-80.
"Die Itzig." In addition, an
Itzig genealogical table
(no. 8), 1723-1888, appears
at end of book. Family of
Berlin. See GENERAL WORKS.
Rosenstein. Unbroken Chain,
pp. 119ff. Genealogical

chart. See GENERAL WORKS.
Schnee. Hoffinanz und Staat,
3. "Stammtafel der
Hoffaktorenfamilie Itzig."
Descendants of Daniel Itzig
(1723-1799), through late
19th century. See GENERAL
WORKS.
————, 1:169-76. "Die Familie
Itzig und ihr Kreis."
Includes genealogical
information on family of
Brandenburg-Prussia, 18th to
19th century. See GENERAL
WORKS.
Spiel, Hilde. Fanny von
Arnstein oder die
Emanzipation. Ein
Frauenleben ander
Zeitenwende, 1758-1818.
Frankfurt am Main: S.
Fischer, 1962. 537 p. One
family tree. Includes Itzig
family.

IVANKA
Kempelen. Magyarországi Zsidó,
1:128, 129. Ivánka family.
See GENERAL WORKS.

IVENECER
Reichel, O. Asher. Isaac
Halevy, 1847-1919: Spokesman
and Historian of Jewish
Tradition. New York: Yeshiva
University Press, 1969.
Genealogical information on
the Ivenecer, Kovner, and
Rabinowitz ancestors of Isaac
Halevy, pp. 15-16. Isaac
Halevy (Rabinowitz) was born
in Ivenets, Province of
Minsk, near Vilna, the son of
R. Eliyahu and Rahel Kovner
Halevy Ivenecer Rabinowitz.
CLU, CSt, CtY, CU, ICU, MB,
MH, NcD, NIC, NjP, NN.

IZAKOWICZ
Bałaban. Żydów w Krakowie,
2:128. Genealogical table of
the descendants of Mojzesz
Izakowicz of Cracow, 17th to
18th century. See GENERAL
WORKS.

JABLONSKI
Rosenstein. Unbroken Chain,
pp. 81ff. See GENERAL WORKS.

JABOTINSKY
Schechtman, Joseph B. Rebel
and Statesman: The Vladimir
Jabotinsky Story, The Early
Years. New York: Thomas
Yoseloff, Inc., 1956. 467 p.
"Family Background,"
pp. 25-31. Jabotinsky
(1880-1940), Zionist
activist, soldier, writer,
poet, and founder of the
Jewish Legion during W.W.II,
was born in Odessa, the son
of Yona and Khava Jabotinsky.
The Russian spelling of the
family name is Zhabotinsky.
CSt, CU, DLC, MB, NcD, NN,
OClW, PP, TxU.

JACHIA
Family tree of Idn-Yahya Jachia
Family, beginning with Don
Yahya, Cordova and Lisboa,
d. 1222. MS, parchment,
72 x 55 cm. Jewish
Theological Seminary Library,
New York City.
JE, 12:583. See GENERAL WORKS.

JACKSON
AMH has family records.
"Descendants of Daniel
(Gedalya) Jackson."
Typescript. Begins with
1787. AJA.
"Genealogies of Mordecai Manuel
Noah and His Wife, Rebecca E.
Jackson." Typescript. AJA.
Jackson, Solomon Henry. "Brief
Genealogical Information,
1787-1896." AJA.
Stern. FAJF. Jackson family
trees beginning in:
(I) Portsmouth, England; and
(II and III) London, England.
See GENERAL WORKS.

JACOB
AMH has family records.
CAJ has family tree from
Germany and Denmark,
1620-1924: Geschichte der
Familie Unna
(Hamburg-Kopenhagen).
Includes Jacob family.
CFM has family records.

JACOBI
AJA has family tree from New
York and South Carolina,
beginning 1790.
Born, Max. My Life:
Recollections of A Nobel
Laureate. New York: Charles
Scribner's Sons, 1975.
308 p. The German physicist
(1882-1970) was born in
Breslau. Genealogical
information about the Jacobi,
Lipstein, and Kauffmann
relatives of the author,
pp. 3-28.
Kempelen. Magyarországi Zsidó,
2:14, 54, 95. See GENERAL
WORKS.
Zielenziger, Georg. Stammbaum
der Familie J. Levin Jacobi.
Bromberg, 1905. Lithogr.
34 x 49 cm. Families of
Levin Jacobi and Mortje
Witkowski from ca. 1750.
LBI.

JACOBOWSKY
Jacobowsky, Carl Vilhelm. En
Jubilerande Firma och des
Grundare. Uddevalla, Sweden:
Jacobowskys Handels, A.B.,
1950. 18 p. Family of
Sweden. Effraim Jacobowsky,
1851-1929, was the firm's
founder. JNUL.

JACOBS
AJA has family tree from
Prussia, beginning 1828.
AMH has family records.
CFM has family records.
"Die Familie Jacobs," Märkische
Heimat Heuruppin 6, no. 12
(1933):96.
Golden, Richard L. and Arlene
A. Golden. "The Mark I.

Jacobs Family: A Discursive
Overview," Western States
Jewish Historical Quarterly
13 (Jan. 1981):99-114.
Descendants of Israel Jacobs,
b. Poland, 18th century; then
migrated to England. Family
cf California and Tucson,
Arizona.
See Stern, FAJF (XVIII) entry
under LEVY.
Stern. FAJF. Jacobs family
trees beginning in: (I and
IX) Amsterdam; (II, V, VIII,
and XI) U.S.; (III) Surinam;
(IV) Dartmouth, England;
(VI) England; (VII) Jamaica;
and (X) St. Denis, Quebec.
See GENERAL WORKS.

JACOBSEN
AMH has family records.

JACOBSOHN
Koerner, Bernhard. "Judentaufe
in Marienwerder Wpr.:
Jacobsohn," Der Deutsche
Roland 25, no. 11/12
(1937):131.

JACOBSON
AMH has family records.
CFM has family records.
JGCT has copy of Jacobson
family reunion family tree of
1954 in Portsmouth, Virginia.
Family originally from
Grenkiske, Lithuania.
Settled mainly in Portsmouth
and Berkley, Virginia.
Brown, R.D. "Two Baltic
Families Who Came to America:
The Jacobsons and the
Kruskals, 1870-1970,"
American Jewish Archives 24
(1972):39-93. Family
originally from Zagare, a
town located on the border
between Latvia and Lithuania.
Jacobson-Kruskal Family; New
York, N.Y.; Chicago, Ill.;
and Washington, D.C.
"Genealogical Information,
Documents, and
Correspondence, 1879-1972;"
Typescript and MS. In

English, German, and Hebrew.
AJA.

Schnee, Heinrich. "Der Geheime
Finanzrat Israel Jacobson, d.
vor Kämpfer d.
Judenemanzipation," Deutsches
Archiv für Landes-und
Volksforschung 8
(1944):45-73.

B. Halberstadt, 1768;
d. Berlin, 1828.
Semi-Gotha, 1:29. See GENERAL
WORKS.

JACOBSON DE JONGE
Schnee. Hoffinanz und Staat,
1:106-109. "Die Familie
Jacobson de Jonge." 17th to
18th century. Family of
Brandenburg-Prussia. See
GENERAL WORKS.

JACOBSSON
Semi-Gotha, 1:152ff. See
GENERAL WORKS.

JACOBUS
Frank. Nashville Jewry,
p. 136. Russian family,
arrived in U.S. in 1860s.
See GENERAL WORKS.

JACOBY
CAJ has family records.
CFM has family records.

JACUBOVICH
CAJ has family records.

JADKONSKY
CAJ has family tree from
Germany.

JAECKEL
LBI has family tree beginning
1757.

JAEGER
Schulte. Bonner Juden, p. 300.
See GENERAL WORKS.

JAEL
AMH has family records.

JAFFE
AMH has family records.

CAJ has family tree from
Germany, 1762-1928.
CFM has family records.
EJ(1972), 9:1259. "Jaffe and
Kook Families." Descendants
of Mordecai b. Abraham Jaffe
"Levush," 1535-1612.
Genealogical table covers
through mid-20th century.
See GENERAL WORKS.
See Japha Family Tree entry
under JAPHA.
JE, 7:53-63. Descendants of
Mordechai Jaffe of Bologna,
15th century, and Mordechai
Jaffe of Posen, 1535-1612.
Family of rabbis, scholars,
and communal leaders, with
members in Germany, Austria,
Russia, Great Britain, Italy,
and U.S. Three Jaffe
pedigree tables appear on
pages 53-55. See GENERAL
WORKS.
LBI has family tree beginning
1650.
"Familie Itzig Jaffe,"
Hebraïsche Bibliographie 4
(1861):72-74.
See Jechiel Freud entry under
BER.
Ginzberg, Eli. Keeper of the
Law: Louis Ginzberg.
Philadelphia: Jewish
Publication Society of
America, 1966. 348 p.
Genealogical information on
Ginzberg and Jaffe ancestors
of Louis Ginzberg
(1873-1953), the
world-renowned Talmud and
Jewish law scholar, pp.
12-34. Louis was born in
Kovno, the son of Isaac Elias
and Zippe Jaffe Ginzberg and
the grandson of Rabbi Asher
Ginzberg. He emigrated to
U.S. in 1899. CLU, DLC, NjP,
OCH.
Stern, Moritz. Der schweriner
Oberrabbiner Mordechai Jaffe,
seine Ahnen und Nachkommen,
Ein Stammbaum. Berlin:
Michel, 1933. 15 p.
Mordechai (Marcus) Jaffe of
Berlin, b. Bohemia, d. 1812;

187

rabbi of Schwerin until 1770.
CAJ; Germania-Judaica: Kölner
Bibliothek zur Geschichte des
deutschen Judentums e. V.,
Josef-Haubrich-Hof 1, 5000
Köln 1, West Germany.
Urisohn, J. "Mordechai Jaffe,"
(In Russian.) Jewrjeskaia
Starina 4 (1912):353-69.
Jaffe-Urisohn family.

JAKAB
Kempelen. Magyarországi Zsidó,
2:73. See GENERAL WORKS.

JAKABFFY
Kempelen. Magyarországi Zsidó,
1:103; 2:31. See GENERAL
WORKS.

JAKOBI
See Kempelen entry under
JACOBI. Jakóbi family.

JAKOBOVICS
Kempelen. Magyarországi Zsidó,
2:90. See GENERAL WORKS.

JAKUBOWICZ
Bałaban. Żydow w Krakowie,
1:159, 161-62, 175, 202.
Genealogical chart of the
descendants of Izak
Jakubowicz, 16th to 17th
century. See GENERAL WORKS.

JALSON
AMH has family records.

JAMAIKER
AMH has family records.

JAMES
AMH has family records.

JANASZ
Reychmann. Szkice
genealogiczne, pp. 99-102.
See GENERAL WORKS.

JANKO
Kempelen. Magyarországi Zsidó,
3:106. Jankó family. See
GENERAL WORKS.

JANKOVICH
Kempelen. Magyarországi Zsidó,
1:83. See GENERAL WORKS.

JANKOVICS
Kempelen. Magyarországi Zsidó,
2:74. See GENERAL WORKS.

JANNER
CAJ has family records.

JANOSI
PD has family records.

JANOVITZ
Kempelen. Magyarországi Zsidó,
1:70, 121. See GENERAL
WORKS.

JAPHA
Japha Family Tree. Unpublished
family tree of Japha family
compiled by Max Japha or one
of his relatives. Family
originally from Fraustadt,
Germany. Descendants of
Mordechai ben Abraham ben
Josef Jeffe (Jaffe?) of
Posen, b. 1530. Includes
Brasch family. JGCT.

JAPHET
CAJ (Call No. P/107) has a file
of loose papers and notes on
Japhet family compiled by
Philipp J. Japhet. Includes
6-page family chart,
1736-1921, starting with Leib
Japhet, b. 1736.

JARETZKI
AMH has family records.

JARMAY
Kempelen. Magyarországi Zsidó,
3:99. Jármay family. See
GENERAL WORKS.

JAROSLAWSKI
Stern, Malcolm H., comp. "The
Descendants of Salomon
Jaroslawski," 1956. Family
of New York City. Family
tree begins in Posen, 1796.
AJA.

JASZ
Kempelen. Magyarországi Zsidó,
3:44. See GENERAL WORKS.

JAVAL
CFM has family records.

JAVEL
AMH has family records.

JECHIEL
See Stern, FAJF (I) entry under
MICHAELS.

JEITELES
EJ (1972), 9:1331. "Jeiteles
Family." Family originally
from Prague. Descendants of
Moses b. Simon (d. 1629),
through early 20th century.
See GENERAL WORKS.
Kempelen. Magyarországi Zsidó,
1:135, 136. See GENERAL
WORKS.

JELLINEK
Kempelen. Magyarországi Zsidó,
1:95; 2:137. See GENERAL
WORKS.
Rosenmann, Moses. Dr. Adolf
Jellinek, sein Leben und
Schaffen; zugleich ein
Beitrag zur Geschichte der
israelitischen Kultusgemeinde
Wien in der zweiten Hälfte
des neunzehnten Jahrhunderts.
Wien: J. Schlesinger, 1931.
232 p. Includes genealogical
table. Dr. Adolf Jellinek
(1820/21-1893), researcher
and scholar, was born in
village near Uhersky Brod
(Ungarisch Brod), Moravia.
CSt, CU, DLC, MB, MH, NIC,
NN, OCH, OU.

JENKINS
AMH has family records.

JEREMIAS
CAJ has family records.

JERESLAW
Rosenthal, Rochelle. "The
Jereslaw Family in America,
1858-1913." Term paper,

Hebrew Union College-Jewish
Institute of Religion,
Cincinnati, Ohio, 1970. AJA.

JERUCHEM
Rosenstein. Unbroken Chain,
p. 541. Jeruchem family
pedigree. See GENERAL WORKS.

JESHURUN
AMH has family records.

JESSEL
CFM has family records.
Burke's Peerage and Baronetage.
Finestein, Israel. "Sir George
Jessel, 1824-1883,"
Transactions of the Jewish
Historical Society of England
18 (1958):243-83. Includes
genealogical tables of Aaron
Jessel and his descendants,
mid-18th century forward, Sir
George Jessel and family,
Edward Jessel and his
children, and Albert Henry
Jessel and his children.

JESSELL
AMH has family records.

JESSURUN
CFM has family records.
LBI has family tree beginning
1748.

JESZENAK
Kempelen. Magyarországi Zsidó,
2:23. Jeszenák family. See
GENERAL WORKS.

JEWELL
AMH has family records.
CFM has family records.

JOACHIM
AMH has family records.
CFM has family records.
PD has family records.

JOACHIMMSEN
Stern. FAJF. Joachimmsen
family tree beginning in
Breslau. See GENERAL WORKS.

JOACHIMSSEN
AJA has genealogical files.

JOACHIMSSOHN
Brilling, Bernhard. "Familie
Joachimssohn," Mitteilungen
der Verbändes ehemaliger
Breslauer und Schlesier in
Israel, no. 42 (Sept. 1977).

JOCHEMS
CFM has family records.

JOEL
See CZACZKES.
AMH has family records.
See Sally David Cramer entry
under CRAMER.
JFF, no. 34. Family history.
Stern. FAJF. Joel family tree
beginning in Ingenheim,
Bavaria. Family tree is
listed in FAJF under "Marx
II."

JOFFE
See DEBORIN.
AJA has genealogical files.
Joffe, Tamara. "American
Jewish History of the Joffe
Family." Louisville, Ky.
Jan. 25, 1975. AJA.

JOHNSON
AMH has family records.
Johnson Family; Cincinnati,
Ohio Family Tree, 1979; MS.
AJA.
Johnson Family Papers,
1794-1957. Family of
Cincinnati. Include
genealogical notes and family
trees. AJA.
Stern. FAJF. Johnson family
tree beginning in Portsmouth,
England. See GENERAL WORKS.

JOHNSTONE
AMH has family records.

JOKAI
Kempelen. Magyarországi Zsidó,
2:28, 29. Jókai family. See
GENERAL WORKS.

JOLOWICZ
Phiebig, Albert J. The
Jolowicz Family. New York,
1948. 32 p. Introductory
Note: "List of descendants of
Abraham Hirsch and Sarah
Jolowicz, based on an old
handwritten 'Stammbaum' in
the Possession of Dr. Ernst
Jolowicz." JNUL.

JOMTOB-BONDI
See Jonas Marcus Bondi entry
under LUCKA. Genealogical
tables.

JONAS
AJA has genealogical files.
AMH has family records.
CFM has family records.
LBI has family trees beginning
1700, 1760, and 19th century.
LBIS has family tree and notes.
See Esmond S. De Beer entry
under BARDEN.
Frank. Nashville Jewry,
pp. 134-35. See GENERAL
WORKS.
Jonas, Abraham. "Papers of
Abraham Jonas and Family, May
1892-August, 1966." 9 vols.
Family of Oakland,
California. Collection
includes obituaries, death
certificates, and wills for
various family members.
WJHC.
Kempelen. Magyarországi Zsidó,
2:94. Jónás family. See
GENERAL WORKS.
Stern. FAJF. Jonas family
tree beginning in Exeter,
England. See GENERAL WORKS.

JONASSOHN
CFM has family records.

JONGH
See I. Rosenwaike entry under
DE YOUNG.

JONES
AMH has family records.
CFM has family records.
Stern. FAJF. Jones family
trees beginning in:

(I) Amsterdam and (II) U.S.
See GENERAL WORKS.

JORDAN
Jordan, Ruth. Daughter of the
Waves: Memories of Growing Up
in Pre-War Palestine. New
York: Taplinger Publishing
Co., 1983. 213 p. "Roots,"
pp. 23-33. Ancestors
originally came to Palestine
from Moravia in 1820s.

JOSEL, JOSELMANN
See JOSSELMANN.

JOSEPH
AJA has family tree, 1852-1952.
AMH has family records.
CFM has family records.
Frank. Nashville Jewry,
p. 139. See GENERAL WORKS.
Gluckstein, Joseph.
Genealogical Tables of the
Gluckstein-Salmon-Joseph-
Abrahams Families, etc.
London: By the Author, 1925.
The Anglo-Jewish Archives of
the Mocatta Library in London
holds "The Family Tree of
Anthony Joseph's Family,"
Compiled by Dr. Anthony P.
Joseph. Supplements have
appeared annualy since the
original edition was
completed in 1958. Covers
late 18th century to date for
this Anglo-Jewish family.
Also covers the descendants
of Barnet Levy (d. 1791) and
Solomon Solomon (1764-1819)
and Betsy Levy (1767-1832).
See David Joseph entry under
BEITMAN.
Joseph, Leopold. Familie
Abraham S. Joseph. London:
Frederick Printing Co., 1912?
72 p. JNUL.
Stern. FAJF. Joseph family
trees beginning in:
(I) Germany; (II) Amsterdam;
and (III and IV) Mannheim,
Germany. See GENERAL WORKS.
Woodley, Edward Carruthers.
The House of Joseph in the
Life of Quebec, the Record of

a Century and a Half.
Quebec: Printed by Quebec
Newspapers, 1946. 706 p.
Canadian family of grocers,
bankers, and financiers. MH,
OCH.

JOSEPHS
AMH has family records.
CFM has family records.

JOSEPHSON
AMH has family records.
CFM has family records.
LBI has family trees beginning
1638 and 1766.
Blomberg, Erik. Ernst
Josephson, Hans LIV.
Stockholm: Wahlström &
Widstrand, 1951. 748 p.
Genealogical information on
the Josephson relatives of
the Swedish painter, Ernst
Abraham Josephson
(1851-1906), pp. 13-50, 695.
The family came to Sweden
from Prenzlau, Brandenburg,
in 1780. DLC, MH, NIC, NjP.
Rothschild. Svenska Israel.
See GENERAL WORKS.
Semi-Gotha, 1:135ff. See
GENERAL WORKS.
Stern. FAJF. Josephson family
tree beginning in Germany.
See GENERAL WORKS.

JOSEPHTHAL
Josephthal Family.
Genealogical Tables:
Stammbaum des Familie
Josephthal, beginning with
the 17th century, including
addenda as of Dec. 31, 1973,
Berlin, Germany, 1932; and
genealogical chart,
"Ancestors of the Sons of
Paul and Emma Josephthal,"
New York, N.Y., 1975. AJA.
The latter is also available
at NN.
See Hans Josephthal entry under
GOLDSCHNEIDER. Twelve
genealogical tables. Table
of descendants of Lazarus
Josephthal of Ansbach,
d. 1657.

JOSEPHY
AMH has family records.

JOSHUA
AMH has family records.
CAJ has family records.
CAJ has family tree, 1817-1947,
of family from Hamburg.
CFM has family records.
"Zur Biographie R. Jakob
Joshuas," MGWJ, 1910, p. 608.

JOSIKA
Kempelen. Magyarországi Zsidó,
1:55. Jósika family. See
GENERAL WORKS.

JOSSELMANN
Stern, Moritz. "Josselmann von
Rosheim und seine
Nachkommen," ZGJD 3
(1889):65-74. Josselmann of
Rosheim (known also as Josel,
Joselmann, Josselin, and
Joseph ben Gershon Loans),
16th-century shtadlan or
advocate of the Jews of
Germany, born probably in
Alsace, around 1480, died in
Rosheim, Germany, 1554.

JOST
CAJ has family records.

JOURDAN
LBI has family trees beginning
1782 and 1819.

JUDA
LBI has family tree beginning
1753.

JUDAH
See FRANKS-JUDAH.
AMH has family records.
Franks and Judah Families.
"Genealogical Information,
1721-1970." AJA.
Hart and Judah Families.
Biographical Material,
1724-1954. Includes
genealogical information.
AJA.
"Descendants of Michael Judah
of Norwalk, Conn." AJA.
Miller, Evelyn. "Samuel Judah:

The First Jewish Graduate of
Queens College (Rutgers)," in
Ruth Marcus Patt's The Jewish
Scene in New Jersey's Raritan
Valley, 1698-1948: 1980
Supplement (New Brunswick,
N.J.: The Jewish Historical
Society of Raritan Valley,
1980), pp. 10-17. "Genealogy
of Family of Samuel Judah,"
pp. 13-17. Samuel Benjamin
Judah, lawyer, b. New York
City, 1799; d. Vincennes,
Indiana, 1869. His father
and grandfather were born in
Portsmouth, England; and his
great-grandfather was born in
Breslau, Germany. Genealogy
covers late 17th century
through 1930s. AJHS, NjR.
Stern. FAJF. Judah family
trees beginning in: (I and
III) Breslau; and (II) U.S.
(probably non-Jewish). See
GENERAL WORKS.

JUDE
AMH has family records.
JFF, no. 22. Family history.

JUDEK
See Richard J. Alperin entry
under BEHRMAN. Includes
Judek family.

JUHASZ
Kempelen. Magyarországi Zsidó,
3:71. Juhász family. See
GENERAL WORKS.

JULIAN
AJA has genealogical files.

JULICH
Schulte. Bonner Juden,
pp. 301, 303. Jülich family.
See GENERAL WORKS.

JULLIUS
CAJ has family records.

JUNGMANN
Bruck, Alfred Julius. The
Jungmann Family: A Historical
Sketch. London, 1948. 63 p.
Pp. 1-13 in English;

pp. 14-21 in German. Family
tables, pp. 22-63, for
descendants of Moses
Jungmann, b. 1770/1800, and
for Ollendorf family, which
is related to Jungmann
family. Tables continue to
1940s. "The Jungmann family
originates from Kobylin and
migrated from there to nearby
Rawitsch." (p. 9.) Ollendorf
family is from Rawitsch.
CAJ, Call No. 2699.

JUNGTAUBEN
Carmoly, Eliakim. Ha-'orvim
u-bene yonah. Rodelheim,
1861. 48 p.

JUNKER
Kempelen. Magyarországi Zsidó,
3:60. Jünker family. See
GENERAL WORKS.

JUSTH
Kempelen. Magyarországi Zsidó,
1:101, 103; 2:31; 3:27. See
GENERAL WORKS.

JUSTUS
Kempelen. Magyarországi Zsidó,
1:23; 3:63. See GENERAL
WORKS.

JUTROSINSKI
Jutrosinski, Richard.
Geschichte der Familie
Jutrosinski. [Berlin, 1928.]
7 p. Family of Posen. LBI.

JUX
Lapointe, Lucienne. "Notes sur
la famille Jux établie à
Soultz depuis le milieu du
XVIIe siècle," Bulletin du
Cercle Généalogique d'Alsace
(Strasbourg), no. 37
(1977):8-11.

KAAN
Kempelen. Magyarországi Zsidó,
2:38. Kaán family. See

GENERAL WORKS.
Stevens, T. "De Familie Kaan
en haar fananciele
activiteiten gedurende vier
eeuwen," Studia Rosenthaliana
4 (1970):43-95.

KAAPLANDER
Hechter, Ruth Kaaplander.
Brenner-Sattenstein-
Kaaplander (Caplan)-Hoff
Family Tree. Brooklyn, N.Y.,
1982. PJAC.

KABAK
See Zevi Shimshi entry under
SHIMSHELEWITZ. Includes
genealogical tables.
Includes Kabak family.

KACENELENBOGEN
See Meyer Ellenbogen entry
under KATZENELLENBOGEN.

KACZ
Kempelen. Magyarországi Zsidó,
3:48, 124. See GENERAL
WORKS.

KADA
Kempelen. Magyarországi Zsidó,
1:53. See GENERAL WORKS.

KADISCH
CAJ has family tree, 1788-1921.

KADISH, KADISHAVITZ
Seligman-Kadishavitz Family
Tree. Compiled for family
reunion in Norfolk in 1978.
Includes Kadishavitz family
as well as descendants who
changed name to Kadish and
Savage. JGCT.

KAFFKA
Kempelen. Magyarországi Zsidó,
3:62, 117. See GENERAL
WORKS.

KAFKA
Benes, J. "Zu Max Brods
Namendeutungen [jüdischer
Familiennamen ... Kafka],"
Beiträge zur Namenforschung 4
(1969):215-16.

Brod, Max. Franz Kafka: A
Biography. 2d enlarged ed.
New York: Schocken Books,
1947, 1960. 267 p. "Parents
and Childhood," pp. 3-38.
Franz Kafka (1883-1924) was
the son of Julie Löwy and
Hermann Kafka (1852-?) of
Prague and grandson of Jacob
Kafka (1814-1889) of the
South Bohemian village of
Wossek.

KAGAN
Nurnberg, Maxwell.
"[Cohen-Kagan.]" Names 14
(Sept. 1966):192. On the
identity of these two names.

KAHLBERG
Ballin. Juden in Seesen,
p. 212. See GENERAL WORKS.

KAHLER
PD has family records.

KAHN
AMH has family records.
CFM has family records.
Kahn Family. Birth, Marriage,
and Death Records, 1862-1902.
AJA.
Kahn Family. Genealogy.
Typescript. AJA.
Kahn Family. "Family Tree,
1890-1970." New Brunswick,
N.J. AJA.
Kahn Family. "Genealogical
Chart, 1759-1961." AJA.
Birmingham. Our Crowd. See
GENERAL WORKS.
Kahn, Coralie Lemann.
Genealogical files. AJA.
Kahn Family, New Mexico.
"Gustav Kahn of Santa Fe's
Memoirs Gives Information on
the Kahn Family." AJA.
Kahn, Lazard (1850-1928).
Papers, 1852-1961. Includes
genealogical information on
the Jacob Lehmann-Lazard Kahn
family of Cincinnati and
Hamilton, Ohio; Donaldson and
New Orleans, Louisiana; and
Selma, Alabama. AJA.
Kahn, Ludwig David. Die

Familie Kahn von
Sulzburg/Baden. Ihre
Geschichte und ihre
Genealogie. Basel: By the
Author, 1963. 206 p. CLU,
DLC, MH, NN, OCH, WU.
Kopp. Jüdischen Alsenz,
pp. 140-41. Genealogical
information on
Sternheimer-Kahn family of
Alsenz. See GENERAL WORKS.
Mirwis, L. Geschichte der
Familie Epstein. N.p., 1927.
80 p. Family table for
Epstein family from
Eichstetten, Germany,
mid-1700s-1920s. Dates of
births, marriages, and deaths
included on family table,
pp. 23-80. Also descendants
of Rabbi Eljakim Picard in
Randegg (His wife, Marie
Epstein, was born in 1838 in
Eischstetten.) and
descendants of Herri Kahn
(1848-1922) in Freiburg.
CAJ, Call No. 5434.
Schulte. Bonner Juden,
pp. 305-306. See GENERAL
WORKS.
Semi-Gotha, 1:137ff.; 2:67ff.
See GENERAL WORKS.
Tänzer. Juden in Tirol,
p. 730. See GENERAL WORKS.
Wildberg, Henriette Kahn, comp.
"Kahn Family Tree,
1822-1960." Arranged and
Drawn by Robert Riese Zimmer.
N.p., 1960. 1 sheet,
70 x 55 cm. The descendants
of Israel and Sarah Bauer
Kahn of Oakland, California.
The family tree does not give
dates. WJHC.

KAHNHEIMER
Kopp. Jüdischen Alsenz,
pp. 131-32. Genealogy of
Mayer-Kahnheimer family of
Alsenz. See GENERAL WORKS.

KAHRSTADT
CAJ has family records.

KAISER
Kempelen. Magyarországi

Zsidó, 3:121. See GENERAL
WORKS.

KALAHORA
LBI has family tree beginning
1495.
Bałaban. Żydów w Krakowie,
1:146; 2:532. Genealogical
chart of the descendants of
Dr. Salomon Kalahora, 16th to
19th century. See GENERAL
WORKS.

KALCHMANN
CAJ has family tree from
Germany.

KALIPHARI
Kaliphari, Salomon, gen.
Posner: Mein Lebensbild in
Anschluss an 7 Ahnenbilder
der Familie Kaliphari.
Landsberg. Aus dem Hebr.
übers. und fortgesetzt v.
Moritz Landsberg. Enth. die
Nachkommen des sephard.
Arztes Salomon Kaliphari,
d. ca. 1600. 1908. LBI.

KALISCH, KALISCHER
CAJ has family records.
CAJ has Fischhoff-Kalisch
family tree. Family from
Galanta in Rumania.
LBI has family tree beginning
17th century.
Hasse, Hermann. Familientafel
Kalischer ... ausgefertigt
für die Gesellschaft für
Jüdische Ahnenforschung ...
und das Archiv Deutscher
Juden. Berlin, 1934-1938.
140 p. JNUL.
Kalisch, Paul. "Zur Geschichte
d. Familie
Kremnitzer-Kalischer," JFF,
no. 40/41 (1936):713-23,
737-41.

KALISH
AMH has family records.

KALKAR
Fischer, Josef Simon. Isac
Kalkar og hans slaegt påa
foranledning af

N. Abrahamsen. København,
1917. 72 p. Printed as MS.
OCH.

KALKER
AMH has family records.

KALLAI
Kempelen. Magyarországi Zsidó,
2:88. Kállai family. See
GENERAL WORKS.

KALLAY
Kempelen. Magyarországi Zsidó,
3:126. Kállay family. See
GENERAL WORKS.

KALLEDEY
Kempelen. Magyarországi Zsidó,
3:70. See GENERAL WORKS.

KALLER
AMH has family records.

KALLIR
LBI has family tree beginning
1792.

KALLMES
LBI has family tree beginning
1550.

KALLOS
Kempelen. Magyarországi Zsidó,
1:91; 3:117. Kallós family.
See GENERAL WORKS.

KALMAN
AMH has family records.
Kempelen. Magyarországi Zsidó,
2:11, 71. Kálmán family.
See GENERAL WORKS.

KALMAR
Kempelen. Magyarországi Zsidó,
1:42. Kalmár family. See
GENERAL WORKS.

KALM-CALMS
Semi-Gotha, 1:15ff. See
GENERAL WORKS.

KALNOKI
Kempelen. Magyarországi Zsidó,
2:100. Kálnoki family. See
GENERAL WORKS.

KALONYMUS
EJ (1928), 9:838-40. See
GENERAL WORKS.
LBI has family tree.

KALVARYSKI
CAJ (Call No. 4318) has the
following family trees:
(1) Simon, Menashe. The
Genealogical Tree of the
Eiger, Margoliot-Kalvaryski
and Simon Families (begins
with Katzenellenbogen,
Germany, 1312 and ends in
1937) on one side and (2) on
the opposite side:
Margolis-Jahrblum, Laura
(Tel-Aviv). Continuation of
the Genealogical Tree of the
Margoliot-Kalvaryski Family,
19th and 20th Century.
Margoliot also written by
Margolis.

KAMINSKY
Kaminska, Ida. My Life, My
Theater. New York:
MacMillan, 1973. 310 p.
"About My Parents," pp.
11-19. An account of her
family and Jewish life in
Poland by the founder of the
Yiddish State Theater in
Warsaw. She was born in
Warsaw in 1899, the daughter
of Abraham Isaac (1867-1918)
and Esther Rachel (1870-1926)
Kaminsky. Abraham was born
in Warsaw, and Esther Rachel
was born in Porozovo.

KAMMER
Kempelen. Magyarországi Zsidó,
1:105. See GENERAL WORKS.

KAMPEN
AMH has family records.

KAMPFA
AMH has family records.

KANDER
AJA has genealogical files.
"Genealogical data of the
Eppstein, Kander, and Ulman
Famailies." June 1974. AJA.

KANDO
Kempelen. Magyarországi Zsidó,
3:79. Kandó family. See
GENERAL WORKS.

KANE
AMH has family records.

KANEFSKY
Kay, George. "A Lucky
Encounter," The Genealogical
Helper 36 (Sept./Oct. 1982).
Genealogical article on
Kanefsky and Kay families of
Philadelphia.

KANITZ
PD has family records.
Kempelen. Magyarországi Zsidó,
1:139; 2:35. Kánitz family.
See GENERAL WORKS.

KANN
AMH has family records.
CAJ has family tree of family
of Frankfurt am Main.
Kann, Eleazar. Autobiographie
van Eleazar Kann. By the
Author. 62 p. Contains
family trees of Kann and Boas
families, 1595-1966. Family
of Germany and Holland.
Kempelen. Magyarországi Zsidó,
1:111; 2:88, 95. See GENERAL
WORKS.
Stevens, Th. "De familie Kann
en haar financiele
Activiteiten gedurende vier
eeuwen," Studia Rosenthaliana
4 (Jan. 1970):43-95. Dutch
banking family originally
from Frankfurt.

KANT
CAJ has family records.

KANTER
Blachman-Berlin Reunion,
November 24-26, 1977.
Norfolk, Va. Includes Kanter
family tree, mid-19th century
onwards, and information on
living descendants. AJA,
AJHS, JGCT.
Kanter, Kenneth Aaron.
"Autobiographical Sketch and

Genealogy." Term paper,
Hebrew Union College-Jewish
Institute of Religion,
Cincinnati, Ohio. May 17,
1976. AJA.

KANTOROWICZ
LBI has family tree beginning
1831.
Bałaban. Żydów w Krakowie,
2:233. Genealogical table of
the Cracow descendants of
Zacharjasz Mendel
Kantorowicz, 17th to 18th
century. See GENERAL WORKS.

KANZI
Poznánski, Samuel. "Il cognome
Kanzi," Rivista Israelitica 9
(1912):115-20, 212-13.

KAO
Leslie, "Chinese-Hebrew
Kaifeng." Includes family
tree of this clan. See
GENERAL WORKS.

KAPFELMAN
Semi-Gotha, 1:22. See GENERAL
WORKS.

KAPLAN
AJA has genealogical files.
Kaplan, Mendel. From Shtetl to
Steelmaking: The Story of
Three Immigrant Families and
a Family Business. Capetown,
S.A.: C. Struik on Behalf of
the Kaplan-Kushlick
Foundation, 1979. 144 p.
Owners of Cape Gate Fence and
Wire Works Co. DLC.
See R. Brock Shanberg entry
under GOLTZ.
Smith, Julha Frances. Aaron
Copeland: His Work and
Contribution to American
Music. New York: Dutton,
1955. 336 p. Pp. 11-14.
The famous American composer
is the son of Harris Kaplan
(b. 1860) and Sarah
Mittenthal (b. 1862) and the
grandson of Sussman and Freda
Kaplan and Aron and Bertha
Mittenthal. The Kaplan

family was originally from
Shavel, Lithuania, near
Kovno; the Mittenthal family
was from Vistinich,
Lithuania, near Königsberg,
Prussia.

KAPLIN
See Sally David Cramer entry
under CRAMER.

KAPLUSHNICK
Sefer Hamishpacha. Ot. Haifa,
Sept. 1964. 110 p. Family
trees of descendants of
Eliezer (d. 1889) and Bluma
(d. 1891) Kaplushnick;
Yitzchok (d. 1908) and Chaya
(d. 1900) Shevetz; Feiga and
Velvel (d. 1918) Mintz from
Smialitz (?); Malka-Raiza
(d. 1935) and Yisrael-Aharon
Monzer from Kamenets-Litovsk.
JNUL.

KAPOSI
Kempelen. Magyarországi Zsidó,
3:70. See GENERAL WORKS.

KAPP
LBI has family tree.

KAPPEL
Kempelen. Magyarországi Zsidó,
2:18. See GENERAL WORKS.

KAPROV
Gillman, Joseph M. The B'nai
Khaim in America: A History
of Cultural Change in a
Jewish Group. Philadelphia:
Dorrance, 1969. 168 p.
Genealogical tables. "A
detailed study of the
acculturation and adjustment
of the American descendants
of Khaim Kaprov, candle-maker
in the Ukraine, their
educational and economic
achievments, and their
attitudes toward matters
Jewish and general."

KARA
Sefer Hayichus Mimichpachat

Kara. Berlin: L. Lamm, 1922.
JNUL.

KARATSON
Kempelen. Magyarországi Zsidó,
1:100. Karátson family. See
GENERAL WORKS.

KARESKI
CAJ has family records.

KARFUNKEL
LBI has family trees beginning
1572 and 1762.

KARGER
Gronemann, Isak Selig.
Familienblätter zur
Erinnerung an unseren
verewigten Vater Raphael J.
Karger in namen der Familie.
Frankfurt am Main, 1898.
YIVO.

KARL
CAJ has family records.

KARLSOHN
Kempelen. Magyarországi Zsidó,
2:66. See GENERAL WORKS.

KARMAN
Kármán, Theodore von. The Wind
and Beyond. Theodore von
Kármán: Pioneer in Aviation
and Pathfinder in Space.
Boston: Little, Brown and
Co., 1967. Especially,
pp. 13-20. The author
(1881-1963) was born in
Budapest, the son of Mór
[Maurice] Kármán (1843-1915),
a university professor from
Szeged who was one of the
great educational innovators
in modern Hungary, and Helen
Konn Kármán. The family name
was originally Kleinmann.
Kempelen. Magyarországi Zsidó,
2:65. Kármán family. See
GENERAL WORKS.

KARO
AMH has family records.

KAROLYI
Kempelen. Magyarországi Zsidó,
3:126. Károlyi family. See
GENERAL WORKS.

KARP
Karp Family Tree. Compiled by
Irwin M. Berent. Family
originally from Bauska,
Latvia. JGCT.

KARPELES
CFM has family records.

KARSAI
Kempelen. Magyarországi Zsidó,
1:144; 2:74. See GENERAL
WORKS.

KARSUNSKY
See Yaffa Draznin entry under
BERNSTEIN.

KASER
AMH has family records.

KASHNICK
See KAPLUSHNICK.

KASNER
AMH has family records.

KASNYA
See ANDAHAZY-KASNYA.

KASS
CAJ has family tree, 1838-1963.

KASSOWITZ
PD has records of family from
Prague.
Toni Stolper Collection.
Includes Kassowitz family
history. Toni Stolper
(1891-   ) was born Antonie
Kassowitz in Vienna. Her
husband was Gustav Stolper,
economist and journalist.
LBI.

KASZAB
Kempelen. Magyarországi Zsidó,
2:39; 3:75, 120. See GENERAL
WORKS.

KATZ
AJA has family tree from
 Russia.
AMH has family records.
CAJ has family records. CAJ
 also has a family tree for
 Bachrach, Blumenfeld, Katz,
 Klebe, and Meierstein
 families of Bremke and Rhina,
 Germany, Israel, and U.S.
 covering 1650-1975.
Katz Family. "Genealogical
 Chart, 1694-1959." In
 German. AJA.
LBI has family tree beginning
 1694.
Ballin. Juden in Seesen,
 p. 213. See GENERAL WORKS.
Katz, Julius. Die Familie Katz
 zwischen Süntel und Deister.
 Ein altes niedersächsisches
 Bauerngeschlecht. Leipzig:
 Degner & Co., 1938. 48 p,
 2 übersichtstafen.
 (Bibliothek glicher.
 Arbeiten, 10.) MH.
Leitner, Isabella Katz.
 Fragments of Isabella: a
 Memoir of Auschwitz. New
 York: Thomas F. Crowell,
 1978. 112 p. Covers family
 life in Kisvárda, Hungary,
 and Auschwitz. Mother was
 Teresa Katz, and her children
 were Isabella, Philip, Poyto,
 Rachel, Chicha, and Cipi.
CAJ (Call No. 5251) has 2-page
 family tree of Sandel Katz
 (1773-1849) from Melsungen by
 Elisabeth S. Plaut.
 Continues to 1981. Family
 tree shows the relationship
 of Katz and Plaut families.
Rosenstein. Unbroken Chain,
 pp. 150ff. "Descendants of
 R. Moses Hakohen Katz." See
 GENERAL WORKS.
————, pp. 252ff. Descendants
 of R. Naftali Katz. See
 GENERAL WORKS.
Schulte. Bonner Juden, p. 307.
 See GENERAL WORKS.
Shapiro. Mishpachot Atikot,
 pp. 241-77. See GENERAL
 WORKS.
See Meir Yizraeli entry under

BIDERMAN.
Zapf. Tübinger Juden, pp.
 53-54, 141-42. See GENERAL
 WORKS.

KATZAN
Kempelen. Magyarországi Zsidó,
 1:115, 142. See GENERAL
 WORKS.

KATZENELLENBOGEN
EJ (1928), 9:1069-1072. See
 GENERAL WORKS.
Eisenstadt and Wiener. Da'at
 Kedoschim. Includes
 Katzenellenbogen family. See
 GENERAL WORKS.
Ellenbogen, Meyer. Ḥevel
 ha-kesef. Added title page:
 Record of the Kacenelenbogen
 Family including Mintz,
 Lurie, Teumin, Samuel, and
 Greenberg. Brooklyn, N.Y.:
 Printed by Moinester Pub.
 Co., 1937. 65, 16 p. In
 Hebrew and English.
 Genealogical table. DLC.
Kahan. 'Anaf 'ez avoth. See
 GENERAL WORKS.
Rosenstein. Unbroken Chain.
 Very detailed genealogical
 study of the Katzenellenbogen
 family and interrelated
 families; an earlier edition
 published under the title
 These are the Generations,
 1967. See GENERAL WORKS.
————. Zarei Yitzchak (The
 Seeds of Isaac): The Ancestry
 and the Descendants of Rabbi
 Joel Isaac Katzenellenbogen
 Including Biographical
 Sketches of Family Members
 from the 15th-20th Centuries.
 Elizabeth, N.J., 1974. 80 p.
Shapiro. Mishpachot Atikot,
 pp. 122-49. See GENERAL
 WORKS.
Wollsteiner, Max.
 Genealogische Übersicht über
 einige zweige der
 Nachkommenschaft des Rabbi
 Meier Katzenellenbogen von
 Padua. 2. Aufl. Berlin: By
 the Author, 1930. 48 p.

KATZENELNBOGEN
Braun, S. "Die Vorfahren von
Karl Marx, Aus der Ahnentafel
der Familie,"
Mitteilungsblatt (Tel Aviv),
no. 44 (10. Nov. 1977).
Includes genealogy of the
Katzenelbogen, Kaznelson,
and Marx families.

KAUFER
Kempelen. Magyarországi Zsidó,
2:133, 134. See GENERAL
WORKS.

KAUFFMAN, KAUFFMANN, KAUFMAN,
KAUFMANN
AMH has Kaufman family records.
CAJ has Kaufmann family tree
beginning 1800 and family
records.
Keneseth Israel. Includes
Kaufmann family. See GENERAL
WORKS.
LBI has Kauffmann family trees
beginning 1693 and 1818.
Born, Max. My Life:
Recollections of A Nobel
Laureate. New York: Charles
Scribner's Sons, 1975.
308 p. The German physicist
(1882-1970) was born in
Breslau. Genealogical
information about the Jacobi,
Lipstein, and Kauffmann
relatives of the author,
pp. 3-28.
Harris. Merchant Princes.
Kaufmann department store
family of Pittsburgh.
Descendants of Jacob Kaufmann
who settled in Pittsburgh in
1868 from Rheinish village of
Viernheim. See GENERAL
WORKS.
Kaufmann, Alfred. "Anshej
Rhenus: A Chronicle of Jewish
Life by the Rhine." Santa
Rosa, California, 1953.
12 p. Includes brief
300-year history of the
Kaufmann (from Viernheim bei
Mannheim), Sternheimer (from
Viernheim), Regensburger
(from Eppingen), and Wolf
(from Rohrbach) families.

LBI.
Kempelen. Magyarországi Zsidó,
2:45. Kaufmann family. See
GENERAL WORKS.
Meredith, Scott. George S.
Kaufman and His Friends.
Garden City, N.Y.: Doubleday
& Co., 1974. "The Family,"
pp. 13-25. George S. Kaufman
(1889-1961), the American
playwright, was born in
Pittsburgh, the son of Joseph
and Henrietta Myers Kaufman.
The Kaufman and Myers
families came to Pittsburgh
from Germany in the 1840s.
Schulte. Bonner Juden,
pp. 310-19.
Kauffmann/Kaufmann family.
See GENERAL WORKS.
See Zevi Shimshi entry under
SHIMSHELEWITZ. Includes
Kaufman family.
Stern. FAJF. Kaufman family
tree beginning in Bingen,
Germany. See GENERAL WORKS.
Tänzer. Juden in Jebenhausen,
pp. 332-33. Kaufmann family
of Jebenhausen. See GENERAL
WORKS.
Ullmann, Elias.
Familien-Register und
Stammtafeln des Ephraim
Grödel und des Löb Cassel
(Cassella) und deren
Nachkommen. Als
Verwandschafts Nachweis
behufs Erhebung v. Ansprüchen
an die Moritz Kaufmann'sche
Familien-Stiftung in Fürth im
königreich Bayern. Frankfurt
am Main, 1872.
Weiner, Robert H. Descendants
of Boruch Ber Kaufman.
[Chevy Chase, Md., 1977.]
253 p. About the American
descendants of family which
originated in Smorgan, White
Russia. AJHS.

KAULLA
LBI has family tree beginning
1740.
Schnee, Heinrich. "Die
Hoffaktorenfamilie Kaulla an
Süddeutschen Fürstenhofen,"

Zeitschrift fur
Württembergische
Landesgeschichte 20, no. 2
(1961):238-67. Family of
Stuttgart. Includes
genealogical table.
————. "Madame Kaulla.
Deutschlands bedeutendste
Hoffaktorin und ihre Familie,
1739-1809," in Lebensbilder
aus Schwaben und Franken,
9.Band. (Stuttgart:
Kohlhammer, 1963),
pp. 85-104.
Schnee. Hoffinanz und Staat,
4:148-78. "Die Hoffaktoren
Familie Kaulla." Also see
genealogical chart, vol. 4,
opp. p. 364. Includes
genealogical information on
family of Stuttgart and
Munich, 18th to 20th century.
See GENERAL WORKS.
Zapf. Tübinger Juden, pp.
54-56. See GENERAL WORKS.

KAUTZKY
Kempelen. Magyarországi Zsidó,
1:80. See GENERAL WORKS.

KAVEN
AJA has family tree of
Kaven-Buckstein family.

KAY
See KANEFSKY.

KAYSER
LBI has family tree beginning
1760.

KAYTON
Kayton, Harmon. "History of
the Kayton Family." Norfolk,
Va.: Bernard Kayton. Begins
in 19th-century Germany.
AJA.
Stern. FAJF. Kayton family
tree beginning in Gelnhausen,
Hesse. Originally Koethen;
next generation changed name
to Kayton. See GENERAL
WORKS.

KAZNELSON
See KATZENELNBOGEN.

KEANE
AMH has family records.

KEELING
AMH has family records.

KEESING
See Esmond S. De Beer entry
under BARDEN.

KEGLEVICH
Kempelen. Magyarországi Zsidó,
1:135; 3:129. See GENERAL
WORKS.

KEILER
LBI has family tree beginning
1573.

KELETI
Kempelen. Magyarországi Zsidó,
3:71. See GENERAL WORKS.

KELLERT
Kempelen. Magyarországi Zsidó,
2:134. See GENERAL WORKS.

KELLNER
Korda, Michael. Charmed Lives:
A Family Romance. New York:
Random House, 1980. 499 p.
Hungarian family originally
from Túrkeul, about ninety
miles east of Budapest.
Original name was Kellner.
Descendants of Henrik Kellner
and Ernesztina Weisz Kellner.
Biography of Vincent,
Alexander, and Zoltán Korda.
Kulik, Karol. Alexander Korda:
The Man Who Could Work
Miracles. London: W.H.
Allen, 1975. 407 p.
Tabori, Paul. Alexander Korda.
New York: Living Books, 1966.
323 p.

KELLY
AMH has family records.

KEMENY
Kempelen. Magyarországi Zsidó,
3:106. Kemény family. See
GENERAL WORKS.

201 KESZNER

KEMPE
Semi-Gotha, 1:133. See GENERAL
WORKS.

KEMPENICH
See CAJ (Call No. P/123) entry
under ECKSTEIN.

KEMPNER
Chapiro, José. Für Alfred
Kerr. Ein Buch der
Freundschaft. Berlin: S.
Fischer, 1928. 181 p. Pages
162ff. are on his ascendants,
the families Kempner and
Calé. CtY, DLC, IEN, MH, NN,
NNC, WU.

KENDE
Kempelen. Magyarországi Zsidó,
2:54. See GENERAL WORKS.

KENDEFFY
Kempelen. Magyarországi Zsidó,
1:54. See GENERAL WORKS.

KENEDY
Kempelen. Magyarországi Zsidó,
1:73. See GENERAL WORKS.

KENEZ-KURLANDER
Kempelen. Magyarországi Zsidó,
2:17, 54. Kenéz-Kurländer
family. See GENERAL WORKS.

KENNARD
AMH has family records.

KEOGH
AMH has family records.

KEPPICH
Kempelen. Magyarországi Zsidó,
2:118, 132; 3:64. See
GENERAL WORKS.

KERB
Schulte. Bonner Juden, p. 321.
See GENERAL WORKS.

KEREKES
Kempelen. Magyarországi Zsidó,
1:75; 2:64, 137. See GENERAL
WORKS.

KERESZTFALVY
Kempelen. Magyarországi Zsidó,
2:104. See GENERAL WORKS.

KERN
Kern, Janet. Yesterday's
Child. Philadelphia:
J.B. Lippincott Co., 1962.
239 p. Story of author's
family life in Chicago, to
W.W.II. Family originally
came from Bohorodczany in
Galicia. Author is daughter
of Maximilian (1890-   ) and
Elaine Hoexter (1901-   )
Kern. Elaine Kern was born
in Chicago of German-Jewish
parents.

KERR
Chapiro, José. Für Alfred
Kerr. Ein Buch der
Freundschaft. Berlin: S.
Fischer, 1928. 181 p. Pages
162ff. are on his ascendants,
the families Kempner and
Calé. CtY, DLC, IEN, MH, NN,
NNC, WU.

KERSON
See KIRSCHEN.

KERTESZ
Kempelen. Magyarországi Zsidó,
1:106. Kertész family. See
GENERAL WORKS.

KERTSMAR
Kempelen. Magyarországi Zsidó,
2:103. Kertsmár family. See
GENERAL WORKS.

KESLER
AMH has family records.

KESSLER
AMH has family records.

KESZLER
Kempelen. Magyarországi Zsidó,
2:76, 137. See GENERAL
WORKS.

KESZNER
Kempelen. Magyarországi Zsidó,
3:83. See GENERAL WORKS.

KESZRANEK
Kempelen. Magyarországi Zsidó,
1:118. See GENERAL WORKS.

KETLY
Kempelen. Magyarországi Zsidó,
3:123. Kétly family. See
GENERAL WORKS.

KEUSCH
Schulte. Bonner Juden, p. 322.
See GENERAL WORKS.

KEYSER
AMH has family records.
CFM has family records.

KEYZER
AMH has family records.

KHALLAS
Havlin, S.Z. "Sur la famille
Khallas et la paternité du
Maggid Mishneh sur Hilkot
Sheḥiṭah de Maïmonide," (In
Hebrew.) Kirjat Sepher 49
(1974):643-56. Covers mainly
15th to 17th century.

KHUNER
Kempelen. Magyarországi Zsidó,
1:56. See GENERAL WORKS.

KIEFER
CAJ has family records.

KILENYI
Kempelen. Magyarországi Zsidó,
2:57, 72; 3:80. Kilényi
family. See GENERAL WORKS.

KIMCHI, KIMHI
Aptowitzer, Vigdor. "Sur la
pronunciation du nom Kimḥi,"
Revue des Études Juives 54
(1907):63.
Dukes, Léopold. "Die Familie
Kimchi," Der Orient
(Supplement Litteraturblatt)
11 (1850):11-14, 21-23,
34-38, 91-93, 133-36, 331-35,
359, 376-80, 389-92.
Frankl, Dr. "Die Familie
Kimchi und ihre Ausbreitung
nach Ländern und Zeiten,"
MGWJ 33 (1884):552-61.

Simonsen, David. "Notizen über
Träger des Namen Kimchi,"
MGWJ 34 (1885):525-26.

KING
AMH has family records.
Stern. FAJF. King family
trees beginning in:
(I) Moravana-Goslin, Prussian
Posen (name changed from
Krulschik to Krolek to King);
and (II and III) U.S. See
GENERAL WORKS.

KING-HALL
AMH has family records.

KINGSLEY
Kingsley, Ralph P. "How Henry
Kissinger Became My Cousin,"
American Jewish Archives 33
(1981):166-69. On history of
Kissinger family. Kingsley
is an Anglicized version.

KINO
AMH has family records.

KIRALDI, KIRALDY
Kempelen. Magyarországi Zsidó,
3:121. Királdi, Királdy
family. See GENERAL WORKS.

KIRCH
See CAJ (Call No. P/123) entry
under ECKSTEIN.

KIRSCHBAUM
AMH has family records.
Kirschbaum, Jacob.
Mi-Yerushalayim 'ad
Yerushalayim. Added title
page: From Jerusalem to
Jerusalem. Jerusalem, 1966.
136 p. CLU, CtY, CU, DLC,
MB, MH, NIC, NjP.
See Daniel Jay Rottenberg entry
under ROTTENBERG.

KIRSCHEN
Carton, Lawrence Howard.
"Notes on the Descendants of
the Kirschen [,] Samuels and
Other Related Families Who
Immigrated to America."
1983. 1 vol. Computer

printout of a short history
of the Kirschen family
(originally of Seduva, Kovno
Gubernia, Lithuania; later
settled in Baltimore,
Maryland; Pennsylvania; North
Carolina; and elsewhere) and
of genealogical charts of the
Kirschen (also spelled Kirsh,
Kerson, and Kirson),
Israelsohn, and Samuels
families. AJHS.

KIRSCHNER
Kempelen. Magyarországi Zsidó,
1:74; 2:16. See GENERAL
WORKS.

KIRSH, KIRSON
See KIRSCHEN.

KIS, KISS
Kempelen. Magyarországi Zsidó,
2:48, 89. See GENERAL WORKS.

KISCH
AMH has family records.
CAJ has family tree and records
from Prague, 17th to 20th
century.
CFM has family records.
JFF, no. 8 (1932):456.
Contains family tree of Dr.
Abraham Kisch (1725-1803).
Kisch, Bruno. Wanderungen und
Wandlungen, Die Geschichte
eines Arztes im 20.
Jahrhundert. Köln: Greven
Verlag, 1966. 360 p.
Genealogical information on
this family of Prague, pp.
25-30. CtY, DLC, ICU.
Kisch, Guido. "Die Familie
Kisch.
Genealogisch-Bibliographische
Überblick über die
vierhundertjährige Geschichte
einer jüdischen Familie,"
Udim (Zeitschrift der
Rabbinerkonferenz in der
Bundesrepublik Deutschland,
Frankfurt) 5 (1974/75):59-73.
————. Die Prager Universität
und die Juden, 1348-1848, mit
Beiträgen zur Geschichte des
Medizinstudiums.

Mährisch-Ostrau: J. Kittes
Nachfolger, 1935. 239 p.
Includes large amount of
information on Kisch family.
CtY, OCH, PPDrop.
Utitz, Emil. Egon Erwin Kisch:
Der klassiche Journalist.
Berlin: Aufbau Verlag, 1956.
211 p. There is a section on
Kisch's family in this work.
Kisch (1885-1948) was a
journalist who was born into
the famous Kisch family of
Prague. He also lived in
Germany and the U.S. CtY,
DLC, NIC, NN, WU.

KISER
Kiser Family. "Genealogical
Chart of the Kiser-Steinfeld
Family, 1856-1953." AJA.

KISFALVY
Kempelen. Magyarországi Zsidó,
2:90. See GENERAL WORKS.

KISS
See KIS, KISS.

KISSING
Brilling, Bernhard. "Die
Vorfahren der Else
Lasker-Schüler," Allgemeine
Wochenzeitung der Juden in
Deutschland (Düsseldorf), 18.
Juni 1965. Else
Lasker-Schüler, 1869-1945,
German poet, was born in the
eminent Schüler family of
Elberfeld, the daughter of
Aron (1825-1897) and Jeanette
Kissing (1857-1890) Schüler
and the granddaughter of
Moses Schüler. The Kissing
family was from Frankfurt am
Main and Kissingen.

KISSINGER
See KINGSLEY.
Ben Chorin, Scholom. "Die
Kissinger aus Kissingen,"
Zeitschrift für die
Geschichte der Juden 11,
no. 1/2 (1974):30-32.
Biographical sketch of Henry
Kissinger and his family.

Mazlish, Bruce. Kissinger: The
European Mind in American
Policy. New York: Basic
Books, 1976. 330 p.
Especially "Beginnings:
Family and Germany,"
pp. 17-35. Family was from
Fürth, Bavaria.

KITSON
AMH has family records.

KITZINGER
Kitzinger, Wilhelm.
Familienerinnerungen. Tel
Aviv, 1942-1943. 19, 2 p.
Bayern family. Family tree
begins 1870. LBI.
Tänzer. Juden in Tirol,
p. 731. See GENERAL WORKS.

KLAAR
Clare, George. Das waren die
Klaars: Spuren einer Familie.
Ins Deutsche übertr. von
Gabriele Grünwald und Frank
Hergun. Berlin: Ullstein,
1980. 319 p. Klaar family
of Vienna. LBI.
————. Last Waltz in Vienna:
The Destruction of a Family,
1842-1942. New York: Holt,
1982. 283 p.

KLABER
Kempelen. Magyarországi Zsidó,
2:10. See GENERAL WORKS.

KLAR
Kempelen. Magyarországi Zsidó,
3:72. Klár family. See
GENERAL WORKS.

KLATZCO
Rosenstein. Unbroken Chain,
pp. 641ff. See GENERAL
WORKS.

KLAUS
LBI has family tree beginning
1630.
Marshuetz Family, Cincinnati,
Ohio and Memphis, Tenn., and
Petersburg, Va. "History of
the Family, written by Leo J.
Marshuetz, Including Material

on the Klaus and Landauer
Families, 1946; and Family
Correspondence, 1870-1903."
Typescript and MS;
photostats. AJA.

KLAUSNER
CAJ has family records.
Shapiro. Internationalen
Verwandtschaftlichen. See
GENERAL WORKS.

KLEBE
CAJ has family tree for
Bachrach, Blumenfeld, Katz,
Klebe, and Meierstein
families of Bremke and Rhina,
Germany, Israel, and U.S.
covering 1650-1975.

KLEBELSBERG
Ello, Anton. "Interessantes
aus dem Stammbaum der
gräflichen Häuser Apponyi und
Klebelsberg," Jüdischer
Archiv 2, no. 5 (1929):3-4.

KLEBERG
Semi-Gotha, 2:93. See GENERAL
WORKS.

KLEE
AJA has genealogical files.
Schulte. Bonner Juden, p. 323.
See GENERAL WORKS.

KLEEFELD
See Hans Josephthal entry under
GOLDSCHEINDER. Includes 12
family trees. Includes
Kleefeld family.

KLEEGMAN
Singer, Joy Daniels. My
Mother, the Doctor. New
York: Dutton, 1970. 224 p.
A memoir of the career of
Anna [Hanna] Kleegman, one of
the first Jewish women
doctors in New York City.
Early part of book deals with
Kleegman family life in
Borschevka, a village near
Kiev. Israel and Elka
Kleegman were the
grandparents of the author.

KLEEMAN
AMH has family records.

KLEIN
AMH has family records.
CAJ (Call No. 3418) has family
tree of family of Berlin.
CFM has family records.
Kempelen. Magyarországi Zsidó,
1:21, 27, 84, 85, 143; 2:57,
67, 91, 134, 136, 141; 3:25,
46, 48, 52, 78, 80, 112, 123.
See GENERAL WORKS.
The Klein Family History: 9
Klein Generations. Part I,
Compiled by Simon Friedman,
and Part II, Compiled by
Harold Weinberger. Los
Angeles: Weinberger, 1980.
312 p. DLC.
See Daniel Jay Rottenberg entry
under ROTTENBERG. Includes
Klein family.

KLEIN-CHEVALIER
See Stammbaum Levinstein entry
under AVELLIS. Includes
Klein-Chavalier families.

KLEINADEL
Reychman. Szkice
genealogiczne, pp. 103-104.
See GENERAL WORKS.

KLEINMANN
See KARMAN.
Kempelen. Magyarországi Zsidó,
2:65. See GENERAL WORKS.

KLEINPENNIG
CAJ has family tree.

KLEMPERER
PD has family records.

KLERCKER
Semi-Gotha, 1:126. See GENERAL
WORKS.

KLINGENSTJERNA
Semi-Gotha, 1:98. See GENERAL
WORKS.

KLINGER
PD has family records.
Kempelen. Magyarországi

Zsidó, 1:49. See GENERAL
WORKS.

KLINGSPOR
Semi-Gotha, 2:115. See GENERAL
WORKS.

KLINTBERG
Semi-Gotha, 1:133. See GENERAL
WORKS.

KLOMPUS
CAJ has family records.

KLOPFER
Kempelen. Magyarországi Zsidó,
1:122, 123. See GENERAL
WORKS.

KLUGAI
See Zevi Shimshi entry under
SHIMSHELEWITZ. Includes
Klugai family.

KMIOTEK
See Judith A. Walters entry
under GRYNSZPAN.

KNER
Papp, János. "A
Kner-Könyukiadás
történétéböl. A
Könyvmüvészeti Kisérletezés
évei," Békesi Élet, no. 3
(1977):307-22. History of
the Kner Jewish printing
family in Hungary.

KNIGHT
AMH has family records.

KNINA
CAJ (Call No. CS/180) has
4-page family tree,
1724-1886, of family of
Prague. In German.

KNOLLER
CAJ has family tree from
Germany.

KNOPF
Schulte. Bonner Juden, p. 324.
See GENERAL WORKS.

KOBER
Kober, Wilhelm. Die Geschichte
meiner Familie. Breslau,
1929. 28, 1 p. LBI.

KOCH
Kempelen. Magyarországi Zsidó,
2:42. See GENERAL WORKS.
Kurzweil, Arthur. "Hizzoner's
Roots," New York, Oct. 29,
1979, pp. 46-48. About the
forebears of New York City
Mayor, Edward I. Koch.
Great-grandparents: Yoel Koch
of Uścieszko, Poland, and
Yisroel Edelstein of Skala,
Poland.
Tänzer. Juden in Jebenhausen,
p. 334. See GENERAL WORKS.

KOCZAN
Kempelen. Magyarországi Zsidó,
1:102. Kóczán family. See
GENERAL WORKS.

KOEN-CANTARINI
Osimo, Marco. Narrazione della
strage compita nel 1547
contro gli Ebre Asolo e cenni
biografici della famiglia
Koen-Cantarini originata da
un ucciso Asolano. Casale
Monferrato: Tipogr. Bertero,
1875. 138 p. OCH, PPDrop.

KOESTLER
Koestler, Arthur. Arrow in the
Blue: An Autobiography. New
York: MacMillan, 1952. 353
p. "The Koestler Saga," pp.
10-22. The Koestler
(originally Köstler) family
from Miskolcz, Hungary.
Arthur Koestler (1905-1983)
was the son of Henrik (d.
1939) and Adéla Koestler and
the grandson of Leopold
Koestler (d. 1911).

KOETHEN
See Stern, FAJF entry under
KAYTON.

KOGAN
CFM has family records.

KOHARI
Kempelen. Magyarországi Zsidó,
1:92; 3:117. Kohári family.
See GENERAL WORKS.

KOHEN
Kempelen. Magyarországi Zsidó,
1:45. See GENERAL WORKS.

KOHLBERG
LBI has family trees beginning
1545 and 1717.
Keeley, Joseph C. The China
Lobby Man: The Story of
Alfred Kohlberg. New
Rochelle, N.Y.: Arlington
House, 1969. 421 p. "Family
Album," pp. 14-26. The
biography of an American
businessman (1887-   ) who
was a strong supporter of
Chiang Kai Shek and was also
the founder of the American
Jewish League Against
Communism. Kohlberg was born
in Annapolis, Md., the son of
Manfred Kohlberg (b. 1856)
and the grandson of Selig and
Rose Kohlberg. Selig
Kohlberg had come to U.S. in
early 1850s from Germany.

KOHLEMAN
See Stern, FAJF entry under
COLEMAN.

KOHLER
Kohler, Kaufmann.
"Genealogical Data." In
German. Family tree begins
1611. AJA.

KOHLMAN
AJA has genealogical files.
Kohlman Family. "Genealogy,
1790-1975." New Orleans, La.
1976. AJA.

KOHN
AMH has family records.
See Esmond S. De Beer entry
under BARDEN.
Kempelen. Magyarországi Zsidó.
Kohn family, 1:70, 90; 2:25,
39, 60, 97, 135; 3:33, 60,
71, 116, 118, 125, 138, 140.

207

KOMOR

Kohn Götz Schwerin family,
2:24. See GENERAL WORKS.
Kohn, Jean. Die Familie Kohn
aus Wassertrüdingen. Paris,
1948. 53 p. Family tree
begins 1771. LBI.
Kohn, Walter A. Illustrated
Family Tree of the Kohn,
Barnett, and Other Related
Families of Albany, N.Y.
Philadelphia, 1946. Family
tree begins 1744 in Bohemia.
AJA.
Kohn, Joseph. "The Story of
Joseph Kohn and His
Descendants, 1744-1945,"
compiled by Sidney C. Singer.
Glendale, Calif., Aug. 21,
1945. AJA; Western Reserve
Historical Society,
Cleveland, Ohio.
See Daniel Jay Rottenberg entry
under ROTTENBERG.
Stern. FAJF. Kohn family tree
beginning in Petersburg,
Bohemia. See GENERAL WORKS.

KOHNER
Az Egyenlöség (Budapest),
Oct. 18, 1896. History of
Kohner family of Hungary, a
leading family of
industrialists and
philanthropists. Family came
to Pest from Leipzig via
Bohemia before 1840.
Kempelen. Magyarországi Zsidó,
1:88; 2:135; 3:79. See
GENERAL WORKS.

KOHNSOM
AMH has family records.

KOHNSTAM
CFM has family records.

KOHNSTAMM
LBI has family tree beginning
1650.
Schulte. Bonner Juden, p. 325.
See GENERAL WORKS.

KOJETANER
Kempelen. Magyarországi Zsidó,
1:127. Kojetáner family.
See GENERAL WORKS.

KOKERNOT
Stern. FAJF. Kokernot family
tree beginning in Amsterdam.
See GENERAL WORKS.

KOKISOW
UJE, 6:440. Karaite family
from Poland and the Crimea.
Also spelled Kukisow.

KOLBL
Kempelen. Magyarországi Zsidó,
1:70. See GENERAL WORKS.

KOLISCH
Kempelen. Magyarországi Zsidó,
3:106. See GENERAL WORKS.

KOLLAR
Kempelen. Magyarországi Zsidó,
2:43. Kollár family. See
GENERAL WORKS.

KOLLER
Kempelen. Magyarországi Zsidó,
1:124. See GENERAL WORKS.

KOLLINSKY
Schachtitz, Jonas, ed. "Dr.
Adolf Kollinsky," Judisches
Archiv, 1, N.F., H. 5/6:1-3,
12-13. Includes family tree.
Family of Weimar and Vienna.

KOLODNY
CAJ has family records.

KOLOSVARY
Kempelen. Magyarországi Zsidó,
1:125. Kolosváry family.
See GENERAL WORKS.

KOMAIKO
Gitelson-Komaiko Family
Association. The Chronicle.
New York, 1961-? YIVO.

KOMLOS
Kempelen. Magyarországi Zsidó,
1:96; 2:66. Komlós family.
See GENERAL WORKS.

KOMOR
Kempelen. Magyarországi Zsidó,
2:97. See GENERAL WORKS.

KONIC
Reychman. Szkice
genealogiczne, pp. 105-110.
See GENERAL WORKS.

KONIG
Kempelen. Magyarországi Zsidó,
2:13, 92; 3:24. König
family. See GENERAL WORKS.
Semi-Gotha, 1:29, 30. See
GENERAL WORKS.

KONIGSBERGER
CAJ has Königsberger family
records.

KONIGSEGG
Kempelen. Magyarországi Zsidó,
1:141. Königsegg family.
See GENERAL WORKS.

KONIGSWARTER
Bloch, Chajim. "Der Ursprung
der freiherrlichen Familie
Königswarter," ZGJT 3
(1931/32):35-39.
"Die Familie Königswarter," in
Geadelte jüdische Familien
(Salzburg, 1891), pp. 45ff.
Family of Frankfurt am Main.
"Die Familie Königswarter,"
Jüdisches/Israelitisches
Gemeindeblatt (u.a.T)
(Frankfurt) 13, no. 13
(1934/35):492.
Gastfreund, Isaac. Toledot Bet
Königswarter. Vienna, 1877.
8 p. LBI, OCH.
Kempelen. Magyarországi Zsidó,
1:39; 2:18, 19. Königswarter
family. See GENERAL WORKS.

KONIGSWATER
Daniel Meyer Papers. Jonas
Hirsch Konigswater Family
Tree, 1760-1887. WJHC.

KONISWARTER
AMH has family records.

KONRAD
Kempelen. Magyarországi Zsidó,
2:142; 3:19, 39. Konrád
family. See GENERAL WORKS.

KONSTANTIN
Kempelen. Magyarországi Zsidó,
3:124. See GENERAL WORKS.

KONTI
Kempelen. Magyarországi Zsidó,
3:137. See GENERAL WORKS.

KONYI
See HAJNAL-KONYI.
Kempelen. Magyarországi Zsidó,
2:137. Kónyi family. See
GENERAL WORKS.

KOOK
EJ (1972), 9:1259. "Jaffe and
Kook Families." Genealogical
table. See GENERAL WORKS.

KOOPMAN
JFF, no. 26. Family history.
Schulte. Bonner Juden,
pp. 326-27. See GENERAL
WORKS.

KOPALD
Rubin Family. "Information on
the Rubin and Kopald
families, families who moved
from Nebraska to San
Francisco. Includes family
Bible with family genealogy
inside, and a business card
of the E.I. Rubin Co., San
Francisco, which was a snack
bar and popcorn equipment
co." WJHC.

KOPPE
CAJ (Call No. 3418) has family
tree of family of Berlin.

KOPPEL
Kempelen. Magyarországi Zsidó,
1:143, 144; 2:35. See
GENERAL WORKS.
Yaoz. Album Shel. See GENERAL
WORKS.

KOPPEL-THURNAUER
Heckscher, Albert Gottlieb.
Stammtafel Koppel (oder
Thurnauer). Copenhagen: S.B.
Salomon, 1883. 24 p. AJA,
OCH.

KOPPELY
Kempelen. Magyarországi Zsidó,
1:43, 143, 144. Koppély
family. See GENERAL WORKS.

KOPPENHAGEN
AMH has family records.

KOPSTEIN
Ballin. Juden in Seesen,
p. 214. See GENERAL WORKS.

KORACH
CAJ has family tree from Italy.

KORAI
Kempelen. Magyarországi Zsidó,
3:44. See GENERAL WORKS.

KORANYI
Kempelen. Magyarországi Zsidó,
1:123. Korányi family. See
GENERAL WORKS.

KORBER
Semigothaisches Taschenbuch.
Genealogical table 12.
Körber family. See GENERAL
WORKS.

KORCZAK
Dauzenroth, E. "Zum Schicksal
Janusz Korczak und seiner
Kinder," Frankfurter Hefte 27
(1972):587-92. Korczak,
noted Polish author,
educator, and social worker,
b. Warsaw, 1878/79; d. 1942.
He was head of the famous
Jewish orphanage. His real
name was Henryk Goldszmidt.

KORDA
See KELLNER.

KOREFF
JFF, no. 29. Family history.

KOREIN
Kempelen. Magyarországi Zsidó,
2:23. See GENERAL WORKS.

KORMOCZI
Kempelen. Magyarországi Zsidó,
1:58. Körmöczi family. See
GENERAL WORKS.

KORN
"Die Ahnen," Judaica
(Pressburg) 2, no. 9/10
(1935):21-22. A. Korn,
1825-1903.

KORNFELD
PD has family records.
Kempelen. Magyarországi Zsidó,
1:123, 130; 2:101. See
GENERAL WORKS.

KORNHABER
Kempelen. Magyarországi Zsidó,
3:76. See GENERAL WORKS.

KORNISS
Kempelen. Magyarországi Zsidó,
1:56; 2:53. See GENERAL
WORKS.

KORNREICH
Conrich, J. Lloyd, comp. "The
Kornreich Family." 1965.
WJHC.

KOROSSY
Kempelen. Magyarországi Zsidó,
1:142; 3:90. Körössy,
Körössy family. See GENERAL
WORKS.

KORWIN
Piotrowski, Ludwik (pseud.:
Ludwik Korwin). Korwinowie.
Krakow, Skl. gl. w. ksieg. S.
Lisowskiego, 1935. 136 p.
DLC, MH.

KOSHLAND
Narell. Our City. Includes
genealogical tables for this
pioneer San Francisco Jewish
family. Descendants of Simon
Koshland (1825-1896). Family
originally from Ichenhousen,
15 miles east of Ulm in
Bavaria. See GENERAL WORKS.

KOSMANOS
See MIRBACH-KOSMANOS.

KOSTERLITZ
CAJ has family records.

KOSTLER
See KOESTLER.

KOTANYI
Kempelen. Magyarországi Zsidó,
1:127. Kotányi family. See
GENERAL WORKS.

KOUDELKA
Kempelen. Magyarországi Zsidó,
2:76. See GENERAL WORKS.

KOVACH, KOVACS
Kempelen. Magyarországi Zsidó,
1:17, 101; 2:25, 56; 3:58.
Kovách, Kovács family. See
GENERAL WORKS.

KOVALSKY
Yaoz. Album Shel. See GENERAL
WORKS.

KOVER
Kempelen. Magyarországi Zsidó,
1:101; 3:105. Kövér family.
See GENERAL WORKS.

KOVESI
Kempelen. Magyarországi Zsidó,
2:67; 3:37, 77. Kövesi
family. See GENERAL WORKS.

KOVNER
Reichel, O. Asher. Isaac
Halevy, 1847-1919: Spokesman
and Historian of Jewish
Tradition. New York: Yeshiva
University Press, 1969.
Genealogical information on
the Ivenecer, Kovner, and
Rabinowitz ancestors of Isaac
Halevy, pp. 15-16. Isaac
Halevy (Rabinowitz) was born
in Ivenets, Province of
Minsk, near Vilna, the son of
R. Eliyahu and Rahel Kovner
Halevy Ivenecer Rabinowitz.
CLU, CSt, CtY, CU, ICU, MB,
MH, NcD, NIC, NjP, NN.

KOZMIN
Kozmin, M. "The Past and
Present of the Siberian
Sabbatarian Sectarians," (In
Hebrew and Russian),
Evreiskaia Starina 6

(1913):3-22, 162-83.
Includes author's genealogy.
He was a Sabbatarian.

KOZUCHOWSKI
Balaban. Żydów w Krakowie,
1:190. Kożuchowski family.
Genealogical table, 16th to
17th century. See GENERAL
WORKS.

KRAEMER
Semi-Gotha, 1:94. See GENERAL
WORKS.

KRAFFT
CAJ has family records.

KRAFT
Stone, Susan Kaplan. Kraft
Family Genealogy: Descendants
of Yosi (Yolick) and Faiga
Kraft. Bellmore, N.Y., 1982.
76 11 illus. AJHS.

KRAININ
Krainin Family, Naples, Maine.
Krainin, Joseph. "The
Krainin Family Saga." 1970;
Typescript; Xerox copy. AJA.

KRAKAUER
Kempelen. Magyarországi Zsidó,
2:123. See GENERAL WORKS.

KRAKENBERGER
LBI has family tree beginning
1785.

KRAMARZ
Kempelen. Magyarországi Zsidó,
1:118. See GENERAL WORKS.

KRAMER
AMH has family records.
CAJ has family records.
PD has family records.
See Sidney Cramer entry under
BINDMAN.
Kempelen. Magyarországi Zsidó,
1:86; 2:68. See GENERAL
WORKS.
Kramer, Simon. Memoirs of
Simon Kramer [1808-1887],
Written on the Occasion of
His Golden Wedding. Chicago:

Aetna Stationers, Inc. 1942.
80 p. A translation of
Goldene Hochzeit und
Autobiographie by Emma
Schemel. DLC.

KRANZLER
Kranzler, David. My Jewish
Roots: A Practical Guide to
Tracing and Recording Your
Genealogy and Family History.
New York: Sepher-Hermon
Press, 1979. 88 p.

KRAUS
AJA has family tree beginning
18th century.
Kraus, Eugene. "History of the
Kraus Family of Columbia
City, Indiana," in Jewish
Life in Indiana (Ft. Wayne?:
Indiana Jewish Historical
Society, Inc., Nov. 1980),
pp. 13-18. Descendants of
Leopold Kraus, b. Geisen,
Germany, 1841; d. 1931; came
to America ca. 1858.
Stern. FAJF. Kraus family
tree beginning in
Demmelsdorf, Bavaria. Also
Krouse originally. See
GENERAL WORKS.

KRAUSE
Kempelen. Magyarországi Zsidó,
2:13. See GENERAL WORKS.

KRAUSZ
Kempelen. Magyarországi Zsidó,
1:86, 140; 2:89, 127, 133,
141, 145; 3:25, 96. See
GENERAL WORKS.

KREIBNER
Kempelen. Magyarországi Zsidó,
1:118. See GENERAL WORKS.

KREMER
Kremer, Abraham M. "Report of
An Interview with Abraham M.
Kremer ... West Los Angeles,
Sept. 9, 1966, by Dr. Norton
B. Stern, and Biographical
Material on Mr. and Mrs.
Maurice Kremer from Other
Sources." [Santa Monica,

Calif.] 1966. Typescript.
5 p. "The interviewee, born
in Los Angeles in 1877, is
the son of Maurice and
Matilda Kremer. This report
includes biographical data on
Abraham, as well as family
genealogical data...." AJA,
WJHC.

KREMNITZER
Kalisch, Paul. "Zur Geschichte
d. Familie
Kremnitzer-Kalischer," JFF,
no. 40/41 (1936):713-23,
737-41.

KRENSKY
The Krensky-Ehrenreich
"Time-Line," Heder Hadorot,
Spertus Museum of Judaica,
2nd floor, 618 S. Michigan
Ave., Chicago, Ill. "This
permanent exhibit is a
documentary and pictorial
history of the
Krensky-Ehrenreich family,
with pictures and diagrams
tracing back 200 years, on
the walls of the Milton J.
Krensky and Rosemary
Ehrenreich Krensky Conference
Room."

KRESNER
AMH has family records.

KRETSCHMAR-BERGER
Kempelen. Magyarországi Zsidó,
2:19. See GENERAL WORKS.

KRIEG
Krieg, Max and Erwin. Chronik
der Familie Krieg. Liegnitz,
By the Author, 1923. Table
of descendants of Naphtali
Hirsch Charig (b. Province of
Posen, ca. 1750).

KRIEGER
See Nathan M. Reiss entry under
EDELMUTH. Includes Krieger
family of Melecz and
Osiek/Oświecim.

KRIEGSMANN
Schulte. Bonner Juden, p. 328.
See GENERAL WORKS.

KRIESHABER
Kempelen. Magyarországi Zsidó,
2:63. See GENERAL WORKS.

KROLECK
See Stern, FAJF (I) entry under
KING.

KRONACHER
LBI has family tree beginning
1725. Also, CAJ has family
tree, 1725-1960.

KRONENBERG
Reychman. Szkice
genealogiczne, pp. 111-15.
See GENERAL WORKS.
Schulte. Bonner Juden, p. 329.
See GENERAL WORKS.

KRONENGOLD
CAJ has family records,
1881-1889.

KRONSTEIN
Kempelen. Magyarországi Zsidó,
2:70; 3:74. See GENERAL
WORKS.

KRONTHAL
LBI has family trees beginning
1694 and 1775.
JFF, nos. 22, 23, and 24.
Family histories.

KROPUSCHIN
AMH has family records.

KROUSE
See Stern, FAJF entry under
KRAUS.

KRUK
Kempelen. Magyarországi Zsidó,
3:99. See GENERAL WORKS.

KRULEWITCH
Krulewitch, Melvin L. Now That
You Mention It. New York:
Quadrangle Press, 1973. 257
p. Genealogical information
on the various U.S. branches

of the Krulewitch families,
pp. 1-11. Autobiography of
an active life as a major
general in the U.S. Marine
Corps, lawyer, bibliophile,
artist, boxing official, and
community leader in New York.
Family came to U.S. during
the Civil War.

KRULSCHIK
See Stern, FAJF (I) entry under
KING.

KRUMAN
Kruman Family Tree. Family
from Jagielnica and Czortkov
in Galicia. JGCT.

KRUSKAL
Jacobson-Kruskal Family; New
York, N.Y.; Chicago, Ill.;
and Washington, D.C.
"Genealogical Information,
Documents, and
Correspondence, 1879-1972;"
Typescript and MS. In
English, German, and Hebrew.
AJA.
Brown, R.D. "Two Baltic
Families Who Came to America:
The Jacobsons and the
Kruskals, 1870-1970."
American Jewish Archives 24
(1972):39-93. Family
originally from Dorpat (the
present-day Tartu), Estonia.

KUBINSKY
PD has family records.

KUBINSZKI
Kempelen. Magyarországi Zsidó,
1:89? (or 2:89 or 3:89?) See
GENERAL WORKS.

KUBINYI
Kempelen. Magyarországi Zsidó,
1:124. See GENERAL WORKS.

KUCHINKA-GAJARI
Kempelen. Magyarországi Zsidó,
2:104. Kuchinka-Gajári
family. See GENERAL WORKS.

KUFFLER
Kempelen. Magyarországi Zsidó,
2:128. See GENERAL WORKS.

KUFFNER
PD has family records.
Kempelen. Magyarországi Zsidó,
3:51. See GENERAL WORKS.

KUGELMANN
Rose. Schöninger Juden. See
GENERAL WORKS.

KUHLBRAND
Kurtzig, Heinrich.
Ostdeutsches Judentum.
Tradition einer Familie.
Stolp: Eulitz, 1927. 164 p.
On his father, Aaron Kurtzig,
1822-1904; his grandfather,
Dr. med. Juda Beinesch, who
later changed name to
Kuhlbrand, b. Fodor, before
1782; d. Jnowraczlaw, before
1853; and other descendants
of his five daughters. DLC,
LBI, MH, NN, OCH. 2 Aufl.
Leipzig: G. Engel, 1930. NN,
PPDrop.

KUHN
Metzger, Hermance. Die
Geschichte der Familie Kuhn.
o.O., 1932. 7 p. Family
from Bisserheim/Pfalz. LBI.

KUKISOW
See KOKISOW.

KUKLANSKI
[Rutenberg, Herman.] "A Tree of
the Rutenberg and Kuklanski
Families." 1959. History of
Kuklanski family of Suvalk,
Poland; and history of
Rutenberg family, originally
of the village of Padumle,
near Kopchevo, State of
Suvalk, Poland. Both cover
mainly 20th century.
Rutenberg family is claimed
to be descended from a branch
of the descendants of Rabbi
Meir of Rothenburg that
settled in Riga, Latvia in
mid-17th century. JGCT.

KULB
AMH has family records.

KULINYI
Kempelen. Magyarországi Zsidó,
3:75. See GENERAL WORKS.

KULP
AMH has family records.
Baer, Berthold. Stammtafeln
der Familie Speyer.
Frankfurt am Main: Kumpf &
Reis, 184f. Includes Kulp
family from Frankfurt,
pp. 104-110. LBI, OCH.
Goldschmidt, Leo S. Die
Familie Kulp. By the Author,
1935. Some ancestors and the
grandchildren of Juda Michael
Kulp, 1796-1867, and his wife
Adelhard, née Mainz,
1801-1892.
Sichel, Jacques V., ed. and
compiler. The Kulp Family: A
Genealogy. Union, N.J.?,
1965. 225 p. Genealogical
tables, group portrait. Very
detailed genealogy of family
originating from Frankfurt am
Main. In English and German.
AJHS, DLC, NN, OCH.

KUN
Kempelen. Magyarországi Zsidó,
3:72. See GENERAL WORKS.

KUNEWALDER
Kempelen. Magyarországi Zsidó,
2:35. See GENERAL WORKS.

KUNFFY
Kempelen. Magyarországi Zsidó,
2:60. See GENERAL WORKS.

KUNOS
Kempelen. Magyarországi Zsidó,
1:108. See GENERAL WORKS.

KUNSTADT
LBI has family tree beginning
1790.

KUNSTADTER
Kempelen. Magyarországi Zsidó,
2:132. Kunstädter family.
See GENERAL WORKS.

KUPPELWIESER
Kempelen. Magyarországi Zsidó,
1:118; 3:94. See GENERAL
WORKS.

KUPPERMAN
Straus, Dorothea. Thresholds.
Boston: Houghton, Mifflin,
1971. 183 p. Memoir's of
author's family, the
Kupperman family in New York,
brewers of Rheingold beer.
Family originally from
Ludwigsburg, Württemberg;
arrived in Brooklyn in 1848.

KURKIN
See R. Brock Shanberg entry
under GOLTZ.

KURLANDER
See KENEZ-KURLANDER.
Kempelen. Magyarországi Zsidó,
2:17, 53, 54. Kurländer
family. See GENERAL WORKS.
Tänzer. Juden in Tirol,
p. 733. Kurländer family.
See GENERAL WORKS.

KURREIN
CAJ has family records from
1905.

KURSCHNER
Kempelen. Magyarországi Zsidó,
3:74. Kürschner family. See
GENERAL WORKS.

KURSHEEDT
CFM has family records.
Stern. FAJF. Kursheedt family
tree beginning in Germany.
See GENERAL WORKS.

KURSLETT
AMH has family records.

KURTZIG
Kurtzig, Heinrich.
Ostdeutsches Judentum.
Tradition einer Familie.
Stolp: Eulitz, 1927. 164 p.
On his father, Aaron Kurtzig,
1822-1904; his grandfather,
Dr. med. Juda Beinesch, who
later changed name to

Kuhlbrand, b. Fodor, before
1782; d. Jnowraczlaw, before
1853; and other descendants
of his five daughters. DLC,
LBI, MH, NN, OCH. 2 Aufl.
Leipzig: G. Engel, 1930. NN,
PPDrop.

KURZWEIL
Kurzweil, Arthur. From
Generation to Generation: How
to Trace Your Jewish
Genealogy and Personal
History. New York: Morrow,
1980. 353 p.
————. The Kurzweil Family
History and Genealogy. New
York, 1976. 135 p. Family
from Dobromil, in Galicia.
AJA, AJHS.

KUSEL
Ballin. Juden in Seesen,
p. 215. See GENERAL WORKS.
Schrag, Paul J. Heimatkunde.
Die Geschichte einer
deutsch-jüdischen Familie.
München: Kindler, 1979.
161 p. Story of Kusel family
in Southern Germany and of
the tobacco factory, Moll &
Schneider, owned 1881-1938 by
Kusel family. LBI.

KUSHLICK
Kaplan, Mendel. From Shtetl to
Steelmaking: The Story of
Three Immigrant Families and
a Family Business. Capetown,
South Africa: C. Struik on
Behalf of the Kaplan-Kushlick
Foundation, 1979. 144 p.
Owners of Cape Gate Fence and
Wire Works Co. DLC.

KUSSY
Kussy, Sarah. The Story of
Gustav and Bella Kussy of
Newark, N.J.: A Family
Chronicle. Newark, N.J.,
1945? 28 p. NjR.

KUTLIK
Bettlheim, Samuel. "Die
Familie Kutlik," Judaica

(Pressburg) 3, no. 19/20
(1936):10-11.

KUTNER
PD has family records.

KUTTNER
CAJ has family records from
1846.

KUYLENTSJERNA
Semi-Gotha, 1:35, 46. See
GENERAL WORKS.

KUZMANN
Kempelen. Magyarországi Zsidó,
1:42. See GENERAL WORKS.

LABAN
Kempelen. Magyarországi Zsidó,
3:120. See GENERAL WORKS.

LABAT
CFM has family records.

LABATT
Stern. FAJF. Labatt family
tree beginning in France.
See GENERAL WORKS.

LABORFALVI
Kempelen. Magyarországi Zsidó,
2:28. See GENERAL WORKS.

LACHMAN
LBI has family tree beginning
1832.
Brilling, Bernhard. "The Names
Lachmann, Bettsack, Sanwil,"
(In Hebrew.) Yeda'-'am 2,
no. 1 (1953):13-15.

LACK
Lack, Ruth. V.H., ed. "You
Can't Live All Your Life": A
Story about Fannie Lack.
[Houston, 1967.] 63 p. AJHS.

LACKENBACH
Kempelen. Magyarországi Zsidó,
3:136. See GENERAL WORKS.

LACKENBACHER
PD has family records.

LACZAI
Kempelen. Magyarországi Zsidó,
3:72. Láczai family. See
GENERAL WORKS.

LACZKO
Kempelen. Magyarországi Zsidó,
2:64. Laczkó family. See
GENERAL WORKS.

LADENBURG
CFM has family records.
Rosenthal, B. Die Familie
Ladenburg. Jüd. Gemeinde
Berlin. Mannheim, 1935.
Family tree begins 1762.
Waldeck, Florian. Alte
Mannheimer Familien.
Mannheim:
Familiengeschichtliche
Vereinigung, 1920. 103 p.
Includes Ladenburg family of
Frankfurt am Main and
Mannheim. NN.

LADESMA
CFM has family records.

LAGER
Brandmark, Bernice. Lager,
Lagzitsky, Lagrzitski.
[Manhasset, N.Y., 1981].
34 ll. illus. Genealogy of
the descendants of Meyer Zvi
Lagrzitski (b. ca. 1830) of
Kruszyna, Poland. AJHS.

LAGERBERG
Semi-Gotha, 1:111. See GENERAL
WORKS.

LAGERCRANTZ
Semi-Gotha, 2:98. See GENERAL
WORKS.

LEGERHJELM
Semi-Gotha, 1:34. See GENERAL
WORKS.

LAGERSPARRE
Semi-Gotha, 1:96. See GENERAL
WORKS.

LAGRZITSKI, LAGZITSKY
See LAGER.

LAIB
Stern. FAJF. Laib family tree
beginning in Bavaria. Also
originally Loeb. See GENERAL
WORKS.

LAIDLEY
AMH has family records.

LAITNER
AMH has family records.

LAKOS
Kempelen. Magyarországi Zsidó,
2:127. See GENERAL WORKS.

LALAND
AMH has family records.

LAMART
AMH has family records.

LAMBERT
LBI has family tree beginning
1699.
Goldstein, Ruth Hartzell.
Herzog and Lambert
Genealogy.... Santa Barbara,
Calif.: ABC-Clio, 1971.
41 p. Includes genealogical
tables. DLC, OCH.

LAMEGO
AMH has family records.
CFM has family records.
Familieminder Tilegnet. Lamego
family, p. 107. See GENERAL
WORKS.

LAMEL
PD has family records.

LAMERT
AMH has family records.

LAMM
Kempelen. Magyarországi Zsidó,
3:119. See GENERAL WORKS.
Lamm, Louis. Durch 3,
Jahrhunderte Stammtafel der
Leviten-Familie Lamm aus
Wittelshofen in Bayern.
Berlin, 1914. Folio. LBI.

Rothschild. Svenska Israel.
See GENERAL WORKS.
Semi-Gotha, 2:77ff. See
GENERAL WORKS.

LA MOTTA
AJA has genealogical files.

LANCZI, LANCZY
Kempelen. Magyarországi Zsidó,
1:74, 86, 105; 2:143.
Lánczi, Lánczy family. See
GENERAL WORKS.

LANDAU
AMH has family records.
JE, 7:606. "Pedigree of Landau
Family." Descendants of
Judah Landau, lived ca. 1480
or 1490, through early 19th
century. Family of Poland
and Russia. See GENERAL
WORKS.
Bałaban. Żydów w Krakowie,
1:178-79; 2:275, 648-49.
Genealogical table of the
descendants of Mojesz Lewita
Landau, 16th to 20th century.
See GENERAL WORKS.
Friedberg, Bernhard. Bene
Landau le-mishpeḥotham.
Added title page: Die Familie
Landau; ihre genealogie und
ihr literarisches wirken vom
XIV. Jahrhundert bis auf die
gegenwart, nach den quellen
bearbeitet von B. Friedberg.
Frankfurt am Main: J.
Kauffmann, 1905. 24 p.
Folding genealogical table.
CtY, DLC, MH, NN.
Kempelen. Magyarországi Zsidó,
1:93. See GENERAL WORKS.
Landau, Herrmann Josef.
Stammbuchblätter.
Erinnerungen aus meinem
Leben. Prag: J.B. Pichl,
1875. 323 p. CU, OCH.
————. Stammbuchblätter.
Erinnerungen aus meinem
Leben. 2. Aufl. Prag, 1879.
MH.
Landau, Ronald M. "In Search
of Mishpokhe," Toledot: The
Journal of Jewish Genealogy
3, no. 4 (1981?):22-24.

Family from Warsaw and Lodz,
Poland.
Margolioth, Ephraim Zalman.
Ma'aloth ha-Yubasin. Edited
by Abraham Segal Ettinger.
Lemberg: A.B. Krochman, 1900.
83 p. Includes Landau
family. DLC, MH.
Shapiro. Mishpachot Atikot.
See GENERAL WORKS.
Rosenstein. Unbroken Chain,
pp. 389ff. "Landau Family
Pedigree." See GENERAL
WORKS.
See Mordechai Rubenstein entry
under FRANKEL.

LANDAUER
AJA has genealogical files.
CAJ has family trees from
Germany, 1833-1939 and
1690-1936.
CFM has family records.
Landauer Family. "Genealogical
Chart, 1690-1959." In
German; Photostat. AJA.
LBI has family trees beginning
1690 and 1776.
Frenkel, Elias Karl. Family
Tree: Elias & Karoline
Landauer (Hürben-Krumbach nr.
Münich). Jerusalem: By the
Author, 1964. 59 p. LBI.
Kempelen. Magyarországi Zsidó,
1:116; 3:118. See GENERAL
WORKS.
See Daniel Nathan Leeson entry
under LEESON.
Marschuetz Family, Cincinnati,
Ohio and Memphis, Tenn., and
Petersburg, Va. "History of
the Family, written by Leo
J. Marshuetz, Including
Material on the Klaus and
Landauer Families, 1946; and
Family Correspondence,
1870-1903." Typescript and
MS; photostats. AJA, AJHS.
Tänzer. Juden in Tirol,
pp. 734-36. See GENERAL
WORKS.

LANDE
LBI has family tree beginning
1780.
Czellitzer, Arthur. "Die Namen

Landé und London," JFF,
no. 46 (1937):862.

LANDER
AJA has genealogical files.
Lander Family. "Genealogy,
1910-1974; and Brief
Biographical Information for
Jacob Joseph Lander and Clara
Shnay Lander." Winnipeg,
Manitoba, Canada, 1975. AJA.
See Yaffa Draznin entry under
BERNSTEIN. Family history.

LANDERBURG
See Daniel Jay Rottenberg entry
under ROTTENBERG.

LANDESBERG
Kempelen. Magyarországi Zsidó,
1:58; 2:30; 3:24. See
GENERAL WORKS.

LANDESBERGER
PD has family records.

LANDMAN
Berkowitz Family. "Letter and
genealogy charts sent to
Rabbi Malcolm H. Stern by his
grandmother, Clara Landman
Berkowitz, Philadelphia, Pa.,
March 19, 1956." AJA.

LANDMANN
LBI has family tree beginning
1748.

LANDSBERG
CAJ has family records.
Kaliphari, Salomon, gen.
Posner: Mein Lebensbild in
Anschluss an 7 Ahnenbilder
der Familie Kaliphari.
Landsberg. Aus dem Hebr.
übes. und fortgesetzt v.
Moritz Landsberg. Enth. die
Nachkommen des sephard.
Arztes Salomon Kaliphari
(d. ca. 1600). 1908. Family
of Posen. LBI.
Landsberg, Solomon. B'nai
Shlomo. Krotoschin, 1870.
77 p. Autobiography and
family history. OCH.

Schulte. Bonner Juden, p. 332.
See GENERAL WORKS.

LANDSHUT
Landshut, Siegfried. Neumark,
Westpreussen und die Familie
Landshut. Kiriat Tivon,
Israel, 1962. 44 p. LBI.

LANG
LBI has family tree beginning
1749.
PD has family records.
Kempelen. Magyarországi Zsidó,
1:55; 2:16, 53, 72. Láng,
Lángh family. See GENERAL
WORKS.

LANGDON
AMH has family records.

LANGE (DE)
Lange, G. de. "De familie de
Lange," Arent Thoe Boecop 3,
no. 4 (1978):1-9.
Descendants of Joseph Levy,
d. 1839. Family from Elburg,
Holland.

LANGENHEIM
CFM has family records.
Langenheim, Kurt. "Die Familie
Langenheim in Ostpreussen,"
Ostdeutsche Familienkunde
(Neustadt/Aisch) 29
(1981):216-17.

LANGENN
Semi-Gotha, 1:140. See GENERAL
WORKS.

LANGH
See Kempelen entry under LANG.

LANGSFELD
Kempelen. Magyarországi Zsidó,
2:131. See GENERAL WORKS.

LANKOROWSKY
Kempelen. Magyarországi Zsidó,
1:38. See GENERAL WORKS.

LANYI
Kempelen. Magyarországi Zsidó,
1:82; 2:131; 3:39. Lányi
family. See GENERAL WORKS.

LAOR
Laor, Eran. "Unbekanntes
Judentum vorfahren,
verwandte, und Geschichte de
Slowakischen Judentums,
1700-1900," Bulletin des Leo
Baecks Instituts, no. 35
(1966):213-77. Includes
account of author's family's
history, training, births,
marriages, deaths.

LAPOWSKI
AJA has family tree.
"Genealogical Information on
the Lapowski-Dillon Family."
AJA.

LARA
See DE LARA.
AMH has family records.
CFM has family records.

LASAR
PD has family records.

LASCH
Krauss, S. "Die böhmische
Familie Lichtenstadt-Lasch,"
ZGJT 2 (1931):147-49.

LASKI
Reychman. Szkice
genealogiczne, pp. 117-18.
See GENERAL WORKS.

LASSAL, LASSALLE
Brann, Marcus. "Die Abstammung
Ferdinand Lassalle," Archiv
für Jüdische
Familienforschung 2
(1916):27-29.
————. "Die Abstammung
Ferdinand Lassalle," MGWJ 62
(1918):270-74. Corrected and
enlarged reprint of above
article.
Heppner, A. "Stammtafel
Ferdinand Lassalle,"
Bresslauer Jud.
Gemeindeblätter 2:37-39.
Ferdinand Lassalle, the
German Socialist leader,
b. Breslau, 1825; d. 1864.
His real name was Lassal.
Mayer, Gustav. "Die vorfahren

Ferdinand Lassalle," Die
Stimme (Vienna) 1, no. 23
(7.6. 1928).

LASZLO
Kempelen. Magyarországi Zsidó,
1:85; 2:147; 3:26. László
family. See GENERAL WORKS.

LATES, LATTES
Roth, Cecil. "An Italian
Family in Oxford in the
Eighteenth Century," in
English Miscellany--A
Symposium of History,
Literature, and the Arts
(Roma, 1958), vol. 9,
pp. 163-72.

LATINOVITS
Kempelen. Magyarországi Zsidó,
1:101. See GENERAL WORKS.

LATZ
Latz, Simon and Family.
[Biographical and
Genealogical Data.] Includes
family tree beginning 1851.
Pioneer California Jewish
family. AJA, WJHC.
Schulte. Bonner Juden, p. 333.
See GENERAL WORKS.

LATZER
Kempelen. Magyarországi Zsidó,
2:126. See GENERAL WORKS.

LATZKO
PD has family records.
Kempelen. Magyarországi Zsidó,
1:137. Latzkó family. See
GENERAL WORKS.
See Ernst Wolf entry under
GOMPERZ. Six family trees.
Includes Latzko family.

LAUB
Kempelen. Magyarországi Zsidó,
2:147; 3:26. See GENERAL
WORKS.

LAUCHHEIMER
Tänzer. Juden in Jebenhausen,
pp. 336-38. See GENERAL
WORKS.

LAURENCE
AMH has family records.

LAUTERBACH
Lauterbach Family, Cincinnati.
Papers and Records. Include
genealogical material. AJA.
Jacob Zallel Lauterbach
(1873-1942; Hebrew Union
College professor of Talmud,
1911-1934). Papers. Contain
some genealogical material.
AJA.
Lauterbach, Leo. Chronicle of
the Lauterbach Family;
Descendants of Jacob Bezalel
Lauterbach of Drohobycz,
1800-1960. New Edition.
Jerusalem: Lauterbach Family
Fund, 1961. 184 p. CtY,
CLU, MH, NN, OCH. Supplement
No. 1 (Jerusalem: Typ.
Hadassah Apprentice School,
1962). 14 p.
──────. The Lives of My
Parents: Pinkas and Anna
Lauterbach: Two Memoirs to
Commemorate the 100th
Anniversaries of Their
Births. Jerusalem: By the
Author, 1956. 78 p.
Genealogical tables. Family
of Galicia. Pinkas
Lauterbach, 1855-1937, and
Anna Lauterbach, 1856-1940.
DLC, NN.

LAUTERSTEIN
Rose. Schöninger Juden. See
GENERAL WORKS.

LAVIN
AMH has family records.

LAWRENCE
AMH has family records.

LAWSON
AMH has family records.

LAYE
AMH has family records.

LAZAR
AMH has family records.
Kempelen. Magyarországi Zsidó,

2:54. Lázár family. See
GENERAL WORKS.

LAZARE
See Nelly Wilson entry under
BERNARD.

LAZARSFELD
Kempelen. Magyarországi Zsidó,
2:105. See GENERAL WORKS.

LAZARUS
AMH has family records.
Calder Family; Wilmington, N.C.
"Records And Recollections of
the Calder Family, Including
Information About the Lazarus
and Mordecai Families of
Charleston, S.C., 1757-1959."
Typescript. Xerox copy.
AJA.
"Genealogy of the Lazarus
Family of North and South
Carolina." AJA.
Keneseth Israel. See GENERAL
WORKS.
Birmingham. The Grandees. See
GENERAL WORKS.
Brilling, Bernhard. "Lazarus
(Breslau) Familie," Beiträge
zur Geschichte d. Breslauer
Juden 1 (1935):6-8.
See Esmond S. De Beer entry
under BARDEN.
Fischer, Josef. Simon Lazarus
og hans efterkommere.
Udgivet påa foranledning af
bogtrykker Paul Hertz.
København: By the Author,
1911.
Harris. Merchant Princes.
Lazarus department store
family of Columbus, Ohio.
Descendants of Simon Lazarus,
who opened a men's clothing
shop in Columbus in 1851.
See GENERAL WORKS.
Joseph, Anthony. "A Jewish
Wedding," Genealogists'
Magazine 13 (1960):200-203.
Marriage of Anglo-Jews, Jonas
Lazarus and Rosceia Nathan,
in 1810, their families and
descendants.
Lazarus, Moritz (1824-1903).
Papers, 1854-1902. Include

family tree of Lazarus
Moritz, German historian and
professor of psychology and
philosophy, b. Filhe, Posen,
1824; d. Meran, Tyrol, 1903.
LBI.
Neumann, Norbert Collection,
York, Pa. "Genealogies of
the Ballin, Lazarus, Schäfer,
and Neumann Families, 11th
Century to Date." AJA.
Schulte. Bonner Juden, p. 334.
See GENERAL WORKS.
Stern. FAJF. Lazarus family
trees beginning in U.S. (I,
II, III, and IV). See
GENERAL WORKS.

LAZARUS-SOLOMONS-YATES
AJA has family trees beginning
1757-1808.

LEAMAN
AMH has family records.

LEAPMAN
AMH has family records.

LEAVITT
See LEVITANSKY.

LEBAIR
See Stern, FAJF entry under
LIEBER.

LEBECK
Frank. Nashville Jewry,
pp. 145-46. Family
originally from near
Frankfurt am Main, arrived in
U.S. in 1840s. See GENERAL
WORKS.

LEBENHART
Lebenhart, Filipp. Die Familie
Lebenhart. Prag, 1922.

LEBENSOHN
See Harry and Nellie Lepsky
entry under CHALEPSKY.

LEBERMAN
Stern. FAJF. Leberman family
tree beginning in Merzbach,
Bavaria. See GENERAL WORKS.

LEBOLD
Lebold, Foreman M., Chicago.
"A Record of the Ancestry and
Collected Relatives of
Foreman M. Lebold," n.d.
Begins 18th century. AJA.

LEBRECHT
AJA has family tree beginning
1700.
LBI has family tree beginning
1700.

LEBUS
AMH has family records.

LEDERER
Kempelen. Magyarországi Zsidó,
2:73; 3:55, 83, 119. See
GENERAL WORKS.

LEDERMANN
LBI has family trees beginning
1700 and 1714.

LEDESMA
Stern. FAJF. Ledesma family
tree beginning in London.
Also originally De Ledesma.
See GENERAL WORKS.

LEDITZKY
Kempelen. Magyarországi Zsidó,
3:116. See GENERAL WORKS.

LEDOFSKY
Kempelen. Magyarországi Zsidó,
3:116. See GENERAL WORKS.

LEDOWSKI
Kempelen. Magyarországi Zsidó,
3:115. See GENERAL WORKS.

LEE
AMH has family records.
CFM has family records.

LEEFSMA
Droege, "Frisian Names". See
GENERAL WORKS.

LEESER
Schulte. Bonner Juden, p. 335.
See GENERAL WORKS.
Stern. FAJF. Leeser family

tree beginning in U.S. See
GENERAL WORKS.

LEESON
Leeson, Daniel Nathan.
"Consists of a photocopy of a
computer printout of the
compilers' (Daniel N. and
Rosanne D. Leeson) ancestors
containing detailed
genealogical charts of the
following families: Singer,
Levy, Landauer, Leeson,
Sendowsky, Gutman, Dreyfuss,
(Dryfuss), Hemmerdinger,
Braun, Lobl, Sandow, and
Stein." Fair Lawn, N.J.
Feb. 21, 1976. 1000 p. AJA.

LEFFMANN
Gronemann. Genealogische
Hannovers, pp. 34-50.
"Stammtafel des Hauses
Leffmann Behrens Cohen,
Hannover." Includes
genealogical table. See
GENERAL WORKS.
Saphra, B. "Leffmann," Ost und
West 11 (1911):1077ff.; 12
(1912):561-66.

LEGUM
Legum Family Tree. Compiled by
Irwin M. Berent. Family
originally from Ligum
(Lygumai), Kovna Gubernia,
Lithuania. Settled mainly
in Baltimore, Md., and
Norfolk and Berkley,
Virginia. Includes two
different Legum families.
The immigrant ancestor of one
of the families was
originally Simon Pose (?)
(Post? or Posner?) who
changed name to Legum. The
other immigrant ancestors
also changed their name to
Legum from a name similar to
Pose. Simon was apparently
not related to the other
Legum family, but married one
of their sisters-in-law in
Europe. Covers mid-19th
century onwards. JGCT.
"Legum Family Circle, Organized

1951, Dedicated in Memory of
Abraham, Aaron and Isaac
Legum." Lists members' names
and addresses. Members are
descendants of these three
brothers. JGCT.

LEHFELD
AMH has family records.

LEHMAN
AMH has family records.
Birmingham. Our Crowd. See
GENERAL WORKS.
"Family Tree of Herbert
Lehman." AJA.
Wechsberg, Joseph. The
Merchant Bankers. Boston:
Little, Brown, 1966. 365 p.
"Lehman Brothers: The
Money-Magicians,"
pp. 279-334.

LEHMANN
AJA has genealogical files of
Lehmann-Bauer family.
CFM has family records.
Friess, Herbert. "Zur
Genealogie der Familie des
gelehrten Johann Gottlob
Lehmann (1719-1761),"
Mitteldeutsche Familienkunde
(Neustadt/Aisch) 20, no. 3
(1979):141-42.
Ginsburger, Moise. "Les
familles Lehmann et Cerf
Berr," Revue des Études
Juives 59 (1910):106-30.
Family of Alsace-Lorraine.
Kahn, Lazard (1850-1928).
Papers, 1852-1961. Include
genealogical information on
Jacob Lehmann-Lazard Kahn
family. Cincinnati, and
Hamilton, Ohio; Donaldson,
and New Orleans, Louisiana;
and Selma, Alabama. AJA.
Lehmann, Ascher Lämle
Weldtsberg, known as. (also
called Ascher Lemuel
Lehmann). Urgrossvaters
Tagebuch. Verden A.d. Aller
1769 bis 1858. Mit dem
Stammbaum der Familie
Lehmann. Hrsg. von Max
Lehmann. Gerwisch b.

Magdeburg, 1936. 59 p.
University of Utah Library,
Salt Lake City, Utah.
————. Tagebuch mit einem
Stammbaum der Familie Lehmann
und einem Vorwort von Max
Lehmann. Gerwisch b.
Magdeburg, 1936. 72 p.
Rabbi Ascher Lehmann,
b. Reckendorf, 1769;
d. Verden, 1858. LBI.
Lehmann, Emil. Gesamm.
Schriften. Hrsg. von seinen
Kindern... 2. Aufl.
Dresden: C. Weiske, 1909.
318 p. Descendants of Elija
Halevy of Essen, 17th
century. Page 134 contains
genealogical information.
DLC, OCH, PPDrop.
————. Der polnische Resident
Berend Lehmann der Stammvater
der israelistischen
Religionsgemeinde zu Dresden.
Dresden: E. Pierson's
Buchhandlung, 1885. 74 p.
Includes genealogical table.
Behrend Lehmann, 1661-1730.
LBI, OCH, PP, PPDrop.
Lehmann, Julian. "Die
Stammtafel einer jüdische
Familie in Deutschland.
Ascher b. Aron Lämle
(Lehmann) und seine
Nachkommen," JFF, no. 45
(1937):829-33.
Lehmann, Richard. Die Familie
Lehmann aus Lubbenau.
Berlin, 1919. 41 p.
1 genealogical table.
Saville, Pierre. Le juif de
cour: histoire du resident
royal Behrend Lehmann.
Paris: Société Encyclopédique
Française, 1970. 277 p.
Includes genealogical table.
Behrend Lehmann, 1661-1730.
CSt, CtY, DLC, MB, NIC, NjP,
NN, WU.
Schnee. Hoffinanz und Staat,
2:169-222. "Hoffaktoren der
Familie Lehmann." Includes
genealogical information,
17th to 19th century. Family
of Poland, Halberstadt, and
Dresden. See GENERAL WORKS.

See Stammbaum Levinstein entry
under AVELLIS. Includes
Lehmann family.
"Wiener Judentaufe Lehmann,"
Der Deutsche Roland 25,
no. 9/10 (1937):120.

LEHNE
Kempelen. Magyarországi Zsidó,
1:102. See GENERAL WORKS.

LEHOCZKY
Kempelen. Magyarországi Zsidó,
3:98. See GENERAL WORKS.

LEHR
LBI has family tree beginning
1774.

LEHRFELD
CAJ has family records from
Germany.

LEHRMANN
Lehrmann, Cuno Ch. "Als der
Grossvater die Grossmutter
nahm (Aus Lehrmanns)
Familienchronik 'Stirb und
Werde', hrsg. von Graziella
Lehrmann," Neue Deutsche
Hefte 161 (1979):89-102.
Author, 1905-1977, was a
rabbi, and professor of
Romance languages, Würzburg.
Zapf. Tübinger Juden, pp.
143-46. See GENERAL WORKS.

LEIB
Eizner, Avraham Abba. Toledot
Hagaon Rav David Lida.
Breslau, 1938. 88 p.
Descendants of David Ben
Aryeh Leib of Lida
(ca. 1650-1696), a famous
rabbi. He was the nephew of
Zvi Naphtali Rivkes. JNUL.

LEIBOWITZ
CAJ (Call No. 5044) has the
following large family trees:
"Family of Philip 'Phievel'
Dan," "Family of Pere Libba
'Lizza' Solomon Dan," and
"History of the Den and
Leibowitz Families." Also
included are a 2-page copy of

1900 census, notes on Philip
Dan and family in Memphis,
Tenn., and pictures of Philip
Dan and brother Solomon Den.
Pere Dan (1862-1944) was the
wife of Philip Dan
(1852-1926). Philip Dan, and
his brother Solomon Den
(1858-1940), both came to
America and were the two sons
of David King Den and Kala
Bossel Den all of whom lived
in Taverick, Lithuania.

LEIDENSDORFER
Jäger-Sunstenau, Haans. "Die
Leidensdorfer. Eine Wiener
Honoratiorenfamilie des 18.
und 19. Jahrhunderts,"
Jahrbuch des Vereine für
Geschichte der Stadt Wien
(Austria) 34 (1978):192-203.
Includes genealogical
information.

LEIDESDORF, LEIDESDORFF
LBI has family tree beginning
1749.
Leidesdorff Family, California.
"Genealogical Information,
1755-1853." Typescript. In
German and English. AJA.
PD has family tree.

LEIFMANN
Schulte. Bonner Juden, p. 346.
See GENERAL WORKS.

LEINDORFER
Kempelen. Magyarországi Zsidó,
1:82; 2:74. Leindörfer
family. See GENERAL WORKS.

LEIPHEIMER
Schwaiger, Karl. Geschichte
der Altertumer Familie
Leipheimer. Hrsg. von Carl
Schwenk. Ulm, 1937. 67 p.
Includes two genealogical
tables.

LEIPNIK
AMH has family records.

LEIPZIGER
Kempelen. Magyarországi

Zsidó, 3:78. See GENERAL
WORKS.

LEITERSDORF
Kempelen. Magyarországi Zsidó,
1:12; 3:114. See GENERAL
WORKS.

LEITERSDORFER
Kempelen. Magyarországi Zsidó,
2:75. See GENERAL WORKS.

LEITNER
AMH has family records.
CFM has family records.
Kempelen. Magyarországi Zsidó,
2:35, 127. See GENERAL
WORKS.

LEITNER-HARANGI
Kempelen. Magyarországi Zsidó,
3:121. See GENERAL WORKS.

LEJA
Rothschild. Svenska Israel.
See GENERAL WORKS.

LEMANN
Lemann, Bernard. The Lemann
Family of Louisiana: An
Account Compiled from
Diaries, Correspondence, and
Personal Reminiscences.
Donaldsonville, La?, 1965.
180 p. Includes "The Lemann
Family Tree, edited by Arthur
A. Lehmann, III," p. 22.
AJA, DLC, LU, NN, OCH.

LEMBERGER
Kempelen. Magyarországi Zsidó,
1:7, 12. See GENERAL WORKS.

LEMEGO
AMH has family records.

LEMMEL
Lemmel, Herbert E. "Zur
geschichte der
erzgebirgisch-vogtländischen
Lemmel im 15.-16
Jahrhundert," Mitteldeutsche
Familienkunde
(Neustadt/Aisch) 21, no. 4
(1980):329-353.

LEMON
AMH has family records.
CFM has family records.

LENEL
LBI has family tree beginning
1500.

LENGYEL
Kempelen. Magyarországi Zsidó,
2:60, 67, 132; 3:99. See
GENERAL WORKS.

LENK
Kempelen. Magyarországi Zsidó,
1:118. See GENERAL WORKS.

LENNHOFF
Schulte. Bonner Juden, p. 336.
See GENERAL WORKS.

LEO
AJA has family tree.
AMH has family records.
CFM has family records.
Kempelen. Magyarországi Zsidó,
1:116. See GENERAL WORKS.
Reychman. Szkice
genealogiczne, pp. 119-20.
See GENERAL WORKS.
Schulte. Bonner Juden, p. 337.
See GENERAL WORKS.
"Stammfolge Leo aus Hamelin,"
Deutsches Geschlechterbuch 89
(1936/37):313-34.
Stern. FAJF. Leo family tree
of descendants of
"Rev. Simon Leo, Hazan,
Denmark Court Synagogue,
London." See GENERAL WORKS.

LEON
See DE LEON.
AMH has family records.
CFM has family records.
Kempelen. Magyarországi Zsidó,
1:95. See GENERAL WORKS.

LEONE
Ravenna, G.F. "Leone Ravenna e
Felice di Leone Ravenna,"
Rassegna Mensile di Israel 36
(1970):407-415.

LEONINO
AMH has family records.

CFM has family records.

LEON PINELO
Lewin, Boleslao. Los León
Pinelo, la ilustre familia
marrana del siglo XVII ligada
a la historia de la
Argentina, Perú, América y
España. Buenos Aires:
Sociedad Hebraica Argentina,
1942. 51 p. DLC, TxU, YIVO.

LEOPOLD
AMH has family records.
Kempelen. Magyarországi Zsidó,
2:15; 3:61. See GENERAL
WORKS.
Semi-Gotha, 1:49ff. See
GENERAL WORKS.

LEPSKY
See Harry and Nellie Lepsky
entry under CHALEPSKY.

LERNER
See Bernát Munkácsi entry under
AUSTERLITZ.

LESINSKY
Fierman, Floyd S. "Jewish
Pioneering in the Southwest:
A Record of the
Freudenthal-Lesinsky-Solomon
Families," Arizona and the
West 2 (Spring 1960):54-72.
————. Some Early Jewish
Settlers on the Southwestern
Frontier. El Paso, Tex.:
Texas Western Press, 1960.
58 p.

LESLIE
AMH has family records.

LESSER
AMH has family records.
Poizer, Anne. "Die Geschichte
einer Familie. Aus dem Leben
einer deutsche Jüdin," Aufbau
(New York), Apr. 29, 1960.
Hedwig Lesser Friedheim.
Reychman. Szkice
genealogiczne, pp. 121-25.
See GENERAL WORKS.

LESSING
CFM has family records.
Lessing, Theodor. Einmal und
nie Wieder. Gütersloh:
Bertelsmann Sachbuchverlag,
1969. 447 p. Reprint of
1935 Prague edition.
"Ahnen," pp. 28-40; "Mein
Vater," pp. 41-72; "Meine
Mutter," pp. 73-78. This
famous German philosopher
(1872-1933) was born in
Hannover and assassinated by
the Nazis in Marienbad. CtY,
CU, DLC, IEN, MH, NcU, NjP,
NN.

LESSNER
Kempelen. Magyarországi Zsidó,
2:128. See GENERAL WORKS.

LESTSCHINSKY
CAJ has family records,
1832-1872.

LESTYAN
Kempelen. Magyarországi Zsidó,
3:35. Lestyán family. See
GENERAL WORKS.

LETAI, LETAY
Kempelen. Magyarországi Zsidó,
1:10; 2:124. Létai, Létay
family. See GENERAL WORKS.

LETERMAN
Leterman Family Tree.
Descendants of b. Simon
Leterman, b. Württemberg,
Germany, 1828;
d. Charlottesville, Va.,
1904. JGCT.

LETOWSKI
Kempelen. Magyarországi Zsidó,
3:115. See GENERAL WORKS.

LEUCCI
CFM has family records.

LEVASON
AMH has family records.

LEVEAUX
CFM has family records.

LEVELEKI
Kempelen. Magyarországi Zsidó,
3:111. See GENERAL WORKS.

LEVENBERG
AMH has family records.

LEVENE
AMH has family records.

LEVENSON
AMH has family records.
Levenson, Sam. In One Era and
Out the Other. New York:
Simon and Schuster, 1973.
190 p. Memories of the late
comedian's immigrant family's
life in New York City.

LEVENSTEIN
Rubinstein, Anton.
Autobiography of Anton
Rubinstein, 1829-1889.
Translated from the Russian
by Alice Delano. Boston:
Little, Brown & Co., 1892.
171 p. Genealogical
information concerning
Levenstein and Rubinstein
families, pp. 1-3. The
famous Russian pianist and
composer was born in
Vykhvatinetz, a village on
the Dniester River, Podolia
Province, the son of Gregori
Romanovich (d. 1846) and
Kaleria Levenstein Rubinstein
and the grandson of Roman
Rubinstein, from Berdichev.
The entire family was
baptized a few years after
Anton was born. DLC, ICJ,
MB, MH, NcU, NN, OCl, TxU.

LEVER
AMH has family records.
CFM has family records.

LEVERER
AMH has family records.

LEVERSON
AMH has family records.
CFM has family records.

LEVERTIN
LBIS has family tree and notes
of family of Sweden.
Rothschild. Svenska Israel.
See GENERAL WORKS.

LEVESON
CFM has family records.

LEVETUS
AMH has family records.

LEVI
See HAMBRO.
AMH has family records.
CAJ, Call No. 3742, has a
two-page letter in German
concerning Levi family of
Kochendorf during 18th and
19th centuries.
CFM has family records.
LBI has family trees beginning
1300, 1498, 1627, 1754, and
1792.
Ballin. Juden in Seesen,
pp. 216-18. See GENERAL
WORKS.
Colbi, Paolo. "Una pagina di
storia ebraica triestina: Di
un'antica famiglia ebraica di
Trieste," Rassegna Mensile di
Israel (Roma) 17
(1951):122-29. 17th to early
20th century.
Dann, Wilhelm. Stammtafel und
Register der Nachkommenschaft
des Samuel Alexander Levi
(Dann) aus Frankfurt-am-Main.
Frankfurt am Main: Drukerei
C. Kruthoffer, 1870. 38 p.
Includes 7 genealogical
tables. CAJ, OCH.
Frister, Roman. Hahagada
Levait Levi. English title:
The House of Levi. Tel Aviv:
Michaelmark Books, 1980.
246 p. About Asher Levy of
Germany, 19th century, and
his descendants. JNUL.
Hyamson, Albert M. "An
Anglo-Jewish Family,"
Transactions of the Jewish
Historical Society of England
17 (1951/52):1-10. Includes
genealogical table,
descendants of Moses Simon

Levi of Cassel (d. before
Feb. 28, 1678). Migrated to
Holland, then to England.
Jacobovits, Moses. Vier
Generationen der
Rabbiner-Familie
Levi-Schopflich. Strasbourg:
La Tribune Juive, 1938.
34 p. Descendants of Rabbi
Hirsch Lévy Schopflich,
1700s, his son Rabbi Anschel
Lévy I, d. 1773, and grandson
Rabbi Anschel II, 1773-1846.
JNUL.
Levi, Giuseppe Raffaele.
Autobiografia di un padre di
famiglia. Firenze: Monnier,
1868. 113 p. MH, NcD, OCH,
YIVO.
See Siegfried Porta entry under
FALKENSTEIN.
Risch, Izhak. Megilat
Mishpaḥtenu. Added title
page: Records Concering the
Ancestry of the Levi,
Berlinger, and Ellinger
Families of the Zvi Branch.
1974. 88 p. CLU, DLC, MB,
NN, WU.
See Stern, FAJF entry under
LIEBER.
Streng Family. "Genealogical
Information Concerning the
Streng, Levi, and Starr
Family, Louisville, Ky. and
Pittsburgh, Pa., 1817-1957."
AJA.
Tänzer. Juden in Jebenhausen,
pp. 340-41.
See Meir Yizraeli entry under
BIDERMAN.

LEVI ALVARES
CAJ (Call No. 5267) has
Carrence family tree for
family of Paris. Includes
Levi Alvares family.

LEVIANSKY
AMH has family records.

LEVIEN
AMH has family records.
CFM has family records.

LEVIN
See ASSER-LEVIN.
See LEVITANSKY.
AMH has family records.
CFM has family records.
Fischer, Josef. Slaegten
Levin-Fridericia. Påa
Foranledning af Martin J.
Levin. Trykt som Mskpt.
54 p. Descendants of Joseph
L. Levin, ca. 1734-1791.
Semi-Gotha, 1:58ff. See
GENERAL WORKS.
Stern. FAJF. Levin family
trees beginning in:
(I) Germany; (II) London; and
(III) U.S. See GENERAL
WORKS.
Winstock, Mordecai. "Genealogy
of Winstock, Levine, and
Levin Families." N.d. AJA.

LEVINE
See LEVITANSKY.
AMH has family records.
Fern, Joan. "The Life Story of
Hyman and Emma Levine." Los
Angeles, 1954. Typescript.
74 p. "The Levines
immigrated to the United
States from Polish-Russia in
1883. After 24 years in New
York City they moved to Los
Angeles in 1907 at which time
Mr. Levine established a
million dollar cooperage."
CLU.
Levine, Julius. Family History
of Jacob and Jennie B.
Levine. Memphis, Tenn.,
1982. 1 vol. Story of
family of Boston. AJHS.
Rosenstein. Unbroken Chain,
pp. 237ff. The descendants
of R. Solomon Zalman
Katzenellenbogen. See
GENERAL WORKS.
Stern. FAJF. Levine family
tree beginning in U.S. See
GENERAL WORKS.
Winstock, Mordecai. "Genealogy
of Winstock, Levine, and
Levin families." N.d. AJA.

LEVINGER
CAJ has family tree for family
of Hungary.

LEVINSON
Draznin, Nathan, ed. and
annotater. Isaac Levinson's
Genealogy. Baltimore, Md.:
Published by the son of the
Author, Saul Levinson, 1948.
29 p. AJA, NjR.

LEVINSTEIN
LBI has family tree beginning
1772.

LEVIS
CFM has family records.

LEVISOHN
Fischer, Josef. "Slaegten
Levisohn fra Hamburg
Mosaisk-Trossamfund
(Maskinskreuet)."
København, 1957. Family
which came to Copenhagen from
Hamburg.

LEVISON
AMH has family records.
See Harry and Nellie Lepsky
entry under CHALEPSKY.
Levinson, Wilhelm (1876-1947).
Papers, 1898-1968. Includes
genealogical material on
Levison and Freundlich
families of England and
Germany. LBI.
Levison, Jacob Bertha.
Memories for My Family. San
Francisco: John Henry Nash,
1933. 282 p. CSt, CU, MH.
Levison, Wilhelm. Die
Siegburger Familie Levison
und verwandte Familien.
Bonn: Röhrscheid, 1952.
187 p. Includes genealogical
tables. DLC, CSt, LU, NN,
NNJ.
Narell. Our City. Includes
genealogical table of pioneer
Jewish family, descendants of
Bertha Levison, b. Virginia
City, Nev., 1862; d. 1947.
See GENERAL WORKS.

LEVISSEUR
AMH has family records.

LEVITA
CAJ has family tree from
Germany.
CFM has family records.

LEVITANSKY
Levitansky Family, Los Angeles,
California. "Genealogy of
Schlaime Itzhock Levitansky,
born 1794, [Suwalki,] Poland,
Tracing the Descendants of
His Eight Children and Their
Families' Immigration to the
United States, All by 1920,
Including Photographs and
Newspaper Articles." 1980.
Typescript. "The family
claims heritage from 15th
century Spain as well as a
clan name 'Baranis.' Among
the descendants are Boris
Leavitt, founder of Lana
Lobell women's mail-order
house, Dr. Samuel A. Levine,
a prominent cardiologist,
Dr. Abraham L. Levin, medical
inventor, and Dr. Max Levine,
bacteriologist...." AJA,
AJHS.

LEVITUS
AMH has family records.

LEVOR
Ballin. Juden in Seesen,
p. 219. See GENERAL WORKS.

LEVY
See BEREND LEVY.
See CALMAN-LEVY.
See CASTLE-LEVY.
See HAMBRO.
"Family Tree of Ezekiel-Levy
Families, Richmond,
Virginia." AJA.
AMH has family records.
CFM has family records.
JE, 8:59. Genealogical table
of family descended from
Benjamin Levy of Philadelphia
through early 20th century.
See GENERAL WORKS.
Cable, Mary and Annabelle

Prager. The Levys of
Monticello: The Jewish Family
that Rescued Jefferson's
Home," American Heritage 29
(Feb./Mar. 1978):30-39. The
role played by Uriah Phillips
Levy and Jefferson Monroe
Levy in preserving the
American national shrine.
Birmingham. The Grandees. See
GENERAL WORKS.
"The Coats of Arms Attributed
to Moses Levy," St. Charles 1
(Jan. 1935):118-22.
Cohn, John Magnus. The Cohn
Family Tree. Swan Hill,
Australia: n.p., Mar. 1963.
32 p. Genealogical table
from 1751-1962. Includes
Levy family of Australia.
More than 400 relatives
listed. The Cohn family is
related to the Ballin family
of Denmark. Four Cohn
brothers migrated to
Australia from Denmark in
mid-19th century. CAJ, Call
No. 1676.
Conrich, J. Lloyd, comp. "The
Levy (Levi or Rechthandt)
Family." 1965. Family of
California. WJHC.
"Diary and Genealogical Notes
Kept by Aaron Levy
(1771-1852)," Publications of
the American Jewish
Historical Society 27
(1920):335-45.
Dobrin, Paul. Stammbaum der
Familie Levy aus Zachan.
Breslau, 1920. 7 p.
Descendants of Moses Levy,
1763-1843. LBI.
Frank. Nashville Jewry,
p. 132. Family originally
from Nassau Province,
Germany. See GENERAL WORKS.
Haan, H. de. Salomon Levy.
Ljonwert: Ufhete Fryske
Akademy, 1961. 315 p.
(Fryske Akademy, Waldrige
Nr. 10). Salomon Levy,
ca. 1749-1796, of Friesland.
Includes genealogical
information.
"Items Relating to the Moses

and Levy Families of New
York," Publications of the
American Jewish Historical
Society 27 (1920):331.
See Moses Jacobovits entry
under LEVI.
Joseph, Anthony P. "Jewry of
South-west England and Some
of its Australian
Connections," Jewish
Historical Society of England
Transactions 24 (1975):24-37.
Includes genealogical tables
of descendants of Zender
Moses Eliezer Hart and
Eleazar Levy, 18th century
forward.
The Anglo-Jewish Archives of
the Mocatta Library in London
holds "The Family Tree of
Anthony Joseph's Family,"
compiled by Dr. Anthony P.
Joseph. Supplements have
appeared annually since the
original edition was
completed in 1958. Covers
late 18th century to date for
this Anglo-Jewish family.
Also covers the descendants
of Barnet Levy (d. 1791),
Solomon Solomon (1764-1819),
and Betsy Levy (1767-1832).
Kopp. Jüdischen Alsenz,
pp. 136-37. Genealogical
information on Rothenberg,
Levy, and Marum families of
Alsenz. See GENERAL WORKS.
Lange, G. de. "De familie de
Lange," Arent Thoe Boecop 3,
no. 4 (1978):1-9. Dutch
descendants of Joseph Levy,
d. 1839. Family from Elburg.
See Daniel Nathan Leeson entry
under LEESON.
Levy, Aaron. "Records of
Births, Deaths, and
Marriages, 1746-1856."
Written into the Bible of
Aaron Levy, Sr. AJA.
"Descendants of Abraham Levy
and Rachel Cornelia Bernard
of Richmond, Va." AJA.
Levy, Abraham R. "Collection;
Records of Births and
Marriages, 1878-1908;
Germany; Athens, Ga.; Austin,

Texas; Chicago; Erie, Pa."
AJA.

Levy, Alphonse. Erlebt.
Erzählungen aus dem jüdischen
Familienleben. Berlin:
Hesperus-Verlag, 1914. 71 p.
Mainly on the forbears of the
author (1838-1917). Family
of Dresden. NN, OCH.

Levy, Harriet Lane. 920
O'Farrell Street. Garden
City, N.Y.: Doubleday and
Co., Inc., 1947. 273 p. The
story of an Orthodox Levy
family in late 19th-century
San Francisco. The author
was the daughter of Benish H.
Levy, who was born in Fordon,
West Prussia.

Morris Levy Family Papers.
Contain family tree. Family
of California. WJHC.

Levy, Nathan. The "Green
Book": Records of the Levy,
Goodwin, Stevenson, and Many
Other Families. Montclair,
N.J., 1931. 41 p. NN.

Levy, Salman Leib. Zichronot
Mibert Aba: Mishpachat Levy
Beyerusalaim. Added title
page: Memories: The Levy
Family in Jerusalem. N.p.,
1960. 43 p. in English and
35 p. in Hebrew. JNUL.

McDavid, Raven I. and Samuel R.
Levin. "The Levys of New
Orleans: An Old Myth and a
New Problem," Names 12 (June
1964):82-88. Attempt to
verify and explain the
assertion by reputable
scholars that "Levy" is the
second most common surname in
New Orleans.

Moss, Sanford A. "Levy-Myers
Families, 1721-1939," Lynn,
Mass. AJA.

"Pearce-Levy Bible Records,"
Maryland Historical Magazine
21 (1926):201-206. Article
reprinted in Maryland
Genealogies: A Compilation of
Articles from the "Maryland
Historical Magazine"
(Baltimore: Genealogical
Publishing Co., 1980),

2:279-84. Contains extracts
from two Bibles which
belonged originally to Judge
Moses Levy (1756-1826) of
Philadelphia. Includes "Levy
Family Hebrew Bible Records"
begun by his grandfather,
Moses Levy (d. 1728) of New
York, and continued by his
father, Samson Levy (b. New
York, 1722; d. Pennsylvania,
1781). Judge Levy married
Mary Pearce, a Christian, of
Poplar Neck, Cecil County,
Md. in 1791. All of their
children were baptized.

Phillips, N. Taylor. "The Levy
and Seixas Families of
Newport and New York,"
Publications of the American
Jewish Historical Society 4
(1896):189.

Richter, John H. The Ancestors
of Emil Louis Meyer and Helen
Levy Meyer of Hannover,
Germany. Ann Arbor, Mich.,
1963. 11 p. LBI.

"Samuel Levy, ein Stiefsohn der
Glückel von Hameln," MGWJ,
1909, p. 480.

Schloss-Levy Family.
"Genealogy, 1801-1964." AJA.

Schnee. Hoffinanz und Staat,
1:230-44. "Die Hoffaktoren
Familie Levy-Delmar."
Includes genealogical
information on family of
Brandenburg-Prussia, 17th to
19th century. See GENERAL
WORKS.

Schulte. Bonner Juden,
pp. 338-44. See GENERAL
WORKS.

Semi-Gotha, 2:93ff. See
GENERAL WORKS.

See Stern, FAJF entry under
FLORANCE.

See Stern, FAJF entry under
HAMBURGER.

See Stern, FAJF (VI) entry
under PHILLIPS.

See Stern, FAJF (I) entry under
PIKE.

Stern. FAJF. Levy family
trees beginning in:
(I) Germany; (II, IX, X,

XIII, XX) U.S.;
(III) Fernholz, Hanover; (IV
and VII) Amsterdam;
(V) Woolwich, England;
(VI) London; (VIII) Holland;
(XI) Zobnau, Poland;
(XII) Montreal, Canada;
(XIV) Surinam; (XV) England;
(XVI) Bodek in Recife;
(XVII) Oxford, England;
(XVIII) London (some members
of later generation changed
names to Jacobs and Israel);
and (XIX) Mogador, Morocco.
See GENERAL WORKS.
Stern, Malcolm H. "Asser
Levy--A New Look at Our
Jewish Founding Father,"
American Jewish Archives 26
(1974):66-77. List of
"Contemporary Descendants of
America's First Jewish
Family," p. 77.
————. "Asher Levy, New
Jersey Revolutionary and His
Colonial Namesakes," New
Jersey History 98
(Fall/Winter 1980):233-36.
Genealogy of Asher Levy of
Philadelphia (b. ca. 1756,
d. 1785), who served in the
First Regiment of New Jersey
during the Revolutionary War;
what is known about him and
other namesakes in colonial
America. Descendants of
Asher Levy (b. in Westphalian
town of Schwelm, ca. 1630;
d. in U.S., 1681/82), who
migrated to Brazil via
Amsterdam and came to U.S. in
1654. Asher Levy of New
Jersey was a
great-great-great-nephew of
the original Asher Levy.
Styker-Rodda, Harriet. "Asser
Levy," New York Genealogical
and Biographical Record 102
(July 1971):129-35;
(Oct. 1971):240-47. Brief
biography of Asser Levy of
New York and detailed
inventory of his estate.
Wolf, Edwin III. "Genealogy of
the Levy and Pollock
Families." Philadelphia.
AJA.

LEVYS
CFM has family records.

LEVYSOHN
AMH has family records.

LEVY-STRASS
Nirtl, J. "Familie
Levy-Strass," ZGJT 4
(1934):48.

LEWALD
LBI has family tree beginning
1700.

LEWANDOWSKI
LBI has family tree beginning
1818.

LEWENBERG
Reychman. Szkice
genealogiczne, pp. 127-29.
See GENERAL WORKS.

LEWENZ
LBI has family tree beginning
1852.

LEWI
AJA has family tree beginning
1783 in Germany.

LEWIN
AMH has family records.
Lewin, Laurance A. "Report of
An Interview ... Los Angeles,
November 10, 1966, by Norton
B. Stern." [Santa Monica,
Calif.] 1966. Typescript.
3 p. "Laurance's father,
Louis Lewin, came to Los
Angeles in 1868 from East
Prussia. This report
contains information on his
mother, Jeanette Lazard
Lewin, his grandparents,
Solomon and Caroline Newmark
Lazard, and other members of
his family." AJA, WJHC.

LEWIN-EPSTEIN
Rosenstein. Unbroken Chain,
pp. 641ff. See GENERAL
WORKS.

LEWINGER
Kempelen. Magyarországi Zsidó,
    2:70. See GENERAL WORKS.

LEWINSKI
Kempelen. Magyarországi Zsidó,
    2:70. See GENERAL WORKS.

LEWIS
AJA has
    Lewis-Goldstone-Hendricks
    genealogical files.
AMH has family records.
CFM has family records.
See Yaffa Draznin entry under
    BERNSTEIN.
AJA has David Lewis family tree
    beginning 18th century.
Stern. FAJF. Lewis family
    trees beginning in:
    (I) Gwinfe, Carmarthe, Wales;
    and (II) Würzburg. See
    GENERAL WORKS.

LEWIS-BARNARD
AMH has family records.

LEWISOHN
AJA has family tree of
    Lewisohn-Eloesser family.
Birmingham. Our Crowd. See
    GENERAL WORKS.
[Lewisohn, Sam.] "Family
    History." 6 p. "Joachim
    (Menachem) Levy of Rendsburg
    was the first ancestor of the
    Lewisohn family residing in
    Hamburg. He was born about
    the year 1700 in
    Rendsburg.... The genealogy
    continues to the children of
    Samuel Lewisohn (1809-1872)."
    JNUL.

LEWISON
AMH has family records.

LEWY
AJA has family tree.
Lewy Family. "Family Tree."
    AJA.
Kempelen. Magyarországi Zsidó,
    3:61. See GENERAL WORKS.

LEYCESTER
AMH has family records.

LEYSER
CAJ has family tree from
    Germany and Holland,
    1720-1959.

LI
Leslie, "Chinese-Hebrew
    Kaifeng." See GENERAL WORKS.

LIBAN
CAJ has family records.

LICHENHEIM
LBI has family tree beginning
    1838.

LICHTBLAU
Kempelen. Magyarországi Zsidó,
    3:111. See GENERAL WORKS.

LICHTEN
Lichten, Hershel
    (ca. 1872-1937). Papers,
    1932. 1 folder. "Photocopy
    of an autobiography, 1932, of
    Hershel Lichten, translated
    by his son, James Lichten.
    Lichten tells about his
    family and life in Russia,
    c. 1872-1913, in great
    detail, until he immigrated
    to Philadelphia where he had
    friends." PJAC.

LICHTENBERG
Kempelen. Magyarországi Zsidó,
    1:96; 2:69. See GENERAL
    WORKS.

LICHTENBERGER
Kempelen. Magyarországi Zsidó,
    2:70. See GENERAL WORKS.

LICHTENFELD
AMH has family records.

LICHTENSTADT
AMH has family records.
CFM has family records.
Krauss, Samuel. "Die böhmische
    Familie Lichtenstadt-Lasch,"
    ZGJT 2 (1931/32):147-49.

LICHTENSTEIN
Kempelen. Magyarországi Zsidó,
    2:13. See GENERAL WORKS.

Lichtenstein, Gaston. The
Virginia Lichtensteins;
Amplified by Historical and
Biographical Data. Richmond,
Va.: H.T. Ezekiel, Printer,
1912. 16 p. AJA, AJHS, DLC,
MWalB, NcD, NN, OCH; Virginia
State Library, Richmond.
Stern. FAJF. Lichtenstein
family tree beginning in
Fordon, Prussian Poland. See
GENERAL WORKS.

LICHTMANN
Kempelen. Magyarországi Zsidó,
3:113. See GENERAL WORKS.

LIEBENBERG
Kempelen. Magyarországi Zsidó,
3:114. See GENERAL WORKS.

LIEBER
Stern. FAJF. Lieber family
tree of the descendants of
George Levi (d. 1855).
Levi's children changed name
to Lieber or Lebair. Later
generations took the name
Lebair. See GENERAL WORKS.

LIEBERG
Lieberg, Moritz. "Geschichte
seiner Familie und seiner
Firma 'Messinghof' bei
Kassel. Aufgezeichnet von
seiner Tochter. Mit einem
Dokumentenanhang."
Stuttgart, 1935. 23, 33 p.
LBI.

LIEBERMANN
LBI has family tree beginning
1748.
Bick-Shauli, "Roots and
Branches." Includes
genealogy of Aaron Samuel
Liebermann, 1845-1880,
pioneer Jewish Socialist and
Hebrew writer, born in
Lithuania, and grew up in
Bialystok and Suwalki,
Poland. See GENERAL WORKS.
Chelminsky-Lajmer, "Jewish
Surnames." See GENERAL
WORKS.
See Ludwig Herz entry under

REICHENHEIM.
Hancke, Erich. Max Liebermann:
Sein Leben und seine Werke.
Berlin: Bruno Cassirer, 1923.
"Abstammung," pp. 11-14.
Haller and Liebermann
families of Berlin. Max
Liebermann (1847-1935),
German painter, was the son
of Louis Liebermann and the
grandson of Joseph
Liebermann, who came to
Berlin in 1824 from the state
of Märkisch-Friedland. The
Haller family was Max
Liebermann's mother's family.
CSt, CtY, CU, DLC, MH, NIC.
Kempelen. Magyarországi Zsidó,
1:62; 2:49; 3:24. See
GENERAL WORKS.
Liebermann, Yosef. Sefer
Shalshelet Hayuchasin.
Jerusalem, 1978. 157 p.
Includes genealogical tables.
Contains genealogy of many
great rabbis within the
family and related families.
JNUL.
See Zevi Shimshi entry under
SHIMSHELEWITZ. Includes
Liebermann family.
Zondek, Theodor. "Die
Liebermanns. Eine
altberliner Familie,"
Jüdische Illustrierte 11,
no. 1 (Juni 1962).

LIEBIG
JFF, no. 27. Family history.

LIEBMAN
AMH has family records.

LIEBMANN
PD has family records.
Neustadt, L. Stammtafeln der
von Liebmann-Schwarzschild
(1555-1594) abstammenden
Familien. Frankfurt, 1886.
Schnee. Hoffinanz und
Staat,1:47-77. "Die Familie
Aaron-Schulhoff-Liebmann in
brandburgischpreussischen
Diensten." Includes
genealogical information,
17th to 18th century. See

GENERAL WORKS.
Zapf. Tübinger Juden, pp.
56-57. See GENERAL WORKS.

LIEBNER
Kempelen. Magyarországi Zsidó,
3:108, 111. See GENERAL
WORKS.

LIECHTENSTEIN
Mess, Walter. "Nachkommen des
1606 in Frankfurt a. M.
getauften Juden Johann Daniel
Liechtenstein," Rheinische
Sippen 1, no. 3 (1937):73-74.

LIEPMANN
Rost, Wilhelm. "Die Nachkommen
des Wolff Nathan Liepmann,
ein Beitrag zur
Liman-Forschung," Genealogie
(Neustadt/Aisch) 29, no. 2
(1980):44-51.

LIEPOLD
Kopp. Jüdischen Alsenz,
pp. 132-33. See GENERAL
WORKS.

LIESER
Kempelen. Magyarországi Zsidó,
2:141. See GENERAL WORKS.

LILIEN
CAJ has family records.

LILLIENFELD
CAJ has family tree from
Germany.

LILIENSTEIN
See Nathan M. Reiss entry under
EDELMUTH. Includes
Lilienstein family of
Rossdorf, Ober-Ramstadt, and
Gräfenhausen.

LILIENTHAL
Halle, Gerhard. "Vorfahren O.
Lilienthal's," Deutsche
Luftwacht 3 (1936):217. Otto
Lilienthal, German inventor
and aeronaut. He was born in
Analam, Pomerania. His
Jewish origins have been
disputed by scholars,
however.
Lilienthal, Anna R. and Gustav.
Die Lilienthals. Stuttgart
und Berlin: Cotta, 1930.
127 p. Otto Lilienthal,
1848-1896, and Gustav
Lilienthal, 1849-1933. CU,
DLC, NN, OC1.
Lilienthal, Lillie Bernheimer.
In Memoriam: Jesse Warren
Lilienthal. San Francisco:
John Henry Nash, 1921.
218 p. CLU, CSt, MH, NIC,
OCH.
Lilienthal, Sophie. The
Lilienthal Family Record.
San Francisco: H.S. Crocker,
1930. 139, 4 p. Includes
genealogical tables. This
history starts in Bavaria in
1632 and traces family up
through early 20th century in
California and the East. MH,
NN.
Narell. Our City. Includes
genealogical table of pioneer
San Francisco Jewish family.
See GENERAL WORKS.
O'Neill, Frederic Gordon, comp.
Ernest Reuben Lilienthal and
His Family, Prepared from
Family Histories, Documents,
and Interviews. [Stanford,
Calif.: Stanford University
Press], 1949. 176 p.
Includes genealogical charts
of forebearers and
descendants. CU, CtY, DLC,
NN, NNJ, WJHC.
Weiss, Mordechai Y. Beit
Lilienthal Beyerushalaim.
Jerusalem: Weiss Press, 1947.
61 p. On Lilienthal family
of Jerusalem. JNUL.

LINDAU
LBI has family tree beginning
1685.
Lindau, Paul (1839-1919).
Papers, 1867-1930. Include
family tree of Paul Lindau,
German theatre critic,
playwright, and stage
director. LBI.

LINDAUER
Tänzer. Juden in Jebenhausen,
    pp. 342-45. See GENERAL
    WORKS.

LINDEN
PD has family records.

LINDENBAUM
Kempelen. Magyarországi Zsidó,
    2:89, 134, 135. See GENERAL
    WORKS.

LINDERER
CAJ has family records.

LINDO
AMH has family records.
CFM has family records.
JE, 8:92. "Pedigree of the
    Lindo Family." English
    family, descendants of Isaac
    (d. 1712) and M. Leah
    (d. 1713) Lindo, through
    mid-19th century. See
    GENERAL WORKS.
Barnes, Lady Eleanor C. Alfred
    Yarrow, His Life and Work.
    London: E. Arnold, 1923.
    328 p. Large amount of
    information about Lindo
    family from which Sir Alfred
    Yarrow was descended. CtY,
    DLC, ICJ, IEN, MB, NN, OCl.
    Popular Edition. London,
    1928. 276 p. NcD.
"Lindo Family, 1796-1810."
    AJA.

LINDSAY
AMH has family records.

LINIK
CAJ has family records.

LINK
Kempelen. Magyarországi Zsidó,
    3:124. See GENERAL WORKS.

LINKS
AMH has family records.
Kempelen. Magyarországi Zsidó,
    1:63; 3:25, 129. See GENERAL
    WORKS.

LINN
See Sidney Cramer entry under
    BINDMAN.

LINYT
AMH has family records.

LINZ
CAJ has family records.

LION
AMH has family records.
Lion, Schlomoh. Stammbaum der
    Familie Lion. Ramat Chen,
    Israel: By the Author, 1967.
    Originally from Ettenheim,
    Germany. Covers 1779-1967.
    CAJ, LBI.
Schulte. Bonner Juden, p. 347.
    See GENERAL WORKS.
Zapf. Tübinger Juden, pp.
    146-48. See GENERAL WORKS.

LIPCHOWITZ
CAJ has family history
    beginning 18th century.
Schulte. Bonner Juden, p. 348.
    See GENERAL WORKS.

LIPINSKI
AMH has family records.

LIPKIN
JE, 8:96. "Pedigree of the
    Lipkin Family." Descendants
    of Samuel, rabbi at Plungian,
    Russia, through late 19th
    century. See GENERAL WORKS.

LIPMAN
AMH has family records.
Lipman Family. Papers and
    Documents, 1857-1901.
    Include genealogical chart
    and history of the families
    of Isaac and Rebecca Harris,
    compiled by Rowena Lipman,
    1969. WJHC.
Kempelen. Magyarországi Zsidó,
    3:113. See GENERAL WORKS.

LIPPERT
AMH has family records.

LIPPMANN
See Nathan M. Reiss entry under

EDELMUTH. Includes Lippmann family.

LIPSCHITZ
Kempelen. Magyarországi Zsidó, 1:12. See GENERAL WORKS.

LIPSCHUTZ
Freudenthal, Max. "Die Mutter Moses Mendelssohns, ZGJD 1 (1929):200. Pedigree of the wife of the grandson of Moses Mendelssohn's brother, derived from Saul Wahl.
Rosenstein. Unbroken Chain, pp. 144ff. See GENERAL WORKS.
————, pp. 285ff. Descendants of R. Solomon Zalman Lipschutz. See GENERAL WORKS.
————, pp. 664ff. See GENERAL WORKS.
Singerman, Felix. "Die Lippman-Tauss"-Synagoge und das Rabbinerhaus der "Lipschütz." Berlin: Selbstv., 1920. 50 p. Family of Polish and German rabbis, descendants of Saul Wahl. NN, OCH.
Waldman, Bess. The Book of Tziril: A Family Chronicle. Marblehead, Mass.: Micah Publications, 1981. 250 p. In narrative form, this book covers the life of some of the descendants of Zalman Yitchok and Dvera Esther Gordon from 1840-1890s in Russia and Jersey City, N.J. Includes the Gordon family of Kafkaz (near Tiflis in the Caucasus region); the Rosenblum family of Kovno (Chana Gordon and Reb Yosef Rosenblum); Yosef Yacov and Tziril Miriam Gordon Wilkimirsky (changed to Friedman in U.S.) of Wilki near Kovno; and Abraham (Alte) and Hinda Dvera Friedman Lipschutz of New Jersey. Abraham Lipschutz was the son of Reb Yeheschel and Rivka Lipschutz of

Vienna. The author is the daughter of Abraham and Hinda Lipschutz. AJA, AJHS, DLC.

LIPSITZ
Stocker, Devera Steinberg. "The Lipsitz Families: Early Jewish Settlers in Detroit," Michigan Jewish History 22 (June 1982).

LIPSKY
See Harry and Nellie Lepsky entry under CHALEPSKY.

LIPSON
AJA has genealogical files. AMH has family records.

LIPSTEIN
Born, Max. My Life: Recollections of A Nobel Laureate. New York: Charles Scribner's Sons, 1975. 308 p. Genealogical information about the Jacobi, Lipstein, and Kauffmann relatives of the author, pp. 3-28. The German physicist (1882-1970) was born in Breslau.

LIPTHAY
Kempelen. Magyarországi Zsidó, 2:105, 106. See GENERAL WORKS.

LISSA
See DE LISSA.
AMH has family records.

LISSAUER
LBI has family tree beginning 1722.

LISSER (DE)
See DE LISSER.

LISSO
AMH has family records.

LIST
"List Family, Genealogy, 1861-1970;" Typescript. AJA.

LITCHFIELD
AMH has family records.

LITVINOV
Bick-Shauli, "Roots and
Branches." Includes
genealogy of Maxim Litvinov,
Russian Revolutionary and
Soviet diplomat,
b. Bialystok, 1867; d. 1951.
He was born Meir Moiseevitch
Wallach. See GENERAL WORKS.

LITZER
AMH has family records.

LIVINGSTON
Livingston Family.
"Genealogical Material
Regarding the Livingston
Family of New York, and
Prussia, Germany, 1837-1944."
AJA.
AJA has Isaac Livingston family
tree from Prussia and New
York, beginning 1837.

LIVINGSTONE
AMH has family records.

LIZARS
AMH has family records.

LIZER
AMH has family records.

LLOYD
AMH has family records.

LOANZ
Epstein, Abraham. Mispaḥat
Lurya. Added title page: Die
Familie Lurie, von ihren
Anfängen bis auf die
Gegenwart, nebst einer
Abhandlung über Elia b. Mose
Loanz. Wien, 1901. 63 p.
Elijah Loanz, 1555-1636.
Name also spelled Luncz or
Luntz. DLC, NN.
Luncz, Judah Loeb. Kovetz
Shoshanim. Warsaw, 1891.
"Toledot Mishpachat Luntz,"
pp. 58-64. MH.

LOB
AMH has family records.
CAJ has family tree.
Schulte. Bonner Juden, p. 354.
Löb family. See GENERAL
WORKS.

LOBATTO
AJA has genealogical files.

LOBEL
CAJ has family records.

LOBL
See Daniel Nathan Leeson entry
under LEESON.

LOBSTEIN
Tänzer. Juden in Jebenhausen,
p. 346. Löbstein family of
Jebenhausen. See GENERAL
WORKS.

LOEB
AMH has family records.
LBI has family tree.
Gerstley-Loeb Family. Papers,
1868-1976. 2 boxes and
photographs. Records of four
generations of a Philadelphia
family of German origin.
Includes genealogical
information. PJAC.
Wolf Family. Papers,
c. 1970-1977. 1 folder.
"Biographical material, 1976,
of Howard A. Wolf (1900-   )
and genealogical information
about his ancestors and those
of his wife, Martha Rosenthal
Wolf, including members of
the Wolf, Rosenthal, Loeb,
Fels, and Price Families,
dating back to the 18th
century." PJAC.
Birmingham. Our Crowd. See
GENERAL WORKS.
See David Joseph entry under
BEITMAN.
Schulte. Bonner Juden,
pp. 349-53. See GENERAL
WORKS.
See Stern, FAJF entry under
LAIB.
Ward, Clare Mc Vicker.
Ancestors and Descendants of

Adeline Moses Loeb. New
York, 1980. One genealogical
chart. AJA, AJHS.

LOEBENSTEIN
Howwald, Albrecht Frhr. v.
"Die Loebenstein.
Erläuterungen zum Semi-Gotha
1913, s. 763f," Der Deutsche
Roland 25, no. 5/6
(1937):93-94.

LOEFFLER
CAJ has family records.

LOEN
CAJ has family records.

LOESER
LBI has family tree beginning
1811.
Kopp. Jüdischen Alsenz,
pp. 133-35. Genealogical
information on
Loeser-Neuberger family of
Alsenz. See GENERAL WORKS.

LOEVINSON
LBI has family tree beginning
1770.

LOEW
AMH has family records.
Loew, Hermann. Stammbaum der
Familie Loew.
Augsburg-Göggingen, Johanna
M. Loew, 1963. 4 Bl. LBI.
Judah Loew Family Tree. WJHC.
"Stammfolge Leo aus Hamelin,"
Deutsches Geschlechterbuch 89
(1936/37):313-34. Includes
Löew and Löwe families.
See Stern, FAJF (III) entry
under HENRY.

LOEWE
AMH has family records.
CAJ has family trees.
Brilling, Bernhard. "Die
Vorfahren des Prof. Heinrich
Löwe [sic]," Allgemeine
Wochenzeitung der Juden in
Deutschland (Düsseldorf),
15.8. 1952. Heinrich Loewe,
historian, folklorist, and
Zionist leader;

b. Wanzeleben, Germany, 1869;
d. 1951.
JFF, nos. 6, 11, and 12.
Reychman. Szkice
genealogiczne, pp. 131-32.
See GENERAL WORKS.

LOEWEN
LBI has family tree beginning
1747.
Valentin, Bruno. Geschichte
der Familien Valentin, Loewen
und Manheimer-Behrend. Rio
de Janeiro, 1963. 82 p.
LBI.

LOEWENGART
Loewengart, Stefan. Aus der
Geschichte meiner Familie.
Die Familie Bing. Der
Familienname Loewengart.
Kiryat Bialick, Israel: By
the Author, 1973. 23 p.
Genealogical tables. The
Bing, Rav Abraham-Loewengart
family. LBI, OCH.
─────── "Der Familien
Loewengart," Israelitische
Religionsgemeinschaft
Württembergs
(halbjahresschrift),
(Sept. 1971):29-30.

LOEWENSTEIN
LBI has family tree beginning
1784.
Reychman. Szkice
genealogiczne, pp. 133-34.
See GENERAL WORKS.

LOEWENTHAL
LBI has family trees beginning
1670 and 1700.

LOEWI
LBI has family tree beginning
1746.

LOEWY
LBI has family tree beginning
1794.

LOFFLER
Kempelen. Magyarországi Zsidó,
3:43. Löffler family. See
GENERAL WORKS.

LOHNSTEIN
LBI has family tree.

LOKE
Kempelen. Magyarországi Zsidó,
3:115. Lőke family. See
GENERAL WORKS.

LOLOSKY
AMH has family records.

LONDON
AMH has family records.
Abravanel-Mickleshanski-
Freedman-London Families,
1762-1948. Printed and
handwritten. AJA.
Chelminsky-Lajmer, "Jewish
Names." See GENERAL WORKS.
Czellitzer, Arthur. "Die Namen
Landé und London," JFF,
no. 46 (1937):862.
Kempelen. Magyarországi Zsidó,
3:30. See GENERAL WORKS.
London, Hannah Ruth. Shades of
Forefathers. Springfield,
Mass.: Pond-Ekberg, Co.,
1941. 199 p. DLC, NNC, PHi,
PP.
London Family, Boston.
Pouzzner, Bessie London.
"Their Exits and Their
Entrances," 1970.
Typescript; Printed copy.
AJA.

LONGUET
Rosenstein. Unbroken Chain,
pp. 150ff. See GENERAL
WORKS.

LONNERSTAEDTER
LBI has family tree beginning
1790.

LONYAY
Kempelen. Magyarországi Zsidó,
1:131; 2:98. Lónyay family.
See GENERAL WORKS.

LOPES
AMH has family records.
CFM has family records.

LOPES-FRANCO
Burke's Peerage and Baronetage,

1922. Family of Ludlow.
Burke's Peerage and Baronetage,
1970. Family of Roborough.

LOPEZ
AMH has family records.
Lopez Family, Charleston, S.C.
"Genealogical Information,
1703-1942;" Typescript. AJA.
Birmingham. The Grandees. See
GENERAL WORKS.
Corraze, R. "Les Lopez,
ancêstres maternels de M. de
Montaigne," Comité des
Travaux Historiques et
Scientifiques, Bulletin
Philologique et Historique 46
(1932/33):283-99.
Friedman, L.M. "Aaron Lopez's
Family Affairs from 'The
Commerce of Rhode Island,'"
Publications of the American
Jewish Historical Society 35
(1939):295-304.
Ginsburger, Ernest. "La Mère
de Montaigne [origine
juive]," La Revue Juive de
Lorraine 4 (1935/36):67-71.
Gutstein, Morris A. Aaron
Lopez and Judah Touro. A
Refugee and a Son of a
Refugee. New York: Behrman's
Jewish Book House, 1939.
118 p. Aaron Lopez,
1731-1782; Judah Touro,
1775-1854. DLC, IEN, MH,
NcD, OCl, OU.
————. "Descriptive Index of
Aaron Lopez Material at the
Newport Historical Society,"
Publications of the American
Jewish Historical Society 37
(1947):153.
Kahn, Daniel. "Le judaïsme de
Montaigne," La Revue Juive de
Lorraine 4 (1928):97-100.
————. "Montaigne et sa
Mère," La Revue Juive de
Lorraine 12 (1936):29-32.
Kohler, Max J. "The Lopez and
Rivera Families of Newport,"
Publications of the American
Jewish Historical Society 2
(1894):101.
Maduro, J.M.L. "A Genealogical
Note on the Pimental, Lopez,

Sasportas and Rivera
Families," Publications of
the American Jewish
Historical Society 42
(1952):303.

Moffat, Abbot Low, comp. "The
Descendants of David Lopez
and Priscilla Moses."
Princeton, N.J., Aug. 11,
1935. Corrected by Harold
Moïse in his The Moïse Family
of South Carolina: An Account
of the Life and Descendants
of Abraham and Sarah Moïse
Who Settled in Charleston,
South Carolina, In The Year
1791 A.D (Columbia, S.C.:
R.L. Bryan Co., 1961), 304 p.
DLC, MB, NN.

Roth, Cecil. "Jewish Ancestry
of Michel de Montaigne," in
his Personalities and Events
in Jewish History
(Philadelphia: Jewish
Publication Society of
America, 1953), pp. 215-25.
AJA, OCH.

Stern. FAJF. Lopez family
trees beginning in: (I) Spain
or Portugal; (II) Malaga,
Spain ("All descendants not
named Eliau [first name]
added Da Fonseca to Lopez");
and (III) Jamaica. See
GENERAL WORKS.

Strowski, F. "La jeunesse de
Montaigne, II. La tribu
Lopez de Villanueva," Revue
des Cours et Conférences 39,
no. 1 (1937/38):681-91.

LO PRESTI
Kempelen. Magyarországi Zsidó,
1:129. See GENERAL WORKS.

LORADO
AMH has family records.

LORAND
Kempelen. Magyarországi Zsidó,
2:90. Lóránd family. See
GENERAL WORKS.

LORD
AMH has family records.
Lord Family, San Antonio,

Texas. "Records of Births,
Marriages, and Deaths,
1829-1965." AJA.

LORENCO
CFM has family records.

LORIA
CFM has family records.
"La famiglia Loria," Il
Vessillo Israelitico 52
(1904):165-168. Family of
Mantova.

LORIN
Bick-Shauli, "Roots and
Branches." Includes
genealogy of Yuri Lorin,
b. Kiev, 1882; d. 1932. He
was an economist, a leader in
the USSR government,
co-author of its Five-Year
Plan, author of The Jews and
Antisemitism in the USSR, and
one of those who developed
the idea of a Jewish Soviet
Republic in the Crimea. See
GENERAL WORKS.

LORSCH
Teller, Chester. Teller Family
in America, 1842-1942: A
Record of a Hundred Years.
Philadelphia: Cousins'
Publications Committee, 1944.
221 p. Descendants of Marx
Teller, 1778-1850, and his
wife, Caroline Lorsch Teller,
1788-1872. DLC, OCH, PP.
————. New Teller
Generations: Sequel to Teller
Family in America.
Philadelphia: Cousins'
Publications Committee, 1953.
64 p. DLC, NN, NNJ, OCH, PP,
PPDrop.

LORYEA
Stern. FAJF. Loryea family
tree beginning in Courland,
Russia. See GENERAL WORKS.

LOSER
Lassally, Oswald and Egon
Flatow. "Die Familie des
Petschierstechers Michael

Löser (1724-1812) zu
Landsberg a.d. Warthe," JFF,
no. 41/42 (1936):749-51,
758-63.

LOSKY
AMH has family records.

LOTH
AJA has family tree beginning
1860.
Loth Family. "Genealogy,
Cincinnati, Ohio, 1860-1961."
AJA.

LOUCHHEIM
Louchheim Family, California
Family Tree, n.d. Typescript
and MS. AJA.

LOUIS
AMH has family records.
Louis, Julius (1833-1892)
Collection, 1778-1965.
Includes genealogical
material dealing with Pollack
family, 1778-1943, and
Bernstein and Louis families,
1840-1965; Baltimore and
Norfolk. AJA.

LOUISSON
AMH has family records.

LOURIA
Rosenstein. Unbroken Chain.
pp. 641ff. See GENERAL
WORKS.

LOURIE
See entry under LURIA, LURIE,
LURYA.

LOUSADA
AMH has family records.
CFM has family records.

LOUVESTEN
AMH has family records.

LOUYET
CFM has family records.

LOUZADA
AMH has family records.
Miller, George J. Collection.

Includes notes on the Louzada
family of Bound Brook, N.J.,
1717-1768. AJA.
Stern. FAJF. Louzada family
tree beginning in London.
See GENERAL WORKS.

LOVAS
Kempelen. Magyarországi Zsidó,
2:101. See GENERAL WORKS.

LOVASSY
Kempelen. Magyarországi Zsidó,
2:104. See GENERAL WORKS.

LOVEDAY
AMH has family records.

LOVELL
AMH has family records.

LOVEMAN
Frank. Nashville Jewry,
p. 138. Hungarian family,
arrived in U.S. in 1850s.
See GENERAL WORKS.

LOVENSTEIN
Lovenstein Family Records,
1861-1973. AJA.

LOVENTHAL
Frank. Nashville Jewry,
p. 143. Family of Prussia.
See GENERAL WORKS.

LOVINSON
Lovinson, Moritz.
Gedenkschrift zur Erinnerung
an die von Dr. Moritz
Lövinson, geboren Danzig
1820-gestorben Berlin 1887,
hinterlassene
Familien-Stiftung.
Zusammengestellt von den über
drei Erdteile verstreuten
überlebenden der Familie.
Philadelphia, 1981. Includes
genealogical table. Moritz
Lovinson was a physician.
LBI, PJAC.

LOW
AMH has family records.
Kempelen. Magyarországi Zsidó,

1:50; 2:129, 134; 3:25. Löw
family. See GENERAL WORKS.

LOW-BEER
Kempelen. Magyarországi Zsidó,
1:84. Löw-Beer family. See
GENERAL WORKS.

LOWE
AMH has family records.

LOWELL
AMH has family records.

LOWENADLER
Semi-Gotha, 1:88. Löwenadler
family. See GENERAL WORKS.

LOWENBERG
Stern. FAJF. Lowenberg family
tree beginning in
Württemberg. Family tree is
listed in FAJF under "Hecht."
See GENERAL WORKS.
Tänzer. Juden in Tirol,
pp. 737-40. Löwenberg
family. See GENERAL WORKS.

LOWENGARD
Tänzer. Juden in Tirol,
pp. 714-43. Löwengard
family. See GENERAL WORKS.

LOWENHEIM
Frank. Nashville Jewry,
p. 131. See GENERAL WORKS.

LOWENHERZ
Philippsohn, Molly. Chronik
der Familie
Friedländer-Lowenherz,
1760-1912. CAJ.

LOWENHJELM
Semi-Gotha, 1:47. Löwenhjelm
family. See GENERAL WORKS.

LOWENROSEN
PD has family records.

LOWENSOHN
Kempelen. Magyarországi Zsidó,
3:115. Löwensohn family.
See GENERAL WORKS.

LOWENSTAMM
Fischer, Josef. Michaelsen og
hustrus forfaeadre.
Køalbenhavn: Hertz, 1913.
31 p. Printed as MS.
Descendants of Lob Saul
Löwenstamm. OCH.
Rosenstein. Unbroken Chain,
pp. 433ff. See GENERAL
WORKS.

LOWENSTEIN
AJA has Lowenstein family tree.
CAJ has family tree from
Germany and Pakistan.
CFM has family records.
See Esmond S. De Beer entry
under BARDEN.
Frank. Nashville Jewry,
pp. 134-35. Family
originally from Frankfurt,
arrived in U.S. in 1860s.
See GENERAL WORKS.
Kempelen. Magyarországi Zsidó,
3:127. Löwenstein family.
See GENERAL WORKS.
See Siegfried Porta entry under
FALKENSTEIN. Includes family
trees. Table of descendants
of Abraham Basch, 1545-1590,
and Marcus Jakob Levi at
Brakel or Ottenberg,
ca. 1648. His children or
grandsons are named Porta,
Steinheim, Falkenstein,
Goldsmith, Löwenstein, and
Rosenberg.
Price-Goldsmith-Lowenstein and
Related Families, edited by
Harriet Stryker-Rodda. From
the Collected Notes of
Katherine Goldsmith
Lowenstein. New York, 1967.
49 p. Genealogical tables.
DLC.
Schulte. Bonner Juden, p. 356.
Löwenstein family. See
GENERAL WORKS.
Tänzer. Juden in Jebenhausen,
p. 347. Löwenstein family.
See GENERAL WORKS.
Wallach, Laura. Die Familien
Alsberg und Löwenstein.
Israel, 1964. 29 p. LBI.
Zapf. Tübinger Juden, pp.
148-57, 189-90, 204-208.

Löwenstein family. See
GENERAL WORKS.

LOWENTHAL
CFM has family records.
Auerbach, Siegfried, comp. The
Descendants of Moritz
Löwenthal of Ladenburg.
London: Perry Press
Production, 1959. 72 p.
Includes genealogical table.
DLC.
JFF, no. 14. Family history.
Kempelen. Magyarországi Zsidó,
2:66. Löwenthal family. See
GENERAL WORKS.
Lowenthal, Marvin M. "Our
Fathers That Begat Us: A
Genealogical Inquiry,"
Menorah Journal 11
(Apr. 1925):133-144; 12
(Feb.-Apr. 1926):22-31,
156-69. German family
originally from Stuttgart,
Ulm, and Buchau-am-Federsee,
Württemberg.

LOWI, LOWY
AMH has Lowy family records.
Brod, Max. Franz Kafka: A
Biography. 2d enlarged ed.
New York: Schocken Books,
1947, 1960. 267 p. "Parents
and Childhood," pp. 3-38.
Franz Kafka (1883-1924) was
the son of Julie Löwy and
Hermann Kafka (1852-?) of
Prague and grandson of Jacob
Kafka (1814-1889) of the
South Bohemian village of
Wossek.
Kempelen. Magyarországi Zsidó,
1:12, 21, 26, 123; 2:26, 127,
128, 132; 3:65, 101. Löwi,
Löwy family. See GENERAL
WORKS.

LOWINGER
Kempelen. Magyarországi Zsidó,
3:96. Löwinger family. See
GENERAL WORKS.

LOWINSKY
CFM has family records.

LOWISOHN
Kempelen. Magyarországi Zsidó,
2:55. Löwisohn family. See
GENERAL WORKS.

LOWY
See LOWI, LOWY.

LOYEV
See Yaffa Draznin entry under
BERNSTEIN.

LUARD
AMH has family records.

LUBELL
Saxe Family; Riverdale, N.Y.
"Family Tree Including Five
Generations; and Also Lubell
Families of New York and
Tulsa, Oklahoma," 1981. MS.
Xerox copy. AJA.

LUBIN
David Lubin Papers (1848-1919).
David Lubin Family Tree.
WJHC.

LUBLIN
AMH has family records.
LBI has family tree beginning
1838.

LUBLINSKI
Richter, John Henry. David
Lublinski in West Prussia. A
Chronicle of the Life of the
Lublinski and Segall Families
in West Prussia, 1850-1881.
Ann Arbor, Mich.: University
Microfilms, 1965. 83 p.
LBI.

LUCAS
AMH has family records.
CFM has family records.
Fischer, Josef. Slaegten
Lucas. Påa foranledning af
Elsa Lucas og Robert Lucas.
Trykt som manuskript.
København, 1948. 31 p. WU.

LUCAS-TOOTH
AMH has family records.

LUCCA

Holzmann, Michael. "Aus dem Ahnensaal der Pauline Lucca; Dr. S.B. Lucca," Jüdische Archiv 1, N.F., no. 1/2 (1928):1-10. Pauline Lucca, world-famous soprano, b. Vienna, 1841; d. Vienna, 1908. She was the niece of Samuel Benedict Lucca (also spelled Lucka), author and physician, b. Prague, 1803; d. Vienna, 1891.

LUCENA

CFM has family records.
See Stern, FAJF entry under NUNEZ.
"The Will of Abraham de Lucena of New York," St. Charles 1 (Jan. 1935):131-32. A genealogical table includes "Families Intermarried with Abraham and Rachel de Lucena and Their Descendants during the 18th and Part of the 19th Centuries."

LUCIA

AMH has family records.

LUCKA

See LUCCA.
Bondi, Jonas Marcus. Zur Geschichte der Familie Jomtob-Bondi in Prag, Dresden und Mainz. Frankfurt am Main: D. Droller, 5681 [1921?]. 33 p. Genealogical tables. Includes Bondi, Fränkel, Jomtob, Lucka, Spira, and Theomim families. OU, PPDrop, PPULC.

LUCKHURST

AMH has family records.

LUCZ

Kempelen. Magyarországi Zsidó, 2:19. See GENERAL WORKS.

LUCZENBACHER

Kempelen. Magyarországi Zsidó, 3:118. See GENERAL WORKS.

LUDASI

Kempelen. Magyarországi Zsidó, 2:137; 3:106. See GENERAL WORKS.

LUDDINGTON

AMH has family records.

LUDLOW

AMH has family records.

LUDWIG

Straunch, Ralph. The Altschuler Family Tree: The Descendants of Moses and Sarah Altschuler; A Genealogical Survey. New York: Ludwig-Field-Altschuler Family Circle, 1975. 1 v. NN, YIVO.

LUEGER

CAJ has family records.

LUFT

LBI has family tree beginning 1775.

LUKACS

Bick-Shauli, "Roots and Branches." Georg Lukács, 1885-1971, of Hungary. See GENERAL WORKS.
Kempelen. Magyarországi Zsidó, 1:102, 134; 2:63; 3:79, 80. Lukács, Lukáts family. See GENERAL WORKS.

LUKATS

See Kempelen entry under LUKACS.

LUMBROZO

Russell, George Ely. "Elizabeth (Wiles) (Lumbrozo) (Browne) Robinson of Charles County, Maryland, 1662," The American Genealogist 55 (July 1979):174-77. "An account of some of the unsavory incidents in the life of the 17th century Dr. Jacob Lumbrozo of Maryland, and the story of his wife and offspring."

LUMLEY
AMH has family records.

LUNCZ
See LOANZ.

LUNKANYI
Kempelen. Magyarországi Zsidó,
3:114. Lunkányi family. See
GENERAL WORKS.

LUNTZ
See LOANZ.
JE, 8:209. Family of Worms,
18th century. See GENERAL
WORKS.

LURIA, LURIE, LURYA
See Meyer Ellenbogen entry
under KATZENELLENBOGEN.
Includes genealogical table.
Epstein, Abraham. Mishpahat
Lurya. Added title page: Die
Familie Lurie, von ihren
Anfängen bis auf die
Gegenwart, nebst einer
Abhandlung über Elia B. Mose
Loanz. Wien, 1901. 63 p.
Elijah Loanz, 1555-1636.
DLC, NN.
Gussow, Dan. Chaia Sonia: A
Family's Odyssey: Russian
Style. New York: Cherry and
Scammel Books, Inc., 1980.
251 p. Life of family from
Pumpian, Lithuania
originally. Chaia Sonia
(Luria) and Simche Gussow
(originally from Kharkov,
Russia).
Lourié, Anton. Die Familie
Lourié (Luria). Wien: Druck
von Stern und Steiner, 1923.
50 p. DLC, MH, NN, OCH,
PPDrop.
Luria, S. "The Luria Family in
Roman Egypt," (In Russian),
Evreiskaia Starina 11
(1924):319-29.
Luria, Yeshayahu. Megillat
Hayuchasin Lemishpachat Luria
Ha'atika Hameforsemet Leshem
Uletiferet. Jerusalem:
Haivri Press, 1965. 32 p.
JNUL.
Saphra, B. "Luria," Ost und

West 12 (1912):561-66.
Shapiro. Mishpachot Atikot,
pp. 56-84. See GENERAL
WORKS.
Stern. FAJF. Luria family
tree beginning in London.
See GENERAL WORKS.

LUSHER
Stern. FAJF. Lusher family
tree beginning in U.S.
Family tree is listed in FAJF
under "Salomon." See GENERAL
WORKS.

LUSKY
Frank. Nashville Jewry,
pp. 132-33. Family of
Warsaw, Poland, arrived in
U.S. in 1850s. See GENERAL
WORKS.

LUSZTIG
Kempelen. Magyarországi Zsidó,
1:26; 2:74, 86; 3:96. See
GENERAL WORKS.

LUXEMBURG
Wistrich, Robert. "The Jewish
Origins of Rosa Luxemburg,"
[In Hebrew.] 'Olam Ho-Omanut
(Tel Aviv), no. 3
(Winter/Spring 1977):3-10.
Rosa Luxemburg (1871-1919),
German Marxist economist and
revolutionary, was born in
Zamosc, Russian Poland, but
she went to school in Warsaw.
Luxemburg eventually
emigrated to Germany where
she participated in various
revolutionary activities.

LUZZATTI
CFM has family records.

LUZZATTO
AMH has family records.
JE, 8:220. Contains
genealogical chart for of
family of Italy, descendants
of Abraham Luzzatto, early
16th century. See GENERAL
WORKS.
Brann, Markus. Die Familie
Luzzatto. 1900. 48 p. OCH,

YIVO.
————. "Die Familie Samuel
David Luzzatto," in
Gedenkbuch David Kaufmann
(Breslau, 1900), p. 48.
Verband der Vereine für
Jüdische Geschichte und
Literatur in Deutschland.
Samuel David Luzzatto: Ein
Gedenkbuch zum hundertsten
Geburtstage, 22 August
1900.... Berlin: A. Katz.
Pages 25-48 contain an essay
by Markus Brann on the
Luzzatto family. CU, DLC,
MH, NN, OCH, PPDrop.
Luzzatto, Isaia. "Notizie
storico-letterarie sulla
famiglia Luzzatto," Mosè
(Corfù) 1 (1878):79-90,
137-42, 178-81, 252-57.
Luzzatto, Samuel David.
Autobiografia preceduta da
alcune notizie
storico-letterarie sulla
famiglia Luzzatto a datare
dal secolo decimosesto e
susseguito da varie appendici
fra cui le tavole
genealogische dei Luzzatto di
S. Daniele. Padova: Tipogr.
Crescini, 1882. 183 p.
Genealogical table. NN, OCH.
Morpurgo, E. "Samuel David
Luzzatto e la sua famiglia,"
Rassegna Mensile di Israel 39
(1973):618-32.
Zoller, Israele. "Note sur la
famille Luzzatto après son
expulsion de San Daniele,"
Revue des Études Juives 94
(1933):50-56.

LWOW
Horowitz, Zvi Hirsch. "Die
Familie Lwow," MGWJ 72
(1928):487-99.
Rosenstein. Unbroken Chain,
pp. 150ff. See GENERAL
WORKS.

LYBARGER
Lybarger, Donald Fisher. The
Story of the
Dowler-Hartshorne,
Fisher-Lybarger Families.

Cleveland, 1938, 1962, 2d ed.
63 p. DLC, OCl.

LYBECK
Semi-Gotha, 1:98. See GENERAL
WORKS.

LYND (VAN DER)
AMH has family records.

LYON
AMH has family records.
CFM has family records.
Semi-Gotha, 2:94ff. See
GENERAL WORKS.
Stern. FAJF. Lyon family
trees beginning in:
(I) Pornak, Posen, Poland;
and (II and III) U.S. See
GENERAL WORKS.

LYONS
AMH has family records.
Stern. FAJF. Lyons family
trees beginning in:
(I) Holland;
(II) Oberelsbach, Germany;
(III) Amsterdam; and
(IV) U.S. See GENERAL WORKS.

LYONS-LEVY-MOSS
AJA has genealogical files.

MAAS
Ullmann, Elias.
Familien-Register und
Stammtafel Michael Isaac Bing
und seiner Nachkommen.
2 Aufl. Frankfurt am Main,
1864. 42 p. "Nathan Maas
und Nachkommen," p. 36.
Family of Frankfurt. LBI.

MAASS
CAJ (Call No. 418) has the
following family trees:
Family tree showing
descendants of Philip Moses
(his children took the name
Maass), d. 1796 , 1 p.;
family tree of Philipp Levin
Maass (grandson of Philip

Moses), b. 1815; d. Berlin,
1886 (last date on tree is
1919); and family tree of
Maass family, dated 1933,
8 p.

MABOVITCH, MABOVITZ
Meir, Golda Mabovitz. My Life.
New York: Putnam, 1975. 480
p. "My Childhood," pp.
13-29. Daughter of Moshe and
Bluma Mabovitch from Kiev and
Pinsk.

MACHADO
AMH has family records.
CFM has family records.
EJ, 8:245. Contains "Family
Tree of the Machado Family of
New York," descendants of
David Mendez Machado,
d. 1753, through early 19th
century. See GENERAL WORKS.
Phillips, N. Taylor. "Family
History of the Rev. David
Mendez Machado," Publications
of the American Jewish
Historical Society 2
(1894):45-61.

MACHIEL, MACHIELS
CAJ has Machiel family tree
beginning 1804 in Amsterdam,
and Machiels family tree,
also from Amsterdam.

MACHINI
CAJ has family records.

MACHLUP
Kempelen. Magyarországi Zsidó,
2:8. See GENERAL WORKS.

MACHOL
AJA has family tree beginning
in Germany, 1831.

MACHORRO
AMH has family records.
CFM has family records.

MacIVER
AMH has family records.

MACK
Mack Family, Cincinnati, Ohio.

"Genealogy, 1875-1948." AJA.
Bachrach, Samuel and Babette.
Collection of Correspondence;
Memoirs, and Genealogical
Material Concerning the
Bloch, Wise, Tandler, and
Mack Families, 1851-1940. In
German and English. AJA.
Barnard, Harry. The Forging of
An American Jew: The Life and
Times of Judge Julian W.
Mack. New York: Herzl Press,
1974. 346 p. Pp. 3-17.
Judge Mack of Chicago
(1866-1943) was born in San
Francisco, the son of William
Jacob Mack who arrived in the
1830s from Ichenhausen,
Bavaria, and Rebecca Tandler
Mack. Mack's mother was the
daughter of Abraham and Fanny
Tandler of Bavaria.

MACNIN
CFM has family records.

MADANSKY
Watters, Gary. "The Russian
Jew in Oklahoma: The May
Brothers," Chronicles of
Oklahoma 53, no. 4
(1976):479-91. Story of
Hyman (d. 1932) and Hanna
Mandanic (name changed to
Madansky and then to May in
U.S.) and their children Max,
Harry, Paul, Jacob, and
Sarah. The family immigrated
to U.S. in 1889 from Galena
Gubernia, about 100 miles
south of Kiev. They operated
clothing stores in Illinois
and eventually in several
cities throughout Oklahoma.

MADARASSY-BECK
UJE, 7:267-68. Family of
Hungarian economists.
Kempelen. Magyarországi Zsidó,
2:26, 64, 141; 3:105. See
GENERAL WORKS.

MADEIRA
CFM has family records.

MADURO

Hartog, Johannes. Her
verhaalder Maduros, en
foto-album van Curaçao,
1837-1962, uitgegeven ter
gelegenheid van het honderd
vijfentwintigjarig bestaan
van S.E.L. Maduro & Sons en
opgedragen aan de bevolking
van de Nederlandse Antillen.
Aruba: D.J. De Witt, 1962.
179 p. Includes genealogical
tables. In Dutch and
English. BR.

Krafft, Arnoldus Johannes
Cornelius. Historie en Oude
Families van de Nederlandse
Antillen het antilliaanse
patriciaat met een
historische inleiding, zestig
uitgewerkte genealogieen,
genealogische aantekeningen,
fragmenten va genealogieen,
ungepubliceerde documenten en
een overzicht van bronnen
zowel gedruchte als in
handschrift. 'S-Gravenhage:
M. Nijhoff, 1951. Includes
genealogy of Maduro family of
Curaçao, pp. 99-118. CU, DLC,
MB, MH, NcD, NN, NNC, OC1,
OU, TxU.

MADZA

Kempelen. Magyarországi Zsidó,
1:73. See GENERAL WORKS.

MAERLE

Kempelen. Magyarországi Zsidó,
2:75. See GENERAL WORKS.

MAGEE

AMH has family records.

MAGNES

CAJ has family records.
Bentwich, Norman de Mattos.
For Zion's Sake: A Biography
of Judah L. Magnes: First
Chancellor and First
President of the Hebrew
University of Jerusalem.
Philadelphia: Jewish
Publication Society of
America, 1954. 329 p. Pp.
9-15. Magnes (1877-1948) was

born in San Francisco, the
son of David and Sophia
Magnes and the grandson of
Judah Leibush Magnes. The
family was from Widoma, a
suburb of Przedborg, near
Lodz.

MAGNIN

AJA has Isaac Magnin family
tree beginning 1842 in
Holland.

MAGNUS

AMH has family records.
CAJ has family records.
CFM has family records.
LBI has family tree beginning
1712.
LBIS has family tree.
Rothschild. Svenska Israel.
See GENERAL WORKS.
Semi-Gotha, 2:98ff. See
GENERAL WORKS.

MAGNUSSON

AMH has family records.

MAGRINI

Kempelen. Magyarországi Zsidó,
3:39. See GENERAL WORKS.

MAGRISH

"Vital Statistics of the
Magrish Family Taken from the
Family Bible, Cincinnati,
Ohio, 1869-1973." AJA.

MAHLER

Grange, Henry-Louis de la.
Mahler. Garden City, N.Y.:
Doubleday & Co., 1973. 982
p. Genealogical information
concerning the relatives of
Gustav Mahler (1860-1911),
the Austrian composer, pp.
5-12. Mahler was the son of
Bernhard (1827?-1889) and
Marie Hermann (d. 1889) and
the grandson of Simon
(1793-1865) and Maria Mahler
and Abraham and Theresa
Hermann. The Hermann family
was from Sniet and the Mahler
family was from Lipnitz

(Lipnice), Iglau (Jihlava),
and Kaliste (Kalischt).

MAIER
Neufeld, S. "Der geadelte
Stuttgarter Rabbiner,"
Israelitische
Religionsgemeinschaft
(Württemberg), Pesach and
Rosh Haschana issues, Apr.
and Sept. 1969, Pp. 17-19 of
both issues. Dr. Joseph von
Maier, 1797-1873, was a
member of the Jewish
Consistory of Württemberg.
This gave him the distinction
of being the first German
rabbi belonging to the
nobility.

MAILATH
Kempelen. Magyarországi Zsidó,
2:76. Mailáth family. See
GENERAL WORKS.

MAILER
LBI has family tree beginning
1794.

MAILERT
Stern. FAJF. Mailert family
tree beginning in Cassel,
Germany. Originally Meylert.
See GENERAL WORKS.

MAIMON
The Maimon Family Reunion,
August, 1974; Commemorating
50 Years in the U.S.A.,
1924-1974. [Seattle, 1974.]
Includes family history,
genealogical data, and
genealogical chart of
Sephardic family in Seattle.
AJHS.
The Maimon Family Re-Reunion
50+5, August 1979. [Seattle,
1979.] Additional data on
family. AJHS.

MAINZ
Goldschmidt, Leo S. Die
Familie Kulp. By the Author,
1935. Some ancestors and the
grandchildren of Juda Michael
Kulp (1796-1867) and his wife

Adelherd, née Mainz
(1801-1892).
Mainz, Isaac. Vorwort zum
Stammbaum der Familie Mainz.
Frankfurt am Main, 1909.
Family tree begins 1622.
LBI.

MAIRS
Stern. FAJF. Mairs family
tree beginning in Budingen.
See GENERAL WORKS.

MAISLER
See Zevi Shimshi entry under
SHIMSHELEWITZ. Includes
Maisler family.

MAITLAND
AMH has family records.

MAJER-LEONARD
LBI has family tree beginning
1756.

MAJINSZKI
Kempelen. Magyarországi Zsidó,
2:66. See GENERAL WORKS.

MAKHIRI
Zuberman, Arthur J. A Jewish
Princedom in Feudal France,
768-900. New York: Columbia
University Press, 1972.
490 p. Includes information
on Makhiri family.

MAKOLDY
Kempelen. Magyarországi Zsidó,
1:117. See GENERAL WORKS.

MALAES
Kempelen. Magyarországi Zsidó,
1:74. See GENERAL WORKS.

MALAMUD
Malamud, Joseph. Bi-sdot
Yizrael. Kfar Giladi, 1970?

MALECZKY
Kempelen. Magyarországi Zsidó,
2:138. See GENERAL WORKS.

MALLON
AMH has family records.

MALMBORG
Semi-Gotha, 2:38. See GENERAL
WORKS.

MALOFSKY
See George M. Gross entry under
GROSS. Family originally
from Minsk gubernia.

MALONE
AMH has family records.

MALOWITZ
See Harry and Nellie Lepsky
entry under CHALEPSKY.

MANDANIC
See MADANSKY.

MANDEL
AMH has family records.
Kempelen. Magyarországi Zsidó,
1:70, 86; 2:35; 3:93, 125.
Mandel, Mandl family. See
GENERAL WORKS.

MANDELOWITCH
See Sidney Cramer entry under
BINDMAN.

MANDELSON
AMH has family records.

MANDEL-THEBEN
PD has family records.
Schay, Max. "Die Familie
Theben-Mandel," JFF, no. 5
(1926):115-24. About members
of family in Pressburg during
18th century.

MANDELBAUM
LBI has family trees beginning
1816 and 1837.

MANDELSHTAM
Bick-Shauli, "Roots and
Branches." Includes
genealogy of Osip
Mandelshtam, Russian poet,
b. Warsaw, 1891; d. ca. 1938.
See GENERAL WORKS.

MANDELSTAM
AMH has family records.

MANDER
Mander, Anica Vesel with Sarika
Finci Hofbauer. Blood Ties:
A Woman's History. Berkeley
and New York: Moon Books and
Random House, Inc., 1976.
297 p. Feminist
autobiography focusing on the
author's birth (1934-   )
and early childhood in
Sarajevo, Yugoslavia,
family's escape to Italy in
1943, emigration to
California in late 1940s.
Interspersed are chapters of
reminiscences of Sarika Finci
Hofbauer, the author's
grandmother, about World Wars
I and II. CtY, DLC, ICarbS,
MB, MH, NN, NNC, OCl, OU,
TxU.

MANDL
See Kempelen entry under
MANDEL.

MANDLBAUM
Kempelen. Magyarországi Zsidó,
1:73. See GENERAL WORKS.

MANDLEBERG
CFM has family records.

MANE
LBI has family tree beginning
1849.

MANHART
Rose. Schöninger Juden. See
GENERAL WORKS.

MANHEIM, MANNHEIM, MANHEIMER,
MANNHEIMER
PD has Manheim family records.
Hecht, Otto. Einige
Erinnerungen der Familie
Hecht. Haifa: Skikmona
Publ., 1973. 277 p.
Includes family tree. Hecht
and Mannheim families. LBI.
Löwe, J. Die Familie Valentin
Manheimer, 1815-1889.
Berlin, 1906. LBI.
Rothschild. Svenska Israel.
Includes Mannheimer family.
See GENERAL WORKS.

Shinedling, Abraham I. "Leo
Mannheimer and His Family: A
Memoir;" and "Correspondence
and Documents Relating to the
Memoir, 1959-1960. Family of
New Mexico. AJA.
Tänzer. Juden in Jebenhausen,
p. 348. Mannheimer family of
Jebenhausen. See GENERAL
WORKS.
Valentin, Bruno. Geschichte
der Familien Valentin, Loewen
und Manheimer-Behrend. Rio
de Janeiro, 1963. 82 p.
LBI.

MANN
Kempelen. Magyarországi Zsidó,
2:87. See GENERAL WORKS.

MANNERFELT
Semi-Gotha, 1:138. See GENERAL
WORKS.

MANNING
AMH has family records.

MANNINGER
Kempelen. Magyarországi Zsidó,
3:123. See GENERAL WORKS.

MANNSWORTH
Kempelen. Magyarországi Zsidó,
1:86. See GENERAL WORKS.

MANOR
PD has family records.

MANSFELD
See COLLOREDO-MANSFELD.
Kempelen. Magyarországi Zsidó,
1:69. See GENERAL WORKS.

MANSFIELD
See COHODAS.

MANTAICA
Kempelen. Magyarországi Zsidó,
2:144. See GENERAL WORKS.

MANUEL
Millner, Joseph. "Les grandes
familles juives de France,"
Le Monde Juif 5, no. 27
(1950):10.

MANUELLE
CFM has family records.

MANVILLE
AMH has family records.

MARACHE
CFM has family records.
Stern. FAJF. Maraché family
tree beginning in Curaçao.
See GENERAL WORKS.

MARAM
Brilling, Bernhard. "Der Name
Maram, Marum. Zur Geschichte
der Familien Guggenheim, Weil
und anderer Nachkommen des
Meir von Rothenburg," in
Forschung am Judentum:
Festschrift zum 60.
Geburtstag von Lothar
Rothschild (Bern, 1970),
pp. 99-125. DLC, ICU.
————. "On the History of the
Name 'Marum.'" (In Hebrew.)
Yeda'-'am 2, no. 4/5
(1954):232-33.

MARATEK
Wincelberg, Shimon and Anita.
The Samurai of Vishograd: The
Notebooks of Jacob Maratek.
Philadelphia: Jewish
Publication Society of
America, 1976. 207 p.
Excerpts from Jacob Maratek's
Yiddish memoirs, retold by
the authors. Covers from
Maratek's birth in 1883 to
the Russo-Japanese War of
1904/1905. Maratek (d. 1950)
was the son of Shloime Zalman
and Rachel Maratek of
Vishogrod.

MARC
Vagts, Alfred. "Die Familie
Marc und der Durchbruch zur
Malerei," Bulletin des Leo
Baeck Instituts, no. 33
(1966):85-96. Family of
Waldeck, then Bamberg,
Germany.

MARCH
Millás Vallicrosa, José María.

"La ascendencia judaica de
Juan Luis Vives y la
ortodoxía de su obra
apologética," Sefarad 25
(1965):59-65. 15Th to 16th
century.
Inquisition. Valencia (City).
Procesos inquisitoriales
contra la familia judía de
Juan Luis Vives.
Introducción y transcripción
paleográfica de Miguel de la
Pinta Llorente y José María
de Palacio. Madrid:
Instituto Arias Montano,
1964-. Vol. 1: Proceso
contra Blanquina March, madre
del humanista. DLC, ICU, MH.

MARCHANT
Stern. FAJF. Marchant family
tree beginning in U.S. See
GENERAL WORKS.

MARCHENA
CFM has family records.

MARCUS
AMH has family records.
LBI has family trees beginning
1690 and 1832.
CAJ, Call No. 3553, has
wall-size family chart of
Marcus and Cohn families from
16th century to 1923.
Descendants of Rabbi Moses
ben David Hacohen, rabbi in
Deutz, Germany, and also in
Cologne in first half of 17th
century. In German and
Hebrew.
Ballin. Juden in Seesen,
p. 220. See GENERAL WORKS.
Harris. Merchant Princes.
Marcus department store
family of Dallas.
Descendants of Herbert
Marcus, b. Louisville,
Kentucky, 1878. See GENERAL
WORKS.
Marcus, Jacob R. (1896-   ).
Papers, 1912-1976. Include
notes on history of Marcus
family. Professor of Jewish
history and director of the
American Jewish Archives.

AJA.
Rader-Marcus Family.
"Genealogical Chart compiled
by Dr. Jacob Rader Marcus,
Cincinnati, Ohio." 1966.
AJA.
Marcus, Robert Reuven.
Stammfolge. N.p., 1973.
14 p. Family table of
descendants of Markus Elias
Marcus, b. Soest, 1767;
d. 1856. Family table covers
1768-1973. CAJ, Call
No. 3442.
Rothschild. Svenska Israel.
See GENERAL WORKS.

MARCUSE
CAJ has family tree from Posen.
LBIS has family tree.
Lövinson, Siegfried. 50 Sterne
am Himmel meiner
Kindheitsjahre. Berlin,
1905. Forebearers and
descendants of Johanna
Marcuse Hirschberg,
1803-1871.

MARCZALI
Kempelen. Magyarországi Zsidó,
1:146. See GENERAL WORKS.

MARE
Semi-Gotha, 1:147; 2:99. Maré
family. See GENERAL WORKS.

MARGARETEN
See HOROWITZ-MARGARETEN.

MARGITTAY
Kempelen. Magyarországi Zsidó,
3:126. See GENERAL WORKS.

MARGO
Kempelen. Magyarországi Zsidó,
3:106. Margó family. See
GENERAL WORKS.

MARGOLIOT
CAJ (Call No. 4318) has the
following family trees:
(1) Simon, Menashe. The
Genealogical Tree of the
Eiger, Margoliot-Kalvaryski
and Simon Families (begins
with Katzenellenbogen,

Germany, 1312 and ends in
1937) on one side and (2) on
the opposite side:
Margolis-Jahrblum, Laura
(Tel-Aviv). Continuation of
the Genealogical Tree of the
Margoliot-Kalvaryski Family,
19th and 20th Century.
Margoliot also written
Margolis.
See Shapiro, Mishpachot Atikot
entry under MARGOLIOTH.

MARGOLIOTH
JE 8:327. Contains descendants
table of Samuel Margolioth,
dayyan of Posen, 1550,
through mid-19th century.
See GENERAL WORKS.
Margolioth, Ephraim Zalman.
Ma'aloth ha-Yubasin. Edited
by Abraham Segal Ettinger.
Lemberg: A.B. Krochmal, 1900.
83 p. DLC, MH, OCH, PPDrop.
Rosenstein. Unbroken Chain,
pp. 288ff. Margolioth
descendants of R. Ari Lieb
Katz. See GENERAL WORKS.
Shapiro. Mishpachot Atikot,
291-99. Margoliot,
Margolioth family. See
GENERAL WORKS.

MARGOLIOUTH
CFM has family records.

MARGOLIS
AJA has family tree.
See CAJ (Call No. 4318) entry
under MARGOLIOT.
Kohn, Zedek J. Schem
we-scheerith. Krakau, 1895.
Includes Margolis family of
Poland and Russia.

MARGULIES
CAJ has family records.
See Jechiel Freud entry under
BER.
Kahan. 'Anaf 'ez avoth. See
GENERAL WORKS.
See Daniel Jay Rottenberg entry
under ROTTENBERG.

MARIANSKY
See Daniel Jay Rottenberg entry

under ROTTENBERG. Family
history.

MARIASSY
Kempelen. Magyarországi Zsidó,
2:76. Máriássy family. See
GENERAL WORKS.

MARILES
Rosenstein. Unbroken Chain,
pp. 601ff. See GENERAL
WORKS.

MARK
See MARC.
AMH has family records.

MARKBREIT
Kempelen. Magyarországi Zsidó,
2:73, 74. See GENERAL WORKS.

MARKBREITER
Kempelen. Magyarországi Zsidó,
1:138, 143; 2:10. See
GENERAL WORKS.
Schnitzler, Arthur. My Youth
in Vienna. Translated from
the German by Catherine
Hunter. New York: Holt,
Rinehart & Winston, 1970.
320 p. Genealogical
information concerning the
Markbreiter (of Vienna),
Schey (of Güns), and
Schnitzler (of Gross-Kanizsa,
Hungary) families, pp. 8-13.
Schnitzler (1862-1931), the
famous Austrian dramatist,
was the son of Dr. Johann
Schnitzler (1835-1893) and
Louise Markbreiter Schnitzler
(1840-1911) and grandson of
Johann (d. 1864) and Rosalie
Schnitzler and Philipp and
Amelia Markbreiter. The
Schey family was also related
to the Markbreiter family.

MARKOVITS
Kempelen. Magyarországi Zsidó,
2:145. See GENERAL WORKS.

MARKOWITZ
AJHS has "...8-generation
family tree (showing first
spiritual leader of first

synagogue in Allentown, Pa."
Compiled by Samuel Apt Marks.

MARKREICH
LBI has family tree beginning
1598.

MARKS
See BARUCH.
See MARKOWITZ.
AMH has family records.
CFM has family records.
See Esmond S. De Beer entry
under BARDEN.
Frank. Nashville Jewry,
pp. 134-35. See GENERAL
WORKS.
Friedman, Lee M. "Description
of the Marks Family,
1818-1948." Typescript.
AJA.
Irwin, Norma Nones.
Descendants of Benjamin A.
Nones and Miriam Marks.
Menlo Park, Calif.: 1979.
One genealogical chart.
AJHS, WJHC.
Marks, Stanley. Genealogical
files. AJA.
Stern. FAJF. Marks family
trees beginning in:
(I) England; (II and
III) London; (IV) U.S.; and
(V) Schwarzwald, Germany.
See GENERAL WORKS.

MARKUS
See MARC.
Kempelen. Magyarországi Zsidó,
2:134; 3:51, 65. See GENERAL
WORKS.
Markus, Anton. Geschichte der
Familie Markus;
schlesisch-mährischen
Ursprunges. Neu-Titschein:
Druck der L.V. Ender'schen
Kunstanstalt, 1931. 80 p.
Includes genealogical table.
DLC.

MARON
LBI has family tree begining
1841.

MARQUES
Stern. FAJF. Marques family

tree beginning in Denmark.
See GENERAL WORKS.

MARQUEZ
CFM has family records.

MARROT
AMH has family records.

MARSCHUETZ
AJA has Leo Marschuetz family
tree from Bavaria.

MARSDEN
AMH has family records.
CFM has family records.

MARSHAK
Bick-Shauli, "Roots and
Branches." Includes
genealogy of Samuel Marshak,
Russian poet and Zionist,
b. Voronezh, 1887; d. 1964.
See GENERAL WORKS.

MARSHALL
WJHC has family tree.
Marshall, Lucinda. The
Marshall Family Tree.
Phoenix, Ariz., after 1970.
Unpaged. Genealogical
tables. JNUL.

MARSHUETZ
Marshuetz Family, Cincinnati,
Ohio and Memphis, Tenn., and
Petersburg, Va. "History of
the Family, written by Leo J.
Marshuetz, Including Material
on the Klaus and Landauer
Families, 1946; and Family
Correspondence, 1870-1903."
Typescript and MS;
photostats. AJA.

MARTIN
AMH has family records.
Deutsch, Hermann. Stammbäume
der Familien Buff und Riegel
Wild und Martin. N.p., 1936?
4 pts. Pt. IV:
"Erlauterungen zur Stammtafel
der Familie Martin aus
Cronheim, 1660-1919." 24 p.
Includes drawings of cemetery
monuments and their

inscriptions. CAJ, Call
No. 2771/3.
Frank. Nashville Jewry,
p. 144. German family,
arrived in U.S. in 1850s.
See GENERAL WORKS.
Kempelen. Magyarországi Zsidó,
1:19. See GENERAL WORKS.

MARTINS
CFM has family records.

MARTON
Kempelen. Magyarországi Zsidó,
1:102; 3:60. See GENERAL
WORKS.

MARTOS
Kempelen. Magyarországi Zsidó,
3:53. See GENERAL WORKS.

MARUM
See MARAM.
Kopp. Jüdischen Alsenz,
pp. 136-37. Genealogical
information on Rothenberg,
Levy, and Marum families of
Alsenz. See GENERAL WORKS.

MARWITZ
LBI has family tree beginning
1854.

MARX
AJA has family trees beginning
1713 and 1750.
Marx Family, Mississippi.
"Genealogical Information and
Newspaper Clippings,
1825-1973." MS and
Typescript; Xerox copies.
AJA.
Braun, S. "Die Vorfahren von
Karl Marx, aus der Ahnentafel
der Familie,"
Mitteilungsblatt,
Wochenzeitung des Irgun Olej
Merkas Europa (Tel Aviv), no.
44 (10. Nov. 1977). Includes
genealogy of the
Katzenelnbogen, Kaznelson,
and Marx families.
Cohen, Arthur. Geschichte der
Familie Cohen mit
Berücksichtigung der Familien
Marx und Pflaum. Mit

ergänzenden Anmerkungen un
einem Stammbaum (1558-1940)
versehen von Willy Cohen.
[München, 1934-1935, and] New
York, 1956. 29 p. LBI.
Laufner, Richard and Albert
Rauch. Die Familie Marx und
die Trierer Judenschaft.
Trier: Karl-Marx-Haus, 1975.
41 p. (Schriften aus dem
Karl-Marx-Haus, No. 14.) DLC,
MWalB, NN, OU, WU.
Padover, Saul K. "The Baptism
of Karl Marx's Family,"
Midstream 24, no. 6
(1978):36-44.
————. Karl Marx: An Intimate
Biography. New York:
McGraw-Hill Book Co., 1978.
667 p. "The Family," pp.
1-12. Contents: Rabbinical
Ancestors; Karl Marx's
Father; Karl Marx's Mother.
"Marx's Paternal Ancestors,"
p. 615; Marx's Maternal
Relatives," p. 616; "Heschel
(Heinrich) Marx's Children,"
p. 617; and "Karl Marx's
Descendants," pp. 618-19.
Karl Marx was the son of
Heschel (Heinrich) and
Henriette Presburg Marx. The
Presburg family (also spelled
Presborg, Presborck) was a
Dutch-Jewish family from
Nijmegen.
Payne, [Pierre Stephen] Robert.
Marx. New York: Simon and
Schuster, 1968. 582 p.
Includes genealogical table
of Karl Marx.
Rauch, A. "Der 'Grosse
Sanhedrin' zu Paris und sein
Einfluss auf die jüdische
Familie Marx in Trier,"
Karl-Marx-Haus, (1975):18-40.
Rosenstein. Unbroken Chain,
pp. 154ff. Genealogical
chart. See GENERAL WORKS.
Schulte. Bonner Juden,
pp. 357-71. See GENERAL
WORKS.
Seckbach, Markus. Eine
Ahnentafel von 27
Generationen bis zum Jahre
1290. Betr. Die Familien

Seckbach, Meyer, Auerbach,
Hirsch, Marx. Bodenheimer U.
a Hamburg: Laubhutte, 1936.
22 p. OCH.
Stein, H. "Der Übertritt der
Familie Heinrich Marx zum
evangelischen Christentum,"
Jahrbücher des Kölnischen
Geschichtsvereins 14
(1932):126-29. The father of
Karl Marx.
Stern. FAJF. Marx family
trees beginning in:
(I) Bremen; and
(II) Engenheim, Bavaria. See
GENERAL WORKS.
Tänzer. Juden in Jebenhausen,
p. 349. See GENERAL WORKS.
Wachstein, Bernard. "Die
Abstammung von Karl Marx," in
Festskrift I-Anledning af
Prof. David Simonsens
70-aarige Fodseldag
(København: Hertz's bogtyr.,
1923), pp. 276-89. Additions
and corrections are contained
in Der Jüdischen Arbeiter
(Organ D. Poale Zion, Wien)
4, no. 14 (1927):8-13. CSt,
CtY, DLC, ICU, MB, MH, NN,
OCH, OU, PP, PPDrop.
Zapf. Tübinger Juden, pp.
158-61, 190-91, 208-213. See
GENERAL WORKS.

MASKILEISON
Harkavi, Zvi. Le-ḥekr
mishpaḥot. Jerusalem, 1953.

MASON
AMH has family records.

MASSEENA
CFM has family records.

MASSENBACHER
Tänzer. Juden in Jebenhausen,
p. 350. See GENERAL WORKS.

MASSIAH
CFM has family records.

MASSIAS
AMH has family records.
CFM has family records.

MASTOW
See Yaffa Draznin entry under
BERNSTEIN. Family history.

MATALHA
AMH has family records.

MATHES
Schulte. Bonner Juden, p. 373.
See GENERAL WORKS.

MATHIAS
CFM has family records.

MATTOS
See DE MATTOS.
AMH has family records.

MATZNER
Kempelen. Magyarországi Zsidó,
1:52. See GENERAL WORKS.

MAUTHNER
LBI has family tree beginning
1817.
Kempelen. Magyarországi Zsidó,
1:49; 3:30. See GENERAL
WORKS.

MAVROGHENI
CAJ has family records.

MAWSON
AMH has family records.

MAXSON
Chamberlain, Mildred and Laura
Clarenbach. Descendants of
Hugh Mosher and Rebecca
Maxson through Seven
Generations. By the Author,
1980. 808 p. AJA, AJHS.

MAY
See MADANSKY.
AMH has family records.
CAJ has family tree from
Hamburg, 1650-1962.
LBI has family trees beginning
1653, 1685, and 1844.
PD has records of family from
Innsbruck, Austria.
JFF, no. 14. Family history.
Kempelen. Magyarországi Zsidó,
1:147; 3:63. See GENERAL
WORKS.

See Nathan M. Reiss entry under
EDELMUTH. Includes May
families of Rossdorf,
Ober-Ramstadt, and
Gräfenhausen.

MAYER
AMH has family records.
CAJ has family trees from
Germany and family records.
CFM has family records.
LBI has family trees beginning
1627, 1762, 1766, 1781, and
1807.
Stein-Mayer Family; Louisiana,
Ohio, Germany, and France.
"Papers, Documents, and Birth
and Death Records of Members
of the Family, 1900-1919;" In
English and German. AJA.
Grotte, Alfred Jakob. "Hermann
Mayer aus Kuttenplan," JFF,
no. 30 (1932):454-56.
See David Joseph entry under
BEITMAN.
Kempelen. Magyarországi Zsidó,
1:12, 28, 65, 112; 2:129;
3:83, 112, 119. See GENERAL
WORKS.
Kopp. Jüdischen Alsenz,
pp. 131-32. Genealogical
information on
Mayer-Kahnheimer family of
Alsenz. See GENERAL WORKS.
Mayer, Fred M. "Family-Tree:
Ancestors and Descendants of
Michael Mayer,
Biebesheim/Rhein." New York,
1967. Ludwig Rosenberger
Collection, University of
Chicago Library.
Mayer, Gustav. Aus der
Geschichte d. Familie Ascher
Mayer in Prenzlau. U/M,
1924. 11 p. Separated from
Uchermärk Kurier (Prenzlau),
no. 175 (1924). LBI.
Mayer, John, New York, and
Natchez, Miss. "Family
Genealogy, and Short Story
Concerning Mayer and His
Wife, Jeanette Reis, during
the Civil War Period, 1929."
Typescript. Family genealogy
begins 1832. AJA.
Mayer, Mrs. Richard. Memoir

and Genealogy of the
Ferdinand and Jette Steiner
Mayer Family, 1832-1971. San
Angelo, Tex., 1972. AJA.
Mayer, Richard. Aus der
Geschichte der Familien Mayer
und Hirschberg. N.p., 1970.
15 p. JNUL.
Schulte. Bonner Juden,
pp. 374, 376. See GENERAL
WORKS.
Stern. FAJF. Mayer family
trees beginning in:
(I) Besançon, France; and
(II) Landau, Bavaria. See
GENERAL WORKS.
Tänzer. Juden in Tirol,
pp. 744-46. See GENERAL
WORKS.
Ullman, Sam. "Aunt Sister's
Book." New York, 1929. AJA.

MAYERSOHN
CAJ has family records.

MAYNES
AMH has family records.

MAZUR
CAJ has family tree, 1788-1921.
See Yaffa Draznin entry under
BERNSTEIN.

McGOWAN
AMH has family records.

McINTOSH
AMH has family records.

MEARS
AJA has genealogical files.
AMH has family records.
Hirsh, Lydia R. "The Mears
Family and Their Connections,
1694-1824," Publications of
the American Jewish
Historical Society 33
(1934):199-210. Anglo-Jewish
family which eventually
settled in New York City in
late 17th or early 18th
century.
Stern. FAJF. Mears family
tree beginning in Jamaica.
See GENERAL WORKS.

MEASURES   258

MEASURES
AMH has family records.

MEBORAK
Poznánski, Samuel. "Il nome
Meborak," Rivista Israelitica
7 (1910):171-79, 214-24; 8
(1911):33.

MECHLOVITS
Kempelen. Magyarországi Zsidó,
1:75. See GENERAL WORKS.

MECKAUER
LBI has family tree beginning
1805.

MECKLENBURG
Semi-Gotha, 1:103-104. See
GENERAL WORKS.

MEDEK
Kempelen. Magyarországi Zsidó,
3:49. See GENERAL WORKS.

MEDELSHEIM
CAJ has family records.

MEDINA
See DE MEDINA.
AMH has family records.
Rabinowicz, Oskar K. Sir
Solomon de Medina and a
Biography of the Author by
Judith K. Tapiero and
Theodore K. Rabb. London:
Jewish Historical Society of
Great Britain, 1974. Medina,
ca. 1650-1730. "Appendix B:
Joseph de Medina's Family,"
pp. 82-93. Anglo-Jewish
family; originally from
Bordeaux, via Amsterdam,
arriving in England in 1672.
CtY, ICarbS, IEN, MnU, NjP,
NN, NNC, OCH, OU, TxU.

MEERS
AMH has family records.

MEGYERI
Kempelen. Magyarországi Zsidó,
2:145. See GENERAL WORKS.

MEHLER
LBI has family tree beginning

1540.
Miller, Saul. Dobromil: Life
in a Galician Shtetl,
1890-1907. New York:
Loewenthal Press, 1980. 83
p. in English; 50 p. in
Yiddish. Genealogical
information on Mehler and
Treiber families, pp. 28-36,
74-76. The author
(1890-   ) was born in
Dobromil, the son of Maier
and Roise-Perl Mehler Treiber
and grandson of
Reuben-Yechiel Mehler. He
came to New York City in 1909
and eventually became an
officer in the I.L.G.W.U.
"R. Judas Mehler II," MGWJ,
1917, p. 285.
Schulte. Bonner Juden, p. 377.
See GENERAL WORKS.

MEIERSTEIN
CAJ has family tree for
Bachrach, Blumenfeld, Katz,
Klebe, and Meierstein
families of Bremke and Rhina,
Germany, Israel, and U.S.
covering 1650-1975.

MEINRATH
See Esmond S. De Beer entry
under BARDEN.

MEISEL, MEISELS
Rosenstein. Unbroken Chain,
pp. 662ff., 237ff. See
GENERAL WORKS.

MEISTERLEIN
Herzog, David. "Die Träger des
Namens 'Meisterlein' in der
Steiermark. Eine
Untersuchung zur jüdischen
Gelehrtengeschichte," MGWJ 79
(1935):31-49.

MELCER
See Judith A. Walters entry
under GRYNSZPAN.

MELCHIOR
AMH has family records.
CFM has family records.
Familieminder Tilegnet. See

GENERAL WORKS.
Melchior?, Margo. Marcus og
Meta Melchior's Efterslaegt.
N.p., 1976. 4 p.
Descendants of Marcus and
Meta Melchior, family of
Denmark. Family table covers
1922-1976. CAJ, Call
No. 4041.
Martin-Meyer, Povl. Moses
Melchior & Søn (Gerson).
7. Januar 1761/1961 (et dansk
handelshus gennem 6
generationer). Redaktion:
Povl Martin-Meyer.
København: Typ. O. Fraenkel,
1961. 56 p. English
summary, pp. 53-56. Moses
Melchior, 1736-1817, arrived
in Denmark from Hamburg in
1750. His son, Gerson
Melchior, 1771-1845, founded
the import-export firm which
bears his name today.
Discusses six generations of
family. CAJ.

MELDOLA
JE, 8:451. Contains
"Genealogical Tree of the
Meldola Family"; descendants
of Isaiah Meldola of Toledo
and Mantua, 1282-1340.
Family tree contains 16
generations of Sephardic
family through early 20th
century. See GENERAL WORKS.
Wolf, "Anglo-Jewish Families."
See GENERAL WORKS.

MELEGHY
Kempelen. Magyarországi Zsidó,
2:75. See GENERAL WORKS.

MELHADO
AMH has family records.

MELLER
Kempelen. Magyarországi Zsidó,
1:74. See GENERAL WORKS.

MELLISH
AMH has family records.

MELRICH
See Daniel J. Cohen entry under

CLEVE. Melrich family of
Altona, pp. 98-100. Includes
family tree, early 1600s to
1728, p 121.

MELUATO
CFM has family records.

MENASCE
Kempelen. Magyarországi Zsidó,
1:84. See GENERAL WORKS.

MENCEL
Kempelen. Magyarországi Zsidó,
1:82. See GENERAL WORKS.

MENDE
Kautz, Herbert.
Familiengeschichte der
Familie Mende aus Leipzig.
Stamm-, Nachfahren- und
Ahnenreihen. Hrsg. vom
Familienarchiv Kautz.
Teil 1: Mit jüdischen
Vorfahren aus Dessau und
Nachfahren der Töchter.
Bochum: Familienarchiv Kautz,
1977. 46, 8 p. LBI.
Kempelen. Magyarországi Zsidó,
2:55. See GENERAL WORKS.
Mende, Käthe. Geschichte der
Familie Mende aus Frankfurt
an der Oder. Berlin, 1950.
104 p. LBI.

MENDEL
AMH has family records.
CFM has family records.
Kempelen. Magyarországi Zsidó,
2:17. See GENERAL WORKS.

MENDELSOHN
AMH has family records.
Semi-Gotha, 2:109. See GENERAL
WORKS.
Tänzer. Juden in Tirol,
pp. 747-49. See GENERAL
WORKS.

MENDELSSOHN
AMH has family records.
CFM has family records.
EJ (1972), 11:1325. Contains
genealogical chart,
1729-1874, descendants of
Mendal Dessau, d. 1766. See

GENERAL WORKS.
JE, 8:476. Contains
"Mendelssohn Family Tree."
See GENERAL WORKS.
LBI has family trees beginning
16th century, 1729, 1740, and
1748.
Ballin, Gerhard. "Die Ahnen
des Komponisten Felix
Mendelssohn-Bartholdy,"
Genealogie 16
(Mar. 1967):646-55.
Bankiers, Künstler und
Gelehrte; unveröffentliche
Briefe der Familie
Mendelssohn aus dem 19.
Jahrhundert. Tübingen:
J.C.B. Mohr (Paul Siebeck),
1975. 328 p. 2 genealogical
tables in pocket. CtY, DLC,
NIC, OCH, OU, TxU, WU.
Freudenthal, Max. "Die Mutter
Moses Mendelssohn," ZGJD 1,
no. 3 (1929):192-200.
Includes genealogial table of
forebears.
Geis, Robert Raphael. "Die
Familie Mendelssohn. Zur
Geschichte der
Judenemanzipation in
Deutschland," in Abraham
unser Vater; Juden und
Christen im Gespräch über die
Bibel. Festschrift für Otto
Michel zum 60. Geburtstag
(Leiden: E.J. Brill, 1963),
pp. 216-21.
Hensel, Sebastian. Die Familie
Mendelssohn, 1729-1847. Nach
Briefen und Tagebüchern.
Gekürzt und bearbeitet von
Karl August Horst.
Dreiburg-München: Verlag Karl
Alber, 1959. 472 p. New
edition of the work first
published in 1879. Includes
genealogical information.
CSt, CtY, DLC, NcU, NjP, OU.
Jacobson, Jacob. "Von
Mendelssohn zu
Mendelssohn-Bartholdy," Leo
Baeck Institute Yearbook 5
(1960):251-61.
Kahn-Wallerstein, Carmen. "Die
Familie Mendelssohn,"
Deutsche Rundschau 70, no. 11

(1947):103-107.
Kanitz, Edwin. Die Familie
Mendelssohn mit ihrem
Stammvater Moses Mendelssohn.
Nach einem Original von
Cecilie Oppenheim, geb. von
Mendelssohn-Bartoldy.
Berlin: By the Author, 1929.
(1 Bl.) Includes "Eine
Nachkommenstafel der
Mannestamme." Descendants
table of the 10 children of
Moses Mendelssohn.
Kohut, Adolph. Moses
Mendelssohn und seine
Familie. Eine Festschrift
zum 100 jahrigen Todestage
Moses Mendelssohn's am 4.
Januar 1886. Dresden:
E. Pierson, 1886. 149 p.
CtY, MH, NN, OCH.
Kupferberg, Herbert. The
Mendelssohns: Three
Generations of Genius. New
York: C. Scribner's Sons,
1972. 272 p.
Mendelssohn, Moses. Denkmal
der Freundschaft:
Stammbuchblätter und
Widmungen von Moses
Mendelssohn. Berlin: Aldus
Druck, 1929. 38 p.
(Soncino-Gesellschaft der
Freunde des Jüdischer Buches.
Sonderpublikation, Nr. 3.)
NN, PPDrop.
Meyer, Herrmann. Die Vorfahren
von Moses und Fromet
Mendelssohn. Jerusalem,
1967. 8 p. JNUL.
"New Light on the Family of
Felix Mendelssohn," Hebrew
Union College Annual 26
(1955):543-65.
Obst, Arthur. "Die Familie
Mendelssohn in Hamburg,"
Hamburger Fremdenblatt 31
(1909).
Petitpierre, Jacques. The
Romance of the Mendelssohns.
New York: Roy, 1950. 251 p.
Pudor. Internationalen
Verwandtschaftlichen. Vol. 2
includes a section on
Mendelssohn family. See
GENERAL WORKS.

Rachel and Wallich. Berliner
Grosskaufleute, 3:98-111.
"Joseph Mendelssohn
(1770-1848)." Also,
"Stammbaum Mendelssohn
(1729-1930)," at end of book.
See GENERAL WORKS.
Reissner, H.G. "Alexander von
Humboldt in Verkehr mit der
Familie Josef Mendelssohns,"
Mendelssohn-Studien (Berlin)
2 (1975):141-82.
Rosenstein. Unbroken Chain,
pp. 119ff. Genealogical
chart. See GENERAL WORKS.
Schneider, Max Ferdinand.
Mendelssohn oder Bartholdy?
Zur Geschichte eines
Familiennamens. Basel:
Internationale
Felix-Mendelssohn-Gesellschaf,
1962. 28 p. CU, MH, NN,
OC1.
Schulte. Bonner Juden, p. 379.
See GENERAL WORKS.
Steiner, Ludwig. "Die Familie
Moses Mendelssohn," B'nai
B'rith: Monatsblätter der
Grossloge für dem
Cechoslowakischen
Staat-J.O.B.B. (Prague) 8,
no. 7 (1929).
Tramer, H. "Die Mendelssohns;
Geschichte einer
deutsch-jüdischen Familie,"
Mitteilungsblatt des Irgun
Olej Merkas Europa (Tel
Aviv), 9. Mai 1975, pp. 5-6.
Werner, E. "New Light on the
Family of Felix Mendelssohn,"
Hebrew Union College Annual
26 (1955):543-65.
Zielenziger. Deutschen
Wirtschaft, pp. 52-63. "Das
Haus Mendelssohn." See
GENERAL WORKS.

MENDES
AMH has family records.
CFM has family records.
JE, 8:487. Contains "Mendes
Pedigree-American Branch."
Descendants of David Pereira
Mendes (1740-1786), who left
Bayonne for Jamaica in 1786,
through late 19th century.

See GENERAL WORKS.
Mendes Family, Savannah,
Georgia. "Mendes Family
Records, 1885-1905." MS;
Xerox copies. AJA.
Emden. Jews of Britain,
pp. 14ff. "The Families of
Mendes and Da Costa." See
GENERAL WORKS.
Ginsburger, Ernest. "Marie de
Hongrie, Charles-Quint, les
veuves Mendes et les
néo-chrétiens," Revue de
Études Juives 89
(1930):179-192.
"Families of Mendes and Da
Costa," Gentleman's Magazine,
January 1812, pp. 21-24.
Roth, Cecil. The House of
Nasi: Doña Gracia.
Philadelphia: Jewish
Publications Society of
America, 1948. 208 p.
"Genealogical table," p. 82;
"The House of Mendes,"
pp. 3-20.
Stern. FAJF. Mendes family
tree beginning in Jamaica.
See GENERAL WORKS.

MENDES DA COSTA
AMH has family records.
Familieminder Tilegnet. Mendes
da Costa family, pp. 105-106.
See GENERAL WORKS.

MENDES-FRANCE
Mendès-France, Pierre. "Mes
Origines," L'Arche 19 (Mai
1976):36-40. Interview with
Victor Malka.
Nantet, Jacques. Pierre
Mendès-France. Paris:
Éditions du Centurion, 1967.
272 p. "La famille et
l'enfance," pp. 19-23. CSt,
DLC, NIC, NN.

MENDESIA
Roth, Cecil. The House of
Nasi: Doña Gracia.
Philadelphia: Jewish
Historical Society of
England, 1948. 208 p. About
Gracia Mendesia,

ca. 1510-1569? Family tree,
p. 82.

MENDES SEIXAS
Lucius Levy Solomons
(1863-1940) of San Francisco
Papers. Contain Abraham
Mendes Seixas family tree.
WJHC.

MENDEZ
AMH has family records.
JE, 8:245. Contains "Family
Tree of the Machado Family of
New York," descendants of
David Mendez Machado,
d. 1753, through early 19th
century. See GENERAL WORKS.
Birmingham. The Grandees. See
GENERAL WORKS.
Phillips, N. Taylor. "Family
History of the Rev. David
Mendez Machado," Publications
of the American Jewish
Historical Society 2
(1894):45-61.
Wolf, "Anglo-Jewish Families."
See GENERAL WORKS.

MENDL
AMH has family records.
CFM has family records.
Kempelen. Magyarországi Zsidó,
2:55. See GENERAL WORKS.

MENDOZA
AMH has family records.
CFM has family records.

MENIR
Leroy, Béatrice. "Une famille
de la judería de Tudela aux
XIIIe et XIVe siècles; les
Menir," Revue des Études
Juives 136 (1977):277-95.
"Indications généalogiques
sur la famille Menir au
Portugal," pp. 292-93. 13th
to 15th century; Navarre.

MENKE
AMH has family records.

MENKEL
Schulte. Bonner Juden, p. 381.
See GENERAL WORKS.

MENKEN
Schulte. Bonner Juden, p. 385.
See GENERAL WORKS.
Solis, Elvira Nathan, d. 1963.
"Correspondence and research
notes for genealogical
studies of the Etting,
Menken, Nathan, and Nones
Families." AJHS.
Stern. FAJF. Menken family
tree beginning in Westphalia.
Originally, name possibly was
Davis. See GENERAL WORKS.

MENKO
CAJ has family tree from
Holland, 1742-1960.
Menko Family. Papers, 1980.
1 folder. Include photocopy
of family tree, 1671 to
present. Family of Bavaria.
PJAC.

MENKO-HARTOGENESIS
Kempelen. Magyarországi Zsidó,
3:79. See GENERAL WORKS.

MENSER
AMH has family records.

MENTZ
Kempelen. Magyarországi Zsidó,
3:133. See GENERAL WORKS.

MENUHIN
Rolfe, Lionel Menuhin. The
Menuhins: A Family Odyssey.
San Francisco: Panjandrum
Books, 1978. 256 p.
Genealogical tables,
pp. xvi-xvii. Original
spelling of name was Mnuchin.
Family from Gomel and
Lubavitch, Russia. CtY, DLC,
ICarbS, N, NjP, NN, NNJ, OCH,
OCl, TxU.

MENZ
Tänzer. Juden in Tirol,
pp. 750-51. See GENERAL
WORKS.

MENZELES
AMH has family records.

MENZIES
AMH has family records.

MERCADO
See DE MERCADO.
CFM has family records.
Samuel, E.R. "Portuguese Jews
in Jacobean London,"
Transactions of the Jewish
Historical Society of England
18 (1958):181.

MERCEDES
Kempelen. Magyarországi Zsidó,
3:27. See GENERAL WORKS.

MEREDITH
AMH has family records.

MERETSKY
Worley, Carolyn Joy. The
Family of the Golden Flag:
100th Anniversary of the
Meretskys in Windsor,
1881-1981. Elberton, Ga.,
1981. 131 p. Consists of
transcriptions of documents,
photographs, and genealogical
forms relating to family of
Windsor, Ontario, Canada.
AJA, AJHS.

MERGULIES
See Daniel Jay Rottenberg entry
under ROTTENBERG.

MERKLER
Kempelen. Magyarországi Zsidó,
3:49. See GENERAL WORKS.

MERLIN
Paul, Albert. Une famille
lorraine: Les Merlin de
Thionville. Metz, 1949.
YIVO.

MERMELSTEIN
See George M. Gross entry under
GROSS. Family originally
from Munkács, Hungary.

MERRY
AMH has family records.

MERSEL
AMH has family records.

MERTON
AMH has family records.
CFM has family records.

MERX
CAJ has family records.

MERZBACH
LBIS has family tree.
Reychman. Szkice
genealogiczne, pp. 135-36.
See GENERAL WORKS.

MERZBACHER
LBI has family trees beginning
1730 and 1845.

MESQUITA
AMH has family records.

MESSEL
CFM has family records.

MESSER
AJA has genealogical files of
family of Eric Brysk.
Includes Messer family.

MESTERTON
Semi-Gotha, 1:130. See GENERAL
WORKS.

MESZAROS
Kempelen. Magyarországi Zsidó,
3:32. Mészáros family. See
GENERAL WORKS.

METZ
See DE METZ.
CAJ has family tree from
Amsterdam.

METZON
Metzon, Hans. Mine forfaeder.
CAJ.

MEXBOROUGH
AMH has family records.

MEYER
See BRANDT-MEYER.
AMH has family records.
CAJ has family tree.
CAJD has family tree from
Germany.
CFM has family records.

LBI has family trees beginning 1680, 1707, 1780, 1797, 1862, and 1875.

LBIS has family tree.

Corwin, Henri Max. "Geslacht Meyler." Oldenzaal, 1960. 19 p. Genealogical table starts with Levy Marcus Meyer, 1720-1800, from Vriezenveen, and continues to 1950s. Family of Holland. BR; CAJ, Call No. 1004.

Frank. Nashville Jewry, p. 147. See GENERAL WORKS.

Meyer, Daniel E. Papers. Peggy Boynton, comp., "Abraham and Elsie Meyer Family Tree, 1825-1938." Family of San Francisco. WJHC.

Meyer, Henry O. A Brief Account of the Family of Oser Meyer and Bertha Michelson Meyer and Its Relationship to the Michelsons.... South San Francisco, Calif., [1969]. 35 p. Typescript. Covers 1824-1969. WJHC.

Meyer, Lewis. Mostly Mama. Garden City, N.Y.: Doubleday, 1971. 216 p. Family in Oklahoma.

Richter, John H. The Ancestors of Emil Louis Meyer and Helen Levy Meyer of Hannover, Germany. Ann Arbor, Mich., 1963. 11 p. LBI.

Schulte. Bonner Juden, pp. 386-97. See GENERAL WORKS.

Seckbach, Markus. Eine Ahnentafel von 27 Generationen bis zum Jahre 1290. Betr. die Familien Seckbach, Meyer, Auerbach, Marx. Bodenheimer u.a. Hamburg: Laubhuttee, 1936. 22 p. OCH.

Semi-Gotha, 2:112. See GENERAL WORKS.

MEYERBEER
See Gerhard Ballin entry under BEER.

MEYER-COHEN
AMH has family records.

MEYERFELD
See Nathan M. Reiss entry under EDELMUTH. Includes Meyerfeld family.

MEYERS
AMH has family records. CAJ has family archives, 1818-1857.

MEYERSTEIN
CFM has family records.

MEYLERT
See Stern, FAJF entry under MAILERT.

MEYSELS
"Das Testament Mardochai Meysels in Prag," MGWJ 1893, p. 25.

MEYUHAS
Ben-Yaacob, Abraham. Jerusalem within Its Walls: The History of the Meyuhas Family. Jerusalem, 1976.

MEZA
Margolinsky, Julius. "Abraham Gotfred de Meza og hans Familie; nogle Studier omkring en glemt Gravsten i Møllegade," Jødisk Samfund (København) 26 (Jan. 1955):12-18. Family of Denmark. YIVO.

MEZEI
Kempelen. Magyarországi Zsidó, 1:31, 32, 33; 3:55. See GENERAL WORKS.

MIARA
AMH has family records.

MICHAEL
AMH has family records. CFM has family records. Duckesz, Eduard. Geschichte des Hauses Michael in Hamburg 1683 bis 1893. Hamburg,

1927. 27 p. LBI.
Geschichte der Familie Unna.
Hamburg, Kopenhagen, n.d.
Includes Michael family.
CAJ.
Michael, M. "Das Leben der
Juden in Hamburg um die Mitte
des 19. Jahrhunderts."
Jerusalem, 1956. 5 p. Brief
history of family in Hamburg,
Berlin, and Frankfurt. LBI.

MICHAEL DAVID
See Gronemann entry under
DAVID.

MICHAELIS
AMH has family records.
CFM has family records.
See Esmond S. De Beer entry
under BARDEN.

MICHAELS
AJA has genealogical files.
AMH has family records.
Stern. FAJF. Michaels family
trees beginning in:
(I) Herzfeld, Germany (also
originally spelled Jechiel,
Mikal, and Michal); and
(II) Montreal. See GENERAL
WORKS.

MICHAELSON
AMH has family records.
Fischer, Josef.
J.C.E. Michaelson og hustrus
forfaedre. København:
Hertz, 1913. 31 p. Printed
as MS. Descendants of Lob
Saul Löwenstamm. OCH.
Semi-Gotha, 1:101. See GENERAL
WORKS.

MICHAL
See Stern, FAJF (I) entry under
MICHAELS.

MICHALOWSKI
Rothmann, Adolph Abraham.
Familiengeschichte.
Karkur/Palästina, 1940.
12 p. Includes Michalowski,
Rothmann, Casper,
Munderstein, and Wolff
families of Posen. LBI.

MICHEL
Kempelen. Magyarországi Zsidó,
1:7, 39; 2:45, 72. See
GENERAL WORKS.
Schnee. Hoffinanz und Staat,
1:23-31. "Der 'Reiche
Michel.'" Family of
Brandenburg-Prussia, 16th to
17th century. See GENERAL
WORKS.

MICHELHAM
AMH has family records.

MICHELSON
Meyer, Henry O. A Brief
Account of the Family of Oser
Meyer and Bertha Michelson
Meyer and Its Relationship to
the Michelsons.... South San
Francisco, Calif., [1969].
35 p. Typescript. Covers
1824-1969. WJHC.
Rosenstein. Unbroken Chain,
pp. 452ff. See GENERAL
WORKS.

MICHIELS
AMH has family records.

MICHL
Kempelen. Magyarországi Zsidó,
2:93. See GENERAL WORKS.

MICHLIN
Yaoz. Album Shel. See GENERAL
WORKS.

MICHOLLS
AMH has family records.
CFM has family records.

MICKLESHANSKI
Abravanel-Mickleshanski-
Freedman-London Families,
1762-1948. Printed and
Handwritten. AJA.

MIER
AMH has family records.

MIESES
Ginzig, E. Toledot Fabius
Mieses. Krakow, 1890.
German and Austrian family of
scholars of 19th century.

MIHALY
Kempelen. Magyarországi Zsidó,
2:72. Mihály family. See
GENERAL WORKS.

MIHELFFY
Kempelen. Magyarországi Zsidó,
2:72. See GENERAL WORKS.

MIKAL
See Stern, FAJF (I) entry under
MICHAELS.

MIKLOS
Kempelen. Magyarországi Zsidó,
1:84, 85, 145. Miklós
family. See GENERAL WORKS.

MIKSZATH
Kempelen. Magyarországi Zsidó,
3:91. Mikszáth family. See
GENERAL WORKS.

MILASSIN
Kempelen. Magyarországi Zsidó,
1:16. See GENERAL WORKS.

MILCH
Kempelen. Magyarországi Zsidó,
2:22. See GENERAL WORKS.

MILHAUD
Labande, L.H. "Familles juives
d'Avignon," Chercheurs et
Curieux 47 (1903):236. On
Milhaud family.
Milhaud, Darius. Notes Without
Music. New York: Alfred A.
Knopf, 1953. 355 p.
Autobiography of the French
composer (1892-1974), a
descendant of an old family
from Aix-en Province.
"Origins," pp. 3-8, and "My
Childhood," pp. 9-20.
Milhaud's mother was born in
Marseilles of the Allatini
family originating in Modena,
Italy.

MILKIN
Rusinek, Alla. Like a Song;
Like a Dream: A Soviet Girl's
Quest for Freedom. New York:
Scribner's Sons, 1973. 267
p. Story of Alla Milkin

Rusinek's discovery of her
Jewish identity and her
efforts to emigrate to
Israel. Her mother was
Polina Glazman (1910-?), the
daughter of Abram and Sarah
Glazman from Dvinsk and
Vologda. Her father was
Tsalik Milkin (1901-1960)
from Tchardjow, Turkmenia.
The author married Yosif
Rusinek, whose family came
from Liepaja, Latvia.

MILLER
See MEHLER.
AMH has family records.
Keneseth Israel. See GENERAL
WORKS.
Miller, Benjamin, 1907-1971.
Papers, 1875, 1952-1975.
1 folder and 1 book.
Genealogical information
about his relatives, the Romm
family, are among the papers.
Dr. Miller was a physician
and author from Cincinnati,
Ohio. PJAC.

MILLHISER
Millhiser family. "The
Descendants of Arkiba
Millhiser." Beth Ahabah
Archives, Richmond, Virginia.

MILLS
AMH has family records.

MILNS
See Esmond S. De Beer entry
under BARDEN.

MINACCIATI
Raphael, F. "La famiglia
ebraica Minacciati," Rassegna
Mensile di Israel 41
(1975):221-45.

MINDEN
AMH has family records.
Hirsch, F. "Das Haus [Georg
und Franka] Minden," in
Gegenwart im Röckblick;
Festgabe für die jüdische
Gemeinde zu Berlin
(Heidelberg: L. Stiehm,

1970), pp. 257-64. CLU, CSt, DLC, IEN, NNJ, WU.

MINDL
CAJ (Call No. 4318) has family chart entitled, "The Feibelmanns from Rulzheim," which lists more than 880 descendants of Jakob Feibelmann (1732-1796). Includes Mindl family.

MINIS
JE, 8:597. Contains "Pedigree of the Minis Family" through early 20th century. Family of U.S., descendants of Abraham Minis, who left England in 1733. See GENERAL WORKS.
Minis Family Papers, 1733-1960. Include genealogical data for family of Georgia. AJA.
"The Minis Family," Georgia Historical Quarterly 1 (1917).
Stern. FAJF. Minis family tree beginning in England. See GENERAL WORKS.

MINTZ
See Meyer Ellenbogen entry under KATZENELLENBOGEN. Includes genealogical table.
"Gaon Reb Judah Mintz [and Descendants]: A Genealogical Chart." N.p., 19- . Includes Rabbinowitz family. NN.
Sefer Hamishpacha. Ot. Haifa, Sept. 1964. 110 p. Family trees for descendants of Eliezer (d. 1889) and Bluma (d. 1891) Kaplushnick; Yitzchok (d. 1908) and Chaya (d. 1900) Shevetz; Feiga and Velvel (d. 1918) Mintz from Smiatitz (?); Leah (d. 1937) and Altar (d. 1926) Kashnich from Smiatitz (?); and Malka-Raiza (d. 1935) and Yisrael-Aharon Monzer from Kamenets-Litovsk. JNUL.

MINZ
JE, 8:604. Contains family tree through mid-19th century. See GENERAL WORKS.
Eisenstadt and Wiener. Da'at Kedoschim. Includes Minz family of Russia. See GENERAL WORKS.
JFF, no. 37. Family history. Rosenstein. Unbroken Chain, pp. 104ff. See GENERAL WORKS.

MIRANDA
CFM has family records.

MIRBACH-KOSMANOS
Kempelen. Magyarországi Zsidó, 2:100. See GENERAL WORKS.

MIREL
AJA has James Mirel family tree from Cincinnati.

MIRELS
AMH has family records.
Löwenstein, L. "Stammbaum der Familie Mirels," Blätter für Jüdische Geschichte und Literatur 4 (1930):1-5, 33-37, 49-54, 113-20, 129, 159-60.

MIRKES
Rosenstein. Unbroken Chain, pp. 237ff. The Mirkes descendants of the R. Solomon Zalman Katzenellenbogen. See GENERAL WORKS.

MITCHELL
AJA has genealogical files.
AMH has family records.
Stern. FAJF. Mitchell family tree beginning in Lissa, Poland. See GENERAL WORKS.

MITFORD
AMH has family records.

MITNICK
Mitnick, Martin Alan. "The Mitnick Family: Four Generations of Baltimore

Lawyers," Generations (Jewish
Historical Society of
Maryland, Baltimore) 2
(Dec. 1981).

MITTELMANN
Kempelen. Magyarországi Zsidó,
3:52. See GENERAL WORKS.

MITTENTHAL
Smith, Julia Frances. Aaron
Copeland: His Work and
Contribution to American
Music. New York: Dutton,
1955. 336 p. Pp. 11-14.
The famous American composer
is the son of Harris Kaplan
(b. 1860) and Sarah
Mittenthal (b. 1862) and the
grandson of Sussman and Freda
Kaplan and Aron and Bertha
Mittenthal. The Kaplan
family was originally from
Shavel, Lithuania, near
Kovno; the Mittenthal family
was from Vistinich,
Lithuania, near Königsberg,
Prussia.

MITTLER
Kempelen. Magyarországi Zsidó,
1:109; 3:138. See GENERAL
WORKS.

MITZ (DE)
See DE MITZ.

MLOCKI-DZIOKOWSKI
Kempelen. Magyarországi Zsidó,
2:101. See GENERAL WORKS.

MNUCHIN
See MENUHIN.

MOBERLY
AMH has family records.

MOCATTA
AMH has family records.
CFM has family records.
JE, 8:636. Contains "Mocatta
Pedigree" through late 19th
century. Anglo-Jewish
family, descendants of Moses
Mocatta, d. London, 1677.
See GENERAL WORKS.

Familieminder Tilegnet.
Mocatta family, pp. 102-104,
108-110. See GENERAL WORKS.
Wolf, "Anglo-Jewish Families."
See GENERAL WORKS.

MOCHIACH
AMH has family records.

MODEL
LBI has family tree beginning
1699.
Löwenstein, L.
"Model-Öttingen," Jahrbuch
für Jüdische Literatur und
Gesellschaft 8
(1910):202-203. Descendants
of Simon Günzburg, d. 1585.

MODENA (DA)
Simonsohn, Shlomo. "Leon da
Modena: A Monograph Based on
Hitherto Unpublished
Manuscripts." Ph.D.
dissertation, University
College, University of
London, 1952. 775 p.
Includes chapter on da Modena
family as well as
genealogical table. Modena
was an Italian rabbi,
scholar, and writer,
1571-1645.

MODIGLIANI
CFM has family records.

MOEREL
Register betreffende de
Families Hollander en Moerel,
1770-1929. [Samengest. door
Magdalena Esther
Polak-Hollander.] Groningen,
1929. Family of Netherlands.
BR.

MOGADOURO
CFM has family records.

MOGALEVITCH
See Harry and Nellie Lepsky
entry under CHALEPSKY.

MOHR
See Esmond S. De Beer entry
under BARDEN.

MOISE
Moïse, Harold. The Moïse
Family of South Carolina: An
Account of the Life and
Descendants of Abraham and
Sarah Moïse Who Settled in
Charleston, South Carolina,
in the Year 1791 A.D.
Columbia, S.C.: R.L. Bryan,
1961. 304 p. DLC; MB; NN;
OCH.
Stern. FAJF. Moise family
tree beginning in Alsace.
See GENERAL WORKS.

MOLEVITZ
See Harry and Nellie Lepsky
entry under CHALEPSKY.

MOLL
LBI has family tree beginning
1516.

MOLLE
See Harry and Nellie Lepsky
entry under CHALEPSKY.

MOLLERSTIERNA
Semi-Gotha, 2:15.
Möllerstierna family. See
GENERAL WORKS.

MOLLERSVARD
Semi-Gotha, 1:76. Möllersvärd
family. See GENERAL WORKS.

MOLNAR
See SIMAY-MOLNAR.
Kempelen. Magyarországi Zsidó,
2:17, 70, 88, 89, 94, 102,
104, 144. Molnár family.
See GENERAL WORKS.

MOMASZTERLY
Kempelen. Magyarországi Zsidó,
2:106. See GENERAL WORKS.

MOMMSEN
CAJ has family records.

MONASCH
Fraenkel, Peter, ed. "The
Memoirs of B.L. Monasch of
Krotoschin," LBI Yearbook 24
(1979):195-223. Includes
genealogical information.

Baer Loew Monasch (1801-1876)
was a printer and publisher
of Jewish books at Krotoschin
(Krotoszyn) in the province
of Posen (Poznán). The
Monasch and Monash families
of Australia are descendants.
Baer Loew was the grandfather
of General John Monash of
Australia.

MONASH
Apple, Raymond. "A Note on the
Jewish Genealogy of Sir John
Monash," Journal and
Proceedings of the Australian
Jewish Historical Society 4
pt. 6 (1957):333-34. Sir
John Monash (1865-1931),
Australian engineer and
soldier who commanded the
Australian forces during
W.W.I. His immigrant family
came from Vienna.

MOND
AMH has family records.
CFM has family records.
Cohen, John Michael. The Life
of Ludwig Mond. London:
Methuen & Co., Ltd., 1956.
295 p. Genealogical chart of
the Anglo-Jewish Mond family,
descendants of Meyer (d.
1820) and Zerlina (1788-1865)
Mond from Cassel, Germany,
p. XV. British family of
chemists and industrialists.
Ludwig Mond, b. Cassel,
Germany, 1839; d. 1909. CtY,
CU, ICU, MH, NIC, NN, OCH,
NjR, WU.
Goodman, Jean. The Mond
Legacy: A Family Saga.
London: Weidenfeld and
Nicolson, 1982. 272 p.
Genealogical table covers
1830-1981.
Heinemann, Leopold.
"Erinnerungen an Mond's,"
Jüd. Wochenzeitung für
Kassel 8, no. 2 (1931):1-3.

MONDOZA
AMH has family records.

MONDSCHEIN
Kempelen. Magyarországi Zsidó,
1:75. See GENERAL WORKS.

MONEY
AMH has family records.

MONFORTE
AMH has family records.
CFM has family records.

MONSANTO
CFM has family records.

MONSOWIZ
CAJ has family records.

MONTAGU
AMH has family records.
CFM has family records.
Montagu, Ivor Goldsmid Samuel.
The Youngest Son:
Autobiographical Sketches.
London: Lawrence and Wishart,
1970. 384 p. Genealogical
information on the
Anglo-Jewish families of
Montagu and Samuel, pp.
17-20, 27-28. Autobiography
covers the years 1904-1927 of
the author's youth. CLU,
CtY, CU, DLC, MH, NjP, NNC.

MONTAGUE
AMH has family records.

MONTALBA
CFM has family records.

MONTALTO
Szancer, Henryk. "De familie
Montalto," De Opbouw, Sept.
1962, pp. 4-7; Apr. 1963,
pp. 28ff.; Sept. 1963,
pp. 54-56; Juni 1964,
pp. 324-25. Sephardic family
from the Netherlands.

MONTBACH
Kempelen. Magyarországi Zsidó,
1:102. See GENERAL WORKS.

MONTEFIORE
See SEBAG-MONTEFIORE.
AMH has family records.
CFM has family records.

EJ, 12:273-74. Contains
genealogical tables.
Descendants of Judah (Leon)
Montefiore, b. ca. 1605,
through mid-20th century.
Anglo-Jewish family mainly.
See GENERAL WORKS.
JE, 8:664-65. "Montefiore
Pedigree." See GENERAL
WORKS.
Battersea, Constance (de
Rothschild) Flower, Baroness.
Reminiscences. London:
Macmillan & Co., Ltd., 1922.
470 p. Includes genealogical
tables. Contains family
pedigree of Montefiore and
Rothschild families.
Bermant. The Cousinhood
Genealogical table of
Anglo-Jewish family.
Burke's Landed Gentry, 1965.
Sebag-Montefiore.
Burke's Peerage and Baronetage,
1935. Bt. of Worth Park.
Burke's Peerage and Baronetage,
1885. Bt. of Isle of Thanet.
Cardozo, David Abraham
Jessurun. Think and Thank:
The Montefiore Synagogue and
College, Ramsgate, 1833-1933:
I. From the Dedication of the
Synagogue to the Death of Sir
Moses Montefiore, bart.,
1833-1885, by D.A. Jessurun
Cardozo. II. The Montefiore
Endowment, 1885-1933, by Paul
Goodman. London: Oxford
University Press, 1933.
200 p. Includes genealogical
table. DLC, NNC, OCH, OCl,
PPDrop.
Cohen, Lucy. Some
Recollections of Claude
Goldsmid Montefiore,
1858-1938. London: Faber &
Faber, 1940. 277 p.
Includes genealogical tables.
DLC, MH, NcD, NN, OCl,
PPDrop.
Crowther, George Rodney.
"Montefiore of Italy,
England, and the U.S.A."
Chevy Chase, Md., 1963.
21 p. Allen County Public
Library, Fort Wayne, Indiana.

Emden. Jews of Britain,
pp. 150ff. "Montefiores."
See GENERAL WORKS.
"The First Montefiore in
Australia," Journal and
Proceedings of the Australian
Jewish Historical Society 2,
pt. 9 (July 1948):467-71.
Goodman, Paul. Moses
Montefiore. Philadelphia:
Jewish Publication Society of
America, 1925. 255 p. "His
Family," pp. 23-29.
"Genealogical Table," p. 228.
DLC, MB, MiU, NcU, NIC, OCH,
OCl, PP, PPDrop, PPRF, TxU.
Munz, Hirsch. Jews in South
Australia, 1836-1936: An
Historical Outline.
Adelaide: Thornquest Press,
1936. 84 p. Includes
section on Montefiore family
in Australia. CtY, DLC, NN.
————. "The Montefiores:
Jews and the Centenary of
South Australia," Australian
Quarterly 9, no. 1
(1937):83-88.
Pudor. Internationalen
Verwandtschaftlichen. Vol. 3
contains section on
Montefiore family.
Wolf, "Anglo-Jewish Families."
See GENERAL WORKS.
Wolf, Lucien. Sir Moses
Montefiore: A Centennial
Biography; With Extracts from
Letters and Journals.
London: J. Murray, 1884.
290 p. Contains genealogical
pedigree. CtY, DLC, ICU, MB,
MH, NcD, NN, OCH, PPDrop.

MONTGOMERY
AMH has family records.
Semi-Gotha, 1:84. See GENERAL
WORKS.

MONZER
Sefer Hamishpacha. Ot. Haifa,
Sept. 1964. 110 p. Family
trees for descendants of
Eliezer (d. 1889) and Bluma
(d. 1891) Kaplushnick;
Yitzchok (d. 1908) and Chaya
(d. 1900) Shevetz; Feiga and

Velvel (d. 1918) Mintz from
Smiatitz (?); Leah (d. 1937)
and Altar (d. 1926) Kashnich
from Smiatitz (?);
Malka-Raiza (d. 1935) and
Yisrael-Aharon Monzer from
Kamenets-Litovsk. JNUL.

MOODS
AJA has genealogical files.

MOON
AMH has family records.

MOOS
Moos, Samuel. The History of
the Family Moos. Melbourne,
Australia, 1964. 97, 75 p.
Family originally from
Haigerloch/Hohenzollern/Rande
g. LBI.
Tänzer. Juden in Tirol,
pp. 752-53. See GENERAL
WORKS.

MORAIS (DE)
See DE MORAIS.

MORALES
AMH has family records.
CFM has family records.

MORALI
CAJ has family records from
Algiers, 1896-1946.

MORANGE
Stern. FAJF. Morange family
tree beginning in Bordeaux.
Family tree is listed in FAJF
under "Menken." See GENERAL
WORKS.

MORAVCSIK
Kempelen. Magyarországi Zsidó,
1:47. See GENERAL WORKS.

MORAWCZYK
Bałaban. Żydów w Krakowie
1:213, 216. See GENERAL
WORKS.

MORDAUNT
AMH has family records.

MORDECAI
AMH has family records.
Calder Family; Wilmington, N.C.
"Records And Recollections of
the Calder Family, Including
Information About the Lazarus
and Mordecai Families of
Charleston, S.C., 1757-1959."
Typescript. Xerox copy.
AJA.
CFM has family records.
Mordecai Family Papers,
1707-1955. Include
genealogical data. Mainly
family of Southern U.S. AJA.
Myers Family Papers, 1790-1900.
Includes genealogical data on
Myers, Mordecai, Hays, and
other Jewish families of
Virginia. Virginia
Historical Society Library,
Richmond, Virginia.
Myers-Mordecai-Hays Collection.
Includes genealogy of the
Judah Hays family, Virginia,
n.d. AJA.
Cohen, Caroline (Myers).
Records of the Myers, Hays,
and Mordecai Families from
1707-1913. Washington, D.C.:
By the Author, 1913? 57 p.
Descendants of Jacob
Mordecai, 1762-1838. DLC,
NN, OCH, PPDrop.
Holland, S.H. "The First
Jewish Child Born in
Washington, D.C., and the
Mordecai Family," The Record
(The Publication of the
Jewish Historical Society of
Greater Washington) 2
(Jan. 1967):2-8. Rosa
Mordecai, 1839-1936.
Mordecai Family. "Biographical
and Genealogical Data,
Supplied by Mrs. Arthur
Kunzelman, St. Louis, Mo.,
1707-1955." Concerning Moses
Mordecai and his descendants.
AJA.
Mordecai, Ellen Mordecai.
Gleanings from Long Ago.
Raleigh, N.C.: Raleigh
Historic Properties
Commission, 1974. 132 p.
"Reprint, with new

introduction and index of the
1933 ed. published by Braid &
Hutton, Savannah." The index
by Elizabeth D. Reid provides
a comprehensive list of the
members of this North
Carolina family with dates of
their life spans. Most
members eventually converted,
however. CtY, DLC, ICN, NcU.
Mordecai, John Brooke.
"Genealogy of the Mordecai
Family of Virginia and North
Carolina." Virginia
Historical Society, Richmond,
Va.
Stern. FAJF. Mordecai family
trees beginning in: (I) Bonn,
Germany; (II) England; and
(III) Teltz, Lithuania. See
GENERAL WORKS.

MOREIRA
CFM has family records.

MOREL
AMH has family records.

MORENA
CFM has family records.

MORENO
Semi-Gotha, 1:154. See GENERAL
WORKS.

MORGAN
"Genealogical chart presented
to Rabbi Merle E. Singer by
Mrs. David J. Morgan, both
sixth-generation descendants
of Rev. Menachem Mendel of
Kotzk." Philadelphia, Pa.,
Oct. 12, 1973. 1 p. Family
tree which traces Singer and
Morgan families from Reb
Menahem Mendel of Kotzk.
AJA.

MORGENSTERN
Kempelen. Magyarországi Zsidó,
1:146. See GENERAL WORKS.
Rosenstein. Unbroken Chain,
pp. 441ff. Chassidic Dynasty
of Morgenstern of Kotsk. See
GENERAL WORKS.

MORISON
AMH has family records.

MORITZ
Semi-Gotha, 1:116ff. See
GENERAL WORKS.

MORLEY
AMH has family records.

MORNER
Semi-Gotha, 1:18, 45. Mörner
family. See GENERAL WORKS.

MORO
AMH has family records.
CFM has family records.

MORON
CFM has family records.
Locker, Zvi. "Simon Isaac
Henriquez Moron: Homme
d'affaires de la Grand'anse;
Esquisse," Revue de la
Société Hatïenne d'Histoire
de Géographie et de Géologie,
no. 125 (décembre
1979):56-69. Moron was in
all probability the founder
of the village of Moron,
Haiti.

MORPURGO
CAJ has family records.
Morpurgo, Edgardo. La famiglia
Morpurgo di Gradisca sull'
Isonzo, 1585-1885. Padova:
Premiata Società Cooperativa
Tipografica, 1909. 110 p.
Contains 6 genealogical
tables. MH, NN, OCH.
———. "Intorno all famiglia
Morpurgo di Gradisca, nuove
ricerche," La Rivista
Israelitica 7 (1910):233-39.
———. Notizie sulle Famiglie
Ebree Esistite a Padova nel
XVI Secolo. Udine: D. del
Bianco, 1909. 27 p.
Reprinted from Corriere
Israelitico, nos. 6-9,
1908-1909. NN, NNJ.

MORRIS
AJA has genealogical files.
AMH has family records.

Morris, Jo Ann. "Genealogy of
the Morris-Brooks Family."
Louisville, Ky., 1975. AJA.
Morris, Margie. "My Family."
Genealogical information
concerning the Morris-Frockt
family. Louisville, Ky.
AJA.

MORRISON
Stern. FAJF. Morrison family
tree beginning in London.
See GENERAL WORKS.

MORTERA
CFM has family records.

MORTIMER
AMH has family records.

MOSBACHER
CAJ, Call No. 4452, has 3-page
list of descendants of
Seligmann Mosbacher,
b. Mosbach, 1826; d. 1910.
Covers 1826-1953.

MOSCATI
CAJ has family records.

MOSCHELES
CFM has family records.

MOSE, MOSSE, MOYSE
Haes, Frank. "Moyse Hall, Bury
St. Edmonds. Whence Its
Name--What It Was--What It
Was Not," Transactions of the
Jewish Historical Society of
England 3 (1899):18-24.
Notes on the name Moyse,
Mose, Mosse in use temp.,
1560-1620, are on pp. 23-24.

MOSELEY
AMH has family records.

MOSELY
AMH has family records.

MOSENTHAL
AMH has family records.
CFM has family records.
Emden. Jews of Britain,
pp. 388-390. "The
Mosenthals." See GENERAL

WORKS.

Lazarus, Felix. "Aus Salomon Herrman Mosenthal's Ahnengalerie," _JFF_, no. 37 (1934):628-31. Salomon Herrmann Mosenthal, 1821-1877, Vienna poet.

MOSES

See MAASS.

AMH has family records.

CFM has family records.

Gratz-Moses Family, Philadelphia. Biographical Information, 1883, 1898, 1900, 1945, 1962, 1980. Includes a Xeroxed family history. PJAC.

LBI has family trees beginning 1600 and 1757.

Moses Family. Papers, 1767-1941. Include genealogical material for family of New York City. AJHS.

Moses Family of New York City Papers, 1767-1941. Includes data and correspondence relating to the genealogy and history of Moses family and related families. AJHS.

Moses Family, New Orleans. "Family History, 1607-1915." 1974. Typescript. AJA.

"The Ancestry of the Children of Henry Phillips Moses and Charlotte Virginia Emanuel," _St. Charles_ 1 (Jan. 1935):83-117. Never completed. 18th to early 19th century.

See Daniel J. Cohen entry under CLEVE. Moses family from Friedrichstadt, Germany, pp. 45-47.

"Diary and Genealogical Notes Kept by Aaron Levy (1771-1852)," _Publications of the American Jewish Historical Society_ 27 (1920):335-45. Includes Moses family of New York, originally of Hesse.

Fischer, Josef and Th. Hauch-Fausboll. _Familien Philipsen i Pilestraede._

København, 1920. 145 p. Descendants of Nathan Moses, d. 1675, Altona, Germany. OCH.

"Items Relating to the Moses and Levy Families, New York," _Publications of the American Jewish Historical Society_ 27 (1920):331.

Moffat, Abbot Low, comp. "The Descendants of David Lopez and Priscilla Moses." AJA. Corrected by Harold Moïse in his _The Moïse Family of South Carolina and Their Descendants._ (See Harold Moïse entry under MOISE.)

Moses, Henry Phillips. "Genealogy of the Moses Family of South Carolina and Georgia." AJA.

See Stern, _FAJF_ entry under MOSS.

Stern. _FAJF._ Moses family trees beginning in: (I) England; (II) Giessen; (III) Bederkese, Hanover; (IV, V, and VI) U.S.; and (VII and VIII) Amsterdam. See GENERAL WORKS.

MOSHER

Chamberlain, Mildred and Laura Clarenbach. _Descendants of Hugh Mosher and Rebecca Maxson through Seven Generations._ By the Authors, 1980. 808 p. AJA, AJHS.

MOSKOWITZ

Kempelen. _Magyarországi Zsidó_, 2:45, 88; 3:93. See GENERAL WORKS.

MOSLER

Salzer-Mosler Family, Cincinnati. "Genealogical Data; [In] English, German and Hebrew." Family from Germany, beginning 1765. AJA.

MOSLEY

AMH has family records.

MOSS
AMH has family records.
CFM has family records.
See Esmond S. De Beer entry
under BARDEN.
AJA has Jacob Moss genealogical
files.
Moss, Sanford. Moss-Harris
Pedigree. Somerville, Mass.,
1934, 1937, 1940, 1943.
AJHS.
Stern. FAJF. Moss family tree
beginning in London.
Originally Moses. See
GENERAL WORKS.

MOSSE
See MOSE, MOSSE, MOYSE.
Neumann, Otto. "Rudolf Mosse's
Ahnen," JFF, no. 38/39
(1935):665-69, 685-87.
Rudolf Mosse, German
publisher and philanthropist,
b. Grätz, Posen, Germany,
1843; d. 1920. He
established his publishing
firm in Berlin.

MOSSERIS
Grunwald, Kurt. "On Cairo's
Lombard Street," Tradition
17, no. 1 (1972):8-22.
Banking family; genealogy
table, ca. 1800-1952.

MOSTYN
AMH has family records.

MOUNTAIN
See Esmond S. De Beer entry
under BARDEN.

MOURADGEA
Semi-Gotha, 1:153ff. See
GENERAL WORKS.

MOURADGEA-D'OHSSON
Semi-Gotha, 1:153.
Mouradgea-d'Ohsson family.
See GENERAL WORKS.

MOVSHOVITZ
CAJ has family records.

MOYSE
See MOSE, MOSSE, MOYSE.

MOYZEY
AMH has family records.

MOZLEY
CFM has family records.

MUALLEM
Muallem, David. Sefer Toledot
Vezichronot David Muallem.
Tel Aviv, 1971. 79 p.,
plus 17 pages of pictures and
documents. Family originated
in Baghdad and came to
Israel. JNUL.

MUEHSAM, MUHSAM
LBI has Muehsam family trees
beginning 1394, 1747, 1785,
and 1840.
Mühsam, Siegfried. Geschichte
des namens Mühsam.
Nachamtlichen Urkunden und
mundlicher überlieferung
aufgezeichnet.
Familien-Chronik. 2. Aufl.
Lübeck: Druck von Werner und
Hörnig, 1912. Family of
Prague, descendants of
Seligmann Pappenheim and his
wife, Hind Crzellitz, early
18th century. MH.

MUGDAN
LBI has family tree beginning
1790.

MUHLHAUS
AMH has family records.

MUHR
Brann, Markus. Abraham Muhr.
Ein Lebensbild [und ein
Beitrag zur Geschichte der
Juden in Scheisen].
[Neuaufl.] O.O. u.J. 65.
1 genealogical table.
Abraham Muhr, 1781-1847.
LBI.

MUHSAM
See MUEHSAM, MUHSAM.

MULLEN
See SALSBURY.

MULLER
CAJ has family records from
Hungary.
Kempelen. Magyarországi Zsidó,
2:24, 134; 3:70, 123. Müller
family. See GENERAL WORKS.

MUNCHEIMER
Reychman. Szkice
genealogiczne, pp. 137-39.
See GENERAL WORKS.

MUNDERSTEIN
Rothmann, Adolph Abraham.
Familiengeschichte.
Karkur/Palästina, 1940.
12 p. Includes Munderstein,
Rothmann, Casper,
Michalowski, and Wolff
families of Posen. LBI.

MUNELES
CAJ has family records.

MUNI
Lawrence, Jerome. Actor: The
Life and Times of Paul Muni.
New York: G.P. Putnam's Sons,
1974. 380 p. Especially
pages 15-60. Paul Muni
(1895-1967) was born in
Lemberg, Austria (now Lwow)
of a Hungarian vaudeville
family. He was born Muni
Weisenfreund, the son of
Nachum Favel and Salche
Weisenfreund.

MUNK
"Identität der Familien Theomin
und Munk," MGWJ 55
(1911):349-57.
Kempelen. Magyarországi Zsidó,
2:95, 124. See GENERAL
WORKS.
See Bernát Munkácsi entry under
AUSTERLITZ.
Wachstein, Bernhard. "Wer sind
die Prager Munk im 16.
Jahr.?" ZGJD 1 (1929):141-51.

MUNKACSI
Kempelen. Magyarországi Zsidó,
2:16, 95. Munkácsi family.
See GENERAL WORKS.

MUNZER
Ballin. Juden in Seesen,
p. 221. Münzer family. See
GENERAL WORKS.

MURAWSKI
Conrich, J. Lloyd. "The
Murawski Family." 1964.
WJHC.

MURAY
Kempelen. Magyarországi Zsidó,
1:73. See GENERAL WORKS.

MURGI
CFM has family records.

MURPHY
AMH has family records.

MURRAY
Semi-Gotha, 1:99, 138. See
GENERAL WORKS.

MUSAPHIA
CFM has family records.

MUSHKIN
AJA has family tree of family
of Milwaukee beginning in
18th-century Russia.

MYCENMACHER
See Judith A. Walters entry
under GRYNSZPAN.

MYER
AMH has family records.
CFM has family records.
See Stern, FAJF (VIII) entry
under MYERS.

MYERS
AMH has family records.
CFM has family records.
Myers Family Papers, 1790-1900.
Includes genealogical data on
Myers, Mordecai, Hays, and
other Jewish families of
Virginia. Virginia
Historical Society Library,
Richmond, Virginia.
Myers-Mordecai-Hays Collection.
Includes genealogy of the
Judah Hays family, Virginia,
n.d. AJA.

Brockman, Herbert. "A Study of the Myers Family of Norfolk: Their Business and Other Activities As Reflected in the Microfilmed Papers in the American Jewish Archives." Term Paper, Hebrew Union College-Jewish Institute of Religion, Cincinnati, Ohio, March 1, 1968. AJA.

Cohen, Caroline (Myers). Records of the Myers, Hays, and Mordecai Families from 1707-1913. Washington, D.C.: By the Author, 1913? 57 p. Descendants of Myer Myers, 1723-1795. DLC, NN, OCH, PPDrop.

"The Family of Major Mordecai Myers," Rhode Island Jewish Historical Notes 5 (Nov. 1968):144. Mordecai Myers, 1776-1871. Transcription from the records of Vale Cemetery in Schenectady, N.Y., through early 20th century.

Frank. Nashville Jewry, p. 139. See GENERAL WORKS.

Mordecai, Julia. "Descendants of Myer Myers of New York, N.Y." Mimeographed. AJA.

Levy-Myers Families, 1721-1939. Chart by Sanford A. Moss, Lynn, Mass. AJA.

Meredith, Scott. George S. Kaufman and His Friends. Garden City, N.Y.: Doubleday & Co., 1974. "The Family," pp. 13-25. George S. Kaufman (1889-1961), the American playwright, was born in Pittsburgh, the son of Joseph and Henrietta Myers Kaufman. The Kaufman and Myers families came to Pittsburgh from Germany in the 1840s.

Myers, Moses. Genealogical files. AJA.

Rosenbaum, Jeanette (Whitehall). Myer Myers Goldsmith, 1723-1795. Philadelphia: Jewish Publication Society of America, 5714-1954. 141 p. "Genealogy," pp. 60-64.

Family of New York.

Stern. FAJF. Myers family trees beginning in: (I, III, VII, and IX) U.S.; (II) Holland; (IV) Amsterdam; (V) Hungary; may have originally been named Benjamin; (VI) London; (VIII) Germany (originally Myer); and (X) Illereichen, Bavaria. See GENERAL WORKS.

MYERS-COHEN
Stern. FAJF. Myers-Cohen family trees beginning in: (I) London and (II) U.S. See GENERAL WORKS.

MYER-SOLOMON
AMH has family records.

NAAR
AJA has family tree beginning 1832.
Stern. FAJF. Naar family tree beginning in Curaçao. See GENERAL WORKS.

NABARRO
AMH has family records.
CFM has family records.

NACHAMSON
Evans, Eli Nachamson and Linda Eve Frankel, eds. "Always Be Good to Each Other:" The Story of the Nachamsons as Told by Jennie B. (1882-1942) and the Nine Children. Durham, N.C.?, 1968? 172 p. Story of East-European family that settled in North Carolina. DLC.

NACHLUP
Kempelen. Magyarországi Zsidó, 1:48, 130. See GENERAL WORKS.

NACHMAN
Semi-Gotha, 2:114ff. See GENERAL WORKS.

NACHMANSON   278

NACHMANSON
Rothschild. Svenska Israel.
See GENERAL WORKS.
Semi-Gotha, 2:118ff. See
GENERAL WORKS.

NADAS
Kempelen. Magyarországi Zsidó,
3:37. Nádas family. See
GENERAL WORKS.

NADLER
Cohen, L. and Dr. Kroner. "Der
Ursprung des Namens 'Nadler,'
Episode aus der Zeit der
Judenverfolgung in Polen
gegen Ende des XV.
Jahrhunderts," Jüdisches
Litteratur-Blatt 14
(1885):150-51, 165-66.

NADOR
Kempelen. Magyarországi Zsidó,
3:30. Nádor family. See
GENERAL WORKS.

NAGEL
Kempelen. Magyarországi Zsidó,
1:85, 87; 2:103. Nágel
family. See GENERAL WORKS.

NAGY
Kempelen. Magyarországi Zsidó,
1:86; 2:28, 29, 48, 73, 89,
125; 3:37. See GENERAL
WORKS.

NAMENYI
Kempelen. Magyarországi Zsidó,
3:69. Naményi family. See
GENERAL WORKS.

NAMIAS
CFM has family records.

NAMIER, NAMIEROWSKI
Namier, Julia. Lewis Namier: A
Biography. London: Oxford
University Press, 1971.
347 p. "Ancestry and Birth",
pp. 3-10. Sir Lewis
Bernstein Namier, famous
English social historian,
philosopher, and Zionist,
b. Wola Okrzejska, Eastern
Galicia, 1888; d. 1960. Real

surname, Namierowski. He
arrived in England in 1908.

NANSIK
AMH has family records.

NAPTALI
AMH has family records.

NASATIR
Nasatir, Abraham P. "The
Nasatir Family in Santa Ana,
California, 1898 to 1915,"
Western States Jewish
Historical Quarterly 15
(Apr. 1983):254-58. Family
of Morris Nasatir, who
emigrated to U.S. in 1888
from Dvinsk, Lithuania. He
became a retail merchant in
Santa Ana. The family left
this town for Los Angeles in
1915.

NASCH
Kempelen. Magyarországi Zsidó,
1:147. See GENERAL WORKS.

NASI
EJ (1972), 12:838. Includes
genealogical table. See
GENERAL WORKS.
Levy, Moritz Abraham. Don
Joseph Nasi, Herzog von
Naxos, seine Familie und zwei
jüdische Diplomaten seiner
Zeit. Eine Biographie nach
neuen Quellen dargestellt.
Breslau: Schletter
(H. Skutsch), 1859. 57 p.
Joseph Nasi, duke of Naxos,
d. 1579. CtY, DLC, OCH, OU,
PP, PPDrop.
Roth, Cecil. The House of
Nasi: The Duke of Naxos.
London, 1948. Reprint: New
York: Greenwood Press, 1970.
250 p.
————. The House of Nasi:
Doña Gracia. Philadelphia:
Jewish Historical Society of
England, 1948. 208 p. About
Gracia Mendesia,
ca. 1510-1569? Family tree,
p. 82.

NASSO
CFM has family records.

NASSY
AJA has documents, letters, and
papers relating to family of
Surinam, 1765-1800. In
Dutch.

NATAFF
CFM has family records.

NATALI
AMH has family records.

NATANSON
Kempelen. Magyarországi Zsidó,
3:28, 30. See GENERAL WORKS.
Reychman. Szkice
genealogiczne, pp. 141-47.
See GENERAL WORKS.

NATHAN
AMH has family records.
CFM has family records.
Cohen Family Papers, 1802-1945.
Includes genealogical data on
Cohen, Gratz, Etting, and
Nathan families of Maryland.
Maryland Historical Society
Library, Baltimore, Maryland.
EJ (1972), 12:849-50. Contains
genealogical tables. Family
of U.S., descendants of Simon
Nathan (1746-1822). See
GENERAL WORKS.
LBI has family tree beginning
1503.
Nathan Family. "Genealogy,
1746-1911." AJA.
Birmingham. The Grandees. See
GENERAL WORKS.
Cardozo, Michael H. IV. Leaves
from a Family Tree. 2d ed.
[Washington, D.C.], 1976.
18 ll. Genealogical charts
on Nathan, Seixas, and
Cardozo families. AJHS.
Cohen, Mendes, Collection.
This collection of family
papers includes genealogy of
Nathan family of Maryland.
Maryland Historical Society,
MS. 251.4.
Hyde, Harford Montgomery.
Strong for Service: The Life

of Lord Nathan of Churt.
London: W.H. Adler, 1968.
280 p. Genealogical
information concerning the
Nathan family, which came to
England from Holland at the
end of the 18th century, pp.
1-7. Baron Harry Louis
Nathan (1889-1963) was a
lawyer and politician who
became a major leader in
world-wide Jewish communal
affairs.
Leverton, B.J.T. "The Nathan
Brothers of
Pietermaritzburg," Jewish
Affairs (Johannesburg) 19
(Nov. 1964):12-16.
Moss, Sanford A. "Genealogy of
the Nathan Family of London,
England, and Charleston,
S.C." AJA.
Mackerras, Catherine. The
Hebrew Melodist: A Life of
Isaac Nathan. Sydney:
Currawong Publishing Co.,
1963. 124 p. Includes
genealogical tables. CtY,
ICN, NIC, OCH.
Marcus M. Nathan, København,
1859-1959. København, 1959.
CAJ.
Nathan, Maud Nathan. Once Upon
A Time And Today. New York:
G.P. Putnam's Sons, 1933.
327 p. Genealogical
information concerning the
Nathan and Seixas ancestors
of the author, pp. 21-24,
315-18. Maud Nathan
(1862-1946) was an American
Jewish communal leader as
well as a leader of the
woman's movement. DLC, OCH,
OCl, MB, NN, NNJ.
Phillips, Olga Somech. Isaac
Nathan: Friend of Byron.
London: Minerva Publishing
Co., 1940. 128 p. An
attempt by the author to
reconstruct Nathan's
genealogy, pp. 13-36. Nathan
(1790?-1864) was a composer,
singer, and writer who was
born in Canterbury, England,
but who gained his greatest

fame after he emigrated to
Australia in 1841.
Solis, Elvira Nathan, d. 1963.
"Correspondence and research
notes for genealogical
studies of the Etting,
Menken, Nathan, and Nones
Families." AJHS.
Stern. FAJF. Nathan family
trees beginning in:
(I) Frome, Somersetshire,
England; (II) Amsterdam; and
(III and IV) U.S. See
GENERAL WORKS.
Wolff, Frances Nathan. Four
Generations. New York:
Colonial Press, 1939. 192 p.
Includes Nathan, Hendricks,
and Wolff families. AJHS.

NATHANS
Stern. FAJF. Nathans family
trees beginning in:
(I) Germany and (II) England.
See GENERAL WORKS.

NATHAN-SEIXAS
Nathan-Seixas Family Records,
1782-1895. AJA.

NATHANSON
LBIS has family tree and notes.
See Yaffa Draznin entry under
BERNSTEIN. Includes
Nathanson family.

NATHORST
Semi-Gotha, 1:55. See GENERAL
WORKS.

NATONEK
Kempelen. Magyarországi Zsidó,
3:96, 132. See GENERAL
WORKS.

NATZLER
Gold. Die Juden und
Judengemeinden Mährens,
p. 182. "Stammbaum
Holzmann-Natzler." The
Holzmann-Natzler descendants
of Rabbi Selig [Salomon]
Holzmann (1769-1824) of
Dambouritz, Germany.

NAUCLER
Semi-Gotha, 1:34. Nauclér
family. See GENERAL WORKS.

NAUMBURG
Naumberg Family Records;
European and American;
Photostats. Records begin
1612. AJA.

NEANDER
Nathan, N.M. "Die Familie des
John Aug. Wilh. Neander,"
JFF, no. 33 (1933):535-36,
564. Descendants of
Gumprecht Jacob, Göttingen,
17th century. Neander
(1789-1850) was a Church
historian.

NEIMAN
Beit Rabi Mordekhai Naiman
Le-mishpahotov. Tel Aviv:
Hamercaz Press, 1957. 118 p.
Collection of writings by
various authors on Mordecai
Neuman (1834-1916/1917; also
spelled Neiman, Nieman) and
his descendants. He and his
wife came to Israel between
1881 and 1884. They were
born in Rumania. DLC, JNUL,
MH, OCH.

NEISSER
Richter, John Henry. The
Neisser Families. The
Descendants of Aron and
Catharina (Breit) Neisser of
Katscher, Dist. of
Leobschütz, Upper Silesia,
Germany. In Memoriam Prof.
Dr. Med. Max Neisser
(1869-1938), First Collector
of Genealogical Data. Ann
Arbor, Mich.: University
Microfilms, 1958. 74 p.
LBI.

NELKE
CFM has family records.

NELSON
AMH has family records.

NEMENYI
Kempelen. Magyarországi Zsidó,
  1:96. Neményi family. See
  GENERAL WORKS.

NEMES
Kempelen. Magyarországi Zsidó,
  1:43, 44; 2:89; 3:71, 88.
  See GENERAL WORKS.

NEMESHEGYI
Kempelen. Magyarországi Zsidó,
  1:101; 2:31. See GENERAL
  WORKS.

NEMIZ
Kempelen. Magyarországi Zsidó,
  2:51. See GENERAL WORKS.

NEMNO
CAJ has family records.

NETGEN
See Richard J. Alperin entry
  under BEHRMAN.

NETIRA
Schreiber, Alexander. "A
  Letter to Abraham b. Isaac
  Netira, from the Geniza
  (Cambridge, T.-S.A.S.
  146.30)," Acta Orientalia
  (Budapest) 33 (1979):113-19.
  Family of Baghdad, 10th to
  11th century. Includes
  identification of family
  members.

NETTER
CAJ has family records.
LBI has family tree beginning
  1777.
Millner, Joseph. "Les grandes
  familles juives de France,"
  Le Monde Juif 4, no. 26
  (1949):19.
Netter, Amy. "Scrapbook of
  Personal Papers and
  Miscellaneous Items,
  Cincinnati, Ohio, 1890-1896."
  Includes genealogical
  information. AJA.

NETTO
CFM has family records.

NEUBERG
AMH has family records.

NEUBERGER
LBI has family tree beginning
  1770.
Kopp. Jüdischen Alsenz,
  pp. 133-35. Genealogical
  information on
  Loeser-Neuberger family of
  Alsenz. See GENERAL WORKS.

NEUBEUER
Kempelen. Magyarországi Zsidó,
  2:78. See GENERAL WORKS.

NEUBURGER
Fraenkel, Abraham Adolf.
  Lebenskreise. Aus den
  Erinnerungen eines jüdischen
  Mathematikers. Stuttgart:
  Deutsche Verlagsanstalt,
  1967. 207 p. "Meine
  Vorfahren," pp. 13-55.
  Genealogical information on
  the Auerbach, Fraenkel, and
  Neuburger relatives of the
  author (1891-1965), who was
  born in Munich. His
  relatives were from Fürth,
  Nürnberg, and Munich.
  Abraham Fraenkel's father was
  Sigmund Fraenkel (1860-1925);
  his grandfather was Wilhelm
  [Wolf] Fraenkel (1830-1907);
  and his great-grandfather was
  Abraham Fraenkel (1792-1858).
  CSt, DLC, NIC, NjP.
Tänzer. Juden in Jebenhausen,
  p. 351. See GENERAL WORKS.

NEUMAIER
Tänzer. Juden in Jebenhausen,
  p. 352. See GENERAL WORKS.

NEUMAN, NEUMANN
See HAUGERMANN. Neumann
  family.
See NEIMAN.
CFM has a Neumann family tree.
See Hans Josephthal entry under
  GOLDSCHNEIDER. Includes
  Neumann family. Descendants
  of Lazarus Josephthal of
  Ansbach, b. 1657.
Kempelen. Magyarországi Zsidó.

Neuman family, 1:104; 2:142.
Neumann family, 1:105, 135;
2:53, 67, 70, 99, 136; 3:69,
77, 78, 92, 96. See GENERAL
WORKS.
Neumann, Norbert Collection,
York, Pa. "Genealogies of
the Ballin, Lazarus, Schäfer,
and Neumann Families, 11th
Century to Date." AJA.

NEUMARK
CAJD has family tree from
Germany, 1696-1908.

NEUMEGEN
AMH has family records.
CFM has family records.
Kempelen. Magyarországi Zsidó,
1:9. See GENERAL WORKS.

NEURENBERG
AMH has family records.

NEUSCHLOSS
Kempelen. Magyarországi Zsidó,
2:25, 124. See GENERAL
WORKS.

NEUSTADT
AMH has family records.
CAJ has family records from
18th century.
CFM has family records.
LBI has family tree beginning
1615.
Neustadt, Ben Z.; Columbus,
Ohio. "The Tree of Life;
Book on the Lives of Rabbi
Isaac E. and Minnie Neustadt
and Their Descendants, 1975."
AJA.

NEUSTADTER
Hart, Neustadter, and
Dannenberg Families' Tree.
Neustadter Family
Miscellaneous Papers.
Contain genealogical chart
for family in New York and
San Francisco, dating from
ca. 1830. WJHC.

NEUSTETEL
CFM has family records.

NEUWELT
Kempelen. Magyarországi Zsidó,
2:45. See GENERAL WORKS.

NEUWIRTH
Kempelen. Magyarországi Zsidó,
2:56; 3:54. See GENERAL
WORKS.

NEVILLE
AMH has family records.

NEWBURN
AMH has family records.

NEWGASS
CFM has family records.

NEWHOUSE
AMH has family records.
Stern. FAJF. Newhouse family
tree beginning in Ettlingen,
Bavaria. See GENERAL WORKS.

NEWMAN
Newman Diamond Jubilee,
1888-1963. Modesto: Belt
Printing and Lithograph Co.,
1963. 80 p. Booklet traces
history of Newman, California
founded by Simon Newman in
1888. Includes large amount
of biographical information
on the Newman family still
active in the community's
affairs. CU; California
State Library, Sacramento.

NEWMARK
Gordon, D. "Charles F. Lummis
and the Newmarks of Los
Angeles," Western States
Jewish Historical Quarterly 7
(1974):32-38.
Narell. Our City. Includes
genealogical chart for
pioneer San Francisco family,
descendants of Joseph Newmark
(1808-1875). See GENERAL
WORKS.
"Nellie Newmark of Lincoln,
Nebraska: A Pictorial Story,"
Western States Jewish
Historical Quarterly 11
(1979):114-18.
Newmark, Harris. Sixty Years

in Southern California,
1853-1913: Containing the
Reminiscences of Harris
Newmark. Edited by Maurice
H. and Marco R. Newmark. 4th
ed., Revised and Augmented
with an Introduction and
Notes by W.W. Robinson. Los
Angeles: Zeitlin & Ver
Brugge, 1970. 744 p. Harris
Newmark (1835-1916) was born
in East Prussia. CSt, CtY,
CU, DLC, ICN, ICU, NjP, WHi.
Newmark, Leo. California
Family Newmark: An Intimate
History. Introduction and
Comentary by William M.
Kramer and Norton B. Stern.
Santa Monica: Norton B.
Stern, 1970. 110 p. NcD,
NjP, NN.
Newmark, Marco. [Scrapbooks of
Newmark Family History ...,
ca. 1892-1957.] 4 vols.
Family of California. AJA,
WJHC.

NEWSALT
AJA has family tree written in
1870.

NEWTON
AMH has family records.
CFM has family records.

NEY
LBI has family tree beginning
1680.

NICHOLL
AMH has family records.

NICHOLLS
AMH has family records.

NICOLSBURGER
Kempelen. Magyarországi Zsidó,
2:35. See GENERAL WORKS.

NICHOLSON
AMH has family records.

NIEDERSUSS
Kempelen. Magyarországi Zsidó,
2:76. Niedersüss family.
See GENERAL WORKS.

NIEMAN
See NEIMAN.

NIEMIROWSKI
See NAMIER.

NIETO
Wolf, "Anglo-Jewish Families."
See GENERAL WORKS.

NIKOLICS
Kempelen. Magyarországi Zsidó,
2:51, 52. See GENERAL WORKS.

NIRNSTEIN
Kempelen. Magyarországi Zsidó,
3:139. See GENERAL WORKS.

NISHRI
See Meir Yizraeli entry under
BIDERMAN.

NISSER
Semi-Gotha, 1:100. See GENERAL
WORKS.

NOAH
"Genealogies of Mordecai Manuel
Noah and His Wife, Rebecca E.
Jackson." Typescript. AJA.
Sarna, Jonathan D. Jacksonian
Jew: The Two Worlds of
Mordecai Noah. New York:
Holmes & Meier, 1981. 233 p.
Genealogical information
concerning the Noah and
Phillips (South Carolina)
families, pp. 1-3. Mordecai
Noah (1785-1851) was born in
Philadelphia, the son of
Manuel Mordecai (1755-1822)
and Zipporah Phillips Noah
(1764-1792). Manual Noah was
a native of Mannheim,
Germany.
Stern. FAJF. Noah family
trees beginning in:
(I) Mannheim, Germany;
(II) Germany; and
(III) Teszchen, Germany. See
GENERAL WORKS.

NOBEL
CAJ has family records.

NODLER
See Richard J. Alperin entry
under BEHRMAN.

NOETHER
LBI has family tree beginning
1686.

NOGUEIRA
CFM has family records.

NONES
CFM has family records.
Nones Family Papers, 1977,
1979. 1 folder. "Computer
printout of Benjamin Nones
(1752-1826) and his
descendants." PJAC.
Irwin, Norma Nones.
Descendants of Benjamin A.
Nones and Miriam Marks.
Menlo Park, Calif., 1981.
1 genealogical chart. Family
originally settled in
Philadelphia. AJA, AJHS,
WJHC.
Solis, Elvira Nathan, d. 1963.
"Correspondence and research
notes for genealogical
studies of the Etting,
Menken, Nathan, and Nones
Families." AJHS.
Stern. FAJF. Nones family
tree beginning in Bordeaux,
France. See GENERAL WORKS.

NOORDEN (VAN)
See VAN NOORDEN.

NORBURY
AMH has family records.

NORDAU
PD has family records.
Molho, M. "Antecedentes
sefardíes de los líderes
sionistas Theodor Herzl y Max
Nordau," Le Judaïsme Sephardi
(London), n.s., 19
(Feb. 1960):843-45.

NORDEN
AMH has family records.
Bick-Shauli, "Roots and
Branches." Includes Albert
Norden, a Communist party

leader of the East German
regime, b. Elberfeld,
Germany, 1912; d. East
Berlin, 1982. See GENERAL
WORKS.
CFM has family records.
See Daniel J. Cohen entry under
CLEVE. Norden family of
Hanau, Altona, Germany,
pp. 91-97. Includes family
tree, 1600s to 1764, p. 120.

NORDENFELDT
Semi-Gotha, 1:105. See GENERAL
WORKS.

NORDENSVAN
Semi-Gotha, 1:84. See GENERAL
WORKS.

NORDHAUS
Hyams Family. "Records of
Births, Marriages, and Deaths
from Family Bibles;
Obituaries; Family Memoirs;
and Notes. Charleston, S.C.;
New Orleans, La.; and San
Antonio, Texas, 1805-1936."
Includes Nordhaus family.
AJA.

NORDWALD
Nordwald Family. "Material
Relating to Nordwald Family
of Chihuahua, Mexico and El
Paso, Texas, 1860-1924." 1
microfilm reel. AJA.

NORMAN-EHRENFELS
Semigothaisches Taschenbuch.
Genealogical table 16. See
GENERAL WORKS.

NORRIS
AMH has family records.

NORSA
CFM has family records.
Norsa, Paolo. "Una famiglia di
banchieri. La famiglia Norsa
(1350-1950)," Bolletino
dell'Archivo Storico del
Banco di Napoli 6
(1953):79ff.; 12
(1959):137ff.

NOTHMAN
"Geschichte der Familie
Nothman," Mitteilungen des
Verbändes ehemaliger
Breslauer und Schlesier in
Israel (Tel-Aviv), nos. 38-42
(1977). Covers 18th to 20th
century.

NOUNAN
AMH has family records.

NOVICH
Gorin, Sadie Novich. "History
of the Novice-Adams Families,
Waco, Texas." AJA.

NOZICK
Hoffman, Madalyn. "50 Years of
a Family Circle," Jewish
Currents 35 (1981):9-13.
About family from Osevetz and
50th Anniversary celebration
of their family circle.

NUNES
AMH has family records.
Lemos, Maximiano. Ribeiro
Sanches: A sua vida e a sua
obra. Porto: Eduardo Tavares
Martins, ed., 1911. 369 p.
Genealogical tables include
ascendants and descendants of
Antonio Nunes Ribeiro
Sanches, a Portuguese Marrano
who fled to Holland and later
became Russian court
physician, b. 1699; d. Paris,
1783. CtY, ICJ, ICN, MH, NN,
OCH, OU.
Samuel, E.R. "Portuguese Jews
in Jacobean England," Jewish
Historical Society of England
Transactions 18 (1958):181.
Includes pedigree chart of
Anglo-Jewish family.

NUNEZ
Rezneck, Samuel. "A Note on
the Genealogy of an
Eighteenth Century Family of
Jewish Origin: The Nunez
Family of Lewes, Delaware,"
American Jewish Archives 30
(1978):20-23.
Stern. FAJF. Nunez family

tree beginning in Portugal.
Originally De Lucena.
Members of later generation
changed name to Nunez. See
GENERAL WORKS.

NURNBERG
CFM has family records.

NUSBAUM, NUSSBAUM
CAJ has Nussbaum family
records.
LBI has Nussbaum family tree
beginning 1833.
Ballin. Juden in Seesen,
pp. 222-24. Nussbaum family.
See GENERAL WORKS.
See David Joseph entry under
BEITMAN.
Kempelen. Magyarországi Zsidó,
3:20. Nussbaum family. See
GENERAL WORKS.
Shane Family, Warsaw, Indiana.
"History of the Shane Family,
Centering upon the Life of
Henry Shane and His Wife,
Henrietta Nusbaum Shane,
1829-1959." AJA.
Nussbaum, Israel.
Familienchronik und Stammbaum
der Familie Israel Nussbaum
in Viersen. Viersen,
1932-1935. 548 p. LBI.

NYSTROEM
AMH has family records.

OBERDORFER
Oberdorfer Family Genealogy.
Compiled by Mrs. Natalie S.
Oberdorfer. Genealogical
information on descendants of
Philip Oberdorfer
(b. Bavaria, ca. 1852) and on
family of David Oberdorfer
who arrived in New York from
Bavaria in early 1840s.
JGCT.

OBERMAYER
PD has family records.

OBERNDOERFFER
LBI has family tree beginning
1760.

OBERSCHALL
Kempelen. Magyarországi Zsidó,
1:106. See GENERAL WORKS.

OBLAT
Kempelen. Magyarországi Zsidó,
1:10, 22; 3:68. See GENERAL
WORKS.

OCHS
AJA has genealogical files.
LBI has family tree beginning
1728.
Sulzberger, Iphigene Ochs, as
told to Susan W. Dryfoos.
From Iphigene: The Memoirs of
Iphigene Ochs Sulzberger.
New York: Dodd, 1981.
Ullman, Elias.
Familien-Register und
Stammtafeln des Seligmann
Sulzbach aus Fürth, des Ruben
Juda Beyfuss, des Moses Isaac
Ochs und des Isaac Jacob Bass
aus Frankfurt am Main und
deren Nachkommen. Frankfurt
am Main, 1875.

ODENHEIMER
Odenheimer Family Records,
Philadelphia, Pa., 1865-1882.
AJA.

OESTREICHER
LBI has family tree beginning
1761.

OETL-PALFFY
Kempelen. Magyarországi Zsidó,
1:96. Oetl-Pálffy family.
See GENERAL WORKS.

OFFENBACH
See EBERT.

OFFENBACHER
Michael Berolzheimer
Collection. Includes
Offenbacher family tree.
LBI.

OFFENHEIMER
Kempelen. Magyarországi Zsidó,
2:35. See GENERAL WORKS.

OFFERMANN
Kempelen. Magyarországi Zsidó,
1:113. See GENERAL WORKS.

OFFNER
Kempelen. Magyarországi Zsidó,
1:132. See GENERAL WORKS.

OGLE
AMH has family records.

OHRENSTEIN
Kempelen. Magyarországi Zsidó,
3:61. See GENERAL WORKS.

OHSSON
See MOURADGEA-D'OHSSON.
Semi-Gotha, 1:154. D'Ohsson
family. See GENERAL WORKS.

OKANYI
Kempelen. Magyarországi Zsidó,
3:103. Okányi family. See
GENERAL WORKS.

OKO
AMH has family records.

OLCOVICH
Joseph Olcovich Miscellaneous
Papers. Contain diary with
four pages of genealogical
information on Olcovich's
family and his wife Hattie's
family, the Isaac Baruchs of
Coulterville, California.
California Historical Society
Library of San Francisco.

OLDENBURG
LBI has family tree beginning
1621.
See Daniel J. Cohen entry under
CLEVE. Oldenburg family from
Altona, Germany, pp. 48-53.
Includes family tree, 1500s
to 1929, p. 114.

OLDENSHAW
AMH has family records.

OLITZKY
Olitzky, Kerry Marc, comp.
"Olitzky Family, Pittsburg,
Genealogy and Family Tree."
AJA.

OLIVEIRA
CFM has family records.

OLIVEN
LBI has family tree beginning
1730.

OLIVETTI
AMH has family records.

OLLESHEIMER
LBI has family tree beginning
1823.

OLOP
Kempelen. Magyarországi Zsidó,
2:133. See GENERAL WORKS.

OLSCHKI
Rosenthal, Bernard M. "Cartel,
Clan, or Dynasty? The
Olschkis and the Rosenthals,
1859-1976," Harvard Library
Bulletin 25 (1977):381-98.
Account of two prominent
families in the rare book and
antiquarian book trade by a
leading member of the current
generation. Discusses
economic situation of
post-World War I Germany and
effects of the rise of Nazism
on Jewish businessmen.
Emigrated to Italy.

OPATOSCHU
CAJ has family records.

OPPENHEIM
AJA has family tree beginning
1600.
AMH has family records.
CAJ has family records.
CFM has family records.
LBI has family trees beginning
1556, 1633, 1676, and 1825.
PD has family records.
Ettlinger, Shlomo.
"Altfrankfurter jüdische
Familien-II," Frankfurter

Jüdische Familienblatt 3,
no. 12 (1957):9.
Frank. See "Bing" heading for
full citation.
Gronemann. Genealogische
Hannovers, pp. 77ff. "Die
Familie Oppenheim." See
GENERAL WORKS.
Jacobson, Jacob.
"Wien-Prag-Berlin: Zur
Entwicklungs-Geschichte einer
Familie," Bulletin für die
Mitglieder der Gesellschaft
der Freunde Leo Baeck
Institut (Tel Aviv) 6 (März
1959):67-72. 17th to
mid-20th century. The
descendants of Jechiel
Oppenheim of Worms. Includes
both Oppenheim and
Oppenheimer members.
Levison, Wilhelm. Die
Siegburger Familie Levinson
und verwandte Familien.
Bonn: Röhrscheid, 1952.
187 p. Includes Oppenheim
family history. CSt, DLC,
LU, NN, NNJ.
[Löwenstein, Leopold.]
Stammbaum Rheinganum,
Oppenheim, Simons. Mannheim,
1908. 38 p. Families of
Mannheim. OCH.
Daniel Meyer Papers. Judah
Oppenheim Family Tree,
1531-1826. WJHC.
Oppenheim, Jeffrey. Jeffrey
Oppenheim Family Tree.
Roslyn Heights, N.Y, 1981.
1 genealogical chart. Chart
traces family to 14th
century, the American
presence to 18th century.
AJHS.
Rapp, Eugen Ludwig and Otto
Böcher. "Bedeutende Träger
der jüdischen Namen Oppenheim
und Oppenheimer," in 1200
Jahre Oppenheim am Rhein
Festschrift (Oppenheim: Stadt
[Verwaltung], 1965),
pp. 106-116. DLC, NIC.
Stern. FAJF. Oppenheim family
tree beginning in Vienna.
Also spelled Oppenheimer.
See GENERAL WORKS.

Stern, Selma. Jud Süss: Ein
Beitrag zur deutschen und zur
jüdischen Geschichte.
München: Gotthold Müller
Verlag, 1973. 346 p.
Genealogical information on
the Oppenheimer family from
Heidelberg, pp. 5-19. Joseph
Süss Oppenheimer (1692 or
1698/99-1738), court Jew and
financial adviser to the Duke
of Württemberg. DLC.
Zapf. Tübinger Juden, pp.
161-64. See GENERAL WORKS.

OPPENHEIMER
See ETTINGHAUSEN.
AJA has family tree beginning
18th century.
AMH has family records.
CAJ, Call No. 2076, has 2-page
family tree of family from
Witzenhausen, 1645-1931.
CFM has family records.
LBI has family trees beginning
1397, 17th century, 1650,
1713, 1745, 1770, 1778, 1807,
and 1876.
Oppenheimer Family, Vancouver,
British Columbia. "From the
Beginning, 1858-1958,
Oppenheimer Brothers and
Company." Typescript; Xerox
copy. AJA.
Brauer, Adalbert. "Der
Südafrikanische
'Diamantenkaiser' Sir Ernest
Oppenheimer aus Hessen,"
Hessisch Familienkunde 4,
no. 3 (1957):149-52; 4, no. 5
(1959):281.
————. "Sir Ernest
Oppenheimer; zu seinem 100
Geburtstag," Genealogie
(Neustadt/Aisch) 29, no. 10
(Okt. 1980):305-308. South
African financier and diamond
industrialist, b. Friedberg,
Hesse, May 22, 1880; d.
Johannesburg, Nov. 25, 1957.
Family went to England.
See Sally David Cramer entry
under CRAMER.
Grünwald, Max. Samuel
Oppenheimer und sein Kreis
(Ein Kapitel aus der

finanzgeschichte
Österreichs). Wien und
Leipzig: W. Braumüller, 1913.
358 p. Samuel Oppenheimer,
1630-1703. DLC, MB, NIC, NN,
OCH, OU.
WJHC's Walter S. Hilborn
"Selected Materials,
1916-1974" collection
contains an 8-page history of
Oppenheimer family of British
Columbia.
See Jacob Jacobson entry under
OPPENHEIM.
Jessup, Edward. Ernest
Oppenheimer: A Study in
Power. London: Rex Collings,
1973. 357 p. "The Family
Tree of Oppenheimer and
History of the Oppenheimer
Family," pp. 326-29. Family
of Hessen. Early 19th to
mid-20th century. DLC.
See David Joseph entry under
BEITMAN.
Kempelen. Magyarországi Zsidó,
1:12, 34, 35, 39; 2:68, 69.
See GENERAL WORKS.
Oppenheimer, Franz. Erlebtes,
Erstrebtes, Erreichtes,
Lebenserinnerungen.
Düsseldorf: Joseph Melzer
Verlag, 1964. 372 p.
"Elternhaus," pp. 33-44.
Franz Oppenheimer
(1864-1943), German and
American sociologist and
economist, was born in
Berlin. His mother's family
was the Benda family of
Berlin. CSt, CtY, CU, DLC,
ICU, NcU, NjP, NNC, OCl.
See Eugen Ludwig Rapp and Otto
Böcher entry under OPPENHEIM.
Reis, Victor. Chronik der
Familie Wolf. Schlüchtern,
1932. 8 p. Five family
trees. Includes Oppenheimer
family.
Rosenthal, B. "Genealogical
Table for Otto Oppenheimer,
Bruchsal." Mannheim, 1938.
18 p. AJA.
See Stern, FAJF entry under
OPPENHEIM.
Stern. FAJF. Oppenheimer

family tree beginning in
Hesse-Darmstadt. See GENERAL
WORKS.
See Ernst Wolf entry under
GOMPERZ. Includes Samuel
Oppenheimer family.

OPPERT
AMH has family records.

OPPLER
PD has family records.

OPPSE
AMH has family records.

ORABUENA
Orabuena, José.
Ebenbild-Spiegelbild.
Erinnerungen. Zürich: Thomas
Verlag, 1962. 656 p. The
German writer (1894-   ) was
born in Córdoba, Spain. CtY.

ORANGE
AMH has family records.

ORAVA
Kempelen. Magyarországi Zsidó,
3:43. See GENERAL WORKS.

ORDODY
Kempelen. Magyarországi Zsidó,
1:83; 2:28. Ordódy family.
See GENERAL WORKS.

ORGELBRAND
Reychman. Szkice
genealogiczne, pp. 149-51.
See GENERAL WORKS.

ORGLER
Orgler Family. "Genealogy of
the Orgler Family, Including
Some Information on Bloch,
and Gratz Families, Tracing
the Ancestry of Rebecca
Gratz, Germany and the United
States, 1650-1939." AJA.

ORNSTEIN
AMH has family records.
Balaban, Meir. Shalshelet
Ha-Jichus.... Warszaw, 1931.
47 p. One genealogical
table. Family of Poland,

descendants of Joel Sirkes,
Rabbi of Krakow, 17th
century.
Kempelen. Magyarországi Zsidó,
3:63. See GENERAL WORKS.
Rose. Schöninger Juden.
Includes Ornstein family.
See GENERAL WORKS.
Rosenstein. Unbroken Chain,
pp. 456ff. See GENERAL
WORKS.

OROBIO
AMH has family records.

OROBIO DE CASTRO
"Balthasar Isaak Orobio de
Castro," MGWJ, 1867, p. 321.
Révah, I.S. "Orobio de Castro
et sa famille aux prises avec
l'Inquisition espagnole,"
Berichten en Mededelingen
v.h. Genootschap voor Joodse
Wetenschappen 9 (1965):87-90.
17th-century Dutch Jewish
family, originally Marranos
from Portugal.

OROSDY
Kempelen. Magyarországi Zsidó,
1:127, 128. See GENERAL
WORKS.

ORSZAG
Kempelen. Magyarországi Zsidó,
2:92. Ország family. See
GENERAL WORKS.

ORTLEPP
AMH has family records.

ORVIETO
CFM has family records.

OSER
CAJ has family history.
See Hans Josephthal entry under
GOLDSCHNEIDER. Includes Oser
family. Descendants of
Lazarus Josephthal of
Ansbach, b. 1657.

OSORIO
AMH has family records.
CFM has family records.

OSTERBERG
LBI has family tree beginning
1786.

OSTERREICHER
Kempelen. Magyarországi Zsidó,
2:136; 3:94. See GENERAL
WORKS.

OSTROGSKI
CAJ has family records from
17th and 18th centuries.

OSTROW
Picon, Molly. So Laugh A
Little, As Told to Eth
Clifford Rosenberg. New
York: Julian Messner, 1962.
175 p. A large part of the
autobiography of this noted
American actress and comic
concerns her family, the
Ostrows and Pyekoons. The
author was the daughter of
Louis and Clara Ostrow
Pyekoon. The Ostrow family
was from Rezshishtchov,
Russia.

OTTENBERG
"The Ottenberg Family," The
Record (The Jewish Historical
Society of Greater
Washington) 10
(Sept. 1979):17-28.
Descendants of Isaac
Ottenberg, originally from
Landau, Germany, who arrived
in U.S. in 1866.

OTTENHEIMER
Tänzer. Juden in Jebenhausen,
pp. 353-57. See GENERAL
WORKS.

OTTER
Semi-Gotha, 1:24. See GENERAL
WORKS.

OTTINGEN
Kaufman, David. "Mordecai
Model Öttingen und seine
Kinder," MGWJ 42
(1898):557-67.
Löwenstein, L.
"Model-Öttingen," JJLG 8

(1910):202-203. Descendants
of Simon Günzburg, d. 1585.

OTTINGER
LBI has Ottinger family tree
beginning 1833.
Ottinger Family of Toledo, Ohio
History, 1834-1956. AJA.
Jakobovits, Tobias. "Die
Verbindung der Prager
Familien Ottinger-Spira
[Wedes]-Bondi," MGWJ 76
(1933):511-19.

OTTOLENGHI
Ottolenghi, Raffaele.
"Documenti storici dell
famiglia Ottolenghi di
Acqui," Rivista di Storia,
Arte e Archeol. di
Alessandria 16 (1912); 21
(1926):45-46.

OTTOLENGUI
Stern. FAJF. Ottolengui
family tree beginning in
Italy. See GENERAL WORKS.

OUCHTERLONY
Semi-Gotha, 1:35. See GENERAL
WORKS.

OVEN
See VAN OVEN.
AMH has family records.

PABLO
CFM has family records.

PACHECO
CAJ has family records.
CFM has family records.

PACIFICO
AMH has family records.
CFM has family records.

PACIFO
AMH has family records.

PADOA
CAJ has a collection of

documents of Padoa family
from Modena, Italy,
1754-1924.

PADRASIC
JGCT has family tree.

PAGEL
Zapf. Tübinger Juden, pp.
214-17. See GENERAL WORKS.
Zielenziger, Georg. Stammbaum
der Familien Pagel und
Boschwitz. Ausgeführt von
Karl Hacker. Berlin, 1907.
BR.

PAGET
AMH has family records.

PAIBA
AMH has family records.
CFM has family records.

PAICOVITCH, PAIKOVITS
Allon, Yigal. My Father's
House. Translated from the
Hebrew by Reuven Ben-Yosef.
New York: Norton, 1976. 204
p. The author (1918-   )
was born in Kefar Tavor
(Mascha), Israel, the son of
Reuven and Chayah-Etil
Shwartz Paicovitch (also
spelled Paikovits) and the
grandson of Yehoshua-Zvi
Paicovitch. The Paicovitch
family was from Grodno and
the Shwartz family from
Safed, Israel.

PAINE
AMH has family records.

PAKE
AJA has family tree from
Mobile, Alabama.

PAKSY
Kempelen. Magyarországi Zsidó,
1:96. See GENERAL WORKS.

PALACHE
AMH has family records.
CFM has family records.
Stern. FAJF. Palaché family

tree beginning in London.
See GENERAL WORKS.

PALAGYI
Kempelen. Magyarországi Zsidó,
3:42. Palágyi family. See
GENERAL WORKS.

PALFFY
See OETL-PALFFY.
Kempelen. Magyarországi Zsidó,
1:127. Pálffy family. See
GENERAL WORKS.

PALGRAVE
AMH has family records.
Edwards, Lewis. "A Remarkable
Family; The Palgraves," in
Remember the Days; Essays on
Anglo-Jewish History
Presented to Cecil Roth by
Members of the Council of the
Jewish Historical Society of
England (London: Jewish
Historical Society of
England, 1966), pp. 303-322.
Sir Frances Palgrave,
1788-1866, and his four sons.
CtY, CU, DLC, ICU, MH.
Palgrave, Derek Aubrey. The
History and Lineage of the
Palgraves. Doncaster, S.
Yorkshire: Palgrave Society,
June 1978. 350 p.

PALIN
Semi-Gotha, 1:154. See GENERAL
WORKS.

PALMAI
Kempelen. Magyarországi Zsidó,
2:56. Pálmai family. See
GENERAL WORKS.

PALMSTJERNA
Semi-Gotha, 1:26, 94. See
GENERAL WORKS.

PALOTAY
Kempelen. Magyarországi Zsidó,
2:69, 126. See GENERAL
WORKS.

PAPPENHEIM
Kempelen. Magyarországi Zsidó,

1:14; 2:10, 11. See GENERAL
WORKS.

PARDO
AMH has family records.
CAJ has family records.
CFM has family records.
"Pardo-Brown Family Tree," in
David de Sola Pool's
Portraits Etched in Stone:
Early Jewish Settlers,
1682-1831 (New York: Columbia
University Press, 1952),
p. 446. Family of New York,
17th to 18th century.
Stern. FAJF. Pardo family
tree beginning in Salonika,
Ottoman Empire. See GENERAL
WORKS.

PARICER
See Richard J. Alperin entry
under BEHRMAN.

PARIENTE
AMH has family records.

PARKER
AMH has family records.

PARLOV
See Meir Yizraeli entry under
BIDERMAN.

PARNAS
Rosenstein. Unbroken Chain,
pp. 252ff. Parnas
descendants of R. Naftali
Katz. See GENERAL WORKS.

PARNICZKY
Kempelen. Magyarországi Zsidó,
3:52. Párniczky family. See
GENERAL WORKS.

PARRAVICINI
Kempelen. Magyarországi Zsidó,
1:138. See GENERAL WORKS.

PARSNER
See LEGUM.

PARTOS
Kempelen. Magyarországi Zsidó,
2:87. Pártos family. See
GENERAL WORKS.

PARTRIDGE
AMH has family records.

PASS
See DE PASS.
AMH has family records.
CFM has family records.

PASTERNAK
Die Familie Pasternak:
Erinnerungen, Berichte,
zusammengestellt und hrsg.
von Paul J. Mark. Genève:
Editions Poésie Vivante,
1975. 167 p. Text in
English, French, and German.
Family of Leonid Osipovich
Pasternak, 1862-1945, and his
son, the Soviet poet and
novelist, Boris Leonidovich
Pasternak, 1890-1960. Family
originally from Odessa; lived
mainly in Moscow.

PATAI
Kempelen. Magyarországi Zsidó,
2:17. See GENERAL WORKS.

PATAKY
Kempelen. Magyarországi Zsidó,
2:98. See GENERAL WORKS.

PATINO
AMH has family records.

PATON
AMH has family records.

PAULI
Semi-Gotha, 1:120. See GENERAL
WORKS.

PAULSCHIFF
Kempelen. Magyarországi Zsidó,
2:19. See GENERAL WORKS.

PAULY
LBI has family tree beginning
1672.

PAYNE
AMH has family records.

PAZ (DE)
See DEPAS.

PEARSON
AMH has family records.

PEAT
AMH has family records.

PECHENIK
Selitzer, Ralph. The Pechenik:
A Genealogy of Dovid Hennock
Pechenik and His Descendants
and Remembrances of Life in
Eastern Europe. Passaic,
N.J.: Cameo Printing Co.,
1969. 62 p. Includes
genealogical tables. DLC,
NN, OU, WHi, YIVO.

PECHY
Kempelen. Magyarországi Zsidó,
1:46; 2:24. Péchy family.
See GENERAL WORKS.

PECSI
Kempelen. Magyarországi Zsidó,
3:35. Pécsi family. See
GENERAL WORKS.

PEEZ
Kempelen. Magyarországi Zsidó,
1:55. See GENERAL WORKS.

PEISER
John Peiser Family Records of
Births and Deaths, Paterson,
N.J., 1842-1860. AJA.

PEISOTY
Pesotta, Rose. Days of Our
Lives. Boston: Excelsior
Publishers, 1958. 262 p.
Family from Derazhnya,
Podolia Gubernia. The author
(1896-1965) was the daughter
of Itzaak and Masya Peisoty.
In the U.S., Rosa Pesotta
eventually became a National
Vice-President of the
I.L.G.W.U. This work covers
the family's history from
1880s to 1914.

PEIXOTTO
AMH has family records.
CFM has family records.
JE, 9:582. American
descendants of Moses Levy

Maduro Peixotto through late
19th century. See GENERAL
WORKS.
Birmingham. The Grandees. See
GENERAL WORKS.
See Samuel Reznick entry under
PHILLIPS.
Stern. FAJF. Peixotto family
trees beginning in:
(I) Amsterdam; Cayenne,
French Guiana; and London.
(II) West Indies.
(III) Jamaica. See GENERAL
WORKS.

PEKARDY
Kempelen. Magyarországi Zsidó,
1:19. Pekárdy family. See
GENERAL WORKS.

PEMBERTON
AMH has family records.

PENFOLD
AMH has family records.

PENHA (DE LA)
See DE LA PENHA.

PENTECOST
AMH has family records.

PERAHIA
Molho, Michael. La famille
Perahia à Thessaloniki.
Thessaloniki, Salonika:
Imprimèrie Acquarone, 1938.
69 p. in French, and 14 p. in
Hebrew. "Arbre généalogique
de la Familie Ha-Cohen,"
starting with Samuel Perahia,
d. 1548, of Italy, p. 67.
Family of Greece and Italy.
JNUL, NN, PPDrop.
Perahia, Josué D. Los origines
de la Fundación del Bicur
Holim y de la familia
Perahia. Conferencia hecha
en el 23 de noviembre 1952 en
la Sociedad la "Hermanidad"
de Salonica. Salonika:
Imprimerìa Behar, 1953.
14 p. JNUL.

PERCZEL
Kempelen. Magyarországi Zsidó,
2:90. See GENERAL WORKS.

PEREIRA
AJA has genealogical files.
AMH has family records.
CFM has family records.
JE, 8:487. "Mendes
Pedigree-American Branch."
Descendants of David Pereira
Mendes (1740-1786), who left
Bayonne, France for Jamaica
in 1786, through late 19th
century. See GENERAL WORKS.
Semi-Gotha, 1:143ff. See
GENERAL WORKS.
Stern. FAJF. Pereira family
tree beginning in Amsterdam.
Originally Rodrigues Pereira.
See GENERAL WORKS.

PEREIRE
Cahen, Isadore. "Grands noms
du judaïsme français: les
Halévy, les Péreire,"
Archives Israélites (de
France) 47 (1886):57-58.
Castille, Charles Hippolyte.
Les frères Péreire. Paris:
E. Dentu, 1861. 62 p. On
the Péreire family of bankers
and financiers of France.
DLC, MH.

PERELES
Pereles, Max (1886-?), Papers,
1891, 1941. Include Pereles
genealogy. PJAC.

PERENYI
Kempelen. Magyarországi Zsidó,
3:126. Perényi family. See
GENERAL WORKS.

PERES
Shankman, Samuel. The Peres
Family. Kingsport, Tenn.:
Southern Publishers, Inc.,
1938. 241 p. Family of
Tennessee. Descendants of
Israel Hyman Peres

(b. Memphis, 1867; d. 1925)
and Hardwig Peres (b. 1859).
Israel Peres, the son of
Jacob J. and Eva Peres, was a
lawyer and Jewish communal
leader. DLC, MB, MH, NcD,
NN, OCH, OCl, PHi, PU, TxU.

PERESZLENYI
Kempelen. Magyarországi Zsidó,
3:95. Pereszlényi family.
See GENERAL WORKS.

PERETZ, PEREZ
Bick-Shauli, "Roots and
Branches." Includes
genealogy of Gregory Peretz,
b. St. Petersburg, 1788; d.
1855. See GENERAL WORKS.
Pribluda, A.S. "Imia i
familia Perez ... Avigdor,"
(In Russian.) Onomastica 18
(1973):261-65.

PERL
Kempelen. Magyarországi Zsidó,
3:124. See GENERAL WORKS.
Steinberg, Sigfrid.
"Perl-Ursinus,"
Familiengeschichtliche
Blätter 33 (1935):271-72.

PERLES
Kempelen. Magyarországi Zsidó,
2:10. See GENERAL WORKS.

PERLHEFTER
See Alfred Julius Bruck entries
under BRUCK.

PERLMUTTER
Panait, Istrati. La famille
Perlmutter. Paris, 1927.
253 p. YIVO.

PERLOW
Rosenstein. Unbroken Chain,
pp. 298ff. Perlow Chassidic
dynasty of Stolin-Karlin.
See GENERAL WORKS.

PERLS
Perls, Maier. Megilath
Yuhasin. Warsaw, 1864, 1869.
Biography of the Maharal of
Prague, 1525-1609, with his

connections to the Perls
family.

PERLSTEIN
Weinbaum, Eleanor Perlstein.
Shalom, America. The
Perlstein Success Story. San
Antonio, Tex.: Naylor, 1969.
152 p. Beaumont, Tex.;
family of Hyman Asher
Perlstein, 1869-1948. DLC,
OCH.

PEROCHON
AMH has family records.

PEROTTI
Kempelen. Magyarországi Zsidó,
1:75. See GENERAL WORKS.

PEROWNA
AMH has family records.

PERUGIA (DA)
Toaff, A. "Note su una
famiglia anconetana del
1700," Rassegna Mensile di
Israel 33 (1967):552-55.

PERWER
Boehmer, Julius. "Was bedeutet
der Name Perwer?"
Jahresbericht des
altmärkischen Vereins für
Väterländische Geschichte zu
Salzwedel 45 (1927):4-17.

PESARO
CFM has family records.
Morpugo, Edgardo. "Notizie in
torno alla famiglia Gentilomo
di Pesaro," Revista
Israelitica (Firenze) 7
(1910):121-24.

PESKO
Kempelen. Magyarországi Zsidó,
3:99. Peskó family. See
GENERAL WORKS.

PESOA
Stern. FAJF. Pesoa family
tree beginning in Kingston,
Jamaica. See GENERAL WORKS.

PESOTTA
See PEISOTY.

PESSOA
CFM has family records.

PETENYI
Kempelen. Magyarországi Zsidó,
2:146. Petényi family. See
GENERAL WORKS.

PETERDI
Kempelen. Magyarországi Zsidó,
3:90. See GENERAL WORKS.

PETITJEAN
Kempelen. Magyarországi Zsidó,
2:99. See GENERAL WORKS.

PETLEY
AMH has family records.

PETLIURA
CAJ has family records.

PETO
Kempelen. Magyarországi Zsidó,
1:102. Pető family. See
GENERAL WORKS.

PETTELMAN
CAJ has family records.

PETTIGREW
AJA has genealogical files.
Stern. FAJF. Pettigrew family
tree beginning in Scotland.
See GENERAL WORKS.

PETZRIK
Kempelen. Magyarországi Zsidó,
1:83. See GENERAL WORKS.

PEVZNER
Pribĺuda, A.S. "O
proiskhozhdenii familii
Pevzner ... Shapiro," (In
Russian.) Onomastica 16
(1971):225-32.

PEYNADO
CFM has family records.

PEYRON
Semi-Gotha, 2:110. See GENERAL
WORKS.

PFEFFER
Chelminsky-Lajmer, "Jewish
Surnames." See GENERAL
WORKS.

PFEIFFER
Kempelen. Magyarországi Zsidó,
3:26, 70, 79, 96. See
GENERAL WORKS.
See Stern, FAJF (III) entry
under PHILLIPS.

PFLAUM
Cohen, Arthur. "Geschichte der
Familie Cohen mit
Berücksichtigung der Familien
Marx und Pflaum. Mit
ergänzenden Anmerkungen und
einem Stammbaum (1558-1940)
versehen von Willy Cohen."
(München, 1934-1935) und New
York, 1956. 29 p. Includes
Pflaum family. LBI.
Scholem, Gershom. From Berlin
to Jerusalem: Memories of My
Youth. Translated from the
German by Harry Zohn. New
York: Schocken Books, 1980.
178 p. "Background and
Childhood (1897-1910)," pp.
1-20. Includes genealogical
information on the Scholem
family and the families of
the author's mother: Hirsch
and Pflaum. The Scholem
family came to Berlin from
Glogau, Lower Silesia, in the
second decade of the
nineteenth century, while the
Hirsch and Pflaum families
came to Berlin from Reetz,
Rawicz, and Lissa.

PFUNGST
CFM has family records.

PHIBBS
AMH has family records.

PHIEBIG
LBI has family tree beginning
1639.

PHILIᴾPI
Tille, Armin. "Eine
Judenfamilie Philippi,"

Familiengeschichtliche
Blätter 33 (1935):270-71.

PHILIPPSON
AMH has family records.
CAJ has family records.
LBI has family tree beginning
1518.
Ballin. Juden in Seesen,
p. 225. Philippson family.
See GENERAL WORKS.
Philippson, Johanna. "The
Philippsons, a German Jewish
Family, 1775-1933," LBI Year
Book 7 (1962):95-118.

PHILIPS
CAJ has family records from
Germany, 1779-1884.
See Esmond S. De Beer entry
under BARDEN.
"Stamboom van de familie
Philips bei Zaltbommel."
[Family Tree of the Philips
Family in Zalt-Bommel].
Document in the International
Institute for Social History,
Amsterdam, The Netherlands.

PHILIPSEN
Fischer, Josef and Th.
Hauch-Fausboll. Familien
Philipsen i Pilestraede.
Kφbenhavn, 1920. 145 p.
Descendants of Nathan Moses,
d. 1675, Altona, Germany.
OCH.

PHILIPSON
AMH has family records.
CFM has family records.
Philipson Family, St. Louis,
Mo. "Biographical Data,
1809-1844." Typescript.
AJA.
Makovsky, Donald I. The
Philipsons, the First Jewish
Settlers in St. Louis,
1807-1858. St. Louis: The
Judaism Sesquicentennial
Committee of St. Louis,
Thanksgiving Day, 1958.
Unpaged. The Philipson
family was originally from
Hamburg. DLC, ICN, NjP, NNJ,
OCH, PHi.

Rothschild. Svenska Israel.
See GENERAL WORKS.
Semi-Gotha, 2:126ff. See
GENERAL WORKS.

PHILLIP
AMH has family records.

PHILLIPS
See FAUDELL-PHILLIPS.
AJA has family tree beginning
in 18th-century Bohemia.
AMH has family records.
CFM has family records.
JE, 10:3. "Pedigree of the
Phillips Family."
Descendants of Jonas
Phillips, b. Germany, 1736;
d. Philadelphia, 1803;
through early 20th century.
See GENERAL WORKS.
Reznick, Samuel. The Saga of
an American Jewish Family
Since the Revolution: A
History of the Family of
Jonas Phillips. Washington,
D.C.: University Press of
America, 1980. 227 p.
Author also shows relations
of family with other Jewish
American families, e.g.,
Machado, Seixas, Cardozo,
Peixotto, and Hendricks.
Sarna, Jonathan D. Jacksonian
Jew: The Two Worlds of
Mordecai Noah. New York:
Holmes & Meier, 1981. 233 p.
Genealogical information
concerning the Noah and
Phillips (South Carolina)
families, pp. 1-3. Mordecai
Noah (1785-1851) was born in
Philadelphia, the son of
Manuel Mordecai (1755-1822)
and Zipporah Phillips Noah
(1764-1792). Manual Noah was
a native of Mannheim,
Germany.
Stern. FAJF. Phillips family
trees beginning in:
(I) Buseck, Germany;
(II) Bohemia; (III) Anspach
(originally named Pfeiffer);
(IV) England; (V and
VII) Amsterdam; and
(VI) London (originally named

Levy). See GENERAL WORKS.
Phillips Family. "Report of An
Interview with Three
Grandchildren of Simon
Phillips, Los Angeles,
Calif., July 8, 1973 by
N.B. Stern," [Santa Monica,
Calif.] 1973. Typescript.
12 p. "This report contains
biographical data on the
Phillips family and
information on their business
interests." Simon Phillips
came to California in the
late 1860s. The Jewish
Community Library, Los
Angeles, Calif.
Wolf, "Anglo-Jewish Families."
See GENERAL WORKS.

PHILLIPSON
AMH has family records.

PIA
AMH has family records.

PICA
PD has family records.

PICARD
AMH has family records.
Picard family Bible, 1831-1884.
AJA.
Mirwis, L. Geschichte der
Familie Epstein. N.p., 1927.
80 p. Family table for the
Epstein family from
Eichstetten, Germany,
mid-1700s-1920s. Dates of
births, marriages, and deaths
included on family table,
pp. 23-80. Also descendants
of Rabbi Eljakim Picard of
Randegg (His wife, Marie
Epstein, was born in 1838 in
Eichstetten.) and descendants
of Herri Kahn (1848-1922) in
Freiburg. CAJ, Call
No. 5434.
See Jacob Picard entry under
BIGARD.

PICHLER
Kempelen. Magyarországi Zsidó,
3:96. See GENERAL WORKS.

PICK
CAJD has family tree from
Germany.
LBIS has family tree.
PD has family records.
Kempelen. Magyarországi Zsidó,
1:126; 2:12, 67, 97. See
GENERAL WORKS.

PICKLES
AMH has family records.

PICON
See PYEKOON.

PIDWELL
AMH has family records.

PIGGOT
AMH has family records.

PIKE
Stern. FAJF. Pike family
trees beginning in: (I) U.S.
(originally Levy); and
(II) Amsterdam. See GENERAL
WORKS.

PILESTRAEDE
Fischer, Josef and Th.
Hauch-Fausboll. Familien
Philipsen i Pilestraede.
København, 1920. 145 p.
Descendants of Nathan Moses,
d. 1675, Altona, Germany.
OCH.

PILZ
AMH has family records.

PIMENTAL
Maduro, J.M.L. "A Genealogical
Note on the Pimental, Lopez,
Sasportas, and Rivera
Families," Publications of
the American Jewish
Historical Society 42
(1952):303.
CFM has family records.

PINCHAS
AMH has family records.

PINCHERLE
AMH has family records.
Rabello, A.M. "Gli ebrei a

Ceneda e a Vittorio Veneto
(con alcuni documenti sulla
famiglia Pincherle),"
Rassegna Mensile di Israel 36
(1970):345-58.

PINCOFTS
CFM has family records.

PINCZOVER
CAJ (Call No. 2067) has two
family trees: Family tree of
Rawitz family of Breslau and
family tree of Wollheim
(formerly Pinczover) family
of Breslau. Neither family
tree provides dates of births
or deaths of family members.

PINCZOWER
"Pinczower," JFF, no. 39
(1935):696. Pedigree of
Elieser Pinczower, Kempen.

PINDER
Kempelen. Magyarországi Zsidó,
3:32. See GENERAL WORKS.

PINERO
CFM has family records.

PINES
Esaguy, Augusto d'. Les Pines,
une famille de médicins et
d'écrivains. Lisboa:
Editorial Império, 1954.
8 p. JNUL.
Pines, Jerome Martin. The
Sermons of Jerome Martin
Pines with a Partial
Genealogy of the Pines
Family. Edited by Wayne L.
Pines. Washington, D.C.: By
the Author, 1978. 100 p.
Pines family is originally
from Kopyl, White Russia.
DLC, NN, OCH.

PINEUS
Semi-Gotha, 1:143ff. See
GENERAL WORKS.

PINHEIRO
Stern. FAJF. Pinheiro family
tree beginning in Amsterdam.
See GENERAL WORKS.

PINKUS
LBI has family tree.
Brilling, Bernhard. "Vier
Generationen der Familie
Pinkus aus Neustadt O/S,"
Aufbau, Apr. 22, 1977.

PINNA (DE)
See DE PINNA.

PINNER (DE)
See DE PINNER.

PINTER
Kempelen. Magyarországi Zsidó,
2:88, 94. Pintér family.
See GENERAL WORKS.

PINTHUS
LBI has family tree beginning
1744.

PINTO
AMH has family records.
CFM has family records.
Révah, I.S. "Généalogie de
l'economiste Isaac de Pinto
(1717-1787)," in Mélanges à
la Mémoire de Jean Sarrailh
(Paris, 1966), 2:265-80.
Salomon, Herman P. "The 'De
Pinto' Manuscript: A 17th
Century Marrano Family
History," Studia
Rosenthaliana 9 (1975):1-62.
Stern. FAJF. Pinto family
tree beginning in U.S. See
GENERAL WORKS.

PINTO DE BUTTO
Samuel, E.R. "Portuguese Jews
in Jacobean England," Jewish
Historical Society of England
Transactions 18 (1958):181.
Pedigree chart of family of
England.

PINZCOWER
CAJ has family history,
1599-1930.

PIO
AMH has family records.

PISA (DA)
Cassuto, Umberto. "Sulla

famiglia da Pisa," Rivista
Israelitica (Firenze) 6
(1909):21-30, 102-113,
160-70, 223-32; 7
(1910):9-19, 72-86, 146-50.
Published separately in 1910.
82 p. PPDrop.
Gutterman, Vita Lindo. The
Chronicle of Joshua Pisa and
His Descendants. New York,
1928. Includes many
documents, genealogies, and
letters. Family hisory,
begining 18th century. AJA.
Kaufmann, David. "Abraham ben
Isaac de Pise," Revue des
Études Juives 32
(1896):130-34.
———. "La famille de Yehiel
'de Pise.'" Revue des Études
Juives 29 (1894):142-47; 31
(1895):62-73.
———. "Notes sur l'histoire
de la famille 'de Pise.'"
Revue des Études Juives 26
(1893):83-96.

PISAR
Pisar, Samuel. Of Blood and
Hope. Boston: Little, Brown,
& Co., 1979. The early part
of the book deals with Pisar
family life in Bialystok
before and during W.W.II.

PISK
CFM has family records.

PISSARRO
Adler, Kathleen. Camille
Pissarro: A Biography. New
York: St. Martin's Press,
1978. 208 p. "Pissarro
Family Tree," p. 8, includes
the descendants of Pierre
Pissarro (b. 18th century,
Bragança, Portugal) who
settled in Bordeaux, France.
[Jacob] Camille Pissarro
(1830-1903), the famous
French artist, was born in
Charlotte Amalie, St. Thomas,
West Indies. Pp. 9-12 also
include Pissarro family
history information.

PITLUCK
Pitluck Family, St. Joseph, Mo.
"The History of the Pitluck
Family," by Mollie Pitluck
Bell, 1974; Typescript. AJA.

PITTE (DE LA)
See DE LA PITTE.

PIZA
AMH has family records.

PLAGER
Kempelen. Magyarországi Zsidó,
3:50. See GENERAL WORKS.
Zyskind, Sara. Stolen Years.
Minneapolis: Lerner
Publications, 1981. 284 p.
Covers 1939-1946. Many
relatives' names are
interspersed throughout the
text. The author (1920-   )
was born in Lodz, the
daughter of Anschel Kalman
Plager. Her father was born
in Drochovitz. DLC.

PLAUEN
Semi-Gotha, 1:100. See GENERAL
WORKS.

PLATNAUER
AMH has family records.

PLATZ
Kempelen. Magyarországi Zsidó,
2:101. See GENERAL WORKS.

PLAU
AJA has family tree beginning
1726 from Sweden.

PLAUR
Kempelen. Magyarországi Zsidó,
2:87. See GENERAL WORKS.

PLAUT
AJA has family tree beginning
in 18th-century Germany.
See CAJ (Call No. P/123) entry
under ECKSTEIN.
CAJ, Call No. 5251, has the
following family histories:
(1) "Frielendorf Plaut
Family." 17 p. History of
Plaut family, data and

biographical notes on family
members, pp. 2-8. Family
tree, pp. 9-17, starts with
Abraham Plaut, early 1700s,
and continues to 1980.
(2) "The Plauts from
Rotenburg/Fulda." 4 p.
Family tree, p. 4, starts
with Heinemann Plaut
(1781/82-1841), who married
Mundel Strauss (1791-1867),
and continues to 1979.
(3) Family tree of Plaut
family of Schmalkalden,
1781-1975. (4) Family tree
of Plaut family from Wehrda,
which starts with Simon Plaut
(1776-1837). Also in same
folder: Family tree showing
descendants of Ruben Moses
Plaut and Simon Plaut, both
of whom were born in second
half of 18th century.
Continues to late 1970s.
(5) "Plaut Family Tree from
Geisa." 15 p. Starts with
Jacob Plaut, late 1600s, and
continues to 1979. All of
the above family trees were
compiled by Elizabeth S.
Plaut.
See Fisher Family entry under
FISHER.
LBI has family trees beginning
1675 and 1843.
Ballin. Juden in Seesen,
p. 226. Plaut family. See
GENERAL WORKS.
Plaut, Elizabeth S. "Scouring
the World for Plauts: The
Making of a Jewish
Genealogist," American Jewish
Archives 32 (1980):137-44.
Family originally of Germany.
W. Gunther Plaut Family Notes,
1830-1908; In Hebrew and
English. Extracted from a
Biblical commentary. AJA.
Plaut, W. Gunther. Descendants
of Rabbi Rudolf Plaut: A
Genealogical Record. Chevy
Chase, Md., 1973. AJA.
Rosenstein. Unbroken Chain,
pp. 81ff. See GENERAL WORKS.

PLESSNER
CAJ has family records.

PLISKAN
Pliskan Family Genealogy, 1946.
1 microfilm reel. Family
history dealing primarily
with Chassidic roots of
Pliskan family in Vilna,
Poland. AJA.

PLOTNICK
Plotnick, Tuvia. B'netivei
Hanedudim. Israel: By the
Author, 1970. 504 p.
History of the author's
family beginning with his
grandfather, Zeev Plotnick,
born in 1842 in village of
Guripka (?) near town of
Starye (?) in the Ukraine.

POCHAPOVSKY
Picker, Howard. Family Tree:
Descendants of Velvel
Pochapovsky, Horodyszcze,
White Russia (c. 1800-?).
Rev. ed. Albany, N.Y., 1971.
45 p. AJA, N.

PODET
AJA has genealogical files.

PODMANICZKY
Kempelen. Magyarországi Zsidó,
1:144; 3:63. See GENERAL
WORKS.

PODRO
CAJ has family records.

POHLY
Ballin. Juden in Seesen,
p. 227. Pohly family. See
GENERAL WORKS.

POLACCO
AMH has family records.

POLACK
AJA has genealogical files.
AMH has family records.
CFM has family records.
Rose. Schöninger Juden.
Includes Polack family. See
GENERAL WORKS.

POLAG
See BOLLAG.

POLAK
AMH has family records.

POLAND
AMH has family records.

POLATSCHEK
CAJ has family records.

POLEVOI
Gray, Betty Anne. Manya's
Story. Minneapolis: Lerners,
1978. 127 p. An account of
the Abramson and Polevoi
families' ordeal in
Revolutionary Russia,
1917-1922. The author's
mother, Manya Polevoi
Abramson (d. 1975), and her
father, Israel Abramson, were
from the Tolne, Ukraine area,
and came to U.S. in 1925.
This work also includes many
photos of the Abramson and
Polevoi families. DLC.

POLIAKOFF
CFM has family records.

POLIANOWSKY
AMH has family records.

POLKE
LBI has family tree beginning
1776.

POLLACK
CAJ has a collection of
material on history of
Pollack family in Silesia
during 18th to 20th century.
LBI has family tree beginning
1772.
Louis, Julius (1833-1892)
Collection, 1778-1965. 1
folder. Includes
genealogical material dealing
with Pollack family,
1778-1943, and Bernstein and
Louis families, 1840-1965.
Baltimore, Md., and Norfolk,
Va. AJA.
Ballin. Juden in Seesen,

p. 228. Family history. See
GENERAL WORKS.

Gold. Juden Mährens, p. 574.
Includes family tree of the
descendants of Friedrich
Pollack, 1831-1914, and
Joshua Pollack, 1829-1905,
both born in Wöking and died
in Vienna. See GENERAL
WORKS.

POLLACSEK, POLLATSEK
Kempelen. Magyarországi Zsidó,
1:66, 91, 94, 104, 142; 3:45,
93. See GENERAL WORKS.

POLLACZEK
Tänzer. Juden in Tirol,
p. 754. See GENERAL WORKS.

POLLAK
CFM has family records.
PD has family records.
Kempelen. Magyarországi Zsidó,
1:131, 137; 2:8, 9, 56, 121,
124, 142; 3:55, 90, 105, 116.
Pollák family. See GENERAL
WORKS.
Zapf. Tübinger Juden, pp.
58-59, 165-68, 217. See
GENERAL WORKS.

POLLATSEK
See POLLACSEK, POLLATSEK.

POLLENSKY
Kempelen. Magyarországi Zsidó,
3:55. See GENERAL WORKS.

POLLITZER
AMH has family records.

POLLOCK
AJA has genealogical files.
Pollock Family. "Genealogical
Information and Family Tree,
1868-1964." AJA.
"David Pollock and His
Descendants." N.p., n.d.
4 p. PHi.
Wolf, Edwin. "Genealogy of the
Levy and Pollock Families."
Philadelphia. AJA.

POLNAY
Kempelen. Magyarországi

Zsidó, 2:142. See GENERAL
WORKS.

POLOCK
AMH has family records.
Stern. FAJF. Polock family
trees beginning in: (I) U.S.
and (II) Amsterdam. See
GENERAL WORKS.
Wolf, Edwin. Rosenbach: A
Biography. Cleveland: World
Publishing Co., 1960. 616 p.
Rosenbach family information
as well as much genealogical
data on the Polock family of
Philadelphia--Rosenbach's
mother's family--on pp.
13-26. Abraham Simon Wolf
Rosenbach (1876-1952) was an
internationally known rare
books dealer in Philadelphia.

POLONYI
Kempelen. Magyarországi Zsidó,
2:94; 3:45. Polónyi family.
See GENERAL WORKS.

POLYA
Kempelen. Magyarországi Zsidó,
1:70, 79; 2:121; 3:71. Pólya
family. See GENERAL WORKS.

POMPER
Kempelen. Magyarországi Zsidó,
1:73. Pompér family. See
GENERAL WORKS.

PONGRACZ
Kempelen. Magyarországi Zsidó,
2:31; 3:27. Pongrácz family.
See GENERAL WORKS.

PONTING
AMH has family records.

POP
See EHRENFELD-POP.
Kempelen. Magyarországi Zsidó,
1:81. SEE GENERAL WORKS.

POPPER
AMH has family records.
PD has family records.
Bató, Ludwig. "Ein jüdisches
Adelsgeschlecht," Menorah
(Frankfurt am Main) 4

303   POSBITYANSKY

(1926):70-72. Joachim Edler
von Popper (b. Bresnitz,
Bohemia, 1720; d. Prague,
1795), merchant, banker, and
philanthropist. He was
enobled in 1790.
Kempelen. Magyarországi Zsidó,
1:52, 86; 2:90, 91; 3:126,
129. See GENERAL WORKS.
Krauss, Samuel. "Die
Primatorenfamilie 'Popper'
und ihre Ausläufer," ZGJT 5
(1938):40-44, 69-84.
Rückler, Günther. "Über meinen
urgrossvater Anton Popper und
die seinen," Sinn und Form
(East Berlin) 33
(1981):1177-91.
Tänzer. Juden in Tirol,
p. 755. See GENERAL WORKS.

POPPERT
See Daniel J. Cohen entry under
CLEVE. Poppert family from
Altona, Germany, pp. 54-58.
Includes family tree, 1600s
to 1883.
Familienminder Tilegnet.
Poppert-Schiff family,
pp. 90-96. See GENERAL
WORKS.

PORAT
Semi-Gotha, 1:108. See GENERAL
WORKS.

PORGES
CFM has family records.
Kempelen. Magyarországi Zsidó,
3:23. See GENERAL WORKS.
Stammbaum der Familien Porges.
Kassel, 1906. Family of
Portheim. OCH.
Tänzer. Juden in Tirol,
p. 756. See GENERAL WORKS.

PORTA
See Siegfried Porta entry under
FALKENSTEIN. Includes family
trees. Table of descendants
of Abraham Basch (1545-1590)
and Marcus Jakob Levi (at
Brakel or Ottenberg,
ca. 1648). His children or
grandchildren are named
Porta, Steinheim,

Falkenstein, Goldsmith,
Löwenstein, and Rosenberg.

PORTALEONE
Colorni, Vittore. "Note per la
biographia di alcuni dotti
ebrei vissuti a Mantova nel
secolo XV," Annuario di Studi
Ebraici, 1934, pp. 169-82.
Luzzatto, L. "Appunti storici
sulla famiglia Portaleone,"
Il Vessillo Israelitico 43
(1895):154ff.
Mortara, Marco. "Un important
document sur la famille des
Portaleone," Revue des Études
Juives. 12 (1886):113-16.

PORTALEONE-SOMMO
Steinschneider, Moritz. "Die
Familie Portaleone-Sommo,"
Hebräische Bibliographie 6
(1863):48ff.

PORTELLO
CFM has family records.

PORTEN
LBI has family tree beginning
1884.

PORTNER
LBI has family tree beginning
1847.

PORTUGALI
Portugali, Yacov. Mishpachat
Haportugalim. Tel Aviv,
N.p., 1979. 146 p. JNUL.

PORUSH
Porush, Elijah. Zikhronot
Rishnim. Jerusalem, 1963.
144 p. A section of the book
is about the author's family.
CLU, DLC, MH.

POS
AMH has family records.

POSBITYANSKY
Urieli, Menachem. B'shuv Banim
Ligvulam. Israel, 1981.
277 p. Includes genealogical
table, potraits. Menachem
Urieli, born in Nevel in the

province of Vitebsk, White
Russia, 1904, came to Israel
in 1923. His father was
Eliezer Posbityansky,
1867-1923. CZA.

POSE
See LEGUM.

POSNER
See LEGUM.
Kempelen. Magyarországi Zsidó,
1:61; 2:30. See GENERAL
WORKS.
Posner, Stanley Irving, Helen
Posner Fuld, and Milton
Posner. The Posner Family
Tree. New York: Posner
Family Circle, 1953. 60 p.
On the Posner Family Circle,
1928-1953, and the origin of
the family as Russian Jews.
DLC, OCH.

POSSE
Semi-Gotha, 1:39, 148. See
GENERAL WORKS.

POST, POSTOLOV
See LEGUM. Post(?) Family.
Post, Ben W. "Brief Genealogy
of the Post (Postolov)
Family." Louisville, Ky.,
1975. AJA.

POWERS
Frank. Nashville Jewry,
p. 140. Family from England.
See GENERAL WORKS.

POZNANSKI
Stern. FAJF. Poznánski family
tree beginning in Storchnest,
Poland. See GENERAL WORKS.

PRAAGH (VAN)
See VAN PRAAGH.

PRADO
AMH has family records.
CFM has family records.

PRAGER
AMH has family records.
CAJ has family records,
1868-1908.

CFM has family records.
LBI has family tree beginning
1503.

PRAGNER
Kempelen. Magyarországi Zsidó,
1:73. See GENERAL WORKS.

PREININGER
Kempelen. Magyarországi Zsidó,
3:99. See GENERAL WORKS.

PREISACH
Kempelen. Magyarországi Zsidó,
1:75. See GENERAL WORKS.

PREISZ
Kempelen. Magyarországi Zsidó,
2:133. See GENERAL WORKS.

PREIZ
See Stern, FAJF entry under
PRICE.

PRENZLAU
Semi-Gotha, 1:106ff. See
GENERAL WORKS.

PRERAUER
LBI has family tree beginning
1814.

PRESBORCK, PRESBORG, PRESBURG
Padover, Saul K. Karl Marx: An
Intimate Biography. New
York: McGraw-Hill Book Co.,
1978. 667 p. "The Family,"
pp. 1-12. Contents:
Rabbinical Ancestors; Karl
Marx's father; Karl Marx's
mother. "Marx's Paternal
Ancestors," p. 615; Marx's
Maternal Relatives," p. 616;
"Heschel (Heinrich) Marx's
Children," p. 617; and "Karl
Marx's Descendants," pp.
618-19. Karl Marx was the
son of Heschel (Heinrich) and
Henriette Presburg Marx. The
Pressburg family (also
spelled Presborg, Presborck)
was a Dutch-Jewish family
from Nijmegen.

PRESCOTT
AMH has family records.

PRESS
See GLASER.

PRESSBURG
AMH has family records.

PRESSBURGER
LBI has family tree beginning
   1630.

PREST
AMH has family records.

PRESTON
AMH has family records.

PREUSS
Preuss, Walter. "Bilder aus
   der Geschichte einer
   jüdischen Familie aus vier
   Jahrhunderten,"
   Mitteilungsblatt (Tel Aviv),
   no. 15/16 (8 Apr. 1960).

PREYER
CAJ has family records.

PREZLMAYER
Kempelen. Magyarországi Zsidó,
   3:24. See GENERAL WORKS.

PRICE
AMH has family records.
Wolf Family. Papers,
   c. 1970-1977. 1 Folder.
   "Biographical material, 1976,
   of Howard A. Wolf (1900-   )
   and genealogical information
   about his ancestors and those
   of his wife, Martha Rosenthal
   Wolf, including members of
   the Wolf, Rosenthal, Loeb,
   Fels, and Price families,
   dating back to the 18th
   century." PJAC.
Lowenstein, Katherine
   Goldsmith.
   Price-Goldsmith-Lowenstein
   and Related Families,
   1700-1967. Edited by Harriet
   Stryker-Rodda. New York,
   1967. 49 p. Genealogical
   tables. DLC.
Stern. FAJF. Price family
   tree beginning in Mainz.

Originally spelled Preiz.
See GENERAL WORKS.

PRILUK
Wolsky, Boris. My Life in
   Three Worlds. Miami Beach,
   Fla.: By the Author, 1979.
   383 p. Includes genealogical
   table. The three worlds of
   the author (1898-   ) are
   turn-of-the-century Domacheva
   and Brest-Litovsk; Paris,
   where he lived from
   1914-1941; and the U.S. after
   1941, where he operated a
   travel agency in New York.
   "My Family," pp. 229-83.
   "Luba's Family," pp. 287-99.
   Luba, the author's wife, came
   from Smolensk and Lachowich,
   Russia. Her maiden name was
   Soloveichik. "The Wolsk
   Family," pp. 303-321. The
   author's uncle shortened
   family name from Wolsky to
   Wolsk. Author's maternal
   grandparents were the Priluk
   family, a history of which is
   covered on pp. 325-38.
   Family was from Kamenitz near
   Brest-Litovsk and later lived
   in Warsaw. DLC, University
   of
   Illinois / Champaign-Urbana
   Library.

PRINCE
AMH has family records.

PRINGSHEIM
LBI has family tree beginning
   1700.
Brilling, Bernhard. "Die
   Vorfahren der Familie
   Pringsheim," Mitteilungen des
   Verbändes ehemaliger
   Breslauer und Schlesier in
   Israel (Tel-Aviv), no. 20
   (Sept. 1966). Bernstadt
   (Schlesien).

PRINS
AMH has family records.
See Ludwig Herz entry under
   REICHENHEIM.

PRINTZ
Keneseth Israel. See GENERAL
WORKS.

PRINTZENSKOLD
Semi-Gotha, 1:26.
Printzensköld family. See
GENERAL WORKS.

PRINZ
AMH has family records.

PRIOR
See Esmond S. De Beer entry
under BARDEN.

PROBST
Rose, Karl. Familienkundliche
Nachrichten über die Familie
Probst mit Tagebuch eines
wandernden
Buchbindergesellen.
Schöningen, 1931. 98 p.
Family of Schöningen. LBI.
Rose. Schöninger Juden. See
GENERAL WORKS.

PROCHOWNIK
JFF, no. 6. Family history.

PRONT
See Stern, FAJF (III) entry
under ISAACS.

PROOPS
AMH has family records.

PROPPER
Kempelen. Magyarországi Zsidó,
1:126; 2:119; 3:48. See
GENERAL WORKS.

PROSCHWITZ
Semi-Gotha, 2:67. See GENERAL
WORKS.

PROSKAUER
LBI has family tree.

PROSZNITZ
Kempelen. Magyarországi Zsidó,
2:36, 73, 75. See GENERAL
WORKS.

PROVENZALI
"La famiglia Provenzali," Il

Vassillo Israelitico 52
(1904):267-69. From Mantova.

PROVUS
See R. Brock Shanberg entry
under GOLTZ.

PRUSS
Raphael, Chaim. A Coat of Many
Colours: Memoirs of a Jewish
Experience. London: Chatto
and Windus, 1979. 240 p.
"The Raphaels [sic] of
Vilkomir," pp. 34-52. Family
name really Pruss; the
author's father, David,
changed name to Rabinovitch
upon arrival in England; the
author in turn changed his
name to Raphael. The U.S.
relatives from Vilkomir,
however, retained the Pruss
family name. Author's
grandfather was Sabbatai
[Shepsi] Pruss.

PRYCE
AMH has family records.

PUISSEUS
Kempelen. Magyarországi Zsidó,
1:51, 55. See GENERAL WORKS.

PULITZER
Kempelen. Magyarországi Zsidó,
1:75. See GENERAL WORKS.

PULVERMACHER
AMH has family records.

PURJESZ
Kempelen. Magyarországi Zsidó,
2:65. See GENERAL WORKS.

PUTTKAMMER
Kempelen. Magyarországi Zsidó,
3:127. See GENERAL WORKS.

PYEKOON
Picon, Molly. So Laugh A
Little, As Told to Eth
Clifford Rosenberg. New
York: Julian Messner, 1962.
175 p. A large part of the
autobiography of this noted
American actress and comic

concerns her family, the
Ostrows and Pyekoons. The
author was the daughter of
Louis and Clara Ostrow
Pyekoon. The Ostrow family
was from Rezshishtchov,
Russia.

PYKE
AMH has family records.
CFM has family records.

PYSZNA
See Judith A. Walters entry
under GRYNSZPAN.

QUARESMA
CFM has family records.

QUIROS
CFM has family records.

QUITTNER
Kempelen. Magyarországi Zsidó,
3:126. See GENERAL WORKS.

QUIXANO
AMH has family records.

RAALTE (VAN)
AMH has family records.

RABA
CFM has family records.

RABBINOWITZ
"Gaon Reb Judah Mintz [and
Descendants]: A Genealogical
Chart." N.p., 19- .
Includes Rabbinowitz family.
NN.

RABHAN
Rabhan, Morris. Our Family
Story: Rabhan (Levites)
1840-1979. Savannah, 1979.
210 p. Story of family which
originated in Szinewa,

Galicia, and settled in
Savannah, Georgia. AJHS.

RABINOVITCH
See Chaim Raphael entry under
PRUSS.

RABINOWITZ
CAJ has family records.
See Yaffa Draznin entry under
BERNSTEIN. Includes family
histories.
Goldstick, Julie. The
Tannenbaum-Rabinowitz Family
Tree. New York, 1979.
Tannenbaum family originally
from Kobrin, Rabinowitz
family originally from
Slutsk, both towns in White
Russia. AJHS.
Rabinowitz, Chaim. Nine
Generations: 200 Years of
Memoirs of Our Family. Tel
Aviv, 1970. YIVO.
Rabinowitz, Mordechai. Book of
the Children of Moses. Tel
Aviv: Ha'aretz, 1928.
33 p. in English, and
45 p. in Hebrew. Mainly, the
genealogy of the descendants
of Rabbi Moses Rabbinowitz,
b. 1817; d. Yedwabno, Poland,
1893.
Rabinowitz, Sholom (pseud.,
Sholom Aleichem). The Great
Fair: Scenes from My
Childhood. New York: Noonday
Press, 1955. 306 p. Sholom
Aleichem (1859-1916) was born
in the village of Voronko,
Poltava, near Pereyaslov, the
son of Reb Nahum Vevik and
Haie-Esther Rabinowitz and
the grandson of Vevik
Rabinowitz.
Reichel, O. Asher. Isaac
Halevy, 1847-1919: Spokesman
and Historian of Jewish
Tradition. New York: Yeshiva
University Press, 1969.
Genealogical information on
the Ivenecer, Kovner, and
Rabinowitz ancestors of Isaac
Halevy, pp. 15-16. Isaac
Halevy (Rabinowitz) was born
in Ivenets, Province of

Minsk, near Vilna, the son of
R. Eliyahu and Rahel Kovner
Halevy Ivenecer Rabinowitz.
CLU, CSt, CtY, CU, ICU, MB,
MH, NcD, NIC, NjP, NN.
Rosenstein. Unbroken Chain,
pp. 232ff. Rabbinowitz
Chassidic dynasty of Radomsk.
See GENERAL WORKS.
————, pp. 542ff. Rabinowitz
Chassidic dynasty of
Linitz-Manisterich. See
GENERAL WORKS.

RABIZANOVICH
See Valentin Senger entry under
SENGER.

RACAH
AMH has family records.

RADER
Rader-Marcus Family.
"Genealogical Chart compiled
by Dr. Jacob Rader Marcus,
Cincinnati, Ohio." 1966.
AJA.

RADIO
Kempelen. Magyarországi Zsidó,
2:101. See GENERAL WORKS.

RADISSICH
Kempelen. Magyarországi Zsidó,
1:102. See GENERAL WORKS.

RADNAY-ROZSAY
Kempelen. Magyarországi Zsidó,
1:41. Radnay-Rozsáy family.
See GENERAL WORKS.

RADO
Kempelen. Magyarországi Zsidó,
2:66, 104; 3:62, 64. Radó
family. See GENERAL WORKS.

RADOS
Kempelen. Magyarországi Zsidó,
2:143. See GENERAL WORKS.

RADZIWILL
CAJ has family records.

RAFALOVICZ
Viertel, Salka. The Kindness
of Strangers. New York:

Holt, Rinehart and Winston,
1969. 338 p. Autobiography.
Especially, pp. 1-9.
Information concerning
Amster, Rafalovicz, and
Steuermann families of
Czernowitz and Sambor near
the town of Wychylowka in
Galicia.

RAFF
AJA has family tree beginning
1699 in Germany.
Tänzer. Juden in Jebenhausen,
pp. 358-61. See GENERAL
WORKS.

RALPH
AMH has family records.

RAMSAY
Semi-Gotha, 1:77, 82, 134. See
GENERAL WORKS.

RANSOHOFF
Ransohoff Family (Cincinnati,
Ohio) Family Tree, 1800-1935;
MS. AJA.

RANTZEN
AMH has family records.

RAPER
AMH has family records.

RAPHAEL
AMH has family records.
CFM has family records.
See Esmond S. De Beer entry
under BARDEN.
Raphael, Alice Pearl. Papers,
1812-1960. Include history
of Raphael family in Canada,
Europe, New York, and Texas
(Brownsville/Matamoros area).
TxU, Texas Archives
Collection.
See Chaim Raphael entry under
PRUSS.
Raphael, Marc L. A Family
Story: Fifty Years in Los
Angeles. Los Angeles?, 1964.
45 p. Typescript. Includes
brief genealogical outlines
of the families. Also
includes Babin family. AJA.

Wolf, "Anglo-Jewish Families."
See GENERAL WORKS.

RAPHAELOWITZ
CAJ has family records.

RAPOPORT
Brann, Markus. "Das Geschlecht
der 'Jungen Raben' (Die
Familie Rapoport)," Jahrbuch
zur Belehrung und
Unterhaltung 38 (1890):3-20.
Family of Breslau.
Carmoly, Eliakim. Ha-'orvim
u-bene yonha. Rödelheim,
1861. 48 p. On Rapoport and
Jungtauben families.
Eisenstadt and Wiener. Da'at
Kedoschim. See GENERAL
WORKS.
Reifmann, Jakob. "Toledot
R. Abraham Menaḥem bar
Ja'aḳob ha-Kohen...,"
Ha-Šaḥar (Vienna) 3
(1870):353-76. Includes a
genealogy of Rapoport family.
Shapiro. Mishpachot Atikot.
See GENERAL WORKS.

RAPPAPORT
Kahan. 'Anaf 'ez avoth. See
GENERAL WORKS.

RAPPOPORT
Bałaban. Dzieje Żydów,
1:162, 164. Genealogical
chart of the descendants of
Gerson Rappoport. See
GENERAL WORKS.
Rosenstein. Unbroken Chain,
pp. 467ff. Rappoport
descendants of the Chacham
Zvi Hirsch Ashkenazi. See
GENERAL WORKS.
————, pp. 288ff. Rappoport
descendants of R. Ari Lieb
Katz. See GENERAL WORKS.

RASHI
Chone [or Huneh(?)], Hayim.
"Mi-geza Rashi [Descendants
of Rashi]," Sinaï 10
(1942?):270-76.

RASKES
Eile Toledot Harav ... Moshe

Raskes. Odessa, n.p., 1865?
8 p. Genealogy of the
descendants of Rabbi Moshe
Raskes. JNUL.

RASO
Kempelen. Magyarországi Zsidó,
2:102. Rásó family. See
GENERAL WORKS.

RAST
Kempelen. Magyarországi Zsidó,
2:98. See GENERAL WORKS.

RATHBONE
AMH has family records.

RATHENAU
Berglar-Schröer, Hans Peter.
Walther Rathenau: Seine Zeit,
Sein Werk, Seine
Persönalichkeit. Bremen:
Schönemann
Universitätsverlag, 1970.
416 p. "Familie und
Freunde," pp. 307-315.
Walter Rathenau (1867-1922),
German engineer,
industrialist, and statesman,
was the son of Emil Rathenau
(1838-1915), the German
engineer who organized the
German telephone and electric
systems, and the grandson of
Moritz Rathenau (1799-1871).
DLC, MH.

RATZENDORFER
Kempelen. Magyarországi Zsidó,
2:68. See GENERAL WORKS.

RAUBENHEIMER
Raubenheimer, Denis, comp.
Familia Raubenheimer. Edited
by R.T.J. Lombard. Pretoria:
Raad vir Geesteswetenskaplike
Navorsing, 1978. 185 p.
"Name Index," pp. 177-82.
"Photo Index," pp. 183-84.
DLC.

RAUSSNITZ
Kempelen. Magyarországi Zsidó,
2:143. See GENERAL WORKS.

RAVA
AMH has family records.

RAVENNA
AMH has family records.
Ravenna, G.F. "Leone Ravenna e
Felice di Leone Ravenna,"
Rassegna Mensile di Israel 36
(1970):407-15.

RAW
AMH has family records.

RAWICZ
See RAWITZ.
LBI has family trees beginning
1725 and 1755.
Reychman. Szkice
genealogiczne, pp. 153-54.
See GENERAL WORKS.

RAWITZ
CAJ (Call No. 2067) Has two
family trees: Family tree of
Rawitz family of Breslau and
family tree of Wollheim
family (formerly Pinczover)
of Breslau. However, neither
of the family trees provides
dates of births and deaths of
family members.

RAY
AMH has family records.

RAYMOND
AMH has family records.

REAL
AMH has family records.

REBELLO
AMH has family records.
CFM has family records.

RECHNITZ
LBI has family tree beginning
1785.

RECHNITZER
Kempelen. Magyarországi Zsidó,
2:92. See GENERAL WORKS.

RECHT
Kempelen. Magyarországi Zsidó,
3:53. See GENERAL WORKS.

RECHTHANDT
Conrich, J. Lloyd, comp. "The
Levy (Levi or Rechthandt)
Family, 1820-." 1965. WJHC.

REDELSHEIMER
Redelsheimer Family.
"Genealogical Chart,
1816-1957." AJA.
Frank. Nashville Jewry,
p. 147. Family originally
from Württemberg. See
GENERAL WORKS.

REDL
Kempelen. Magyarországi Zsidó,
2:129. Rédl family. See
GENERAL WORKS.

REDLICH
PD has family records.
Kempelen. Magyarországi Zsidó,
2:130; 3:61, 318. Rédlich
family. See GENERAL WORKS.

REE
CFM has Reé family tree.
Fischer, Josef. Hartvig Philip
Rée og hans slaegt. Udgivet
paa Foranledning
af ... E. Rée. København:
Hertz, 1912. 74 p. In
Danish, French, and German.
Printed as MS. Danish
family, originally from
Hamburg. OCH, LBI.

REES
AMH has family records.

REEVES
See Esmond S. De Beer entry
under BARDEN.

REGENSBURGER
Kaufmann, Alfred. "Anshej
Rhenus: A Chronicle of Jewish
Life by the Rhine." Santa
Rosa, Calif., 1953. 12 p.
Includes brief 300-year
history of the Kaufmann (from
Viernheim bei Mannheim),
Sternheimer (from Viernheim),
Regensburger (from Eppingen),
and Wolf (from Rohrbach)
families. LBI.

Tänzer. Juden in Jebenhausen,
pp. 362-63. See GENERAL
WORKS.

Sallis-Freudenthal, Margarette.
Ich habe mein Land gefunden;
Autobiographischer Rüchlbick.
Frankfurt-am-Main: Josef
Knecht, 1977. 207 p.
Pp. 1-15 and "Familienchronik
aus meiner mütterlichen
Familie," pp. 166-74. Author
was born in Speyer, Germany
in 1893. Mother's family
surname was Regensburger; the
family was from Eppingen,
Baden. DLC.

REGNER
Kempelen. Magyarországi Zsidó,
1:44. See GENERAL WORKS.

REH
Reh, Alfred. "L'arbre
généalogique d'une famille
alsacienne," Bull. De Nos
Comm. 8, no. 10 (1952):10-11;
no. 11 (1952):10-11. Jochil
(Joachim) Reh, from end of
18th century. Also published
in Amif (Paris) 2
(Apr. 1953):46-57.

REHBINDER
Semi-Gotha, 1:78. See GENERAL
WORKS.

REICH
Kempelen. Magyarországi Zsidó,
2:133; 3:68, 92. See GENERAL
WORKS.
Yaoz. Album Shel. See GENERAL
WORKS.
See Meir Yizraeli entry under
BIDERMAN.

REICHENBACH
CFM has family records.
LBI has family tree beginning
1825.
Tänzer. Juden in Tirol,
pp. 757-61. See GENERAL
WORKS.

REICHENBERG
Kempelen. Magyarországi Zsidó,
1:87. See GENERAL WORKS.

REICHENHEIM
Herz, Ludwig. N. Reichenheim
und Sohn. Geschichte eines
werkes und einer Familie.
Als Privatschrift zur für den
engsten Familienkreis
bestimmt. Berlin, 1936.
132 p. Family of
Bernburg/Anhalt and Berlin.
Includes Berend, Eisner,
Herz, Liebermann, Prins,
Reichenheim, and Sanders
families. LBI.

REICHMANN
Kempelen. Magyarországi Zsidó,
3:124. See GENERAL WORKS.

REIK
Kempelen. Magyarországi Zsidó,
3:51. See GENERAL WORKS.

REIMANN
Kempelen. Magyarországi Zsidó,
2:97. See GENERAL WORKS.

REINACH
CAJ has family records.

REINAUER
Zapf. Tübinger Juden, pp.
218-20. See GENERAL WORKS.

REINBERT
AMH has family records.

REINER
Kempelen. Magyarországi Zsidó,
3:60. See GENERAL WORKS.

REINES
CAJ has family records.
Rosenstein. Unbroken Chain,
pp. 237ff. The Reines
descendants of R. Solomon
Zalman Katzenellenbogen. See
GENERAL WORKS.

REINFELD
Kempelen. Magyarországi Zsidó,
2:134. See GENERAL WORKS.

REINGANUM
AMH has family records.

REINHEIMER-STERN
Kopp. Jüdischen Alsenz,
pp. 135-36. See GENERAL
WORKS.

REINHERZ
Pétrement, Simone. Simone
Weil: A Life. Translated
from the French by Raymond
Rosenthal. New York:
Pantheon, 1977. 577 p.
"Family and Childhood
(1909-1925)," pp. 3-24.
Biography of the noted
philosopher (1909-1943) who
converted to Catholicism. Her
parents were Dr. Bernard
(1872-1955) and Selma
[Salomea] Reinherz Weil
(1879-1965); her grandparents
were Abraham and Eugénie Weil
and Adolphe Reinherz (d. 1906).
The Weil family came
to Paris from Alsace, the
Reinherz family from
Rostov-an-Don, Russia and
Galicia.

REINITZ
Kempelen. Magyarországi Zsidó,
2:70, 102, 122, 129. See
GENERAL WORKS.

REINWALD
CAJ has family records.

REIS
AJA has genealogical files.
LBI has family trees beginning
1670 and 1780.
Mayer, John; New York and
Natchez, Miss. "Family
Genealogy and Short Story
Concerning Mayer and His
Wife, Jeanette Reis, during
the Civil War Period." 1929.
Typescript. AJA.
Semi-Gotha, 1:89ff. See
GENERAL WORKS.

REISNER
Semi-Gotha, 1:139ff. See
GENERAL WORKS.

REISS
See SPRING.

AMH has family records.
CFM has family records.
Hirsch, Louis.
"Familiengeschichte und
Lebenserinnerungen."
Stuttgart, 1937. 149 p.
Family of Stuttgart.
Forbears and children of
Louis Hirsch, 1858-1941, and
his wife, Helene Reiss. LBI.
Kempelen. Magyarországi Zsidó,
2:35. See GENERAL WORKS.
See Nathan M. Reiss entry under
EDELMUTH. Includes Reiss
family of Ulrichstein.
Semi-Gotha, 1:89. See GENERAL
WORKS.
Ullmann, Elias.
Familien-Register und
Stammtafel des Michael Isaac
Bing und seiner Nachkommen.
Nebst beigefügtem auszuge aus
dem Testamente seiner
Enkelin, Gütche Worms geb.
Mendler-Oetingen, die
Stiftung eines
Brautvermächtnisses zu
Gunsten ihrer Anverwandten
betreffund. Frankfurt am
Main, 1864. 42 p. Bing
family of Frankfurt am Main
covers 1625-1864. History of
family of Abraham Reiss,
p. 22. Family of Frankfurt
am Main.

REISSNER
Reissner, Hanns. Familie auf
Wanderschaft. Berlin: Von
Trupp, 1938. 43 p.
(Jüdische Wirklichkeit Heute,
eine Schriftenreihe, Heft 3.)
DLC, NN, OCH.

REISZ
Kempelen. Magyarországi Zsidó,
2:88, 121; 3:101. See
GENERAL WORKS.

REITLINGER
PD has family records.

REITMANN
Kempelen. Magyarországi Zsidó,
1:142. See GENERAL WORKS.

REITZENBERGER
See Friedrich Carl Tuchmann
entry under BING.

REITZES
PD has family records.

REITZLINGER
Kempelen. Magyarországi Zsidó,
2:10. See GENERAL WORKS.

REIZCHE
AMH has family records.

REIZENSTEIN
CAJD has family tree from
Germany.

RELLE
Kempelen. Magyarországi Zsidó,
2:138. See GENERAL WORKS.

REMAK
Kronthal, Arthur. "Der Name
Remak," JFF, no. 47
(1937):872-76.

REMENYI
Kempelen. Magyarországi Zsidó,
1:75; 2:131. Reményi family.
See GENERAL WORKS.

RENARD
CAJ has family records.

RENDALL
AMH has family records.

RENDEL
AMH has family records.

RENDES
Kempelen. Magyarországi Zsidó,
1:58. See GENERAL WORKS.

RENNER-RUBEN
Ruben, Moritz. Stammtafeln der
Hamburger Familie
Renner-Ruben, ca. 1650-1913.
Stockholm: Bokindustri A.-b.:
s. boktryckeri, 1913. 3 p.
Folded genealogical table.
NN.

RENYI
Kempelen. Magyarországi Zsidó,

1:48. Rényi family. See
GENERAL WORKS.

RESNIK
Resnik Family Tree. Compiled
by Irwin M. Berent. Family
originally from Popelany,
Lithuania. JGCT.

RESOFSZKY
Kempelen. Magyarországi Zsidó,
3:124. See GENERAL WORKS.

RETHI, RETHY
Kempelen. Magyarországi Zsidó,
1:47, 75; 3:49, 50. Réthi,
Réthy family. See GENERAL
WORKS.

REUBEN
AMH has family records.

REUCHLEIN
CAJ has family records.

REUSS
Kempelen. Magyarországi Zsidó,
1:142. See GENERAL WORKS.
Semi-Gotha, 1:100. See GENERAL
WORKS.

REUTER
CFM has family records.
Semi-Gotha, 1:141ff. See
GENERAL WORKS.

REUTERBORG
Semi-Gotha, 2:16. See GENERAL
WORKS.

REUTERCRONA
Semi-Gotha, 1:94. See GENERAL
WORKS.

REUTERSKIOLD
Semi-Gotha, 1:95, 155.
Reuterskiöld family. See
GENERAL WORKS.

REUTERSWARD
Semi-Gotha, 1:135, 136; 2:77,
94. Reuterswärd family. See
GENERAL WORKS.

REV
Kempelen. Magyarországi Zsidó,

2:124. Rév family. See
GENERAL WORKS.

REVAYA
Romano, David. "Estudio
histórico de la familia
Revaya, bailes de los reyes
de Aragón en el siglo XIII."
Unpublished thesis, Escuela
de Estudios Hebraicos de
Barcelona, 1952.

REVEL
AJA has genealogical files.

REVESZ
Kempelen. Magyarországi Zsidó,
2:50. Révész family. See
GENERAL WORKS.

REWALD
CAJ has family records.

REY
CFM has family records.

REYCHMAN
Reychman. Szkice
  genealogiczne, pp. 155-61.
See GENERAL WORKS.

REYNOLDS
AMH has family records.

REZNIKOFF
Reznikoff, Charles. Family
  Chronicle. New York:
Universe Books, 1971. 311 p.
Family from Elizavetgrad and
Znamenka, Russia. Settled in
Brooklyn. Charles Reznikoff
(1894-1976), poet, novelist,
and historian. His parents
were Nathan and Sarah
Reznikoff.

RHEINGANUM
[Löwenstein, Leopold.]
  Stammbaum Rheinganum,
  Oppenheim, Simons. Mannheim,
1908. 38 p. Families of
Mannheim. OCH.

RHINE
AMH has family records.

RIBARY
Kempelen. Magyarországi Zsidó,
3:92. Ribáry family. See
GENERAL WORKS.

RIBBING
Semi-Gotha, 1:83; 2:41, 95,
112. See GENERAL WORKS.

RIBEIRO
Lemos, Maximiano. Ribeiro
  Sanches: A sua vida e a sua
  obra. Porto: Eduardo Tavares
Martins, editor, 1911.
369 p. Genealogical tables
include ascendants and
descendants of Antonio Nunes
Ribeiro Sanches, a Portuguese
Marrano who fled to Holland
and later became Russian
court physician, b. 1699;
d. Paris, 1783.

RICARDO
AMH has family records.
CFM has family records.
Burke's Landed Gentry, 1972.
Anglo-Jewish family of
Gatcome House.
Weatherall, David. David
  Ricardo: A Biography. The
Hague: Martinus Nijhoff,
1977. 201 p. "The Jewish
Heritage," pp. 1-7, deals
with the Israel and Ricardo
ancestors of David Ricardo
(1772-1823), the famous
English economic theorist.
His father, Abraham Israel
Ricardo, came to England
about 1759 from Amsterdam.
The Israel family originated
in Livorno, Italy.

RICE
Keneseth Israel. See GENERAL
WORKS.

RICH
Keneseth Israel. See GENERAL
WORKS.
Harris. Merchant Princes.
Rich department store family.
Descendants of Morris Rich,
b. Kaschau (now Kosice in
Czechoslovakia) in the

315

Austro-Hungarian Empire, came
to U.S. in 1859. See GENERAL
WORKS.

RICHARDS
AMH has family records.
Kempelen. Magyarországi Zsidó,
1:56. See GENERAL WORKS.

RICHARDSON
AMH has family records.

RICHLEY
AMH has family records.

RICHTER
LBI has family tree beginning
1823.
Kempelen. Magyarországi Zsidó,
1:103; 2:136. See GENERAL
WORKS.

RIDDERSTOLPE
Semi-Gotha, 2:31. See GENERAL
WORKS.

RIEGEL
Deutsch, Hermann. Stammbäume
der Familien Buff und Riegel
Wild und Martin. Cronheim,
N.p., 1936? 4 Pts. Pt. II:
Erlauterungen zur Stammtafel
der Familie Riegel aus
Cronheim, 1688-1936. 32 p.
CAJ, Call No. 2771/3.

RIEGER
Rieger, Shay. Our Family. New
York: Lothrop, Lee & Shepard,
1972. 64 p. Author uses
photographs of her relatives
and her sculptures to
describe the life of her
family.

RIES, RIESS, RIESSER
See CAJ (Call No. P/123) entry
under ECKSTEIN. Includes
Riess family.
Neufeld, S. "Vom Riesgau über
Wien nach Elbing. Die
Wanderungen einer jüdischen
Familie," Mitteilungsblatt,
Wochenzeitung des Irgun Olej
Merkas Europa (Tel-Aviv),
no. 41 (13 Okt. 1961). Also

in Allgemeine Wochenzeitung
der Juden in Deutschland
(Düsseldorf) 16, no. 28
(Okt. 6 1961). Ries and
Riesser families.
Ries, Estelle H. Elias E.
Ries, Inventor. New York:
Philosophical Library, 1951.
369 p. Genealogical
information, pp. 1-5. Elias
Elkan Ries (1862-1928) was
born in Randegg, near
Stuttgart, Germany, the son
of Elkan and Bertha Weil
Ries. The Weil family came
from Oberdorfer, near
Stuttgart. The Ries family
came to Brooklyn in 1865 and
moved to Baltimore in 1872.
Elias Ries became a noted
patent lawyer, electric
engineer, and inventor of
electricity-related products.
CU, DLC, ICJ, MH, NN, TxU.
Rosenstein. Unbroken Chain,
pp. 78ff. Riesser family.
See GENERAL WORKS.
See Stammbaum Levinstein entry
under AVELLIS. Includes
Riess family.

RIETI (DA)
AMH has Rieti family records.
Cassuto, Umberto. Gli Ebrei a
Firenze nell'età del
Rinascimento. Firenze: Tip.
Galletti e Cocci, 1918.
Includes genealogy of Rieti
family of Italy, p. 349,
no. 6. CU, DLC, ICN, MB, MH,
NcD, NcU, NIC, NN, OCH,
PPDrop.
"La famiglia Rieti di Bologna,"
Il Vessillo Israelitico 53
(1905):507-509.
Simonsohn, Shelomo. "I
banchieri da Rieti in
Toscana," Rassegna Mensile di
Israel 38 (1972):406-23,
487-99.
————. "On the History of the
Rieti Family in Tuscany," in
Festschrift in Honor of Dr.
George S. Wise (Tel Aviv
University, Publication
Dept., 1981), pp. 301-15.

————. Toledot ha-Yehudim
be-Dukasut Mantovah. Added
title page: History of the
Jews in the Duchy of Mantua.
Israel, 1962-1964. 2 vols.
Genealogy of Rieti family,
p. 544, no. 305. DLC.

RIETTI
CFM has family records.

RINDSKOPF
CAJD has family tree from
Germany.
Michael Berolzheimer
Collection. Includes
Rindskopf family tree. LBI.
Fisher-Hecht Family Papers,
Cincinnati, Ohio and
Wheeling, W. Va., 1845-1852.
Includes genealogical
material on Fisher, Hecht,
and Rindskopf families. AJA.

RING
Kempelen. Magyarországi Zsidó,
3:135. See GENERAL WORKS.

RINGELBLUM
CAJ has family records.

RINGOLD
Cohen Family. "Genealogical
Chart of the Descendants of
Alex Cohen and Anna Ringold,
1852-1959." AJA.

RINK
Kempelen. Magyarországi Zsidó,
2:102. See GENERAL WORKS.

RINTEL
AMH has family records.
Kempelen. Magyarországi Zsidó,
1:106. See GENERAL WORKS.

RIS
"Die Nachkommen des Rabbiner
Raphael Ris (Israelitischer
Wochenblatt)." CAJ.

RISSIK
AMH has family records.

RITTENBERG
Rittenberg Family, New Orleans,

La. "Family Tree of Rabbi
Isaac Rittenberg and Miriam
Rittenberg, 1834-1973."
Typescript. AJA.

RITTER
CAJ (Call No. 3841) has 13
documents on this family of
Hamburg, covering 1854-1933.
PD has family records.

RITTERBAND
Stern. FAJF. Ritterband
family tree beginning in
Poland. See GENERAL WORKS.

RITZWOLLER
See Yaffa Draznin entry under
BERNSTEIN. Family history.

RIVERA
Kohler, Max J. "The Lopez and
Rivera Families of Newport,"
Publications of the American
Jewish Historical Society 2
(1894):101.
Maduro, J.M.L. "A Genealogical
Note on the Pimental, Lopez,
Sasportas and Rivera
Families," Publications of
the American Jewish
Historical Society 42
(1952):303.

RIVLIN
Rivlin, Avraham Binyamin.
"Shiva Dorot Shel Rivlinim
Be'eretz Yisrael." 2 p.
Article appeared in the
Israeli newspaper Davar at
the time of the 27th Zionist
Congress, June 9, 1968.
JNUL.
Rivlin, Eliezer. Sefer ha-Hem
Lemishpahat Rivlin.
Jerusalem, 1935-1940. OCH.
Rivlin, Yosef Yoel. "The
Rivlin Family in Eretz
Israel," in Yosef Y. Rivlin
Memorial Volume (Ramat-Gan,
Israel: Bar-Ilan University,
Institute for Research on the
History of the Yishuv, 1964),
pp. 47-77.

ROBEL
Semi-Gotha, 1:111ff. Röbel
family. See GENERAL WORKS.

ROBERTS
AMH has family records.

ROBERTSON
See Esmond S. De Beer entry
under BARDEN.

ROBINSON
AMH has family records.
Rosenstein. Unbroken Chain,
pp. 641ff. See GENERAL
WORKS.

ROBITSEK
Kempelen. Magyarországi Zsidó,
2:36. See GENERAL WORKS.

ROBLES
AJA has family tree.
CFM has family records.
Athias Family. "Genealogical
Chart of the Athias-Robles
Family." 1971. AJA.

ROBOZ
Kempelen. Magyarországi Zsidó,
2:66. See GENERAL WORKS.

ROCAMORA
CFM has family records.

ROCHELLE
Stern. FAJF. Rochelle family
tree beginning in Hamburg.
Originally spelled
Rothschild. See GENERAL
WORKS.

ROCHFORD
AMH has family records.

RODER
Kempelen. Magyarországi Zsidó,
2:105. Róder family. See
GENERAL WORKS.

RODRIGUES
CFM has family records.
See Stern, FAJF entry under
PEREIRA.

RODRIGUEZ
AMH has family records.
Stern. FAJF. Rodriguez family
tree beginning in Bordeaux.
See GENERAL WORKS.

ROESSEL
See Stern, FAJF entry under
RUSSELL.

ROGER
Kempelen. Magyarországi Zsidó,
1:141. Róger family. See
GENERAL WORKS.

ROHLING
CAJ has family records.

ROHR
Semi-Gotha, 1:140. See GENERAL
WORKS.

ROHRBACHER
Tänzer. Juden in Jebenhausen,
pp. 364-65. See GENERAL
WORKS.

ROHSS
Semi-Gotha, 1:16. Röhss
family. See GENERAL WORKS.

ROJOK
See Yaffa Draznin entry under
BERNSTEIN. Family history.

ROKEACH
CAJD has family tree from
Germany.
Eisenstadt and Wiener.
Da'at-kedoschim. See GENERAL
WORKS.
Rosenstein. Unbroken Chain,
pp. 641ff. See GENERAL
WORKS.
See Mordechai Rubinstein entry
under FRANKEL.
Shapiro. Mishpachot Atikot,
pp. 371-86. See GENERAL
WORKS.

ROKESCH
Kempelen. Magyarországi Zsidó,
3:42. See GENERAL WORKS.

ROLFE
Rolfe, Lionel Menuhin. The

Menuhins: A Family Odyssey.
San Francisco: Panjandrum
Books, 1978. 256 p.
Genealogical tables,
pp. xvi-xvii. Original
spelling of name was Mnuchin.
Family from Gomel and
Lubavitch, Russia. CtY, DLC,
ICarbS, NjP, NN, NNJ, OC1,
OCH, OU, TxU.

ROLLAND
CAJ has family records.

ROM, ROMM
Chelminsky-Lajmer, "Jewish
Surnames." See GENERAL
WORKS.
Miller, Benjamin, 1907-1971.
Papers, 1875, 1952-1975.
1 folder and 1 book.
Dr. Miller was a physician
and author from Cincinnati,
Ohio. Included among the
papers is genealogical
information about his
relatives, the Romm family.
PJAC.

ROMAIN
AMH has family records.

ROMANZINI
CFM has family records.

ROMEISTER
Kempelen. Magyarországi Zsidó,
1:85. See GENERAL WORKS.

ROMM
See ROM, ROMM.

RONAI
Kempelen. Magyarországi Zsidó,
2:145. Rónai family. See
GENERAL WORKS.

RONSHEIM
AJA has family tree beginning
1750 in Germany.

ROOS
Semi-Gotha, 1:74, 107, 137.
See GENERAL WORKS.

ROSA
See DA SILVA ROSA.
Kempelen. Magyarországi Zsidó,
1:62. Rósa family. See
GENERAL WORKS.

ROSANES
Rosanes, Salomon Abraham. La
généalogie de la familie
Rosanes. Roustschouck:
D.M. Drobnyak, 1885. OCH.

ROSAUER
Kempelen. Magyarországi Zsidó,
2:132. See GENERAL WORKS.

ROSE
AMH has family records.

ROSEMAN
AJA has family tree beginning
1684.

ROSEN
AMH has family records.
See Yaffa Draznin entry under
BERNSTEIN.
Sack, Sallyann Amdur and Mark
Weiss Shulkin, eds. Search
for the Family: A Chronicle
of the Tzvi Hirsch Shulkin
and Gelye Devorah Rosen
Family and Those Related to
Them. Bethesda, Md.: Marsal
Press, 1980. 176 p. Family
of Polotzk (Plock), Poland
area. AJHS, DLC, MH, WiH,
YIVO.
Reychman. Szkice
genealogiczne, pp. 163-67.
See GENERAL WORKS.

ROSENAU
Keneseth Israel. See GENERAL
WORKS.

ROSENBACH
Deutsch, Helene [Hala].
Confrontations with Myself:
An Epilogue. New York:
Norton, 1973. 217 p.
Especially, pp. 19-92. The
author (1884-   ), the noted
psychoanalyst and
psychiatrist, was born in
Przemyśl, Galicia, the

daughter of Wilhelm
Rosenbach, a lawyer and
Jewish community leader, and
Regina Fass Rosenbach. She
settled in U.S. in 1935.
Wolf, Edwin. Rosenbach: A
Biography. Cleveland: World
Publishing Co., 1960. 616 p.
Abraham Simon Wolf Rosenbach
(1876-1952) was an
internationally known rare
books dealer in Philadelphia.
Includes Rosenbach family
information as well as much
genealogical data on the
Polock family of
Philadelphia--Rosenbach's
mother's family--on pp.
13-26.

ROSENBAUM
AMH has family records.
LBI has family trees beginning
1660, 1748, 1776, and 1790.
Ballin. Juden in Seesen,
p. 229. See GENERAL WORKS.
Rose. Schöninger Juden. See
GENERAL WORKS.
Rosenbaum, Isaac. La cronica
de Isaac Rosenbaum (Una
familia hebrea en Polonia).
Caracas: Edreca Editores,
1973. 193 p. Family from
Draznievo and Sterdyn,
Poland. The author is a son
of Nathan and Rivka
Rosenbaum, a grandson of
Jacob Rosenbaum, and a
great-grandson of Ephraim
Rosenbaum. DLC, OCH.
Rosenbaum-Zell, Mendel.
Familientafel der Nachkommen.
Tel Aviv: Ha-Aretz Press,
1958. CAJ.
Semi-Gotha, 2:132ff. See
GENERAL WORKS.
Strauss, Berthold Baruch. The
Rosenbaums of Zell: A Study
of a Family. London:
Hamakrik Book and Binding
Co.; New York: P. Feldheim,
1962. 177 p. Family of
Bavaria. CLU, DLC, LBI, MB,
MH, NcD, NN, NNC, OCH, OU,
WU.
Tachauer, David. Familentafel

der Nachkommen von Mendel
Rosenbaum Zell. Tel Aviv:
Typ. Ha'aretz, 1958. 40 p.
Rabbi Mendel Rosenbaum
(1782-1868) of Zell, Bavaria.

ROSENBERG
AMH has family records.
CFM has family records.
Kempelen. Magyarországi Zsidó,
1:62, 63, 123; 2:89, 91, 120.
See GENERAL WORKS.
See Siegfried Porta entry under
FALKENSTEIN.
Abraham and Alice Rosenberg
Family Papers,
ca. 1850-ca. 1943. Contain
family tree. Abraham
Rosenberg was a partner in
Rosenberg Brothers of San
Francisco, a dried fruit
firm. WJHC.
Rosenberg, Gabriel S.
Familienchronik. Augefertigt
im November 1908. Frankfurt
am Main, 1928. 31 p.
Descendants of Gabriel
Rosenberg, 1755-1849. Family
of Frankfurt. LBI.
Zapf. Tübinger Juden, pp. 59.
See GENERAL WORKS.

ROSENBLUM
CAJ has family records.
Reychman. Szkice
genealogiczne, pp. 169-72.
See GENERAL WORKS.
Waldman, Bess. The Book of
Tziril: A Family Chronicle.
Marblehead, Mass.: Micah
Publications, 1981. 250 p.
In narrative form, this book
covers the life of some of
the descendants of Zalman
Yitchok and Dvera Esther
Gordon from 1840-1890s in
Russia and Jersey City, N.J.
Includes the Gordon family of
Kafkaz (near Tiflis in the
Caucasus region); the
Rosenblum family of Kovno
(Chana Gordon and Reb Yosef
Rosenblum); Yosef Yacov and
Tziril Miriam Gordon
Wilkimirsky (changed to
Friedman in U.S.) of Wilki

near Kovno; and Abraham
(Alte) and Hinda Dvera
Friedman Lipschutz of New
Jersey. Abraham Lipschutz
was the son of Reb Yeheschel
and Rivka Lipschutz of
Vienna. The author is the
daughter of Abraham and Hinda
Lipschutz. AJA, AJHS, DLC.

ROSENFELD
AJA has family tree beginning
  1741 in Russia.
AMH has family records.
LBI has family trees beginning
  1756 and 1781.
Kempelen. Magyarországi Zsidó,
  1:41, 62, 146; 2:8, 102, 124;
  3:24, 25, 108, 126. See
  GENERAL WORKS.
Rosenstein. Unbroken Chain,
  pp. 506ff. The Rosenfeld
  descendants of Halberstam
  Chassidic dynasty of Sanz.
  See GENERAL WORKS.
Tänzer. Juden in Jebenhausen,
  p. 366. See GENERAL WORKS.

ROSENGARD
Taylor Family Papers,
  1908-1976. Include
  genealogy, documents, and
  photos relating to history of
  Taylor, Tatelbaum and
  Rosengard families in U.S.
  AJHS.

ROSENGARDT
LBI has family tree beginning
  1803.

ROSENGARTEN
Stern. FAJF. Rosengarten
  family tree beginning in U.S.
  See GENERAL WORKS.

ROSENHEIM
AMH has family records.
Stern. FAJF. Rosenheim family
  tree beginning in U.S. See
  GENERAL WORKS.
Tänzer. Juden in Jebenhausen,
  pp. 367-71. See GENERAL
  WORKS.

ROSENKRANTZ
Rosenkrantz, Aharon ben Shlomo.
  Sefer Yuchasin. Warsaw,
  1885. 18 p. Genealogy of
  the great rabbis in
  Rosenkrantz family. JNUL.

ROSENSTEIN
Rosenstein Family. "Brief
  Genealogical Information."
  Cincinnati, Ohio, 1930. AJA.
Ballin. Juden in Seesen,
  p. 230. See GENERAL WORKS.
Gotthelfft, Richard.
  Erinnerungen aus guter alter
  Zeit. Kassel: By the Author,
  1922. Rosenstein family of
  Cassel. LBI.
Rosenstein, Conrad. "Der
  Brunnen. Eine
  Familienchronik." Israel,
  1958. 64 p. Family of
  Lithuania and Posen. LBI.

ROSENSTOCK
Kempelen. Magyarországi Zsidó,
  1:137. See GENERAL WORKS.

ROSENTHAL
AJA has family tree from
  Germany and Philadelphia
  beginning 1790.
AMH has family records.
CAJ has family records.
CFM has family records.
LBI has family tree beginning
  1706.
PD has family records.
Rosenthal-Salus Family.
  Papers, 1859, 1898. 1 folder
  and photograph. Include
  genealogical information as
  well as marriage records,
  etc. spanning two
  generations. PJAC.
Greenwald, Leopold. Toledot
  Mishpaḥat Rosenthal.
  Budapest: Katzburg-Nyomda,
  1920. 103 p. DLC, OCH.
"Die Rosenthals, München," in
  Fritz Homeyer's Deutsche
  Juden als Bibliophilen und
  Antiquare (Tübingen:
  J.C.B. Mohr [Paul Siebeck,
  1963]), pp. 31-34. Family of
  antiquarian booksellers.

Kaufmann, David. "Le-toldoth
R. Mordechai Benet
Rosenthal," Haasif 5
(1889):130-39.
Kempelen. Magyarországi Zsidó,
1:142; 2:45; 3:37, 124, 127.
See GENERAL WORKS.
Rosenthal, Bernard M. "Cartel,
Clan, or Dynasty? The
Olschkis and the Rosenthals,
1859-1976," Harvard Library
Bulletin 25 (1977):381-98.
Antiquarian booksellers in
U.S., England, Netherlands,
France, etc.
Rosenthal, Heinrich. "Chronik
und Stammbaum der Familie
Rosenthal (bis 1933)."
[Dortmund]. 25 p. Family
from Geseke, Germany. Wiener
Library, London.
Rosenthal, Johanna. "Einiges
aus unserem gemeinsamen
Leben: Berthold Rosenthal und
Johanna geb. Benzian 9. Juli
1914-16. Dezember 1957."
Dayton, Ohio, 1959. 35 p.
Includes brief history of
Rosenthal family of Hamburg
and Mannheim. The author and
her husband came to U.S. in
1940. LBI.
Rosenthal, Ludwig. Zur
Geschichte der Juden im
Gebiet der ehemaligen
Grafschaft Hanau unter
besonderer Berücksichtigung
der Juden in Bergen bei
Frankfurt am Main und der
dortigen Vorfahren des
Verfassers vom 17. bis 19.
Jahrhundert. Ein Beitrag zur
Geschichte der Deutschen
Juden. Hanau, 1963. 295 p.
(Veröffentlichungen des
Hanauer Geschichtsvereins
e.V., Band 19).
1 genealogical table.
Includes chapter on history
of author's family of Hanau,
1667-1943. CU, LBI, MnU,
NIC, OCH.
Wolf Family. Papers,
c. 1970-1977. 1 folder.
"Biographical material, 1976,
of Howard A. Wolf (1900-   )

and genealogical information
about his ancestors and those
of his wife, Martha Rosenthal
Wolf, including members of
the Wolf, Rosenthal, Loeb,
Fels, and Price families,
dating back to the 18th
century." PJAC.
Aronson-Rosenthal Family Papers
(1878-   ). Include Solomon
Rosenthal-David Aronson
family tree. WJHC.
Tänzer. Juden in Jebenhausen,
pp. 372-74. See GENERAL
WORKS.
Tänzer. Juden in Tirol,
pp. 762-65. See GENERAL
WORKS.

ROSENTHALER
Rosenthaler Family. "Ancestry
of the Rosenthaler Family,
Including Documentation of
Births, Genealogical Charts,
and Other Records, Ansbach,
Bavaria, 1803-1900." AJA,
LBI.

ROSENWALD
AJA has family tree beginning
1740 in Bavaria.
AMH has family records.
Rosenwald Family, Las Vegas,
N.M. Historical Data,
including genealogy,
1833-1870. AJA.
Harris. Merchant Princes. The
Rosenwald family connected
with the Sears, Roebuck Co.
See GENERAL WORKS.

ROSENWASSER
AJA has family tree of family
of Cleveland beginning 1756.
Rosenwasser, Frieda. "Von
Oberschlesien nach Samarkand:
Schicksal einer Familie."
N.p., n.d. 8 p. Family of
Beuthen, Oberschlesien,
Germany. LBI.
Singer, Sidney C. "Rosenwasser
Family Tree." Typescript.
Aug. 1, 1942. 18 p. AJA;
Western Reserve Historical
Society, Cleveland, Ohio.

ROSENWATER
AJA has family tree from
Nebraska beginning 1865.

ROSENZWEIG
LBI has family tree beginning
1746.
Horwitz, Ludwig. "Zur
Geschichte der Familie
Rosenzweig," Jüdische
Wochenzeitung (Kassel) 6,
no. 49 (1929).
JFF, no. 33, p. 532. Family
history.
Kempelen. Magyarországi Zsidó,
3:74, 124. See GENERAL
WORKS.
Lazarus, Felix. "Aus Franz
Rosenzweig's [1886-1929]
Ahnensaal," JFF, no. 33
(1933):531-34. Family of
Frankfurt am Main.
Rosenzweig, Franz. Briefe.
Berlin: Schocken, 1935.
742 p. Genealogical table,
pp. 722-23. Franz
Rosenzweig, German Jewish
theologian, b. Kassel, 1886;
d. 1929. CtY, DLC, ICU, OCH.

ROSEWATER
Rosewater Collection,
1854-1937. Vol. 5: Rosewater
family, 1841-1935. Birth and
marriage certificates;
genealogy; and family
history. AJA.

ROSHEIM
Stern, Moritz. "Josselmann von
Rosheim und seine
Nachkommen," ZGJD 3
(1889):65-74.

ROSSEL
CFM has family records.

ROSSELLI
Rosselli, Carlo. Epistolario
familiare, 1914-1937 di
Carlo, Nello Rosselli e la
madre. Milano: Sugar Co.
Edizioni, 1979. 590 p.
Carlo Rosselli, b. 1899, and
his brother Nello Rosselli,
were Socialist writers and
economists and active
opponents of fascism. They
were assassinated by the
Italian Fascist government in
France, 1937.

ROSSI
AMH has family records.
Levi, Isaia. "La famiglia
De-Rossi," Il Vessillo
Israelitico 49 (1901):382-84.
From Mantova.

ROSSITER
AMH has family records.

ROSSLER
Kempelen. Magyarországi Zsidó,
3:30. See GENERAL WORKS.

ROSTY
Kempelen. Magyarországi Zsidó,
2:103. See GENERAL WORKS.

ROSZNER
Kempelen. Magyarországi Zsidó,
2:103, 104. See GENERAL
WORKS.

ROTENBURG
Fischel, W.J. "The Rotenburg
Family in Dutch Cochin of the
18th Century," Studia
Rosenthaliana 1, no. 2
(1957):32-44.

ROTH
CFM has family records.
Roth Family. Prayer Book with
Family Genealogy. Amsterdam,
Holland, 1799-1841. AJA.
Drapkin, Frita Roth. Papa's
Golden Land. New York:
Comet, 1960. 182 p. Story
of a Hungarian family which
settled in Michigan. Author
closes her account with her
high school graduation and
mother's citizenship.
PPDrop.
Kempelen. Magyarországi Zsidó,
1:42, 80; 2:25, 92, 134, 137;
3:37, 44. Róth family. See
GENERAL WORKS.

ROTHBAND
CFM has family records.

ROTHBAUM
Kempelen. Magyarországi Zsidó,
3:49, 50. See GENERAL WORKS.

ROTHCHILD
CAJ has family records.

ROTHENBERG, ROTHENBURG
Brilling, Bernhard. "Der Name
Maram, Marum. Zur Geschichte
der Familien Guggenheim,
Weil, und anderer Nachkommen
des Meir von Rothenburg," in
Forschung am Judentum:
Festschrift zum 60.
Geburtstag von Lothar
Rothschild (Bern, 1970),
pp. 99-125. DLC, ICU.
"Der Grabstein R. Mëirs
Rothenburg und Alexander
Wimpfons in Worms," MGWJ,
1896, p. 126.
Kopp. Jüdischen Alsenz,
pp. 136-37. See GENERAL
WORKS.
"La famille de Meir de
Rothenburg," Revue des Études
Juives 12 (1886):91-94.

ROTHER
LBI has family tree beginning
1765.

ROTHFELD
Kempelen. Magyarországi Zsidó,
3:64. See GENERAL WORKS.

ROTHGIESSER
Rose. Schöninger Juden. See
GENERAL WORKS.

ROTHMANN
Rothmann, Adolph Abraham.
Familiengeschichte.
Karkur/Palästina, 1940.
12 p. Includes Rothmann,
Casper, Michalowski,
Munderstein, and Wolff
families of Posen. LBI.
Rothmann, Samuel. Stammbaum
der Familie Rothmann.
Berlin, 1913. 12 p.

ROTHMULLER
Kempelen. Magyarországi Zsidó,
2:133. Róthmüller family.
See GENERAL WORKS.

ROTHSCHILD
"Records from the Family Bible,
1801-1954." On Rothschild
family of Baltimore. AJA.
AMH has family records.
CFM has family records.
EJ (1972), 14:335. Descendants
of Mayer Amschel Rothschild,
1744-1812, through mid-20th
century. See GENERAL WORKS.
JE, 10:491-93. "Rothschild
Pedigree." Descendants of
Moses Rothschild and Mayer A.
Rothschild, through early
20th century. See GENERAL
WORKS.
LBI has family trees beginning
1546, 1730, and 1803.
Achterberg, Erich. Frankfurter
Bankherren. Frankfurt am
Main: F. Knapp, 1956. 99 p.
"Die fünf Rothschilds,"
pp. 68-89. ICU, NIC, NN, WU.
Balla, Ignác. The Romance of
the Rothschilds. London:
E. Nash, 1913. 295 p. DLC,
MB, MH, NN.
Battersea, Constance (de
Rothschild) Flower, Baroness.
Reminiscences. London:
Macmillan & Co., 1922.
470 p. Contains family
pedigree of Montefiore and
Rothschild families. CtY,
DLC, MB, NIC, NjP, NN, OCH,
OCl, PP.
Ben Menachem, ? Di Geshichte
foon der Familia Rothschild.
Lodz, 1932. 25 p. JNUL.
Berghoeffer, Christian Wilhelm.
Mayer Amschel Rothschild, der
Gründer des Rothschildschen
Bankhauses. 2 aufl.
Frankfurt am Main: Englert
und Schlosser, 1923. 244 p.
CtY, CU, ICN, MH, NjP, NN,
NNC, OU, WU.
Birmingham. Our Crowd. See
GENERAL WORKS.
Brewitz, Walther. Die Familie
Rothschild. 2. durchgesehene

Aufl. Stuttgart und Berlin:
W. Kohlhammer, 1943. 192 p.
5 genealogical tables. CU,
CtY, DLC, LBI, NjP, OCH.
Bermant. The Cousinhood.
Genealogical table of
Anglo-Jewish Rothschild
branch. See GENERAL WORKS.
Bouvier, Jean. Les Rothschild.
Paris: Fayard, 1967. 349 p.
Includes genealogical tables,
mainly for the French branch.
CtY, DLC, ICU, NjP, NN, WU.
Burke's Peerage and Baronetage,
1970. Family of England.
Canfield, Cass. Outrageous
Fortunes: The Story of the
Medici, The Rothschilds, and
J. Pierpont Morgan. New
York: Harcourt Brace
Jovanovich, 1981. 108 p.
Cohen, Lucy. Lady de
Rothschild and Her Daughters,
1821-1931. London:
J. Murray, 1935. Includes
genealogical tables. Lady
Louisa (Montefiore)
Rothschild, 1821-1910;
Baroness Constance (de
Rothschild) Flower Battersea,
1843-1931; Hon. Mrs. Annie
(de Rothschild) Yorke,
1844-1926. CtY, CU, DLC,
ICU, NN, OCl, OCU, PPDrop,
TxU.
Corti, Egon Caesar, Conte. The
Rise of the House of
Rothschild. Translated from
the German by Brian and
Beatrix Lunn. London:
V. Gollancz, Ltd., 1928.
463 p. CtY, DLC, ICN, NIC,
NjP.
Cowles, Virginia. The
Rothschilds: A Family of
Fortune. New York: Knopf,
1973. 304 p.
"Das Stammhaus der Familie
Rothschild in Frankfurt am
Main," Der Israelit
(Frankfurt am Main) 28, no. 8
(1887):137-39.
Demachy, Edouard. Les
Rothschild: Une famille de
financiers juifs aux XIXe
siècle. Paris: Chez

d'auteur, 1896. 2 vols.
Includes genealogical tables.
CtY, DLC, MH, NjP, NN, OCH.
Dienemann, Max and Siegfried
Guggenheim. Stammbaum der
Familie Guggenheim aus Worms.
(Rothschild-Dienemann-Guggenh
im). Offenbach a.M.:
H. Cramer, 1926. 21 p.
7 genealogical tables. DLC,
NN, OCH.
Dietz, Alexander. Stammbuch
der Frankfurter Juden.
Frankfurt am Main:
J. St. Goar, 1907. 481 p.
Rothschild family,
pp. 244-50.
———. "Die Vorfahren der
Freiherren v. Rothschild,
1567-1812," Der Israelit
(Frankfurt am Main) 42,
no. 63 (1901):1395ff.
Druck, David. Baron Edmond
Rothschild: The Story of a
Practical Idealist. New
York: Printed at the Hebrew
Monotype Press, 1928. DLC,
OCH, OCl, PPDrop, TxU.
Druon, Maurice. Les Messieurs
de Rothschild (1817-1967).
Paris: P. Tisné, 1967. 60 p.
Includes genealogical table.
Rothschild family of France.
MH.
Escott, T.H.L. "The House of
Rothschild," Quarterly Review
231 (Apr. 1919):430-44.
Rothschild family of England.
Freimann, Aron. Stammtafeln
der Freiherrlichen Familie
von Rothschild. Frankfurt am
Main: Kumpf & Reis, 1906.
74 p. OCH.
Gille, Bertrand. Histoire de
la Maison Rothschild.
Genève: Droz, 1965-1967.
2 vols. Works cover through
1870. CSt, CtY, CU, ICU, MH,
NIC, NjR, NN, NNC.
Heilbrunn, Rudolf M. "Der
Anfang des Hauses Rothschild:
Wahrheit und Dichtung,"
Jahrbuch des Instituts für
Deutsche Geschichte (Tel
Aviv) 2 (1973):209-38.
Henrey, Robert. A Century

Between. New York: Longmans,
Green & Co., 1937. 325 p.
Story of the English
descendants of Nathan
Rothschild (1777-1836). CtY,
CU, DLC, MB, NN, OCH, OCl,
PPDrop.

Huber, Heinrich. "Bayern und
das Haus Rothschild: eine
geschichtliche Betrachtung,"
Allgemeine Wochenzeitung der
Juden in Deutschland
(Düsseldorf) 11, no. 50,
(1957).

See David Joseph entry under
BEITMAN.

Lehman-Wilzig, Sam N. "The
House of Rothschild:
Prototype of the
Transnational Organization,"
Jewish Social Studies 40
(1978):251-70.

Morton, Frederic. The
Rothschilds: A Family
Portrait. New York:
Atheneum, 1962. 305 p.
Contains genealogical table.

Muhlstein, Anka. Baron James:
The Rise of the French
Rothschilds. New York:
Vendome Press (Viking Press),
1982. 208 p. On James Jacob
Rothschild, 1792-1868. The
author is Baron Rothschild's
great-great-great
granddaughter.

N.M. Rothschild, 1777-1836.
Nathan Ma[e]yer Rothschild.
London, 16.9.1977. 25 p.
Includes genealogical table.
N.M. Rothschild was the
founder of the English branch
of the family. LBI.

Palin, Ronald. Rothschild
Relish. London: Cassell,
1970. 192 p. Rothschild
family of England.

Phiebig, Albert J. Die
Nachkommen des Simon und der
Maria Anna Rothschild.
Berlin, 1936. 11 p. JNUL.

Ravage, Marcus Eli. Five Men
of Frankfort: The Story of
the Rothschilds.... New
York: The Dial Press, 1928.
341 p. DLC, NcD, OCl, PP.

Reeves, John. The Rothschilds.
London: Sampson, Low,
Marston, Searle and
Rivington, 1887. 381 p.
CtY, ICU, MH, OCH, PP, PPFR,
PU.

Reynaud, Léonce. Les français
israélites. Paris: Imp.
générale Lahure, 1901. "La
famille Rothschild,"
pp. 380-421. MH.

Roth, Cecil. The Magnificent
Rothschilds. London: Robert
Hale Ltd., 1939. 381 p.
Includes genealogical tables
of English branch. CtY, DLC,
OCH, OU, PPDrop, PU.

Rothschild Family Tree,
1450-1973. London: Curwen
Press, 1963. 26 p. OCH.

Rothschild, Henri James
Nathaniel Charles, baron de.
La lignée française de la
famille de Rothschild,
1792-1942: étude historique
et biographique. Pôrto:
Costa Carregal, 1943. 160 p.
JNUL.

Rothschild, James de, Mrs. The
Rothschilds at Waddesdon
Manor. London: Collins,
1979. 175 p. Includes
genealogical table. DLC.

Rubens, A. "The Rothschilds in
Caricature," Transactions of
the Jewish Historical Society
of England 22 (1970):76-87.

Scherb, Friedrich Elder von.
Geschichte des Hauses
Rothschild. Berlin:
G.A. Dewald, 1892? 147 p.
NcD.

Schnee, Heinrich. Rothschild:
Geschichte eine Finanz
Dynastie. Göttingen:
Musterschmidt-Verlag, 1961.
87 p. DLC, ICU, NcD, NjP,
NN.

Semigothaisches Taschenbuch.
Genealogical table 17.
Includes Frankfurt, London,
Paris, and Vienna branches.
See GENERAL WORKS.

Steen, Hans. Die Rothschilds
in Paris. Dresden: Franz
Müller, Verlag, 1943. 170 p.

CtY, CU, DLC, ICU, NcD, NjP,
NN, NNC.
Steinmann, Friedrich Arnold.
Das Haus Rothschild. 2 vs.
Prag und Leipzig: I.L. Kober,
1857. CtY, DLC, NN, OCH.
See Stern, FAJF entry under
ROCHELLE.
Tänzer. Juden in Jebenhausen,
pp. 375-77. See GENERAL
WORKS.
Verity, W. "The Rise of the
Rothschilds," History Today
18 (1968):225-33.
"Von Rothschild," Geadelte
Jüdische Familien (Salzburg,
1891), pp. 69ff.
Wechsberg, Joseph. The
Merchant Bankers. Boston:
Little, Brown, 1966. 365 p.
"Rothschilds: The Young
Generation," pp. 335-65.
Wolf, Lucien.
"Rothschildiana," in his
Essays in Jewish History
(London, 1934), pp. 261-308.
Wolf, "Anglo-Jewish Families."
See GENERAL WORKS.

ROTHSCHILD-EMMERICH
LBI has family tree beginning
1649.

ROTHSTEIN
CAJ has family records.

ROTSCHILD
Kempelen. Magyarországi Zsidó,
2:49; 3:85. See GENERAL
WORKS.

ROTT
Kempelen. Magyarországi Zsidó,
1:91, 126; 3:124. See
GENERAL WORKS.

ROTTEN
CAJ has family records.

ROTTENBERG
Rottenberg, Daniel Jay.
Yesterday, Today, and
Tomorrow. A History of the
Rottenberg, Rubin, Goldstein
[and Other] Families. And
All Other Ancestors and

Relatives of Lisa Heidi
Rottenberg and Julie Lynn
Rottenberg. Philadelphia,
1977. 291 p. Updated
version of Rottenberg's A
Link with the Future,
(Chicago, 1969). Includes
Cohen, Goldstein, Gralnick,
Grapf, Gudelsky, Guralnik,
Kirschbaum, Klein, Kohn,
Landerburg, Margulies,
Mariansky, Rottenberg, Rubin,
Schwartz, Sicherman, Sobel,
Steinfeld, Tamarin,
Vinshnupsky, and Wiesenberg
families. AJA, AJHS.

ROTTER
Kempelen. Magyarországi Zsidó,
1:81; 3:129. See GENERAL
WORKS.

ROTWAND
Reychman. Szkice
genealogiczne, pp. 173-77.
See GENERAL WORKS.

ROWE
AMH has family records.

ROWLAND
Stern. FAJF. Rowland family
tree beginning in U.S. See
GENERAL WORKS.

ROXAS
CFM has family records.

ROZELAAR
AMH has family records.

ROZEN
See Judith A. Walters entry
under GRYNSZPAN.

ROZENTAL
Reychman. Szkice
genealogiczne, pp. 179-82.
See GENERAL WORKS.

ROZMITAL
Rokycana, Jaroslav.
"Rozmital," ZGJT 1
(1930):41-50. Bohemian
family of nobility,
1447-1542.

ROZSAHEGYI
Kempelen. Magyarországi Zsidó,
1:30, 31, 122. Rózsahegyi
family. See GENERAL WORKS.

ROZSAI
Kempelen. Magyarországi Zsidó,
1:41. Rózsai family. See
GENERAL WORKS.

ROZSAMEZEI
Kempelen. Magyarországi Zsidó,
3:17. Rózsamezei family.
See GENERAL WORKS.

ROZSAY
See RADNAY-ROZSAY.

RUBEN
Ruben, Moritz. Stammtafeln der
Hamburger Familie
Renner-Ruben: ca. 1650-1913.
Stockholm: Bokindustri
A.-b.:s. Boktryckeri, 1913.
3 p. Includes genealogical
table. NN.
Semi-Gotha, 2:135ff. See
GENERAL WORKS.

RUBENS
CFM has family records.

RUBENSON
Rothschild. Svenska Israel.
See GENERAL WORKS.

RUBENSTEIN
AMH has family records.

RUBIN
Rubin Family. "Information on
the Rubin and Kopald
families, families who moved
from Nebraska to San
Francisco. Includes family
bible with family genealogy
inside, and a business card
of the E.I. Rubin Co., San
Francisco, which was a snack
bar and popcorn equipment
co." WJHC.
Kempelen. Magyarországi Zsidó,
3:119. See GENERAL WORKS.
Rosenstein. Unbroken Chain,
pp. 601ff. See GENERAL
WORKS.

See Daniel Jay Rottenberg entry
under ROTTENBERG.

RUBINSTEIN
CAJ has family records.
Kempelen. Magyarországi Zsidó,
2:87. See GENERAL WORKS.
Rosenstein. Unbroken Chain,
pp. 321ff. Genealogical
chart. See GENERAL WORKS.
Rubinstein, Anton.
Autobiography of Anton
Rubinstein, 1829-1889.
Translated from the Russian
by Alice Delano. Boston:
Little, Brown & Co., 1892.
171 p. Genealogical
information concerning
Levenstein and Rubinstein
families, pp. 1-3. The
famous Russian pianist and
composer was born in
Vykhvatinetz, a village on
the Dniester River, Podolia
Province, the son of Gregori
Romanovich (d. 1846) and
Kaleria Levenstein Rubinstein
and the grandson of Roman
Rubinstein, from Berdichev.
The entire family was
baptized a few years after
Anton was born. DLC, ICJ,
MB, MH, NcU, NN, OCl, TxU.
Rubinstein, Charles. Tales of
Yesterday and an Introduction
to Our Family History.
Atlantic City?, 1967. 202 p.
Cherkassy Province, Russia.
DLC.
Rubinstein, Mordecai. Nite'e
nëemanah. Jerusalem, 1910.
62 p. DLC, MH.
See Mordechai Rubinstein entry
under FRANKEL.

RUBNER
Kempelen. Magyarországi Zsidó,
1:150. See GENERAL WORKS.

RUDBECK
Semi-Gotha, 2:38. See GENERAL
WORKS.

RUDEN
Stern. FAJF. Ruden family

tree beginning in U.S. See
GENERAL WORKS.

RUDINGER
Kempelen. Magyarországi Zsidó,
2:47. See GENERAL WORKS.

RUDNYANZSKY
Kempelen. Magyarországi Zsidó,
3:50, 71, 118. Rudnyánzsky
family. See GENERAL WORKS.

RUDOLPH
AMH has family records.

RUDOMIN
Hautzig, Esther Rudomin. The
Endless Steppe: Growing Up in
Siberia. New York:
Thomas Y. Crowell, 1968.
215 p. Describes 1941-1945,
when Esther Rudomin and her
parents and grandmother were
deported by the Russians from
their home in Vilna, Poland
to Siberia. CtY, CU, DLC,
NcD, NIC, NN, NNC, WU.

RUNKEL
Semi-Gotha, 2:47. See GENERAL
WORKS.

RUPERT
Kempelen. Magyarországi Zsidó,
2:65. See GENERAL WORKS.

RUPPIN
Ruppin, Arthur. "Die
Vorfahren." 2 p. Forbears
of Arthur Ruppin going back
to late 1700s. Arthur Ruppin
(b. Rawitsch [Rawicz], Posen,
Prussia, 1876; d. 1943),
Zionist leader, economist and
sociologist, and "father" of
settlement in Eretz Israel,
emigrated to Palestine in
1907 from Berlin. CAJ, Call
No. 5546.

RUSKAY
Ruskay, Sophie. Horsecars and
Cobblestones. New York: The
Beechhurst Press, 1948.
240 p. Family of New York.
DLC, PP.

RUSSELL
AJA has family tree from
Winder, Georgia.
AMH has family records.
CFM has family records.
Stern. FAJF. Russell family
tree beginning in Oberfelt,
Germany. Name originally
spelled Roessel. See GENERAL
WORKS.

RUST, RUSZTI
Kempelen. Magyarországi Zsidó,
2:144. See GENERAL WORKS.

RUTENBERG
Rutenberg Family Tree. In
Hebrew. Ca. 1800-1940.
Compiled by South African
descendant of Rutenberg
family of Popelany,
Lithuania. Claimed to be
descended originally from
Rabbi Meir of Rothenburg.
JGCT.
[Rutenberg, Herman.] "A Tree of
the Rutenberg and Kuklanski
Families." 1959. History of
Kuklanski family of Suwalki,
Poland; and history of
Rutenberg family, originally
of the village of Padumle,
near Kopchevo, Province of
Suwalki, Poland. Both
histories cover mainly 20th
century. Rutenberg family is
claimed to be descended from
a branch of the descendants
of Rabbi Meir of Rothenburg
that settled in Riga, Latvia
in mid-17th century. JGCT.
Rutenberg, M.L., as told to
K.E.F. Gardner. "The
Remarkable Story of the
Rutenberg Family," South
African Jewish Times,
Oct. 1967, pp. 64-66.
General history of Rutenberg
family starting with Rabbi
Meir of Rothenburg; deals
mainly with family from
Popelany, Lithuania, some
members of whom settled in
South Africa. JGCT.

RUTTENBERG
See Meir Yizraeli entry under
BIDERMAN.

RUTTKAI
Kempelen. Magyarországi Zsidó,
2:120, 121. See GENERAL
WORKS.

RUZHIN
EJ (1972), 14:526-32. Family
tree of Ukrainian Hasid
Israel Ruzhin (1797-1851)
also known as Israel Friedman
of Ruzhin. See GENERAL
WORKS. Rosenstein. Unbroken Chain,
pp. 512ff. Genealogical
chart. See GENERAL WORKS.

RYAN
AMH has family records.

RYDINGSWARD
Semi-Gotha, 2:67. Rydingswärd
family. See GENERAL WORKS.

RYNARZEWSKI
CAJ has family records.

SAA
CFM has family records.

SAAFELD
CFM has family records.

SAALFELD
AMH has family records.

SABBATAI
Friedberg, Bernhard. Kather
Kehunah. Added title page:
Keser Kehuna; enthaltend:
geschichte des stammbaumes
des berühmten casulsten
Sabbatai Kohen ... seinen
biographie, nebst biographien
seiner enkel und seiner
ganzen Nachkommenschaft.
Drohobycz, 1898. 41 p.
History of the pedigree of
Sabbatai ben Meir ha-Kohen

(1621-1663), his biography,
and the biographies of his
descendants.

SACH
Rothschild. Svenska Israel.
See GENERAL WORKS.

SACHI
CFM has family records.

SACHS
AJA has genealogical files.
CAJ has family records.
LBI has family trees beginning
1700, 1759, 1760, 1789, and
1807.
Kempelen. Magyarországi Zsidó,
1:112; 2:82, 134. See
GENERAL WORKS.
"Michael Sachs," MGWJ 1908,
pp. 385, 540. Michael Sachs,
German Rabbi and scholar,
b. Glogau, Silesia, 1808;
d. 1864. He finished his
rabbinical career in Berlin,
where he also served as
dayyan at the bet din.
Sachs, Hans Joseph. "Aus der
Geschichte der Zahnheilkunde.
Drei Generationen Sachs,"
Zahnärztliche Mitteilungen
(Köln, Deutscher
Arzte-Verlag), nos. 2, 3, 4
(1966):86-92, 130-37, 183-87.
Sachs, Semmy. "Dob Joel Sachs,
1771, Glogau-1834,
Labischin," JFF, no. 10.
———. "Die Ersten
Oberlandesrabbiner der Märk
Brandenburg und ihre
Verwandten," JFF, no. 13/15
(1928):13-19, 37-42, 67-72.
———. "Die Ursprünge der
Familie Sachs," JFF,
no. 35/36 (1934):581-85,
608-612.
———. "Die Familie Sachs und
ihre Verwandten in Glogau im
17. und 18. Jahr," JFF,
no. 26/27 (1931):355-60,
389-92.
Semi-Gotha, 2:141ff. See
GENERAL WORKS.

SACUTO
CFM has family records.

SAENGER
CAJ (Call No. 5136) has the
following family trees:
(1) Saenger, Adolf (in
Jerusalem) and Franz X.
Neuner (in Munich). "Familie
Saenger-Sänger." N.p., 1980.
3 p. Starts with Jakob
Sänger, a cantor,
b. Fischach, 1755;
d. Buttenwiesen, 1842/43;
continues to 1980.
(2) "Stammbaum Sänger." 1 p.
Starts with Jakob Sänger.
(3) "Familie Saenger." 1 p.
(4) Listing of members and
genealogical data. 29 p.

SAFRANSKY
AJA has Kurt Safransky
genealogical files.

SAFRIN
Rosenstein. Unbroken Chain,
pp. 618ff. Discussion of
Eichenstein and Safrin
Chassidic dynasties of
Zhidachov and Komarno. See
GENERAL WORKS.

SAGARIN
Sagarin, James L.
"Autobiographical Sketch and
the Wallace Family." Term
paper submitted to Hebrew
Union College-Jewish
Institute of Religion,
Cincinnati, Ohio. May 20,
1976. AJA.

SAGER
Tänzer. Juden in Tirol,
p. 766. Säger family. See
GENERAL WORKS.

SAGO
Kempelen. Magyarországi Zsidó,
2:56. Sagó family. See
GENERAL WORKS.

SAIDEL
Sack, Sallyann Amdur and Mark
Weiss Shulkin, eds. Search

for the Family: A Chronicle
of the Tzvi Hirsch Shulkin
and Gelye Devorah Rosen
Family and Those Related to
Them. Bethesda, Md.: Marsal
Press, 1980. 176 p. Family
of Polotzk (Plock) area.
AJHS, DLC, MH, NN, WiH, YIVO.

SAISSET
AMH has family records.

SAKHEIM
LBI has family tree beginning
1660.

SAKOL
See R. Brock Shanberg entry
under GOLTZ.

SAKOLSKY
See R. Brock Shanberg entry
under GOLTZ.

SALEMFELS
PD has family records.

SALA
CFM has family records.

SALAMAN
AMH has family records.
CFM has family records.

SALAMANS
AMH has family records.

SALAMON
AMH has family records.
CFM has family records.

SALAZAR
CFM has family records.

SALDANA
CFM has family records.

SALGO
Kempelen. Magyarországi Zsidó,
1:113. Salgó family. See
GENERAL WORKS.

SALIMAN
CFM has family records.

SALINGER
AMH has family records.
CFM has family records.
Reychman. Szkice
genealogiczne, pp. 183-85.
See GENERAL WORKS.

SALK
Zalke of Trascun; Genealogy;
MS. Zalke of Trascun,
Lithuanian ancestor of
Dr. Jonas E. Salk. AJA.

SALLER
Kempelen. Magyarországi Zsidó,
3:74. See GENERAL WORKS.

SALMON
AMH has family records.

SALOM
AMH has family records.
CFM has family records.

SALOMON
AMH has family records.
CFM has family records.
JE, 10:652. Includes
genealogical chart of the
descendants of the financier
of the American Revolution,
Haym Salomon, b. Lissa,
Poland, 1740?;
d. Philadelphia, 1785,
through late 19th century.
See GENERAL WORKS.
Benjamin, Heinrich. Chronik
der Familie
Herz-Salomon-Fuld.
Jerusalem, 1944. 36 p.
Families of Frankfurt am
Main. LBI.
Carter, Muriel Schaeffer.
"Hyam Salomon Genealogical
and Biographical Data."
Galveston, Tex., 1951. AJA.
See Daniel J. Cohen entry under
CLEVE. Family of
Salomon-Moses from
Friedrichstadt, Germany,
p. 45-47.
Rose. Schöninger Juden.
Includes genealogy of Salomon
family. See GENERAL WORKS.
Salomon, Mordechai. Sefer
Sheloshah dorot ha-Yishuv

[Three Generations in the
Yishuv]. Jerusalem, 1938 or
1939. 240 p. On
Zoref-Salomon family.
Abraham Salomon Zalman Zoref,
1785-1851; Mordecai
Zoref-Salomon, 1806-1865; and
Joel Moses Salomon,
1838-1912.
Stern. FAJF. Salomon family
tree beginning in Lissa,
Poland. See GENERAL WORKS.
Wolf, "Anglo-Jewish Families."
See GENERAL WORKS.

SALOMONS
AMH has family records.
CFM has family records.
Emden. Jews of Britain,
pp. 193-198. "David Salomons
and His Ancestors." See
GENERAL WORKS.
Parkes, James William. The
Story of Three David Salomons
at Broom Hill. Edinburgh:
Typ. T. and A. Constable,
195? 29 p. Sir David
Salomons, 1797-1873; Sir
David Lionel Salomons,
1851-1925; and Capt. David
Reginald Salomons, 1885-1915.
Sir David Salomons was a
banker and the first Jewish
Lord Mayor of London. His
nephew, Sir David Lionel
Salomons, was a pioneer of
electrical engineering and
automobiles. JNUL, OCH.

SALOMONSEN
Fischer, Josef. Slaegten
Salomonsen (Nyborg).
København, 1927. 159 p.
NN.

SALOMONSOHN
Zielenziger, Kurt. Deutschen
Wirtschaft, pp. 112-124.
"Die Familie Salomonsohn."
Family of Adolph Salomonsohn,
co-owner of the Disconto
Gesellschaft Bank in Berlin,
b. Inowrazlaw, Posen, 1831;
d. Berlin, 1919. See GENERAL
WORKS.

SALOMONSON
CFM has family records.

SALSBURY
Salsbury Family Tree. Compiled
by Irwin M. Berent. Family
originally from Grenkoshik
(?) or Padbirz (?),
Lithuania. Name taken from
Salisbury, Maryland; may have
originally been Mullen.
JGCT.

SALTIEL
CFM has family records.

SALTZBERG
Gabow, Lois and Beverly Murphy,
comps. "Aharonisky,
Saltzberg, (Shultzberg):
Family History." Edited by
Alvin Shultzberg.
Philadelphia, 1982. PJAC.

SALUS
Rosenthal-Salus Family.
Papers, 1859, 1898. 1 Folder
and photograph. Includes
genealogical information as
well as marriage records,
etc. spanning two
generations. PJAC.

SALUSINSZKI
Kempelen. Magyarországi Zsidó,
3:93. See GENERAL WORKS.

SALVADOR
AMH has family records.
CFM has family records.
"Genealogy of the Salvador
Family." AJA.
Stern. FAJF. Salvador family
tree beginning in Spain. See
GENERAL WORKS.

SALZBURG
Salzburg-Siegel Family Tree.
Compiled by Mrs. Sarah Streen
Japha. Mainly members in
Norfolk, Virginia. JGCT.

SALZEDO
CFM has family records.

SALZER
Salzer-Mosler Family,
Cincinnati. "Genealogical
Data; [In] English, German
and Hebrew." Family from
Germany, beginning 1765.
AJA.
Kempelen. Magyarországi Zsidó,
1:132. See GENERAL WORKS.

SAMELSDORF
See Stern, FAJF entry under
SAMSON.

SAMMES
AMH has family records.

SAMPAYO
CFM has family records.
Cassuto, A. "Die Familie des
Don Diego Senior Texeira de
Sampayo," JFF, no. 17.

SAMPSON
AMH has family records.
Stern. FAJF. Sampson family
tree beginning in Bury
St. Edmonds, England. See
GENERAL WORKS.

SAMSON
AMH has family records.
CFM has family records.
LBI has family trees beginning
1697, 1765, and 1813.
LBIS has family tree and notes.
Berliner, Moritz. Stammbaum
der Samonschen Familie.
3. Aufl, Hannover, 1912.
31 p. Fourteen family trees
containing more than 3,000
names. Samson family of
Wolffenbüttel, descendants of
Marcus Gumpel Fulda,
16??-1733. MWalB, OCH.
Corwin, Henry Max. Geslacht
Hartz Samson Cohen.
Oldenzaal, Netherlands, N.p.,
1960. 41 p. Family history
starting with Hartz Samson
(1735/40-1808) and his son
Hartz Samson Cohen
(1768-1839). BR; CAJ, Call
No. 1053.
Samonscher Legatenfonds.
Stammbaum der Samonschen

Familie. Hannover: Im
Selbstverlage der
Administration des
Samsonschen Legatenfonds,
1912. 31 p. 13 genealogical
tables. NN, PPDrop, PP.
Samson Family. Papers, 1978.
1 Folder. Include Xerox copy
of family history of the
descendants of Lazar
Samsonovich, prepared be
David Samson. PJAC.
Schulze, Hans. Beiträge zur
Geschichte der jüdischen
Gemeinde in Wolfenbüttel.
Wolfenbüttel, 1964. 87 p.
Genealogies of Gumpel and
Samson families, pp. 4-36,
81-84. LBI.
Stern. FAJF. Samson family
tree beginning in Bavaria.
Name originally spelled
Samelsdorf. See GENERAL
WORKS.

SAMSONOVICH
See Samson Family entry under
SAMSON.

SAMUDA
AMH has family records.
CFM has family records.

SAMUEL
AMH has family records.
CFM has family records.
"Genealogy of the Families of
Samuel and Yates of
Liverpool, England, and New
York." AJA.
Ballin. Juden in Seesen,
p. 231. Samuel family
genealogy. See GENERAL
WORKS.
Bermant. The Cousinhood.
Genealogical table of family
of England. See GENERAL
WORKS.
Bowle, John. Viscount Samuel:
A Biography. London: Victor
Gollancz, Ltd., 1957. 367 p.
"Family Background," pp.
9-16. Herbert Lord Samuel
(1870-1963), British
statesman and philosopher,
was the great-grandson of

Menachem Samuel, who was born
in Kempen, Posen, and came to
London in 1775. CLU, DLC,
NcD, NIR, NjR, NN, OCH, OCl,
PP, TxU.
Brilling, Bernhard. "Von der
Vorfahren Viscount
Samuels-Der Weg der Familie
Montague (aus
Breslau-Kempen),"
Mitteilungsblatt
Wochenzeitung des Irgun Olej
Merkas Europa (Tel Aviv),
Apr. 20, 1951. Viscount
Herbert Louis Samuel,
1870-1963, first Palestine
High Commissioner under the
British Mandate, 1920-1925.
Edelmann, Hirsch. Gedullat
Sha'ul (The Greatness of
Saul, and Progeny of David:
Being a Biography of the
Eminent Saul Wahl, Containing
Also a Genealogical and
Chronological Sketch of His
Ancestry, and Descendants,
Down to Denis M. Samuel ...
And His Relations Residing
Here). London: Shaw,
Printer, 1854. 5 p. DLC,
NN.
See Meyer Ellenbogen entry
under KATZENELLENBOGEN.
Genealogical table.
Hart, Ronald James D'Arcy, ed.
The Samuel Family of
Liverpool and London from
1755 Onwards: A Biographical
and Genealogical Dictionary
of the Descendants of Emanuel
Samuel. London: Routledge &
Paul, 1958. 118 p.
Genealogical tables. DLC,
MB, MH, NIC, NNJ, OCU, OU.
———. ———. Supplement.
London, 1966? 92 p.
Henriques, Robert David
Quixano. Bearsted: A
Biography of Marcus Samuel,
First Viscount Bearsted and
Founder of "Shell" Transport
and Trading Co. New York:
Viking Press, 1960. 676 p.
Includes genealogical chart.
DLC, MnU, NN, OCH, PP.
Kempelen. Magyarországi Zsidó,

2:120. Sámuel family. See
GENERAL WORKS.
Lewin, M. "Die österreich.
Ahnen des Sir Herbert
Samuel," Archiv für Jüdischen
Familien 2 (1916):39-41.
Montagu, Ivor Goldsmid Samuel.
The Youngest Son:
Autobiographical Sketches.
London: Lawrence and Wishart,
1970. 384 p. Genealogical
information on the
Anglo-Jewish families of
Montagu and Samuel, pp.
17-20, 27-28. Autobiography
covers the years 1904-1927 of
the author's youth. CLU,
CtY, CU, DLC, MH, NjP, NNC.
Pudor. Internationalen
Verwandtschaftlichen. Vol. 3
contains section on Samuel
family. See GENERAL WORKS.
Rosenstein. Unbroken Chain,
pp. 39ff. Discussion of the
Samuel and related families
of London and Philadelphia.
See GENERAL WORKS.
Samuel, E. "The Samuels and
the House of Lords," The
Gates of Zion (London) 19,
no. 3 (Apr. 1965):7-9, 31.
Samuel, J. Bunford. Records of
the Samuel Family; Collected
from Essays, Mss., and Other
Sources. Philadelphia:
J.B. Lippincott, 1912. 56 p.
DLC, ICN, MB, PPDrop, PP,
OCH, PPRF.
————. ————. 2d ed. Lynn,
Mass., 1939. Blueprint of 2
genealogical tables. "A New
Edition of the Family Tree in
the Original Volume, From
Mr. Samuel's Notes of
Additional Research...."
DLC.
Samuel, Sir Stuart Montagu.
History and Genealogy of the
Jewish Families of Yates and
Samuel of Liverpool, from
Materials Collected by Stuart
M. Samuel. Edited, with an
Introduction, Additions, and
Notes by Lucien Wolf.
London: By the Author, 1901.
69 p. OCH.

Stern. FAJF. Samuel family
trees beginning in:
(I) Strelitz or Kissingen;
and (II) London. See GENERAL
WORKS.

SAMUELS
AMH has family records.
Carton, Lawrence Howard.
"Notes on the Descendants of
the Kirschen [,] Samuels and
Other Related Families Who
Immigrated to America."
1983. 1 vol. Computer
printout of a short history
of the Kirschen family
(originally of Seduva, Kovno
Gubernia, Lithuania; later
settled in Baltimore,
Maryland; Pennsylvania; North
Carolina; and elsewhere) and
of genealogical charts of the
Kirschen (also spelled Kirsh,
Kerson, and Kirson),
Israelsohn, and Samuels
families. AJHS.

SAMUELSON
CFM has family records.

SAMULON
Cohn, Willy. "Aus der
Geschichte der Familie
Samulon in Osterode in
Ostpreussen," JFF, no. 18
(1929):152-54.

SANCHES
CFM has family records.
Lemos, Maximiano. Ribeiro
Sanches: A sua vida e a sua
obra. Pôrto: Eduardo Tavares
Martins, editor, 1911.
369 p. Genealogical tables
include ascendants and
descendants of Antonio Nunes
Ribeiro Sanches, a Portuguese
Marrano who fled to Holland
and later became Russian
court physician, b. 1699;
d. Paris, 1783.

SANCHEZ COTA
Cantera Burgos, Francisco. El
poeta Ruy Sánchez Cota
(Rodrigo Cota) y su familia

de judíos conversos. Madrid:
Universidad de Madrid,
Cátedra de Lengua Hebrea e
Historia de los Judíos, 1970.
155 p. Genealogical tables.
Rodrigo de Cota, fl. 15th
century. DLC, MH.

SANCHEZ DE CEPEDA
Alonso Cortés, N. "Pleitos de
los Cepedas," Boletín de la
Real Academia Española 25
(1946):85-110. Sánchez de
Cepeda.
Ciadoncha, Marqués de. "Los
Cepeda, linaje de Santa
Teresa ensayo genealógico,"
Boletín de la Real Academia
de la Historia 99
(1931):607-652. Sánchez de
Cepeda.
Serís, Homero. "Nueva
genealogía de Santa Teresa
(artículo-resena)," Nueva
Revista de Filología
Hispánica 10 (1956):364-84.
Sánchez de Cepeda. Converso
family.

SANCT GOAR
Baer, Berthold. Stammtafeln
der Familie Speyer.
Frankfurt am Main: Kumpf &
Reis, 1896. 184 p. Includes
Sanct Goar family,
pp. 130-34. Antiquarian book
dealers of Frankfurt am Main.
LBI, OCH.

SANDAU
AMH has family records.

SANDBERG
Sandberg, Sara. My Sister
Goldie. New York: Doubleday
& Co., 1968. 202 p.
--------. Mama Made Minks.
Garden City, N.Y.: Doubleday
& Co., 1964. 182 p. Family
of New York. For years,
owners of F.M. Sandberg's
Furs in Harlem.

SANDEBERG
Semi-Gotha, 1:39, 150. See
GENERAL WORKS.

SANDELS
LBIS has family tree.

SANDER
Ballin, Gerhard. "Die Familie
Sander in Völksen/Deister."
N.p., n.d. 3 p. Family
chart of family starting with
Raphael Sander, (d. Völksen,
between 1836 and 1844). Last
date on chart is 1961.
Author is from Seesen,
Germany. CAJ, Call No. 1270.
Sander, Emil. Familien und
Geschäftserinnerungen.
Stuttgart, 1931. 18, 10 p.
Family of Darmstadt. Family
tree begins 1773. LBI.

SANDERS
See Ludwig Herz entry under
REICHENHEIM.

SANDHEIM
AMH has family records.

SANDOR
Kempelen. Magyarországi Zsidó,
1:142. Sándor family. See
GENERAL WORKS.

SANDOW
See Daniel Nathan Leeson entry
under LEESON.

SANGER
See SAENGER.
Harris. Merchant Princes,
pp. 158-67. Sanger
department store family of
Dallas, Texas. Descendants
of Messrs. Isaac, Lehman, and
Philip Sanger, who came to
U.S. in 1851, 1854, and 1856
respectively. See GENERAL
WORKS.

SANGUINETTI
CFM has family records.

SANQUINETTI
Emanuel-Sanquinetti-Stein
Family. Papers. Includes a
partial family tree of this
family of Philadelphia,
prepared in 1981. PJAC.

SANTA MARIA
Cantera Burgos, Francisco.
Alvar García de Santa María y
su familia de conversos;
historia de la judería de
Burgos y de sus conversos más
egregios. Madrid: Instituto
Arias Montano, 1952. 624 p.
15th to 16th century.
Includes genealogical tables
for Cartagena, García de
Santa María, and Santa María
families. CtY, ICN, NcD, NN,
OCH, OC1W, OU, NNC, TxU.

SANTANGEL
Cabezudo Astrian, José. "Los
conversos de Barbastro y el
apellido 'Santangel.'"
Sefarad 23 (1963):265-84.

SANTELJANO
Hoek Ostende, J.H. van den.
"Het appendix op Het geslacht
der Santeljano's,"
Amstelodamum 48 (1961):58-61.
Family of Holland.

SAPHIR
Kempelen. Magyarországi Zsidó,
2:134; 3:37. See GENERAL
WORKS.

SAPORTAS
CFM has family records.

SAQUI
AMH has family records.

SARBO
Kempelen. Magyarországi Zsidó,
3:142. Sarbó family. See
GENERAL WORKS.

SARERA
"R. Isaak ben Mose Or Sarera
aus Wien," MGWJ, 1871,
p. 136.

SARFATI
CFM has family records.

SARKADI
Kempelen. Magyarországi Zsidó,
2:95. See GENERAL WORKS.

SARKANY
Kempelen. Magyarországi Zsidó,
1:101. Sárkány family. See
GENERAL WORKS.

SARMENTO
CFM has family records.

SARZEDAS
Stern. FAJF. Sarzedas family
tree beginning in Jamaica.
See GENERAL WORKS.

SAS
Kempelen. Magyarországi Zsidó,
3:91. See GENERAL WORKS.

SASPORTAS
Maduro, J.M.L. "A Genealogical
Note on the Pimental, Lopez,
Sasportas, and Rivera
Families," Publications of
the American Jewish
Historical Society 42
(1952):303.
Stern. FAJF. Sasportas family
tree beginning in Bordeaux.
See GENERAL WORKS.

SASSOON
AMH has family records.
CFM has family records.
EJ (1972), 14:897-98. Contains
genealogical charts of family
of England, descendants of
Sheikh B. Salah Sassoon
(1750-1830). See GENERAL
WORKS.
JE, 11:66. "Pedigree of the
Sassoon Family." Descendants
of David Sassoon (1792-1864),
through late 19th century.
Family of England. See
GENERAL WORKS.
Bermant. The Cousinhood.
Genealogical table of family
of England. See GENERAL
WORKS.
Emden. Jews of Britain,
pp. 324ff. "The Sassoons of
India." See GENERAL WORKS.
Hauser, Ernest Otto. Shanghai:
City for Sale. New York:
Harcourt, Brace & Co., 1940.
"The Sassoon Family,"
pp. 273-80. Indian branch of

family, and their financial
connections and investments
in India and China.
Jackson, Stanley. The
Sassoons. New York: Dutton,
1968. 304 p.
Pudor. Internationalen
Verwandtschaftlichen. Vol. 3
contains section on Sassoon
family. See GENERAL WORKS.
Roth, Cecil. The Sassoon
Dynasty. London: R. Hale,
Ltd., 1941. 280 p. Includes
many genealogical tables.
Descendants of David B.
Sassoon (1793-1864), Baghdad.
Sassoon, David Solomon. A
History of the Jews in
Baghdad. Letchworth,
England: By the Author, 1949.
236 p. Includes history of
the Sassoon family in
Baghdad. CU, DLC, ICU, IEN,
MB, MH, NcD, NcU, NN, NNC,
OCl, PPDrop, TxU.

SAUMELIN
Robert E. Levinson Papers. Jon
Stedman, "Joseph
Goldschmidt-Fromet Saumelin
Family Tree," 1967. Family
of California. WJHC.

SAUNDERS
AMH has family records.

SAVAGE
See KADISH.

SAVETSKY
See Yaffa Draznin entry under
BERNSTEIN.

SAVILE
AMH has family records.

SAVILLE
AMH has family records.

SAVORY
AMH has family records.

SAX-COHEN
AMH has family records.

SAXE (DE)
See DE SAXE.
Saxe Family; Riverdale, N.Y.
"Family Tree Including Five
Generations and Also Lubell
Families of New York and
Tulsa, Oklahoma," 1981. MS.
Xerox copy. AJA.

SCARATOWSKY, SCARR
Scarr, Jacob. Listen My
Children: A Grandfather's
Legacy. Philadelphia:
Dorrance, 1974. 274 p.
"Family Tree," pp. 8-10.
Author tells his life story,
a childhood in the Ukraine
(Zhitomir and Chudnov),
immigration to America,
experience in a variety of
jobs around Newark, N.J., and
his eventual purchase of a
chicken farm.

SCHAAP
Schaap, H.P. "De geboorte van
een wapenspreuk," Da
Navorscher: Nederlands
Archief voor Genealogie en
Heraliek, Heemkunde en
Geschiedens 98, no. 3
(1958):68-75. Family of
Lazarus Joseph Schaap,
1755-1847. Family of
Holland. JNUL.
Schaap, Louis, comp. Records
of the Schaap Family of
Amersfoort. Amsterdam:
Elsevier, 1938. 72 p.

SCHAAR
PD has family records.

SCHACHTER
Kempelen. Magyarországi Zsidó,
3:114. Schächter family.
See GENERAL WORKS.

SCHACK
Kempelen. Magyarországi Zsidó,
2:124. See GENERAL WORKS.

SCHADOW
UJE, 9:387. German family of
artists. Descendants of
Johann Gottfried Schadow

(1764-1850).
JFF, no. 18. Family history.

SCHAEF
See SCHAIFF.

SCHAEFER
LBI has family tree beginning
1693.
Untermeyer, Sophie Guggenheimer
and Alex Williamson. Mother
is Minnie. Garden City,
N.Y.: Doubleday, 1960. 213
p. A biography of Mrs.
Charles S. Guggenheimer.
Includes German Schaefer
family of New York City.

SCHAEFFER
LBI has family tree beginning
1824.

SCHAER
See SCHAIFF.

SCHAF
See SCHAIFF.

SCHAFER
Neumann, Norbert Collection,
York, Pa. "Genealogies of
the Ballin, Lazarus, Schäfer,
and Neumann Families, 11th
Century to Date." AJA.
Zapf. Tübinger Juden, pp. 60,
168-69, 220-21. Schäfer
family. See GENERAL WORKS.

SCHAFFER
Kempelen. Magyarországi Zsidó,
1:138; 2:25, 93. Schäffer
family. See GENERAL WORKS.

SCHAFFGOTSCH
CAH has family records.
Kempelen. Magyarországi Zsidó,
1:51, 55; 2:52. See GENERAL
WORKS.

SCHAFIER
CAJ has family records.

SCHAIER
CAJ has family records.

SCHAIFF
Kober, Adolf. "Vier
Generationen einer jüdischen
Familie am Rhein um 1400," in
Festschrift Dr. Jakob
Freimann zum 70. Geburtstag
gewidmet von der Jüdischen
Gemeinde zu Berlin und dem
Rabbinerseminar zu Berlin
sowie einem Kreise seiner
Freunde und Verehrer (Berlin:
Buchdruckerei "Viktoria,"
1937), pp. 106-118.
Variants: Schoyf, Schaef,
Schaer, Schaf. CtY, NN.

SCHAILER
AMH has family records.

SCHAK
Kempelen. Magyarországi Zsidó,
3:124. See GENERAL WORKS.

SCHALPRINGER
AMH has family records.

SCHAPIRO
AMH has family records.
Rubinstein, Zvi Hirsch. The
Schapiros: A Page of Jewish
History. New York: By the
Author, 1950. Families of
Slavita, Kovno, Lublin, and
Grodzinsk. DLC, NN.

SCHAPRINGER
Kempelen. Magyarországi Zsidó,
2:133. See GENERAL WORKS.

SCHARFENBERG
CAJD has family tree from
Germany.

SCHARTENBERG
CAJ has family records.

SCHARY
Zimmer, Jill Schary. With a
Cast of Thousands: A
Hollywood Childhood. New
York: Stein and Day, 1963.
252 p. Autobiography by the
oldest daughter of Dore
[Isadore] Schary (1905-1980),
U.S. film writer and
producer. Discusses the life

of the Schary family from the
mid-1930s to 1960s.

SCHAUBECK
See BRUSSEL-SCHAUBECK.

SCHAUER
Kempelen. Magyarországi Zsidó,
1:90; 2:40. See GENERAL
WORKS.

SCHAY
LBI has family tree beginning
1515.
Kempelen. Magyarországi Zsidó,
2:16. See GENERAL WORKS.

SCHAZKI
CAJ has family records.

SCHEER-THOSS
Kempelen. Magyarországi Zsidó,
1:52. See GENERAL WORKS.

SCHEINBERGER
Kempelen. Magyarországi Zsidó,
2:136. See GENERAL WORKS.

SCHEINER
See Jechiel Freud entry under
BER.

SCHENK
PD has family records.
Kempelen. Magyarországi Zsidó,
3:127. See GENERAL WORKS.

SCHERZ
Kempelen. Magyarországi Zsidó,
1:8; 3:34. See GENERAL
WORKS.

SCHERZER
CAJ has family records.

SCHEUER
Blun (Bluen) Family.
"Scheuer-Blun Family
Genealogical Chart." 1952.
AJA.
CAJ has records for family of
Gelnhausen, 1837-1900.

SCHEY
CFM has family records.
PD has family records.

Kempelen. Magyarországi Zsidó,
3:135. See GENERAL WORKS.
Schnitzler, Arthur. My Youth
in Vienna. Translated from
the German by Catherine
Hunter. New York: Holt,
Rinehart & Winston, 1970.
320 p. Genealogical
information concerning the
Markbreiter (of Vienna),
Schey (Güns), and Schnitzler
(of Gross-Kanizsa, Hungary)
families, pp. 8-13. The
author (1862-1931), the
famous Austrian dramatist,
was the son of Dr. Johann
Schnitzler (1835-1893) and
Louise Markbreiter Schnitzler
(1840-1911) and grandson of
Johann (d. 1864) and Rosalie
Schnitzler and Philipp and
Amelia Markbreiter. The
Schey family was also related
to the Markbreiter family.

SCHEYER
AMH has family records.
Hertz, Irene. "Die Scheyer von
Koschmin [Posen],"
Israelitisch Wochenblatt
(Zürich), 2. Okt. 1970.
Ullmann, Elias.
Familien-Register und
Stammtafel des Michael Isaac
Bing und seiner Nachkommen.
Nebst beigefügten auszuge aus
dem Testamente seiner
Enkelin, Gütche Worms geb.
Mendler-Oetingen, die
Stiftung eines
Brautvermächtnisses zu
Gunsten ihrer Anverwandten
betreffend. Frankfurt am
Main, 1864. 42 p. Covers
1625-1864. "Löb Samuel
Scheyer und Nachkommen,"
pp. 15-18. Family of
Frankfurt am Main. LBI.

SCHICK
Schick, Salomon (Schueck).
Mi-Mosheh 'ad Mosheh. Added
title page: Der Stammbaum der
Familie Schick mit den
hauptzweigen.... Munkács,
1903. 89 p. DLC.

Šik, Jaroslav. "Beiträge zur
Genealogie der Familie Schick
[Šik]," JFF, nos. 13 and 14
(1928):6-8, 47-51.

SCHIDLOW
Stein, Gottlieb. Familie
Schidlow. Die Geschichte
einer jüdischen Bürgerfamilie
des 18. und 19. Jahrhunderts.
Prag: Im Selbstverlag des
Verfassers, 1925. 363 p.
Genealogical table. Family
of Kolin in Bohemia. The
founder of the family was
Benjamin Benisch, a resident
of Kolin, d. 1749. His son,
Nissanh Benesch (1725-1805),
chose the name Nathan
Schidlow. LBI, OU.

SCHIE
LBI has family tree beginning
1751.

SCHIFF
AMH has family records.
CAJ has biography of family of
Breslau, end 19th to 20th
century.
CFM has family records.
JE, 11:97. "Schiff Pedigree."
Descendants of Jacob Kohen
Zedek Schiff, b. Frankfurt am
Main, ca. 1370, through late
19th century. See GENERAL
WORKS.
LBI has family trees beginning
1627 and 1716.
Birmingham. Our Crowd. See
GENERAL WORKS.
Kempelen. Magyarországi Zsidó,
2:49. See GENERAL WORKS.
Kopp. Jüdischen Alsenz,
pp. 129-31. Genealogical
information on
Kiebe-Kahn-Schiff family of
Alsenz. See GENERAL WORKS.
Mayer, Eugen. "Die Familie
Schiff," Mitteilungsblatt,
Wochenzeitung des Irgun Olej
Merkas Europa (Tel-Aviv),
no. 13 (30. März 1962). Also
in Allgemeine Wochenzeitung
der Juden in Deutschland
(Düsseldorf), no. 46

(9. Feb. 1962).
Neufeld, Siegbert. "Die Family
Schiff. Zur jüdischen
Familienkunde,"
Mitteilungsblatt,
Wochenzeitung des Irgun Olej
Merkas Europa (Tel-Aviv),
no. 3 (19. Jan. 1962).
————. "Sie Kamen aus
Frankfurt am Main: Die
Familie Schiff," Allgemeine
Wochenzeitung der Juden in
Deutschland (Düsseldorf) 16,
no. 46 (1961/62):3.
Pudor. Internationalen
Verwandtschaftlichen. Vol. 3
contains section on "Jacob
Schiff und die Warburgs und
das New Yorker Bankhaus Kuhn,
Loeb und Co." See GENERAL
WORKS.
"Two Branches of the Schiff
Family in Frankfurt," Jewish
Quarterly Review 10:450;
11:385.
Ullman, Elias.
Familien-Register des Jacob
Hirsch Schiff und seiner
Nachkommen. Aufgestellt auf
Grund amtlicher Erhebungen
und privater Mitteilungen.
Frankfurt am Main: Druck von
R. Morgenstern, 1885. 8 p.
DLC.

SCHIFFER
Kempelen. Magyarországi Zsidó,
3:62. See GENERAL WORKS.

SCHIFFMANN
CAJ has album which depicts
history of family in Germany,
1770-1937.
Kempelen. Magyarországi Zsidó,
3:25. See GENERAL WORKS.

SCHILLE
Tänzer. Juden in Jebenhausen,
p. 381. See GENERAL WORKS.

SCHILLER
AJA has family tree.
Kempelen. Magyarországi Zsidó,
3:96. See GENERAL WORKS.
Schiller, Barbara (Mrs. Lloyd
A.). "Genealogy." Valley

Stream, N.Y., Oct. 17, 1964.
AJA.

SCHIMSCHI
See Zevi Shimshi entry under
SHIMSHELEWITZ. 1 family
tree. Family of Russia and
Israel.

SCHINKEL
Semi-Gotha, 1:75. See GENERAL
WORKS.

SCHALPRINGER
PD has family records.

SCHLEGEL
Semi-Gotha, 2:109. See GENERAL
WORKS.

SCHLESINGER
AJA has genealogical files of
˜Schlesinger-Hirsch family.
AMH has family records.
CAJD has family tree from
Germany, 1600-1936.
CFM has family records.
LBI has family trees beginning
1707, 1784, and 1780.
Czellitzer, Arthur. Geschichte
meiner Familie. (Holland),
1942. 121 + 7 p. MS
genealogy beginning 1815.
Family from Breslau and
Chrzelitz bei
Zülz/Oberschlesien. Arthur
Czellitzer (1871-1943?) was
an ophthalmic surgeon in
Berlin and also the founder
of the Gesellschaft für
jüdische Familienforschung in
Berlin. This work also
includes history of the
Schlesinger family, the
author's mother's family.
LBI.
Familiengeschichte
Hamburger-Schlesinger.
Teil I: Familie (Adolf)
Hamburger. Teil II: Familie
Schlesinger. O.O.
Privatdruck, 1974. 58 p.
Adolf Hamburger, b. Hanau,
1841; d. Frankfurt am Main,
1920. Ros'chen Schlesinger
née Hamburger, b. Hanau,

1844; d. Berlin, 1932. Sofie
Diamant née Schlesinger,
b. Mainz, 1880; d. Kibbuz
Yawne, 1972. LBI.
Kempelen. Magyarországi Zsidó,
1:31, 87, 112, 121; 2:8, 9,
15, 68, 74, 89, 128; 3:37,
46. See GENERAL WORKS.
Tänzer. Juden in Tirol,
pp. 767-68. See GENERAL
WORKS.

SCHLIPPENTOCH
CAJ has family records.

SCHLOESSER
CFM has family records.

SCHLOSS
AJA has family tree beginning
1801.
AMH has family records.
CFM has family records.
Schloss Family. "Genealogical
Chart." New York, N.Y.,
1946. AJA.
Schloss Family. "Genealogical
Chart." 1972. AJA.
Schloss Family.
"Simson-Wolf-Schloss
Genealogical Chart." 1972.
AJA.
Schloss-Levy Family.
"Genealogy, 1801-1964." AJA.

SCHMERLING
Semigothaisches Taschenbuch.
Genealogical table 18.
Family of nobility. See
GENERAL WORKS.

SCHMIDL
Kempelen. Magyarországi Zsidó,
2:96. See GENERAL WORKS.

SCHMIDT
Kempelen. Magyarországi Zsidó,
1:58; 2:56. See GENERAL
WORKS.
Semi-Gotha, 1:77. See GENERAL
WORKS.

SCHMITZ
Moloney, Brian. "Svevo as a
Jewish Writer," Italian
Studies 28 (1973):52-65.

Italo Svevo, 1861-1928, was
from Trieste, Italy. His
real name was Ettore Schmitz.
Includes information on his
family origins.

SCHNABEL
PD has family records.

SCHNAPPER
LBI has family tree beginning
1714.

SCHNEERSOHN
EJ (1972), 14:981-82.
Descendants of Shneor Zalman
ben Baruch of Lyady
(1747-1812), founder of Habad
Hassidism, through mid-20th
century. See GENERAL WORKS.
Heilprin, S.A., comp. Sefer
ha-Tze-atza-im [Book of
Descendants: Family Tree of
the Descendants of Rabbi
Shneor Zalman ben Baruch,
1742-1812 of Lyady, founder
of Habad Hassidism].
Jerusalem, 1980. 566 p.
Includes Zalman, Slonim, and
Schneersohn families. JNUL.
Rolfe, Lionel Menuhin. The
Menuhins: A Family Odyssey.
San Francisco: Panjandrum
Books, 1978. 256 p.
Genealogical tables for
Rolfe, Menuhin, and
Schneersohn families,
pp. xvi-xvii.
Slonim, Menahem. Toledot
Mishpahat ha-rav mi-Ladi
[History of the Family of the
Rabbi of Lyady]. Tel-Aviv,
1946. 302 p. Includes
Slonim, Schneersohn, and
Zalman families. DLC, NN,
OCH.

SCHNEIDER
AMH has family records.
CAJ has family records.
Kempelen. Magyarországi Zsidó,
2:8. See GENERAL WORKS.

SCHNEYER
See Richard J. Alperin entry
under BEHRMAN.

SCHNITZER
See Richard J. Alperin entry
under BEHRMAN.

SCHNITZLER
AMH has family records.
Kempelen. Magyarországi Zsidó,
1:143. See GENERAL WORKS.
Schnitzler, Arthur. My Youth
in Vienna. Translated from
the German by Catherine
Hunter. New York: Holt,
Rinehart & Winston, 1970.
320 p. Genealogical
information concerning the
Markbreiter (of Vienna),
Schey (of Güns), and
Schnitzler (of Gross-Kanizsa,
Hungary) families, pp. 8-13.
The author (1862-1931), the
famous Austrian dramatist,
was the son of Dr. Johann
Schnitzler (1835-1893) and
Louise Markbreiter Schnitzler
(1840-1911) and grandson of
Johann (d. 1864) and Rosalie
Schnitzler and Philipp and
Amelia Markbreiter. The
Schey family was also related
to the Markbreiter family.
Schnitzler, Heinrich, Christian
Brandstätter and Reinhard
Urbach. Arthur Schnitzler:
Sein Leben, Sein Werk, Sein
Zeit. Frankfurt am Main: S.
Fischer, 1983. 368 p. "Die
Vorfahren," pp. 12-13. DLC,
University of
Illinois/Urbana-Champaign.

SCHOBER
Kempelen. Magyarországi Zsidó,
1:139. See GENERAL WORKS.

SCHOCKEN
"Die Familie Schocken," in
Adolf Diamant's Zur Chronik
der Juden in Zwickau; dem
Gedenken einer kleinen
jüdischen Gemeinde in Sachsen
(Frankfurt am Main: Im
Selbstverlag, 1971),
pp. 28-36. DLC.
Poppel, S.M. "Salman Schocken
und der Schocken Verlag,"

Philobiblon (Hamburg) 17
(Dez. 1973):231-56.

SCHOENFLIES
LBI has family tree beginning
1667.

SCHOHL-BRAUMANN
Schohl-Braumann, Hela. Sieger
gleibt die Liebe. Dortmund,
1961. MH.

SCHOLEM
Scholem, Gershom. From Berlin
to Jerusalem: Memories of My
Youth. Translated from the
German by Harry Zohn. New
York: Schocken Books, 1980.
178 p. "Background and
Childhood (1897-1910)," pp.
1-20. Includes genealogical
information on the Scholem
family and the families of
the author's mother: Hirsch
and Pflaum. The Scholem
family came to Berlin from
Glogau, Lower Silesia, in the
second decade of the
nineteenth century, while the
Hirsch and Pflaum families
came to Berlin from Reetz,
Rawicz, and Lissa.

SCHOMBERG
AMH has family records.
CFM has family records.
Emden. Jews of Britain,
pp. 33ff. "The Schombergs."
See GENERAL WORKS.

SCHON
Kempelen. Magyarországi Zsidó,
2:27, 90. Schön family. See
GENERAL WORKS.

SCHONBERG
See Hans Josephthal entry under
GOLDSCHNEIDER. Table of
descendants of Lazarus
Josephthal of Ansbach,
b. 1657. Includes Schönberg
family.
See Siegfried Porta entry under
FALKENSTEIN. Includes
Schönberg family.

SCHONEMANN
Tänzer. Juden in Tirol,
p. 769. Schönemann family.
See GENERAL WORKS.

SCHONFELD
AMH has family records.
Kempelen. Magyarországi Zsidó,
1:84, 121; 2:8, 10.
Schönfeld family. See
GENERAL WORKS.

SCHOPFLICH
Jacobovits, Moses. Vier
Generationen der
Rabbiner-Familie
Levi-Schopflich. Strasbourg:
La Tribune Juive, 1938.
34 p. Descendants of Rabbi
Hirsch Lévy Schopflich
(1700s), his son Anschel
Lévy I (d. 1773) of Rosheim,
and grandson Rabbi Anschel II
(1773-1846). JNUL.

SCHOR
Kratuschinsky, Wolf. Ateret
Tiferet Israel. Wien, 1883.
Contains incomplete genealogy
of Israel Schor, 1823-1899.
See Mordechai Rubinstein entry
under FRANKEL.
Sefer Toldoth Mishpahath Schor.
Added title page: Geschichte
der familie Schor; ihre Leben
und literarisches Wirken von
der mitte des 15.
Jahrhunderts bis auf die
Gegenwart, dargestellt und
mit kritischen Anmerkungen
versehen von Bernhard
Friedberg. Frankfurt am
Main: Verlag von I. Kaufmann,
1901. 22 p. DLC, OCl.
Shapiro. Mishpachot Atikot.
See GENERAL WORKS.

SCHORR
Kahan. 'Anaf 'ez avoth. See
GENERAL WORKS.

SCHORSTEIN
CFM has family records.

SCHOSBERGER, SCHOSSBERGER
PD has Schossberger family

records.
Az Egyenlöség (Budapest),
Mar. 23, 1890, pp. 3-5. An
account of Schossberger
family from Pest, Hungary.
Kempelen. Magyarországi Zsidó.
Schosberger family: 2:38, 64,
79. Schosberger,
Schossberger family: 1:31,
87, 112, 121; 3:107, 118.
See GENERAL WORKS.

SCHOTT
Ballin. Juden in Seesen,
pp. 232-33. See GENERAL
WORKS.
Wolf, Grete and Hans Wolf.
"Max Wolf und Frau Ida Wolf
geb. Schott." Frankfurt am
Main, 1929. 24 p. Starts
with Jakob Wolf, b. 1781;
d. Osterberg, 1864; and Simon
Schott, b. between 1780-1810,
lived in Rüsselsheim. CAJ,
Call No. 4893.

SCHOTTLANDER
Lederman, Lisbeth. Die
Schottländer'sche
Familienstiftung. O.O. u.J.
14 p. Family from
Münsterberg/Schlesien. LBI.
Tänzer. Juden in Jebenhausen,
p. 381. Schlottländer family
of Jebenhausen. See GENERAL
WORKS.

SCHOYF
See SCHAIFF.

SCHRECKER, SCHREKER
Schöny, Heinz. "Von der
Vorfahren des komponisten
Franz Schreker (1878-1934),"
Genealogie no. 5
(1981):542-546. The
composer's father, Isak
Schrecker,
b. Goltsch-Jenikau, Bohemia,
1834; d. Ungenach near
Vocklabruck, 'K.K.
Hofphotograph' in Vienna;
changed his name after
baptism to Ignaz Schreker.

SCHREIBER
LBI has family tree beginning
1735.
Bałaban. Żydów w Krakowie,
2:697-720. Genealogical
table of the descendants
(19th century) of Mosze Sofer
(Schreiber). See GENERAL
WORKS.
Kempelen. Magyarországi Zsidó,
2:134; 3:117. See GENERAL
WORKS.
Schreiber, Benjamin. Ketov zot
Zikaron. New York, 1957.
350 p. Genealogical table.
CLU, MH, NN, OCH.
Schreiber, Hermann. Stammbaum
d. Familie Schreiber.
Potsdam, 1914.

SCHREKER
See SCHRECKER, SCHREKER.

SCHREYER
Kempelen. Magyarországi Zsidó,
2:102. See GENERAL WORKS.

SCHRODER
CFM has family records.

SCHUBACH
AMH has family records.

SCHUGLEIT
See Richard J. Alperin entry
under BEHRMAN.

SCHUL
Raphael, F. "Un arbre
généalogique," Tribune Juive,
supplement au no. 150 (20 mai
1971):vii-ix. Family
originally from Westhouse,
Bas-Rhin.

SCHULENBURG
Semi-Gotha, 1:140. See GENERAL
WORKS.

SCHULER
See LASKER-SCHULER.
AMH has family records.
Brilling, Bernhard. "Die
Vorfahren der Else
Lasker-Schüler," Allgemeine
Wochenzeitung der Juden in

Deutschland (Düsseldorf), 18.
Juni 1965. Else
Lasker-Schüler, 1869-1945,
German poet, was born in the
eminent Schüler family of
Elberfeld, the daughter of
Aron (1825-1897) and Jeanette
Kissing (1857-1890) Schüler
and the granddaughter of
Moses Schüler. The Kissing
family was from Frankfurt am
Main and Kissingen.

SCHULHOFF
Kempelen. Magyarországi Zsidó,
1:126; 2:26. See GENERAL
WORKS.
Schnee. Hoffinanz und Staat,
1:47-77. "Die
Aaron-Schulhoff-Liebman in
brandenburgisch-preussichen
Diensten." Includes
genealogical information,
17th to 18th century. See
GENERAL WORKS.

SCHULKIN
See Sallyann Amdur Sack and
Mark Weiss Shulkin entry
under SHULKIN.

SCHULLER
Kempelen. Magyarországi Zsidó,
2:56. See GENERAL WORKS.

SCHULTZ
Kempelen. Magyarországi Zsidó,
3:118. See GENERAL WORKS.

SCHULTZBERG
See Lois Gabow and Beverly
Murphy entry under SALTZBERG.

SCHUSTER
AMH has family records.
CAJ has family records from
Germany, beginning 1790.
CFM has family records.
Schuster, Helen. "The Adolf
Schuster Family." [Santa
Monica, Calif.] 1972.
Typescript. 19 p. The
interviewee was born in 1900
in Holbrook, Arizona, the
daughter of Adolf Schuster.

Family came to Los Angeles
1901. WJHC.

SCHUTSTER
AMH has family records.

SCHUTZ
Kempelen. Magyarországi Zsidó,
1:74. Schütz family. See
GENERAL WORKS.

SCHUTZE
AMH has family records.

SCHUTZER
Kempelen. Magyarországi Zsidó,
3:43. Schützer family. See
GENERAL WORKS.

SCHWAB
LBI has family tree beginning
1495.
Kempelen. Magyarországi Zsidó,
1:74; 2:68, 130. See GENERAL
WORKS.

SCHWABACH
CAJ has family records.
PD has family records.
Kempelen. Magyarországi Zsidó,
1:22. See GENERAL WORKS.

SCHWABACHER
Aron Family; New Orleans, La.
"Genealogical Information of
the Aron and Schwabacher
Families, 1700-1964." MS.
AJA.

SCHWABE
CFM has family records.

SCHWABEN
CAJ has family records.

SCHWARCZ
Kempelen. Magyarországi Zsidó,
2:66, 73, 85, 92, 104, 120,
128, 133, 144; 3:50, 58, 64,
80, 106, 124. Schwarcz,
Schwartz, Schwarz family.
See GENERAL WORKS.

SCHWARTZ
See SCHWARCZ.
Fierman, Floyd S. "The

Schwartz Family of El Paso:
The Story of a Pioneer Jewish
Family in the Southwest,"
S.W. Studies, no. 61
(1980):5-76. Also published
as monograph, (El Paso: Texas
Western Press, 1980), 64 p.
"Genealogy of the Schwartz
Family," pp. 64-68. The
Schwartz family included the
founders and owners of the
"Popular," a department store
in El Paso, Texas. Family
originally from Stropko (now
in Czechoslovakia), a village
near Miskolc and Kassa.
Frank. Nashville Jewry,
p. 141. Family of Poland.
See GENERAL WORKS.
See Daniel Jay Rottenberg entry
under ROTTENBERG. Includes
Schwartz family.
Schwartz, Walter. Roots and
Leaves: A Personal History.
Miami Beach, Fla.? 1978.
364 p. Includes genealogical
tables. JNUL.

SCHWARTZADLER
Ettlinger, Shlomo.
"Altfrankfurter jüdische
Familiennamen,"
Jüdisches/Israelistisches
Gemeindeblatt (Frankfurt am
Main, U.A.T.) 3, no. 11
(1957):7.

SCHWARTZBAND
CAJ has family records.

SCHWARTZBART
CAJ has family records.

SCHWARTZENBERG
AJA has family tree.

SCHWARZ
See SCHWARCZ.
See SZASZY-SCHWARZ.
CAJ has records of family from
France, 1876-1952, and of
families from Hungary and
Portugal.
Schwarz, Karl. Meine familie.
Die Geschichte der Familie
Schwarz in Deutschland.

Israel, 1950. 89 p. Family
from Hürben. Family history
covers 250 years.
Tänzer. Juden in Tirol,
pp. 770-71. See GENERAL
WORKS.

SCHWARZCHILD
See Sally David Cramer entry
under CRAMER.

SCHWARZENBERG
CAJ has family records.
Kempelen. Magyarországi Zsidó,
3:32. See GENERAL WORKS.

SCHWARZENBURG
"Genealogical Notes on the
Schwarzenburg and Colman
Families, 1959 and 1964,"
Typescript and MS. Families
of Los Angeles. AJA.

SCHWARZENFELD
Kempelen. Magyarországi Zsidó,
1:42. See GENERAL WORKS.

SCHWARZFELD
CAJ has family records.

SCHWARZSCHILD
LBI has family trees beginning
1490 and 1555.
JFF, no. 18 (1929):134-38.
Neustadt, Louis. Stammtafeln
der von Liebmann
Schwarzschild in Frankfurt am
Main, 1555-1594, abstammenden
Familien. Frankfurt am Main,
1886. Folio.

SCHWEDER
CFM has family records.

SCHWEICH
"La familie Schweich à Metz,"
Revue des Études Juives 47
(1903):128-31.

SCHWEIGER
Kempelen. Magyarországi Zsidó,
1:70, 132, 138; 2:42; 3:115.
See GENERAL WORKS.

SCHWEITZER
LBI has family tree beginning

1724.
Kempelen. Magyarországi Zsidó,
3:100. See GENERAL WORKS.

Schweitzer, Peter H. "Family
History: My Life and My
Roots." Term paper submitted
to Hebrew Union
College-Jewish Institute of
Religion, Cincinnati, Ohio,
May 25, 1976. Includes
genealogical chart. AJA.

Tänzer. Juden in Tirol,
p. 772. See GENERAL WORKS.

SCHWERIN
See KOHN GOTZ SCHWERIN.
LBI has family tree beginning
1780.
Semi-Gotha, 2:110. See GENERAL
WORKS.

SCHWIMMER
Kempelen. Magyarországi Zsidó,
2:56. See GENERAL WORKS.

SCITOVSZKY
Kempelen. Magyarországi Zsidó,
1:102, 103; 2:31. See
GENERAL WORKS.

SCOTT
AMH has family records.

SEBAG
AMH has family records.
CFM has family records.
EJ (1972), 12:273-74. Includes
genealogical table of the
Montefiore-Sebag family.
Descendants of Judah (Leon)
Montefiore, b. ca. 1605,
through mid-20th century.
See GENERAL WORKS.
Burke's Landed Gentry, 1965.
Sebag-Montefiore family.
Burke's Peerage and Baronetage,
1935. Bt. of Worth Park.
Burke's Peerage and Baronetage,
1885. Bt. of Isle of Thanet.
Also, Burke's Authorised
Arms.

SEBAG-MONTEFIORE
AMH has family records.

SEBESI
Kempelen. Magyarországi Zsidó,
1:75. See GENERAL WORKS.

SEBESTYEN
Kempelen. Magyarországi Zsidó,
1:84, 116; 3:59, 107, 118.
Sebestyén family. See
GENERAL WORKS.

SEBOK
Kempelen. Magyarországi Zsidó,
3:115. Sebők family. See
GENERAL WORKS.

SEBOK-FORTI
Kempelen. Magyarországi Zsidó,
3:115. Sebők-Forti family.
See GENERAL WORKS.

SECKBACH
Seckbach, Markus. Eine
Ahnentafel von 27
Generationen bis zum Jahre
1290. Betr. die Familien
Seckbach, Meyer, Auerbach,
Hirsch, Marx. Bodenheimer
u.a. Hamberg: Laubhuttee,
1936. 22 p. OCH.

SEE
Ginsburger, Moïse. "La famille
Sée en Lorraine et en
Alsace," Souvenir et Science
2 (1931), no. 2, pp. 12-13;
no. 3, p. 8; 3 (1932), no. 2,
p. 5; no. 5, p. 11; no. 6,
pp. 10-12; no. 7, pp. 9-10;
no. 8, pp. 6-10; no. 9,
pp. 8-9; no. 10, pp. 9-12; 4
(1933), no. 1, pp. 3-9;
no. 2, p. 8.

SEELIG
LBIS has family tree.

SEELIGMAN VON EICHTHAL
UJE, 9:458. Industrialist
family of Germany.
Descendants of Aaron
Seeligman (18th century).
Part of the family converted
to Christianity in 19th
century. This part of the
family was ennobled.

SEFTON
AMH has family records.

SEGAL
See CHAGAL, CHAGALL.

SEGALL
LBI has family tree beginning
1734.
Richter, John Henry. David
Lubinski in West Prussia. A
Chronicle of the Life of the
Lubinski and Segall Families
in West Prussia, 1850-1881.
Translated, edited,
annotated, and introduced by
John Henry Richter. Ann
Arbor, Mich.: University
Microfilms, 1965. 83 p.

SEIFENSIEDER
Kempelen. Magyarországi Zsidó,
2:145. See GENERAL WORKS.

SEIFERTH
Brody Family. "Genealogy of
the Brody-Seiferth Family,
1764-1976." New Orleans,
La., 1976. AJA.

SEINSHEIMER
Seinsheimer Family, Cincinnati,
Ohio. "Genealogy,
1830-1966." MS. AJA.

SEIPT
Kempelen. Magyarországi Zsidó,
3:97. See GENERAL WORKS.

SEISIAS
CFM has family records.

SEITZ
Kempelen. Magyarországi Zsidó,
2:36. See GENERAL WORKS.

SEIXAS
AMH has family records.
De Leon Family, Charleston,
S.C. "Biographical and
Genealogical Records,
Indicating the Relationships
between the Seixas, Cardoza,
and De Leon Families,
1708-1888." AJA.
Nathan-Seixas Family. "Records

of Births, Marriages, and
Deaths, 1782-1895." MS and
photostats. Extracted from
family Bible. AJA.
"Seixas Family (only) to 1920."
WJHC.
Seixas Family. "Records of
Births and Deaths of the
Seixas, Cardozo, and De Leon
Families, 1753-1900." AJA.
Solomons Family. Lucius L.
Solomons Collection,
1725-1925. Includes
genealogical records of
Seixas and Solomons families.
AJA.
Birmingham. The Grandees. See
GENERAL WORKS.
Cardozo, Michael H., IV.
Leaves from a Family Tree.
2d ed. [Washington, D.C.],
1976. 18 ll. Genealogical
charts of Nathan, Seixas, and
Cardozo families. AJHS.
"Members of the Seixas Family
Mentioned in These Records,"
in David de Sola Pool's
Portraits Etched in Stone:
Early Jewish Settlers,
1682-1831 (New York: Columbia
University Press, 1952),
p. 347. 18th to early 19th
century. Family of New York.
Mac Leod, Celeste, comp.,
"Seixas [-] Gershoms [-]
Solomons Family Tree," 1969.
WJHC.
Nathan, Maud Nathan. Once Upon
A Time And Today. New York:
G.P. Putnam's Sons, 1933.
327 p. Genealogical
information concerning the
Nathan and Seixas ancestors
of the author (1862-1946),
pp. 21-24, 315-18. Maud
Nathan was an American Jewish
communal leader as well as a
leader of the women's
movement. DLC, MB, NN, NNJ,
OCH, OCl.
See Samuel Reznick entry u..der
PHILLIPS.
"Abraham Mendes Seixas Family
Tree." WJHC.
Stern. FAJF. Seixas family

tree beginning in Portugal.
See GENERAL WORKS.

SELBY
AMH has family records.
See Esmond S. De Beer entry
under BARDEN.

SELIG
AMH has family records.
CFM has family records.

SELIGMAN, SELIGMANN
AMH has Seligman family
records.
CFM has Seligman and Seligmann
family trees.
JE, 11:166-67. Contains a
"Seligmann Pedigree,"
descendants of Abraham
Seligmann (b. ca. 1715;
d. July 11, 1775), through
late 19th century. Includes
New York, Paris, London, and
Frankfurt branches. See
GENERAL WORKS.
JGCT has copy of
Kadish-Kadishavitz-Savage and
Seligman family tree from
these families' reunion in
Norfolk, Virginia in 1978.
LBI has family tree beginning
1628.
PD has family records.
Birmingham. Our Crowd.
Includes Seligman family.
See GENERAL WORKS.
Hellman, George S. The Family
Register of the Descendants
of David Seligman.
Baltimore, Md., 1913. 93 p.
AJHS, NN.
————. "The Story of the
Seligmans." New York, 1945.
329 p. MS. NN.
[Herz, Ludwig.]
Seligman-Familie: 1680-1930.
Die vierteltausendjährige
Geschichte der Familie
Seligman. Berlin: Druck O.
Groner, 1935. 134 p.
2 genealogical tables plus
6 plates. Family originally
from Baiersdorf. Includes
family of U.S. CtY, LBI.
Mott, Harper Stryker. "Isaac

N. Seligman," New York
Genealogical and Biographical
Register 94 (1918):321-26.
Muir, Ross L. and Carl J.
White. Over the Long Term:
The Story of J. & W. Seligman
& Co., 1864-1964. New York:
J. & W. Seligman, 1964.
172 p. Includes material on
the lives of the eight
Seligman brothers. CtY, CLU,
DLC, MH, N, NiC, NjR, WHi.
R., A. Verzeichniss der von
David Seligman aus Baiersdorf
stammenden familien. N.p.,
1889. 21 p. Covers 17th
century to time of
publication. Long Island
Historical Society, Brooklyn,
N.Y.
Rosenstein. Unbroken Chain,
pp. 92ff. See GENERAL WORKS.

SELIGMANN-EICHTHAL
Schnee, Heinrich. "Die Familie
Seligmann-Eichthal als
Hoffinanziers an süddeutschen
Fürstenhöften," Zeitschrift
für Bayerische
Landesgeschichte 25
(1962):163-201. Includes
genealogical table. NIC.
Also: Schnee. Hoffinanz und
Staat, 4:213-41. "Die
Familie Seligmann-Eichthal."
See GENERAL WORKS.

SELIGSOHN
Seligsohn, Hermann. Geschichte
der Familie Seligsohn zu
Samotschin, Provinz Posen.
Berlin, 1903-1915. 2 vols.
LBI.

SELIM
AMH has family records.

SELISBERG
AMH has family records.

SELLO
LBI has family tree beginning
1780.

SELMAN
Emanuel, Victor Rousseau. The

Selmans. New York: The Dial
Press, 1925. 372 p. DLC,
NN, OCH, OCl, YIVO.

SELTZER
CAJ has family records.
Keneseth Israel. See GENERAL
WORKS.

SELVIN
Selvin Family, Tooele, Utah.
"Historical Sketch by Dave
Selvin." AJA.

SEMON
CFM has family records.

SENATOR
CAJ has family records.

SENDOWSKY
See Daniel Nathan Leeson entry
under LEESON.

SENGER
Senger, Valentin. No. 12
Kaiserhofstrasse. New York:
Dutton, 1980. 238 p. Family
of Frankfurt am Main.
Family's real name was
Rabizanovich. The family
immigrated to Germany via
Switzerland from Odessa. The
author was the son of Moishe
and Olga Senger
[Rabizanovich].

SENIGAGLIA
Kempelen. Magyarországi Zsidó,
2:57; 3:106. See GENERAL
WORKS.

SENIOR
AJA has genealogical files.
CAJ has family records.
CFM has family records.
Cassuto, A. "Die Familie des
Don Diego Senior Texeira de
Sampayo," JFF, no. 17.

SENTURIA
Senturia Family, St. Louis, Mo.
"Family History and
Genealogical Information,"
1978. Typescript, Printed
copy. AJA.

SEQUEIRA
CFM has family records.

SEQUIEIRA
AMH has family records.

SERENA
CFM has family records.

SERENI
Bondy, Ruth. The Emissary: A
Life of Enzo Sereni.
Translated from the Hebrew by
Shlomo Katz. Boston: Little,
Brown, 1977. 265 p.
Genealogical information
concerning the Sereni family
of Rome, Italy, pp. 1-8.

SERGEL
Semi-Gotha, 1:97. See GENERAL
WORKS.

SERLIN
See R. Brock Shanberg entry
under GOLTZ.

SERRA
AMH has family records.
CFM has family records.

SETH
Semi-Gotha, 1:23. See GENERAL
WORKS.

SEWILL
AMH has family records.

SEY
Kempelen. Magyarországi Zsidó,
2:74. See GENERAL WORKS.

SEYDL
Kempelen. Magyarországi Zsidó,
1:103. See GENERAL WORKS.

SEYNES
Semi-Gotha, 1:95. See GENERAL
WORKS.

SHAFSKY
"The Shafsky Brothers of Fort
Bragg: A Mendocino County
[California] Vignette,"
Western States Jewish
Historical Quarterly 9 (Oct.

1976):49-54. Story of the
children of Kopel and Cheva
Yarashafsky (name changed to
Shafsky in U.S.) from
Kishinev, Russia. The
children were: Abraham Harry,
Albert, Samuel, Louis, and
Rose. Abraham Harry and
Samuel opened a general
merchandise store in
Ft. Bragg, California.

SHAIKEVITSCH
Zunser, Miriam Shomer.
Yesterday: A Memoir of a
Russian Jewish Family.
Edited by her Granddaughter,
Emily Wortis Leider. New
York: Harper & Row, 1978.
Family of Pinsk.
Nochim-Mayer Shaikevitsch,
1849-1905.

SHAINES
Shaines Family, Portsmouth and
Dover, New Hampshire.
Schlager, Rabbi Milton I.
"Biography of the Shaines
Family," 1962. Typescript
and photographs. AJA.

SHAMBERG
Amdursky-Shamberg Family.
Papers, 1868, 1964, 1969.
1 folder. Genealogy, 1969,
and photocopies, 1868, 1964,
of information about members
of Amdursky and Shamberg
families. PJAC.
See R. Brock Shanberg entry
under GOLTZ.

SHAMES
RMJHS has family tree.

SHANBERG
See R. Brock Shanberg entry
under GOLTZ.

SHANE
Shane Family, Warsaw, Indiana.
"History of the Shane Family,
Centering upon the Life of
Henry Shane and His Wife,
Henrietta Nusbaum Shane,
1829-1959." AJA.

SHAPIRO
Shapiro Family Tree. Compiled
by Irwin M. Berent. Early
19th century to 1980. Family
originally from Chorzelle,
Poland. Called Shpirka in
Polish records. JGCT.
Dessler, Julia Shapiro. Eyes
on the Goal. New York:
Vantage, 1954.
Autobiography. Family of
Lithuania. DLC, NN, PPDrop.
See George M. Gross entry under
GROSS. Family originally
from Poltava gubernia.
Pribłuda, A.S. "O
proiskhozhdenii familii
Pevzner ... Shapiro," (In
Russian.) Onomastica 16
(1971):225-32.
Rosenstein. Unbroken Chain,
pp. 655ff. Shapiro Chassidic
Dynasty of
Lyzhansk-Mogielnica-Grodzisk.
See GENERAL WORKS.
See Mordechai Rubinstein entry
under FRANKEL.
Shapiro. Mishpachot Atikot,
pp. 19-47. See GENERAL
WORKS.

SHAW
AMH has family records.

SHEBY
Sheby, David. "In Search of a
Sephardic Tradition: A Family
Named Sheby," Toledot: The
Journal of Jewish Genealogy 2
(1978/79):15-18. Family from
Gallipoli, Turkey.

SHEFTALL
Sheftall Family. "Records from
Family Bible, 1783-1947."
AJA.
Abrahams, Edmund H. "Some
Notes on the Early History of
the Sheftalls of Georgia,"
Publications of the American
Jewish Historical Society 17
(1909):167.
Morgan, D.T. "The Sheftalls of
Savannah," American Jewish
Historical Quarterly 62
(1973):348-61.

Sheftall, John Mc Kay. "A
Christian Student of Jewish
Genealogy," Toledot: The
Journal of Jewish Genealogy 1
(Spring 1978):8-10.
Stern. FAJF. Sheftall family
tree beginning in Prussia.
See GENERAL WORKS.
Stern, Malcolm H. "The
Sheftall Diaries: Vital
Records of Savannah Jewry,
1733-1808," American Jewish
Historical Quarterly 54
(1965):243.

SHEFTMAN
See Yaffa Draznin entry under
BERNSTEIN. Includes Sheftman
family.

SHEKLOW
Sheklow, Edna. So Talented My
Children. Cleveland: World,
1966. 160 p. A playwright
and advertising writer
describes her childhood in a
New York family of thirteen
during the Depression years.

SHEMASKY
J. Lloyd Conrich, comp., "Louis
Charmak/Annie Shemasky Family
Tree," 1965. WJHC.

SHEPHERD
AMH has family records.

SHER
See Yaffa Draznin entry under
BERNSTEIN. Includes Sher
family.

SHERBORNE
AMH has family records.

SHERENBECK
CFM has family records.

SHERESHOVSKY
Rosenstein. Unbroken Chain,
pp. 104ff. See GENERAL
WORKS.

SHERMAN
Sherman Family Trees. Compiled
by Philip Sherman, Irwin M.

Berent, and Mrs. Edith
Morganstein. Family
originally from Shavel
(Siauliai), and Pakroy
(Pakruojis), Lithuania.
JGCT.

SHEVETZ
Sefer Hamishpacha. Ot. Haifa,
Sept. 1964. 110 p. Family
trees for descendants of
Eliezer (d. 1889) and Bluma
(d. 1891) Kaplushnick;
Yitzchok (d. 1908) and Chaya
(d. 1900) Shevetz; Feiga and
Velvel (d. 1918) Mintz from
Smiatitz (?); Leah (d. 1937)
and Altar (d. 1926) Kashnich
from Smiatitz (?);
Malka-Raiza (d. 1935) and
Yisrael-Aharon Monzer from
Kamenets-Litovsk. JNUL.

SHEWELL
AMH has family records.

SHICK
Shick, Maete Gordon. The
Burden and the Trophy: An
Autobiography, translated by
Mary J. Reuben. New York:
Pageant, 1957. 209 p. The
author (1885-   ) discusses
her Lithuanian childhood and
adolescence in order to
provide cultural roots for
her grandchildren. DLC, OCH.

SHIFRIN
AJA has genealogical files.
Shifrin Family. "Family Tree,
Tracing the Shifrin Family
Genealogy from Its Russian
Immigrant Beginnings,
1812-1972." AJA.

SHIH
Leslie, "Chinese-Hebrew
Kaifeng." Includes family
tree of this Chinese clan.
See GENERAL WORKS.

SHIMSHELEWITZ
Shimshi, Zevi. Megilat
Yuḥasin. Jerusalem, 1957.
45 p. Genealogical tables.

Author's original name Zevi
Shimshelewitz. Includes
Ben-Zvi, Carmon, Kabak,
Kaufman, Klugai, Liebermann,
Maisler, Shimshelewitz, and
Shimshi families. NN, OCH.

SHIMSHI
See SHIMSHELEWITZ.

SHINEDLING
Shinedling, Moses. "Page from
his family Bible, including
family biography, 1891-1931."
MS. In English and Hebrew.
Photostat. AJA.

SHIRLEY
AMH has family records.

SHKOORATERSKY
See SCARATOWSKY.

SHLAFERMAN
AJA has genealogical files.
Shlaferman, Joe. "The Joe
Shlaferman Family: Genealogy
of the Shlaferman-Snyder
Family." Louisville, Ky.,
Jan. 19, 1975. AJA.

SHLICHTER
Rosenstein. Unbroken Chain,
pp. 321ff. Genealogical
chart. See GENERAL WORKS.

SHOMER
Zunser, Miriam Shomer.
Yesterday. New York:
Stackpole Sons, 1939. 271 p.
Three generations of the
author's family. Pinsk area
of Russia. CU, DLC, NcD, NN,
OCH, PPDrop.

SHOR
Rosenstein. Unbroken Chain,
pp. 265ff. Shor descendants
of R. Jacob Shor. See
GENERAL WORKS.
Shapiro. Mishpachot Atikot,
pp. 281-88. See GENERAL
WORKS.

SHOYER
Stern. FAJF. Shoyer family

tree beginning in U.S. See
GENERAL WORKS.

SHPIRKA
See Shapiro Family Tree entry
under SHAPIRO.

SHRAGAI
Shragai, Shlomo Zalmen and
Miriam Shragai. Min Hayamim
Hahame Ad Hazmin Hazeh.
Jerusalem, 1978. 52 p. Book
traces authors' descendants
and forbears. Includes
Feivalavitz family. JNUL.

SHRAGYA
AMH has family records.

SHULKIN
Sack, Sallyann Amdur and Mark
Weiss Shulkin, eds. Search
for the Family: A Chronicle
of the Tzvi Hirsch Shulkin
and Gelye Devorah Rosen
Family and Those Related to
Them. Bethesda, Md.: Marsal
Press, 1980. 176 p. Family
of Polotzk (Plock) area.
AJHS, DLC, MH, NN, WiH, YIVO.

SHULTZBERG
See SALTZBERG.

SHUTER
AMH has family records.

SHUTZE
AMH has family records.

SHWARTZ
Allon, Yigal. My Father's
House. Translated from the
Hebrew by Reuven Ben-Yosef.
New York: Norton, 1976. 204
p. The author (1918-   )
was born in Kefar Tavor
(Mascha), Israel, the son of
Reuven and Chayah-Etil
Shwartz Paicovitch (also
spelled Paikovits) and the
grandson of Yehoshua-Zvi
Paicovitch. The Paicovitch
family was from Grodno, and
the Shwartz family from
Safed, Israel.

SHWAYDER
Berry, Hannah Shwayder. "A
Colorado Family History,"
Western States Jewish
Historical Quarterly 5
(1973):158-65. Chronicles
the history of the Isaac and
Rachel Shwayder family, from
their emigration from Poland
(Suwalki Province) in 1865,
to their successful business
activities in Denver in 1916.
Shwayder family includes
founders of Samsonite Luggage
Co.

SHYER
Frank. Nashville Jewry,
p. 132. Family originally
from Hesse. See GENERAL
WORKS.

SICHEL
AMH has family records.
CAJ has family records.
CFM has family records.
Baer, Berthold. Stammtafeln
der Familie Speyer.
Frankfurt am Main: Kumpf &
Reis, 1896. 184 f.
Descendants of Joseph Lazarus
Speyer oo Jeanette geb.
Ellissen and of Ruben
Gumpertz Ellissen oo Jeanette
geb. Speyer. Sichel family
of Frankfurt am Main,
pp. 113ff. LBI, OCH.

SICHERMAN
Kempelen. Magyarországi Zsidó,
3:47. See GENERAL WORKS.
See Daniel Jay Rottenberg entry
under ROTTENBERG. Family
from Slovakia.

SICHROVSKY
PD has family records.

SIDON
PD has family records.

SIEBENSCHEIN
Kempelen. Magyarországi Zsidó,
3:47. See GENERAL WORKS.

SIEBENSTEIN
Moses, L. "Die Familie
Siebenstein in Mähren," JFF,
no. 42/44 (1936/37):768-75,
798-803.

SIEFF
Sieff, Israel. Memoirs.
London: Weidenfeld and
Nicolson, 1970. 214 p. "My
Family and Its Origins,"
pp. 1-16, and "My Childhood
in Manchester," pp. 17-28.
Anglo-Jewish family,
originally from Eiregola and
Siady, near Kovno, Lithuania.
The author, Lord Israel Moses
Sieff (1889-1972), was a
Manchester retail merchant,
industrialist, and English
Zionist leader. He was the
son of Ephraim Sieff and the
grandson of Rabbi Chaim
Sieff. Variants: Ziev, Ziff.
DLC, ICU, NcU, WU, William
and Mary College Library.

SIEGEL
PD has family records.
Siegel, Moritz F. "Meine
Familiengeschichte."
Meiningen, 1900-1917. 4 vs.
MS. Family from Walldorf.
LBI.
Salzburg-Siegel Family Tree.
Compiled by Mrs. Sarah Streen
Japha. Mainly members in
Norfolk, Virginia. JGCT.

SIELBERFELD
Kempelen. Magyarországi Zsidó,
3:24. See GENERAL WORKS.

SIELBERMANN
Kempelen. Magyarországi Zsidó,
2:89. See GENERAL WORKS.

SIELBERSPITZ
Kempelen. Magyarországi Zsidó,
3:35. See GENERAL WORKS.

SIENIAWSKI
CAJ has family records from
Poland, 1689-1940.

SIERRA
See DE LA SIERRA.
CFM has family records.

SIK
See SCHICK.

SIKLOSSY
Kempelen. Magyarországi Zsidó,
2:86. Siklóssy family. See
GENERAL WORKS.

SILBER
AMH has family records.
CFM has family records.
Kempelen. Magyarországi Zsidó,
2:87. See GENERAL WORKS.

SILBERER
Kempelen. Magyarországi Zsidó,
1:137. See GENERAL WORKS.

SILBERFELD
Rosenstein. Unbroken Chain,
pp. 321ff. Genealogical
chart. See GENERAL WORKS.

SILBERGLEIT
Auerbach, Anna. Die Chronik
der Familie Silbergleit.
Jena, 1905. 77 p. Family of
Breslau. LBI.

SILBERMANN
Silbermann, Karl. Chronik d.
Familie Silbermann. München,
1922. Descendants of
Jonathan Silbermann,
1822-1900.

SILBERSTEIN
LBI has family tree.

SILFVERHJELM
Semi-Gotha, 1:116. See GENERAL
WORKS.

SILFVERSTOLPE
Semi-Gotha, 1:79, 80, 83. See
GENERAL WORKS.

SILVA
See CALVO DE SILVA.
See DA SILVA.
See DA SILVA ROSA.
See SOLIS-COHEN (DA SILVA)

See VAS DA SILVA.
AMH has family records.
CFM has family records.
See JE entry under SOLIS.
Da Costa, Isaac. Noble
Families among the Sephardic
Jews. By Isaac da Costa.
With Some Account of the
Capadose Family (Including
their Conversion to
Christianity). By Bertram
Brewster. And An Excursus on
their Jewish History. By
Cecil Roth. London: Oxford
University Press, 1936.
219 p. Includes Silva
family. CtY, CU, DLC, MB,
NcD, NNC, NNJ, PPDrop.
See Stern, FAJF entry under
SOLIS.

SILVEIRA
AMH has family records.

SILVERA (DE LA)
See DE LA SILVERA.

SILVERSTONE
AMH has family records.

SILVIERA
CFM has family records.

SIMAY-MOLNAR
Kempelen. Magyarországi Zsidó,
2:79. See GENERAL WORKS.

SIMEON
AMH has family records.

SIMMOND
AMH has family records.
Weiss, Gertrude Marks.
"Collection of Harrer Simmond
Papers: Biography, 1829-1895;
Family Tree, 1777-1932;
Correspondence and Other
Material, 1777-1939." AJA.

SIMMONDS
AMH has family records.

SIMMONS
AMH has family records.

SIMON

AMH has family records.
CAJ (Call No. 4318) has the
following family trees:
(1) Simon, Menashe. The
Genealogical Tree of the
Eiger, Margoliot-Kalvaryski
and Simon Families (begins
with Katzenellenbogen,
Germany, 1312, and ends in
1937) on one side and (2) on
the opposite side:
Margolis-Jahrblum, Laura
(Tel-Aviv). Continuation of
the Genealogical Tree of the
Margoliot-Kalvaryski Family,
19th and 20th Century.
Margoliot also written
Margolis.
CAJD has family tree from
Germany.
CFM has family records.
LBI has family trees beginning
930, 1655, 1732, 1782, and
1818.
Simon Family. "Birth,
Marriage, and Death Records,
Chicago, Illinois, and St.
Louis, Mo., 1817-1886." AJA.
Simon, Steinman and Bloch
Families' Tree (1798-   ).
WJHC.
Ballin. Juden in Seesen,
pp. 234-35. See GENERAL
WORKS.
Kempelen. Magyarországi Zsidó,
1:150; 2:15, 22. See GENERAL
WORKS.
Simon, Fritz. Schalscheleth
ha-Juchasin, Eger,
Margoliouth, Calvariski,
Simon. Jerusalem, 1941. 1
leaf gr. folio.
Simon, Joseph. "Family Tree."
Lancaster, Pa., n.d. AJA.
Simon, Moritz.
Stiftungs-Urkunde betreffend
die Moritz Simonsche
Familien-Stiftung.
Königsberg: A. Hausbrand's
Nachf., 1890. 14 p. A
pedigree of Simon family is
attached. Moritz Alexander
Simon (1837-1905) was a
Hannover banker. OCH.
Simon, Solomon. My Jewish

Roots: A Personal Record.
Philadelphia: Jewish
Publications Society of
America, 1956. 274 p.
Recollections of a boyhood in
Russia. MB, MH, NcD, NN,
NNJ, OCH, OC1.
Stern. FAJF. Simon family
tree beginning in U.S. See
GENERAL WORKS.
Zondek, Theodor. "Die Familien
Veit und Simon.
Aufzeichnungen aus einer
altberliner Chronik,"
Allgemeine Wochenzeitung der
Juden in Deutschland-Jüdische
Illustrierte (Düsseldorf) 10,
no. 4 (März 1962).

SIMONIS

LBI has a copiously illustrated
family tree.

SIMONS

AMH has family records.
CFM has family records.
[Löwenstein, Leopold.]
Stammbaum Rheinganum,
Oppenheim, Simons. Mannheim,
1908. 38 p. Family of
Mannheim. OCH.
Simons, Karl. Stammbaum der
Familie Michael Simons.
Düsseldorf, 1905. 49 p.
OCH.
Stern. FAJF. Simons family
tree beginning in London.
See GENERAL WORKS.

SIMONSEN

Fischer, Josef. Jacob Simonsen
og Hustru Rose født Hahn og
deres Forfaedre, hundrede Aar
efter Jacob Simonsens Fødsel
udgivet af S.H. Simonsens
Børn, ved. Josef Fischer.
København: H. Meyers
Bogtrykkeri, 1923. 87 p.
Includes genealogical table.
Family in Denmark and
Germany. Jacob Simonsen,
1821-1880; Rose (Hahn)
Simonsen, 1826-1869. The
founder of the family was
Simon David Levy, the
so-called Höllander,

1760-1833. NN, OU.
"Prof. David Simonsen's
Vorfahren," in Festschrift in
Anledning af David Simonsen,
70 aarige fodselsdag
(København: Hertz's bogtr,
1923), pp. 311-79. David
Jacob Simonsen, Danish Rabbi,
scholar, and bibliophile,
b. Copenhagen, 1853; d. 1932.
He was the son of Jacob
Simonsen, a banker and leader
of the Jewish community.
Includes one family tree.
CSt, CtY, DLC, ICU, MB, MH,
NN, OCH, OU, PP, PPDrop.

SIMONSON
CFM has family records.

SIMONSSOHN
LBI has family tree beginning
1730.

SIMONVEIT
LBI has family tree beginning
1827.

SIMONYI
Kempelen. Magyarországi Zsidó,
3:95, 96. See GENERAL WORKS.

SIMOPOULOS
AMH has family records.

SIMPSON
AMH has family records.
Stern. FAJF. Simpson family
tree beginning in U.S. See
GENERAL WORKS.

SIMSON
AMH has family records.
Schloss Family.
"Simson-Wolf-Schloss
Genealogical Chart." 1972.
AJA.
Buchmann, Ehrich. Von der
jüdischen Firma Simson zur
nationalsozialistischen
Industriestiftung
Gustloff-Werke. Mit 10 Abb.
und einer Stammliste der
Familie Simson. Erfurt:
Boding-Verlag, 1944. 36 p.
(Thüringer Untersuchungen zur

Judenfrage, Heft 10).
Stern. FAJF. Simson family
tree beginning in Germany.
See GENERAL WORKS.

SINAUER
CFM has family records.

SINCLAIR
AMH has family records.

Semi-Gotha, 1:94; 2:30. See
GENERAL WORKS.

SINGER
AJA has family tree that traces
the Singer and Morgan
families from Reb Menahem
Mendel of Kotzk.
AMH has family records.
LBI has family trees beginning
1719 and 1836.
Hamburger, Karl. Legende zum
Stammbaum der Familien
Hamburger-Singer. Wien,
1928. 29 p. Families of
Prossnitz. LBI.
Hiller, Kurt. Leben Gegen die
Zeit. v. 1: Logos. Reinbek
bei Hamburg: Rowohlt Verlag,
1969. 422 p. "Herkunft und
Kindheit," pp. 11-23. The
author (1885-1972) was a
German socialist
theoretician. He was born in
Berlin, the son of Hartwig
Hiller (1854-1897) and Ella
Singer Hiller (1862-1936) and
the grandson of Joel Hiller
and Julius and Sophie Singer.
The Hiller family came to
Berlin from Bentschen
(Posen). CLU, CSt, CtY, CU,
DLC, ICU, IEN, MH, NIC, NjP.
Kempelen. Magyarországi Zsidó,
1:96; 2:67, 88, 94, 143;
3:55, 71, 79, 80, 83. See
GENERAL WORKS.
Kresh, Paul. Isaac Bashevis
Singer: The Magician of West
86th Street: A Biography.
New York: Dial Press, 1979.
441 p. Genealogical
information on the Singer and
Zylberman families, pp.
16-22.

See Daniel Nathan Leeson entry
under LEESON.
Singer, Isaac Bashevis. In My
Father's Court. New York:
Farrar, Straus, and Giroux,
1966. 307 p. "The Family
Tree," pp. 43-48. The Nobel
Prize-winning author
(1904-   ) was born in
Leoncin, Province of Warsaw,
the son of Reb Pinchas Mendel
Singer, who was born in
Tomaszow, and the grandson of
Reb Samuel and Bathsheba
Zylberman Singer. Bathsheba
Zylberman was from Bilgoray
in the Province of Lublin and
was the daughter of Rabbi
Jacob Zylberman.
————. A Day of Pleasure:
Stories of a Boy Growing Up
in Warsaw. New York: Farrar,
Straus and Giroux, 1969. 227
p. Covers 1908-1918.
Singer, Israel Joshua. Of A
World That is No More: A
Tender Memoir. Translated by
Joseph Singer. New York: The
Vanguard Press, 1970. 253 p.
A Singer family memoir by
Isaac Bashevis Singer's older
brother, who was also a
famous author.
"Genealogical chart presented
to Rabbi Merle E. Singer by
Mrs. David J. Morgan, both
sixth-generation descendants
of Rev. Menachem Mendel of
Kotzk." Philadelphia, Pa.,
Oct. 12, 1973. 1 p. AJA.

SINGTON
AMH has family records.
CFM has family records.

SINSHEIM
See Wilhelm and Rudolf Frank
entry under BING.

SINSHEIMER
"Family Tree ... Sinsheimer."
N.p., n.d. 1 p. Starts with
Simcha, b. Germany, 1650, and
his son, Boruch, b. Weiler,
near Sinsheim (Baden,
German), 1680; d. Heppenheim

on the Bergstrasse, 1752.
Many descendants lived in
Mannheim, Bürstadt, and now
in U.S. Last date on family
tree is 1955. CAJ, Call
No. 5132.
Stern, Norton B. and William M.
Kramer. "The Sinsheimers of
San Luis Obispo," Western
States Jewish Historical
Quarterly 6 (Oct. 1973):3-32.
Pioneer German-Jewish family
of California. Originally
from Bürstadt, Darmstadt, and
Weiler, near Sinsheim, and
Heppenheim.

SINTZHEIM
CAJ has family records.

SINZHEIM
PD has family records.
See Wilhelm and Rudolf Frank
entry under BING.

SIPOCZ
Kempelen. Magyarországi Zsidó,
2:75. Sipőcz family. See
GENERAL WORKS.

SIPRUT
CFM has family records.

SIRKES
Bałaban, Meir. Shalshelet
Ha-Jichus.... Warsaw, 1931.
47 p. 1 genealogical table.
Family of Poland, descendants
of Joel Sirkes, Rabbi of
Krakow, 17th century.
Schochet, Elijah Judah.
Bach = Rabbi Joel Sirkes: His
Life, Works, and Times. New
York: Feldheim Publishers,
1971. 265 p. "Family," pp.
15-18. On Rabbi Joel ben
Samuel Sirkes (1561-1640).
DLC.

SIRKIN
Shapiro. Mishpachot Atikot,
pp. 324-48. Sirkin, Sirkis,
Sirkus family. See GENERAL
WORKS.

SIRKIS
CAJ has family records.
See Shapiro, Mishpachot Atikot
entry under SIRKIN.
See Meir Yizraeli entry under
BIDERMAN.

SIRKUS
See Shapiro, Mishpachot Atikot
entry under SIRKIN.

SITKEY
Kempelen. Magyarországi Zsidó,
2:79. See GENERAL WORKS.

SJOCRONA
Semi-Gotha, 1:106. Sjöcrona
family. See GENERAL WORKS.

SKALLER
Skaller, Ulrich. The Family
History of Nicholas Paul
Alexander. London, 1972.
34 p. Includes Skaller
family. YIVO.

SKENE
AMH has family records.

SKERLETZ
Kempelen. Magyarországi Zsidó,
2:141. See GENERAL WORKS.

SKIOLDEBRAND
Semi-Gotha, 1:85. Skiöldebrand
family. See GENERAL WORKS.

SKIPPER
AMH has family records.

SKLARINSKY
Hurwit, Doris Schwarz. Max and
His Rose. Hartford, Conn.,
1979. 179 p. The story of
Max and Rose Sklarinsky and
their family who arrived in
Hartford in 1902. AJA, AJHS.

SKURATOWSKY
See SCARATOWSKY.

SKUTCH
See Sydney M. Cone entry under
AMBACH.

SKUTSCH
Friedländer, Siegfried.
Geschichte der Familie
Friedländer. 1-2. Breslau
1912 und Potsdam 1921.
110, 111 p. MS. Includes
Skutsch family of Schlesien.
LBI.

SLATER
AMH has family records.

SLAZENGER
CFM has family records.

SLOMAN
AMH has family records.
CFM has family records.

SLONIM
Slonim, Menachem. Toledot
Mishpaḥat ha-rav mi-Ladi.
Tel-Aviv, 1946. 302 p.
Slonim, Schneersohn, and
Zalman families. Descendants
of Shneor Zalman ben Baruch
of Lyady (1747-1812), founder
of Habad Hassidism. DLC, NN,
OCH.
Heilprin, S.A., comp. Sefer
ha-Tze-atza-im [Book of
Descendants: Family Tree of
the Descendants of Rabbi
Shneor Zalman ben Baruch,
1742-1812 of Lyady, founder
of Habad Hassidism].
Jerusalem, 1980. 566 p.
Includes Slonim, Schneersohn,
and Zalman families. JNUL.

SLOSS
Narell. Our City. Includes
genealogical charts of Sloss
family, originally from the
Bavarian village of
Untereisenheim on the Main
River. See GENERAL WORKS.

SLUSZ
CAJ has family records.

SMAUZ
Kempelen. Magyarországi Zsidó,
2:91. See GENERAL WORKS.

SMITH
See ARCH-SMITH.
See BROOK-SMITH.
AMH has family records.
See Esmond S. De Beer entry
  under BARDEN.

SNAPPER
AMH has family records.
Kempelen. Magyarországi Zsidó,
  1:39. See GENERAL WORKS.

SNEIDERN
Semi-Gotha, 2:132. See GENERAL
  WORKS.

SOARES
AMH has family records.
CFM has family records.

SOBEL
AJA has genealogical files.
Frank. Nashville Jewry,
  pp. 145-46. See GENERAL
  WORKS.
See Daniel Jay Rottenberg entry
  under ROTTENBERG. Includes
  Sobel family.

SOFER
See SPRING.
EJ (1972), 15:76. Contains
  genealogical chart for the
  descendants of Samuel Sofer
  (Schreiber), 1715-1798,
  through mid-20th century.
  See GENERAL WORKS.
Reinitz, Samuel. Olelot
  Efraim. Munkács: Druck von
  Kahn und Fried, 1914. 36 p.
  Deals with Zusman Sofer, his
  son, Efraim Fischel Sofer,
  and the latter's children,
  all from Pressburg, Hungary.
  JNUL.
Roth, Ernest. "Die
  Blutbeschuldigung in Trient
  von 500 Jahren, zugleich die
  Genealogie einer Sofer
  Familie aus Heidelberg," Udim
  6 (1975/76):79-85.

SOHER
Stern. FAJF. Soher family
  tree beginning in U.S. See
  GENERAL WORKS.

SOKOL
See R. Brock Shanberg entry
  under GOLTZ.

SOL
Semi-Gotha, 2:118. See GENERAL
  WORKS.

SOLA (DA)
See DA SOLA.

SOLA (DE)
JE, 11:430-34. Contains a
  pedigree of 25 generations
  showing the "various branches
  and chief members of the De
  Sola family." See GENERAL
  WORKS.

SOLAS
CFM has family records.

SOLIS (DE or DA)
AMH has Solis family records.
JE, 11:435. "Solis Pedigree."
  Descendants of Solomon da
  Silva Solis, from 17th to
  late 19th century. Family of
  England and Holland. See
  GENERAL WORKS.
Birmingham. The Grandees.
  Includes Solis family. See
  GENERAL WORKS.
Stern. FAJF. Solis family
  tree beginning in Lisbon.
  Name originally Da Silva and,
  possibly, Da Silva Solis.
  See GENERAL WORKS.

SOLIS-COHEN (DA SILVA)
EJ, 15:96. Contains
  genealogical chart of the
  descendants of Jacob da Silva
  Solis, 1780-1829, through
  mid-20th century. Family of
  U.S. See GENERAL WORKS.

SOLLEDOR
CAJ has family records.

SOLOMON
See MYER-SOLOMON.
AMH has family records.
CAJ (Call No. 5044) had the
  following large family trees:
  "Family of Philip 'Phievel'"

Dan," "Family of Pere Libba
'Lizza' Solomon Dan," and
"History of the Den and
Leibowitz Families." Also
included are a 2-page copy of
1900 census, notes on Philip
Dan and family in Memphis,
Tenn., and pictures of Philip
Dan and brother Solomon Den.
Pere Dan (1862-1944) was the
wife of Philip Dan. David
King Den and his wife, Kala
Bossel Den, lived in
Tavirick, Lithuania, and had
two sons who came to America:
Philip Dan, 1852-1926, and
Solomon Den, 1858-1940.
CFM has family records.
Solomon Family, Helena,
Arkansas. "Birth and Death
Records, 1867-1927." AJA.
See Richard J. Alperin entry
under BEHRMAN.
Fierman, Floyd S. "Jewish
Pioneering in the Southwest:
a Record of the
Freudenthal-Lesinsky-Solomon
Families," Arizona and the
West 2 (1960):54-72. Isador
Elkan Solomon settled in
Arizona at Pueblo Viejo and
expanded from merchant to
banker. He was born in
Posen, Poland.
The Anglo-Jewish Archives of
the Mocatta Library in London
holds "The Family Tree of
Anthony Joseph's Family,"
compiled by Dr. Anthony P.
Joseph. Supplements have
appeared since the original
edition was completed in
1958. Covers late 18th
century to date for this
Anglo-Jewish family. Also
covers the descendants of
Barnet Levy (d. 1791),
Solomon Solomon (1764-1819),
and Betsy Levy (1767-1832).
Solomon, Ezekiel. "Genealogy."
AJA.
Solomon, Israel, born 1803.
Records of My Family. New
York: By the Author, 1887.
17 p. AJA, NN.
Solomon Family, New York, N.Y.

"Genealogy, 1835-1968; and
'Records of My Family,' by
Israel Solomon, 1887." MS
and printed; Xerox copy and
photostat. AJA.
Solomon, Joseph.
"Autobiography," American
Jewish Archives 28
(Apr. 1976):51-58. Covers
the family's life in New York
City from 1905, the year of
Solomon's birth, to 1929. He
was the son of Abraham and
Rebecca Solomon (real name
Szylkowski), who came to U.S.
from Grodno in 1902.
According to the author, all
other family members who came
to U.S. adopted the surname
Solomon.
Stern. FAJF. Solomon family
tree beginning in Germany.
See GENERAL WORKS.
Wolf, Abraham. "A Family
Record." 1948. Typescript.
Family of New York City.
AJA.

SOLOMONS
AMH has family records.
CFM has family records.
"Solomons Family Genealogical
Notes and Records of Births,
Marriages, and Deaths." MS.
AJA.
"Solomons Genealogy." Family
of California. WJHC.
"Items Relating to the Solomons
Family, New York,"
Publications of the American
Jewish Historical Society 27
(1920):376.
Mac Leod, Celeste, comp.
"Seixas [-] Gershoms [-]
Solomons Family Tree," 1969.
Families of California.
WJHC.
Solomons Family. Lucius L.
Solomons Collection,
1725-1925. Includes
genealogical records of
Seixas and Solomons families.
AJA.
Lucius Levy Solomons Papers and
Documents. Contain materials
on Solomons' ancestors, the

Solomons and Seixas families,
as well as on his
descendants. Of particular
interest are the following
items: a genealogy of the
Seixas and Solomons families,
1738-1963, and another for
the family of Lucius Levy
Solomons himself. WJHC.
Stern. FAJF. Solomons family
trees beginning in:
(I) Montreal; (II and
III) London; (IV) Amsterdam;
and (V) Germany. See GENERAL
WORKS.

SOLOMONSON
Solomonson, Herman. "The
Solomonson Family: A
History." N.p., n.d. 56 p.
Located at Genealogical Forum
of Portland, Oregon.

SOLOVEICHIK
EJ (1972), 15:127. Contains
genealogical chart of the
descendants of Joseph Ha-Levi
Soloveichik, Lithuanian
rabbi, 17th to mid-20th
century. See GENERAL WORKS.
Wolsky, Boris. My Life in
Three Worlds. Miami Beach,
Fla.: By the Author, 1979.
383 p. Includes genealogical
tables. The three worlds of
the author (1898-   ) are
turn-of-the-century Domacheva
and Brest-Litovsk; Paris,
where he lived from
1914-1941; and the U.S. after
1941, where he operated a
travel agency in New York.
"My Family," pp. 229-83.
"Luba's Family," pp. 287-99.
Luba, the author's wife, came
from Smolensk and Lachowich,
Russia. Her maiden name was
Soloveichik. "The Wolsky
Family," pp. 303-21.
Author's uncle shortened
family name from Wolsky to
Wolsk. The author's maternal
grandparents were the Priluk
family, a history of which is
covered on pp. 325-38.
Family was from Kamenitz near

Brest-Litovsk, and later
lived in Warsaw. DLC;
University of
Illinois / Champaign-Urbana
Library.

SOLT
Kempelen. Magyarországi Zsidó,
2:42. See GENERAL WORKS.

SOMAN
CFM has family records.

SOMECH
Ben-Yacov, Avraham. Toledot
Harav Avdala Somech. Gadol
Rabbenai Bavel B'dorot
Ha'acharonim. Jerusalem:
Matmon, 1950. 96 p. CZA.

SOMERSALL
AMH has family records.

SOMJEN
Kempelen. Magyarországi Zsidó,
2:129; 3:100. Sömjén family.
See GENERAL WORKS.

SOMMER
Kempelen. Magyarországi Zsidó,
3:100. See GENERAL WORKS.

SOMMERGUTH
Sommerguth, Ludwig. Chronik
der Familien Sommerguth,
Weinzweig, Brandus. Berlin:
By the Author, 1933. 18 p.
Folio. LBI.

SOMMERSTEIN
Namier, Julia. Lewis Namier: A
Biography. London: Oxford
University Press, 1971.
347 p. "Ancestry and Birth,"
pp. 3-10. Sir Lewis
Bernstein Namier, famous
English social historian,
philosopher, and Zionist,
b. Wola Okrzejska, 1888;
d. 1960. Real surname,
Namierowski. He arrived in
England in 1908.

SOMMO
Steinschneider, Moritz. "Die
Familie Portaleone-Sommo,"

Hebräische Bibliographie 6
(1863):48ff.

SONCINO
CAJ has family records.
EJ (1972), 15:141. Contains
genealogical chart of the
Soncino descendants of Moses
of Speyer (mid-15th century),
through late 16th century.
Family of Hebrew printers
active in Italy, Turkey, and
Egypt in the 15th and 16th
centuries. See GENERAL
WORKS.
Freimann, Aron. "Die Familie
Soncino," Soncino-Blätter 1
(1925):9-12.
Habermann, Abraham Meir.
Ha-madpisim bene Soncino.
Added title page: Die Drucker
aus der Familie Soncino.
Wien: Buchhandlung David
Fränkel, 1933. 80 p.
Includes a genealogical
table. DLC.

SONDER
Sonder, Alfred. Ahnentafel der
Kinder des Nathan Weill (Sohn
des Löw Weill) in Kippenheim.
Frankfurt am Main: Schirmer &
Machlau, 1935. 50, 6 p.
Four genealogical tables.
Includes Sonder family. NN.

SONDHEIM
Stern. FAJF. Sondheim family
tree beginning in Germany.
See GENERAL WORKS.

SONDHEIMER
Kempelen. Magyarországi Zsidó,
2:134. See GENERAL WORKS.
Rosenthal, Ludwig. Der Hanauer
Rabbiner Mosche Tobias (Raw
Mosche Tuvje) Sondheimer
(1775-1830) und seine
Nachfahren in der ehemaligen
Frankfurter Metallfirma von
Weltruf Beer, Sondheimer &
Co. Hanau: Kittsteiner, 1975?
44 p. Includes genealogical
table. LBI.

SONNEBORN
Behrend-Sonneborn Family.
Papers, 1907, 1911, 1940,
1942, 1978-79. 1 folder.
Family papers, including
genealogies, newspaper
clippings, and correspondence
of Sonneborn and Behrend
families. Behrend family
genealogy, 1942. Sonneborn
Family, 1978. PJAC.
Kober, A. Sonneborn
Beginnings. New York, 1978.
20 p. Story of family from
Breidenbach, Hessen, Germany,
whose descendants initially
settled in Baltimore and New
York. AJHS.

SONNENBERG
Kempelen. Magyarországi Zsidó,
1:68; 3:87. See GENERAL
WORKS.

SONNENFELD
Kempelen. Magyarországi Zsidó,
2:73; 3:73. See GENERAL
WORKS.

SONNENFELS
CAJ has family records, 18th to
19th century.
LBI has family tree beginning
1680.
JFF, no. 13 (1928):13-19.
Includes family history.
Nirtl, Joseph. "Die Freiherren
von Sonnenfels," ZGJT 3
(1933):224-25.

SONNENSCHEIN
CFM has family records.

SONSINO
CFM has family records.

SONTHEIMER
Tänzer. Juden in Jebenhausen,
pp. 378-79. See GENERAL
WORKS.

SOOS
Kempelen. Magyarországi Zsidó,
1:124. Soós family. See
GENERAL WORKS.

SOPHER
AJA has family tree.
Sopher, Ira. "Sequence of the
Generations for the Hacohen
Family from Which Mr. Sopher
is Descended." 1922. AJA.

SORA
CFM has family records.

SOREPH
CAJ (Call No. 5267) has family
tree of Carrence family of
Paris. Includes Soreph
family.

SORIA
AJA has genealogical files.
Stern. FAJF. Soria family
tree beginning in Bordeaux.
See GENERAL WORKS.

SOSNA
Kempelen. Magyarországi Zsidó,
2:19. See GENERAL WORKS.

SOUSA
CFM has family records.

SOUZA
Stern. FAJF. Souza family
tree beginning in Bayonne,
France. See GENERAL WORKS.

SPADA
CAJ has family records,
1600-1938.

SPALLETTI-TRIVELLO
Kempelen. Magyarországi Zsidó,
1:44. See GENERAL WORKS.

SPANIER
LBI has family trees beginning
16th century and 1676.
Stern. FAJF. Spanier family
tree beginning in Wundsdorf,
Hanover. See GENERAL WORKS.

SPANJAARD
Citroën, K.A. The Spanjaard
Family: A Survey of the
Descendants of Salomon Jacob
Spanjaard (1783-1861) and
Sara David van Gelder
(1793-1882). 2d rev. and

augmented ed. Borne,
Holland: Family Association
"Berith Salom," 1981. 286 p.
AJHS.

SPATZ
LBI has family tree beginning
1794.
Kempelen. Magyarországi Zsidó,
2:88. See GENERAL WORKS.

SPECTOR
See Yaffa Draznin entry under
BERNSTEIN. Includes Spector
family.

SPEKTOR
CAJ has family records.

SPELMAN
AMH has family records.

SPEOL
AMH has family records.

SPERANS
J. Lloyd Conrich, "The Sperans
Family," 1964. WJHC.

SPEYER
AMH has family records.
CFM has family records.
JE, 11:507. "Speyer Pedigree."
Descendants of Agatha zur
Sonnen (d. 1556), through
late 19th century. See
GENERAL WORKS.
Baer, Berthold. Stammtafeln
der Familie Speyer.
Frankfurt am Main: Kumpf &
Reis, 1896. 184 p.
Descendants of Joseph Lazarus
Speyer oo Jeanette geb.
Ellissen and of Ruben
Gumpertz Ellissen oo
Jeannette geb. Speyer. LBI,
OCH.
Kempelen. Magyarországi Zsidó,
1:39. See GENERAL WORKS.
Pudor. Internationalen
Verwandtschaftlichen. Vol. 3
has section on Speyer family.
See GENERAL WORKS.
Renus, Georg. "Eine deutsche
Familie von Weltbankiers.
Frankfurt, die Wiege der

Hochfinanz. Ein Naher
Verwandter: Diamantenkönig
Sir Otto Bert aus Hamburg,"
Frankfurter Zeitung,
1 Mai 1932, p. 3.

SPIEGEL
AJA has family tree from
Chicago, beginning 1828.
CAJ has family records.
Barbie, Lizzie J.
"Autobiography." 1934.
Includes Greenbaum-Spiegel
genealogy, ca. 1719-1931.
AJA.
Cowan, Paul. An Orphan in
History: Retrieving a Jewish
Legacy. New York: Doubleday,
1982. 246 p. The author is
the son of Louis Cowan,
former President of CBS-TV.
Family's original name was
Cohen, and the family was
from Lithuania. The author's
mother's family was the
famous Spiegel family of
Chicago.

SPIEGELBERG
UJE, 10:2-3. Family of New
Mexico. Descendants of
Solomon Jacob Spiegelberg who
came to U.S. from Natzungen,
Westphalia in 1842.
Fierman, Floyd S. The
Spiegelbergs of New Mexico,
Merchants and Bankers,
1844-1893. El Paso, Tex.:
Texas Western College Press,
1964. 48 p. (Southwestern
Studies, vol. 1, no. 4.)
Jones, Hester. "The
Spiegelbergs and Early Trade
in New Mexico," El Palacio
38, no. 15/17 (1935):81-89.
Latimer, Roman L. "Spiegelberg
Brothers: Bankers and
Merchants to New Mexico
Territory," Numismatic
Scrapbook Magazine 38,
no. 432 (Feb. 1972). 10 p.

SPIEGL
Kempelen. Magyarországi Zsidó,
2:89. See GENERAL WORKS.

SPIELBERG
Shragai, Shlomo Zalmen and
Miriam Shragai. Min Hayamim
Hahame Ad Hazmin Hazeh.
Jerusalem, 1978. 52 p. Book
traces authors' descendants
and forbears. Includes
Feivalavitz and Spielberg
families. JNUL.

SPIELMAN
AMH has family records.

SPIELMANN
CFM has family records.

SPIELMANN
Spielmann, Percy Edwin. The
Early History of the
Spielmann Family and of
Marion Harry Alexander
Spielmann (1858-1948) to the
Year of His Marriage (1880)
Together with Some Associated
Excursions and Diversions.
Reading, England: By the
Author, 1951. 62 p. OCH.
————. ————. Additions and
Corrections. N.p., 1953?
CLU, DLC, NN.

SPIER
AMH has family records.
CAJ has genealogical material
for family of Netherlands.

SPIERO
LBI has family tree beginning
1700.

SPIERS
AMH has family records.
CFM has family records.

SPINGARN
Kempelen. Magyarországi Zsidó,
1:87. See GENERAL WORKS.

SPINOZA
Bab, Arturo. "Spinozas Ahnen,"
JFF 6, no. 4 (1930).
Gebhartm, Karl. "Der Name
Spinoza," Chronicon
Spinozanum 1 (1921):272-76.
Vaz Diaz, A.M. and W.G. Van der
Tak. De firma Bento y

Gabriel de Spinoza. Leiden:
Brill, 1934. 23 p. ICU, MH,
NNC, OCH.
————. Spinoza Mercator et
Autodidactus. Oorkonden en
andere authenticke Documenten
betreffende des Wijsgeers
jengd en Diens betrekkingen.
's Gravenhage: Martinus
Nijhoff, 1933. 100 p. CU,
ICU, MB, NcD, NN, OCH, OU.
Warynski, T.; Myślicki, I.; and
Gebhardt, Karl. "Le nom de
Spinoza," Chronicon
Spinozanum 2 (1922):251-54.

SPIRA
LBI has family tree beginning
1630.
See Jonas Marcus Bondi entry
under LUCKA. Genealogical
tables. Includes Spira
family.
"Die Grabschriften der Familie
Frankel-Spira in Prag," MGWJ,
1902, pp. 450, 556.
Jüdische Centralblatt 7
(1888):78. Family history of
Spira family of Jungbunzlau.
Kempelen. Magyarországi Zsidó,
3:124. See GENERAL WORKS.
Rosenstein. Unbroken Chain,
pp. 660ff. Discussion of
Spira Chassidic dynasty of
Munkács-Dynow. See GENERAL
WORKS.

SPIRE
"Les grandes familles
françaises: la famille Spire,"
La Revue Juive de Lorraine,
n.s., 5, no. 41 (1952):1-4.

SPIRO
PD has family records.
Kempelen. Magyarországi Zsidó,
3:125. See GENERAL WORKS.
Stern. FAJF. Spiro family
tree beginning in Prussia.
See GENERAL WORKS.
Zapf. Tübinger Juden, pp.
60-61, 169-71, 221-223. See
GENERAL WORKS.

SPITTEL
CAJ has records for family of

Naumburg and Aachen,
1775-1907.

SPITZ
Kempelen. Magyarországi Zsidó,
2:9. See GENERAL WORKS.
See Bernát Munkácsi entry under
AUSTERLITZ.
See Ernst Wolf entry under
GOMPERZ.

SPITZER
Bronner, Jakob. "Zur
Genealogie des
Achtundvierziger Karl H.
Spitzer," Jüdischer Archiv 1,
no. 6 (1927):16-18. Karl
Heinrich Spitzer, 1830-1848,
first Jewish victim of the
March 1848 Revolution in
Vienna, was born in Bzenec
(Bisenz), Moravia, where the
family had settled after the
expulsion of the Jews in
Vienna in 1670.
Kempelen. Magyarországi Zsidó,
1:122; 2:8, 35, 73; 3:37, 54,
74, 92, 99. See GENERAL
WORKS.
Röder, Julius. Die Nachkommen
von Moses (Josef) Zweig.
Olmütz, 1932. Family from
Olomouc, Moravia. YIVO.
————. Die Nachfahren des
Moses Zweig. Olmütz, 1932.
Contains 6 family trees; more
than 500 names which belong
to 8 generations of this
family. Family of Olomouc,
Moravia. CAJ, YIVO.

SPIVAK
See Yaffa Draznin entry under
BERNSTEIN. Includes Spivak
family.

SPLENYI
Kempelen. Magyarországi Zsidó,
2:93. See GENERAL WORKS.

SPRATKIN
Keneseth Israel. See GENERAL
WORKS.

SPRING
Spring, Chaim. Zicherman,

Intrater, Reiss, Sofer.
Rehovot, Israel: By the
Author, 1979. Includes
genealogical tables. JNUL.

SPRINGER
PD has family records.
Kempelen. Magyarországi Zsidó,
1:39. See GENERAL WORKS.

SPRINZENSTEIN
PD has family records.

SPROAT
AMH has family records.

SPYER
AMH has family records.
CFM has family records.

SPYERS
AMH has family records.
CFM has family records.

STADECKER
Kempelen. Magyarországi Zsidó,
2:127. See GENERAL WORKS.

STAITZKER
AMH has family records.

STALHAMMAR
Semi-Gotha, 1:87. See GENERAL
WORKS.

STAMMERS
AMH has family records.

STAMPFER
CAJ has family records.

STANCOMB
AMH has family records.

STANGEL
Kempelen. Magyarországi Zsidó,
1:122. See GENERAL WORKS.

STARGARDT
LBIS has family tree and notes.

STARK
Kempelen. Magyarországi Zsidó,
2:89, 118, 134. See GENERAL
WORKS.

STARKENSTEIN
Starkenstein, Emil.
Familienforschung. Prag,
n.D. (ca. 1928). LBI.

STARR
Streng Family. "Genealogical
Information Concerning the
Streng, Levi, and Starr
Family, Louisville, Ky. and
Pittsburgh, Pa., 1817-1957."
AJA.

STATMAN
AMH has family records.

STAURIANU
CAJ has family records.

STEARNS
AMH has family records.

STECKERL
LBI has family tree.

STEEL
AMH has family records.

STEG
Herz, Emil. Denk ich an
Deutschland in der Nacht, die
Geschichte des Hauses Steg.
2. Aufl. Berlin: Ullstein,
1953. 329 p. Family of
Warburg. Descendants of
Rabbi Samuel Steg (mid-18th
century). CU, DLC, LBI, NN,
NNJ, OCH, OCl.

STEIERMANN
Berney, Albert. Descendants of
Zodik Hochshild Born 1792,
Died 12-26-1858 Married
Rikkel Steiermann.
Westcliffe, Colorado, 1977.
9 p. AJA.

STEIN
AJA has family tree from
Philadelphia, beginning 1795.
CFM has family records.
LBI has family trees beginning
1700, 1756, and 1766.
Emanuel-Sanquinetti-Stein
Family. Papers. Includes a
partial family tree of this

family of Philadelphia,
prepared in 1981. PJAC.
Stein-Mayer Family, Louisiana,
Ohio, Germany, and France.
"Papers, Documents, and Birth
and Death Records of Members
of the Family, 1900-1919."
In English and German. AJA.
Cohn, Rose B. Stein, Bergman,
and Cohn Families
(1787-1954). Baltimore: Ida
Wilkins Foundation, 1954.
21 p. Includes genealogical
tables. NN.
Dickinson, John K. German and
Jew: The Life and Death of
Sigmund Stein. Chicago:
Quadrangle Books, 1967. 338
p. "Jewish Children in a
Hessian Village," pp. 1-26.
Sigmund Stein (1896-1945), a
German lawyer and communal
leader, was born in
Bachdorf-on-the-Frieden, the
son of Isaac and Dela Stein,
the grandson of Benedict
Stein, and the great-grandson
of Isaac Stein. The Stein
family was from Niederhausen.
Sigmund Stein later moved to
Hochburg-on-the-Felsen.
Kempelen. Magyarországi Zsidó,
1:86, 95, 134; 2:144; 3:74,
75, 107. See GENERAL WORKS.
Koplowitz, Hannah. "Stein
Family of Reichensachsen and
Their Descendants."
Cincinnati, Ohio, 1975. 8 p.
Allen County Public Library,
Ft. Wayne, Indiana.
See Daniel Nathan Leeson entry
under LEESON.
See Bernát Muncácsi entry under
AUSTERLITZ.
Stein, Edith. Aus dem Leben
einer jüdischen Familie; das
Leben Edith Steins. Vol. 1:
Kindheit und Jugend.
Louvain: E. Nauwelaerts,
1965. 292 p. (Edith Steins
Werke, 7.) Edith Stein
(1891-1942) was born into a
Jewish family of Breslau.
She converted to Catholocism
in 1922. MH.
Stein, Jon. "Letters from

Stein to His Family and
Friends Concerning His
Activities in European
Theatre of Operations during
World War II, Oct. 1943 To
Dec. 1945; And His Family
Tree, 1968." AJA.
Stein, Nathan.
"Lebenserinnerungen." New
York, n.D. ca. 400 pp.
Includes brief history of
family of the author
(1881-1966) from Worms,
Baden. LBI.
Yaoz. Album Shel. See GENERAL
WORKS.

STEINACH
Tänzer. Juden in Tirol,
p. 773. See GENERAL WORKS.

STEINART
AMH has family records.

STEINBACH
Tänzer. Juden in Tirol,
p. 774. See GENERAL WORKS.

STEINBERG
Bick-Shauli, "Roots and
Branches." Includes
genealogy of Isaac Nahman
Steinberg, Russian
revolutionary, jurist,
writer, and leader of the
Territorialist Movement,
b. Dvinsk (Daugavpils)
Latvia, 1888; d. 1957. See
GENERAL WORKS.
Friedberg, Bernhard. Sefer
ha-yahas min mispaḥath
Steinberg. Added title page:
Généalogie de la famille
Steinberg d'après des sources
authentiques remontant au
XIV. Siècle, retracée par B.
Friedberg. Anvers, 1934.
26 p. CU, DLC, NN, OCH.
Newman, Peter Charles. Flame
of Power: The Story of
Canada's Greatest
Businessmen. Toronto:
Mc Clelland and Stewart,
1959. 255 p. "The Steinberg
Brothers (1905-   ),"
chap. 8, pp. 171-82.

Developers of the largest
food supermarkets across
Quebec, Canada.

STEINER
AJA has family tree beginning
1832.
Kempelen. Magyarországi Zsidó,
2:44, 89, 90, 128, 134; 3:95,
96, 121, 124. See GENERAL
WORKS.
Mayer, Mrs. Richard. Memoir
and Genealogy of the
Ferdinand and Jette Steiner
Mayer Family, 1832-1971. San
Angelo, Tex., 1972. AJA.
Steiner, Sebastian. "Als erste
Emigranten familie in
Hongkew," Shanghai Jewish
Chronicle, March 1940, p. 27.
Family of Austria which fled
in late 1930s to Shanghai,
China.
Tänzer. Juden in Tirol,
pp. 775-76. See GENERAL
WORKS.

STEINFELD
Kempelen. Magyarországi Zsidó,
1:87, 129; 2:94. See GENERAL
WORKS.
Kiser Family. "Genealogical
Chart of the Kiser-Steinfeld
Family, 1856-1953." AJA.
See Daniel Jay Rottenberg entry
under ROTTENBERG.
Zachariah, Brian. "A History
of the Zachariah Family:
Genealogy of the
Zachariah-Steinfeld Family."
Louisville, Ky., Feb. 2,
1975. AJA.

STEINFURTER
Tänzer. Juden in Jebenhausen,
p. 382. See GENERAL WORKS.

STEINHARDT
AMH has family records.

STEINHEIM
LBI has family tree beginning
1789.
See Siegfried Porta entry under
FALKENSTEIN. Includes family
trees. Table of descendants

of Abraham Basch, 1545-1590,
and Marcus Jakob Levi at
Brakel or Ottenberg,
ca. 1648. His chldren or
grandsons are named
Falkenstein, Goldsmith,
Lowenstein, Porta, Rosenberg,
and Steinheim.
Steinheim, Salomon Ludwig.
Salomon Ludwig Steinheim zum
Gedenken: Ein Sammelband.
Hrsg. von Hans-Joachim
Schoeps. Leiden: E.J. Brill,
1966. 359 p. Includes
genealogical information on
Salomon Ludwig Steinheim,
German poet, physician, and
religious philosopher,
b. Bruchhausen, Westphalia,
1789; d. 1866. He lived most
of his life first in Altona
and then in Rome. CLU, CU,
DLC, ICU, MH, NcD, NIC, OCH,
WU.

STEINHERZ
CAJ has family records.

STEINITZ
LBI has family trees beginning
1751 and 1796.

STEINITZER
Kempelen. Magyarországi Zsidó,
2:94. See GENERAL WORKS.

STEINMAN
Simon, Steinman, and Bloch
Families' Tree (1798-   ).
WJHC.

STEINMETZ
Steinmetz, Charles P.
Schenectadt, N.Y.
"Information on the Ancestry
of Dr. Steinmetz, 1964."
Typescript. Charles Proteus
Steinmetz, U.S. electrical
engineer, b. Breslau, 1865;
d. 1923. He immigrated to
U.S. in 1889. AJA.

STEINTHAL
LBI has family tree beginning
1720.
Herz, Ludwig. Fünfhundert

Jahre Familiengeschichte,
1430-1930. Includes Herz and
Steinthal families. LBI.
Kempelen. Magyarországi Zsidó,
2:90. See GENERAL WORKS.

STEKL
Kempelen. Magyarországi Zsidó,
2:90. See GENERAL WORKS.

STENBOCK
Semi-Gotha, 1:142. See GENERAL
WORKS.

STERN
See DE STERN.
AJA has family tree from
Germany, Delaware, and
Philadelphia.
AMH has family records.
CAJ has family records.
See CAJ (Call No. P/123) entry
under ECKSTEIN.
CFM has family records.
Goldmark Family, Pest, Hungary
and Philadelphia, Pa.
"Goldmark-Stern Letters,
1845-1870." Pamphlet.
Contains family letters and
genealogical information.
AJA.
LBI has family trees beginning
17th century, 1807, 1829, and
1860.
PD has family records.
Ballin. Juden in Seesen,
pp. 236-38. See GENERAL
WORKS.
Burke's Landed Gentry, 1952.
Family of Highdown Tower.
Burke's Peerage and Baronetage,
1970. Family of Michelham.
Burke's Peerage and Baronetage,
1933. Family of Bt. of
Chertsey.
See Jechiel Freud entry under
BER.
Friedericks, Henry F.
"Frankfurter Ahnen von
Anthony Armstrong-Jones,"
Hessiche Familienkunde 5,
no. 3 (1960/61):156-58.
Bingen and Stern families.
Fruchter, Shlomo ben Yisrael.
Egeret Shlomo. Jerusalem,
1960. 138 p. The lineage of

3 brothers: Rabbi Shlomo
Fruchter, Rabbi Mordechai
Stern, and Rabbi Avraham
Adler. JNUL.
Houwald, Albrecht Frh. V. "Das
Geschlecht Stern zu Frankfurt
am Main (Berichtigg. Zum
Semi-Gotha)," Der Deutsche
Roland 25, no. 7/8
(1937):105.
JFF, no. 13 (1928):25. Family
histories of family of
Hoppstädten, A.D. Nahe,
Saarbrücken, etc.
Descendants of Sender
Lazarus, 1692-1756.
See David Joseph entry under
BEITMAN.
Kempelen. Magyarországi Zsidó,
1:49, 62, 117, 141; 2:45,
119, 133, 141; 3:35, 44, 63,
75, 87, 100, 122, 135. See
GENERAL WORKS.
Kopp. Jüdischen Alsenz,
pp. 135-36. Genealogical
information on the
Stern-Rheiheimer family of
Alsenz. See GENERAL WORKS.
————, pp. 138-40.
Genealogical information on
the Abraham-Stern family of
Alsenz. See GENERAL WORKS.
Laurence, Alfred. "Zwei alte
Soester Portraits," Soester
Zeitschrift 83
(1971):101-109. On Süsskind
Stern (1610-1687) and his
descendants. Family of
Frankfurt. Includes Bingen
and Stern families.
Lejeune, Fritz W. and Eckart
Lejeune. "Die Frankfurter
Judenfamilien Bingen und
Stern," Hessiche
Familienkunde 7, no. 2
(1964/65):75-83.
Stern. FAJF. Stern family
trees beginning in:
(I) Odenkirchene;
(II) Schwetzingen, Baden;
(III) Miltenberg, Bavaria;
and (IV) Cologne, Germany
(name was changed to Sterne).
See GENERAL WORKS.
Stern, Alfred. Zur
Familiengeschichte. Clärchen

zum 22. März 1906 gewidmet.
Zürich, 1906. 78 p.
Families of Göttingen and
Frankfurt-am-Main. Stern
(1846-1936) was a historian
who emigrated to Switzerland
at the end of the 19th
century. LBI.
Stern, Arthur. Stammtafel der
Familie Abraham Stern.
Jerusalem: By the Author,
1961? LBI.
Stern, Gerson. Chronik der
Familie Stern aus Holzminden.
Kiedrich im Rheingau, 1933.
39, 7 p. Family of
Holzminden/Braunschweig.
Author (b. Holzminden, 1874;
d. Jerusalem, 1956) describes
eight generations of his
family, the descendants of
Itzig Stern who came to
Holzminden in 1722. LBI.
Stern, Howard E. Papers,
1886-1971. Include family
genealogies of Howard E.
Stern. PJAC.
Stern-Bamberger Families.
"Genealogical Chart of the
Ancestors of Morris Stern and
the descendants of both Stern
and His Wife, Mathilda
Bamberger, Compiled and
Charted by Howard Stern,
grandson of Morris Stern,
Germany, Delaware, and
Philadelphia, Pa., Feb. 16,
1973." AJA.
Ullman, Elias.
Descendenz-Register des Jacob
Samuel Hayum Stern u. Dessen
Ehefrau Theresa geb. Wohl.
Frankfurt am Main, 1876.
Zapf. Tübinger Juden, pp.
61-62. See GENERAL WORKS.

STERNBERG
AMH has family records.
CAJD has family tree from
Germany.
LBI has family tree beginning
1762.

STERNE
Sterne Family, Georgia and
Alabama. Papers. Include

family history, 1861-1967.
Family of Germany. AJA.
See Stern, FAJF (IV) entry
under STERN.

STERNECK
Kempelen. Magyarországi Zsidó,
1:81. See GENERAL WORKS.

STERNHEIMER
LBI has family tree beginning
1640.
Kaufmann, Alfred. "Anshej
Rhenus: A Chronicle of Jewish
Life by the Rhine." Santa
Rosa, Calif., 1953. 12 p.
Includes brief 300-year
history of the Kaufmann (from
Viernheim bei Mannheim),
Sternheimer (from Viernheim),
Regensburger (from Eppingen),
and Wolf (from Rohrbach)
families. LBI.
Kopp. Jüdischen Alsenz,
p. 129. Genealogical
information on the
Honig-Sternheimer family of
Alsenz. See GENERAL WORKS.
————, pp. 140-41.
Genealogical information on
the Sternheimer-Kahn family
of Alsenz. See GENERAL
WORKS.

STERNTHAL
Kempelen. Magyarországi Zsidó,
2:35. See GENERAL WORKS.
Sternthal, Alfred.
"Erinnerungen eines Alten
Arztes." Chicago, 1937.
295 p. The author
(b. Koethen, 1862;
d. Chicago, 1942) describes
the Sternthal family of
Anhalt and Braunschweig.
LBI.

STETTAUER
LBI has family tree beginning
1821.

STETTINER
AMH has family records.

STETTLER
Kempelen. Magyarországi

Zsidó, 3:43. See GENERAL
WORKS.

STEUART
AMH has family records.

STEUER
Kempelen. Magyarországi Zsidó,
2:129; 3:100. See GENERAL
WORKS.

STEUERMANN
Viertel, Salka. The Kindness
of Strangers. New York:
Holt, Rinehart and Winston,
1969. 338 p. Autobiography.
Especially, pp. 1-9.
Information concerning
Amster, Rafalovicz, and
Steuermann families of
Czernowitz and Sambor near
the town of Wychylowka in
Galicia.

STEWART
AMH has family records.

STEYER
Kempelen. Magyarországi Zsidó,
3:135. See GENERAL WORKS.

STIBBE
Stibbe, David Wollie.
Geslachtsregister der Familie
Stibbe. Amsterdam: Heynes,
1912.

STIEBEL
AMH has family records.
CFM has family records.
Semi-Gotha, 2:154ff. See
GENERAL WORKS.
Straus, Heinrich Joseph.
Verzeichnis der von Hirsch
Herz Straus (1723-1800),
Iette geb. Stiebel
(1736-1814), aus Frankfurt am
Main stammenden Familien,
1854. Erneuert hrsg. v.
Elias Ullmann. Frankfurt am
Main, 1880.

STIEGLITZ
LBI has family trees beginning
1710 and 1770.
Brilling, Bernhard. "Die

Familie Stieglitz aus
Arolsen: Unbekannte
Heine-Nachkommen,"
Mitteilungsblatt,
Wochenzeitung des Irgun Olej
Merkas Europa (Tel-Aviv), 3.
Mai, 1957.
Maydell, Bodo Freiherr von. Im
Baume des Tikkun. Ein
wiedergewonnenes geistiges
Erbe. Grafenau: Morsak,
1979. 81 p. Genealogical
tables. LBI.
————. "Die Stieglitz aus
Arolsen, ihre Vorfahren und
Nachkommen (die Familie der
St. Stammt aus Laasphe),"
Deutsches Familienarchiv 5
(1956):49-126; supplement in
Deutsches Familienarchiv 15
(1960):228-41.
Spanjaard, Barry. Don't Fence
Me In! An American Teenager
in the Holocaust. Saugus,
Calif.: B. & B. Publishing
Co., 198? 206 p. The author
was only two years old when
his parents left New York
City to return to their
native Holland. He describes
his family's life in
Amsterdam and their life in
the infamous Bergen-Belsen
concentration camp.

STILLER
Kempelen. Magyarországi Zsidó,
1:95. See GENERAL WORKS.

STIRBEY
Kempelen. Magyarországi Zsidó,
1:55. See GENERAL WORKS.

STIX
Aurelia Stix Rice. "The
Genealogy of the Stix
Family." St. Louis, Mo.,
1921. Family tree beginning
1750. AJA.
Stern. FAJF. Stix family tree
beginning in Demmelsdorf,
Bavaria. See GENERAL WORKS.

STJERNBERG
Semi-Gotha, 2:17. See GENERAL
WORKS.

STJERNSTEDT
Semi-Gotha, 1:124. See GENERAL
WORKS.

STJERNSVARD
Semi-Gotha, 1:75. Stjernsvärd
family. See GENERAL WORKS.

STOCKLER
See Richard J. Alperin entry
under BEHRMAN.

STOCKLEY
AMH has family records.

STOERK
PD has family records.

STORA
CAJ has family records of
family of Algeria.

STRAATEN (VAN)
AMH has family records.

STRAKOSCH
PD has family records.

STRANDERS
AMH has family records.

STRASS
See LEVY-STRASS.

STRASSER
Kempelen. Magyarországi Zsidó,
2:16, 48, 104; 3:96. See
GENERAL WORKS.

STRASSNER
PD has family records.

STRAUCHER
CAJ has family records.

STRAUS, STRAUSS
AMH has Strauss family records.
CAJ (Call No. 5251) has the
following Plaut family
histories: (1) "Frielendorf
Plaut Family." 17 p.
History of Plaut family,
data, and biographical notes
on family members, pp. 2-8;
family tree starting with
Abraham Plaut, early 1700s to

1980, pp. 9-17. (2) "The
Plauts from Rotheburg/Fulda."
4 p. Family tree, starting
with Heinemann Plaut
(1781/82-1841), who married
Mundel Strauss (1791-1867),
continues to 1979, p. 4.
(3) Family tree for the
Plauts of Schmalkalden
(1781-1975). (4) Family tree
for the Plauts from Wehrda,
which starts with Simon Plaut
(1776-1837). Also in same
folder: Family tree showing
descendants of Ruben Moses
Plaut and Simon Plaut, both
of whom were born in second
half of 18th century,
continues to late 1970s.
(5) "Plaut Family Tree from
Geisa." 15 p. Starts with
Jacob Plaut, late 1600s, and
continues to 1979. All of
the above family trees were
compiled by Elizabeth S.
Plaut. The collection of
Plaut family trees contains a
5-page family tree of Strauss
family from Riedenburg,
Germany; covers from 1800s to
1980.
CAJ has list of descendants of
Strauss family from Hesse,
1636-1910.
CAJD has family tree from
Germany.
CFM has family records.
LBI has family trees beginning
1470 and 1815.
PD has family records of family
of Pressburg (Bratislava).
Strauss Family Book of the
Strauss Family of Grombach,
Germany, 1718-1892. Printed
copy. AJA.
Straus Family of Georgia and
New York. "Information on
Members of the Family," 1966.
AJA.
Ballin. Juden in Seesen,
p. 239. See GENERAL WORKS.
Birmingham. Our Crowd.
Includes Straus family. See
GENERAL WORKS.
Cray, Ed. Levi's: The
"Shrink-to-Fit" Business that

Stretched to Cover the World.
Boston: Houghton, Mifflin,
1978. 286 p. Includes
pictures, portraits, and name
index. History of family of
San Francisco's Levi Strauss
and Co.
Harris. Merchant Princes,
pp. 237-39. Family of San
Francisco. Descendants of
Levi Strauss, who came to
America from Bavaria in 1850.
See GENERAL WORKS.
Harris. . The Strauss
department store family of
New York. See GENERAL WORKS.
Kopp. Jüdischen Alsenz,
p. 141. Genealogical
information on
Strauss-Federlein-Frank
family of Alsenz. See
GENERAL WORKS.
Levy, Edwin L. The Descendants
of Emanuel Straus and Fanny
Heller Straus. Richmond,
Va., 1972. 11 p. Family of
Richmond, Virginia. AJA,
AJHS.
Noren, Catherine Hanf. The
Camera of My Family. New
York: Knopf, 1976. 240 p.
100-year album of a
German-Jewish family.
Includes Strauss family,
descendants of Samuel Strauss
(1847-1922), born in the
Prussian town of Solzingen,
lived in Bochum, and died in
Düsseldorf. Also includes
Hanf and Wallach families.
Paul, Roland and Hans
Steinebrei. "Die
Straus-Familie, in Otterberg
geboren, in den U.S.A. zu
Ehre, Reichtum und Ansehen
gelangt," in Otterberg,
1581-1981; 400 Jahre Stadt
(Otterberg, 1981), pp. 48-56.
Lazarus Straus, 1808-1898,
emigrated with his family in
1852 to U.S.; partner and
later owner of the R.H. Macy
department store in New York.
Straus, Eli. "Eine Stammtafel
Unserer Familie," LBI
Bulletin (Tel-Aviv), no. 21

(1963):52-66. Includes
genealogical table.
Straus, Heinrich Joseph.
Verzeichnis der von Hirsch
Herz Straus (1723-1800),
Iette geb. Stiebel
(1736-1814), aus Frankfurt am
Main stammenden Familien,
zuerst aufgestellt von
Heinrich Joseph Straus, 1854.
Erneut unter Berücksichtigung
der inzwischen eingetretenen
veränderungen von Elias
Ullman. Frankfurt am Main:
Morgenstern, 1880. 63 p.
BR.
Straus, Isaak and Salomon
Koppel. Anleitung zum
Stammbaum der Familie Straus.
Marburg, 1910. 25 p. LBI.
CAJ (Call No. 3454) has family
tree of Isaac Herxheimer
(d. 1833), which includes 5
generations of his
descendants and 4 generations
of the descendants of Israel
Strauss. Last date on family
tree is 1931.
Straus, Robert K. Straus
Genealogical Miscellany.
N.p.: By the Author, 1973.
AJA, AJHS.
Charles Moses Strauss
(1840-1892) Papers. Nathan
Strauss Family Tree. WJHC.
Strauss, Emil. Die Familie
Strauss im Wandel der
Jahrhunderte. Josef Strauss
zum 70. Geburtstag. Prag,
1927. LBI.

STRAUSZ
Kempelen. Magyarországi Zsidó,
2:42, 67, 126; 3:117, 124.
See GENERAL WORKS.

STRELISKER
Rosenstein. Unbroken Chain,
p. 265. See GENERAL WORKS.

STRENG
AJA has family tree from
Louisville and Pittsburgh,
beginning 1817.
Streng Family. "Genealogical
Information Concerning the

Streng, Levi, and Starr
Family, Louisville, Ky. and
Pittsburgh, Pa., 1817-1957."
AJA.

STROSS
Kempelen. Magyarországi Zsidó,
2:66. See GENERAL WORKS.

STRUPP
Schunk, Betty. Aus alten
Tagebüchern und Erinnerungen
der Familien Hirsch, Worms,
Strupp, Eisenberg.
Absgeschrieben, illustriert
und mit vier Stammtafeln
versehen von Alexander
Eisenberg. Meiningen, 1924.
24 p. Hirsch family from
Cochem, and Worms family from
Karlsruhe. LBI.

STUART
See CRICHTON-STUART.
Semi-Gotha, 1:152. See GENERAL
WORKS.

STUCKHART
LBI has family tree beginning
16th century.

STUMPF
Semi-Gotha, 1:139. See GENERAL
WORKS.

STURM
Kempelen. Magyarországi Zsidó,
1:29, 38. See GENERAL WORKS.

STURMAN
Kushnir, Shimon. Men of
Basalt: The Sturmans. Tel
Aviv, 1975.

STYER
AMH has family records.

SUARES
Stern. FAJF. Suares family
tree beginning in U.S. See
GENERAL WORKS.

SUASSO
AMH has family records.
CFM has family records.

SUBER
Semi-Gotha, 1:138ff. See
GENERAL WORKS.

SUGAR
Kempelen. Magyarországi Zsidó,
1:139; 3:136. Sugár family.
See GENERAL WORKS.

SULEMA
CFM has family records.

SULKIN
See Sallyann Amdur Sack and
Mark Weiss Shulkin entry
under SHULKIN.

SULZBACH
Ullman, Elias.
Familien-Register und
Stammtafeln des Seligmann
Sulzbach aus Fürth, des Ruben
Juda Beyfuss, des Moses Isaac
Ochs und des Isaac Jacob Bass
aus Frankfurt am Main und
deren Nachkommen. Frankfurt
am Main, 1875.

SULZBACHER
Frank. Nashville Jewry,
p. 142. Family originally
from Bavaria. See GENERAL
WORKS.
Kempelen. Magyarországi Zsidó,
3:93. See GENERAL WORKS.

SULZBERGER
JE, 11:585. "Sulzberger
Pedigree." Descendants of
Eliezer Sussman Sulzberger,
fl. ca. 1600, through late
19th century. American
family originally from
Bavaria. See GENERAL WORKS.
LBI has family tree beginning
1570.
Simpson, Robert. "Genealogical
Data on the Sulzberger Family
of Germany, Philadelphia, and
New York." AJA.
Stern. FAJF. Sulzberger
family tree beginning in
Odenheim, Germany. See
GENERAL WORKS.
Sulzberger, Iphigene Ochs as
told to Susan W. Dryfoos.

From Iphigene: The Memoirs of
Iphigene Ochs Sulzberger.
New York: Dodd, 1981.

SULZER
AMH has family records.
Tänzer. Juden in Tirol,
p. 777. See GENERAL WORKS.

SUMBEL
AMH has family records.
Bobe, Louis. "Familien Sumbel
fra Marokko og dens
Forbindelser med Denmark,"
Tidsskrift for Jødisk
Historie og Literatur 1
(1917):37-50.

SUMEGI
Kempelen. Magyarországi Zsidó,
3:33. Sümegi family. See
GENERAL WORKS.

SUMMERFIELD
AMH has family records.

SUNDO
AMH has family records.

SUNGER
See SAENGER. Sünger family.

SUNNESHEIM
See Wilhelm and Rudolf Frank
entry under BING.

SUPINE
AMH has family records.

SUPINO
CFM has family records.

SURINAM
Dentz, Fredrik Oudschans. "The
Name of the Country Surinam
as a Family Name,"
Publications of the American
Jewish Historical Society 48
(1958/59):19-27, 262-64.

SUSMANN
LBI has family tree beginning
1801.

SUSMANOVITZ
CAJ has family records.

SUSSKIND
Chelminsky-Lajmer, "Jewish
Surnames." Includes Süsskind
family. See GENERAL WORKS.
Pfeilsticker, Walther. "Zur
Frage des jüdischen Ursprungs
der württembergischen
Süsskind," Archiv für
Sippenforschung 12, no. 1
(1935):26-27.

SUSSMANN
LBI has family trees beginning
1755 and 1774.
Cohn, Warren I. "The Moses
Isaac Family Trust," LBI Year
Book 18 (1973):267-79.
Includes genealogical chart
of the Fliess and Sussmann
families of Berlin.

SUTHLERLAND
AMH has family records.

SUTRO
AJA has genealogical files.
AMH has family records.
CFM has family records.
See Hans Josephthal entry under
GOLDSCHNEIDER.

SUTTON
AJA has family tree.
AMH has family records.

SVAB
Az Egyenlöség (Budapest),
July 5, 1885. An account of
Sváb family of Hungary.
See Kempelen entry under
SCHWAB.
Kempelen. Magyarországi Zsidó,
1:131, 138; 3:78. Sváb
family. See GENERAL WORKS.

SVERDLOV
Bick-Shauli, "Roots and
Branches." Includes
genealogy of Yakov Sverdlov,
Russian revolutionary and
Communist leader,
b. Nizhni-Novgorod (now
Gorki) 1885; d. 1919. See
GENERAL WORKS.

SVEVO
See Brian Maloney entry under
SCHMITZ.

SWALBEY
AMH has family records.

SWARTS
Stern. FAJF. Swarts family
tree beginning in Osterburg,
Bavaria. See GENERAL WORKS.

SWAYTHLING
AMH has family records.

SWIFT
AMH has family records.

SYDOW
Semi-Gotha, 1:18, 40, 41. See
GENERAL WORKS.

SYLVESTER
CFM has family records.

SYMONS
AMH has family records.
CFM has family records.

SYNDER
Shlaferman, Joe. "The Joe
Shlaferman Family: Genealogy
of the Shlaferman-Synder
Family." Louisville, Ky.,
Jan. 19, 1975. AJA.

SYRKIN
AJA has family tree.

SZABO
Kempelen. Magyarországi Zsidó,
2:67; 3:69, 72. Szabó
family. See GENERAL WORKS.

SZABOLCSI
Kempelen. Magyarországi Zsidó,
3:31. See GENERAL WORKS.

SZAKY
Kempelen. Magyarországi Zsidó,
1:16. Száky family. See
GENERAL WORKS.

SZALACSY
Kempelen. Magyarországi Zsidó,
1:124. See GENERAL WORKS.

SZALAI
Kempelen. Magyarországi Zsidó,
1:142, 143; 3:80. See
GENERAL WORKS.

SZALARDY
Kempelen. Magyarországi Zsidó,
2:140. Szalárdy family. See
GENERAL WORKS.

SZALATNAY
Kempelen. Magyarországi Zsidó,
1:19. See GENERAL WORKS.

SZALAY
Kempelen. Magyarországi Zsidó,
2:105. See GENERAL WORKS.

SZAMECZ
Kempelen. Magyarországi Zsidó,
3:108. See GENERAL WORKS.

SZANTO
Kempelen. Magyarországi Zsidó,
2:75; 3:35, 96. Szántó
family. See GENERAL WORKS.

SZAPIRO
See A.S. Pribluda entry under
SHAPIRO.

SZASZ
Kempelen. Magyarországi Zsidó,
2:86, 89. Szász family. See
GENERAL WORKS.

SZASZY
PD has records of family of
Hungary.

SZASZY-SCHWARZ
Kempelen. Magyarországi Zsidó,
2:86, 106. Szászy-Schwarz
family. See GENERAL WORKS.

SZAVOZD
Kempelen. Magyarországi Zsidó,
2:97. Szávozd family. See
GENERAL WORKS.

SZEBEN
Kempelen. Magyarországi Zsidó,
2:145. See GENERAL WORKS.

SZECHENYI
Kempelen. Magyarországi Zsidó,

1:119. Széchenyi family.
See GENERAL WORKS.

SZECHENYI-ERDODY
Kempelen. Magyarországi Zsidó,
2:141. Széchenyi-Erdődy
family. See GENERAL WORKS.

SZECSI
Kempelen. Magyarországi Zsidó,
2:89; 3:115. Szécsi family.
See GENERAL WORKS.

SZEDERKENYI
Kempelen. Magyarországi Zsidó,
3:52. Szederkényi family.
See GENERAL WORKS.

SZEGER
Kempelen. Magyarországi Zsidó,
1:117. See GENERAL WORKS.

SZEGVARI
Kempelen. Magyarországi Zsidó,
2:140. Szegvári family. See
GENERAL WORKS.

SZEKACS
Kempelen. Magyarországi Zsidó,
3:81. Székács family. See
GENERAL WORKS.

SZEKELY
Kempelen. Magyarországi Zsidó,
2:89; 3:46, 57, 81, 119.
Székely family. See GENERAL
WORKS.

SZELL
Kempelen. Magyarországi Zsidó,
1:109. Széll family. See
GENERAL WORKS.

SZEMERE
Kempelen. Magyarországi Zsidó,
2:98; 3:93. See GENERAL
WORKS.

SZENDE
Kempelen. Magyarországi Zsidó,
1:92; 3:70. See GENERAL
WORKS.

SZENDREI
Kempelen. Magyarországi Zsidó,
3:63. See GENERAL WORKS.

SZENES
Kempelen. Magyarországi Zsidó,
2:104. See GENERAL WORKS.

SZENTIVANYI
Kempelen. Magyarországi Zsidó,
1:100, 101. Szentiványi
family. See GENERAL WORKS.

SZEPESI, SZEPESSY
Kempelen. Magyarországi Zsidó,
2:52; 3:112. See GENERAL
WORKS.

SZERENCSES
Kempelen. Magyarországi Zsidó,
2:80. Szerencsés family.
See GENERAL WORKS.

SZILAGYI
Kempelen. Magyarországi Zsidó,
2:74. Sziglágyi family. See
GENERAL WORKS.

SZILASI, SZILASSY
Kempelen. Magyarországi Zsidó,
1:55; 2:101; 3:72, 97, 99.
See GENERAL WORKS.

SZIRMAI
Kempelen. Magyarországi Zsidó,
2:122. See GENERAL WORKS.

SZIRMAY
Kempelen. Magyarországi Zsidó,
2:126. See GENERAL WORKS.

SZITANYI
Kempelen. Magyarországi Zsidó,
1:96; 2:30; 3:27, 95.
Szitányi family. See GENERAL
WORKS.

SZIVESSY
Kempelen. Magyarországi Zsidó,
3:36. See GENERAL WORKS.

SZMEIDLER
See Richard J. Alperin entry
under BEHRMAN.

SZOFER
Vadász, Ede. Adalékok A
Wahrmann-, gorlicei Weiss-,
Szófer-(Schreiber)-Es
Fischmann-Családok.

379

Budapest: Athanaeum, 1907.
32 p. JNUL.

SZOKE
Kempelen. Magyarországi Zsidó,
2:74. Szőke family. See
GENERAL WORKS.

SZOLD
PD has family records.
Levin, Alexandria Lee. The
Szolds of Lombard Street: A
Baltimore Family, 1859-1901.
Philadelphia: Jewish
Publication Society of
America, 1960. 418 p.
Biography of the family which
produced Henrietta Szold and
Marcus and Joseph Jastrow.
Family originally from
Nemiskert, Hungary.
Genealogical tables,
biographical appendix,
bibliography, and
illustrations.

SZOLLOSY
Kempelen. Magyarországi Zsidó,
2:147. Szőllősy family. See
GENERAL WORKS.

SZOMAHAZY
Kempelen. Magyarországi Zsidó,
3:121. Szomaházy family.
See GENERAL WORKS.

SZOMMER
Kempelen. Magyarországi Zsidó,
2:134. See GENERAL WORKS.

SZONYI
Kempelen. Magyarországi Zsidó,
3:87. Szönyi family. See
GENERAL WORKS.

SZOYER
Kempelen. Magyarországi Zsidó,
3:52. See GENERAL WORKS.

SZTERENYI
Kempelen. Magyarországi Zsidó,
1:117. Szterényi family.
See GENERAL WORKS.

SZTOJANOVITS
Kempelen. Magyarországi

Zsidó, 1:83. See GENERAL
WORKS.

SZTYNBERG
See Richard J. Alperin entry
under BEHRMAN.

SZUNYOGH
Kempelen. Magyarországi Zsidó,
2:48. See GENERAL WORKS.

SZURDAI, SZURDAY
Kempelen. Magyarországi Zsidó,
1:47. See GENERAL WORKS.

SZUSZKIND
Kempelen. Magyarországi Zsidó,
1:22; 3:35. Szüszkind
family. See GENERAL WORKS.

SZUTS
Kempelen. Magyarországi Zsidó,
1:112. Szüts family. See
GENERAL WORKS.

SZYLKOWSKI
See Joseph Solomon entry under
SOLOMON.

TABORI
Kempelen. Magyarországi Zsidó,
3:54. Tábori family. See
GENERAL WORKS.

TACHAU
Tachau, Paul. My Memoirs.
2 Pts. Chicago, 1933-1964.
395 p. Pt. 1: From My Family
Chronicle. Pt. 2: My Own
Recollections. Family of
Frankfurt am Main. CAJ, LBI.

TAKACSY
Kempelen. Magyarországi Zsidó,
1:105. Takácsy family. See
GENERAL WORKS.

TAKATS
Kempelen. Magyarországi Zsidó,
2:48. See GENERAL WORKS.

TALLIAN
Kempelen. Magyarországi Zsidó,
1:145. Tallián family. See
GENERAL WORKS.

TAMARIN
See Daniel Jay Rottenberg entry
under ROTTENBERG.

TAMARINA
Kempelen. Magyarországi Zsidó,
3:83. See GENERAL WORKS.

TAMM
Semi-Gotha, 1:25. See GENERAL
WORKS.

TAMWORTH
AMH has family records.

TANDLER
Keneseth Israel. See GENERAL
WORKS.
Bachrach, Samuel and Babette.
Collection of Correspondence,
Memoirs, and Genealogical
Material Concerning the
Bloch, Wise, Tandler, and
Mack Families, 1851-1940. In
German and English. AJA.
Barnard, Harry. The Forging of
An American Jew: The Life and
Times of Judge Julian W.
Mack. New York: Herzl Press,
1974. 346 p. Pp. 3-17.
Judge Mack of Chicago
(1866-1943) was born in San
Francisco, the son of William
Jacob Mack, who arrived in
the 1830s from Ichenhausen,
Bavaria, and Rebecca Tandler
Mack. Mack's mother was the
daughter of Abraham and Fanny
Tandler of Bavaria.

TANG
AMH has family records.

TANNENBAUM
Goldstick, Julie. The
Tannenbaum-Rabinowitz Family
Tree. New York, 1979.
Tannenbaum family originally
from Kobrin; Rabinowitz
family from Slutsk; both
towns in White Russia. AJHS.

TANZER
CAJ has records of Tänzer
family.
Tänzer. Juden in Tirol,
p. 778. See GENERAL WORKS.

TARAJOSSY
Kempelen. Magyarországi Zsidó,
1:16. See GENERAL WORKS.

TARTAS
CFM has family records.

TASHKER
Kaufman, Louis, Barbara
Fitzgerald, and Tom Sewell.
Moe Berg: Athlete, Scholar,
Spy. Boston: Little, Brown
and Co., 1975. 274 p. "The
Family," pp. 29-39. Moe Berg
(1902-1972) was born in New
York City, the son of Bernard
and Rose Tashker Berg.
Bernard was the son of Mendel
Berg of Kamnets, Ukraine, and
Rose was the daughter of
Simon Tashker of Zaleschiki.

TATELBAUM
Taylor Family Papers,
1908-1976. Includes
genealogy, documents, and
photos relating to history of
Taylor, Tatelbaum and
Rosengard families in U.S.
AJHS.

TAUB
Kempelen. Magyarországi Zsidó,
2:91. See GENERAL WORKS.

TAUBER
Kempelen. Magyarországi Zsidó,
3:54. See GENERAL WORKS.

TAUSEN
AMH has family records.

TAUSK
LBIS has family tree.

TAUSS
Kempelen. Magyarországi Zsidó,
2:35. See GENERAL WORKS.

TAUSSIG
Kempelen. Magyarországi Zsidó,
2:64; 3:110. See GENERAL
WORKS.

TAWSSIG
CAJ has family records.
PD has family records.

TAXIS
See THURN-TAXIS.
Kempelen. Magyarországi Zsidó,
1:131. See GENERAL WORKS.

TAYLOR
AMH has family records.
Taylor Family Papers,
1908-1976. Includes
genealogy, documents, and
photos relating to history of
Taylor, Tatelbaum and
Rosengard families in U.S.
AJHS.

TEDESCO
CFM has family records.
Kempelen. Magyarországi Zsidó,
1:12, 121; 2:12, 13. See
GENERAL WORKS.

TEICH
Kempelen. Magyarországi Zsidó,
2:80. See GENERAL WORKS.

TEICHHOLZ
CAJ has family records.

TEILLES
CFM has family records.

TEIM
See Stern, FAJF entry under
TIM.

TEITELBAUM
Kempelen. Magyarországi Zsidó,
1:31; 2:139. See GENERAL
WORKS.
Rosenstein. Unbroken Chain,
pp. 664ff. Teitelbaum
Chassidic dynasty. See
GENERAL WORKS.

TEIXEIRA
Cassuto, Alfonso. "Die Familie
des Dom Diego Senior Teixeira

de Sampayo," JFF, no. 17
(1929):115-17.
David, Ernest. "Les Teixeira,"
Archives Israélites
(de France) 42 (1881):334-40,
349-50, 364-65, 381-82,
397-98, 409-410, 429-30,
438-39; 43 (1882):13, 21, 27.
Grunwald, Max. "Zur Geschichte
der Familie Teixeira," Archiv
für Judische
Familienforschung no. 1
(1912):5-10.
Lucassen, Th. R. Valck. Het
Geslacht Teixeira in
"Nederlandes' Adelsboek."
's-Gravenhage, 1919. BR,
NNC. Offprint from:
Maandblad van het
Genealogisch-Heraldisch
Genootschap: "De
Nederlandsche Leeuw" 37
(Apr. 1919):138-90.
Silbergleit, R. "Manuel
Teixeira," JFF, no. 17
(1929):117-18.
Teixeira de Mattos, Ed.
Critiek op het artikel van
Th. R. Valck Lucassen in "De
Neder1. Leeuw," dd. Mei 1918,
over het geslacht Teixeira in
het "Nederl. Adelsboek."
Bijdrage tot de geschiedenis
betreffende
oud-Spaansch-Portugeesche
geslachten in Nederland.
Uitslvitend naar authentieke
en officieele bescheiden.
Rotterdam, 1918. 93 p.
Includes genealogical table.
BR, NNC.

TELEKI
Kempelen. Magyarországi Zsidó,
1:54. See GENERAL WORKS.

TELESZKI
Kempelen. Magyarországi Zsidó,
1:135. See GENERAL WORKS.

TELKES
Kempelen. Magyarországi Zsidó,
2:39; 3:119. See GENERAL
WORKS.

TELLER

Bondy, Ottilie. Ein Beitrag zu einer Familiengeschichte des Hauses Michael Beerman Teller. O.O., 1937. 54 p. Family of Prague. LBI.

Teller, Charles. Teller Family in America, 1842-1942: A Record of a Hundred Years. Philadelphia: Cousins' Publications Committee, 1944. 221 p. Descendants of Marx Teller (1778-1850) and his wife, Caroline Lorsch Teller (1788-1872). Family of Bavaria. DLC, OCH, PHi, PP.

————. New Teller Generations: Sequel to Teller Family in America. Philadelphia: Cousins' Publication Committee, 1953. 64 p. DLC, NN, NNJ, OCH, PP, PPDrop.

TELLI

Kempelen. Magyarországi Zsidó, 1:80. See GENERAL WORKS.

TELTSCHER

PD has family records.

TEMESVARI

Kempelen. Magyarországi Zsidó, 3:93. Temesvári family. See GENERAL WORKS.

TEMPLE

AMH has family records.

TENSCH

AMH has family records.

TENZER

Batkin, Stanley I., ed. The Tenzer Family Tree Including the Feiler and Zahl Families. New Rochelle, N.Y.: S.I. Batkin, Co., 1977. 1 portfolio (54 leaves). Family originally of Southern Galicia. Covers 1690-1977. AJA, AJHS, DLC, MH, NN.

Kersten, Solomon, comp. and ed. Jubilee Volume of the Michael Tenzer Family Circle, Tenth Anniversary

(5687-5697)-(1927-1937); A Record of the Activities and Achievments of the ... Circle Including Articles on the Jewish Family by Outstanding Rabbis and Scholars. New York: Typ. Ginsberg Linotyping Co., 5697-1937. 205 p. DLC, JNUL, WHi.

TEOMIN

Rosenstein. Unbroken Chain, pp. 169ff. Genealogical chart. See GENERAL WORKS. See Shapiro, Mishpachot Atikot entry under THEOMIM, THEOMIN.

TEPER

Goldstein, Louis L. "The Goldstein Family History," in Jewish Life in Indiana (Fort Wayne, Indiana: Indiana Jewish Historical Society, Inc., November 1980), pp. 19-42. Author is descendant of Max Goldenstein of Savron, Russia, and Hannah Teper of Teraspol, Rumania. Author's father was David Goldstein (1878-1963). Family settled in Indianapolis and Rushville, Indiana in 1904/05.

TERBOCZ

Kempelen. Magyarországi Zsidó, 3:63. Terbócz family. See GENERAL WORKS.

TERNES

Kempelen. Magyarországi Zsidó, 2:20. Hattburg von Ternes family. See GENERAL WORKS.

TERQUEM

Menkis, Richard. "Les frères Elie, Olry et Lazar Terquem," Archives Juives 15, no. 3 (1979):58-61. Family of France. Olry Terquem (b. Metz, 1782; d. 1862), French mathematician, was the only member of his family who did not convert to Catholicism.

TERRAMARE
PD has family records.

TETIEVSKY
See Yaffa Draznin entry under
BERNSTEIN. Tetievsky family.

TEUMIN
See Meyer Ellenbogen entry
under KATZENELLENBOGEN.
Genealogical table.

TEUTSCH
LBI has family trees beginning
1590 and 1725.
Teutsch, Albert. Geschichte
der Juden der Gemeinde
Venningen in Baden, bes. D.
Familie Teutsch, 1590-1936.
Karlsruhe, 1936. 112, 23 p.
13 family trees. Descendants
of Gerson Aschkenasy. LBI.

TEVEN
Kempelen. Magyarországi Zsidó,
3:26. Téven family. See
GENERAL WORKS.

TEXEIRA
CFM has family records.

THALMANN
Birmingham. Our Crowd. See
GENERAL WORKS.

THALMESSINGER
LBI has family tree beginning
1772.

THAM
Semi-Gotha, 1:26. See GENERAL
WORKS.

THAVONAT
Kempelen. Magyarországi Zsidó,
1:51, 55; 2:52, 53. See
GENERAL WORKS.

THEBEN
PD has family records.
Schay, Max. "Die Familie
Theben-Mandel," JFF, no. 5
(1926):115-24. About members
of family in Pressburg during
the 18th century.

THEMAL
LBI has family tree beginning
1773.

THEMANS
CAJ has family tree from the
Netherlands, 1745-1956.
Corwin, Henri Max. "Het
geslacht Themans."
Oldenzaal, 1960. Family of
Holland. BR.

THEOMIM, THEOMIN
AMH has Theomin family records.
PD has family records.
See Jonas Marcus Bondi entry
under LUCKA. Genealogical
tables. Includes
Theomim-Fränkel family.
See Esmond S. De Beer entry
under BARDEN. Includes
Theomim family.
JFF, no. 1 (1925):77-78.
Theomim-Fränkel family of
Breslau, descendants of Saul
Wahl.
Kaufmann, David. "R. Chajjim
Jona Theomin-Fränkel," MGWJ
42 (1898):322-28.
Löwenstein, Leopold. "Die
Familie Theomin," MGWJ 57
(1913):341-62.
Shapiro. Mishpachot Atikot,
pp. 228-38. Teomin, Theomim
family. See GENERAL WORKS.
Wachstein, B. "Die Identität
der Theomim und Munk," MGWJ
55 (1911):355.
———. "Weitere Bemerkungen
zu Löwenstein, Die Familie
Theomin," Jahrbuch der
Jüdisch-Lit. Geschichte 16
(1924):174-76.

THIEL
Rothschild. Svenska Israel.
See GENERAL WORKS.

THOMAN
Kempelen. Magyarországi Zsidó,
3:19. Thomán family. See
GENERAL WORKS.

THOMPSON
AMH has family records.

See Esmond S. De Beer entry
under BARDEN.

THOMSON
AMH has family records.

THORMAN
Stern. FAJF. Thorman family
tree beginning in Unsleben,
Bavaria. See GENERAL WORKS.

THORNEYCROFT
AMH has family records.

THORSCH
LBI has family trees beginning
1771, 1809, and 1861.
Hirschfeld, Alfred.
"Erinnerungen." Berlin,
1916. 52 p. Includes brief
histories of the Hirschfeld
banking family of Berlin and
the Thorsch banking family of
Vienna and Prague (the family
of author's mother). LBI.

THOSS
See SCHEER-THOSS.

THRIFT
AMH has family records.

THROSBY
AMH has family records.

THUMIM
Rosenstein. Unbroken Chain,
pp. 213ff. Thumim family of
Zalischick. See GENERAL
WORKS.
————, pp. 185ff. Thumim
family of Krisnapol,
Vilkatsch, Kolomya, Zbariz,
Buczacz, Zlatchou, and
Stanislau. See GENERAL
WORKS.

THURNAUER
Heckscher, Albert. Stammtafel
Koppel (oder Thurnauer).
Copenhage: S.B. Salomon,
1883. 24 p. OCH.

THURN-TAXIS
Kempelen. Magyarországi Zsidó,
2:146. See GENERAL WORKS.

TIBBON
"Ein Eheprozess in der Familie
Ibn-Tibbon," MGWJ, 1887,
p. 49.

TICHAUER
Zapf. Tübinger Juden, pp.
171-72. See GENERAL WORKS.

TIETZ
Tietz, Georg. Hermann Tietz:
Geschichte einer Familie und
ihrer Warenhäuser.
Stuttgart: Deutsche
Verlags-Anstalt, 1965.
212 p. Hermann Tietz
(1837-1907), a member of the
famous Tietz family of
department store owners in
Germany. CLU, CsT, CtY, DLC,
MB, MH, NjR, NN, NNC, OCH.
Zielenziger. Deutschen
Wirtschaft, pp. 206-220.
"Die Familie Tietz." Family
of Berlin. See GENERAL
WORKS.

TIGERMANN
Kempelen. Magyarországi Zsidó,
2:43. See GENERAL WORKS.

TIGERSCHIOLD
Semi-Gotha, 1:125.
Tigerschiöld family. See
GENERAL WORKS.

TIHANYI
Kempelen. Magyarországi Zsidó,
2:43, 140. See GENERAL
WORKS.

TIKTIN
CAJ has family trees.

TILLER
Kempelen. Magyarországi Zsidó,
2:61; 3:53. See GENERAL
WORKS.

TIM
Stern. FAJF. Tim family tree
beginning in Hamburg,
Germany. Originally spelled
Teim. See GENERAL WORKS.

TINNEY
AJA has genealogy, compiled by
Thomas Milton Tinney (1971),
of family of Utah.

TISCHLER
Brilling, Bernhard. "Makkabäer
Nachkommen,"
Mitteilungsblatt,
Wochenzeitung des Irgun Olej
Merkas Europa (Tel-Aviv),
Dec. 24, 1948. Reprinted in
Die Lupe (Bern), no. 94
(1949):23-24. Family from
Gross-Wartenberg, Schlesien.

TIVOLI
Cassuto, Umberto. "La famiglia
di David da Tivoli," Il
Corriere Israelitico
(Trieste) 45
(1906/07):149-52, 261-64,
297-301.
———. La famiglia di David
da Trivoli. Trieste, 1907.
7 p. OCH.

TOBACK
Malkin, Carole. The Journeys
of David Toback as Retold by
His Granddaughter Carole
Malkin. New York: Schocken
Books, 1981. 216 p. Covers
1888-1898. Toback, the son
of Leibish Hershik and Chaya
Sarah, lived originally in
Shumbar and Shumsk in the
Ukraine and came to U.S. in
1898.

TOBERT
Kempelen. Magyarországi Zsidó,
2:9. See GENERAL WORKS.

TOBIAS
AMH has family records.
CFM has family records.
"Records of Births, Marriages,
and Deaths, 1770-1928." From
the Tobias family bible.
AJA.
Birmingham. The Grandees. See
GENERAL WORKS.
Stern. FAJF. Tobias family
trees beginning in:
(I) Liverpool, England; and

(II) U.S. See GENERAL WORKS.
Tobias, Thomas J. Collection,
Vols. I-II, 1764-1893.
Photostats. Includes notes
on Tobias family of South
Carolina (records of births
and marriages) in their
family Bible, beginning in
1761. AJA.

TOBIASON
Stern. FAJF. Tobiason family
tree beginning in England.
See GENERAL WORKS.

TOBY
AMH has family records.

TODESCO, TODESKO
PD has family records.
Jäger-Sunstenau, Hanns. "Die
geadelten Judenfamilien im
vormärzlichen Wien." Ph.D.
dissertation, Universität
Wien, 1950. Pp. 174-75.
JNUL, Michigan State
University (East Lansing)
Library.
Kempelen. Magyarországi Zsidó,
1:137; 2:12, 13; 3:67. See
GENERAL WORKS.
See Kempelen entry under
TEDESCO.

TOEPLITZ
Reychman. Szkice
genealogiczne, pp. 187-92.
See GENERAL WORKS.

TOFFLER
Kempelen. Magyarországi Zsidó,
3:140. See GENERAL WORKS.

TOLEDANO
EJ (1972). Genealogical table
of the descendants of Daniel
B. Joseph Toledano,
ca. 1570-1640. See GENERAL
WORKS.

TOOTH
See LUCAS-TOOTH.

TORFIN
Bernardi, Jack. My Father the
Actor. New York:

W.W. Norton, 1971. 233 p.
The story of the Yiddish
actor, Berel Bernardi (born
Berel Torfin) and his family,
originally from Galicia.

TORNAI, TORNAY
PD has family records.

TORNERHJELM
Semi-Gotha, 1:87. Tornérhjelm
family. See GENERAL WORKS.

TORNYA
Kempelen. Magyarországi Zsidó,
3:37. See GENERAL WORKS.

TORNYAI, TORNYAY
Kempelen. Magyarországi Zsidó.
Tornyai, Tornyay family,
2:38. Tornyay family, 2:56.
See GENERAL WORKS.

TORNYAY-SCHOSBERGER
Kempelen. Magyarországi Zsidó,
1:112, 130, 134; 3:92. See
GENERAL WORKS.

TORRES
CFM has family records.

TOSCANO
Milano, Attilio. "La vita
privata di una famiglia di
banchieri ebrei a Roma nel
seicento," Rassegna Mensile
di Israel 14 (1948):261-69,
303-311, 359-68, 396-406.

TOSZEGHY
Kempelen. Magyarországi Zsidó,
1:69; 3:87. Tószeghy family.
See GENERAL WORKS.

TOTH
Kempelen. Magyarországi Zsidó,
1:119. Tóth family. See
GENERAL WORKS.

TOTHVARADJAY-ASBOTH
Kempelen. Magyarországi Zsidó,
2:27. Tóthváradjay-Asbóth
family. See GENERAL WORKS.

TOURO
Gutstein, Morris Aaron. The

Touro Family in Newport.
Bulletin of the Newport
Historical Society, no. 94.
Newport, R.I., 1935. 44 p.
DLC, NN, OCH.
"Items Relating to the Touro
Family, Newport,"
Publications of the American
Jewish Historical Society 27
(1920):417.
Stern. FAJF. Touro family
tree beginning in Holland.
See GENERAL WORKS.

TRADGARDH
Semi-Gotha, 2:98. Trädgardh
family. See GENERAL WORKS.

TRAJTENBERG
CAJ has family records.

TRASKENOFF
Chotzinoff, Samuel. A Lost
Paradise. New York: Knopf,
1955. The author, a music
critic and classical pianist,
b. Vitebsk, 1889; d. 1964;
the son of Mayshe Bear and
Rachel Traskenoff Chotzinoff.
The family came to U.S. in
1896.

TRATTNER
Kempelen. Magyarországi Zsidó,
3:93. See GENERAL WORKS.

TRAUBE
CAJ has records for family of
Breslau.

TRAUGOTT
LBIS has family tree.

TREBITSCH
CAJ has family records.
Kempelen. Magyarországi Zsidó,
1:12; 2:35, 68, 133. See
GENERAL WORKS.
Shapiro. Mishpachot Atikot,
pp. 90-114. See GENERAL
WORKS.

TREIBER
Miller, Saul. Dobromil: Life
in a Galician Shtetl,
1890-1907. New York:

Loewenthal Press, 1980. 83
p. in English; 50 p. in
Yiddish. Genealogical
information on Mehler and
Treiber families, pp. 28-36,
74-76. The author
(1890-   ) was born in
Dobromil, the son of Maier
and Roise-Perl Mehler Treiber
and grandson of
Reuben-Yechiel Mehler. He
came to New York City in 1909
and eventually became an
officer in the I.L.G.W.U.

TREIBISH
Shapiro. Mishpachot Atikot.
See GENERAL WORKS.

TRENKLER
Kempelen. Magyarországi Zsidó,
1:118. See GENERAL WORKS.

TREUENWART
PD has family records.

TREVES
AMH has family records.
CFM has family records.
JE, 12:244. "Treves Pedigree."
Descendants of Johann Treves,
13th to late 16th century.
Italian branch. See GENERAL
WORKS.
Brüll, Nehemiah. "Das
Geschlecht der Treves,"
Jahrbücher für Jüdische
Geschichte und Literatur 1
(1874):87-122, 242; 2
(1876):209-210. 13th to
mid-19th century.
Chone, Heymann. "Rabbi Joseph
von Schlettstadt, zur
Geschichte der Familie
Treves," ZGJD 6, no. 1
(1935):3-16.
Lopez, G. "Infanzia e
giovinezza di un grande
editore: Emilio Treves
(1834-1916)," Rassegna
Mensile di Israel 36, no. 7/9
(1970):213-31. Includes
genealogical information.
This information is corrected
in the author's "Una
precisazione sui fratelli

Treves," Rassegna Mensile di
Israel 37, no. 3 (1971):186.
Wolf, Lucien. "The Treves
Family in England: A
Genealogical Sketch," in his
Essays in Jewish History
(London: Jewish Historical
Society of England, 1934),
pp. 145-65. Contents: I. The
Alleged Descent from Rashi.
II. Miscellaneous Treveses in
the English Jewry.
III. Joseph Treves of Mincing
Lane. IV. The Two
Pellegrins.

TREVOR
AMH has family records.

TRIER
LBI has family tree beginning
1807.

TRINDER
AMH has family records.

TRIVELLO
See SPALLETTI-TRIVELLO.

TROTZER
Kempelen. Magyarországi Zsidó,
2:87. See GENERAL WORKS.

TROYES
Carmoly, Elkiam. "La famille
Troyes," Archives Israélites
(de France) 17 (1856):261-69.

TROYT
Davis, M.D. "Troyt: An
Anglo-Jewish Name," Jewish
Quarterly Review 9
(1897):361-62.

TRUBOFF
"Birth Announcement of Zachary
Winiker Truboff," Toledot:
The Journal of Jewish
Genealogy 3, no. 4 (1981?):4.
Four-generation chart of the
Truboff and Winiker families.

TSANIN
CAJ has family records.

TSCHERIKOWER
CAJ has family records.

TUBA
Kempelen. Magyarországi Zsidó,
2:127. See GENERAL WORKS.

TUCHLER
Kempelen. Magyarországi Zsidó,
2:92. Tüchler family. See
GENERAL WORKS.

TUCHMANN
LBI has family tree beginning
1774.
Tuchmann, Friedrich Carl.
Stammbaum und Chronik d.
Familie Tuchmann aus Uhlfeld
bei Neustadt a.d. Aisch,
Ferner enth. d. Fam. Hopf,
Winkler, Reitzenberger, Bing
und Iglauer nach dem Stande
vom 1.1. 1928. 47 lfs.
folio. AJA, LBI.

TUCK
AMH has family records.

TUCKETT
AMH has family records.

TUESKI
CFM has family records.

TUKORY
Kempelen. Magyarországi Zsidó,
1:52. Tüköry family. See
GENERAL WORKS.

TULLOCH
AMH has family records.

TULMAN
Tulman, David. Going Home.
Translated from the French by
Eileen Finletter. New York:
Times Books, 1977. 302 p.
This work mainly deals with
the Tulman family's life in
Hungary before W.W.II.
Tulman was born in 1906 in
the village of Kurtakeszi,
between the Danube and the
Sajo Rivers in Hungary. The
family lived also in the

towns of Sajo-Kesznyetem,
Petrozseny, Bakuny-Tamasi,
Oroszvár, and Nemes-Szalok.

TURAI
Kempelen. Magyarországi Zsidó,
3:31. See GENERAL WORKS.

TURKSEMA, TURKSMA
Droege, "Frisian Names." See
GENERAL WORKS.

TURNER
AMH has family records.

TURRILL
AMH has family records.

TUSZKAI
Kempelen. Magyarországi Zsidó,
1:65. See GENERAL WORKS.

TWEEDIE
AMH has family records.

TWERSKI, TWERSKY
Rosenstein. Unbroken Chain,
pp. 697ff. Twersky Chassidic
family genealogical chart.
Twerski, Aaron. Sefer Ha-yahas
mi-Tschernobil ve-rosin.
Jerusalem, 1966. On Frydman
and Twerski families. AJHS.

TYPULA
Kempelen. Magyarországi Zsidó,
2:38. See GENERAL WORKS.

TYROLER
Kempelen. Magyarországi Zsidó,
2:31, 129. See GENERAL
WORKS.

UFFENHEIM
Kempelen. Magyarországi Zsidó,
1:39. See GENERAL WORKS.

UFFENHEIMER
Tänzer. Geschichte in Tirol,
pp. 780. See GENERAL WORKS.

UGGLA
Semi-Gotha, 1:27, 98. See
GENERAL WORKS.

UGGLAS
Semi-Gotha, 1:97, 102. See
GENERAL WORKS.

UHLFELDER
LBI has family tree beginning
1712.

UJHELYI
Kempelen. Magyarországi Zsidó,
3:112. See GENERAL WORKS.

UJVARI
Kempelen. Magyarországi Zsidó,
3:91. Ujvári family. See
GENERAL WORKS.

ULLMANN
See Hans Josephthal entry under
GOLDSCHNEIDER.
Kempelen. Magyarországi Zsidó,
1:21, 22, 57, 90, 94, 96,
104; 2:30, 50; 3:94, 95. See
GENERAL WORKS.
Tänzer. Geschichte der Tirol,
p. 780. See GENERAL WORKS.

ULLSTEIN
LBI has family trees beginning
1503 and 1792.
Ullstein, Hermann. The Rise
and Fall of the House of
Ullstein. New York: Simon
and Schuster, 1943. 308 p.
Ullstein publishing family of
Berlin. DLC, NN, OCH.

ULMAN, ULMANN
CFM has family records.
"Genealogical data of the
Eppstein, Kander, and Ulman
Families." June 1974. AJA.
Ullman, Elias.
Familien-Register und
Stammtafel des Michael Isaac
Bing und seiner Nachkommen.
Nebst beigefügten auszuge dem
Testamente seiner Enkelin,
Gütche Worms geb.
Mendler-Oetingen, die
Stiftung eines
Brautvermächtnisses zu

Gunsten ihrer Anverwandten
betreffend. Frankfurt am
Main, 1864. 42 p. "Elias
Ullmann und Nachkommen,"
p. 34. Bing family of
Frankfurt; covers 1625-1864.
Ullmann, 1812-1888, was a
book dealer and compiler of
genealogies as well as a
leader of the
Frankfurt-am-Main Jewish
community.
Willstätter, Richard. From My
Life: The Memories of Richard
Willstätter. Translated from
the German edition by Lilli
S. Hornig. New York: W.A.
Benjamin, Inc., 1965. 461 p.
"My Ancestors," pp. 1-11.
Richard Willstätter
(1872-1942), German organic
chemist and Nobel Prize
winner, was born in
Karlsruhe. His maternal
ancestors were the Ulmann
family of Pfersee near
Augsburg and Fürth. His
mother was Sophie Ulmann (b.
1849), his grandfather was
Moritz Ulmann (1814-1890),
and his great-grandfather was
Beer [Bernhard] Ulmann
(1751-1837). The Willstätter
family was from Karlsruhe
since 1720. The author's
father was Max W.
(1840-1912), his grandfather
Maximilian [Meier] W.
(1810-1872), his
great-grandfather Ephraim W.
(1761-1829), and his
great-great-grandfather Elias
W. (d. 1795). DLC, MiU, WU.

ULMO
Fischer, Josef. Jacob Simonsen
og Hustru Rose født Hahn og
deres Forfaedre. Hundrede
aar efter Jacob Simonsen
fødsel, udgivet af S.H.
Simonsen børn, ved. Josef
Fischer. København: H.
Meyers Bogtrykkeri, 1923.
87 p. Includes Ulmo family.
NN, OU.
Kempelen. Magyarországi

Zsidó, 2:68. See GENERAL
WORKS.

UMSTADTER
Stern. FAJF. Umstadter family
tree beginning in Hanover,
Germany. See GENERAL WORKS.

UNGAR
Kempelen. Magyarországi Zsidó,
1:74; 3:70, 83, 118, 119.
See GENERAL WORKS.

UNGE
Semi-Gotha, 1:132. See GENERAL
WORKS.

UNGER
AMH has family records.
Kempelen. Magyarországi Zsidó,
1:19; 2:88, 118, 132, 134.
See GENERAL WORKS.
Rosenstein. Unbroken Chain,
pp. 679ff. Includes Unger
Chassidic dynasty.

UNKELHAUSER
Kempelen. Magyarországi Zsidó,
1:58. See GENERAL WORKS.

UNNA
CFM has family records.

URI
AJA has family tree beginning
1819.
Uri Family. "Genealogical
Information on the Uri and
Wallerstein Families,
Cincinnati, Ohio, Los
Angeles, Cal., and Ky.,
1819-1963." AJA.

URIELI
Urieli, Menachem. B'shul Banim
Ligvulam. Israel, 1981.
277 p. Includes genealogical
table, portraits. Menachem
Urieli (1904-   ) was born
in Nevel in the province of
Vitebsk, White Russia. He
came to Israel in 1923. His
father was Eliezer
Posbityansky (1867-1923).
CZA.

URISOHN
Urisohn, J. "Mordechai Jaffe,"
(In Russian.) Jewrjeskaia
Starina 4 (1912):353-69.
Jaffe of Urisohn, descendant
of R. Mordechai Jaffe (=Baal
Lewuschim).

URSINUS
Steinberg, Sigfrid.
"Perl-Ursinus,"
Familiengeschichtliche
Blätter 33 (1935):271-72.

URY
AMH has family records.

UZZIELLI
CFM has family records.

VAALY
Kempelen. Magyarországi Zsidó,
1:30. Vaály family. See
GENERAL WORKS.

VADNAY
Kempelen. Magyarországi Zsidó,
2:86. See GENERAL WORKS.

VAGO
Kempelen. Magyarországi Zsidó,
2:144; 3:107. Vágó family.
See GENERAL WORKS.

VAHL (DE)
See DE VAHL.

VAJDA
Kempelen. Magyarországi Zsidó,
2:70; 3:111. See GENERAL
WORKS.

VAJKAY
Kempelen. Magyarországi Zsidó,
2:20. See GENERAL WORKS.

VALENCIN
CFM has family records.

VALENTIA
CFM has family records.

VALENTIN
CAJ has family records, 1810 to
1883.
LBI has family trees beginning
1430 and 1683. Valentin, Bruno. Geschichte
der Familien Valentin, Loewen
und Manheimer-Behrend. Rio
de Janeiro, 1963. 82 p.
LBI.

VALENTINE
AMH has family records.
Stern. FAJF. Valentine family
tree beginning in London.
See GENERAL WORKS.

VALLE
AMH has family records.

VALLENTINE
AMH has family records.

VALVERDE
CFM has family records.
Stern. FAJF. Valverde family
tree beginning in Recife,
Brazil. See GENERAL WORKS.

VAMBERY
Kempelen. Magyarországi Zsidó,
1:40. Vámbéry family. See
GENERAL WORKS.

VAN BIEMA
AMH has family records.
Droege, "Frisian Names." See
GENERAL WORKS.

VAN BRUNT
See Stern, FAJF (III) entry
under ISAACS.

VANDAM
AMH has family records.

VAN DEN BERG, VAN DEN BERGH
See BERGH (VAN DEN).

VANDER
Kempelen. Magyarországi Zsidó,
1:74. See GENERAL WORKS.

VANDERLYN
AMH has family records.

VAN DER LYND
AMH has family records.

VANDERMOOLEN
AMH has family records.

VAN DER WALDE
See Esmond S. De Beer entry
under BARDEN.

VAN EMBDEN
Hes, H. "Rof'im u-Madpisim
Benei Mishpaḥat Van Embden
be-Amsterdam (The Van Embden
Family as Physicians and
Printers in Amsterdam),"
Koroth (Israel) 6, no. 11/12
(1975):719-24. Covers
1226-1836.

VAN GELDER
AMH has family records.
Citroën, K.A. The Spanjaard
Family: A Survey of the
Descendants of Salomon Jacob
Spanjaard (1783-1861) and
Sara David van Gelder
(1793-1882). 2d revised and
augmented ed. Borne,
Holland: Family Association
"Berith Salom," 1981. 286 p.
AJHS.

VAN GRUISEN
CFM has family records.

VANICK
Kempelen. Magyarországi Zsidó,
3:71. See GENERAL WORKS.

VAN NOORDEN
AMH has family records.

VAN OVEN
CFM has family records.

VAN PRAAGH
CFM has family records.

VAN RAALTE
AMH has family records.
CFM has family records.

VAN STRAATEN
AMH has family records.

VARICAS
AMH has family records.
CFM has family records.

VARJASSY
Kempelen. Magyarországi Zsidó,
1:100. See GENERAL WORKS.

VARNAI
Kempelen. Magyarországi Zsidó,
3:90. Várnai family. See
GENERAL WORKS.

VARRO
Kempelen. Magyarországi Zsidó,
2:135. Varró family. See
GENERAL WORKS.

VASARHELYI
Kempelen. Magyarországi Zsidó,
1:101. Vásárhelyi family.
See GENERAL WORKS.

VAS DA SILVA
CFM has family records.

VASZILIEVITS
Kempelen. Magyarországi Zsidó,
3:100. See GENERAL WORKS.

VAUGHAN
AMH has family records.

VAY
Kempelen. Magyarországi Zsidó,
3:126. See GENERAL WORKS.

VAZ
CFM has family records.

VAZ DIAS
UJE, 10:396-97. Dutch family
of Marrano descent.

VAZSONYI
Kempelen. Magyarországi Zsidó,
1:136; 3:68. Vázsonyi
family. See GENERAL WORKS.

VEASEY
AMH has family records.

VECINHO
"The Astronomers of the Vecinho
Family," in Cecil Roth's
Gleanings: Essays in Jewish

History, Letters, and Art
(New York: Hermon Press for
Bloch Publishing Co., 1967).
Roth, Cecil. "A Note on the
Astronomers of the Vecinho
Family," Jewish Quarterly
Review 27 (1936/37):233-36.
Family of Portugal, 15th to
17th century. Some family
members went to Italy.

VEGH
Kempelen. Magyarországi Zsidó,
1:145. Végh family. See
GENERAL WORKS.

VEGHELY
Kempelen. Magyarországi Zsidó,
3:99. Véghely family. See
GENERAL WORKS.

VEIL (DE), VEILLE (DE)
Weill, Ernest B. Weil-De Veil:
A Genealogy, 1360-1956.
Weil, Weill, Weyl, De Veil,
De Veille, De Weille.
Important Figures among the
Descendants of Juda Weil,
Generations of Rabbis,
Teachers, Priests, Ministers,
Writers, and a Composer; A
Guide to German, Dutch, and
English Sources with Special
Emphasis on Their
Interrelationships.
Scarsdale, N.Y.: By the
Author, 1967. 44 p.
Includes genealogical tables.
CLU, CtY, ICN, MH, NN, OCH,
PHi, WHi.

VEIT
CAJ has family records.
LBI has family trees beginning
1669 and 1758.
Reissner, H.G. "Gebrüder Veit,
Berlin (1780-1931)," in
Rückblick: Festgabe für die
Jüdische Gemeinde zu Berlin
(Heidelberg: L. Stiehm,
1970), pp. 257-64. CLU, CSt,
DLC, IEN, NNJ, WU.
Veit, Uhde. "Reisbriefe des
Uhde Veit aus dem Jahre 1833.
Mitgeteilt und mit e. Einl.
über die Familie Veit (zur

veitschen Familiengeschichte)
versehen v. Theodor Zondek,"
Bulletin des Leo Baeck
Instituts, no. 15
(1961):171-220; no. 16
(1961):336-41.
Zondek, Theodor. "Die Familien
Veit und Simon.
Aufzeichnungen aus einer
altberliner Chronik,"
Allgemeine Wochenzeitung der
Juden in Deutschland
(Düsseldorf)-Jüdische
Illustrierte 10 (März 1962).

VEITEL
CAJ has family records.

VEITH (VON)
AMH has family records.

VELENTSZEI
Kempelen. Magyarországi Zsidó,
1:30. See GENERAL WORKS.

VENETIANER
Kempelen. Magyarországi Zsidó,
1:29. See GENERAL WORKS.

VENTURA
CFM has family records.

VERCELLI
CAJ has family records.

VERES
Kempelen. Magyarországi Zsidó,
3:71. See GENERAL WORKS.

VERLENGO
AMH has family records.

VERO
Kempelen. Magyarországi Zsidó,
1:116; 3:106. Verő family.
See GENERAL WORKS.

VERSCHVOVSKY
Bronner, Barbara. "The
Bronners and the
Verschvovskys: Genealogy of
the Bronner-Verschvovsky
Family." Louisville, Ky.,
1975. AJA.

VESEL
Mander, Anica Vesel with Sarika
Finci Hofbauer. Blood Ties:
A Woman's History. Berkeley
and New York: Moon Books and
Random House, Inc., 1976.
297 p. Feminist
autobiography focusing on
author's birth (1934-   );
her early childhood in
Sarajevo, Yugoslavia; and the
family's escape to Italy in
1943 and emigration to
California in the late 1940s.
Interspersed are chapters on
the reminiscences of Sarika
Finci Hofbauer, the author's
grandmother, about World Wars
I and II.

VESINHO
AMH has family records.

VESZI
Kempelen. Magyarországi Zsidó,
2:70, 143, 144. Vészi
family. See GENERAL WORKS.

VIDA
Kempelen. Magyarországi Zsidó,
2:117. See GENERAL WORKS.

VIDOR
Kempelen. Magyarországi Zsidó,
1:126; 2:88, 89, 119. See
GENERAL WORKS.

VIERFELDER
Vierfelder, Moriz.
Familiengeschichte des Hauses
Vierfelder. Buchau und
Youngstown, Ohio um
1939-1957. 1 vol. Genealogy
begins 1693. Family of
Buchau am
Federsee/Württemberg. LBI.

VIERTEL
Viertel, Salka. The Kindness
of Strangers. New York:
Holt, Rinehart and Winston,
1969. 338 p. Autobiography.
Especially, pp. 1-9.
Information concerning
Amster, Rafalovicz, and
Steuermann families of

Czernowitz and Sambor near
the town of Wychylowka in
Galicia.

VIGEVENA
CFM has family records.

VILLA REAL, VILLAREAL
AMH has family records.
CFM has family records.

VILLIERS
AMH has family records.

VINCE
Kempelen. Magyarországi Zsidó,
1:30; 3:130. See GENERAL
WORKS.

VINEBERG
AMH has family records.

VINSHNUPSKY
See Daniel Jay Rottenberg entry
under ROTTENBERG.

VIOLA
Kempelen. Magyarországi Zsidó,
3:45. See GENERAL WORKS.

VIRANYI
Kempelen. Magyarországi Zsidó,
3:97. Virányi family. See
GENERAL WORKS.

VISCHL
Kempelen. Magyarországi Zsidó,
2:9. See GENERAL WORKS.

VISONTAI
Kempelen. Magyarországi Zsidó,
3:100. See GENERAL WORKS.

VITERBI
CAJ has family histories.

VITTA
Laurent, Général. "Une grande
famille juive de Lyon: les
Vitta," Rive Gauche 17,
no. 18 (1966):11-21.

VIVANTI
CAJ has family records.

VIVES
Inquisition. Valencia (Spain).
City. Procesos
inquisitoriales contra la
familia judía de Juan Luis
Vives. Introdución y
transcripción paleográfica de
Miguel de la Pinta Llorente y
José María de Palacio y de
Palacio. Madrid: Instituto
"Arias Montano," 1964-   .
Vol. 1. Proceso contra
Blanquina March, madre del
humanista. DLC, ICU, MH.
Millás Valliciosa, José María.
"La ascendencia judaica de
Juan Luis Vives y la
ortodoxía de su obra
apologética," Sefarad 25
(1965):59-65. 15th to 16th
century.

VOGEL
AMH has family records.
CFM has family records.

VOGELSTEIN
LBI has family tree beginning
1729.
Braun, Julie Vogelstein. Was
Niemäls Stirbt. Gestalten
und Erinnerungen. Stuttgart:
Deutsche Verlagsanstalt,
1966. 428 p. Memoirs of the
Vogelstein rabbinical family,
many of whose members were
rabbis in various German
communities. CSt, DLC, LBI,
NjP.

VON GELDEREN
AMH has family records.

VON HALLE
Von Halle Family. Papers, n.d.
1 folder. Include
genealogical information, in
German, of family beginning
ca. 1600. Includes names of
family members, places of
residence, and dates of
birth, death, and marriage.
PJAC.

VON HOLDERN
AMH has family records.

VON VEITH
AMH has family records.

VOOS
AMH has family records.

VOROS
Kempelen. Magyarországi Zsidó,
1:145. Vörös family. See
GENERAL WORKS.

VOS
AMH has family records.

VRIES
See DE VRIES.
Laansma, S. Genealogie van het
geslacht Vries. Renswoude,
1969. 11 p. DLC.

WAAG
Stern. FAJF. Waag family tree
beginning in Frankfurt. See
GENERAL WORKS.

WACHENHAUSEN
Kempelen. Magyarországi Zsidó,
1:39. See GENERAL WORKS.

WACHSNER
Weissbluth, Gertrude. "Es soll
die Spur von ihren Erdentagen
nicht in äonen untergehen
Entwurf einer
Familiengeschichte."
Cleveland, Ohio, 1955.   12 p.
Family of Beuthen and
Oberschlesien. LBI.

WACHTLER
Kempelen. Magyarországi Zsidó,
1:43, 44. See GENERAL WORKS.

WACHTMEISTER
Semi-Gotha, 1:27.   See GENERAL
WORKS.

WAERN
Semi-Gotha, 2:30.   See GENERAL
WORKS.

WAGENFELT
Semi-Gotha, 2:15.   See GENERAL
WORKS.

WAGG
AMH has family records.
CFM has family records.
Dietz, Alexander. Stammbuch
der Frankfurter Juden.
Frankfurt am Main: J. St.
Goar, 1907. 481 p. Family
chart of Wagg family, p. 313.

WAGHALTER
UJE, 10:438-39. Family of
musicians. German and Polish
descendants of Laibisch
Waghalter (1790-1868).

WAGNER
CAJ has family history.
See Daniel J. Cohen entry under
CLEVE. Wagner family of
Friedrichstadt, pp. 29-44,
111-13. Includes family tree
which starts with Ahron
Wagner (d. 1831), and
continues to 1954. Also,
family tree of the
descendants of Hirsch Wagner,
17th century to 1957.

WAGSCHAL
Rosenstein. Unbroken Chain,
pp. 655ff. See GENERAL
WORKS.

WAHL
AMH has family records.
LBI has family tree beginning
1617.
Czellitzer, Arthur. "Der jüd.
Polen-König Saul Wahl und s.
Nachfahren," JFF, no. 1
(1925).
Edelmann, Hirsch. Gedullat
Sha'ul (The Greatness of
Saul, and Progeny of David:
Being a Biography of the
Eminent Saul Wahl, Containing
Also a Genealogical and
Chronological Sketch of His
Ancestry, and Descendants,
Down to Denis M. Samuel ...
and His Relations Residing
Here). London, Shaw,

Printer, 1854. DLC, NN.
"English Descendants of Saul
Wahl," Jewish Chronicle
(London), Oct. 18, 1889.
Translated into German:
"Englische Nachkommen d.
Wahl," Jüd. Lit-Bl. 21
(1890):139-40.
Freudenthal, Max. "Die Mutter
Moses Mendelssohns," ZGJD 1
(1929):200. Pedigree derived
from Saul Wahl.
Kempelen. Magyarországi Zsidó,
2:102. See GENERAL WORKS.
Singermann, Felix. "Die
Lippman-Tauss"-Synagogue und
das Rabbinerhaus der
"Lipschütz." Berlin:
Selbstv., 1920. 50 p.
Family of Polish and German
rabbis, descendants of Saul
Wahl. NN, OCH.
Wahl, Saul and Raphael.
Modehaus, Barmen. Hundert
Jahre im Dienste der Mode,
1821-1921. Verfasst von
Albert Herzog. Barmen, 1921.
52 p. LBI.
Wettstein, Feivel Hirsch.
"Ursprung des Familiennamens
Wahl," MGWJ 45 (1901):92-94,
272, 450, 571.
Wollsteiner, Max. "Wie ich
meine Ahnen suchen ging,"
JFF, no. 1 (1925):74-77.
Also, family history of
Fränckel of Breslau,
descendants from Saul Wahl,
pp. 77-78.

WAHREN
LBIS has family tree.
Semi-Gotha, 1:77, 132ff., 134.
See GENERAL WORKS.

WAHRING
Rothschild. Svenska Israel.
See GENERAL WORKS.

WAHRMANN
PD has family records.
Kempelen. Magyarországi Zsidó,
1:139, 146; 2:38, 146. See
GENERAL WORKS.
Vadász, Ede. Adalékok A
Wahrmann-, gorlicei Weiss-,

Szófer-(Schreiber)-Es
Fischmann-Családok.
Budapest: Athenaeum, 1907.
32 p. JNUL.

WAISZ
Kempelen. Magyarországi Zsidó,
1:116. See GENERAL WORKS.

WAKE
AMH has family records.

WAKSMAN
Waksman, Selman Abraham. My
Life with the Microbes. New
York: Simon and Schuster,
1954. 364 p. Pp. 14-50.
The author (1888-1973), a
Nobel Prize-winning (1952)
microbiologist, was born in
Novaia-Priluka, forty miles
from Berdichev, Kiev
Gubernia. His father, the
son of Abraham Waksman, was
born in Vinnitsa. Selman
Waksman emigrated to U.S. in
1910.

WALDBERG
PD has family records.

WALDE (VAN DER)
See VAN DER WALDE.

WALDER
Kempelen. Magyarországi Zsidó,
2:118. See GENERAL WORKS.

WALDMAN
CAJ has family records.

WALDMANN
Schmidt, Ernst-Heinrich.
"Zürndorf-Waldmann: das
Schicksal einer Familie
deutscher Frontkämpfer
jüdischer Abstammung und
jüdischen Glaubens,
1914-1945," in Deutsche
jüdische Soldaten, 1914-1945
(Freiburg i Br.:
Militärgeschichtlichen
Forschungsamt zur
Sonderausstellung im
Wehrgeschichtlichen Museum
Schloss Rastatt, 1981),

pp. 40-48. Family from
Zürndorf, Austria.

WALEY
AMH has family records.
CFM has family records.

WALFORD
AMH has family records.
CFM has family records.

WALKER
AMH has family records.

WALKO
Kempelen. Magyarországi Zsidó,
3:71. Walkó family. See
GENERAL WORKS.

WALLACE
Sagarin, James L.
"Autobiographical Sketch and
the Wallace Family." Term
paper submitted to Hebrew
Union College-Jewish
Institute of Religion,
Cincinnati, Ohio. May 20,
1976. AJA.

WALLACH
AMH has family records.
Back, M. "Zur Herkunft des
Namens 'Wallach.'" JFF,
no. 33 (1933):530; no. 34
(1933):551-57.
Barlev, Jehuda [original name:
Kurt Herzberg]. "Neues zur
jüdischen Familiengeschichte:
die Familie Wallach in Rheda
und Wiedenbrück," Gütersloher
Beiträge zur Heimat-und
Landeskunde (Gütersloh
Heimatverein), no. 58/59
(1980):1169-71.
Bick-Shauli, "Roots and
Branches." Includes
genealogy of Maxim Litvinov,
Russian revolutionary and
Soviet diplomat, b. Meir
Moiseevitch Wallach in
Bialystok, 1867; d. 1951.
See GENERAL WORKS.
See Esmond S. De Beer entry
under BARDEN.
Noren, Catherine Hanf. The
Camera of My Family. New

York: Knopf, 1976. 240 p.
100-year album of German
family. Descendants of
Heinemann Wallach (d. 1899),
born in Weidenbruck, lived in
Geseke, and died in
Bielefeld, Germany. Also
includes Hanf and Straus
families.

WALLEEN
Semi-Gotha, 1:81. See GENERAL
WORKS.

WALLEGA
Droege, "Frisian Names." See
GENERAL WORKS.

WALLER
AMH has family records.

WALLERSTEIN
CAJ has family records.
Schick, Salamon. Mi-Mosheh' ad
Mosheh. Added title page:
Der Stammbaum der Familie
Schick mit den Hauptzweigen
Wallerstein, Heller.
Munkács, 1903. Includes
genealogical tables. BR,
DLC.
Uri Family. "Genealogical
Information of the Uri and
Wallerstein Families,
Cincinnati, Ohio, Los
Angeles, Cal., and Ky.,
1819-1963." AJA.

WALLICH
JE, 12:460. "Wallich
Pedigree." Descendants of
Moses Joshua Wallich of
Worms, through early 19th
century. See GENERAL WORKS.
See Daniel J. Cohen entry under
CLEVE. Worms-Wallich family,
pp. 59-78, 116-17.
"Die Familie Wallich,"
Hebraïsche Bibliographie 7
(1864):82-83.
Schultze, H. "Geschichte der
Familie Wallich," MGWJ 49
(1905):57, 183, 454-58,
571-80.
Zwei Generationen im deutschen
Bankwesen (1833-1914).

Hermann Wallich: Aus meinem
Leben. Paul Wallich:
Lehr-und Wanderjahre eines
Bankiers (Einfuehrung von
Henry C. Wallich). Frankfurt
am Main: F. Knapp, 1978.
432 p. Family of bankers and
economists of Berlin. LBI.

WALLIS
AMH has family records.

WALSCH
Tänzer. Juden in Tirol,
p. 781. Wälsch family. See
GENERAL WORKS.

WALSRODE
CAJ has family tree beginning
in 16th-century Germany.
See Daniel J. Cohen entry under
CLEVE. Includes family tree
of Cohen-Walsrode family from
Altona, pp. 5-28, 109-110.

WALTER
AMH has family records.

WALZER
AJA has family tree from
Stratford, Connecticut.

WAMOSCHER
Kempelen. Magyarországi Zsidó,
2:27. See GENERAL WORKS.

WANDSWORTH
AMH has family records.
Burke's Peerage and Baronetage,
1912.

WANNEFRIED
Kempelen. Magyarországi Zsidó,
2:10, 11. See GENERAL WORKS.

WARBURG
AMH has family records.
CFM has family records.
LBI has family tree.
Birmingham. Our Crowd. See
GENERAL WORKS.
Farrer, David. The Warburgs.
The Story of a Family. New
York: Stein & Day, 1975.
255 p. Includes family tree.
400-year-old family history;

descendants of Simon Warburg,
a moneylender.
Geschichte des
Geschlechts/Warburg.
Bearbeitet von Eduard Duckesz
und Otto Hintze. Neu
bearbeitet von Salomon Fürth.
Altona und Winsen a.d. Luhe,
1929. Stocksund, Stockholm,
1941-1942. 300 p. LBI.
Hoffman, Paul Theodor. Neues
Altona, 1919-1929. Zehn
Jahre Aufbau einer deutschen
Grosstadt. Dargestellt im
Auftrage des Magistrates der
Stadt Altona. Jena: Eugen
Diederichs Verlag, 1929.
2 vols. "Warburg Family,"
pp. 240-44. CtY, ICU.
JFF, no. 29. Family history.
Pudor. Internationalen
Verwandtschaftlichen. Vol. 3
contains section on "Jacob
Schiff und die Warburgs und
das New Yorker Bankhaus Kuhn,
Loeb und Co."
Rosenbaum, E. and A.J. Sherman.
M.M. Warburg and Co.,
1798-1938: Merchant Bankers
of Hamburg. New York: Holmes
and Meier Publishers, 1979.
190 p. Includes genealogical
table.
Rothschild. Svenska Israel.
See GENERAL WORKS.
Semi-Gotha, 2:161ff. See
GENERAL WORKS.
Stamm-und Nachfahrentafeln der
Familie Warburg,
Hamburg-Altona. Hamburg,
1937, 1953. OCH.
Vagts, Alfred. Bilanzen und
Balancen: Aufsätze zur
internationalen Finanz und
internationalen Politik.
Hrsg. von Hans-Ulrich Wehler.
Frankfurt am Main: Syndicat,
1979. 307 p. "M.M. Warburg
& Co.: ein Bankhaus in der
deutschen Weltpolitik,
1905-1933," pp. 36-94,
251-68.
Warburg, Felix M. of New York.
"Miscellaneous Letters."
Contains genealogical chart
of family up to 1894. AJA.

Warburg, Ferdinand Samuel. Die
Geschichte der Firma R[uben]
D[aniel] Warburg & Co., ihre
Teilhaber und deren Familien.
Berlin, 1914. 208 p. Family
of Hamburg. Genealogical
table contains about 2850
names. LBI, MH.
Warburg, James P. The Long
Road Home: The Autobiography
of A Maverick. Garden City,
New York: Doubleday & Co.,
1964. 314 p. Information on
the Altona-Hamburg and New
York banking relatives of
James Paul Warburg
(1896-1969), pp. 5-18. He
was the son of Paul Moritz
Warburg (1868-1932).
Wechsberg, Joseph. The
Merchant Bankers. Boston:
Little, Brown, 1966. 365 p.
"Warburg: The Nonconformist,"
pp. 164-226. DLC.
Wenzel, Gertrud. Broken Star:
The Warburgs of Altona, Their
Life in Germany and Their
Death in the Holocaust.
Smithtown, N.Y.: Exposition
Press, 1981. 216 p.
Translation of Granny Greta
Warburg und die Ihren.
Hamburger Schicksale
(Hamburg: Christian, 1976.
238 p.) Author is descendant
of family of Hamburg and
Altona, Germany. DLC, LBI.

WARD
AMH has family records.

WARFIELD
AMH has family records.

WARING
AMH has family records.

WARRE
AMH has family records.

WARTMAN
Bar-Zvi, G. Mishpachteinu,
Mirav Rafael Mibareshad Od
Yameinu. Tel Aviv, n.p.,
1975. 43 p., plus 6 pages of
pictures. A section of the

book is devoted to family of
Zvi (1859-1915) and Chana
(1861-1929) Wartman. JNUL.

WASSER
Chelminsky-Lajmer, "Jewish
Surnames." See GENERAL
WORKS.
See Stern, FAJF entry under
WATTERS.

WASSERMAN
AMH has family records.

WASSERMANN
LBI has family trees beginning
1635, 1720, 1760, and 1807.
PD has Wasserman and Wassermann
family records.
Wassermann, David. Geschichte
der Wassermann'schen Familie
soweit nach Geburts-und
Sterberegister in der
Gemeinde Harburg/Riess,
Sulzbürg in der Oberpfalz und
Akten des Fürstlich
Wallerstein'schen Archivs
ersichtlich. Family of
Salzbürg and Harburg. LBI.

WASSERZUG
Wasserzug, Mosche. Memoiren
eines pol. Juden. Hrsg. v.
Heinrich Loewe. Berlin,
1911. 4, 6, 28 p. Separate
from JJLG, vol. 9.

WATERMAN
Waterman Family, Vancouver,
B.C. "Information Pertaining
to Various Family Members,
1966." Typescript. AJA.
Stern. FAJF. Waterman family
tree beginning in Amsterdam.
Some members took the surname
Abraham. See GENERAL WORKS.

WATKINS
AMH has family records.

WATTERS
Stern. FAJF. Watters family
tree beginning in Pomerania.
Originally spelled Wasser.
See GENERAL WORKS.

WATTS
AMH has family records.

WAWELBERG
Reychman. Szkice
genealogiczne, pp. 193-195.
See GENERAL WORKS.

WAY
AMH has family records.

WEBB
AMH has family records.

WEBBER
AMH has family records.

WEBSTER
Crohn, Lawrence W. We
Remember: Saga of the
Baum-Webster Family Tree,
1842-1964. New York?, 1964.
105 p. Genealogical tables.
AJHS, OCH.

WECHSBERG
Wechsburg, Joseph. Homecoming.
New York: Alfred A. Knopf,
1946. Story of the author's
attempt to find family and
friends after World War II,
interspersed with stories on
family life in
Moravská-Ostrana,
Czechoslovakia. Wechsberg
emigrated to U.S. in 1928.
DLC, MB, NIC, NN, OCl, PP,
TxU.
————. Sweet and Sour.
Boston: Houghton Mifflin Co.,
1948. Boston: Houghton
Mifflin Co., 1948. 268 p.
Recollections of author's
boyhood and adolescence in
Moravská-Ostrana and later in
Paris. DLC, MB, OCl, PP,
TxU, WU.

WECHSLER
Kempelen. Magyarországi Zsidó,
3:124. See GENERAL WORKS.
Wechsler, Benjamin, New York.
"Family History and
Genealogy, 1795-1963." AJA.

WEDELES
AMH has family records.
Jakobovits, Tobias. "Die
Verbindung der Prager
Familien
Oettinger-Spira-Wedeles-
Bondi" MGWJ 76 (1933):511-19.

WEGLER
Wegler, Stanley. The Wegler
Family. Montreal, n.p.,
1976. 20 p. History of
family from village of Kozlow
(Galicia), 2 miles from
Tarnopol. Family fold-out
chart starts with Wolfe
Wegler (1795-1898) and
continues to 1976.
Descendants are living in
U.S., South America, Israel,
and Canada. CAJ, Call
No. 4217.

WEHLE
LBI has family tree.
PD has family records.
Bałaban, Majer. "Zur
Geschichte der Familie Wehle
in Prag," ZGJT 3
(1932/33):113-15.
Goldmark, Josephine. Pilgrims
of '48: One Man's Part in the
Austrian Revolution of 1848,
and a Family Migration. New
Haven: Yale University Press,
1930. 311 p. Part two
includes discussion of Wehle
family which came to America
in 1849.
Wehle Family. "Genealogy of
the Wehle Family of Prague,
1700-1898." AJA.

WEHLI
PD has family records.

WEIDA
Semi-Gotha, 1:100. See GENERAL
WORKS.

WEIDINGER
Kempelen. Magyarországi Zsidó,
3:77. See GENERAL WORKS.

WEIDENHJELM
Semi-Gotha, 1:41. See GENERAL
WORKS.

WEIDMANN
Kempelen. Magyarországi Zsidó,
1:42. See GENERAL WORKS.

WEIDNER
PD has family records.
Diamant, Paul J. Paulus
Weidner v. Billerburg,
1525-1585, Kaiserl. Leibarzt
und Rektor d. Universität
Wien. Wien, 1933. 8 p.
1 pl. Reprint from Mitt. d.
Vereine für Geschichte d.
Stadt Wien, vs. 13/14.

WEIGERT
LBI has family trees beginning
1700.

WEIJEL, WEIJL
Barendregt, H.J. Het
Hederlands Joods geslacht
Weijel (Weijl, Whyl). N.p.,
1972? 33 p. Offprint from:
Nederlandsche Leeuw 88
(1971):203-23. Family of
Holland. DLC.

WEIK
Kempelen. Magyarországi Zsidó,
2:134. See GENERAL WORKS.

WEIL
AJA has family tree beginning
1777.
AMH has family records.
LBI has family trees beginning
1750, 1756, 1792, and 1806.
Weil Family. "Genealogical
Data, 1777-1956;" and "Record
and History of the Weil
Family," 1914. AJA.
Brilling, Bernhard. "Der Name
Maram, Marum. Zur Geschichte
der Familien Guggenheim, Weil
und anderer Nachkommen des
Meir von Rothenburg," in
Forschung am Judentum.
Festschrift zum 60.
Geburtstag von Lothar
Rothschild (Bern, 1970),
pp. 99-125. DLC, ICU.

Frank. Nashville Jewry,
pp. 145-46. Family
originally from St. Dieu,
France. See GENERAL WORKS.
Kahn, Daniel. "Le judaïsme de
Marcel Proust," La Revue
Juive de Lorraine 12
(1936):113-16. Proust's
mother's family was the Weil
family.
Kempelen. Magyarországi Zsidó,
1:137; 3:117. See GENERAL
WORKS.
Löwenstein, Leopold. Nathanael
Weil, Oberrabiner in
Karlsruhe und seine Familie.
Frankfurt am Main: Kauffmann,
1898. 85 p. (Beiträge zur
Geschichte der Juden in
Deutschland, 2.)
Mesnil-Amar, Jacqueline.
"Jeanne Proust et son fils
[Marcel Proust]," Les
Nouveaux Cahiers 28
(Printemps 1972):50-57.
Jeanne-Clémence Weil was the
mother of Marcel Proust
(1871-1922), French writer,
and the daughter of Nathée
and Adèle Weil. This
Parisian family originally
came from Metz and then went
to Alsace-Lorraine.
Pétrement, Simone. Simone
Weil: A Life. Translated
from the French by Raymond
Rosenthal. New York:
Pantheon, 1977. 577 p.
"Family and Childhood
(1909-1925)," pp. 3-24.
Biography of the noted
philosopher (1909-1943) who
converted to Catholicism.
Her parents were Dr. Bernard
(1872-1955) and Selma
[Salomea] Reinherz Weil
(1879-1965); her grandparents
were Abraham and Eugénie Weil
and Adolphe Reinherz (d.
1906). The Weil family came
to Paris from Alsace, the
Reinherz family from
Rostov-an-Don, Russia and
Galicia.
Ries, Estelle H. Elias E.
Ries, Inventor. New York:

Philosophical Library, 1951.
369 p. Genealogical
information, pp. 1-5. Elias
Elkan Ries (1862-1928) was
born in Randegg, near
Stuttgart, Germany, the son
of Elkan and Bertha Weil
Ries. The Weil family came
from Oberdorfer, near
Stuttgart. The Ries family
came to Brooklyn in 1865 and
moved to Baltimore in 1872.
Elias Ries became a noted
patent lawyer, electric
engineer, and inventor of
electricity-related products.
CU, DLC, ICJ, MH, NN, TxU.

Roundtree, Moses. Strangers in
the Land: The Story of Jacob
Weil's Tribe. Philadelphia:
Dorrance, 1969. 177 p.
Biography of German family,
owners of department store in
Goldsboro, N.C. for over a
century. DLC, N, NcD.

Shapiro. Mishpachot Atikot.
See GENERAL WORKS.

Tänzer. Juden in Jebenhausen,
p. 383. See GENERAL WORKS.

Tänzer. Juden in Tirol,
pp. 782-85. See GENERAL
WORKS.

Weil, Bruno (1883-1961).
Papers, 1892-1964. Include
genealogical material of this
lawyer and politician of
Germany and New York City.
LBI.

Weil, Emma. Chronik der
Familien Weil, Gutmann und
Einstein. London, 1962.
102 p. Family of Stuttgart.
LBI.

Weill, Ernest B. Weil-De Veil:
A Genealogy, 1360-1956.
Weil, Weill, Weyl, De Veil,
De Veille, De Weille.
Important Figures among the
Descendants of Juda Weil,
Generations of Rabbis,
Teachers, Priests, Ministers,
Writers, and a Composer; A
Guide to German, Dutch, and
English Sources with Special
Emphasis on Their
Interrelationships.

Scarsdale, N.Y.: By the
Author, 1967. 44 p.
Includes genealogical tables.
CLU, CtY, ICN, MH, NN, OCH,
PHi, WHi.

Weille, Gerardus Johannes de
and Gustaaf Alexander Weille.
Het Geslacht De Weille (Weil,
Weill, De Veille, De Veil).
Weesp [Holland]:
Drukkerij-boekhandel G.A. de
Weille, 1936. 160 p.
Genealogical table. NN, OCH.

Zapf. Tübinger Juden, pp.
62-63, 172-81, 223-26. See
GENERAL WORKS.

WEILEN
PD has family records.

WEILER
Kempelen. Magyarországi Zsidó,
3:124. See GENERAL WORKS.

Tänzer. Juden in Tirol,
p. 786. See GENERAL WORKS.

WEILHEIMER
PD has family records.

WEILL, WEILLE
AJA has family tree from
Oakland, California.
CAJ has family records.
LBI has family trees beginning
1790.

Sonder, Alfred. Ahnantafel der
Kinder des Nathan Weill (Sohn
des Löw Weill) in Kippenheim.
Frankfurt am Main: Schirmer &
Mahlau, 1935. 50 p.
Genealogical tables.
Descendants of Marum Weyl in
Stuhlingen (d. ca. 1659) and
of Nathan Löw Weill. NN,
OCH.

Weill, Alphonse. "Letter from
his daughter, Blanche C.
Weill, including a family
tree." Oakland, Calif.,
Nov. 21, 1968. AJA.

Weill, Ernest B. Weil-De Veil:
A Genealogy, 1360-1956.
Weil, Weill, Weyl, De Veil,
De Veille, De Weille.
Important Figures among the
Descendants of Juda Weil,

Generations of Rabbis,
Teachers, Priests, Ministers,
Writers, and a Composer; A
Guide to German, Dutch, and
English Sources with Special
Emphasis on Their
Interrelationships.
Scarsdale, N.Y.: By the
Author, 1967. 44 p.
Includes genealogical tables.
CLU, CtY, ICN, MH, NN, OCH,
PHi, WHi.
Weille, Gerardus Johannes de
and Gustaaf Alexander Weille.
Het Geslacht De Weille (Weil,
Weill, De Veille, De Veil).
Weesp [Holland]:
Drukkerij-boekhandel G.A. de
Weille, 1936. 160 p.
Genealogical table. NN, OCH.

WEILLER
AMH has family records.

WEIN
Rosenstein. Unbroken Chain,
pp. 193ff. See GENERAL
WORKS.

WEINBAUM
Frank. Nashville Jewry, p.137.
Family of Poland. See
GENERAL WORKS.

WEINBERG
AMH has family records.
Weinberg Family; Memphis, Tenn.
"Letter from Amelia Kopald to
Dr. Jacob R. Marcus
describing her family,
Including Family Tree, 1981."
MS. AJA.
Rosenstein. Unbroken Chain,
pp. 211ff. See GENERAL
WORKS.
"Weinberg," Gothaisches
Genealogisches Taschenbuch
der Adeligen Häuser: Alter
Adel und Briefadel (Gotha) 19
(1927):899ff.; 21
(1929):711ff. Family of
Frankfurt am Main.

WEINBERGER
Kempelen. Magyarországi Zsidó,
2:40, 41, 59; 3:20, 24, 49,

100, 112, 125. See GENERAL
WORKS.
Rosenstein. Unbroken Chain,
pp. 573ff. See GENERAL
WORKS.

WEINER
AJA has genealogical files.
AMH has family records.
Kempelen. Magyarországi Zsidó,
1:86, 131. See GENERAL
WORKS.

WEINKOP
CAJ has family records.

WEINLANDER
Kopp. Jüdischen Alsenz,
p. 119. Genealogical
information on Weinländer
family of Alsenz. See
GENERAL WORKS.

WEINLAUB
LBI has family tree beginning
1850.

WEINSBERG
CAJ has family records from
15th-century Germany.

WEINSCHENK-BENDER
Kopp. Jüdischen Alsenz,
p. 141. See GENERAL WORKS.

WEINSHENKER
AJA has genealogical files.

WEINSTEIN
Weinstein Family Tree.
Ca. 1850-1960. Only names;
no dates provided. JGCT.
Kempelen. Magyarországi Zsidó,
3:31. See GENERAL WORKS.

WEINTRAUB
Kempelen. Magyarországi Zsidó,
1:15. See GENERAL WORKS.

WEINZWEIG
Kempelen. Magyarországi Zsidó,
2:89. See GENERAL WORKS.
Sommerguth, Ludwig. Chronik
der Familien Sommerguth,
Weinzweig, Brandus. Berlin:

By the Author, 1933. 18 p.
LBI.

WEISE
PD has family records.

WEISENFELD
PD has family records.

WEISENFREUND
See MUNI.

WEISER
Kempelen. Magyarországi Zsidó,
2:91. See GENERAL WORKS.

WEISGAL
Weisgal, Meyer Wolf. Meyer
Weisgal ... So Far, An
Autobiography. New York:
Random House, 1971. 404 p.
Especially, pp. 1-33, 50-54.
The author (1894-   ), a
famous American Zionist
leader, was born in Kikl or
Kokol near Lipno, Poland in
the province of Plotsk, a son
of Shlomo Chail Weisgal
(d. 1921), the hamlet's
chazan. The whole family
came to U.S. between 1903 and
1905 from Kikl and the
near-by hamlet of Sherpz.

WEISS
AMH has family records.
LBI has family tree beginning
1700.
PD has family records.
Gold. Juden Mährens,
pp. 510-11. Families from
Pullitz. See GENERAL WORKS.
Kempelen. Magyarországi Zsidó.
Weiss family, 1:11, 138;
3:87. Weiss, Weisz family,
1:47, 49, 69, 85, 115, 140;
2:27, 64, 79, 89, 135, 136;
3:70, 90, 109, 111, 124, 139.
See GENERAL WORKS.
Schachtel, Hugo. Stammbuch der
Familie Weiss aus
Sulmirschültz. Breslau,
1914. 19 p. JNUL.
Vadász, Ede. Adalékok A
Wahrmann-, gorlicei Weiss-,
Szófer-(Schreiber)-Es

Fischmann-Családok.
Budapest: Athenaeum, 1907.
32 p. JNUL.
Weiss, Emil (1896-?). Papers,
ca. 1950. 1 folder. Include
autobiography, ca. 1950,
written by Emil Weiss of
Philadelphia, about his life
in Focsani, Rumania, and his
children before he immigrated
to U.S. A sequel covers his,
and his family's, life from
1907 in U.S. PJAC.
Weiss, Gertrude Marks.
"Collection of Harrer Simmond
Papers: Biography, 1829-1895;
Family Tree, 1777-1932;
Correspondence and Other
Material, 1777-1939." AJA.

WEISSBLUM
Rosenstein. Unbroken Chain,
pp. 655ff. See GENERAL
WORKS.

WEISSBLUTH
Weissbluth, Gertrude. "Es soll
die Spur von ihren Erdentagen
nicht in änen untergehen
Entwurf einer
Familiengeschichte."
Cleveland, Ohio, 1955. 12 p.
Family of
Beuthen/Oberschlesien. LBI.

WEISSBURG
Weiss, Roger. The Weissburgs:
A Social History. Chicago:
Kimbark Press, 1975. 129 p.
Family of Erdöbénye, Hungary;
descendants of Moses Joseph
Weissburg, (b. Weissenburg,
Alsace, 1744; d. Zemplén,
Hungary.) DLC, OCH.

WEISSENFELD
Kempelen. Magyarországi Zsidó,
2:141. See GENERAL WORKS.

WEISSHEIMER
Weissheimer, Hermann.
Geschichte der Familie
Weissheimer. Andernach: By
the Author, 1936. 16 p.
Includes genealogical tables.

WEISSMANN
Klein, Gerda Weissmann. All
but My Life. New York: Hill
and Wang, 1957. 246 p.
Autobiography covers 1930s to
1946 in Poland. Author is
daughter of Julius and Helene
Weissmann.

Weissmann, Frieda. Ausschnitt
aus dem Leben der Familie
Weissman. Jerusalem, 1956.
11 p. Family of
Kieferstädtel/Oberschlesien/B
eslau. LBI.

WEISSWEILER
AMH has family records.

WEISWEILLER
CFM has family records.

WEISZ
See CAJ (Call No. P/123) entry
under ECKSTEIN.
Berend, Ivan and György Ránki.
Csepel Története [The History
of Csepel]. Budapest:
Kossuth, 1965. Extensive
scholarly account of history
of Weisz family of Hungary,
pp. 33ff.
See Bernát Munkácsi entry under
AUSTERLITZ.
See Kempelen entry under WEISS.

WEISZBURG
Kempelen. Magyarországi Zsidó,
3:81. See GENERAL WORKS.

WEISZFELD
Kempelen. Magyarországi Zsidó,
1:136; 3:68. See GENERAL
WORKS.

WEISZKOPF
Kempelen. Magyarországi Zsidó,
2:39. See GENERAL WORKS.

WEISZMAYER
Kempelen. Magyarországi Zsidó,
1:21, 22, 94, 95; 2:133, 134.
See GENERAL WORKS.

WEITHEIMER
AMH has family records.

WEITZ
AMH has family records.

WEIZEL
AMH has family records.

WEJNTROP
See Judith A. Walters entry
under GRYNSZPAN.

WEKERLE
Kempelen. Magyarországi Zsidó,
1:53. See GENERAL WORKS.

WELBY
AMH has family records.

WELFARE
AMH has family records.

WELI
AMH has family records.

WELLENSTEIN
PD has family records.

WELLINS
See Sidney Cramer entry under
BINDMAN.

WELLISCH
Kempelen. Magyarországi Zsidó,
1:48, 57, 58, 96. See
GENERAL WORKS.

WELSH
CAJ has family records from
Czechoslovakia.
PD has family records.

WENDEL
"Wendel family biographical
data." AJA.

WENDT
Semi-Gotha, 1:77. See GENERAL
WORKS.

WENGER
Frank, Ivie A. The Wenger
History: Descendants of Jacob
Wenger and Hannah Brenneman
Wenger. N.p., 1970. 66 p.
NN.

WERNER
AMH has family records.

WERTHAN
Frank. Nashville Jewry,
p. 146. See GENERAL WORKS.

WERTHEIM
Reychman. Szkice
genealogiczne, pp. 197-99.
See GENERAL WORKS.

WERTHEIMBER
LBI has family tree beginning
1588.
Baer, Berthold. Stammtafeln
der Familie Speyer.
Frankfurt am Main: Kumpf &
Reiss, 1896. 184 f.
"Familie Wertheimber,"
pp. 10-18. Descendants of
Joseph Lazarus Speyer oo
Jeanette geb. Ellissen and of
Ruben Gumpertz Ellissen oo
Jeanette geb. Speyer. Family
of Frankfurt am Main. LBI,
OCH.
Franz-Schneider, Lucia.
Erinnerungen an das
Schopenhauerhaus Schöne
aussicht Nr. 16 in Frankfurt
am Main. Niedergeschrieben
im Jahre 1911. Frankfurt am
Main: Krammer, 1959. 60 p.
"Familie Wertheimber,"
pp. 25-35, 37-50. CtY, NN.

WERTHEIMER
AJA has family tree from
Dayton, Ohio, and Denver,
beginning 1815.
AMH has family records.
CAJ has family records.
CFM has family records.
LBI has family trees beginning
17th century, 1721, 1738, and
1770.
PD has family records.
Aron, Willy. "Zur
Familiengeschichte von R.
Akiba Wertheimer," JFF,
no. 38 (1935):663-64. Rabbi
Akiba ben Awigdor Wertheimer
(b. Breslau, ?; d. Altona,
Germany, 1838) served as
rabbi in Moislingen, Lübeck,

and Altona.
"Die Bösinger Linie der Familie
Wertheimer. Zum 70.
Geburtstage S. Wertheimers,"
Judaica (Pressburg) 2,
no. 15/16 (1935):18-21.
Grunwald, M. "Die Deszendenten
Simon Wertheimers," JFF,
nos. 7-10 (1926/27). Also
descendants of Samuel
Wertheimer.
————. "Deszendenten-Tafel
der Familie Isak Wertheimer,"
Archiv für Jüdische
Familien-Forschung (Vienna)
1, no. 1 (1912):12-13.
Kaufmann, David. Urkundliches
aus dem Leben Samson
Wertheimers. Wien:
C. Konegan, 1892. 142 p.
CU, DLC, MH, OCH, PP. Also
Budapest: Druck von
A. Alkalay, Pressburg, 1891.
142 p. CtY, DLC, MH, NN,
OCH.
————. Samson Wertheimer, der
Oberhoffactor und
Landesrabbiner, 1658-1724 und
seine Kinder. Wien: F. Beck,
1888. 113 p. (Zur
Geschichte jüdischer
Familien, 1.) CtY, DLC, MH,
NN, NNJ, OCH, OU, PP.
Kempelen. Magyarországi Zsidó,
1:33; 2:8, 9, 18, 47. See
GENERAL WORKS.
Landmann, Martha Wertheimer.
Chronicle of the Wertheimer
Family. Washington, D.C.: By
the Author, 1977. 175 p.
Story of family from Baden
which arrived in U.S. during
World War II. AJHS, DLC.
Tänzer. Juden in Jebenhausen,
p. 384. See GENERAL WORKS.
Wertheimer, Emanuel. "Family
Records of Births and
Marriages, 1826-1870."
Family of San Francisco.
AJA.

See Ernst Wolf entry under
GOMPERZ. Includes the
descendants of Samson
Wertheimer.

WERTHEIMSTEIN
Holzer, Rudolf. Villa
  Wertheimstein. Haus der
  Genien und Dämonen. Mit
  unveröffentlichten Gedichten,
  Briefen, und
  Tagebuch-aufzeichnungen.
  Wien: Bergland Verlag, 1960.
  139 p. (Österreich-Reihe,
  Bd. 118/120.) Family of
  Vienna. Their salon was a
  meeting-place of writers and
  poets. NIC, OCH.
Kempelen. Magyarországi Zsidó,
  1:38, 39; 2:48, 49; 3:67.
  See GENERAL WORKS.

WERTHER
PD has family records.

WERTHNER
Kempelen. Magyarországi Zsidó,
  2:128. See GENERAL WORKS.

WESSELLS
AMH has family records.

WESSELS
CFM has family records.

WESSELY
CAJ has family records.

WESSLIG
PD has family records.

WESTERFELD
LBI has family tree beginning
  1783.

WESTFRIED
Kempelen. Magyarországi Zsidó,
  1:82. See GENERAL WORKS.

WESTHEIMER
See HEINSHEIMER-WESTHEIMER.
Westheimer Family. "Family
  Tree of the Family of
  Ferdinand Westheimer." N.p.,
  Aug. 30, 1970. AJA.
Westheimer Family, Cincinnati.
  "Family Chart compiled by
  Julius Westheimer, n.d."
  Typescript. AJA.

WETZLAR
Kempelen. Magyarországi Zsidó,
  1:39; 2:75. See GENERAL
  WORKS.

WETZLAU
Diamant, Paul J. "Die
  Descendenz des Karl Abraham
  Freiherrn von Wetzlau,"
  Archiv für Jüdische
  Familien-Forschung (Vienna)
  1, no. 2/3 (1913):10-16; 1,
  no. 4/6 (1913):2-17.
Wachstein, Bernhard, ed. Das
  Testament der Baronin
  Eleonora Wetzlau von
  Plankenstern. Vienna, 1913.
  8 p. Aristocratic Austrian
  family, most of whose members
  converted to Catholocism in
  18th century. LBI, OCH.

WEYL
See WEIL.
Hirschel, Levie. Iets over
  Jacob Michaël Weyl
  (1776-1856) en zijn familie.
  Amsterdam, n.p., 1933. 11 p.
  Offprint from: Nieuw. Isr.
  Weekblad 69, nos. 14-17
  (1933). BR.

WEYLANDT
Semi-Gotha, 2:114. See GENERAL
  WORKS.

WHEELER
AMH has family records.

WHELI
AMH has family records.

WHITE
AMH has family records.

WHITEHEAD
"Ist die Familie Whitehead
  jüdisch?," Nachrichten der
  Gesellschaft für
  Familienkunde in Kurhessen
  und Waldeck 10, no. 1
  (1935):24-25.

WHITING
Cohn, John Magnus. The Cohn
  Family Tree. Swan Hill,

Australia: n.p., Mar. 1963.
32 p. Genealogical table
from 1751-1962. More than
400 relatives listed. Cohn
family is related to Ballin
family of Denmark. Four Cohn
brothers migrated to
Australia from Denmark in
mid-19th century. Includes
Whiting family. CAJ, Call
No. 1676.

WHYL
See WEIJEL, WEIJL.

WICH
Kempelen. Magyarországi Zsidó,
2:51, 52. See GENERAL WORKS.

WIDDER
Kempelen. Magyarországi Zsidó,
2:86, 102, 104, 118; 3:96.
See GENERAL WORKS.

WIDRONOVITS
Kempelen. Magyarországi Zsidó,
3:124. See GENERAL WORKS.

WIELEN
Berg, Samuel van den. The Life
of Simon Van den Bergh and
Elisabeth van der Wielen.
Portrayed for Their
Descendants. London, 1911.
BR.

WIENER
AMH has family records.
CFM has family records.
The Jewish Chronicle (London),
Feb. 25, 1977, p. 22.
Contains a letter by Maxa
Nordau concerning the
founders of the Wiener family
of Krotoschin (Krotoszyn),
Posen (Poznán).
Kempelen. Magyarországi Zsidó,
2:133. See GENERAL WORKS.

WIENIAWSKI
Reychman. Szkice
genealogiczne, pp. 201-203.
See GENERAL WORKS.

WIENSKOWITZ
LBI has family tree beginning
1774.

WIESBADEN
Kempelen. Magyarországi Zsidó,
2:8. See GENERAL WORKS.

WIESENBERG
See Daniel Jay Rottenberg entry
under ROTTENBERG.

WIESENFELD
Wiesenfeld Family, Baltimore,
Md. "Materials and
biographical data concerning
the Wiesenfeld family and the
Baltimore Fireworks Company,
including a number of
photographs of the family and
the early business buildings,
1977." Typescript and
photographs; Xerox copies.
AJA.

WIESENTHAL
LBI has family tree beginning
1781.
Schwartz, Helene E. "A
Photograph Comes to Life: A
JGS Directory Success Story,"
Jewish Genealogical Society
Newsletter (New York) 1,
no. 5 (Feb. 1980):1-2. Brief
genealogical information on
the children of Yitzchak and
Chana Wiesenthal Herzog of
Skala and Jagielnica,
Galicia.

WIESNER
PD has family records.

WIGODER
Sefer Zikaron: Genealogy of
Myer Joel Wigoder. Leeds,
England, 1931. 13 p. In
Hebrew. Anglo-Jewish family
originally from Kovno,
Lithuania. Meir Joel Wigoder
was a rabbi. NN.
Wigoder, Myer Joel. My Life.
Translated by Louis E.
Wigoder. Edited by Samuel

Abel. Leeds: J. Porton &
Sons, Printers, 1935. 174 p.
Includes genealogical tables.
NN, OCH.

WIJK
Semi-Gotha, 1:41. See GENERAL
WORKS.

WILD
AMH has family records.
Deutsch, Hermann. Stammbäume
der Familien Buff und Riegel
Wild und Martin. Cronheim,
n.p., 1936? 4 pts. Pt. III:
Erlauterungen zur Stammtafel
der Familie Wild aus
Cronheim, 1632-1913. 26 p.
CAJ, Call No. 2771/3.

WILDENBRUCH
CAJ has family records.

WILDENSTEIN
Ginsburger, Moses. Les
families Wildenstein à
Fegersheim. Strasbourg,
1937.

WILHELM
CAJ has family records.
Kempelen. Magyarországi Zsidó,
2:8. See GENERAL WORKS.

WILKENSON
AMH has family records.

WILKIMIRSKY
Waldman, Bess. The Book of
Tziril: A Family Chronicle.
Marblehead, Mass.: Micah
Publications, 1981. 250 p.
In narrative form, this book
covers the life of some of
the descendants of Zalman
Yitchok and Dvera Esther
Gordon from 1840-1890s in
Russia and Jersey City, N.J.
Includes the Gordon family of
Kafkaz (near Tiflis in the
Caucasus region); the
Rosenblum family of Kovno
(Chana Gordon and Reb Yosef
Rosenblum); Yosef Yacov and
Tziril Miriam Gordon
Wilkimirsky (changed to

Friedman in U.S.) of Wilki
near Kovno; and Abraham
(Alte) and Hinda Dvera
Friedman Lipschutz of New
Jersey. Abraham Lipschutz
was the son of Reb Yeheschel
and Rivka Lipschutz of
Vienna. The author is the
daughter of Abraham and Hinda
Lipschutz. AJA, AJHS, DLC.

WILKINSON
AMH has family records.

WILKS
AMH has family records.

WILLEBRAND
Semi-Gotha, 1:83. See GENERAL
WORKS.

WILLENSKY
AMH has family records.

WILLIAMS
AMH has family records.

WILLIS
AMH has family records.

WILLSTAETTER
LBI has family tree beginning
1720.

WILLSTATTER
Willstätter, Richard. From My
Life: The Memories of Richard
Willstätter. Translated from
the German edition by Lilli
S. Hornig. New York: W.A.
Benjamin, Inc., 1965. 461 p.
"My Ancestors," pp. 1-11.
Richard Willstätter
(1872-1942), German organic
chemist and Nobel Prize
winner, was born in
Karlsruhe. His maternal
ancestors were the Ulmann
family of Pfersee near
Augsburg and Fürth. His
mother was Sophie Ulmann (b.
1849), his grandfather was
Moritz Ulmann (1814-1890),
and his great-grandfather was
Beer [Bernhard] Ulmann
(1751-1837). The Willstätter

family was from Karlsruhe
since 1720. The author's
father was Max W.
(1840-1912), his grandfather
Maximilian [Meier] W.
(1810-1872), his
great-grandfather Ephraim W.
(1761-1829), and his
great-great-grandfather Elias
W. (d. 1795). DLC, MiU, WU.

WILMERSDOERFER
LBI has family tree beginning
1730.

WILNER
AMH has family records.

WIMBLE
AMH has family records.

WIMMER
Kempelen. Magyarországi Zsidó,
3:122. See GENERAL WORKS.

WIMPFEN
Kempelen. Magyarországi Zsidó,
3:62, 63. See GENERAL WORKS.

WINDMUEHL-COHEN
LBI has family tree beginning
1706.

WINDMUELLER, WINDMULLER
CAJ has Windmüller family
records, 1763-1866.
LBI has Windmueller family tree
beginning 1690.
Windmueller, Ida S., Inge W.
Horowitz, and Rita J.
Horowitz. The Windmueller
Family Chronicle, 1680-1980.
Richmond, Va.: Windmill Press
Associates. 268 p. Story of
the Levite branch of
Windmueller [Windmüller]
family, 1680-1980. Includes
300-year annotated genealogy,
essays, family documents,
letters, 165 photographs,
charts, maps, and section
devoted to the 120 family
members who died in the
Holocaust. Also includes
alphabetical index to the
2259 names in the book, an

index to current locations of
family members, and current
addresses of heads of
households. Covers the
descendants of Levi
Windmüller
(ca. 1680-ca. 1750). Family
from Westphalian towns of
Beckum and Rheda.
Translation and continuation
of Chronik der Familie
Windmüller-Geschichte der
Gemeinde Beckum by Fritz
Windmüller, Frankfurt am
Main, 1938. 116, 30 p.
Family of Beckum. LBI, OCH.

WINDMUHL
AMH has Windmühl family
records.

WINDT
Kempelen. Magyarországi Zsidó,
1:120. See GENERAL WORKS.

WINE
Wine, Jacob David. The Wine
Family in America.
Forestville, Va., 1952-1971?
3 sections. DLC, ICN, NcD,
NN.

WING
AMH has family records.

WINGARD
Semi-Gotha, 1:16. See GENERAL
WORKS.

WINIKER
"Birth Announcement of Zachary
Winiker Truboff," Toledot:
The Journal of Jewish
Genealogy 3, no. 4 (1981?):4.
Four-generation chart of
Truboff and Winiker families.

WINKLER
LBI has family tree beginning
1795.
Ballin. Juden in Seesen,
p. 240. Family history. See
GENERAL WORKS.
Kaufmann, David. "Un siècle de
l'existence d'une famille de
médecins juifs de Vienne et

de Posen; Dr. Leo, Dr. Jacob,
Dr. Isaac, Dr. Wolf Winkler,"
Revue des Études Juives 20
(1890):275-81. 16th to 18th
centuries.
Kempelen. Magyarországi Zsidó,
2:95, 123. See GENERAL
WORKS.
See Friedrich Carl Tuchmann
entry under BING.

WINKOOP
CAJ has family records.

WINOGRADSKY
See GRADE.

WINSKI
Winski Family, Lafayette,
Indiana. "Family History,
1818-1975." Typescript.
AJA.

WINSLOE
Kempelen. Magyarországi Zsidó,
2:63. See GENERAL WORKS.

WINSTANLEY
AMH has family records.

WINSTOCK
Gross, Evelyn Rosenberg. "The
Winstocks of South Carolina."
Greenwood, S.C., 1961-1962.
AJA.
Winstock, Mordecai. "Genealogy
of Winstock, Levine, and
Levin Families." N.d. AJA.

WINSTON
Keneseth Israel. See GENERAL
WORKS.

WINTER
PD has family records.

WINTERNITZ
Kempelen. Magyarországi Zsidó,
2:10. See GENERAL WORKS.

WISCHNITZER
CAJ has family records.

WISE
AMH has family records.
Bachrach, Samuel and Babette.

Collection of Correspondence,
Memoirs, and Genealogical
Material Concerning the
Bloch, Wise, Tandler, and
Mack Families, 1851-1940. In
German and English. AJA.
Heller, James G. Isaac M.
Wise: His Life and Thought.
New York: The Union of
American Hebrew
Congregations, 1965. 819 p.
"Family, Childhood, and Early
Education," pp. 49-58. Rabbi
Wise (1819-1900), a pioneer
of Reform Judaism in
Cincinnati (Congregation
B'nai Jeshurun) and the U.S.,
was born in Steingrub,
Bohemia. He also lived in
Prague, Vienna, and Radnitz,
Bohemia, before coming to
U.S. in 1846. CSt, CU, DLC,
MB, MH, MnU, N, NcD, NjP, NN,
OCl.

WISHNIPOLSKY
See Yaffa Draznin entry under
BERNSTEIN. Includes
Wishnipolsky family.

WITKOWSKI
LBI has family tree beginning
1737.
Zielenziger, Georg. Stammbaum
der Familie Levin Jacobi.
Bromberg, 1905. 34 x 49 cm.
Descendants of Levin Jacobi,
ca. 1750, and Mortje
Witkowski. LBI.

WITTGENSTEIN
PD has family records.

WITZENHAUSEN
CAJ has family records.
Frenkel, Elias Karl, comp.
Family Tree of R. Moshe
Witzenhausen. Ancestors and
Descendants, Collected by His
Great-Great Grandson Elias
Karl Frenkel. Jerusalem:
Polypress, 1969. 65, 19 p.
Genealogical tables. Rabbi
Moshe Witzenhausen of
Westphalia changed his name

to Frenkel at the time of
Napoleon. CAJ, CLU, DLC.

WIX
PD has family records.

WOCHENMARK
Zapf. Tübinger Juden, pp.
182-84, 226-27. See GENERAL
WORKS.

WODIAMER
PD has family records.

WODIANER
UJE, 10:551. Family of
Hungary, descendants of
Woidzislaw who came to
Hungary in 1750. Some of
family embraced Christianity.
Jäger Sunstenau, Hanns. "Die
geadelten Judenfamilien im
vormärzlichen Wien." Ph.D.
dissertation, Universität
Wien, 1950. Pp. 186-87.
JNUL. Michigan State
University (East Lansing)
Library.
Kempelen. Magyarországi Zsidó,
1:42, 100, 144; 2:23, 24;
3:58. See GENERAL WORKS.

WOHL
Ullmann, Elias.
Descendenz-Register des Jacob
Samuel Hayum Stern u. dessen
Ehefrau Theresia geb. Wohl.
Frankfurt am Main, 1876.

WOHLAUER
LBI has family tree beginning
1789.

WOHLGENANNT
Tänzer. Juden in Tirol,
pp. 787-89. See GENERAL
WORKS.

WOHLWILL
LBI has family tree beginning
1799.
Ballin. Juden in Seesen,
pp. 241. Family history.
See GENERAL WORKS.
Wohlwill, Friedrich Joachim.
"Erinnerungen" [Fragment].

N.p., n.d. 21 p. The author
(b. Hamburg, 1881; d.
Boston,
1958) includes brief history
of family from his
grandfather, Immanuel
Wohlwill, and father, Emil
Wohlwill. LBI.

WOIDISLAV
Kempelen. Magyarországi Zsidó,
1:42. See GENERAL WORKS.

WOIDZISLAW
UJE, 10:551. Family of
Hungary, descendants of
Woidzislaw who came to
Hungary in 1750. Some of
family embraced Christianity.

WOLF
AMH has family records.
CAJ has history of family from
Essen. CAJ also has the
memoirs of Werner Wolf,
concerning his family and the
community of Aurich, 19th to
20th century.
LBI has family trees beginning
1659, 1786, and 1808.
Schloss Family.
"Simson-Wolf-Schloss
Genealogical Chart." 1972.
AJA.
Böhm, Erich. "Die Eisenstädter
Wolf-Familie," in Hugo Gold
Gedenkbuch der
untergegangenen
Judengemeinden des
Burgenlandes. (1970).
Frank. Nashville Jewry,
p. 147. See GENERAL WORKS.
JFF, no. 5. Family history.
Kaufmann, Alfred. "Anshej
Rhenus: A Chronicle of Jewish
Life by the Rhine." Santa
Rosa, Calif., 1953. 12 p.
Includes brief 300-year
history of the Kaufmann (from
Viernheim bei Mannheim),
Sternheimer (from Viernheim),
Regensburger (from Eppingen),
and Wolf (from Rohrbach)
families. LBI.
Kopp. Jüdischen Alsenz,
pp. 142-43. See GENERAL
WORKS.

Reis, Victor. Chronik der
Familie Wolf. Schluchtern,
1932.
Stern. FAJF. Wolf family
trees beginning in: (I) U.S.;
and (II) Altstrelitz,
Mecklenberg. See GENERAL
WORKS.
Wachstein, Bernhard. "Zur
Genealogie der Familie Wolf
in Eisenstadt," in Die
Grabschriften des alten
Judenfriedhofes in
Eisenstadt, 1679-1874 (Wien,
1922), pp. 621, 867, 891,
1019. Family of Hungary.
See Ernst Wolf entry under
GOMPERZ.
"Wolf Family Chronicle." San
Francisco?, 1980. 54 p.
Genealogical tables of the
descendants of Aron ben
Schneor of Schluchtern,
Germany. This is the English
version of Chronik der
Familie Wolf, first published
in 1932, new edition in 1955,
now revised by Fred (Fritz)
Wolf. LBI.
Wolf, Grete and Hans Wolf.
"Max Wolf und Frau Ida Wolf
geb. Schott." Frankfurt am
Main, 1929. 24 p. Begins
with Jakob Wolf, born 1781,
died 1864 in Osterberg, and
Simon Schott, probably born
between 1780-1810, lived in
Rüsselsheim. CAJ, Call
No. 4893.
Wolf Family. Papers, c.
1970-1977. 1 folder.
"Biographical material, 1976,
of Howard A. Wolf (1900-   )
and genealogical information
about his ancestors and those
of his wife, Martha Rosenthal
Wolf, including members of
the Wolf, Rosenthal, Loeb,
Fels, and Price Families,
dating back to the 18th
century." PJAC.

WOLFE
See BARUCH. Family of South
Carolina.
AMH has family records.

Stern. FAJF. Wolfe family
trees beginning in: (I) U.S.;
and (II) Neustadt, Prussia.
See GENERAL WORKS.

WOLFERS
Feibes, J., Hrsg. Stammbaum
der Familien Itzig (aus
Burgensteinfurt) und Feibes
(Lengerich). Münster, 1887.
46 p. Family tree begins
1720 and includes Wolfers
family. LBI.

WOLFES
Schragenheim, Willi.
Geschichte der Familie
Wolfes. Hannover: By the
Author, 1936. 17 p.
Genealogical tables begin in
1690. Descendants of Wolf
Lazarus, b. ca. 1690. LBI.

WOLFESOHN
AMH has family records.

WOLFF
AJA has genealogical files.
AMH has family records.
CFM has family records.
JE, 12:551. Contains family
tree of Wolff family of U.S.,
descendants of Daniel Robler
de Fonseca of Surinam, Dutch
Guiana, through early 20th
century. See GENERAL WORKS.
LBI has family trees beginning
1681 and 1800.
Kempelen. Magyarországi Zsidó,
1:12; 2:10, 61, 130; 3:26,
138. See GENERAL WORKS.
Reychman. Szkice
genealogiczne, pp. 205-212.
See GENERAL WORKS.
Rose. Schöninger Juden. See
GENERAL WORKS.
Rothmann, Adolf Abraham.
Familiengeschichte.
Karkur/Palästina, 1940.
12 p. Includes Wolff,
Rothmann, Casper,
Michalowski, and Munderstein
families of Posen.
See Stammbaum Levinstein entry
under AVELLIS. Includes
Wolff family.

Stern. FAJF. Wolff family
tree beginning in Germany.
See GENERAL WORKS.
Wolff, Frances Nathan. Four
Generations. New York:
Colonial Press, 1939. 192 p.
Includes Hendricks, Nathan,
and Wolff families. AJHS.

WOLFFENSTEIN
LBI has family tree beginning
1759.

WOLFFING
CAJ has family records.

WOLFFRAM
Semi-Gotha, 2:115. See GENERAL
WORKS.

WOLFFSTERN
LBI has family tree beginning
1817.

WOLFNER
PD has family records.
Kempelen. Magyarországi Zsidó,
1:88; 2:19; 3:92. See
GENERAL WORKS.

WOLFSDORF
Ballin. Juden in Seesen,
p. 242. Family history. See
GENERAL WORKS.

WOLFSKEHL
CAJ has family tree, 18th to
20th century.
Hesse. Landesbibliothek. Karl
Wolfskehl, 1869-1969: Leben
und Werk in Dokumenten
(Ausstellung der Hessischen
Landes-und
Hochschulbibliothek ..., 1969;
Konzeption und Katalog:
Manfred Schlosser).
Darmstadt: Agora Verlag,
1969. 396 p. (Agora, 22).
Includes genealogical table.
Karl Wolfskehl, German poet,
b. Darmstadt, 1869; d. 1948.
He claimed he was a
descendant of the famous
Kalonymus family. DLC, OCH.

WOLKIN
Sack, Sallyann Amdur and Mark
Weiss Shulkin, eds. Search
for the Family: A Chronicle
of the Tzvi Hirsch Shulkin
and Gelye Devorah Rosen
Family and Those Related to
Them. Bethesda, Md.: Marsal
Press, 1980. 176 p. Family
of Polotzk (Plock) area.
Includes Wolkin family.
AJHS, DLC, MH, NN, WiH, YIVO.

WOLLEY
AMH has family records.

WOLLHEIM
See CAJ (Call No. 2067) entry
under PINCZOVER.

WOLLNER
Kempelen. Magyarországi Zsidó,
2:36. See GENERAL WORKS.

WOLLSTEINER
Rosenstein. Unbroken Chain,
pp. 81ff. See GENERAL WORKS.
Wollsteiner, Max. "Wie ich
meine Ahnen suchen ging,"
JFF, no. 1 (1925):74-77.

WOLSELEY
AMH has family records.

WOLSK, WOLSKY
Wolsky, Boris. Yizkor. Added
title page: Iscor; A Memorial
Dedicated to Thirteen Members
of the Wolsky Family Who Were
Tragic victims of Nazi
Atrocities. New York, 1950.
66 p. AJHS, DLC, NN.
————. My Life in Three
Worlds. Miami Beach, Fla.:
By the Author, 1979. 383 p.
Includes genealogical table.
The three worlds of author
(1898-   ) are
turn-of-the-century Domacheva
and Brest-Litovsk; Paris,
where he lived from
1914-1941; and the U.S. after
1941, where he operated a
travel agency in New York.
"My Family," pp. 229-83,
"Luba's Family," pp. 287-99.

Luba, the author's wife, came from Smolensk and Lachowich, Russia. Her maiden name was Soloveichik. "The Wolsk Family," pp. 303-321. The author's uncle shortened family name from Wolsky to Wolsk. Author's maternal grandparents were the Priluk family, a history of which is covered on pp. 325-338. Family was from Kamenitz near Brest-Litovsk, and later lived in Warsaw. DLC; University of Illinois / Champaign-Urbana Library.

WOODBURNE
AMH has family records.

WOODFORD
AMH has family records.

WOOLF
AMH has family records.
CFM has family records.
Stern. FAJF. Woolf family tree beginning in U.S. See GENERAL WORKS.
Woolf, Leonard Sidney. Sowing: An Autobiography of the Years, 1880-1904. London: The Hogarth Press, 1960. 206 p. Especially, pp. 11-26. The author (1880-1969), an English publisher and writer, was the son of Solomon Rees Sydney Woolf (1844-1892) and Marie De Jongh Woolf and the grandson of Benjamin (1808-1870) and Isabella Woolf (1808-1878). Author's mother was born in Amsterdam of an old Dutch Jewish family. CLU, CSt, CtY, DLC, ICN, MnU, NcD, NN, NNC, NjR, TxU.

WOOLSTONE
AMH has family records.

WORKUM
Stern. FAJF. Workum family tree beginning in Workum, Holland. See GENERAL WORKS.

"Genealogical Data Concerning the Family of Jacob L. Workum of Cincinnati and Related Families." AJA.
Workum, Ruth I. "Marriage, Birth, and Death Records of Prominent Cincinnati Families, 1942." Includes Workum family. AJA.

WORMS
AMH has family records.
CFM has family records.
JE, 12:565. "Worms Pedigree." English and German descendants of Aaron Worms, fl. ca. 1750, through late 19th century. See GENERAL WORKS.
Benas, Bertram B. "Genealogical Notes upon the Family of Baron Henry de Worms, Sometime Member of Parliament for East Toxteth," Transactions of the Historical Society of Lancashire and Cheshire 91 (1940):143-58. Lord Pirbright.
See Daniel J. Cohen entry under CLEVE. Worms-Wallich family, pp. 59-78. Includes family tree starting with Moses Abraham Wallich (d. 1587), and continuing to 1810, pp. 116-17. Family originally from Worms.
Ginsburger, Moses. "Rabbin de l'Empereur, Jacob de Worms et sa famille," Revue des Études Juives 82 (1926):461-68. 16th-century Germany. Family originally from Ensisheim, B-Rhin.
Kempelen. Magyarországi Zsidó, 2:13. See GENERAL WORKS.
Pudor. Internationalen Verwandtschaftlichen. Vol. 3 includes section on Worms family. See GENERAL WORKS.
Schunk, Betty. Aus alten Tagebuchern und Erinnerungen der Familien Hirsch, Worms, Strupp, Eisenberg. Abgeschrieben, illustriert und mit vier Stammtafeln

versehen von Alexander
Eisenberg. Meiningen, 1924.
24 p. Worms family of
Karlsruhe. LBI.

Ullmann, Elias. Genealogical
History of the Family of de
Worms. Frankfurt am Main,
1886. Descendants of Hirsch
Amschel Mendler Ottingen,
1644-1720, oo. Ester
Flörsheim, 1654-1728. LBI.

Wolf, "Anglo-Jewish Families."
See GENERAL WORKS.

WORMSER
AMH has family records.

Frintrop, H.W.F. Stammboom
Wormser-Ettlinger. 1954.
4 p. The two families came
to the Netherlands from
Worms. The family tree
starts with Samuel Dudenhofen
(d. 1590) from Dudenhofen.
Gemeente Archief Amsterdam,
Amstelkade, Amsterdam,
Private Archive
No. 578, 8 G6.

WORTHINGTON
AMH has family records.

WOTTITZ
Kempelen. Magyarországi Zsidó,
1:96. See GENERAL WORKS.

WRANGEL
Semi-Gotha, 1:88. See GENERAL
WORKS.

WREDE
Semi-Gotha, 1:46. See GENERAL
WORKS.

WULF
Rosenstein. Unbroken Chain,
pp. 119ff. Genealogical
chart. See GENERAL WORKS.

WULFF
Fischer, Josef. Slaegten
Wulff, fra Fredericia og
Randers; Carl Wulff og hans
efterkommere. På
foranledning af Sofus
Oppenheim, påbegyndt af Josef
Fischer, afsluttet af Michael

Hartvig. København, 1953.
153 p. MH.

Freudenthal, Max. Aus der
Heimat Mendelssohns: Moses
Benjamin Wulff und seine
Familie, die Nachkommen des
Moses Isserls. Berlin:
Lederer, 1900. 304 p. Moses
Benjamin Wulff, 1661-1729.
Dessau. Moses Isserles
b. Israel Isser, 1520-1572 in
Cracow. DLC, LBI, MH, NN,
OCH, PP, PPDrop.

Rachel and Wallich. Berliner
Grosskaufleute, 2:393-429.
"Liepmann Meyer Wulff."
Includes genealogical
information for Liepmann
Wulff (1745-1812) family.
See GENERAL WORKS.

Siersted, P.R. Stamtavle over
Familien Wulff af
Stubbekjobing. 2. udg.: Ved.
Th. Siersted, 1904. 20 p.
Family of Denmark.

WUNDERLICH
LBI has family tree.

WURZBURGER
LBI has family trees beginning
1689 and 1730.

Tänzer. Juden in Jebenhausen,
p. 387. See GENERAL WORKS.

WYZANSKI
AJA has genealogical files.

XIMENES
AMH has family records.
CFM has two family trees.

YACHIA
See YAHIA.

YAFFE
Shapiro. Mishpachot Atikot.
See GENERAL WORKS.
Yacobi, Paul Yisrael.

"Megillat Hayachas
Lemichpacha Yaffe." Israel,
1978. 9 p. Genealogy of
Yaffe family. JNUL.
Yaoz. Album Shel. See GENERAL
WORKS.

YAHIA
See JACHIA.
Carmoly, Eliakim. Sefer divre
ha-yamim le-bene Yaḥia.
Frankfurt am Main, 1850.
43 p.

YAMPOLSKY
See Yaffa Draznin entry under
BERNSTEIN. Includes family
history.

YARASHAFSKY
See SHAFSKY.

YARROW
Barnes, Lady Eleanor. Alfred
Yarrow, His Life and Work.
London: E. Arnold, 1923.
328 p. Anglo-Jewish family.
Sir Alfred Fernandez Yarrow
(1842–1922), engineer and
shipbuilder, was created a
baronet in 1916. CtY, DLC,
ICJ, IEN, MB, NN, OCl.

YATES
AMH has family records.
"Genealogy of the Families of
Samuel and Yates of
Liverpool, England and New
York." AJA.
JE, 11:32–33. "Samuel and
Yates Pedigree." German,
English, and American
branches, early 18th to late
19th century. See GENERAL
WORKS.
"Yates–Samuel–Lazarus–and Levy
Records, 1788–1901." AJA.
Samuel, Sir Stuart Montagu,
bart. History and Genealogy
of the Jewish Families of
Yates and Samuel of
Liverpool, from Materials
Collected by Stuart M.
Samuel. Edited with an
introduction, addition, and
notes by Lucien Wolf.

London: By the Author, 1901.
69 p. OCH.
Stern. FAJF. Yates family
tree beginning in Liverpool.
See GENERAL WORKS.

YELLIN
EJ (1972), 16:736.
Genealogical table,
descendants of David
Yellin-Tavia, 1803–1863,
through mid-20th century.
Israeli family originally
from Poland. See GENERAL
WORKS.
Yellin, Jehoshua. Zikhronot
le-ben Yerushalem.
Jerusalem, 1924.
6, 3, 202, 8 p. One family
tree. DLC.

YEO
AMH has family records.

YIZRAELI
See Meir Yizraeli entry under
BIDERMAN.

YOUNG
See DE YOUNG.
AMH has family records.

YOUNGMAN
Youngman Family, Fremont, Ohio.
"Biographical Data: Birth,
Marriage, and Death Record
from the Family Prayer Book,
and Newspaper Obituary
Notices, 1824–1938." In
German, English, Hebrew, and
Yiddish. AJA.

ZABARRA
Sobrequés Vidal, Santiago.
"Contribución a la historia
de los judíos de Gerona:
Familias hebreas gerundenses;
Los Zabarra y los Caravita,"
Anales del Instituto de
Estudios Gerundenses 2
(1947):68–98.

ZABARSKI

Bick-Shauli, "Roots and
Branches." Boris Zabarski,
b. Podolsk (Kamenets), 1917.
Member of the USSR Medical
Academy. Under his
supervision, Lenin's body was
embalmed. See GENERAL WORKS.

ZACHARIAH

AJA has genealogical files.
AMH has family records.
Zachariah, Brian. "A History
of the Zachariah Family:
Genealogy of the
Zachariah-Steinfeld Family."
Louisville, Ky., Feb. 2,
1975. AJA.

ZACUTO

Cantera Burgos, Francisco.
Abraham Zacuto, siglo XV.
Madrid: M. Aguilar, 1935.
225 p. Includes genealogical
tables. Abraham ben Samuel
Zacuto, astronomer and
mathematician, b. Salamanca?,
ca. 1450; d. Damascus,
1510/1515. DLC, ICN, NcD,
OU, PPDrop, TxU.
Meekman, J. "Moses Zacuto en
zijn familie," Studia
Rosenthaliana 3
(1969):145-55.

ZADOK

AMH has family records.

ZAHL

Batkin, Stanley I., ed. The
Tenzer Family Tree Including
the Feiler and Zahl Families.
New Rochelle, N.Y.:
S.I. Batkin Co., 1977.
1 portfolio (54 leaves).
Family originally from
Southern Galicia. Covers
1690-1977. AJA, AJHS, DLC,
MH, NN.

ZALAN

Kempelen. Magyarországi Zsidó,
2:60. Zalán family. See
GENERAL WORKS.

ZALAY

Kempelen. Magyarországi Zsidó,
3:137. See GENERAL WORKS.

ZALKA

Kempelen. Magyarországi Zsidó,
2:102. See GENERAL WORKS.

ZALKE

See Zalke of Trascun entry
under SALK.

ZALMAN

AMH has family records.
Heilprin, S.A., comp. Sefer
ha-Tze-atza-im [Book of
Descendants: Family Tree of
the Descendants of Rabbi
Shneor Zalman ben Baruch,
1742-1812 of Lyady, founder
of Habad Hassidism].
Jerusalem, 1980. 566 p.
Includes Slonim, Schneersohn,
and Zalman families. JNUL.
Slonim, Menahem Samuel.
Toledot Mishpaḥat ha-Rav
mi-Ladl [History of the
Family of the Rabbi of
Lyady.] Tel-Aviv, 1946. On
the descendants of Shneor
Zalman ben Baruch of Lyady
(1747-1812), founder of Habad
Hassidism. DLC, NN.

ZALTER

AMH has family records.

ZAMENHOF

Fechter, J. "Le docteur Louis
Lazare Zamenhof et les autres
membres de la famille," Revue
d'Histoire de la Médicine
Hébraïque 3 (Mai 1949):63-69.
Ludwik Lazar Zamenhof, Polish
physician, philologist, and
creator of Esperanto,
b. Bialystok, 1859; d. 1917.
Wiessenfeld, Edvardo. Galerio
de Zamenhofoj. Horrem bei
Koln: Heroldo de Esperanto,
1925. 40 p., plus 19 pages
of portraits of the Zamenhof
family members. In
Esperanto. JNUL.

ZAMIRA
AMH has family records.

ZANGWILL
AMH has family records.
Wohlgelernter, Maurice. Israel
   Zangwill. New York: Columbia
   University Press, 1964. 344
   p. Especially, pp. 16-19.
   Zangwill (1864-1926) was born
   in London, England, the son
   of Moses Zangwill, who
   emigrated from Rybinishki, a
   small Latvian town
   thirty-five miles north of
   Dvinsk.

ZAPPERT
CAJ has family records of
   family from Prague, 18th and
   19th centuries.
PD has family records.

ZARFATI
MGWJ, 1873, pp. 282 ff. Family
   history.

ZDEKAUER
PD has family records.

ZEBI
AMH has family records.

ZECHARIAH
AMH has family records.

ZECKENDORF
Fierman, Floyd S. "The
   Spectacular Zeckendorfs," The
   Journal of Arizona History 22
   (1981):387-414. Brief
   genealogy, p. 414. An early
   New Mexican and Arizona
   mercantile family. Family
   originally from Hannover,
   Germany. Aaron Zeckendorf
   arrived in Santa Fe, New
   Mexico in 1853.

ZEFFERT
AMH has family records.

ZEITMAN
Kiefer, Karl. "Stammbaum der
   Familie Zeitmann in Frankfurt
   am Main," Frankfurter

Familienblätter für
Familiengeschichte 6, no. 8
   (1913):122; 7, no. 3
   (1914):39. Family of Hans
   Zeitman.

ZERBONI
CAJ has family records.

ZEYK
Kempelen. Magyarországi Zsidó,
   1:54. See GENERAL WORKS.

ZHABOTINSKY
See JABOTINSKY.

ZHITLOWSKY
Bick-Shauli, "Roots and
   Branches." Includes
   genealogy of Chaim
   Zhitlowsky, Yiddish
   philosopher and writer,
   socialist, and chief
   threoretician of galut
   ("diaspora") nationalism and
   Yiddishism, b. near Vitebsk
   in Russia, 1865; d. 1943.
   See GENERAL WORKS.

ZICHERMAN
Spring, Chaim. Zicherman,
   Intrater, Reiss, Sofer.
   Rehovot, Israel: By the
   Author, 1979. 43 p.
   Includes genealogical tables.
   JNUL.

ZICHERMANN
Kempelen. Magyarországi Zsidó,
   3:48. See GENERAL WORKS.

ZICHY
Kempelen. Magyarországi Zsidó,
   1:87, 129, 143; 3:71, 111,
   112. See GENERAL WORKS.

ZIEGLER
CAJ has family records from
   Hungary and Germany.

ZIELENZIGER
LBI has family tree beginning
   1701.
Zielenziger, Georg.

"Stammtafel der Familie
Zielenziger." Berlin, 1937.
1 p. JNUL.

ZIEV
See SIEFF.

ZIFF
See SIEFF.

ZILTZER
Kempelen. Magyarországi Zsidó,
2:35. See GENERAL WORKS.

ZIMBLER
See Yaffa Draznin entry under
BERNSTEIN. Includes family
history.

ZIMMER
Zimmer, Max. "Report of An
Interview with Mr. Max
Zimmer, Los Angeles, Calif.,
Jan. 27, 1973, by Norton B.
Stern." [Santa Monica,
Calif.] 1973. Typescript.
19 p. Contains biographical
information about the Zimmer
family. Max Zimmer was born
in Austria in 1895, and came
to Los Angeles in 1923 where
he became a successful
building contractor. WJHC.

ZIMMERMAN
AMH has family records.
CFM has family records.

ZIMMERMANN
Kempelen. Magyarországi Zsidó,
3:81. See GENERAL WORKS.

ZINKIN
Zinkin, Taya. Odious Child.
London: Chatto & Windus,
1971. 218 p. Includes
genealogical table. DLC.

ZINNER
Kempelen. Magyarországi Zsidó,
2:57. See GENERAL WORKS.

ZIPPERT
LBI has family tree.

ZIVI
Zapf. Tübinger Juden, pp.
184-87. See GENERAL WORKS.

ZOFFANY
CFM has family records.

ZOLD
Kempelen. Magyarországi Zsidó,
2:123. Zöld family. See
GENERAL WORKS.

ZOLKI
AMH has family records.

ZOLTAN
Kempelen. Magyarországi Zsidó,
1:84. Zoltán family. See
GENERAL WORKS.

ZOMBORI, ZOMBORY
Kempelen. Magyarországi Zsidó,
Zombori family, 3:107;
Zombori, Zombory family,
1:143, 144; 3:83. See
GENERAL WORKS.

ZOREF
Salomon, Mordechai. Sefer
Sheloshah dorot ha-Yishuv.
[Three Generations in the
Yishuv.] Jerusalem, 1938 or
1939. 240 p. On
Zoref-Salomon family.

ZORNDORFER
Tänzer. Juden in Jebenhausen,
p. 388. Zörndorfer family of
Jebenhausen. See GENERAL
WORKS.

ZOSSENHEIM
AMH has family records.
CFM has family records.

ZSOLNA
PD has family records.

ZSORY
Kempelen. Magyarországi Zsidó,
3:121. Zsóry family. See
GENERAL WORKS.

ZUBOVICS
Kempelen. Magyarországi Zsidó,
1:82. See GENERAL WORKS.

ZUCKERMAN
Bick-Shauli, "Roots and
  Branches." Includes
  genealogy of Eliezer
  Zuckerman, pioneer socialist
  in Russia, b. Mogilev, 1852;
  d. 1887. See GENERAL WORKS.

ZUKER
Zuker-Bujanowska, Liliana.
  Liliana's Journal: Warsaw,
  1939-1945. New York: Dial
  Press, 1980. 162 p. Family
  of the author (1928-   ) was
  from Kalisz, Poland. During
  the War they lived in Warsaw.
  Except for Lillian, who went
  underground, all family
  members perished. Author's
  underground name was Stefania
  Bujanowska.

ZUMOFF
Zumoff, Nathan, ed. Our
  Family: A History of Five
  Generations in Pictures and
  Script, 1831-1956. Includes
  4 genealogical tables. New
  York: Printed by Academy
  Photo-Offset, 1956 or 1957.
  NN, YIVO.

ZUMSKY
Zumoff, Nathan, ed. Our
  Family: A History of Five
  Generations in Pictures and
  Script, 1831-1956. Includes
  4 genealogical tables. New
  York: Printed by Academy
  Photo-Offset, 1956 or 1957.
  NN, YIVO.

ZUNSER
Zunser, Miriam Shomer.
  Yesterday. New York:
  Stackpole Sons, 1939. 271 p.
  Three generations of author's
  family. CU, DLC, NcD, NN,
  OCH, PPDrop.

ZUNTZ
Stern. FAJF. Zuntz family
  tree beginning in Westphalia.
  See GENERAL WORKS.

ZUNZ
"Alexander Zunz, Rabbi in
  Austerlitz," MGWJ, 1899,
  p. 191.
Brann, Markus. "Dr. Leopold
  Zunz und seine frankfurter
  Ahnen," MGWJ 38
  (1894):493-500.
Brann, Markus and David
  Kaufmann. Leopold Zunz und
  seine Familie. Ein
  Gedenkblatt an sein erster
  Centennarium (10. Aug. 1894).
  Breslau (Trier, S. Mayer),
  1895. 32 p. 1 genealogical
  table. CtY, PP.
Kaufmann, David. "Die Familie
  Zunz," MGWJ 38 (1894):481-93.
————. "R. Lob Zunz," MGWJ 38
  (1894):500-504.

ZUSSMAN
Rosenstein. Unbroken Chain,
  pp. 467 ff. Zussman
  descendants of the Chacham
  Zvi Hirsch Ashkenazi. See
  GENERAL WORKS.

ZWAAB
CAJ has family records.

ZWACK
Kempelen. Magyarországi Zsidó,
  2:102. See GENERAL WORKS.

ZWART
AMH has family records.

ZWEIG
Röder, Julius. Die Nachfahren
  des Moses Zweig. Olmütz,
  1932. 40 p. Contains six
  family trees; more than 500
  names among 8 generations of
  family of Olomouc, Moravia.
  CAJ, YIVO.

ZWEIGBERGK
Semi-Gotha, 1:145. See GENERAL
  WORKS.

ZYDOWER
Zapf. Tübinger Juden, pp.
  187-89. See GENERAL WORKS.

ZYDOWSKY
JFF, no. 6. Family history.

ZYLBERMAN
Kresh, Paul. Isaac Bashevis
   Singer: The Magician of West
   86th Street: A Biography.
   New York: Dial Press, 1979.
   441 p. Genealogical
   information on the Singer and
   Zylberman families, pp.
   16-22.
Singer, Isaac Bashevis. In My
   Father's Court. New York:
   Farrar, Straus, and Giroux,
   1966. 307 p. "The Family
   Tree," pp. 43-48. The Nobel
   Prize-winning author
   (1904-   ) was born in
   Leoncin, Province of Warsaw,
   the son of Reb Pinchas Mendel
   Singer, who was born in
   Tomaszow, and the grandson of
   Reb Samuel and Bathsheba
   Zylbereman Singer. Bathsheba
   Zylberman was from Bilgoray
   in the Province of Lublin and
   was the daughter of Rabbi
   Jacob Zylberman.
────────. A Day of Pleasure:
   Stories of a Boy Growing Up
   in Warsaw. New York: Farrar,
   Straus and Giroux, 1969. 227
   p. Covers 1908-1918.
Singer, Israel Joshua. Of A
   World That is No More: A
   Tender Memoir. Translated by
   Joseph Singer. New York: The
   Vanguard Press, 1970. 253 p.
   A Singer family memoir by
   Isaac Bashevis Singer's older
   brother, who was also a
   famous author.